Y0-ABY-444

SAN RAFAEL PUBLIC LIBRARY
3 1111 01962 3493

The Auto Guide 2002

Published by Firefly Books Ltd., 2001

First Printing

National Library of Canada Cataloguing in Publication Data

Duval, Jacques
[Auto Guide (2002)]
Auto Guide

Annual.
2002-
Continues: Duquet, Denis. Auto guide, ISSN 0839-1068.
ISSN 0839-1068
ISBN 1-55297-533-9 (2002 edition)

1. Automobiles—Purchasing—Periodicals. I. Duquet, Denis
II. Title. III. Title: Auto Guide (Agincourt) IV. Title: Auto Guide (Markham)
V. Title: Auto Guide (Willowdale)

Publisher Cataloguing-in-Publication Data (U.S)

Duval, Jacques.
The Auto Guide 2002 / Jacques Duval and Denis Duquet. -- 1st ed.
[526] p. : col. photos. ; cm.
Includes index.
Summary: An illustrated buyer's guide to cars, trucks, minivans and SUVs.
Includes tips on buying used cars, prototype vehicles, and road tests.
ISBN 1-55297-533-9
1. Automobiles -- purchasing. 2.Trucks -- Purchasing. 3.Vans -- Purchasing.
I.Duquet, Denis. II. Title.
629.222/ 029 21 CIP TL162.D88 2001

Published in Canada in 2001 by
Firefly Books Ltd.
3680 Victoria Park Avenue
Willowdale, Ontario M2H 3K1

Published in the United States in 2001 by
Firefly Books (U.S.) Inc.
P.O. Box 1338, Ellicott Station
Buffalo, New York 14205

Printed in Canada

Translation: My-Trang Nguyen,
assisted by Pierre-Yves Le Dilicocq
Editor: Michael Ballantyne
Coordinator: Brigitte Duval
Scanner operator: Mélanie Sabourin

Photos: Denis Duquet, Jacques Duval,
Michel Fyen-Gagnon, (email: fyengagnon@lr.cgocable), Alain Raymond

The authors of *The Auto Guide* used AGFA Agfachrome film for their photographs.
Our thanks to Denis Dubois.

The Auto Guide test drivers trust Shell.

The following individuals and organizations contributed to this edition.
Our thanks to them all.

Patrice Attanasio (Palm Advertising)
Denis Boisvert
Lucie Boisvert
Mathieu Bouthillette
Marc Cantin
Claude Carrière
Luigi Chinetti Junior
Robin Choinière
Yves Day
Paul Deslauriers (Autodrome St. Eustache, Quebec)
Francine Tremblay-Duval
François Duval
Dominic Fortier
Jacques Guertin (Sanair)
Gene McGovern
Richard Petit
Blainville Test Centers, New West, PMG Technologies, Ferrari Québec
Mikes Restaurants, TransOr

Participants in our comparison tests:
Charles-André Bilodeau
Mathieu Bouthillette
Claude Carrière
Alexandre Doré
Jean-François Doré
Carole Dugré
François Forgues
Yvan Fournier
Bertrand Gahel
Éric Gariepy
Robert Gariepy
Antoine Joubert
Stéphane Lessard
François Macret
Pierre-Louis Mongeau
Alain Morin
Éric Nolin
Mario Petit
Vincent Poirier
Pierre G. Verge

A final and very personal "thank-you" to
Monique, for having once said to me:
"Why don't you do an auto guide?"
Jacques Duval

Jacques
DUVAL
and Denis Duquet

FIREFLY BOOKS

Jacques Duval

Although he's better known in Quebec as a journalist and top-flight auto expert, Jacques Duval first made his name as a radio and television presenter, hosting a variety of programs devoted to music and the Canadian record industry.

A former race driver, Duval won the Quebec Championship three times and was the first Canadian to win the GT class of the 24 Hours of Daytona. In 1990, he returned to auto-racing and took part in 16 races across Canada. He finished second at Mosport in August 1991 during the Firehawk Series.

In 1966, Jacques Duval's popular TV show *Prenez le volant* [Let's Get Behind the Wheel] led him to write the first edition of what was to become a classic and all-time best-seller in the annals of Canadian publishing: *Le Guide de l'auto* [The Auto Guide]. The veteran columnist hosts a weekly 90 minutes TV Show called "The Auto Guide" and he can also be heard on several radio stations in Montreal and elsewhere.

Denis Duquet

A former teacher of Roman history (and a lifelong car enthusiast), Denis Duquet forsook his interest in classical chariots to pursue a different career – writing about more up-to-date conveyances. He began his journalistic career in the early 1970s as a sportswriter and magazine editor, including a tour of duty with CAA – Québec Touring magazine.

In 1980, Jacques Duval asked Denis to join the team at *Le Guide de l'auto* and since then their collaboration has grown steadily. His responsibilities include organizing comparison tests, taking photographs to accompany the text, and writing up many of the road tests themselves.

In recent years, this activity has become a full-time commitment, thanks to the constant growth and popularity of *Le Guide de l'auto* and the successful TV program of the same name.

Contents

Index

Price List

The prices shown ($CDN / $US) refer to models without optional equipment.

ACURA
- 1.7 EL Premium ....23,500 / n.a.
- 1.7 EL Touring ....21,500 / n.a.
- 3.2 CL Type S ....40,000 / 30,810
- 3.2 TL.................................37,000 / 29,360
- 3.2 TL Type S ....41,000 / 31 710
- 3.5 RL ....54,000 / 43,630
- MDX...................................47,000 / 34,850
- NSX-T...............................140,000 / 88,845
- RSX M ....24,000 / n.a.
- RSX M Premium ....28,000 / n.a.
- RSX M6 Type S..........................31,000 / n.a.

ASTON MARTIN
- DB7 ....206,700 / n.a.
- DB7 Volante ....207,760 / 154,350
- Vanquish ....375,000 / n.a.

AUDI
- A4 1.8T 5-speed ....37,225 / 27,225
- A4 3.0 6-speed....................44,495 / 32,665
- A4 Avant 1.8 5 speed ....38,675 / 28,225
- A4 Avant 3.0 6 speed ....45,945 / 33,665
- A6 2.7T 6-speed..................58,830 / 40,325
- A6 3.0 5-speed Tiptronic ......54,335 / 37,725
- A6 4.2 5-speed Tiptronic ......71,175 / 50,225
- A6 Avant 3.0 5-speed Tiptronic ....55,900 / 38,925
- A8 4.2 LW............................95,450 / 67,775
- A8 4.2 ....86,500 / 62,775
- Allroad 6-speed man.............58,800 / 40,475
- Allroad Tiptronic ....59,990 / n.a.
- S4 5-speed or automatic ......57,200 / 41,075
- S6 Avant...................................88,500 / n.a.
- S8 5-speed Tiptronic ....102,500 / 73,075
- TT 1.8 180 hp 5-speed ....50,400 / 33,525
- TT 1.8 225 hp 5-speed ....54,900 / 36,675
- TT Roadster 180 hp Traction..50,500 / 33,775
- TT Roadster 220 hp 6-speed ....59,000 / 39,475

BMW
- 320i 34,500
- 325Ci 41,200
- 325Ci convertible ....52,800 / 36,635
- 325i ....38,900 / 27,635
- 325iT 40,400
- 325Xi 42,100
- 325XiT 43,600
- 330Ci ....48,500 / 35,635
- 330Ci convertible ....62,900 / 43,045
- 330i ....45,900 / 34,635
- 330Xi 49,700
- 525i auto..................................56,400 / n.a.
- 525i man. ....55,200 / 36,045
- 525i Touring ....57,600 / 37,845
- 530i auto..................................64,400 / n.a.
- 530i man. ....63,200 / 40,045
- 540i auto. ....74,400 / 51,745
- 540i man. ....74,400 / 54,545
- 540i Touring ....76,800 / 54,125
- M Coupe ....67,900 / 45,635
- M Roadster ....67,900 / 46,635
- M3 cabrio ....83,500 / 54,045
- M3 coupe ....73,500 / 46,045
- M5 ....105,500 / 70,045
- 7 Series ....n.a.
- X5 3.0 ....56,800 / 39,470
- X5 4.4 ....68,800 / 49,970
- Z3 3.0 ....55,900 / 38,345
- Z8 ....195,000 / 128,745

BUICK
- Century Custom....................25,325 / 20,725
- Century Limited....................28,045 / 23,725
- LeSabre Custom ....32,960 / 24,975
- LeSabre Limited ....38,580 / 30,675
- Park Avenue ....43,700 / 34,015
- Park Avenue Ultra ....48,820 / 38,525
- Regal GS.............................32,970 / 27,725
- Regal LS ....29,080 / 23,670
- RendezVous CX ....30,995 / 25,499
- RendezVous CX AWD ....34,995 / 28,027
- RendezVous CXL AWD................40,095 / n.a.

CADILLAC
- Catera.................................42,485 / 31,945
- Catera Sport ....44,790 / n.a.
- CTS ....n.a.
- DeVille ....52,555 / 43,070
- DeVille DHS.........................62,025 / 48,000
- DeVille DTS ....63,575 / 48,000
- Eldorado Touring Coupe ....57,450 / 45,745
- Escalade ....72,700 / 51,980
- Escalade EXT.......................65,900 / 49,990
- Seville SLS ....59,450 / 44,269
- Seville STS ....67,015 / 49,625

CHEVROLET
- Astro...................................26,940 / 21,448
- Astro AWD...........................29,870 / 23,848
- Avalanche 4X2 ....38,960 / 30,965
- Avalanche 4X4 ....42,205 / 33,965
- Avalanche 4X4 North Face ....46,680 / 38,409
- Blazer 2-door 4X4 ....28,455 / 22,770
- Blazer LS 4-door 4X4............34,585 / 27,505
- Camaro...............................26,995 / 18,455
- Camaro Z28 ....30,795 / 22,870
- Camaro Z28 convertible........39,225 / 29,965
- Cavalier LS sedan ....21,275 / 15,375
- Cavalier VL coupe ....15,100 / n.a.
- Cavalier Z24 sedan ....22,475 / 17,120
- Cavalier Z24 coupe ....22,575 / 17,020
- Corvette convertible.............69,665 / 47,975
- Corvette coupe ....62,400 / 41,450
- Corvette hardtop Z06............70,780 / 50,150
- Impala.................................24,875 / 20,495
- Impala LS ....29,410 / 24,195
- Malibu ....22,760 / 17,970
- Malibu LS ....25,215 / 20,175
- Monte Carlo LS ....26,525 / 20,595
- Monte Carlo SS ....29,220 / 23,395
- S-10 standard/short bed ......17,060 / 14,210
- S-10 extended cab/short bed ....19,200 / n.a.
- Silverado 4X2 ....24,100 / 17,888
- Silverado 4X4 ....25,915 / 20,873
- Suburban LS 4X2 ....45,875 / 35,863
- Suburban LT 4X4..................54,655 / 40,376
- Tahoe LS 4X2 ....41,695 / 33,094
- Tahoe LT 4X4 ....51,625 / 35,910
- Tracker 4-door 4X4 ....22,250 / 18,105
- Tracker convertible 4X4 ....20,575 / 17,415
- TrailBlazer LS 4X2 ....34,600 / 25,755
- TrailBlazer LS 4X4 ....38,170 / 27,980
- Venture LS AWD ....36,440 / 30,725
- Venture SW Value Van ....25,195 / 21,935
- Venture Warner Bros ....37,865 / 31,055

CHRYSLER
- 300M ....39,900 / 28,995
- 300M Special ....43,305 / n.a.
- Concorde LX ....29,690 / 22,995
- Concorde LXi..........................31,200 25,600
- Intrepid ES ....27,210 / 23,125
- Intrepid R/T..........................31,970 / 27,240
- Neon LE ....18,505 / 12,730
- Neon LX ....20,530 / 14,505
- Neon R/T.............................23,140 / 16,680
- Prowler ....63,740 / 44,700
- PT Cruiser...........................23,650 / 18,480
- Sebring LTD convertible ....37,505 / 29,390
- Sebring LX ....23,320 / 18,300
- Sebring LX convertible ....34,495 / 23,670
- Sebring LX coupe ....28,195 / 20,615
- Sebring LXi ....27,780 / 22,305
- Town & Country AWD............50,015 / 38,515
- Town & Country LTD.............47,005 / 36,190
- Town & Country LXi ....41,815 / 29,830

DAEWOO
- Lanos S 3-door auto...................14,100 / n.a.
- Lanos S 3-door man. ....13,100 / 9,659
- Lanos S 4-door auto...................14,900 / n.a.
- Lanos S 4-door man. ....13,900 / 10,559
- Leganza CDX ....25,300 /19,659

- Leganza SX ....21,000 / 18,159
- Nubira SX sedan auto. ....18,100 / 12,500
- Nubira SX sedan man. ....17,000 / 11,699
- Nubira SX wagon auto..........19,200 / 13,650
- Nubira SX wagon man...........18,100 / 12,500

DODGE
- Caravan ES ....37,270 / 33,375
- Caravan SE ....25,430 / 19,795
- Dakota ....21,480 / 16,440
- Dakota 4X4 ....22,775 / 18,990
- Dakota 4X2 Quad Cab ....25,255 / 21,010
- Dakota 4X4 Quad Cab ....28,955 / 23,775
- Durango SLT ....40,375 / 29,695
- Durango SLT 5.9-liter...........43,350 / 32,305
- Grand Caravan Sport ....29,505 / 24,930
- Grand Caravan Sport AWD ....42,085 / 30,480
- Ram 4X2 short wheelbase ....23 255 / 17,670
- Ram 4X4 short wheelbase ....27,395 / 21,930
- Ram Quad Cab 4X2 short wheelbase...........................26,960 / 22,865
- Ram Quad Cab 4X4 short wheelbase...........................30,365 / 26,065
- Viper GTS coupe ....110,285 / 70,000
- Viper RT/10.......................106,515 / 73,000

FERRARI
- 360 6-speed ....229,050 / 148,000*
- 360 F1 ....236,737/ n.a.
- 360 Spyder ....262,966 / 165,000*
- 456 6-speed ....351,161 / 230,000*
- 456 auto. ....356,699 / n.a.
- 550 Barchetta.........................394,000 / n.a.
- 550 Maranello ....329,295 / 245,000*

FORD
- Escape XLS 4X2 ....21,510 / 18,725
- Escape XLS AWD ....24,160 / 20,200
- Escape XLT AWD ....30,010 / 21,750
- Expedition Eddie Bauer..........50,865 / 41,565
- Expedition XLT ....41,255 / 30,910
- Explorer Eddie Bauer ....45,060 / 34,655
- Explorer Limited...................46,810 / 34,655
- Explorer Sport 4X4................30,280 / 24,655
- Explorer Sport Trac 4X2 ....28,440 / 22,510
- Explorer Sport Trac 4X4 ....32,330 / 25,280
- Explorer XLS ....37,370 / 24,620
- Explorer XLT ....39,105 / 28,330
- F-150 ....22,730 / 17,960
- F-150 SuperCrew ....34,125 / 31,665
- Focus LX.............................15,970 / 13,220
- Focus SE.............................17.955 / 14,810
- Focus SE wagon ....18,995 / 17,015
- Focus ZTS...........................20,780 / 16,030
- Focus ZTW ....21,780 / 18,195
- Focus ZX3...........................17,390 / 12,905
- Focus ZX5...........................20,780 / 16,105
- Mustang ....22,795 / 17,695
- Mustang Bullitt ....37,055 / n.a.
- Mustang convertible.............27,465 / 19,490
- Mustang GT coupe ....31,055 / 24,480
- Mustang GT convertible ....35,020 / 28,735
- Ranger XL ....15,995 / 12,695
- Ranger XLT Supercab 4X2 ....21,195 / 17,150
- Ranger XLT Supercab 4X4 ....21,695 / n.a.
- Taurus LX ....24,550 / 19,175
- Taurus SE ....26,175 / 19,950
- Taurus SE wagon ....27,285 / 21,105
- Taurus SEL wagon ....28,690 / 22,450
- Thunderbird..........................51,550 / 36,495
- Thunderbird hardtop ....56,550 / 38,995
- Windstar Limited ....41,535 / 39,360
- Windstar LX.........................25,995 / 22,840
- Windstar SEL.......................33,685 / 31,770
- Windstar Sport ....31,400 / n.a.

GMC
- AMG Hummer ....121,250 / 76,800
- Envoy SLE 4X2 ....37,955 / 29,420
- Envoy SLE 4X4 ....41,275 /31,645
- Jimmy SLS 2-door 4X4 ....28,455 /
- Jimmy SLS 4-door 4X4 34,585
- Safari SL ....26,440 / 21,668
- Safari SL AWD ....26,940 / 24,068
- Sierra short bed....................22,565 / 17,410
- Sierra extended bed.............22,855 / 17,710
- Sonoma SL 4X4...................24,775 / 19,924
- Sonoma SL short bed...........17,060 / 14,224
- Yukon Denali AWD ....60,850 / 47,280
- Yukon SLE...........................42,210 / 33,982
- Yukon SLE 4X4 ....45,790 / 36,565
- Yukon XL SLE ....46,400 / 36,922
- Yukon XL SLE 4X4 ....49,980 / 39,505

HONDA
- Accord sedan EX LTH ....27,300 / 23,090
- Accord sedan EX V6.............31,100 / 25,740
- Accord sedan LX ....23,000 / 19,330
- Accord sedan Special Edition ..24,800 / 21,290
- Accord sedan Special Edition V6 ..28,300 / n.a.
- Accord coupe EX-L ....27,300 / 23,090
- Accord coupe EX V6.............31,100 / 25,740
- Accord coupe Special Edition ..24,800 / 21,290
- Civic sedan DX ....15,900 / 13,450
- Civic sedan LX.....................19,100 / 15,550
- Civic coupe DX ....15,900 / 13,250
- Civic coupe LX.....................18,100 / 15,350
- Civic coupe Si ....19,900 / n.a.
- CR-V EX ....28,300 / 21,190
- CR-V LX ....26,300 / 19,590
- Insight hybrid coupe 26,000
- Odyssey EX ....34,900 / 27,190
- Odyssey EX LTH ....36,900 / n.a.
- Odyssey LX ....31,900 / 24,690
- S2000 ....48,500 / 32,740

HYUNDAI
- Accent 3-door GS ....12,395 / 9,894
- Accent 3-door Gsi ....14,495 / n.a.
- Accent sedan GL ....13,795 / 10,394
- Elantra GL ....15,295 / 12,994
- Elantra GT ....18,495 / n.a.
- Elantra GT Premium ....20,495 / n.a.
- Elantra VE.................................16,995 / n.a.
- SantaFe GL 4L.....................21,060 / 16,994
- SantaFe GL V6 4RM.............26,795 / 21,294
- SantaFe GL V6.....................23,495 / 19,794
- SantaFe GLS V6 4WD ....29,250 / 21,294
- Sonata GL ....21,195 / 15,494
- Sonata GL V6 ....22,695 / 17,494
- Sonata GLX ....25,695 / 18,819
- XG350 ....31,995 / 25,500

INFINITI
- G20 ....29,900 / 21,900
- G20 Sport ....31,200 / 24,640
- I35 ....39,500 / 29,295
- I35 Sport.............................42,500 / 32,000
- Q45L ....73,000 / 49,500
- Q45 Premium ....79,800 / 51,100
- QX4 ....48,000 / 36,000

ISUZU
- Rodeo LS ....36,900 / 23,820
- Rodeo S ....31,935 / 21,395
- Trooper Limited ....44,565 / 35,333
- Trooper LS...........................40,325 / 31,285
- Trooper S ....35,695 / 28,140

JAGUAR
- S-Type V6 ....59,960 / 44,250
- S-Type V8 ....70,950 / 49,950
- Super 8.............................104,950 / 71,845
- Vanden Plas ....91,950 / 69,345
- XJ8.....................................82,950 / 62,950
- XJR 97,950/ 71,845
- XK8 convertible ....104,950 / 75,545
- XK8 coupe ....95,950 / 70,545
- XKR convertible ....116,950 / 87,495
- XKR coupe ....107,950 / 81,545
- X-Type 2.5 ....42,950 / 30,545
- X-Type 3.0 ....49,950 / 36,545

JEEP
- Grand Cherokee Laredo 4X4 ..39,095 / 27,995
- Grand Cherokee Limited 4X4 ..44,885 / 33,300
- Grand Cherokee Overland ....51,850 / 37,430
- Liberty Limited.....................26,680 / 21,795
- Liberty Sport 4X4.................22,880 / 18,545
- TJ Sahara ....28,120 / 23,000
- TJ SE convertible 4X4 ....19,975 / 15,475
- TJ Sport convertible 4X4 ......23,675 / 19,740

KIA
- Magentis LX ....21,295 / n.a.
- Magentis LX Sport.....................23,295 / n.a.

- Magentis LX V6 ....24,295 / n.a.
- Magentis LX V6 Sport ....26,995 / n.a.
- Magentis SE V6....29,095 / n.a.
- Rio S....12,095 / 9,390
- Rio RS ....13,095 / n.a.
- Rio RX-V....15,095 / n.a.
- Rio RX-V Sport ....14,695 / n.a.
- Sedona EX ....27,595 / n.a.
- Sedona EX De Luxe....29,595 / n.a.
- Sedona LX ....24,595 / n.a.
- Spectra....14,595 / 11,740
- Spectra GS-X 5-door ....17,595 / 13,940
- Spectra LS ....16,595 / n.a.
- Sportage ....22,095 / n.a.
- Sportage EX auto. ....25,595 / n.a.
- Sportage EX man. ....24,095 / 19,840

LAMBORGHINI

- Diablo GT ....500,000 / n.a.
- Diablo Roadster ....404,000 / n.a.
- Diablo VT....386,000 / 300,000*
- Murciélago ....n.a.

LAND ROVER

- Discovery SD....47,000 / 34,600
- Discovery SE....52,000 / 37,600
- Freelander S....34,800 / n.a.
- Freelander SE....38,800 / n.a.
- Range Rover 4.6 HSE....98,000 / 69,300

LEXUS

- ES 300 ....44,000 / 32,080
- GS 300....61,600 / 39,150
- GS 430....71,600 / 47,950
- IS 300 auto. ....39,440 / n.a.
- IS 300 man. ....37,820 / n.a.
- IS 300 Sportcross ....49,450 / n.a.
- LS 430 ....81,900 / 54,750
- LS 430 Premium....94,600 / n.a.
- LS 430 Touring ....83,900 / n.a.
- LX 470....90,600 / n.a.
- RX 300 ....48,000/ n.a.
- SC 430 ....84,000 / 59,000

LINCOLN

- Continental ....51,920 / 38,555
- LS V6 auto. ....41,350 / 32,900
- LS V6 man. ....40,870 / 34,355
- LS V8 auto. ....41,175 / 36,930
- LS V8 Sport package ....49,195 / 38,485
- Navigator 4X4 ....66,415 / 48,580
- Town Car Cartier L ....66,415 / 49,605
- Town Car Executive ....50,700 / 40,540
- Town Car Signature ....52,030 / 42,710

MAZDA

- 626 ES ....31,165 / 23,415
- 626 LX ....23,470 / 20,415
- Millenia....42,150 / 31,500
- MPV DX ....25,505 / 21,155
- MPV ES....33,855 / 26,760
- MPV LX....29,450 / 23,280
- MX-5 Miata....27,695 / 21,660
- Protegé5 ....19,895 / n.a.
- Protegé ES ....17,795 / 16,015
- Protegé LX ....16,695 / 14,635
- Protegé MP3 ....23,795 / n.a.
- Protegé SE ....15,795 / n.a.
- B Series SX....16,765 / n.a.
- B Series SE Cab Plus 4X4 ....25,590 / 20,515
- B Series SX Cab Plus....22,330 / n.a.
- Tribute DX ....22,450 /17,750
- Tribute DX V6....24,525 / 20,085
- Tribute DX 4RM ....25,065 /19,450
- Tribute DX V6 4RM....27,715 / 21,485

MERCEDES-BENZ

- C32 AMG ....65,900 / n.a.
- C240 A Classic ....39,450 / n.a.
- C240 M Classic....37,950 / 30,000
- C240 Sport man. ....47,500 / n.a.
- C320 ....50 600 / n.a.
- C320 wagon ....52,850 / 37,500
- C320 Sport wagon ....57,400 / n.a.
- C320 Sport....55,150 / n.a.
- C Coupe Kompressor M....33,950 / n.a.
- C Coupe Kompressor Sport ....35,450 / n.a.
- CL500C ....132,500 / 88,000
- CL600C ....174,850 / 118,000
- CLK55 AMG ....96,400 / 68,000
- CLK55 convertible AMG....107,500 / n.a.
- CLK320 ....59,900 / 42,600
- CLK320A convertible ....70,550 / 49,500
- CLK430 ....71,350 / 50,300
- CLK430A convertible ....79,250 / 57,200
- E55 AMG ....101,600 / 70,900
- E320 4Matic wagon....73,250 / 52,000
- E320 wagon ....69,200 / 49,300
- E430 ....76,150 /53,850
- E430 4Matic ....79,950 / 56,700
- ML55 AMG ....92,850 / 66,500
- ML320 Elegance ....55,600 / 36,500
- ML500....65,250 / n.a.
- S55 ....140,500 / 98,650
- S430L....101,850 / 71,500
- S500 ....116,950 / 79,600
- S600 ....171,100 / 114,700
- SLK32 AMG ....76,900 / n.a.
- SLK230 man. ....55,100 / 39,500
- SLK320 auto. ....62,250 / 44,500
- SLK320 man. ....61,050 / n.a.
- SL500R ....116,500 / 84,500
- SL600R ....169,000 / 129,600

MERCURY

- Cougar S Coupe ....30,845 / 20,395
- Cougar V6....23,655 / 17,495
- Grand Marquis GS ....34,125 / 24,325
- Grand Marquis LS ....35,490 / 27,800

MINI

- Mini Cooper ....27,500 / 17,250 *

NISSAN

- Altima SE ....32,798 / 22,889
- Altima S ....23,498 / 18,539
- Altima SL ....28,998 / 22,439
- Frontier KC XE....23,998 / 19,089
- Frontier CC SE-V6 ....29,498 / 23,339
- Maxima GLE ....36,900 / 26,989
- Maxima GXE ....33,900 / 21,789
- Maxima SE ....37,900 / 27,689
- Pathfinder LE....44,500 / 32,039
- Pathfinder XE ....35,900 / 28,189
- Sentra GXE ....17,998 / 14,039
- Sentra SE-R ....19,998 / n.a.
- Sentra SE-R Spec V....21,498 / n.a.
- Sentra XE ....15,598 / 12,189
- Xterra SE-SC....33,298 / 25,639
- Xterra XE....29,498 / 21,589

OLDSMOBILE

- Alero GL sedan ....23,100 / 19,380
- Alero GL coupe ....23,345 / 19,380
- Alero GLS sedan/coupe ....27,670 / 22,500
- Alero GX sedan ....21,480 / 17,795
- Alero GX coupe ....21,745 / 17,795
- Aurora 3.5....40,030 / 31,289
- Aurora 4.0....46,570 / 35,464
- Bravada ....46,455 / 34,767
- Intrigue GL ....30,165 / 24,880
- Intrigue GLS ....33,680 / 27,245
- Intrigue GX ....28,365 / 23,125
- Silhouette GL ....33,060 /27,295
- Silhouette GLS....37,025 / 31,160
- Silhouette GLS AWD ....41,045 / n.a.
- Silhouette Premiere ....44,135 / 33,960

PONTIAC

- Aztek ....29,255 / 24,660
- Aztek GT ....32,895 / 27,465
- Bonneville SE....32,365 / 25,875
- Bonneville SLE....36,530 / 28,845
- Bonneville SSEi ....42,805 / 33,215
- Firebird ....27,695 / 20,090
- Firebird Trans Am coupe....36,375 / 28,065
- Firebird Trans Am Ram Air conv. ....46,590 / 32,135
- Firebird Trans Am Ram Air coupe ....41,020 / n.a.
- Grand Am GT ....26,375 / n.a.
- Grand Am GT sedan/coupe....26,595 / 21,000
- Grand Am GTi sedan/coupe ..27,830 / 22,400
- Grand Am SE sedan/coupe....21,405 / 16,900

- Grand Am SEI sedan/coupe ..23,055 / 18,600
- Grand Prix GT sedan/coupe ..28,275 / 22,600
- Grand Prix GTP sedan/coupe 32,400 / 26,150
- Grand Prix SE ....26,385 / 21,100
- Montana SE AWD.................37,010 / 27,380
- Montana 2WD ....27,870 / 25,040
- Montana Vision ....41,555 / 32,990
- Sunfire GT coupe..................22,975 / 17,065
- Sunfire GTX sedan ....21,950 / n.a.
- Sunfire SL coupe........................15,390 / n.a.
- Sunfire SLX coupe......................18,235 / n.a.
- Sunfire SLX sedan......................18,090 / n.a.

PORSCHE

- Boxster ....60,500 / 42,865
- Boxster S ....73,300 / 50,965
- 911 Carrera convertible 113,4/ 76,76500
- 911 Carrera coupe ....99,300 / 67,265
- 911 Carrera 4 convertible ..121,900 / 82,265
- GT2 ....253,000 / n.a.
- Turbo Coupe ....168,400 / 111,765

SAAB

- 9_3 hatchback 3-door ....32,000 / 27,070
- 9_3 hatchback 5-door ....36,500 / 27,570
- 9_3 convertible ....52,000 / n.a.
- 9_3 SE convertible HO ....58,000 / 40,570
- 9_3 SE hatchback HO 5-door....42,390 /33,170
- 9_3 Viggen 3-door ....51,300 / 38,570
- 9_3 Viggen 5-door ....51,300 /38,570
- 9_3 Viggen convertible ....65,000 / 45,570
- 9_5 Aero sedan ....54,900 / 40,750
- 9_5 Aero wagon 56,400/ 41,450
- 9_5 Arc sedan.............................52,000 / n.a.
- 9_5 Arc wagon ....53,500 / n.a.
- 9_5 Linear sedan.........................41,500 / n.a.
- 9_5 Linear wagon ....43,000 / n.a.

SATURN

- L100....................................21,125 / 16,795
- L200....................................23,325 / 18,185
- L300....................................26,580 / 20,845
- LW200 ....25,200 / 19,580
- LW300 ....29,400 / 22,775
- SC1 ....16,765 / 13,230
- SC2 ....22,045 / 16,410
- SL..14,245 / 11,035
- SL1......................................15,215 / 12,180
- SL2......................................18,125 / 13,665
- VUE ....26,500 / 16,600 *

SUBARU

- Forester L ....28,395 / 20,820
- Forester S.................................31,795 / n.a.
- Forester SE..............................29,995 / n.a.
- Forester S Limited.....................35,495 / n.a.
- Forester Sport...........................33,495 / n.a.
- Impreza Outback Sport..........26,395 / 19,220
- Impreza RS sedan ....26,995 / 19,520
- Impreza TS wagon ....21,995 / 18,020
- Impreza WRX sedan.............34,995 / 24,520
- Impreza WRX wagon ....34,995 /24,0020
- Legacy Brighton wagon ....24,295 / n.a.
- Legacy GT...........................30,395 / 23,390
- Legacy GT wagon ....32,495 / 24,290
- Legacy GT Limited...............34,395 / 24,899
- Legacy L ....27,395 / 19,790
- Legacy L wagon ....26,995 / 20,490
- Outback ....31,995 / 23,390
- Outback H6 3.0 ....39,995 / n.a.
- Outback H6 3.0 sedan ....41,995 / n.a.
- Outback H6 VDC ....43,995 / 32,390
- Outback Limited ....36,995 / 26,490

SUZUKI

- Esteem GL ....15,695 / 13,679
- Esteem GL wagon ....16,195 / 14,179
- Esteem GLX ....18,795 / 14,479
- Esteem GLX wagon ....19,795 / 17,179
- Grand Vitara ....31,495 / n.a.
- Grand Vitara JLX...................27,295/ 21,279
- Grand Vitara JX.........................24,495 / n.a.
- Vitara JA convertible ....18,695 / n.a.
- Virara JX 4-door ....20,995 / 17,579
- Vitara JX convertible ....19,795 / 15,969
- XL.7 ....28,995 / n.a.
- XL.7 Plus ....31,995 / n.a.
- XL.7 Touring ....33,595 / n.a.

TOYOTA

- 4Runner Badlands V6 ....36,250 / n.a.
- 4Runner Limited ....49,465 / 36,585
- Avalon XL ....38,365 / 27,120
- Avalon XLS ....45,135 / 30,760
- Camry LE ....23,755 / 20,870
- Camry SE ....30,715 / n.a.
- Camry XLE V6 ....32,570 / 26,680
- Camry Solara convertible ......39,105 / 30,970
- Camry Solara SE ....27,580 / 19,420
- Camry Solara V6 ....30,650 / 22,130
- Celica GT ....24,645 / 17,570
- Celica GT-S ....30,860 / 22,040
- Celica TRD ....33,985 / n.a.
- Corolla CE...........................15,765 / 13,023
- Corolla XLE...............................21,365 / n.a.
- Corolla Sport.............................20,640 / n.a.
- Echo 2-door ....14,085 / 10,480
- Echo 4-door ....14,420 / 12,070
- Highlander ....31,990 / 25,790
- Highlander AWD V6 ....36,190 / 27,370
- Matrix.................................24,000 / 15,000 *
- Prius..................................29,990 / 20,450
- RAV4 4-door AWD ....26,315 / 18,435
- Sequoia ....51,200 / n.a.
- Sequoia Limited...................45,570 / 39,735
- Sequoia SR5 ....58,205 43,055 / 43,055
- Sienna CE ....29,335 / 24,385
- Sienna LE ....32,985 / 26,235
- Tacoma 4X2 Prerunner Double Cab ....30,775 / 19,000
- Tacoma 4X2 XTRA CAB ....23,795 / 15,050
- Tacoma 4X4 Double Cab ......33,385 / 22,630
- Tacoma regular cab 4X2 ......21,920 / 12,410
- Tundra Access 4X4 V8 ....34,385 / 26,785
- Tundra Access 4X2 V8 ....30,595 / 23,455

VOLKSWAGEN

- EuroVan GLS ....41,795 / 26,815
- EuroVan MV ....44,190 / 28,315
- Golf Cabrio GL......................28,530 / 20,150
- Golf Cabrio GLS....................29,750 / 21,150
- Golf Cabrio GLX....................32,250 / 22,850
- Golf GL 2-door......................19,230 / 15,600
- Golf GL 4-door......................19,530 / 15,800
- Golf GL TDI 2-door................21,110 / 16,895
- Golf GL TDI 4-door................21,410 / 17,095
- Golf GLS ....22,280 / 17,150
- Golf GLS TDI ....23,800 / 18,200
- Golf GTI 1.8T........................25,895 / 19,460
- Golf GTI VR6 ....27,530 / 20,845
- Jetta GL ....21,490 / 17,400
- Jetta GLS 1.8T ....25,930 / 20,100
- Jetta GLS VR6 ....26,840 / 20,750
- Jetta GLX VR6 ....33,875 / 25,250
- New Beetle 1.8T ....28,875 / 19,750
- New Beetle 1.8T GLX............28,885 / 22,050
- New Beetle GL......................21,950 / 16,450
- New Beetle TDI ....24,300 / 18,450
- Passat GLS ....29,550 / 22,300
- Passat GLS wagon................30,725 / 23,100
- Passat GLS V6......................33,050 / 24,800
- Passat GLS V6 wagon ....34,225 / 25,600
- Passat GLX...............................39,175 / n.a.
- Passat GLX wagon 4Motion ....44,480 / n.a.
- Passat GLX V6 4Motion ....43,305 / 32,125
- Passat W8 ....55,000 / 34,500*

VOLVO

- C70 ....49,995 / 37,575
- C70 convertible ....59,595 / 44,175
- C70 HT convertible ....63,995 / 46,175
- S40 ....31,495 / 28,025
- S60 2.4 ....36,395 / 27,175
- S60 AWD ....43,995 / 30,475
- S60 T5 ....46,495 / 32,475
- S80 ....54,895 / 38,775
- S80 T6 ....62,895 / 49,375
- V40....................................32,495 / 29,025
- V70 2.4...............................37,920 / 30,075
- V70 2.4 AWD 46,470 / 33,075
- V70 T5 49,315 / 34,875
- V70 XC 49,470 / 35,575

*: *estimated*

Please note that many of the prices listed are for 2001 models, and they are given for information only and refer to models without optional equipment. These prices are those in effect as of October 1, 2001 and are subject to change without notice during the year.

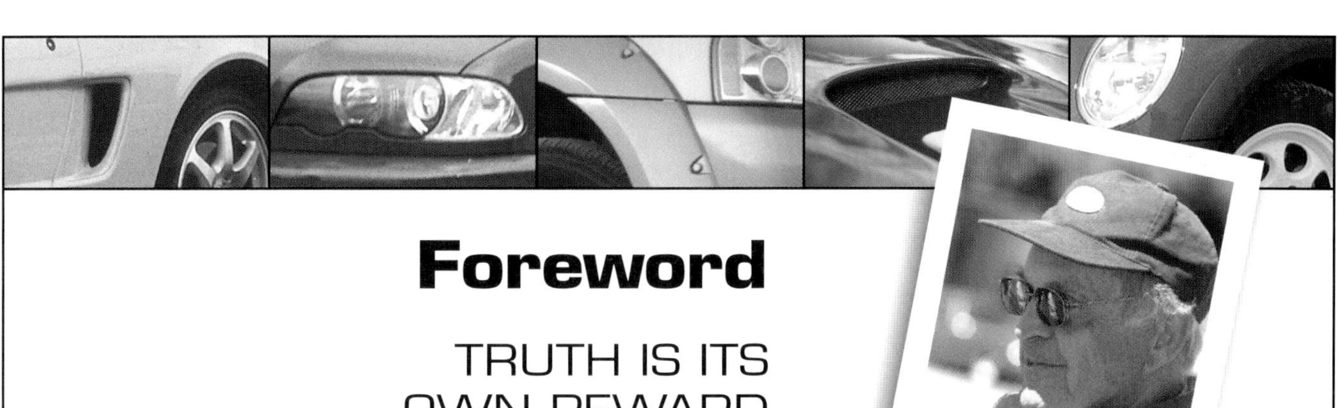

Foreword

TRUTH IS ITS OWN REWARD

I have been writing about cars for the past 36 years and my guidelines have remained constant: to stick to what I believe is the truth and to inform the reader, listener or television audience to the best of my ability. Apparently, this recipe has worked because *The Auto Guide* sold a record 85,000-plus copies last year. The secret of this success was given to me by a television producer who wants to remain anonymous but who confided that he could not find a single sponsor for a television broadcast on cars that he was about to program. As soon as the news got out that I was going to be the moderator, people became extremely nervous. In other words, my frankness, my integrity and my core belief that "the truth should always be told" was a disturbing prospect. They had no desire to be associated with someone who might make negative comments about the cars in question, whether it be tires, oil or spare parts.

This nervousness struck me as flattering and it provided clear proof of the extent to which I have achieved my goals: to tell the public exactly what's going on, even at the risk of making enemies in the automobile world. It's precisely this unwillingness to play footsy with the manufacturers that allows us this year to cross the border and offer an English-language version of *The Auto Guide* designed to reach the whole of North America. The two editions share a common denominator, that is test-driving most of the vehicles (sedans, sport-utes, wagons and pickups) sold in Canada and the United States. The information collected on the performance of each vehicle is complemented by comparison tests among the various models within a given category. Frankly, it's no small job to set up all the elements needed for this type of evaluation. As an example, take our comparison between the new Jeep Liberty and nine of its rivals. In total, ten vehicles were brought together at the same time, in the same place, as well as some 20 individuals who were invited to drive and test each of the models, then fill out evaluation charts. Moreover, we had to find an off-road track and make sure that there were two photographers, a cameraman and a mechanic – and, of course, to prepare lunches for the entire crew. So may I take this opportunity to thank Denis Duquet, the ringmaster of these meetings, as well as all those enthusiastic and dedicated people who volunteered.

For the 2002 edition, Denis Duquet did not rest on his laurels. In addition to the compact 4-wheel drive tests, he also put together the small wagon test, and those involving the mini sports cars and all-wheel drive sedans. While all this hard work was going on, I was happily enjoying myself at the wheel of the Ferrari lineup (Ferrari Festival), testing the AMG lineup ("Six Mercedes on the Loose") and organizing the Porsche Boxster – Subaru Impreza WRX head-to-head road test. I hope you'll have as much fun reading about these special road tests as I did doing the driving. For those readers who have to think seriously about their pocketbooks, Alain Morin's sense of humor may put a smile on your face as you choose the second-hand car best suited to your circumtances. *The Auto Guide 2002* might also have added the 2003 model year to its title as we've included so many cars that are still waiting in the wings. I'm thinking, for instance, of the MINI Cooper that Alain Raymond road-tested in Italy and the Mazda M6 that Denis Duquet drove in Japan. One fine new member of our crew is photographer Michel Fyen-Gagnon. Without him, you probably would never have seen a Ferrari skidding on three wheels or a Mercedes-Benz CLK55 stirring up a smokescreen in a high-speed skid-control maneuver. This time around, I also benefited from the much appreciated support of several contributors, including Jean-Georges Laliberté, François Duval, Mathieu Bouthillette and Louis Butcher. Nor dare I omit to mention my new right-hand person, Brigitte Duval who, in her own way, has played a key role in the production of this year's *Auto Guide.*

As for me, I still intend to frighten people in the car industry and will probably make more enemies with my underlying conviction that honesty is always the best policy. Happy motoring!

Jacques Duval

AUTO GUIDE Best Buys for 2002

SUB-COMPACTS

(less than $20,000)

1 MAZDA PROTEGÉ/PROTEGÉ5

Best Buys

2 HONDA CIVIC

3 NISSAN SENTRA

Nominated

- Chevrolet Cavalier / Pontiac Sunfire
- Chrysler Neon
- Daewoo Lanos / Nubira
- Honda Civic
- Hyundai Accent / Elantra
- Kia Rio / Spectra
- Mazda Protegé / Protegé5
- Nissan Sentra
- Saturn SL1
- Suzuki Esteem
- Toyota Echo

COMPACTS

($20,000 to $25,000)

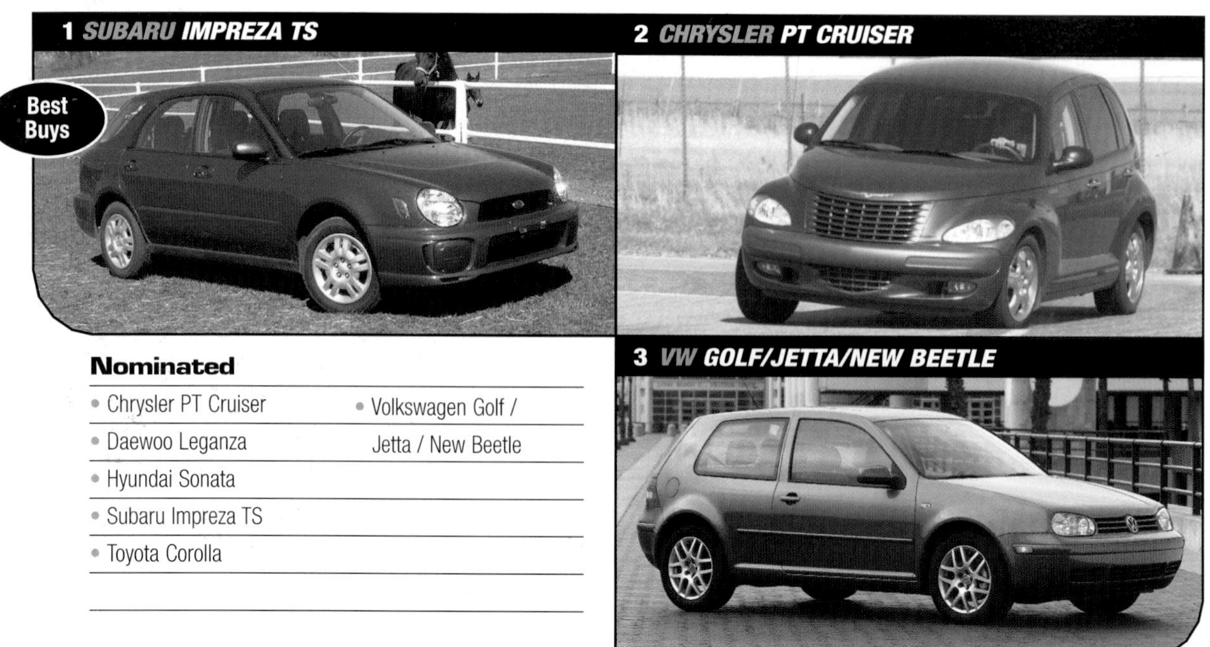

1 SUBARU IMPREZA TS

Best Buys

2 CHRYSLER PT CRUISER

3 VW GOLF/JETTA/NEW BEETLE

Nominated

- Chrysler PT Cruiser
- Daewoo Leganza
- Hyundai Sonata
- Subaru Impreza TS
- Toyota Corolla
- Volkswagen Golf / Jetta / New Beetle

LARGE COMPACTS

($25,000 to $30,000)

1 TOYOTA CAMRY

Best Buys

2 NISSAN ALTIMA

3 HONDA ACCORD

Nominated

- Buick Century / Regal / Chevrolet Malibu
- Chrysler Sebring
- Ford Taurus
- Honda Accord
- Infiniti G20
- Kia Magentis
- Mazda 626
- Nissan Altima
- Oldsmobile Alero
- Pontiac Grand Am
- Saturn L
- Subaru Legacy
- Toyota Camry

INTERMEDIATE AND LARGE SEDANS

(less than $45,000)

1 NISSAN MAXIMA

Best Buys

2 ACURA TL

3 TOYOTA AVALON XL

Nominated

- Acura TL
- Buick Le Sabre / Chevrolet Impala
- Chrysler Concorde / Intrepid
- Hyundai XG350
- Mazda Millenia
- Mercury Grand Marquis
- Nissan Maxima
- Oldsmobile Intrigue
- Pontiac Grand Prix / Bonneville
- Toyota Avalon XL

SPORT LUXURY SEDANS

(less than $50,000)

1 AUDI A4 1.8 QUATTRO

Best Buys

2 M-BENZ C320 & VW PASSAT 4MOTION

3 BMW 330

Nominated

- Audi A4 1.8 Quattro
- BMW 325 / 330
- Chrysler 300 M
- Infiniti I35
- Jaguar X-Type
- Lexus ES 300 / IS 300
- M-Benz C240 / C320
- Oldsmobile Aurora
- Saab 9^3 / Viggen
- Volkswagen Passat 4Motion
- Volvo S60 / S60 AWD

LUXURY CARS

(more than $50,000)

1 BMW 540i

Best Buys

2 AUDI A6 2.7T QUATTRO

3 INFINITI Q45

Nominated

- Acura RL
- Audi A6 3.0 Quattro / 2.7T Quattro
- BMW 5 Series
- Buick Park Avenue / Cadillac Seville
- Infiniti Q45
- Jaguar S-Type
- Lexus LS 430
- Lincoln LS V8
- Mercedes-Benz E Class
- Saab 9^5
- Volkswagen Passat W8
- Volvo S80

SPORTS CARS

(less than $35,000)

1 MERCEDES-BENZ COUPE C230

Best Buys

2 SUBARU IMPREZA WRX & ACURA RSX TYPE S

3 VOLKSWAGEN GOLF GTI/JETTA 1.8T

Nominated

- Acura RSX Type S
- Ford Focus ZX3
- Honda Civic Si
- Mazda MP3
- Mercedes-Benz Coupe C230
- Mercury Cougar
- Nissan Sentra SE-R
- Saturn SC
- Subaru Impreza WRX
- Toyota Celica
- Volkswagen Golf GTI / Jetta 1.8T

CONVERTIBLES, ROADSTERS AND GT'S

(less than $60,000)

1 VOLKSWAGEN CABRIO

Best Buys

2 BMW 325Ci

3 MAZDA MIATA

Nominated

- Audi TT
- BMW Z3 / 325Ci
- Chevrolet Camaro / Pontiac Firebird
- Ford Mustang / Thunderbird
- Honda S2000
- Mazda Miata
- Mercedes-Benz SLK
- Saab 9³ cabriolet
- Volkswagen Cabrio
- Volvo C70

SPORTS CARS AND CONVERTIBLES

($60,000 to $200,000)

1 PORSCHE 911 / 911 TURBO

Best Buys

2 LEXUS SC 430

3 CHEVROLET CORVETTE Z06

Nominated

- Acura NSX-T
- BMW Z8
- Chevrolet Corvette Z06
- Dodge Viper
- Jaguar XK8
- Lexus SC 430
- Mercedes-Benz CLK 430 / CL 500
- Porsche 911 / 911 Turbo

MINIVANS

1 HONDA ODYSSEY

Best Buys

2 CHRYSLER TOWN & COUNTRY/DODGE CARAVAN

3 MAZDA MPV

Nominated

- Buick RendezVous / Pontiac Aztek
- Chevrolet Venture / Pontiac Montana / Oldsmobile Silhouette
- Chrysler Town & Country / Dodge Caravan
- Ford Windstar
- Honda Odyssey
- Kia Sedona
- Mazda MPV
- Toyota Sienna
- Volkswagen EuroVan

COMPACT SPORT UTILITY VEHICLES

(less than $35,000) **See Comparison match on page 39**

SPORT UTILITY VEHICLES

($35,000 to $55,000)

1 *ACURA* MDX

Best Buys

2 *CHEVROLET* TRAILBLAZER/*GMC* ENVOY

3 *LEXUS* RX 300 & *M-BENZ* ML320

Nominated

- Acura MDX
- Chevrolet TrailBlazer / GMC Envoy
- Dodge Durango
- Ford Explorer / Expedition
- Infiniti QX4
- Jeep Grand Cherokee
- Land Rover Discovery / Freelander
- Lexus RX 300
- Mercedes-Benz ML320
- Nissan Pathfinder
- Toyota 4Runner

HYBRID WAGONS

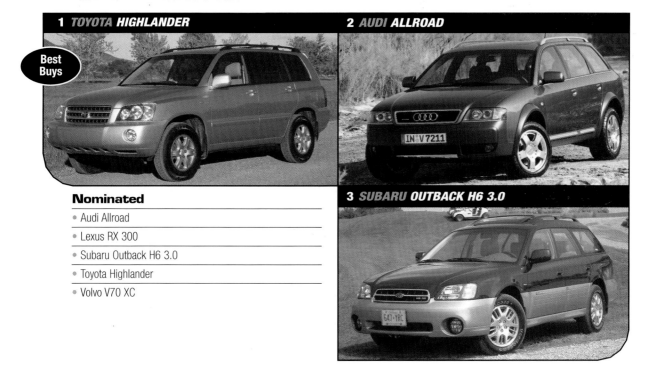

1 *TOYOTA* HIGHLANDER

Best Buys

2 *AUDI* ALLROAD

3 *SUBARU* OUTBACK H6 3.0

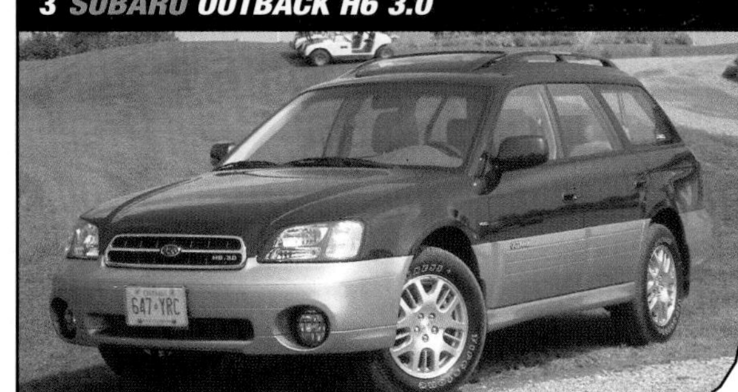

Nominated

- Audi Allroad
- Lexus RX 300
- Subaru Outback H6 3.0
- Toyota Highlander
- Volvo V70 XC

CAR OF THE YEAR

Candidates

- Acura RSX
- Audi A4
- Audi S8
- Chevrolet TrailBlazer / GMC Envoy
- Ford Thunderbird
- Infiniti I35
- Infiniti Q45
- Jaguar X-Type
- Jeep Liberty
- Kia Sedona
- Lexus ES 300
- Mazda Protegé/Protegé5
- Mercedes-Benz Coupe C230
- Nissan Altima
- Subaru Impreza WRX
- Toyota Camry
- Volkswagen Passat

Nominated

- Audi A4
- Ford Thunderbird
- Jeep Liberty
- Mazda Protegé5
- Mercedes-Benz Coupe C230
- Nissan Altima
- Subaru Impreza WRX

MAZDA PROTEGÉ5

The Winner

Which one do you like? red or blue?

BY ALAIN MORIN

In real life the time always comes when the big decisions have to be made. "Should I wait a while longer before changing my 1985 Hyundai Stellar?" agonizes one undecided soul. "Honey, as soon as we get up this morning, we're going to get a new car!" says Mrs. Go-Getter. No matter what camp you belong to, *The Auto Guide* has compiled the following tables in the hope of helping to make your choices a little easier.

The tables provide information about the pros and cons of various makes, as well as pointing out pitfalls that could ruin your bank balance. We also include a brief summary of major recalls for vehicles affected with a serious mechanical problem. On this subject, Transport-Canada's website is a useful source of information (www.tc.gc.ca). For its part, the NHTSA (National Highway Traffic Safety Administration) offers complete crash-test reports and recall notices on its own site, www.nhtsa.dot.gov.

The price list represents ballpark figures – the lowest refer to cars with minimum equipment and a lot of mileage, while at the other end of the spectrum you'll find prices for high-end cars with few miles on the odometer. But chances are you can still find cheaper or more expensive cars, since not every option has been considered here. As always, the most sensible thing to do is to rely on your own informed judgement. The information provided in these pages deals, of course, in generalities. A Toyota Corolla always gets high marks for reliability, but if the previous owners didn't take care of it and drove it as if it were a 4X4, then a less familiar vehicle will make a better choice. When all's said and done, it's your decision.

ACURA INTEGRA

Recommended model years:

- 1995 - 2000.

Best features:

- Above-average reliability.
- Suitable for sport-driving.

Worst features:

- Cost of some parts unacceptably high.
- Frequent repairs after the first 4 or 5 years.

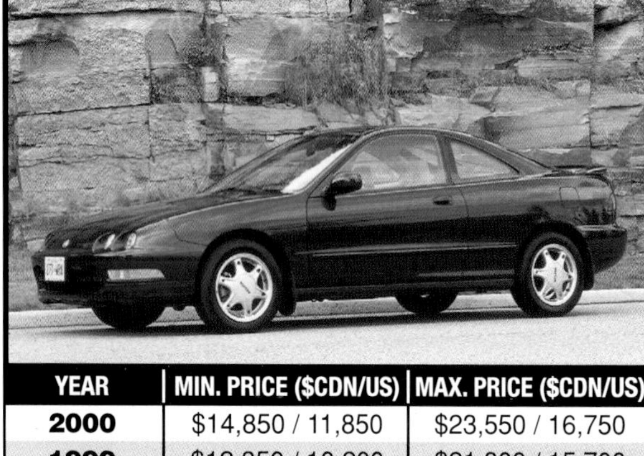

YEAR	MIN. PRICE ($CDN/US)	MAX. PRICE ($CDN/US)
2000	$14,850 / 11,850	$23,550 / 16,750
1999	$12,850 / 10,200	$21,300 / 15,700
1998	$9,800 / 7,400	$19,800 / 14,250
1997	$8,600 / 6,400	$16,950 / 13,600
1996	$6,650 / 5,250	$14,500 / 12,250
1995	$5,800 / 3,900	$12,250 / 11,050

Add 5% for a GS-R and 15% for a Type R.

What you should know:

- Climate-control air compressor has very short life expectancy.
- Alternator has short lifespan.
- Brakes wear out quickly (for a sports car, this means frequent replacements, and that adds up fast!)

Major recalls:

- None.

Occupant safety:

- Front crash: 7 stars out of 10.
- Side crash: n.a.

***Auto Guide* Verdict:**

- If the car in question has been well maintained, grab it!

ACURA TL

Recommended model years:

- 1996 - 2000 (new model in 1999).

Best features:

- Very, very, very reliable. Can't repeat it often enough.

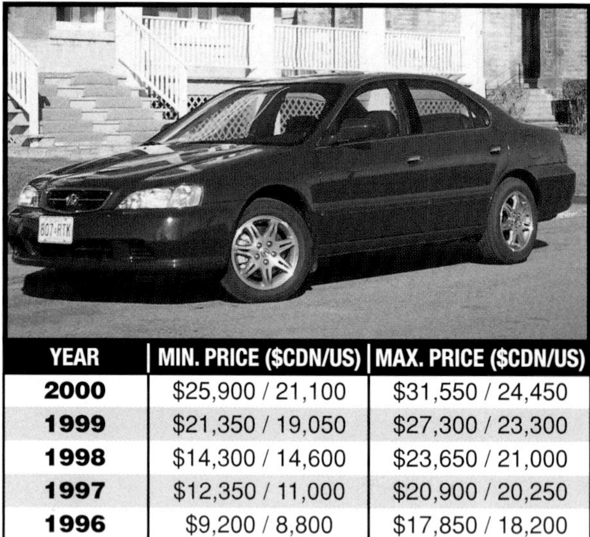

YEAR	MIN. PRICE ($CDN/US)	MAX. PRICE ($CDN/US)
2000	$25,900 / 21,100	$31,550 / 24,450
1999	$21,350 / 19,050	$27,300 / 23,300
1998	$14,300 / 14,600	$23,650 / 21,000
1997	$12,350 / 11,000	$20,900 / 20,250
1996	$9,200 / 8,800	$17,850 / 18,200

Worst features:

- Uneven finish, dashboard presentation sometimes erratic.
- Rear seats do not fold, making trunk space limited.

What you should know:

- Problems are few and far between.
- "Check engine" warning light may illuminate for no apparent reason, possibly due to a defective sensor.
- One owner warns about a problem with the headlight switch, another complains about windows that "whistled."

Major recalls:

- 1) Acura 2.5 TL (1996 -1998 models): Replacement of front-suspension lower ball joints on 10,190 units;
  2) Acura 3.2 TLS (1996 -1998 models): new transmission's case bolts on 5689 units.

Occupant safety:

- Front crash: 7 stars out of 10.
- Side crash: n.a.

***Auto Guide* Verdict:**

- Has one of the best quality/price ratios on the market.

BMW 3 SERIES

Recommended model years:

- 318i: 1995 - 1999
- 323i: 1998 - 2000
- 328i: 1996 - 2000
- M3: 1997 - 2000

Best features:

- Unsurpassed driving pleasure.
- Solid build.

Worst features:

- Reliability not always impressive after five years.
- Exorbitant maintenance and repair costs.

What you should know:

- A few electrical problems on models built before 1998.
- Fragile climate-control compressor.
- Requires more frequent maintenance after five years.

Major recalls:

- More than 17,000 BMWs, built between 1994 and 1997 (and not just the 3 Series) have been recalled for their inadequate cruise control.

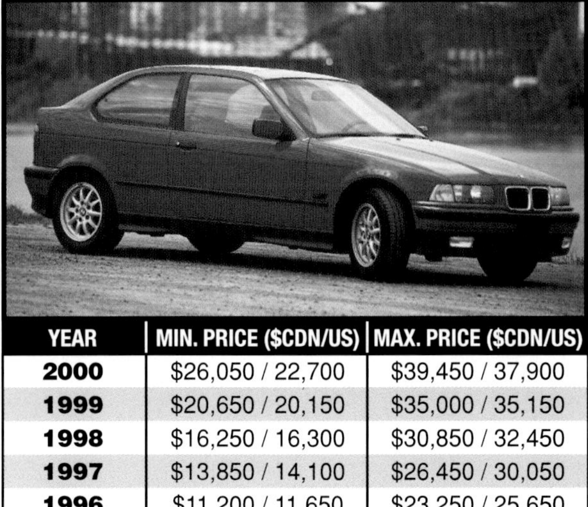

YEAR	MIN. PRICE ($CDN/US)	MAX. PRICE ($CDN/US)
2000	$26,050 / 22,700	$39,450 / 37,900
1999	$20,650 / 20,150	$35,000 / 35,150
1998	$16,250 / 16,300	$30,850 / 32,450
1997	$13,850 / 14,100	$26,450 / 30,050
1996	$11,200 / 11,650	$23,250 / 25,650
1995	$9,200 / 9,850	$18,600 / 22,400

Exclusivity has its own cost. So expect to shell out an extra 35% for an M3, but deduct 15% for a Ti. You're in for an excellent deal!

Occupant safety:

- Front crash: 8 stars out of 10.
- Side crash: n.a.

***Auto Guide* Verdict:**

- Extended warranty highly recommended, but you'll enjoy the drive!

CADILLAC DEVILLE

Recommended model years:

- 1995 - 2000 (new model in 2000).

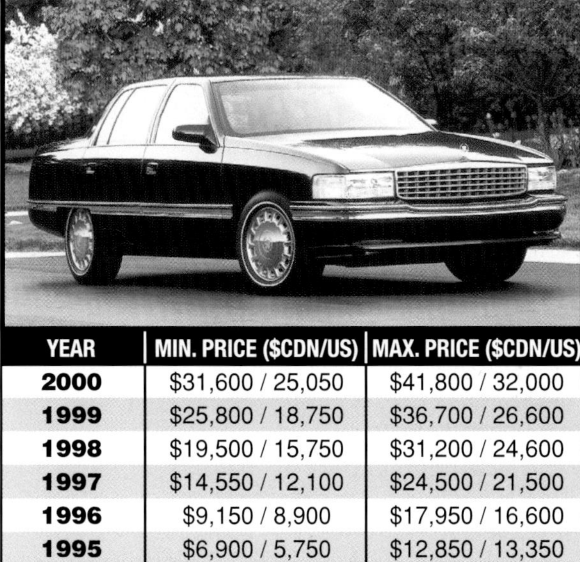

YEAR	MIN. PRICE ($CDN/US)	MAX. PRICE ($CDN/US)
2000	$31,600 / 25,050	$41,800 / 32,000
1999	$25,800 / 18,750	$36,700 / 26,600
1998	$19,500 / 15,750	$31,200 / 24,600
1997	$14,550 / 12,100	$24,500 / 21,500
1996	$9,150 / 8,900	$17,950 / 16,600
1995	$6,900 / 5,750	$12,850 / 13,350

Best features:

- "Certified" roominess.
- Excellent finish.

Worst features:

- Oversized body.
- Significant depreciation.

What you should know:

- Unreliable engine-temperature gauge.
- Otherwise, little information is available. But since it's a GM car, it's safe to expect only average reliability at best.

Major recalls:

- 1) 1997 model: New electronic brake control module on 7303 units; 2) 1998-1999 models: The Side Impact Sensor Modules in 5245 units may have flaws that can cause the driver or passenger airbag to deploy inadvertently.

Occupant safety:

- Front crash: 6 stars out of 10. (worse than a Pontiac Firefly!).
- Side crash: 8 stars out of 10.

***Auto Guide* Verdict:**

- A good deal only if you don't mind the Cadillac brand's senior-citizen aura.

CHEVROLET CAVALIER /PONTIAC SUNFIRE

Recommended model years:

- 1995 - 2000.

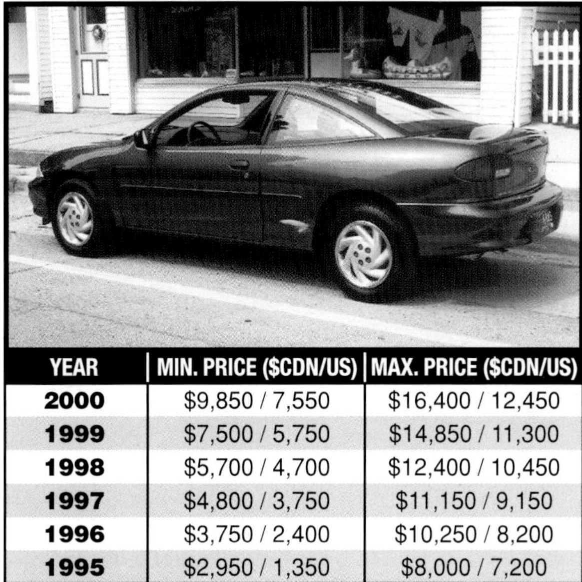

YEAR	MIN. PRICE ($CDN/US)	MAX. PRICE ($CDN/US)
2000	$9,850 / 7,550	$16,400 / 12,450
1999	$7,500 / 5,750	$14,850 / 11,300
1998	$5,700 / 4,700	$12,400 / 10,450
1997	$4,800 / 3,750	$11,150 / 9,150
1996	$3,750 / 2,400	$10,250 / 8,200
1995	$2,950 / 1,350	$8,000 / 7,200

You might have to fork over an extra 20% for a convertible. In other words, more money for less car...

Best features:

- Good handling.
- Cost of parts generally reasonable.

Worst features:

- Uneven construction quality.
- Unpleasant ABS brakes.

What you should know:

- Totally unreliable alternator.
- Steering rack and climate-control compressor are perpetual problems.
- For more information, contact the Automobile Protection Association (APA).

Major recalls:

- Too many, and not just for minor problems.

Occupant safety:

- Front crash: 8 stars out of 10.
- Side crash: 4 stars out of 10.

***Auto Guide* Verdict:**

- Buying a Cavalier or a Sunfire is like trying to cross a busy highway. So make sure you look both ways before plunging in.

CHEVROLET CORVETTE

Recommended model years:

- 1995 - 2000 (new model in 1997).

Best features:

- Sports car with a capital S.
- Unbeatable price/quality ratio.

Worst features:

- Roller-coaster comfort (cars built before 1997).
- Uneven finish.

What you should know:

- Some cases of water penetration in the cockpit.
- The clutch (manual transmission, of course) may slip or not engage properly, even in new or slightly used cars.
- Oil leakage between the axles and the transmission.

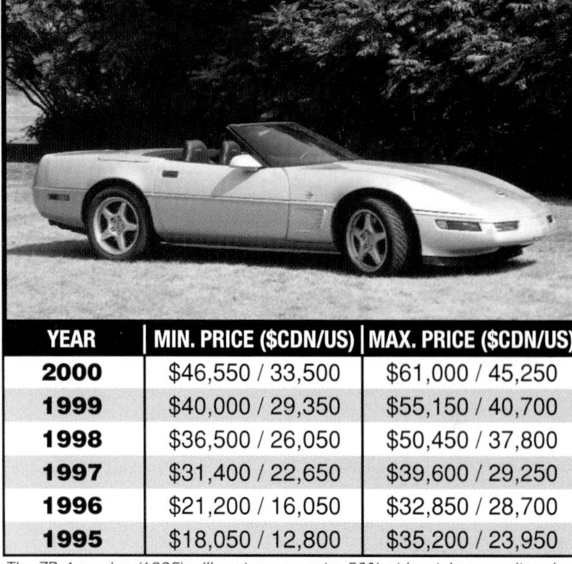

YEAR	MIN. PRICE ($CDN/US)	MAX. PRICE ($CDN/US)
2000	$46,550 / 33,500	$61,000 / 45,250
1999	$40,000 / 29,350	$55,150 / 40,700
1998	$36,500 / 26,050	$50,450 / 37,800
1997	$31,400 / 22,650	$39,600 / 29,250
1996	$21,200 / 16,050	$32,850 / 28,700
1995	$18,050 / 12,800	$35,200 / 23,950

The ZR-1 version (1995) will cost you an extra 50% at least, because its value will appreciate with time. Think of it as an investment!

Major recalls:

- Nothing significant. 2288 units (1997 to 2000 models) were recalled so dealers could install new seat belt retractor guides.

Occupant safety:

- Front crash: n.a.
- Side crash: n.a.

***Auto Guide* Verdict:**

- Take heart, it's not as small as you think.

CHEVROLET METRO/PONTIAC FIREFLY/SUZUKI SWIFT

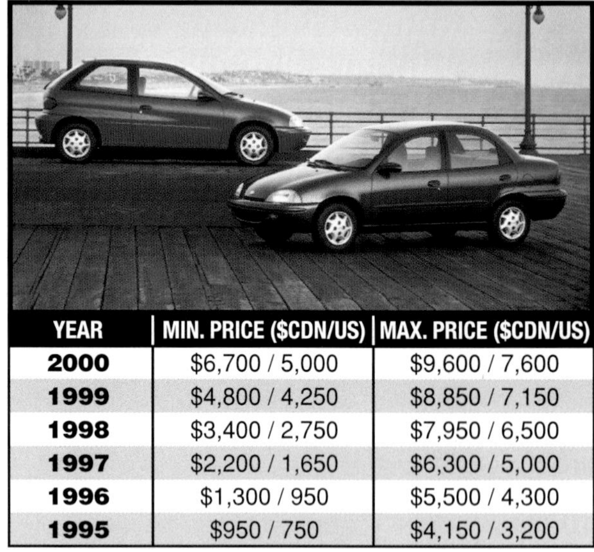

YEAR	MIN. PRICE ($CDN/US)	MAX. PRICE ($CDN/US)
2000	$6,700 / 5,000	$9,600 / 7,600
1999	$4,800 / 4,250	$8,850 / 7,150
1998	$3,400 / 2,750	$7,950 / 6,500
1997	$2,200 / 1,650	$6,300 / 5,000
1996	$1,300 / 950	$5,500 / 4,300
1995	$950 / 750	$4,150 / 3,200

Recommended model years:

- Geo Metro: 1995 - 1997
- Chevrolet Metro: 1998 - 2000.
- Firefly and Swift: 1995 - 2000.

Best features:

- Extremely low fuel consumption.
- Impressive cabin space, considering the car's exterior dimensions.

Worst features:

- For city driving only.
- Lifeless 3-cylinder engine.

What you should know:

- High-maintenance 3-cylinder engine.
- Brakes (disc/drum) need regular maintenance.
- Flimsy rear suspension.
- Cost of parts can be high. Shop around.

Major recalls:

- Replacement of the automatic-transmission gear selection mechanism on 2724 Metro, Swift and Firefly.

Occupant safety:

- Front crash: 8 stars out of 10.
- Side crash: n.a.

***Auto Guide* Verdict:**

- Perfect car in terms of fuel economy. Otherwise...

CHEVROLET S-10/GMC SONOMA /ISUZU HOMBRE

Recommended model years:

- Chevrolet S-10 / GMC Sonoma: 1995 - 2000.
- Isuzu Hombre: 1998 - 2000.

Best features:

- Excellent handling.
- Improved reliability.

Worst features:

- GM finish (that is, highly uneven).

What you should know:

- Fuel pump frequently malfunctions.
- Fragile front suspension and steering mechanism, even when not abused.
- Inadequate electric system.

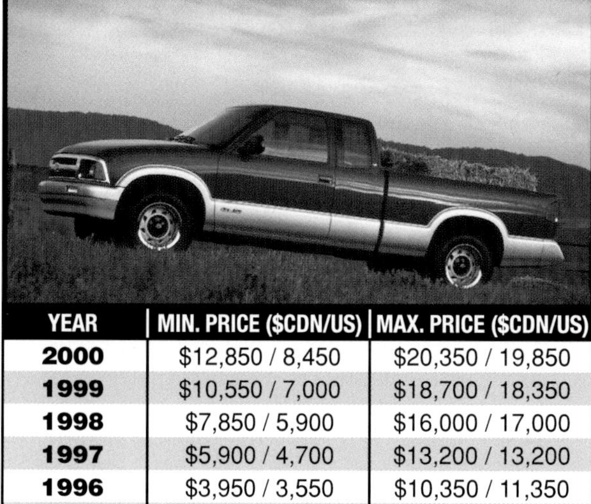

YEAR	MIN. PRICE ($CDN/US)	MAX. PRICE ($CDN/US)
2000	$12,850 / 8,450	$20,350 / 19,850
1999	$10,550 / 7,000	$18,700 / 18,350
1998	$7,850 / 5,900	$16,000 / 17,000
1997	$5,900 / 4,700	$13,200 / 13,200
1996	$3,950 / 3,550	$10,350 / 11,350
1995	$3,250 / 2,450	$8,000 / 9,250

The lowest prices apply to two-wheel drive pickups and the highest to four-wheel drive models.

Major recalls:

- More than 70,000 4WD models were recalled so dealers could replace the back pressure module valve assembly. These units may have had an ABS motor containing an out-of-specification spring clip.

Occupant safety:

- Front crash: 6 stars out of 10.
- Side crash: 4 stars out of 5.

***Auto Guide* Verdict:**

- Despite the many options designed to enhance driving pleasure, the S-10 remains essentially a workhorse.

CHRYSLER CIRRUS/DODGE STRATUS/PLYMOUTH BREEZE

Recommended model years:

- Cirrus: 1995 - 2000.
- Stratus: 1995 - 1999.
- Breeze: 1996 - 1999.

Best features:

- Nice-looking automobiles.
- Affordable prices.

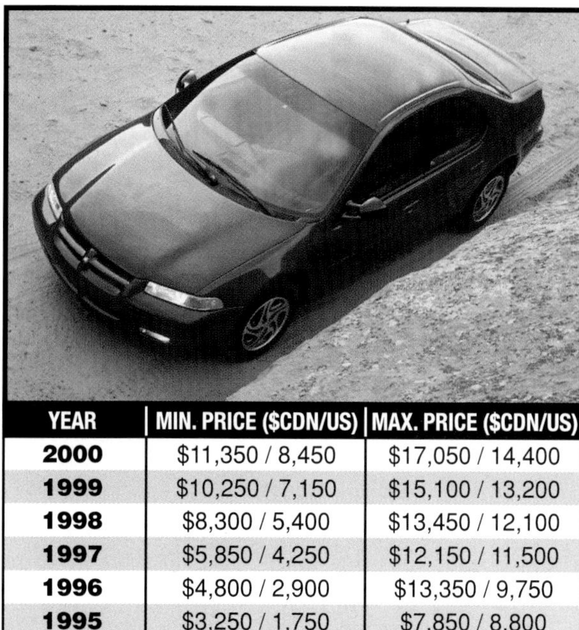

YEAR	MIN. PRICE ($CDN/US)	MAX. PRICE ($CDN/US)
2000	$11,350 / 8,450	$17,050 / 14,400
1999	$10,250 / 7,150	$15,100 / 13,200
1998	$8,300 / 5,400	$13,450 / 12,100
1997	$5,850 / 4,250	$12,150 / 11,500
1996	$4,800 / 2,900	$13,350 / 9,750
1995	$3,250 / 1,750	$7,850 / 8,800

Worst features:

- Poor resale value.
- 2.0-liter 4-cylinder engine.

What you should know:

- Front brakes overheat easily.
- Rear wheel bearings fragile and expensive to repair.
- Unreliable air conditioner.
- Troublesome cylinder head (2.0-liter engine).

Major recalls:

- 1) 1995-1998 models: Replacement of the shifter-ignition switch interlock mechanism in more than 60,000 units ; 2) 1995-1997 models: 53,000 units were recalled because the lower control arm ball joint was found to be at risk of breaking due to loss of lubrication, a situation that could result in a loss of vehicle control.

Occupant safety:

- Front crash: 7 stars out of 10.
- Side crash: 5 stars out of 10.

***Auto Guide* Verdict:**

- If you're really that fond of these hot-looking cars, at least avoid the 1995 and 1996 models, as well as those equipped with the 2.0-liter engine.

CHRYSLER CONCORDE, INTREPID/EAGLE VISION

Recommended model years:

- Chrysler Concorde, Intrepid: 1995 - 2000 (new model in 1998).
- Eagle Vision: 1995 - 1997.

Best features:

- First-rate comfort.
- Generous trunk space.

Worst features:

- Not terribly reliable.
- Lightning-speed depreciation.

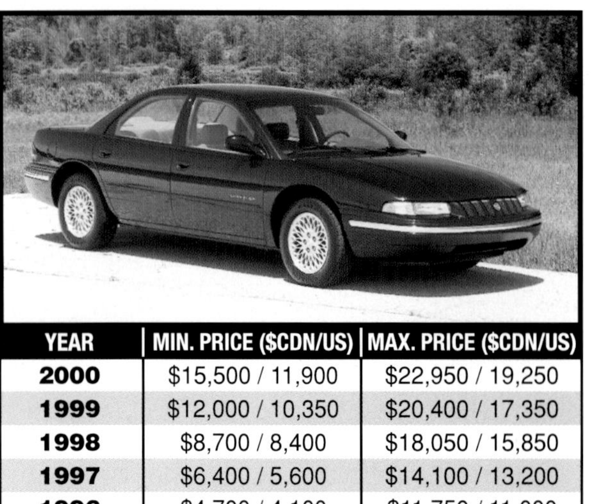

YEAR	MIN. PRICE ($CDN/US)	MAX. PRICE ($CDN/US)
2000	$15,500 / 11,900	$22,950 / 19,250
1999	$12,000 / 10,350	$20,400 / 17,350
1998	$8,700 / 8,400	$18,050 / 15,850
1997	$6,400 / 5,600	$14,100 / 13,200
1996	$4,700 / 4,100	$11,750 / 11,000
1995	$3,400 / 2,350	$9,100 / 8,500

What you should know:

- Electrical system barely adequate.
- 3.5-liter engine overheats easily, has weak timing belt.
- High repair bills.
- Unreliable steering rack-and-pinion mechanism.

Major recalls:

- 1) 1993-1997 models: The fuel injection system in 58,470 units received a new gasket; 2) 1993-1997 models:17,530 units were recalled to be fitted with a new safety belt anchor.

Occupant safety:

- Front crash: 8 stars out of 10.
- Side crash: 7 stars out of 10.

***Auto Guide* Verdict:**

- "The flesh is weak..." The Concorde, Intrepid and Vision are so good-looking that you can forgive almost everything. Unfortunately.

CHRYSLER TOWN & COUNTRY /DODGE CARAVAN/PLYMOUTH VOYAGER

Recommended model years:

- 1995 - 2000 (new model in 1996).
- Plymouth Voyager discontinued in 2000.

Best features:

- Roomy and comfortable.
- Used spare parts readily available and generally at reasonable cost.

Worst features:

- Uneven quality of finish.
- Inadequate 4-cylinder engine.
- Attractive to car thieves.

What you should know:

- Saddled with many problems : fragile steering rack and pinion, 4-speed automatic transmission, differential, air conditioner, you name it. Check with APA.

YEAR	MIN. PRICE ($CDN/US)	MAX. PRICE ($CDN/US)
2000	$15,800 / 10,850	$26,400 / 26,850
1999	$12,300 / 8,650	$23,050 / 21,750
1998	$9,400 / 7,300	$19,950 / 18,950
1997	$7,750 / 6,000	$16,700 / 17,450
1996	$4,950 / 4,450	$13,850 / 13,300
1995	$3,750 / 3,300	$10,900 / 10,950

The more upscale Chrysler Town & Countrys may cost 20 to 30% more.

Major recalls:

- 180,000 units (1996 to 2000 models) were recalled so they could be fitted with a new gasket to prevent fuel leakage; another 130,000 units experienced electrical problems relating to the airbags. For information on other recalls, consult the Transport Canada and NHTSA websites.

Occupant safety:

- Front crash: 8 stars out of 10.
- Side crash: 10 stars out of 10.

***Auto Guide* Verdict:**

- Make sure your bank account is well lined, just in case.

DODGE NEON

Recommended model years:

- Dodge Neon: 1995 - 1999.
- Chrysler Neon: 2000.

Best features:

- Stylish body.
- New Neon 2000.

Worst features:

- The following points concern first-generation models (1995-1999):
- Flimsy construction.
- Phenomenal depreciation.

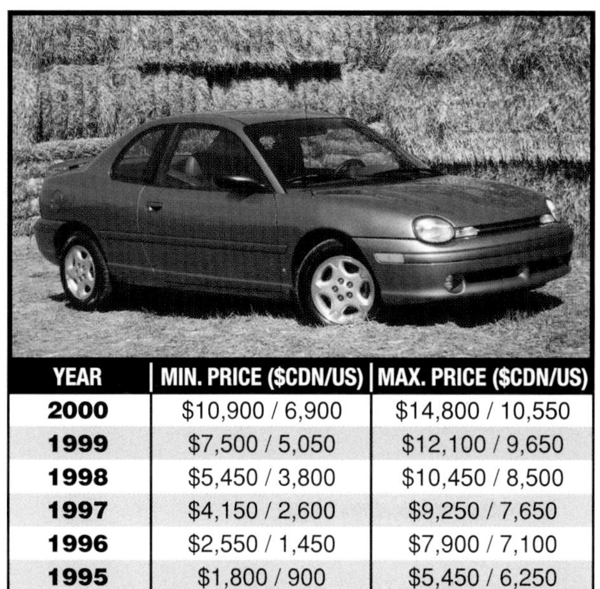

YEAR	MIN. PRICE ($CDN/US)	MAX. PRICE ($CDN/US)
2000	$10,900 / 6,900	$14,800 / 10,550
1999	$7,500 / 5,050	$12,100 / 9,650
1998	$5,450 / 3,800	$10,450 / 8,500
1997	$4,150 / 2,600	$9,250 / 7,650
1996	$2,550 / 1,450	$7,900 / 7,100
1995	$1,800 / 900	$5,450 / 6,250

What you should know:

- Water pump, electric system, automatic transmission, cylinder head (2.0-liter engine), air conditioner, paint job – all leave something to be desired.
- Consult the APA, NHTSA and Transport Canada websites.

Major recalls:

- 59,641 units of the 1995 model were recalled because of an inadequate steering column coupling, while almost 35,000 other units were found to have fuel and rear-brake lines that were too easily corroded.

Occupant safety:

- Front crash: 8 stars out of 10.
- Side crash: 6 stars out of 10.

***Auto Guide* Verdict:**

- The 2000 models are far and away the best. Earlier Neons are too risky.

FORD ESCORT

Recommended model years:

- 1995 - 2000.

Best features:

- Escorts built in 1997 and thereafter enjoy excellent reliability.
- For models up to 1996, spare parts are readily available at reasonable cost.

Worst features:

- Noisy engine.
- Assembly quality subpar at times.

What you should know:

- Automatic transmission (courtesy of Mazda) can be unreliable, especially after 60,000 miles (100,000 km). Be prepared for significant maintenance costs.
- Disc brakes do not last long.
- Frequent leaks in engine and transmission main seals.

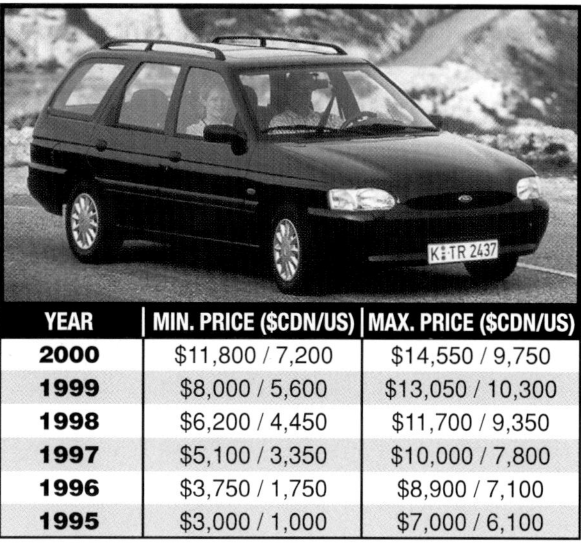

YEAR	MIN. PRICE ($CDN/US)	MAX. PRICE ($CDN/US)
2000	$11,800 / 7,200	$14,550 / 9,750
1999	$8,000 / 5,600	$13,050 / 10,300
1998	$6,200 / 4,450	$11,700 / 9,350
1997	$5,100 / 3,350	$10,000 / 7,800
1996	$3,750 / 1,750	$8,900 / 7,100
1995	$3,000 / 1,000	$7,000 / 6,100

Major recalls:

- Only two campaigns, affecting less than 8000 units (1995-2000 models).

Occupant safety:

- Front crash: 6 stars out of 10.
- Side crash: 6 stars out of 10.

***Auto Guide* Verdict:**

- The best Escorts were made in 1997 and after. Earlier models were not always up to standard.

FORD MUSTANG

Recommended model years:

- 1995 - 2000.

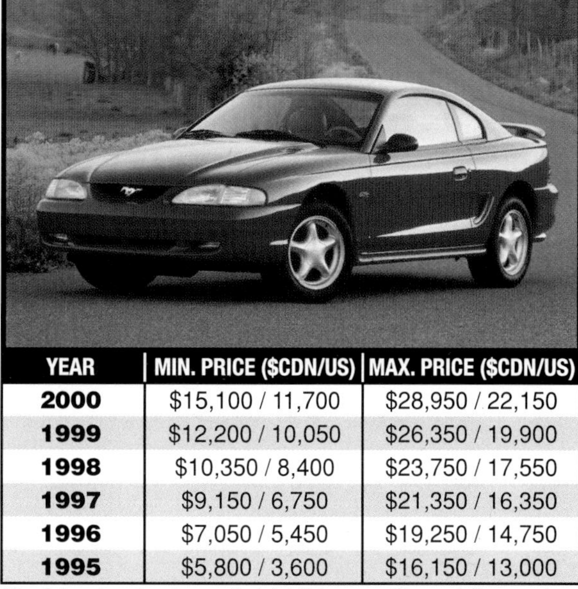

YEAR	MIN. PRICE ($CDN/US)	MAX. PRICE ($CDN/US)
2000	$15,100 / 11,700	$28,950 / 22,150
1999	$12,200 / 10,050	$26,350 / 19,900
1998	$10,350 / 8,400	$23,750 / 17,550
1997	$9,150 / 6,750	$21,350 / 16,350
1996	$7,050 / 5,450	$19,250 / 14,750
1995	$5,800 / 3,600	$16,150 / 13,000

King Cobras have long been extinct, but Cobras are still around. If you want one, add 15% to the highest prices, 25% for an SVT.

Best features:
- Reasonable cost of spare parts.
- First-rate performance (V8).

Worst features:
- Poor traction on wet or slippery surfaces.
- May have been driven (too) hard.

What you should know:
- Several steering rack problems.
- Anti-freeze leakage between engine block and intake manifold (V6).
- Rod ends tend to wear out prematurely.

Major recalls:
- 62,645 units were recalled because the bond between the hood and inner insulation pad was at risk of separating. Additional adhesive was subsequently applied. Another recall involved 35,668 units, which were fitted with a new cruise control cable.

Occupant safety:
- Front crash: 8 stars out of 10.
- Side crash: 6 stars out of 10.

***Auto Guide* Verdict:**
- Sports cars are addictive, but for your own sake, don't get carried away. An in-depth inspection is a must.

FORD F SERIES

Recommended model years:
- 1995 - 2000 (new model in 1996).

Best features:
- Very reliable.
- Comfortable vehicle.

Worst features:
- Gas guzzler.
- Uneven finish.

What you should know:
- Starter has short lifespan.
- A few cases of corrosion affecting the hydraulic fluid containers.
- Dashboard tends to crack in cold weather.

YEAR	MIN. PRICE ($CDN/US)	MAX. PRICE ($CDN/US)
2000	$16,550 / 10,050	$20,150 / 22,600
1999	$13,600 / 8,550	$18,450 / 21,000
1998	$9,750 / 7,600	$15,950 / 19,350
1997	$8,050 / 6,400	$13,650 / 17,550
1996	$6,200 / 5,350	$11,000 / 14,100
1995	$5,150 / 3,900	$8,800 / 12,400

Expect to fork over an extra $800 for an XL or XLT, and up to $1100 for an Eddie Bauer. And as for SVTs (1999-2000), hang on to your wallet. They're worth almost twice as much as the highest quotes here.

Major recalls:
- 1) 1997-1998 models: 141,580 units (F-150 and F-250) received new, stronger wheel nuts; 2) 1999-2000 models: 114,791 units were recalled because the circuit controlling the daytime running headlights tended to corrode. Other recalls were not as significant.

Occupant safety:
- Front crash: 9 stars out of 10.
- Side crash: 5 stars out of 5.

***Auto Guide* Verdict:**
- A bona fide workhorse.

FORD WINDSTAR

Recommended model years:
- 1995 - 2000.

YEAR	MIN. PRICE ($CDN/US)	MAX. PRICE ($CDN/US)
2000	$16,500 / 12,700	$26,600 / 24,250
1999	$13,250 / 10,650	$23,700 / 20,850
1998	$9,850 / 8,000	$20,050 / 17,500
1997	$8,500 / 7,250	$15,850 / 14,300
1996	$6,650 / 5,200	$13,200 / 11,450
1995	$4,700 / 4,200	$10,600 / 11,150

For the humbler Cargo version, deduct 10%.

Best features:
- Ultra safe minivan.
- Huge cockpit.

Worst features:
- Rust-prone body.
- Not always reliable.

What you should know:
- Fragile cylinder head gaskets (3.8-liter engine). Check with APA about extended warranty or special repair discounts.
- Automatic transmission (1995-1996 models) wears out as fast as miles are accumulated on the odometer (once again, APA is an excellent source on the subject).

Major recalls:
- 166,223 were recalled so a maintenance instructions sticker could be stuck on the front of the brake fluid reservoir. As

with the Ford Mustang, the bond between the hood panel and inner insulation pad on some units was at risk of separating. For other recalls, consult Transport Canada and NHTSA websites.

Occupant safety:
- Front crash: 10 stars out of 10.
- Side crash: 10 stars out of 10.

***Auto Guide* Verdict:**
- Maybe, as long as you avoid the 1995 - 1997 models.

HONDA ACCORD

Recommended model years:
- 1995 - 2000 (new model in 1998).

Best features:
- Surefire reliability.
- Guaranteed quality.

Worst features:
- Unacceptably high asking price.
- Popular with car thieves.

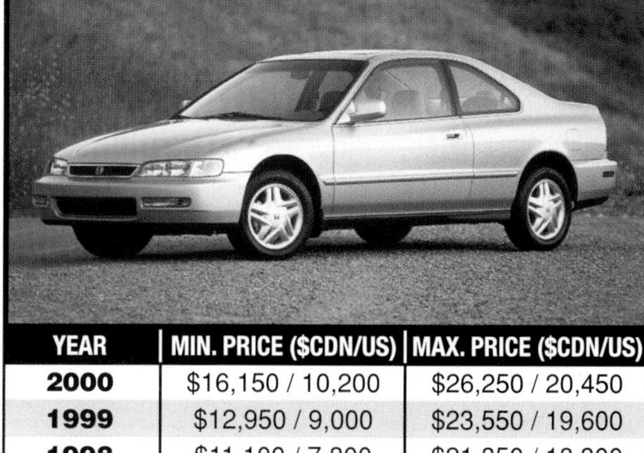

YEAR	MIN. PRICE ($CDN/US)	MAX. PRICE ($CDN/US)
2000	$16,150 / 10,200	$26,250 / 20,450
1999	$12,950 / 9,000	$23,550 / 19,600
1998	$11,100 / 7,800	$21,850 / 18,300
1997	$9,100 / 6,500	$18,950 / 17,150
1996	$6,900 / 5,450	$16,000 / 15,650
1995	$6,200 / 4,050	$12,900 / 13,950

What you should know:
- Risk of defective air conditioner after four or five years.
- Front end of exhaust system not all that resistant.
- Steering rack bound to wear out long before the other components.

Major recalls:
- 1) 1995-1997 models: 50,466 units received a new air-conditioner wire harness; 2) 1998 model: 10,000 units were given new front-suspension ball joints.

Occupant safety:
- Front crash: 8 stars out of 10.
- Side crash: 9 stars out of 10.

***Auto Guide* Verdict:**
- You're more likely to wear out before the Accord. Beware if the asking price seems abnormally low: you're probably dealing with a car that was rebuilt after a major crash.

HONDA CIVIC

Recommended model years:
- 1995 - 2000 (new model in 1996).

Best features:
- Honda reliability.
- Excellent fuel economy.

Worst features:
- Popular with car thieves.
- Usually high price.

What you should know:
- The rubber boots protecting the CV-joints tend to crack prematurely.
- Fragile exhaust system (between catalytic converter and auxiliary muffler).
- Rear suspension bearings wear out too quickly.

Major recalls:
- 21,000 units of the 1996 model were recalled to clean a hose in the power-brake system, while 3000 others saw their passenger-side airbag module repaired.

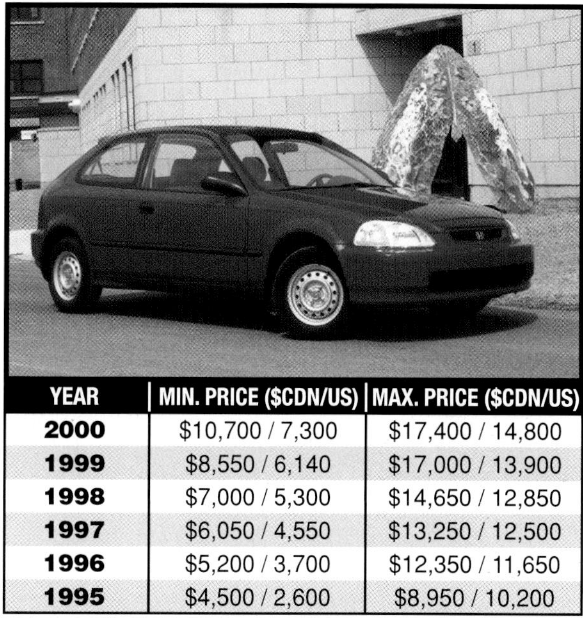

YEAR	MIN. PRICE ($CDN/US)	MAX. PRICE ($CDN/US)
2000	$10,700 / 7,300	$17,400 / 14,800
1999	$8,550 / 6,140	$17,000 / 13,900
1998	$7,000 / 5,300	$14,650 / 12,850
1997	$6,050 / 4,550	$13,250 / 12,500
1996	$5,200 / 3,700	$12,350 / 11,650
1995	$4,500 / 2,600	$8,950 / 10,200

For the gorgeous Si-R and Del Sol, add 10 and 20% respectively.

Occupant safety:
- Front crash: 8 stars out of 10.
- Side crash: 6 stars out of 10.

***Auto Guide* Verdict:**
- Excellent buy. If the price is too low, watch out. If you want to buy a Si, check insurance rates before signing anything.

HYUNDAI ACCENT

Recommended model years:
- 1995 - 2000.

Best features:
- Perfect car for low-budget buyers.
- Engine shines.

Worst features:
- Rust-prone body.
- Poor resale value.

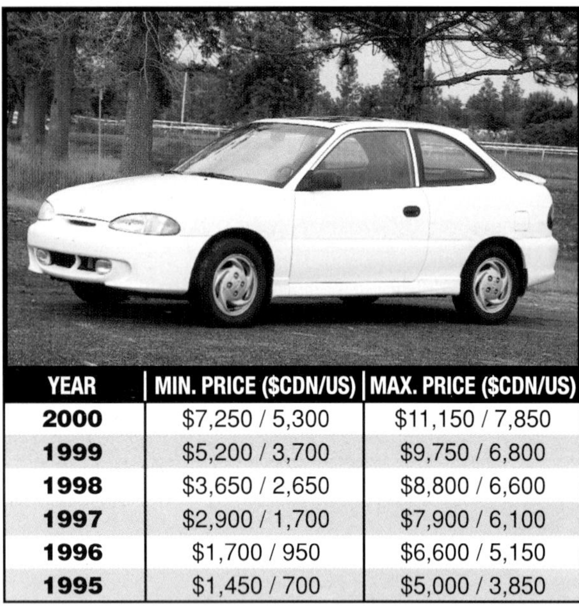

YEAR	MIN. PRICE ($CDN/US)	MAX. PRICE ($CDN/US)
2000	$7,250 / 5,300	$11,150 / 7,850
1999	$5,200 / 3,700	$9,750 / 6,800
1998	$3,650 / 2,650	$8,800 / 6,600
1997	$2,900 / 1,700	$7,900 / 6,100
1996	$1,700 / 950	$6,600 / 5,150
1995	$1,450 / 700	$5,000 / 3,850

What you should know:
- Suspension comfortable but not durable.
- Exhaust and brake systems have short lifespan.

Major recalls:
- 1) 1995 - 1997 models: 25,575 units received protection to prevent broken front-suspension pieces from damaging the tire. 2) 1996 - 1997 models: 14,087 Accents and Elantras were recalled because the windshield wiper motor electrical contacts were found to be contaminated with soldering flux.

Occupant safety:
- Front crash: 7 stars out of 10.
- Side crash: n.a.

***Auto Guide* Verdict:**
- Who cares if it's not as exciting as a Ferrari. The price is right!

HYUNDAI ELANTRA

Recommended model years:
- 1995 - 2000 (new model in 1997).

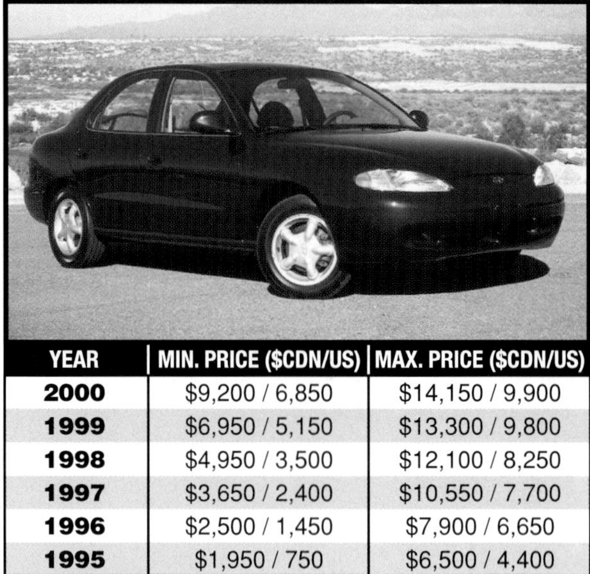

YEAR	MIN. PRICE ($CDN/US)	MAX. PRICE ($CDN/US)
2000	$9,200 / 6,850	$14,150 / 9,900
1999	$6,950 / 5,150	$13,300 / 9,800
1998	$4,950 / 3,500	$12,100 / 8,250
1997	$3,650 / 2,400	$10,550 / 7,700
1996	$2,500 / 1,450	$7,900 / 6,650
1995	$1,950 / 750	$6,500 / 4,400

Best features:
- Complete equipment.
- Poor fuel economy.

Worst features:
- Not always reliable.
- Barely average resale value.

What you should know:
- Design and build of electrical circuits below par.
- Starter tends to fail in extreme cold.
- Front shock absorber brackets can break at the welds.

Major recalls:
- See Hyundai Accent regarding the campaign involving 14,087 Hyundais. Furthermore, 12,654 Elantras and Tiburons had their fuel-filler caps replaced.

Occupant safety:
- Front crash: 9 stars out of 10.
- Side crash: 9 stars out of 10.

N. B.: Other side-crash tests conducted on Elantras not equipped with side-impact airbags, yielded only 4 out of ten stars.

***Auto Guide* Verdict:**
- The Korean automaker is a quick study. Since 1997, Elantras have improved significantly.

JEEP GRAND CHEROKEE

Recommended model years:
- 1995 - 2000 (new model in 1999).

Best features:
- Impressive off-road capabilities.
- Guaranteed comfort.

Worst features:
- Ridiculously unreliable.
- Fuel and maintenance costs out of this world.

YEAR	MIN. PRICE ($CDN/US)	MAX. PRICE ($CDN/US)
2000	$19,250 / 13,550	$29,700 / 21,800
1999	$15,150 / 11,100	$26,250 / 19,600
1998	$12,300 / 9,050	$23,650 / 19,050
1997	$9,750 / 7,500	$19,850 / 15,800
1996	$7,800 / 6,200	$16,550 / 14,200
1995	$5,500 / 4,750	$13,050 / 12,300

What you should know:

- Automatic transmission, air conditioner, ABS, alternator, you name it, they all badly need work. And that's just the beginning...

Major recalls:

- 1) 1996-1998 models: 47,393 units received new front disc brakes ; 2) 1997 model: 22, 825 units had their electronically-controlled fuel gauges replaced; 3) 1999-2000 models: 17,530 units were given new safety belt anchor bolts.

Occupant safety:

- Front crash: 6 stars out of 10.
- Side crash: 9 stars out of 10.

***Auto Guide* Verdict:**

- Deluxe version of a Lada Niva

JEEP WRANGLER, TJ, YJ

Recommended model years:

- YJ: 1995 - 1996.
- TJ: 1997 - 1999.
- Wrangler: 2000.

Best features:

- Guaranteed all-terrain aptitudes.
- Magnetic-looking and timeless vehicle.

Worst features:

- Bumper-car comfort.
- Rust-prone paint job.

What you should know:

- Exhaust and fuel systems have short lifespans.
- Fragile differentials.
- Leak-prone clutch slave cylinder.

Major recalls:

- Certain 1997 Jeep TJs were recalled to replace their air bag electronic control module.

Occupant safety:

- Front crash: 8 stars out of 10.
- Side crash: n.a.

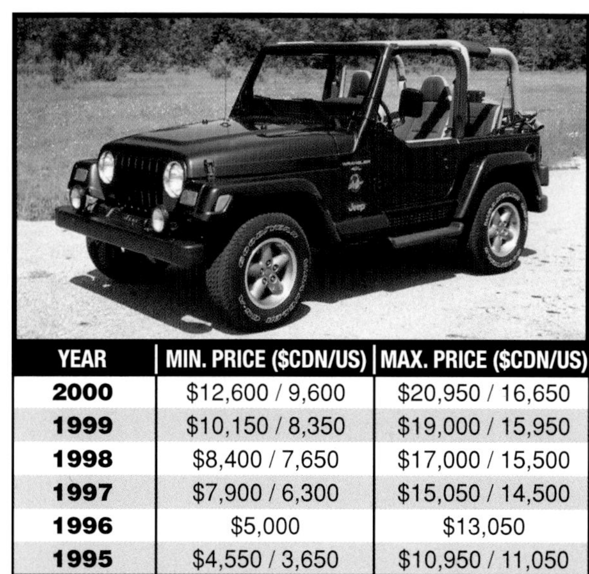

YEAR	MIN. PRICE ($CDN/US)	MAX. PRICE ($CDN/US)
2000	$12,600 / 9,600	$20,950 / 16,650
1999	$10,150 / 8,350	$19,000 / 15,950
1998	$8,400 / 7,650	$17,000 / 15,500
1997	$7,900 / 6,300	$15,050 / 14,500
1996	$5,000	$13,050
1995	$4,550 / 3,650	$10,950 / 11,050

***Auto Guide* Verdict:**

- Strictly for cavorting in the mud ...

MAZDA MIATA

Recommended model years:

- 1995 -1997, 1999 - 2000 (new model in 1999).

Best features:

- 2200 lbs (1000 kg) of undiluted pleasure.
- And reliable, to boot!

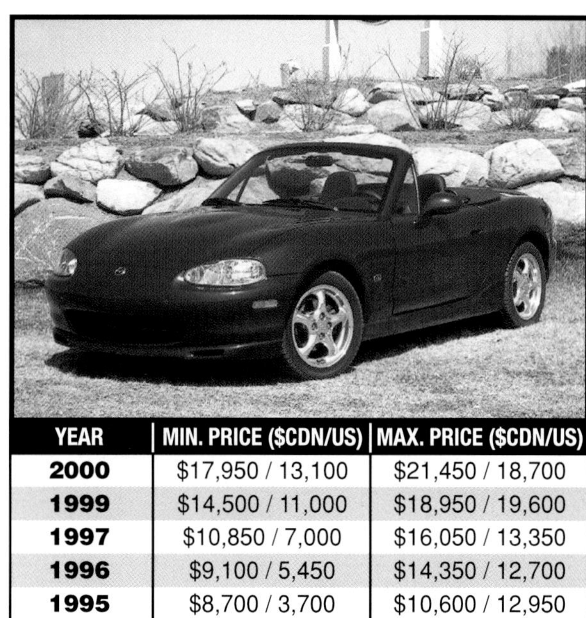

YEAR	MIN. PRICE ($CDN/US)	MAX. PRICE ($CDN/US)
2000	$17,950 / 13,100	$21,450 / 18,700
1999	$14,500 / 11,000	$18,950 / 19,600
1997	$10,850 / 7,000	$16,050 / 13,350
1996	$9,100 / 5,450	$14,350 / 12,700
1995	$8,700 / 3,700	$10,600 / 12,950

* The Miata was not produced in 1998

Worst features:

- Only two seats.
- Steep price.

What you should know:

- Tiny cockpit.
- Trunk is barely bigger than your lunchbox. Generally reliable car, except for cracks that may develop in the dashboard. In 1999, Mazda celebrated the Miata's 10th anniversary with a special edition that was well worth the extra 30% cost.

Major recalls:

- 1795 Miatas were recalled, some because of a faulty fuel injector ramp, others to receive a new fuel filler one-way valve.

Occupant safety:

- Front crash: 7 stars out of 10.
- Side crash: n.a.

***Auto Guide* Verdict:**

- It's a good thing that pleasure is no longer considered a sin.

MAZDA PROTEGÉ

Recommended model years:

- 1995 - 2000.

Best features:

- Highly reliable.
- 3-year/50,000-mile (80,000 km) warranty.
- Often less expensive than a Honda Civic or Toyota Corolla, with no reduction in quality.

YEAR	MIN. PRICE ($CDN/US)	MAX. PRICE ($CDN/US)
2000	$10,950 / 6,850	$14,950 / 11,200
1999	$8,600 / 5,700	$13,450 / 10,450
1998	$6,900 / 4,500	$12,150 / 9,500
1997	$5,450 / 3,650	$10,850 / 9,050
1996	$4,150 / 2,500	$9,300 / 7,700
1995	$3,850 / 1,650	$8,200 / 7,500

Worst features:

- High cost of some spare parts (especially brakes).
- Inadequate sound insulation.

What you should know:

- Fragile automatic transmission. • Muffler has short lifespan.
- Rust-prone body.

Major recalls:

- Insignificant. A mere 3820 Protegés –1999 vintage – were recalled so the air-conditioner wiring could be modified.

Occupant safety:

- Front crash: 8 stars out of 10.
- Side crash: 7 stars out of 10.

***Auto Guide* Verdict:**

- Strange name, but a totally conventional car. Well bred, though.

MERCEDES-BENZ C CLASS

Recommended model years:

- C220: 1995 - 1996.
- C230: 1997 - 2000.
- C280: 1995 - 2000.

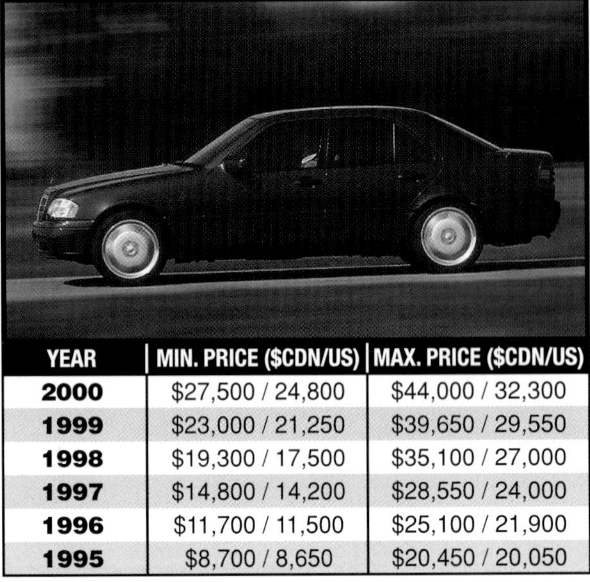

YEAR	MIN. PRICE ($CDN/US)	MAX. PRICE ($CDN/US)
2000	$27,500 / 24,800	$44,000 / 32,300
1999	$23,000 / 21,250	$39,650 / 29,550
1998	$19,300 / 17,500	$35,100 / 27,000
1997	$14,800 / 14,200	$28,550 / 24,000
1996	$11,700 / 11,500	$25,100 / 21,900
1995	$8,700 / 8,650	$20,450 / 20,050

Best features:

- Unbeatable long-term reliability.
- Slow depreciation (on the one hand...)

Worst features:

- Steep price (on the other...)
- High maintenance costs.

What you should know:

- A few cases involving broken front suspension coils springs.
- Central computer tends to fail after 50,000 miles (80,000 km), and its repair cost can go as high as a couple of thousand dollars. Check with APA to see if there might be some hidden warranty.

Major recalls:

- None

Occupant safety:

- Front crash: n.a.
- Side crash: 7 stars out of 10.

***Auto Guide* Verdict:**

- You've never driven a Mercedes? That's too bad.

NISSAN ALTIMA

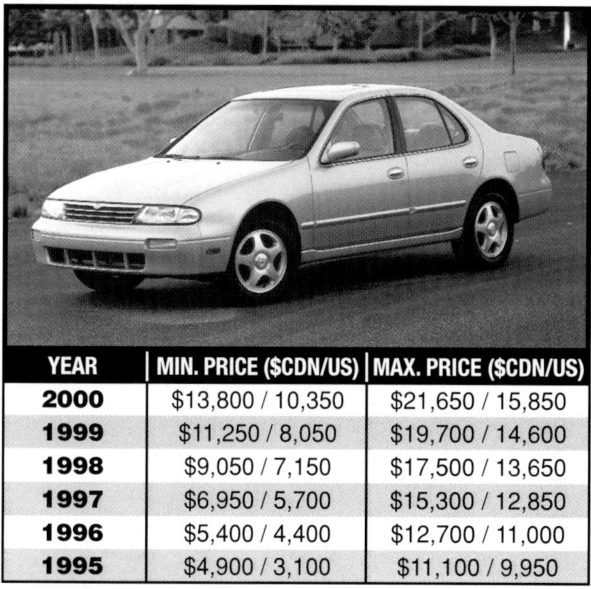

YEAR	MIN. PRICE ($CDN/US)	MAX. PRICE ($CDN/US)
2000	$13,800 / 10,350	$21,650 / 15,850
1999	$11,250 / 8,050	$19,700 / 14,600
1998	$9,050 / 7,150	$17,500 / 13,650
1997	$6,950 / 5,700	$15,300 / 12,850
1996	$5,400 / 4,400	$12,700 / 11,000
1995	$4,900 / 3,100	$11,100 / 9,950

Recommended model years:

- 1995 - 2000.

Best features:

- Solid build.
- Generally affordable prices.

Worst features:

- Spare parts more expensive than the competition (Accord, Camry, Mazda 626).
- Unresponsive steering.

What you should know:

- Rear drums tend to overheat.
- High oil consumption in certain Altimas with 87,500 miles (140 000 km) and up on the odometer.

Major recalls:

- 1132 Altimas (1997 model) received new rear-seat safety belts.

Occupant safety:

- Front crash: 9 stars out of 10.
- Side crash: 6 stars out of 10.

***Auto Guide* Verdict:**

- An ideal car if you want to travel incognito.

NISSAN MAXIMA

Recommended model years:

- 1995 - 2000 (new model in 2000).

Best features:

- Simple and reliable mechanicals.
- Affordable parts.

Worst features:

- Asking price sometimes unrealistic.
- Low feedback in the steering wheel.

What you should know:

- Muffler dislikes working overtime.
- Brakes not all that durable.
- Electric system often fails after 62,500 miles (100 000 km).

Major recalls:

- None.

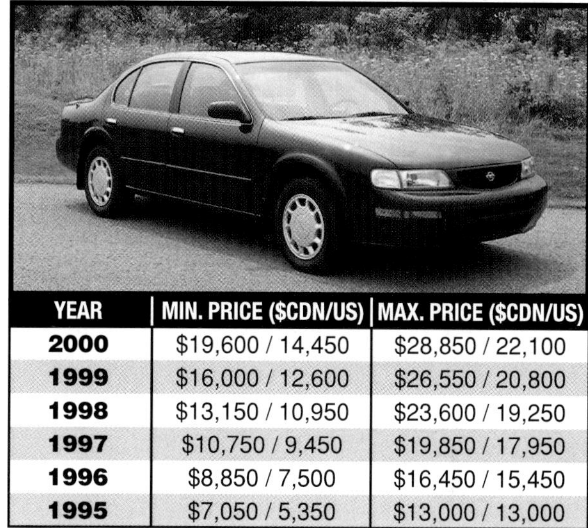

YEAR	MIN. PRICE ($CDN/US)	MAX. PRICE ($CDN/US)
2000	$19,600 / 14,450	$28,850 / 22,100
1999	$16,000 / 12,600	$26,550 / 20,800
1998	$13,150 / 10,950	$23,600 / 19,250
1997	$10,750 / 9,450	$19,850 / 17,950
1996	$8,850 / 7,500	$16,450 / 15,450
1995	$7,050 / 5,350	$13,000 / 13,000

Occupant safety:

- Front crash: 9 stars out of 10.
- Side crash: 6 stars out of 10.

***Auto Guide* Verdict:**

- Give me one good reason why you shouldn't buy a Maxima. "Too expensive?" Well, all right. Is there another reason? I'm waiting.

NISSAN PATHFINDER

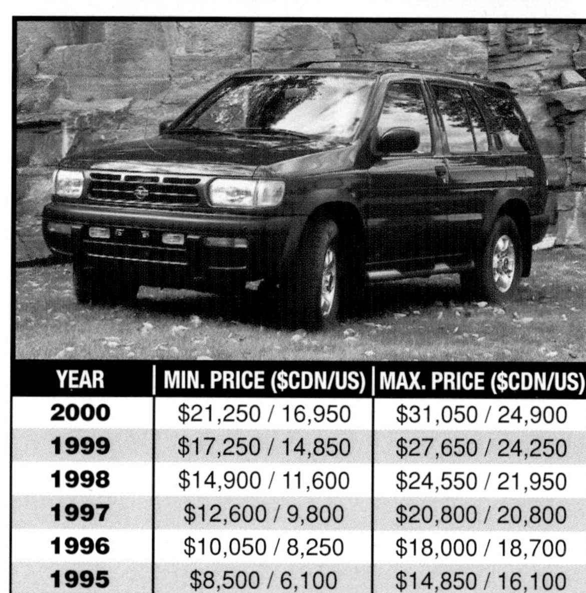

YEAR	MIN. PRICE ($CDN/US)	MAX. PRICE ($CDN/US)
2000	$21,250 / 16,950	$31,050 / 24,900
1999	$17,250 / 14,850	$27,650 / 24,250
1998	$14,900 / 11,600	$24,550 / 21,950
1997	$12,600 / 9,800	$20,800 / 20,800
1996	$10,050 / 8,250	$18,000 / 18,700
1995	$8,500 / 6,100	$14,850 / 16,100

Recommended model years:

- 1995 - 2000 (new model in 1996).

Best features:

- First-rate finish.
- Comfortable vehicle.

Worst features:

- Listless engines.
- Barely adequate brakes.

What you should know:

- Fragile CV-joints, especially during off-road driving.
- Rust-prone body.
- Oxygen sensors have limited lifespan.

Major recalls:

- Nothing to worry about. 357 Pathfinders (1996 model) were recalled because of two defects: 1) thick carpet padding risked interfering with the pedal system, and 2) steering wheel hard to turn at low speeds.

Occupant safety:

- Front crash: 9 stars out of 10.
- Side crash: 10 stars out of 10.
- These data apply strictly to the 1999 and 2000 models. Passive safety on earlier models was a contradiction in terms.

***Auto Guide* Verdict:**

- Not for heavy-duty off-road activities. Otherwise, why not?

NISSAN SENTRA

Recommended model years:

- 1995 - 2000 (new model in 1996).

Best features:

- Good, honest car. Generally less expensive than its competitors (Civic, Corolla and Protegé).

YEAR	MIN. PRICE ($CDN/US)	MAX. PRICE ($CDN/US)
2000	$9,500 / 7,200	$17,400 / 12,200
1999	$7,300 / 6,150	$15,900 / 11,800
1998	$5,300 / 4,650	$11,900 / 11,200
1997	$4,000 / 3,800	$11,450 / 10,200
1996	$1,800 / 2,600	$10,200 / 8,800
1995	$1,300 / 1,500	$8,100 / 7,950

Worst features:

- Nondescript appearance.
- Noisy engine.

What you should know:

- Stabilizer bar's ball joints don't always wear well.
- Water penetration in the trunk.
- Front brakes tend to seize easily.

Major recalls:

- 1) 1995-1999 models: the wiper pivots on 12,168 units were found to be too rust-prone. 2) 1995-1997 models: 11,322 units were recalled because the throttle linkage could stick. 3) 1994-1996 models (2-door only): The front coil springs on 11,100 units were replaced with springs coated with zinc phosphate.

Occupant safety:

- Front crash: 7 stars out of 10.
- Side crash: 6 stars out of 10.

***Auto Guide* Verdict:**

- For those who prefer long-term value to short-term passion.

SATURN SL

YEAR	MIN. PRICE ($CDN/US)	MAX. PRICE ($CDN/US)
2000	$8,950 / 7,300	$15,300 / 12,700
1999	$6,100 / 5,900	$13,900 / 11,800
1998	$4,300 / 4,650	$11,350 / 10,500
1997	$3,350 / 4,000	$9,850 / 9,600
1996	$2,450 / 2,950	$9,400 / 8,900
1995	$2,150 / 1,650	$8,500 / 7,500

Recommended model years:

- 1995 - 2000.

Best features:

- Cost of replacement parts lower than average.
- Anti-rust body.

Worst features:

- Base models unappealing.
- Deafening engines.

What you should know:

- High fuel consumption (base 100-hp engines) after 50,000 miles (80,000 km). Potential oil leaks from manual transmission. Air conditioner compressor bearings tend to fail after three years.

Major recalls:

- Very infrequent, the most important involved a faulty horn assembly in 4294 units of the 1997 model.

Occupant safety:

- Front crash: 10 stars out of 10.
- Side crash: 6 stars out of 10.
- (Contrary to what some people may have thought, only the body was made of composite, not the chassis!)

***Auto Guide* Verdict:**
- An ordinary car, made more attractive by Saturn's terrific after-sales service.

SUBARU LEGACY

Recommended model years:
- 1995 - 2000 (new model in 2000).

Best features:
- Exceptional traction for a car.
- First-rate finish.

Worst features:
- High maintenance and spare-parts costs.
- Engines need Viagra more than they need gas.

YEAR	MIN. PRICE ($CDN/US)	MAX. PRICE ($CDN/US)
2000	$15,200 / 11,950	$27,900 / 21,100
1999	$9,900 / 8,600	$24,6800 / 17,950
1998	$8,500 / 7,400	$22,350 / 14,100
1997	$7,950 / 6,100	$18,450 / 13,900
1996	$6,800 / 5,650	$15,050 / 14,100
1995	$4,250 / 3,300	$12,35s0 / 12,350

What you should know:
- Too few dealers.
- Exhaust Y-junction pipe very expensive to replace.
- Ultra fragile CV-joint rubber boots.
- Oil leaks between transmission and engine.

Major recalls:
- 1) 1998-1999 models: 16,710 units were affected by a brake master cylinder that seized up in extreme cold.
  2) 1995 model: Front tow hooks on 3442 vehicles were installed so low down that the air bags were activated when the car hit a curb.

Occupant safety:
- Front crash: 4 stars out of 10.
- Side crash: n.a.

***Auto Guide* Verdict:**
- Not recommended for high-performance or off-road activities. Otherwise an excellent car, unbeatable in wintertime.

SUZUKI ESTEEM

Recommended model years:
- 1996 - 2000.

Best features:
- Reasonable fuel economy.
- Family-friendly wagon.

Worst features:
- Rust-prone.
- Poor resale value (but that's an excellent selling point).

What you should know:
- Tires wear out prematurely.
- Ditto the front brakes.
- There have been few complaints, perhaps due to the fact that very few Esteems were sold.

Major recalls:
- 7458 Esteems (1995-1998 models) were recalled so they could be fitted with a new block heater.

YEAR	MIN. PRICE ($CDN/US)	MAX. PRICE ($CDN/US)
2000	$9,650 / 6,200	$15,200 / 9,850
1999	$6,600 / 4,950	$12,500 / 8,950
1998	$5,000 / 3,350	$11,150 / 8,450
1997	$3,950 / 2,250	$9,000 / 6,650
1996	$2,950 / 1,400	$7,650 / 5,900
1995	$800	$4,250

Occupant safety:
- Front crash: n.a.
- Side crash: n.a.

***Auto Guide* Verdict:**
- Esteems are not all that exciting, but they're not bad either.

TOYOTA CAMRY

Recommended model years:
- 1995 - 2000 (new model in 1997).

Best features:
- Guaranteed reliability.
- Comfortable.

Worst features:

- Steep price.
- Not built for driving pleasure.

What you should know:

- Watch automatic transmission after 75,000 miles.
- Fallible water pump.
- Air conditioner compressor not tough enough.

Major recalls:

- 1) 1997 model: 23,281 units received a new module preventing the ignition key from being removed until the gearshift lever is set at "Park." 2) 1998 model: 21,454 units were recalled so that the steering-wheel retaining nut could be properly tightened.

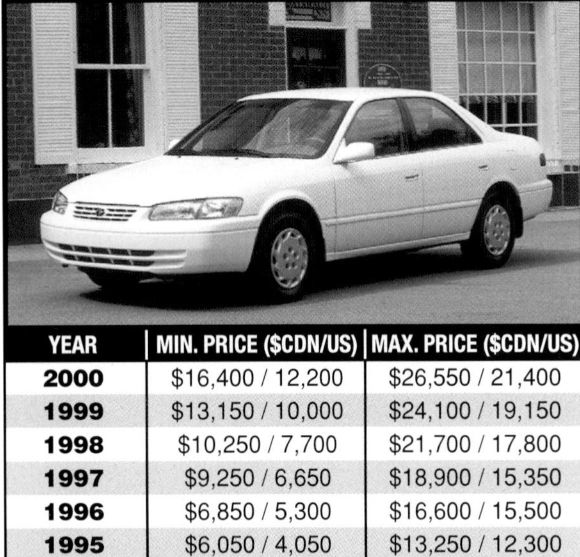

YEAR	MIN. PRICE ($CDN/US)	MAX. PRICE ($CDN/US)
2000	$16,400 / 12,200	$26,550 / 21,400
1999	$13,150 / 10,000	$24,100 / 19,150
1998	$10,250 / 7,700	$21,700 / 17,800
1997	$9,250 / 6,650	$18,900 / 15,350
1996	$6,850 / 5,300	$16,600 / 15,500
1995	$6,050 / 4,050	$13,250 / 12,300

Occupant safety:

- Front crash: 9 stars out of 10.
- Side crash: 6 stars out of 10.

***Auto Guide* Verdict:**

- An excellent choice if the asking price isn't too high. Otherwise you're better off buying a new car, especially if there's a sale.

TOYOTA COROLLA

Recommended model years:

- 1995 - 2000 (revamped model in 1998).

Best features:

- Paragon of reliability.
- Little maintenance.

Worst features:

- Not built for driving pleasure.
- Popular with car thieves.

What you should know:

- Loud water pump.
- Wiper pivots use older technology.

Major recalls:

- 1997 model: 3598 units were recalled because their airbag electronic control module had a potential for inadvertent deployment.

Occupant safety:

- Front crash: 8 stars out of 10.
- Side crash: 7 stars out of 10.

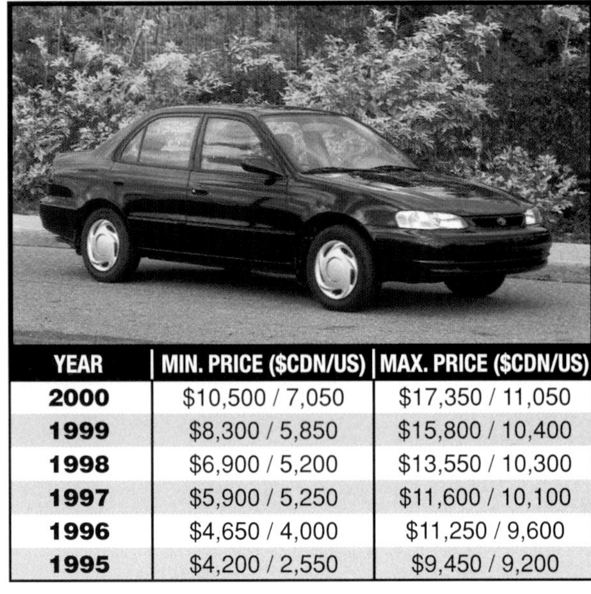

YEAR	MIN. PRICE ($CDN/US)	MAX. PRICE ($CDN/US)
2000	$10,500 / 7,050	$17,350 / 11,050
1999	$8,300 / 5,850	$15,800 / 10,400
1998	$6,900 / 5,200	$13,550 / 10,300
1997	$5,900 / 5,250	$11,600 / 10,100
1996	$4,650 / 4,000	$11,250 / 9,600
1995	$4,200 / 2,550	$9,450 / 9,200

***Auto Guide* Verdict:**

- No other car will give you more peace of mind.

TOYOTA RAV4

Recommended model years:

- 1997 - 2000.

Best features:

- Super-solid reliability.
- Slow depreciation.

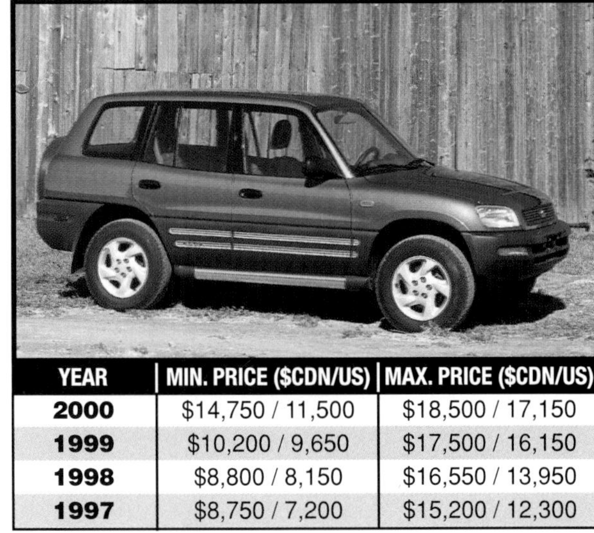

YEAR	MIN. PRICE ($CDN/US)	MAX. PRICE ($CDN/US)
2000	$14,750 / 11,500	$18,500 / 17,150
1999	$10,200 / 9,650	$17,500 / 16,150
1998	$8,800 / 8,150	$16,550 / 13,950
1997	$8,750 / 7,200	$15,200 / 12,300

Worst features:
- Not for off-road driving.
- Lackluster performance.

What you should know:
- Exhaust leaks between catalytic converter and muffler.
- Rudimentary rust protection.

Major recalls:
- 1997 model: 1144 units were sold without the electronic module controlling the daytime and night-time headlight settings.

Occupant safety:
- Front crash: 8 stars out of 10.
- Side crash: 10 stars out of 10.

***Auto Guide* Verdict:**
- The RAV4's sole redeeming qualities are its first-rate reliability and interesting design. But are they worth the asking price?

TOYOTA TERCEL

Recommended model years:
- 1995 - 1999.

Best features:
- Legendary reliability.
- Good fuel economy.
- Low running costs.

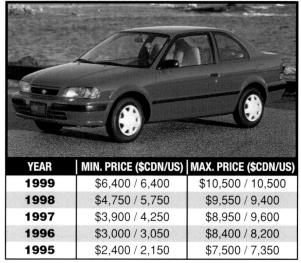

YEAR	MIN. PRICE ($CDN/US)	MAX. PRICE ($CDN/US)
1999	$6,400 / 6,400	$10,500 / 10,500
1998	$4,750 / 5,750	$9,550 / 9,400
1997	$3,900 / 4,250	$8,950 / 9,600
1996	$3,000 / 3,050	$8,400 / 8,200
1995	$2,400 / 2,150	$7,500 / 7,350

* Not available in the U.S. in 1999.

Worst features:
- Asking price often excessive.
- Cabin noise.

What you should know:
- Heater fan motor bearings cop out too early in life.
- The gear selector cable (manual transmission) tends to snap or jam easily.
- The water pump has short lifespan.
- Increased oil consumption over 81,250 miles (130,000 km).

Major recalls:
- None.

Occupant safety:
- Front crash: 7 stars out of 10.
- Side crash: n.a.

***Auto Guide* Verdict:**
- Excellent car. Its replacement, the Echo, is so bizarre that the Tercel seems more attractive than ever.

VOLKSWAGEN GOLF

Recommended model years:
- 1995 - 2000 (new model in 1999).

Best features:
- Guaranteed driving pleasure.
- Complete equipment.

Worst features:
- Unreliable.
- Ultra high maintenance costs.

What you should know:
- Failure-prone electricals; locks jam in cold weather; excessive oil consumption (2.0-liter engine); weak wiper motor; rear disc brakes require constant and costly maintenance, to name just a few problems.

Major recalls:
- 1993-1996 models: 64,460 units (Golf and Jetta) so that their hood latch system could be inspected or replaced.

Occupant safety:
- Front crash: 10 stars out of 10.
- Side crash: n.a.

***Auto Guide* Verdict:**
- Strictly for buyers who enjoy surprises.

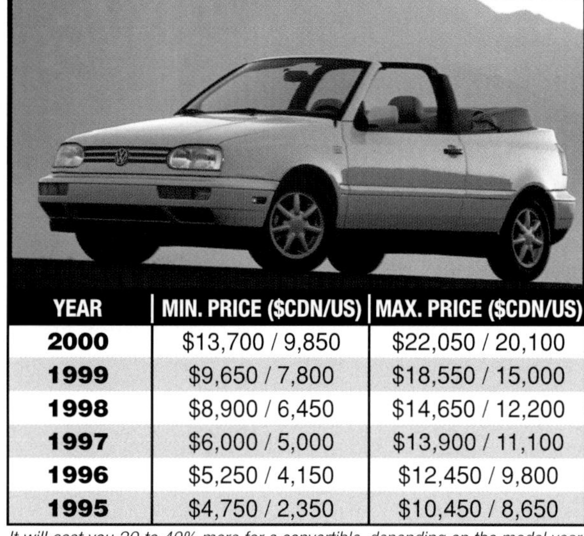

YEAR	MIN. PRICE ($CDN/US)	MAX. PRICE ($CDN/US)
2000	$13,700 / 9,850	$22,050 / 20,100
1999	$9,650 / 7,800	$18,550 / 15,000
1998	$8,900 / 6,450	$14,650 / 12,200
1997	$6,000 / 5,000	$13,900 / 11,100
1996	$5,250 / 4,150	$12,450 / 9,800
1995	$4,750 / 2,350	$10,450 / 8,650

It will cost you 20 to 40% more for a convertible, depending on the model year. Add another 20% for the VR6 version.

VOLKSWAGEN JETTA

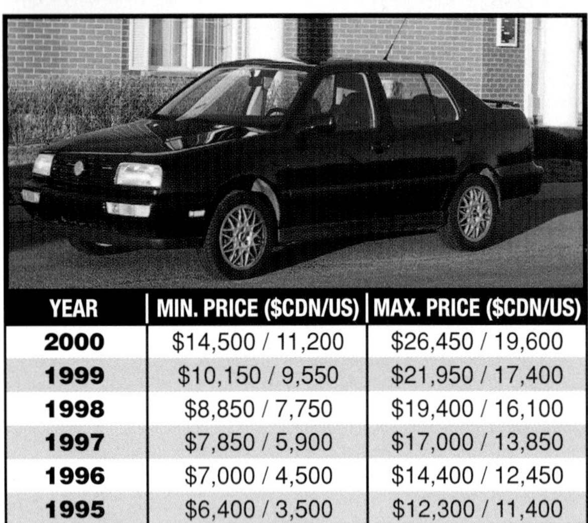

YEAR	MIN. PRICE ($CDN/US)	MAX. PRICE ($CDN/US)
2000	$14,500 / 11,200	$26,450 / 19,600
1999	$10,150 / 9,550	$21,950 / 17,400
1998	$8,850 / 7,750	$19,400 / 16,100
1997	$7,850 / 5,900	$17,000 / 13,850
1996	$7,000 / 4,500	$14,400 / 12,450
1995	$6,400 / 3,500	$12,300 / 11,400

Recommended model years:
- 1995 - 2000 (new model in 1999).

Best features:
- Comfortable.
- Good handling.

Worst features:
- Barely reliable.
- Inconceivably high maintenance costs.

What you should know:
- Inadequate electric system.
- Both starter and wiper motor have short lifespans.
- Oil leaks in power-steering pump.
- Flimsy heater fan motor. Check with APA for more complete report.

Major recalls:
- Oddly enough, there have been few recalls, the most important of which involved 4583 units of the 1999 model. They were found to contain a substandard piece of sound-insulation material.

Occupant safety:
- Front crash: 10 stars out of 10.
- Side crash: 8 stars out of 10.

***Auto Guide* Verdict:**
- Driving a Jetta is like living with a glamorous partner who spends all your money on expensive trifles. But love is blind, as the saying goes.

VOLKSWAGEN NEW BEETLE

Recommended model years:
- 1998 - 2000.

Best features:
- Eye-catching design.
- Uncommonly comfortable.

Worst features:
- Reliability, Volkswagen-style.

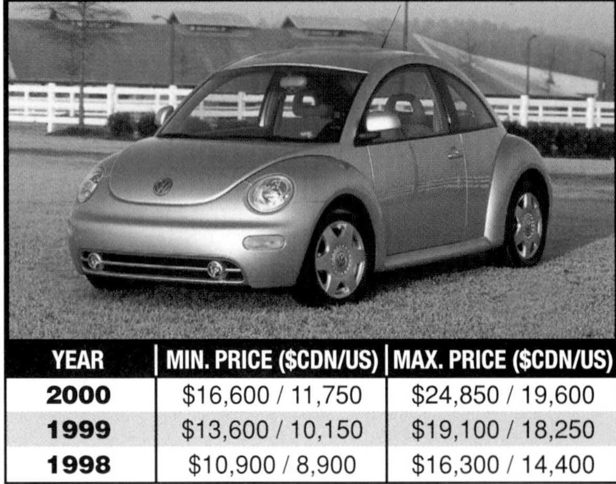

YEAR	MIN. PRICE ($CDN/US)	MAX. PRICE ($CDN/US)
2000	$16,600 / 11,750	$24,850 / 19,600
1999	$13,600 / 10,150	$19,100 / 18,250
1998	$10,900 / 8,900	$16,300 / 14,400

- Outrageously short warranty – 2 years/15,000 miles (24,000 km).

What you should know:
- The New Beetle is based on the Golf platform, and shares both its mechanical components and problems. See text on the Golf.

Major recalls:
- 1998 model: 1515 units were recalled because some electrical wiring was found rubbing against the battery support.

Occupant safety:
- Front crash: 8 stars out of 10.
- Side crash: 8 stars out of 10.

***Auto Guide* Verdict:**
- Four years after its launch, the New Beetle still looks ravishing. But its "unfaithfulness" may ruin the love-affair.

JEEP LIBERTY FACES UP TO ITS RIVALS

What's the Best Compact SUV?

BY DENIS DUQUET PHOTO: MICHEL FYEN-GAGNON

The arrival this year of the Jeep Liberty marks the beginning of a new era. It was, after all, its ancestor – the 4-door Jeep Cherokee – that spearheaded the compact SUV boom, way back in 1984. Since that time, however, newer, more up-to-date and stylish models have come along, relegating the Cherokee to the bottom of the heap, as confirmed by the results of our last compact-SUV comparison test in 1999.

This time around, there's no excuse. The Liberty embodies the very best that Jeep can produce, in terms of style, mechanicals and of course, off-road capability. Whether it can unseat the Subaru Forester and take over first place remains to be seen. And then there are newcomers to contend with, like the Ford Escape, Mazda Tribute and Toyota RAV4. Have they got what it takes to be serious contenders?

To answer to all these questions, we brought ten compact SUVs to a sand quarry near Knowlton, Quebec. Our colleague Robin Choinière, a stuntman and four-wheel-drive specialist, came along to give us a hand. Not only did he submit these vehicles to a far tougher test than usual, but he devised a special test run that helped us all to evaluate the off-road performance of these vehicles more accurately. Another part of the test was to drive the vehicles over an approximately 20-mile circuit (30 km), consisting of unpaved surfaces, winding mountain roads and, finally, a stretch of highway.Many of the 15 test drivers were veterans of the 1999 trial and were therefore in a position to detect any change – for better or for worse – in the behavior of certain vehicles, as well as assess the new participants in this comparison test: Ford Escape, Hyundai SantaFe, Jeep Liberty, Kia Sportage, Mazda Tribute, Suzuki XL7 and the new-generation Toyota RAV4. It was regrettable that Honda Canada chose to announce – after completion of the test – that a new model, available in December, would be replacing the CR-V model we tested. In view of what happened, you'll find a short article elsewhere in the *Auto Guide* describing the new CR-V and comparing its qualities and shortcomings with those of the other participants.The new Land Rover Freelander was one of the noticeable absentees. While its size and technical specifications amply qualified it for the test, its sticker price put it in a different category altogether. To accommodate new models, the *Auto Guide*'s ranking system has evolved significantly from years past. Also worth mentioning is the fact that new models generally scored high in the rankings. Here's how the ten compact SUVs fared in a demanding on- and off-road comparison test.

OFF-ROAD RANKINGS

Robin Choinière, noted 4X4 test driver, recently put ten vehicles through a series of demanding off-road trials. When the dust settled, his rankings were as follows:

1	Subaru Forester	**6**	Toyota RAV4
2	Jeep Liberty	**7**	Suzuki XL7
3	Nissan Xterra	**8**	Hyundai SantaFe
4	Mazda Tribute	**9**	Honda CR-V
5	Ford Escape	**10**	Kia Sportage

1

JEEP LIBERTY

SPECTACULAR PERFORMANCE

The new Jeep leaped into first place, a few points ahead of the Subaru Forester, last year's winner of the comparison test. Once again, the implacable law of numbers prevailed. Not only did the Liberty gain first place as the testers' choice, but its looks were much appreciated and its interior design was considered the most elegant.

The Liberty is propelled by the most powerful engine in this group, a 210-hp 3.7-liter V6 plus a new rack-and-pinion steering and an independent front suspension that will make you forget the rustic character of the defunct Cherokee. These improvements are no match to the Subaru in terms of driving enjoyment and roadholding, but the results are however very impressive. Only the Forester and the Mazda Tribute are slightly ahead of it in this slot.

The off-road part of this test once again enabled the Subaru Forester to reveal its surprising agility. However, the Liberty proved to be a far stronger contestant than its Japanese rival. Moreover, its mechanical components are protected by sheet metal under the chassis and its all-wheel-drive system is more in keeping with the enthusiasts' expectations.

Jeep wanted to preserve the sturdiness of the Cherokee and to introduce a vehicle which could handle America's most celebrated track, the Rubicon Trail, a benchmark in terms of toughness. Through it all, the Liberty stands as the best compromise between extreme off-road requirements and those of everyday driving. It is the best in its category and is most capable of handling the worst off-road conditions anytime, anywhere.

What really impressed our testers were the Liberty's looks, which were modeled on the archetypal Jeep lines. They have been adapted to a more modern frame and are more attractive. The cockpit was the most elegant of the group despite its roughrider nature. However, things are far from perfect. The lack of space, the lack of a left-footrest for the driver were mentioned by all. Many considered that rear legroom was a little too tight. Finally, some were worried about the reliability of this Jeep. The Liberty will be an extraordinary success if DaimlerChrysler could put to rest the reliability problems normally associated with Jeep in a convincing manner.

Curiously, the combination tailgate and swinging tire rack was neither acclaimed nor criticized by testers. All appreciated the disappearance of the spare wheel, which used to be attached to the side of the cargo space. With its great looks, competitive price and much improved road behavior, the Jeep Liberty is a very pleasant surprise. As for its reliability, only time will tell.

What they said:

▲ PRO

Ah yes! Marvelous! A very lovely vehicle, which is as pleasant to drive as it is to watch. Super!

▼ CON

I still wonder about Jeep's bad reputation in terms of reliability.

2

SUBARU FORESTER

FAULTY LOOKS

When the difference between two vehicles is just a few points, it's difficult to declare a winner and a loser. Having won the previous contest, the Forester loses its title to the brand new, freshly designed Jeep Liberty. Chalk it up to age. Yet this incredible hybrid has lost nothing of its off-road qualities, a category in which it won easily. Its road behavior and performance still put it ahead of the winner in this department. On the other hand, the Liberty won hands down in terms of style and interior design. The Forester isn't bad looking, but it couldn't compete with the Liberty's innovative style – a fact that caused it to lose a few points here and there, enough to push it to second place.

Yet this second place is not a defeat. The Forester is still the best hybrid vehicle in its class. Despite its origins as a road vehicle, the ease with which it graduated from a road vehicle to off-road standards is impressive. Robin Choinière, an off-road specialist, placed the Forester ahead of the Jeep Liberty in his four-wheel drive rankings. The reason: "It is ahead of all the others off-road and just stays ahead on the road. It is quite exceptional!"

For years, Subaru's trademark Boxer engine was more anemic than anything else. This is not the case of the Forester, powered by a 165-hp engine which is well matched to the size of the vehicle. It works well with the all-wheel-drive system, ensuring linear distribution of the torque, and its thirst for fuel is far less than the V6 engined models.

In fact, if riding comfort and road-holding are important to you, then you will be impressed by the Forester. However, its mechanical design, derived from standard automobile engineering, does have some limitations when you leave the road for forest tracks and fields. Still, it takes extreme conditions before a Forester meets an obstacle it cannot handle.

As a colleague claimed: "Quick, a stylist! It's urgent!" Although most Subaru models have improved in looks over the past few years, the Forester is the exception in this carmaker's model line-up. It was badly penalized by its blown-up wagon look, which may have turned some prospective buyers off. During the course of this comparison test, one of the testers exclaimed: "Wow! Judging by its looks, I would never have

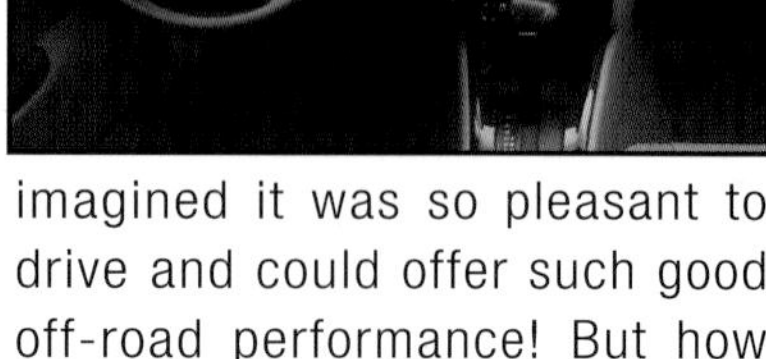

imagined it was so pleasant to drive and could offer such good off-road performance! But how ugly!"

There is nothing much more to be said as to why it came in second.

What they said:

▲ PRO

Excellent performance on the road – very solid off-road – Subaru offers the best of both worlds for those who don't want a truck.

▼ CON

A new interior design would be an improvement, as it's beginning to look dated. Both the interior and exterior are a little too discreet.

3

FORD ESCAPE

BARELY ON THE PODIUM

Just half a point separates the Ford Escape from the Toyota RAV4! Five tenths of the more than 400 points available, that's the lead which allows to put it on the lowest rung of the podium. Enough to argue that the RAV4 could easily have beat the Escape on gas consumption alone. However, the Escape won its bronze medal fair and square. As it turned out, its behavior was almost a perfect compromise between the open road and the forest track. Its all-wheel drive is well suited to highway driving, while its ability to get into a 50/50 mode at the simple flick of a switch is very useful. Furthermore, even though its gas consumption is high, the 200-hp V6 can be most appropriate when the going gets tough, far from any paved road, while the 148-hp of the RAV4 may be just a little short.

If you belong to that group of enthusiasts who just love to knock American-made products, you will be pleased to know that this vehicle was almost entirely designed by Mazda, while Ford supplied the V6 and provided its assembly line in Michigan.

The next question is why does the Mazda Tribute not share the same ranking, as the two vehicles are very similar to each other, give or take a few details. Mind you, it's just these few differences that allowed the Escape to outdo its Japanese sibling. We'll explain this difference in a little more detail when we comment on the Tribute. But just remember that these two vehicles suffer from the same diabolical gear shifter which obstructs access to the radio controls.

What worked in favor of the Escape was its balanced approach. It doesn't outdo many other vehicles in any given category, but it doesn't suffer from any major ailment on-road or off-road either. There are of course a few irritating aspects, like the gear shifter and a rather uninspired interior design. However, this doesn't penalize its standing in the overall assessment. It is precisely this balance between style, interior comfort and performance on the one hand, and overall strength of the platform on the other that won it the necessary points to achieve third place.

The reason the Escape did not obtain first place is simple, it's because it did not have the wherewithal to best both the Subaru and the Jeep, which set new standards in their own right. There's also its high gas consumption, and a lack of driving enjoyment. The Escape hasn't got the spark which brought the Liberty to the fore nor the

excellent roadholding that the Forester sustains on forest tracks.

In conclusion, the Ford Escape is a solid well-designed vehicle, fitted with an original all-wheel drive. But it lacks a little something in terms of driveability and roadholding.

What they said:

▲ PRO

A European look, which I very much enjoyed. A pleasant vehicle overall, and a choice well worth considering.

▼ CON

Interesting overall, it does however lack that little something which would make it stand out. It lacks a little panache.

4 TOYOTA RAV4

MISTAKES CORRECTED

The first generation RAV4 was quite content to be an attractive sport utility and an anemic engine. So much so that it finished last in our previous comparison test. Its feeble engine, coupled with an all-wheel drive that's primitive at best, made the Mount Glenn climb particularly trying.

Fortunately, Toyota redesigned the RAV4 last fall and it is with a renewed vitality that it joined the starting line. The all-new 4-cylinder 2.0-liter engine now produced 148 hp. Nothing to write home about, but it still is a lot more muscle than the original 120 hp. However, apart from the Honda CR-V and the Kia Sportage, it's the least powerful vehicle in the group.

The secret of the RAV4's success lies in its overall balance. The 140 hp is always present, no matter what the engine speed, and the impression is that they are always available just under your right foot. It seems that the system of continuous variable timing with intelligence is very efficient. The 4-speed automatic gearbox was also awarded high marks. Despite some indications leaning toward pessimism, this Toyota is far livelier than its technical specifications might let on.

The first generation looked like a blown-up Tonka toy. This time around, the lines are a little more mature, enough to challenge the Jeep Liberty. Although the first-generation dashboard made us mention "Toyota" and "cheap workmanship" in the same sentence, it is no longer the case for this new offspring. Not only has the quality of materials and workmanship improved, so has the design of the dashboard.

More powerful, more attractive, better assembled than ever and forever agile, this Toyota regains lost ground in a convincing manner. However, one should always allow for the fact that its all-wheel drive is not necessarily designed for the most inhospitable parts of the planet. On occasion, the torque does not operate with the same finesse as it does on the Subaru Forester, while the 148 hp are barely adequate in deep slush or sand.

Toyota is very much aware of this vehicle's limitations in off-road conditions, but the target buyers are not Indiana Jones. Granted, its drivetrain will provide the driver with everything he wants if the road is slippery, but he must be more cautious when driving over bumps and drainage ditches.

The RAV4 is solid, reliable, elegant – an interesting choice for those who

wish to take advantage of its adaptability, reasonable gas consumption and reliability. But the tailgate needs to be improved.

What they said:

▲ PRO

One of my favorites, because of its lines and its interior. The quality of its workmanship must be underlined.

▼ CON

Engine power a little wanting, a cockpit a little too tight, designed more like a Baby-boom box, that is what penalized the cutest of the cute.

5

MAZDA TRIBUTE

JUST THREE LITTLE POINTS!

The experts foresaw a dead heat between the Tribute and the Ford Escape. However, there is a small difference. Just a piffling three points, in fact. Rather strange, come to think of it, as both share the same platform and have the same mechanical components. However, these siblings are different enough to come up with a few points between them. More interesting is the different perceptions that testers had of the Tribute and the Ford Escape.

Both share the same lines and interior design. While the more macho look of the Ford gave it a slight advantage, the Tribute won points on its workmanship. True or false? Does Mazda impose a more rigorous quality control? The facts are there. However, both have the same gear shifter which restricts access to the radio controls. On the other hand, those among us who like to adjust the reclining steering wheel at its highest setting will not have this problem.

As the Tribute doesn't have the same rear suspension tuning as the Escape, it's at a slight advantage on the open road. However, both score the same in the off-road test.

The only noticeable difference is in the testers' favorite choice, where the Escape won two points more than the Escape.

Anyway, it's practically Tweedledum and Tweedledee. Mazda wanted its Tribute to have the allure of a more refined vehicle, built more for the road than running across fields. Cockpit design is drawn from the same inspiration. A slightly more adventurous look in the Ford Escape seems to have found better favor with our testers. They did not fail to notice the 3-liter engine's thirst. They all appreciated the all-wheel drive and the ingenious and efficient mechanism going from all-wheel drive to 50/50 torque transfer mode at the flick of a switch on the dashboard.

In spite of this very attractive compromise, the tandem did not score on all points, even though the Escape eventually found itself on the podium. Why? Simply because both lack that little something that makes the heart beat faster. Everything is in good order, well balanced, but doesn't create much of a stir. This is even less likely of the Tribute, whose "politically correct" nature dulls the senses.

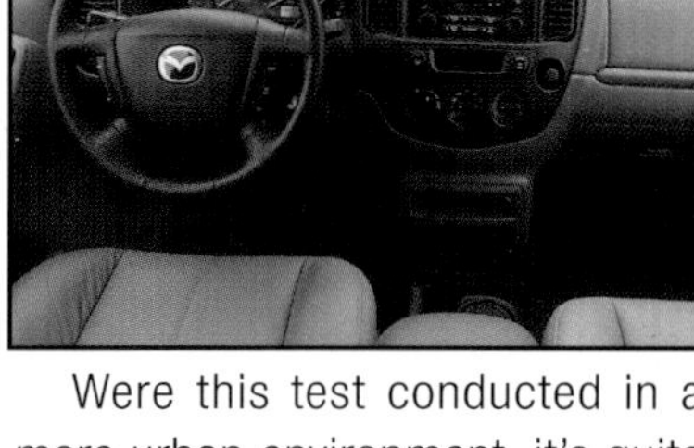

Were this test conducted in a more urban environment, it's quite possible that these two siblings would have switched places. We leave it to you, whatever your preference, either the livelier allure of the Escape, or the finesse of the Tribute.

What they said:

▲ PRO

A dead heat with the Ford Escape. I like its looks and its smooth engine. It is equally at ease everywhere.

▼ CON

Its high gas consumption and awkward gear shifter take away points. I prefer the Ford Escape.

6

NISSAN XTERRA

SIGNS OF AGING!

One of the great surprises of this comparison test on sand and pavement was the ranking of the Xterra. It dropped five places since we last tested it in our 2000 comparison test. The reason is simple. All the vehicles which placed ahead of it were new or had been completely redesigned. Competition is so strong in this class that after just a few months, one can lose ground as more modern, more comfortable and more efficient off-road vehicles are introduced. The comparison parameters which cost the Nissan the most points were riding comfort, roadholding, and the responsiveness and performance of the engine. In effect, the failings come from its origins as a truck: its platform is the same one as the Frontier, which was reworked for use in a front-wheel driver. On top of that, the 170 hp of the 3.3-liter V6 engine worked on paper only. In practice, however, it quickly gets short of breath and becomes a little noisy at higher revs. On the other hand, its reliability is beyond reproach.

While the acclaim of the Hyundai SantaFe's styling was far from unanimous, the lines of the Xterra drew a lot of positive comments. If you like the rugged look, then this Nissan is for you. The dashboard was improved last year, although the new components do not fit too well with the rest of the design. One of the major irritants of this vehicle are the bucket seats which are far too low and dictate an unusual driving position. Moreover, their comfort is just average. The same can be said about the rear bench seat, set unnecessarily low with very thin padding.

Some vehicles are deceiving because of the expectancy generated by their design, but that is not the case of the Nissan with its broad, brawny look. It really has the allure of a genuine four-wheel drive off-road vehicle. Don't be seduced by its attractive lines if you have no intention of driving on barely passable backroads, or if you don't want to ride through a snowstorm to take advantage of ideal skiing conditions. These are the drivers who are most likely to appreciate this genuine four-wheel drive. In the off-road test it conceded defeat only to the Jeep Liberty and to the Subaru Forester.

It's probably the most specialized vehicle of the group and no doubt wilderness campers and extreme sports enthusiasts will prefer it to the other vehicles. However, as competition becomes more prevalent, its specialized nature lowers its ranking in comparison to vehicles that are more adaptive and homogeneous. However, third place in the tester's choice says a lot for the attractive nature of the Xterra.

What they said:

▲ PRO

The macho machine of the lot: tough, powerful, extremely strong off-road and fairly comfortable. A real four-wheel drive!

▼ CON

Not bad, but there are a few things that must be improved before one should consider a purchase. The interior is particularly unattractive.

7

SUZUKI XL7

A STRANGE ANIMAL

As opposed to all the other vehicles in this comparison test, the Suzuki XL7 stands quite apart. First, it's the only one to have a third bench, it's the longest, and its price is among the highest. Besides, although the designers saw its vocation as an off-road minivan, they kept the ladder-type chassis of the Grand Vitara and its part-time four-wheel drive. Anticipating heavier cargo, they installed a 170-hp 2.7-liter V6 that throbs quietly under the hood. That's 15 hp more than the 2.5-liter V6 of the Grand Vitara.

Suzuki doesn't hide the origins of this vehicle. The letters XL stand for "eXtra Long" while the number 7 indicates that it can welcome seven occupants. However, pushing the chassis in too many directions does set this vehicle quite apart from the others. For example, its 110.2-inch wheelbase (280 cm) is the longest of all the vehicles in the test. This helps to accommodate two extra passengers on the third benchseat and improves the riding comfort of the suspension. Off-road performance however, is quite a different story. In fact, with this rather unusual length between the axles, the XL7 is likely to scrape its midriff on bumps and rocks. An inexperienced driver runs the risk of getting caught on an apex, neither capable of moving forward nor backward. Moreover, a rather imprecise steering doesn't help matters. Actually, the XL7 was at the bottom of the group because of its off-road performance.

Strangely, despite technical specifications that place it among true-blue SUVs, this stretched version of the Grand Vitara is much more at ease in an urban setting. Its longer wheelbase ensures a satisfying level of riding comfort while driver-vision and a responsive engine will carry your family from the house to the arena with the greatest of ease.

However, the rather high price of this Suzuki is its main handicap; reflecting mainly the mechanical modifications brought to the Grand Vitara chassis and increased engine power, given that the cockpit just looks average. On top of that, the quality of the materials and the accessories do not quite suit the asking price, although they may seem comparable to those of the competition. Finally, the dashboard could do with a more elegant look as it is very basic.

Like the Nissan Xterra, the Suzuki XL7 targets a specific group of buyers. If you don't feel included, you may feel a little unsatisfied and end up with a higher than-average invoice.

What they said:

▲ PRO

Aesthetics of a small bus, but lots of space. Rear access is easy thanks to the largest doors in the group. Guaranteed practicality, thanks to folding rear seats.

▼ CON

This vehicle does nothing for me. It's too big and lacks personality. Moreover, the interior is old-fashioned and not very comfortable.

8

HYUNDAI SANTAFE

CONTROVERSIAL LOOK

This Hyundai is an unusual vehicle. It is in fact the wagon version of the Sonata sedan, to which an all-wheel drivetrain has been fitted, with an increased ground clearance. Add to the ingredients a 181-hp 2.7-liter V6 coupled to a Sportshift automatic transmission and, presto, you're at the wheel of a sport utility. If you want to keep up with the Jones without breaking your piggy bank, and drive an all-terrain all-wheel-drive vehicle, the SantaFe is an interesting alternative, given that it behaves a little more like a road-going car than an off-roader.

But you may have to accept some unfavorable features. Most of the comments gathered during this comparison test were not terribly positive, which is rather contradictory given the opinions expressed in prior tests. Whatever the issue, the design is either liked or disliked, no ifs and buts. One thing is certain: wherever you go with this charming Korean, you will be noticed.

As a first time entry in this field for Hyundai, it's a success. The carmaker was wise enough to put together a vehicle that is more at ease on the open road than on the forest track. A logical option, as only a small proportion of owners of such vehicles really go off road. And all the better for it, as the performance of the SantaFe on our test track was rather discreet. The 60/40 weighted all-wheel drive is too restrictive for you to play the explorer when things start getting tough. You shouldn't be too adventurous as you may find it difficult to extricate 3750 lbs (1700 kg) of Korean metal out of a rut.

On the open road, the smoothness of the V6 engine is much appreciated while the automatic gearbox is a little lazy, a characteristic trait from this carmaker. As to the Sportshift system which permits gear changing manually, it doesn't prove to be more practical or pleasant than any other. Moreover, it's too easy to accidentally engage the system just by pressing your hand on the gearshift lever. In spite of the V6 engine under the hood, performance is not electrifying: the 181 hp has to work hard to get this heavy vehicle on the move.

In effect, this Hyundai is mostly an urban vehicle capable of good traction in snow and mud, while its riding comfort level is closer to that of an ordinary car than that of a sport utility. Several testers considered the workmanship to be average at best, but enjoyed the ease of access to the cargo space and the good loading capacity. However, the complicated controls, minuscule radio buttons and inverted ventilation controls were seriously criticized.

As a first effort, the SantaFe is good enough, though it couldn't compete with the leaders. The SantaFe is mostly intended for people who are looking for an intermediate wagon with all-wheel drive, at an average price.

What they said:

▲ PRO

A very smooth V6 engine, rather soft suspension. A more urban vehicle, a family wagon more than a four-wheel drive.

▼ CON

The overall look is neither that of a sedan, nor that of a sport utility, which I find perplexing. Interior space could be greater, given its size.

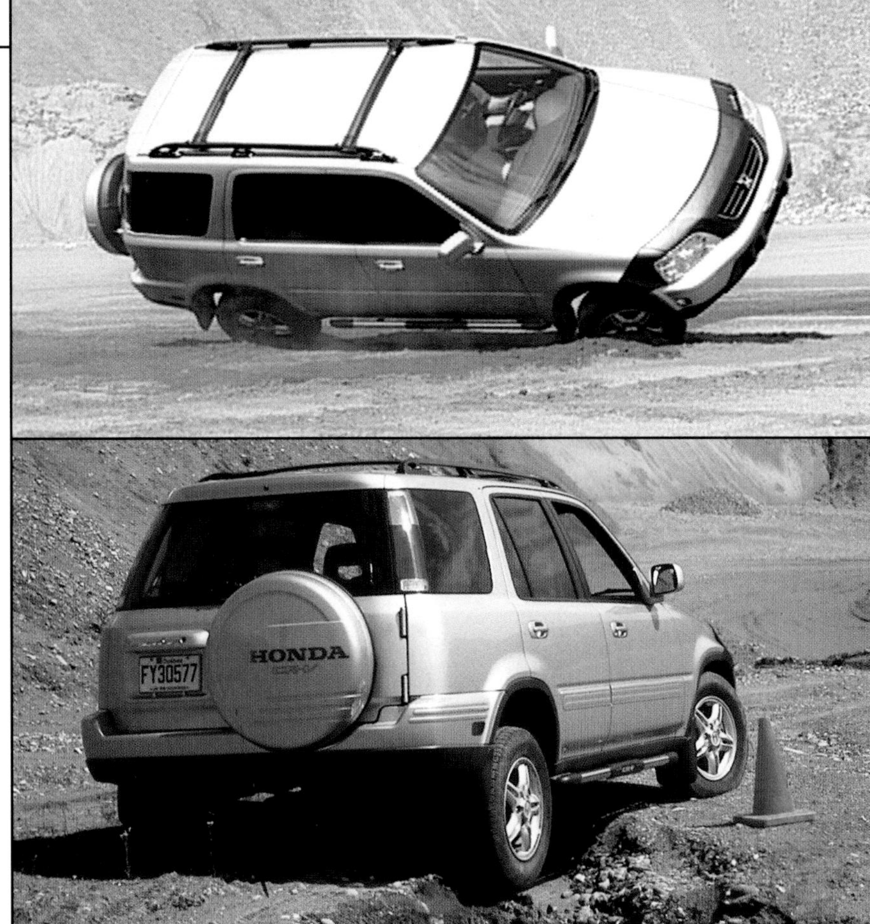

9

HONDA CR-V

BEING IMPROVED

Once again, the Honda organization has played a nasty trick on us. While we were asking about the availability of the new CR-V, our inquiries met with evasion. In the end we decided to organize the compact four-wheel drive comparison test at the end of June. Pow! A few hours after all the results were brought in, Honda announced that it would unveil the new CR-V a few weeks later, adding that this model would be put on sale in December. Here then, is what the "old" CR-V is worth next to its rivals. If you want to know more about the 2002 model, see our special test-drive.

This comparison test confirms without any doubt that the CR-V has reached the end of its tether. Its weak engine, unspectacular all-wheel drive system and so-so look drove the Honda down toward the lower ranks. Fortunately its low gas consumption and legendary Honda reliability tilted the balance in its favor. And, talking about tilt, the CR-V's rather weak lateral stability performed surprisingly well during our testing. Our stunt driver almost rolled the vehicle. Better still, the offside front wheel left an imprint on the sand before the CR-V could get back on its four wheels. This was scary. No other vehicle in this group exhibited similar unruliness.

One only need compare it with the Toyota RAV4 to realize to what point this Honda needs major revisions. A mostly urban vehicle, it remained a rather unconvincing participant as far as our testers were concerned. On the open road, the engine seemed strained just following traffic, while one must be fairly careful about choosing an off-road route.

All in all, the CR-V is just a large Civic wagon, with an economical engine and a rather rudimentary all-wheel drive system, very much at ease in the city. And if the vehicle is still very popular today, it is due more to Honda's reputation than to its performance. The dashboard looks dated and the controls are in serious need of modernization.

There's not much need to go on, as Honda has recognized the superior behavior of the Toyota RAV4 by designing a new model along the same lines as the RAV4, with more power, revised looks and better fuel economy. The CR-V was ranked second in a similar comparison test in 1998, then fourth in 2000. In 2002, it dipped to ninth out of ten. Fortunately, its replacement will be ready by December 2001.

What they said:

▲ PRO

Like all Honda products, the workmanship and the reliability are beyond reproach. I enjoyed the road vision and the overall looks of this CR-V.

▼ CON

I couldn't believe I would be so disappointed. Driving the CR-V is no fun and leaves no desire to go any distance. Greatly disappointed.

10

KIA SPORTAGE

IT'S UNANIMOUS

Any of our testers found it difficult to decide the rankings of one particular model compared with another. This definitely was not the case with the Sportage. They unanimously decided that it should be in tenth place in terms of their personal choice and it received a good drubbing in most other categories of the test. But first, let's start with the good news. This Korean four-wheel drive bested its rivals Hyundai and Suzuki in terms of looks and was their equal in terms of safety. Better still, the Kia manufacturers will be happy to learn that our testers gave it a better mark than the Honda CR-V in the category "other considerations." These victories don't however determine which vehicle obtains the best ranking, but which one will avoid the tailgate position.

However, the Sportage finished last in most categories. Its looks are rather attractive, the interior design is acceptable, but its chassis is old-fashioned and the engine anemic. The automatic gearbox doesn't help in any way. It's hesitant at best and inefficient most of the time. Still, the Sportage's engine/transmission duo made us realize the progress accomplished in the course of these last few years. This road-and-track Kia is handicapped by mechanicals dating back to the 70's and doesn't fare too well as a comparison.

Although our specialist did not seem overly impressed by this Korean in off-road driving, several of our testers took the trouble to mention that it was more at ease on off-road tracks than it was on the road. Its part-time four-wheel drive system is not revolutionary, but it gets the job done. However, the engine doesn't help matters in terms of performance.

In spite of this verdict, one should emphasize that this vehicule reveals better workmanship in terms of construction than the first models introduced in 1999, as 2000 models, like other Kia models. As far as the Sportage is concerned, your best bet is the base model with a manual gearbox. It's really not worth adding accessories and equipment.

If Kia manages to harmonize the quality of its mechanicals with that of its looks, it will definitely graduate from the bottom of the class.

What they said:

▲ PRO

Attractive, good price/equipment ratio and an off-road behaviour which isn't bad.

▼ CON

Nada! Old-fashioned steering, weak roadholding, interior design looking like something out of the 80s. As to the engine, one wonders what it's up to.

CONCLUSION

THE FINAL CHOICE

The Jeep Liberty wins this comparison test on sand and track. The venerable Cherokee had its supporters, but its replacement will make us forget it very quickly. More so, as the price of this new and improved Jeep is very competitive. One should not forget the Subaru Forester. The previous champion in this category finished well, just a few wheel spins from first place. Some may have raised an eyebrow when they found out that the Ford Escape was ranked third, and the Mazda Tribute came in fifth place, even though they appear practically identical. The differences are slight, but our testers seemed to appreciate the qualities of the Ford more. The RAV4 from Toyota managed to squeeze in between the two, thanks to its new-found elegance and more powerful engine.

The Nissan Xterra hasn't really changed much and the new kids on the block got the jump on it. Its looks are still appreciated, but its truck-like behavior is less attractive since other vehicles, just as sturdy, surpass its road-going qualities. Moreover, Nissan offers, as optional equipment for 2002, a supercharged engine. Our test vehicle had a normally aspirated V6, a model which will always be a little more in demand.

Although the Suzuki XL7 ranked seventh, this score doesn't just reflect its on- or off-road qualities, but its rather special configuration as well. Essentially a stretched version of the Grand Vitara – in order to accommodate seven occupants – the XL7 will be hard pressed to meet most buyers' demands. Its ladder-type chassis, part-time four-wheel drive and the 170 horses of its V6 will definitely argue in its favor.

The Hyundai SantaFe is a little out of place. Like the Subaru Forester, its origins are those of a sedan. Moreover, its all-wheel-drive system is rather basic. Which meant that the profile of our test course, being evenly balanced between road and track, put the SantaFe at a dis-

advantage. It should really be considered more as an all-wheel drive wagon with a high ground clearance, rather than a genuine sport utility vehicle.

During the course of these trials, the Honda CR-V continued its downward journey in the rankings. Of course, the new model has just been announced, but it will still be a few more months before it is ready for delivery.

Finally, the Kia Sportage finished last. Blamed for its dated mechanicals, one should not neglect the more economical models, particularly if your "shopping list is Sportage or nothing." Moreover, this vehicle has been greatly improved in terms of workmanship and construction since its arrival on the market. It needs a more powerful engine and a more modern suspension.

Carmakers are drawn closer to this category of compact SUVs and in just a few months they have flooded the market with new models. As proven by the lower rankings of some veteran models, it is no exaggeration the compact SUV is more sophisticated and more refined than ever.

CR-V 2002

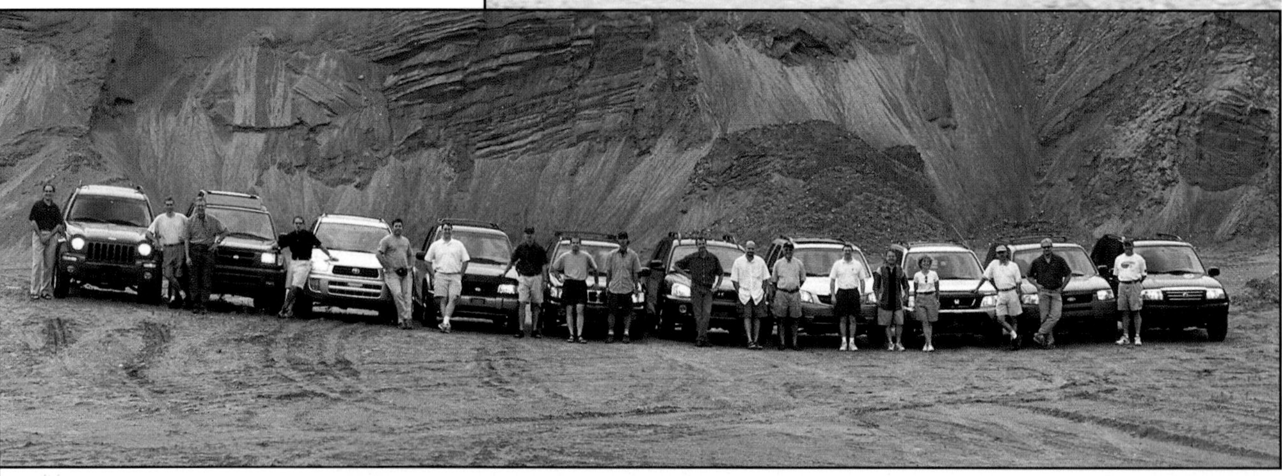

Specifications

	Ford Escape	Honda CR-V	Hyundai SantaFe	Jeep Liberty	Kia Sportage	Mazda Tribute	Nissan XTerra	Subaru Forester	Suzuki XL7	Toyota RAV4
• Wheelbase	103.1 in	103.1 in	103.1 in	104.3 in	104.3 in	103.1	104.3 in	99.2 in	110.2 in	98 in
• Length	172.8 in	177.6 in	177.2 in	174.4 in	170.1 in	177.6 in	178 in	175.6 in	183.5 in	165 in
• Width	70.1 in	68.9 in	71.7 in	71.7 in	68.1 in	70.9 in	70.4 in	68.1 in	70.1 in	68.1 in
• Height	66.9 in	65.7 in	65.7 in	70.9 in	65 in	66.9 in	72 in	62.6 in	67.7 in	66.1 in
• Weight	3252 lb (1475 kg)	3082 lb (1398 kg)	3726 lb (1690 kg)	4116 lb (1867 kg)	3373 lb (1530 kg)	3455 lb (1567 kg)	4131 lb (1874 kg)	3142 lb (1425 kg)	3704 lb (1680 kg)	2877 lb (1305 kg)
• Transmission	automatic	automatic	automatic	automatic	automatic	automatic	automatic	automatic	automatic	automatic
• Number of gears	4	4	4	4	4	4	4	4	4	4
• Engine	V6	4L	V6	V6	4L	V6	V6	4L	V6	4L
• Displacement	3.0-liter	2.0-liter	2.7-liter	3.7-liter	2.0-liter	3.0-liter	3.3-liter	2.5-liter	2.7-liter	2.0-liter
• Horsepower	200-hp	147-hp	181-hp	210-hp	130-hp	200-hp	170-hp	165-hp	170-hp	148-hp
• Front suspension	independent	independent	independent	independent	independent	independent	independent	independent	independent	independent
• Rear suspension	independent	independent	independent	rigid axle	rigid axle	independent	rigid axle	independent	rigid axle	independent
• Front brakes	disc	disc	disc	disc	disc	disc	disc	disc	disc	disc
• Rear brakes	disc	drum	disc	drum	drum	drum	drum	drum	drum	drum
• ABS	yes	yes	yes	yes	yes	yes	yes	yes	yes	yes
• Tires	P225/70R15	P205/70R15	P225/70R16	P225/75R15	P205/75R15	P235/70R16	P265/70R15	P215/60R16	P235/60R16	P235/60R16
• Steering	rack-and-pinion	rack-and-pinion	rack-and-pinion	rack-and-pinion	recirculating-ball	rack-and-pinion	recirculating-ball	rack-and-pinion	rack-and-pinion	rack-and-pinion
• Turning circle	35.4 feet	34.8 feet	37.1 feet	39.4 feet	36.7 feet	35.4 feet	35.4 feet	38.4 feet	38.7 feet	35.1 feet
• Air bags	front/side	front	front	front/side	front	front/ side	front	front	front	front
• Fuel tank	15.4 gallons	15.6 gallons	17.2 gallons	18.6 gallons	15.9 gallons	16.2 gallons	19.3 gallons	15.9 gallons	17 gallons	14.8 gallons
• Trunk	64.8 cu. ft	33.6 cu. ft	78 cu. ft	68.9 cu. ft	50.3 cu. ft	64.8 cu.ft	65.6 cu. ft	54 cu. ft	73.1 cu. ft	16.2 cu. ft
• Acceleration 0-60 mph	11.4 sec	11.4 sec	12.2 sec	10.4 sec	15.8 sec	11,4 sec	10.1 sec	9.5 sec	9.2 sec	11.4 sec
• Maximum speed	112 mph (180 km/h)	99 mph (160 km/h)	112 mph (180 km/h)	115 mph (185 km/h)	109 mph (175 km/h)	112mph (180 km/h)	109 mph (175 km/h)	115 mph (185 km/h)	112 mph (180 km/h)	106 mph (170 km/h)
• Fuel consumption (L/100 km)	14.2 mpg (16.5)	20 mpg (11.7)	16.1 mpg (14.6)	15.8 mpg (14.8)	20.9 mpg (11.2)	14.5 mpg (16.2)	17 mpg (13.8)	19.5 mpg (12)	17 mpg (13.8)	20.8 mpg (11.3)
• Price $CDN/US	$31,495/ 21,750	$31,250/ 23,240	$29,995/ 22,494	$28,895/ 23,305	$25,695/ 19,840	$29,995/ 23,970	$31,495/ 25,639	$31,495/ 24,420	$33,595/ 26,750	$31,495/ 18,245

HOW WOULD THE NEW HONDA CR-V 2002 COMPARE?

After having spoken to the people at Honda Canada in early April, we were left with the impression that the redesigned version of the CR-V would not be introduced before January 2002, which explains the presence of the CR-V 2001 in this test. But after driving the 2002 edition in a preview test run, we wondered how it would have shaped up had it been part of our test in the first place.

Although this road test ruled out comparison with the others, we're pretty sure that it would not have upset the ranking of the top three. The CR-V 2002 is definitely more powerful, its interior roominess is greater and its suspension has been improved. But that still would not have been enough to remove the Jeep Liberty's first place or the Subaru's Forester's second place finish. All things being equal, it would probably have finished between the Toyota RAV4 and the Nissan Xterra, which came in fifth. After all, that's a lot better than the ninth place finish of the 2001 edition!

One must remember that this Honda is not really a true-blue four-wheel drive vehicle. Its roadholding qualities have improved, however, but its off-road qualities have not changed much. As our comparison test emphasized off-road driveability, the CR-V was penalized on account of its greater suitability for urban travel.

Denis Duquet

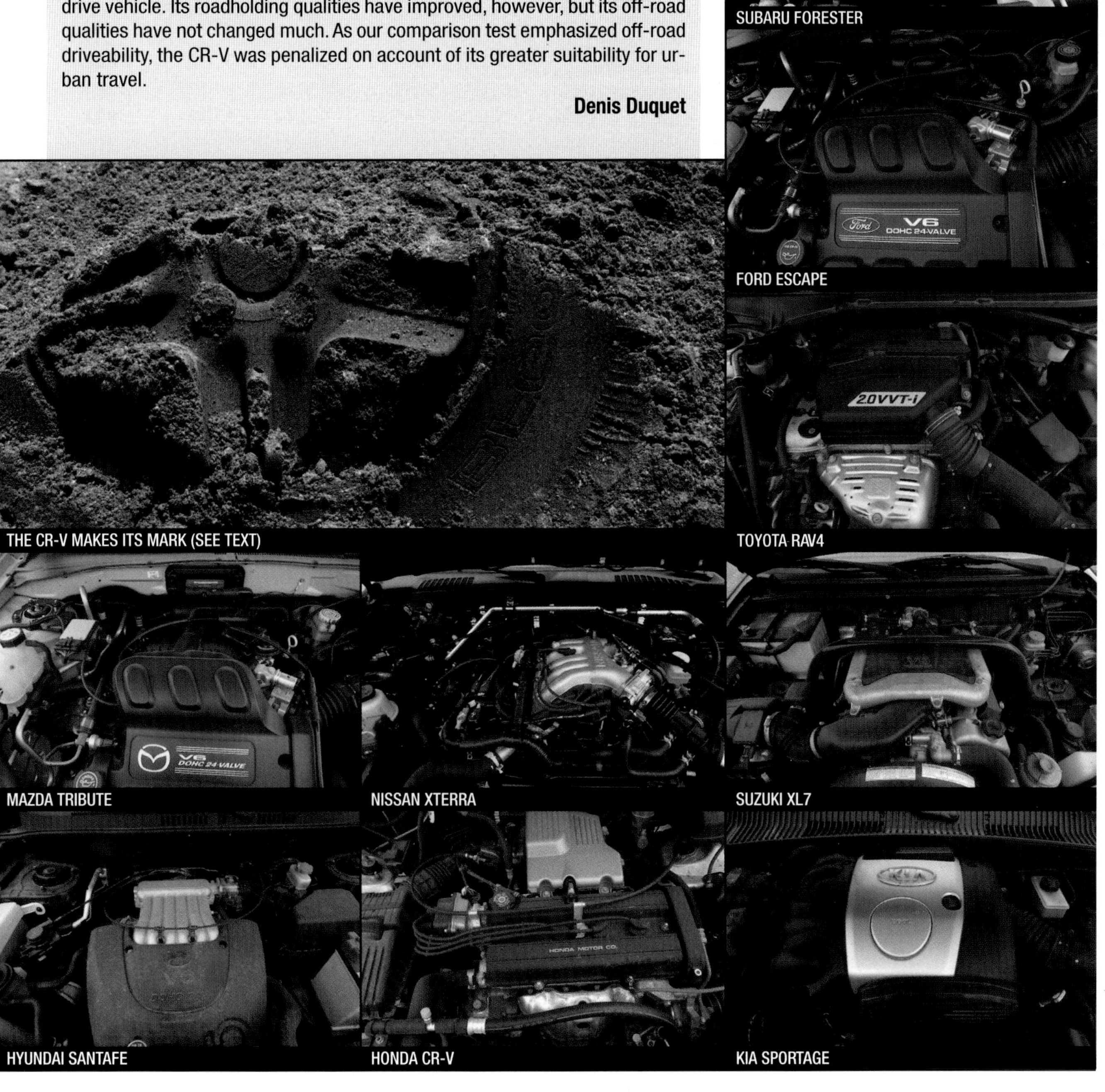

JEEP LIBERTY

SUBARU FORESTER

FORD ESCAPE

THE CR-V MAKES ITS MARK (SEE TEXT)

TOYOTA RAV4

MAZDA TRIBUTE

NISSAN XTERRA

SUZUKI XL7

HYUNDAI SANTAFE

HONDA CR-V

KIA SPORTAGE

Evaluation Sheet

Evaluation Sheet		Ford Escape	Honda CR-V	Hyundai SantaFe	Jeep Liberty	Kia Sportage	Mazda Tribute	Nissan Xterra	Subaru Forester	Suzuki XL7	Toyota RAV4
Esthetics											
• Exterior	10	7.6	7.3	6.0	8.2	7.0	7.2	8.5	6.2	6.9	8.5
• Interior	10	7.0	6.4	6.5	8.9	6.7	6.4	7.4	7.8	5.5	7.2
• Ext. finish	10	7.3	7.5	6.5	8.2	6.2	8.1	7.6	7.4	7.0	8.3
• Int. finish	10	6.8	7.3	6.5	7.6	6.0	7.5	6.6	7.9	6.8	8.4
	40 pts	**28.7**	**28.5**	**25.5**	**32.9**	**25.9**	**29.2**	**30.1**	**29.3**	**26.2**	**32.4**
Accessories											
• Number and practicality	10	7.2	7.4	6.4	8.5	6.2	7.1	6.3	7.8	7.3	7.5
• Storage space	10	7.1	6.5	6.8	7.3	5.8	7.3	7.2	6.9	7.1	7.6
• Instruments/Controls	10	7.4	7.5	6.2	7.8	6.0	7.2	6.4	7.7	6.3	7.2
• Ventilation/Heating	10	7.6	7.4	6.6	8.0	7.1	7.6	7.2	7.8	6.1	7.7
	40 pts	**29.3**	**28.8**	**26.0**	**31.6**	**25.1**	**29.2**	**27.1**	**30.2**	**26.8**	**30.0**
Body											
• Front access/space	15	13.0	12.8	13.5	12.0	10.9	13.0	12.5	12.3	11.8	13.6
• Rear access/space	15	12.8	12.2	12.3	12.6	9.8	12.8	11.1	10.1	9.5	10.8
• Trunk: access & volume	5	4.1	4.0	2.4	4.0	3.0	4.1	4.3	4.7	3.1	3.6
• Mechanical system access	5	2.5	3.5	4.0	4.0	4.0	2.5	4.0	4.0	4.5	4.6
	40 pts	**32.4**	**32.5**	**32.2**	**32.6**	**27.7**	**32.4**	**31.9**	**31.1**	**28.9**	**32.6**
Comfort											
• Suspension	10	8.2	6.2	6.7	8.3	5.0	7.8	7.0	8.5	6.8	8.1
• Noise level	10	8.0	6.0	7.6	8.2	5.0	7.6	7.4	7.8	7.4	7.5
• Seats	10	7.3	6.8	6.7	8.0	6.2	7.5	6.9	9.3	7.0	7.8
• Driving position	10	7.4	6.8	6.8	7.8	6.5	7.7	7.4	8.8	7.4	8.2
	40 pts	**30.9**	**25.8**	**34.0**	**32.3**	**22.7**	**30.6**	**28.7**	**34.4**	**28.6**	**31.6**
Engine/Transmission											
• Efficiency	15	12.1	8.9	10.3	12.1	8.2	12.2	11.5	13.0	11.2	11.6
• Performance	15	12.0	8.0	9.5	12.4	7.3	12.0	10.6	12.3	11.0	10.6
• Gearshift lever	5	2.5	2.7	3.6	3.8	3.3	2.5	3.7	4.4	3.8	4.0
• Gearshifting	5	4.0	3.0	3.4	4.1	2.4	4.0	3.6	4.1	3.6	4.0
	40 pts	**30.6**	**22.6**	**26.8**	**32.4**	**21.2**	**30.7**	**29.4**	**33.8**	**29.6**	**30.2**
Handling											
• Road adherence	20	16.2	14.2	14.7	16.5	12.3	16.5	14.3	17.3	13.9	14.9
• Steering	10	8.0	7.2	7.1	7.5	5.8	8.1	6.5	8.6	8.2	9.0
• Brakes	10	7.9	7.3	7.1	8.3	6.0	7.9	7.5	7.6	7.0	8.0
	40 pts	**32.1**	**28.7**	**28.9**	**32.3**	**24.1**	**32.5**	**28.3**	**33.5**	**29.1**	**31.9**
Safety											
• Airbags	15	10.0	10.0	10.0	10.0	10.0	10.0	10.0	10.0	10.0	10.0
• Visibility	10	7.6	8.1	7.0	8.1	6.7	7.6	7.5	8.7	7.3	8.2
• Sideview mirrors	5	3.9	4.0	3.8	4.3	3.7	3.9	3.6	3.5	4.2	4.2
	30 pts	**21.5**	**22.1**	**20.8**	**22.4**	**20.4**	**21.5**	**21.1**	**22.2**	**21.5**	**22.4**
Performance											
• Off-road	30	26.0	22.0	23.0	28.0	22.0	26.0	28.0	30.0	25.0	24.0
• Acceleration	15	13.0	13.0	12.0	14.0	11.0	13.0	14.0	14.0	15.0	13.0
• Braking	15	15.0	12.0	13.0	13.0	11.0	13.0	12.0	12.0	12.0	13.0
	60 pts	**54.0**	**47.0**	**48.0**	**55.0**	**44.0**	**52.0**	**54.0**	**56.0**	**52.0**	**50.0**
Other criteria											
• Baggage space	10	8.0	6.0	8.0	7.0	6.0	8.0	10.0	8.0	9.0	7.0
• Test drivers' choice	50	47.0	43.0	42.0	50.0	41.0	45.0	47.0	48.0	44.0	46.0
• Price	10	8.0	7.0	8.0	8.0	10.0	8.0	7.0	8.0	6.0	8.0
	70 pts	**63.0**	**56.0**	**58.0**	**65.0**	**57.0**	**61.0**	**64.0**	**64.0**	**59.0**	**61.0**
Grand Total	**400 pts**	**322.5**	**292.0**	**300.2**	**336.5**	**268.1**	**319.1**	**314.5**	**334.5**	**301.7**	**322.0**
RANKING		**3**	**9**	**8**	**1**	**10**	**5**	**6**	**2**	**7**	**4**

THE WAR OF the Mini Muscle Cars

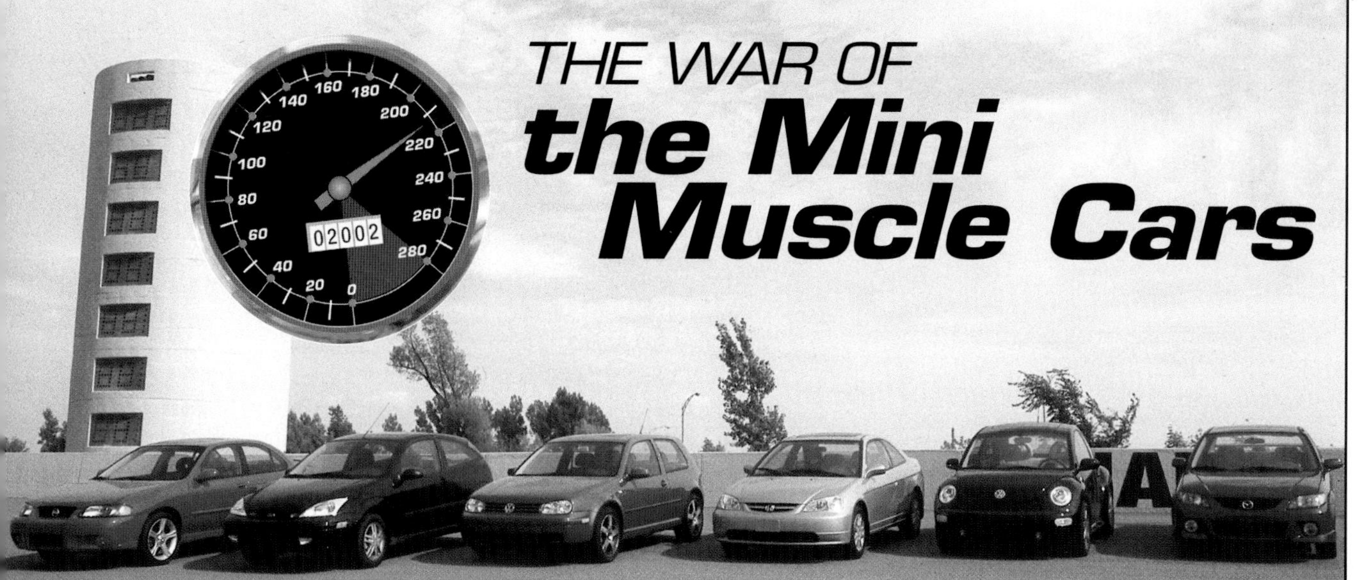

● BY DENIS DUQUET

The muscle car era has been gone for decades. But the enjoyment of performance cars has not disappeared. There are always people (mostly young people) who are looking for a real thrill. But instead of relying on massive cubic inches to power the car, it is now a game of finesse, where sub-compacts emphazise roadholding and driving precision. Compared to the deep-throated roar of the monster V8s, the acceleration of the small performance cars of the new millennium is less spectacular. Their road behavior, however, is a definite improvement, while their agile nature allows for higher speed cornering without drama or worries about flying uncontrollably off the road.

The sub-compact market is generally that of drivers who look for economy cars and who don't want to spend too much money on their driving. Given this definition, it would be surprising to find interesting cars to drive in this slot. But as young drivers are not generally well off, and as they appreciate sporty driving, several carmakers have increased the performance of some of their production cars. The most obvious example in this category is the new Nissan Sentra SE-R Spec V whose 175-hp engine and 17-inch wheels don't really suit buyers who are looking for economy. The Mazda Protegé is another compact sedan that attracts buyers because of its balanced road manners and its competitive price. However, the MP3 version of this model offers practically everything an enthusiast would want in terms of equipment and style. The Ford Focus three-door is not part of this category: this hatchback model has not been fitted with accessories such as those found on the MP3. This is a standard model with a 130-hp engine, sports seats and alloy wheels. Naturally, its price is lower. Only time will tell how this simple approach will turn out.

The Honda Civic is the car that started this trend toward small performance compacts. Its advanced engine, efficient suspension and incredible reliability have made the Civic the obvious choice for tuners and accessory specialists. The disappearance of the hatchback version in 2002 was a disappointment for some as this model was always associated with performance driving among the sub-compacts. In the meantime, while we await the arrival of the 160-hp SiR hatchback models in the spring of 2002, the only model capable of defending Honda colors in this category is the Coupe Si with its 127-hp engine.

The Volkswagen Golf GTI is another model which has been a great contributor to the popularity of high-performance sub-compacts. It was the first cult car before the Civic came along, to create a new market for performance parts and accessories. This caused the division of the performance accessory market into two segments, one centered on the Civic and the other on the Golf. Contrary to Honda, who sometimes had doubts about this type of car, abandoning its hatchback model for a few months, Volkswagen has stayed the course while developing its GTI. It can now be ordered with the formidable VR6 2.8-liter engine and fetches a fairly high price. This test at least enables one to compare what each company has to offer in this category and how they compare in terms of speed and equipment.

The New Beetle is a sub-compact. And it is not necessarily as economical to buy as are some of the models which are part of this comparison test. Its styling and its design as a fun car should disqualify it from this test. But here again we have a car which can in fact give a good account for itself with the 1.8T engine version. Anyway, we included it in just in case.

Once again, we brought everybody to the racetrack so that we could really see what these cars were made of. A slalom, a few laps around the track and driving around the local back roads gave our testers a chance to discover what they were like. Everything was set for a performance car war. Let's find out who the winner is.

VOLKSWAGEN GOLF GTI

ARMED TO THE TEETH

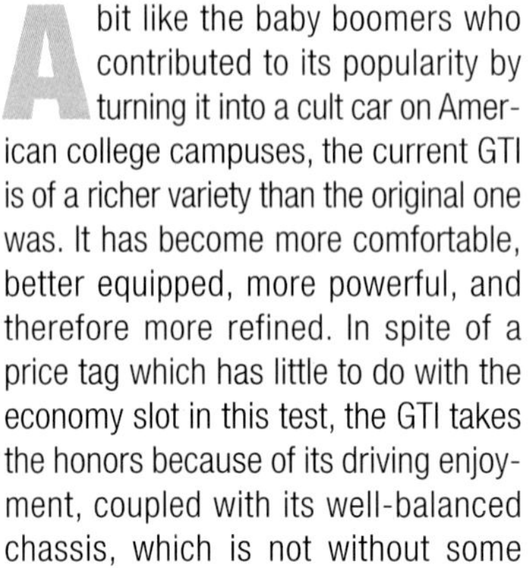

A bit like the baby boomers who contributed to its popularity by turning it into a cult car on American college campuses, the current GTI is of a richer variety than the original one was. It has become more comfortable, better equipped, more powerful, and therefore more refined. In spite of a price tag which has little to do with the economy slot in this test, the GTI takes the honors because of its driving enjoyment, coupled with its well-balanced chassis, which is not without some faults, and because of its interior appointments. It is from the outset the most convincing car of the lot.

It is certain that the 174-hp VR6 engine gives it a distinct advantage. But power is not the answer to all things. For example, the Nissan Sentra with its 175-hp engine did not overwhelm its rivals. Even the V6 engine of the Golf turned out to be a handicap in terms of roadholding, as it put too much weight on the front end, causing strong understeer when pushed in slower corners. The 1.8T engine would definitely have helped the Golf obtain a better balance and therefore its advantage over the Mazda Protegé MP3 would probably have been greater. However, one could also argue that the MP3, fitted with a 160-hp engine, would have blown away the opposition thanks to its better chassis and accessories.

Sheer power is not paramount. The Golf did very well in the slalom test and its general driving manners were very pleasing to our testers. They appreciated the roadholding, the lumbar support of the seats, its look, its interior design; and it was well liked by all our drivers. In other words, this Golf offered performance and above average roadholding. And it did so with relative ease, without making too many demands on the driver and without being a strain on the passengers. It is therefore possible to indulge in sporty driving without having to push things too hard.

But that comes at a price. To top things off, the Golf has acquired creature comforts over the years and some deplore that it has lost its true-blue sports car characteristics which are evident in the Mazda MP3 and the Nissan Sentra SE-R. Let's be politically correct and instead of talking about the GTI acquiring middle-class comforts, let's use balanced terms to indicate that this motor car has reached a "sophisticated level of development," contrary to some of the other participants in this comparison test, in which some were going to battle for the first time.

Anyway, the Golf GTI is no usurper, if its first place in the "Tester's First Choice" category is proof of its quality and integrity. And in order to bolster its position, Volkswagen will increase the power of the 1.8-liter turbo engine within the next six months, taking it from 150 to 180 hp. Also, prices have been revised downward. A rear spoiler would probably give it a more aggressive style, but, nothing's perfect!

PRO

I like this mix of solidity, steering and suspension feedback. This GTI is like my mother's carrot cake!

CON

I enjoyed its roadholding and the sheer driving fun. However, responsiveness, gear selection and its soft suspension should be revised.

MAZDA MP3

FOR THE WANT OF A FEW HORSES

The Golf seduced everyone thanks to its well-balanced approach and the power of its V6 engine. The Mazda MP3 charmed us with its lively presentation and its appointments which made it look like a performance-tuned car with a chassis whose quality is enough to make all the other contestants green with envy. All you need is to look at it for a few seconds, get into the driver's seat and you will be enchanted and mesmerized. Are you a music enthusiast? Just listen to the Kenwood system which will play CDs taken from an MP3 CD burner and you will be even more impressed. In fact, the Mazda has really only one chink in its armor: an engine that just does not quite cut the cake. Its 140 horses don't quite all seem to make the call. Quite often, one is surprised by the engine's lack of response, which always seems to be struggling. Moreover, the acceleration times claimed by Mazda are a little optimistic, which effectively adds to the initial disappointment.

It's too bad, as this sub-compact has a very good overall balance which is almost without equal. As mentioned previously, its chassis is excellent and the use of the lowered suspension on 17-inch wheels and better quality shock absorbers explains its second placing in the slalom. I had faster lap times on the track than the Golf, in spite of the longish straightaways which made the 140-horsepower 2.0-liter engine work very hard.

PRO

Excellent improved package by Mazda. The solid chassis, suspension and roadholding are hyper super, as is the audio system.

CON

It really lacks any real punch. A more powerful engine would make it a much better car.

What is really interesting about the car is that Mazda had great fun modifying one of its production cars, as an enthusiast would have done if he'd gone to buy accessories from a performance shop. The most obvious changes are the front strut tower crossbars which strengthen the front end considerably, the exclusive alloy rims, a more free-flowing exhaust system and a really special paint job. Several air flow add-ons give it a really unique profile, making people notice and stare as it goes by. A few carbon fiber and aluminium fixtures which really look very good have also enhanced the cockpit. Of a more practical nature, aluminium pedals and a Nardi steering wheel are convincing arguments for the performance character of this car. However, one must deplore the absence of ABS brakes, which made the front tires wear out in no time.

Actually, it would have been easy for Mazda to turn this Protégé into an overly decorated sporty Christmas tree. Yet all the add-on elements fit together very well. Unfortunately, it feels as though the audio system is more powerful than the engine is. I'm sorry to harp on this point, but it really is the only significant weakness of this small Japanese car which, in spite of that handicap, has managed to climb to the second rung of the podium. In fact, the MP3 is living proof that a well-balanced motor car does not need to have a large engine.

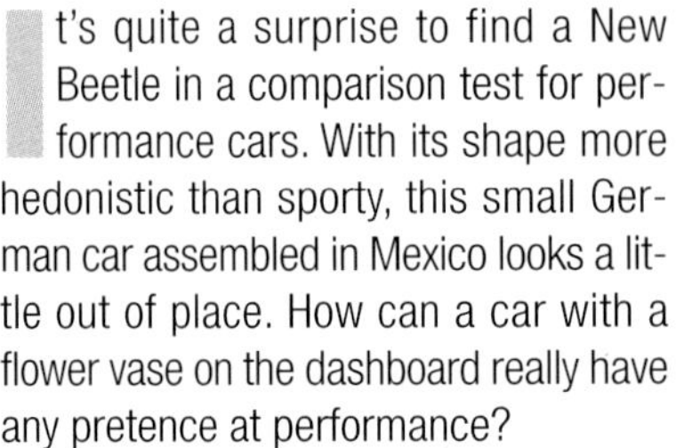

VOLKSWAGEN NEW BEETLE

DECEPTIVE APPEARANCE

It's quite a surprise to find a New Beetle in a comparison test for performance cars. With its shape more hedonistic than sporty, this small German car assembled in Mexico looks a little out of place. How can a car with a flower vase on the dashboard really have any pretence at performance?

With its roundish shape, it does not seem to have what it takes to be part of this group. But surprises are nothing new for the New Beetle which, when it was unveiled, had surprised everyone with its roadholding and its performance, just as everyone was expecting the worst. Made up of rounded shapes and without any visible bumpers, many questions had been raised about its safety. Yet, crash tests have revealed that this sedan has the best safety results for its occupants.

Here again, the New Beetle has struck another blow during this test. Just seeing these playpen lines and its New Age look, it was difficult to anticipate the results, which got it on the third step of the podium. This car does everything well, without ever seeming to be hard pressed. The explanation is very simple. This car is but a Golf onto which one has grafted a fantasy body shell. It has therefore kept the qualities of its older sister. Moreover, the 1.8-liter turbo engine which propels it, is considered by many to have better driveability than the heavier VR6. With its 150 hp, this engine has to concede 24 hp to the VR6 of the Golf GTI, but its power is always there at the right time, in any circumstances, and it always works like a charm.

The fact that this fantasy car, reminiscent of a past era, recorded the quickest lap times, leaves no doubt whatsoever about its performance. And as if this were not enough, it was "best of class" in terms of responsiveness in passing acceleration. All that attests to the qualities of both the engine and the chassis. Surprisingly, this car also achieved first place in terms of overall performance. Odd, but figures don't lie.

This is not the only contradiction. In general, performance cars are penalized in terms of creature comforts and interior roominess, as the designers have had to sacrifice something to performance. In the New Beetle, the fact that rear legroom is only average and that the rear seats are difficult to get to is explained by the stylist's desire to revive the lines from the legendary Beetle whose arched roof practically obliterated rear headroom.

This test confirms that the Wolfsburg engineers were not satisfied with a token design that would just bring back memories of its glorious past. They have put together a car with very real road-going qualities, capable of doing battle with the best, both on the road and the racetrack. It is impossible to find a car that is both more anachronistic and more balanced than the New Beetle.

PRO

I never liked the New Beetle but this test changed my mind. It's not a small car, it's a high performance sports car. The 1.8T engine is superb.

CON

Superb road going car, its only drawbacks are a few sloppy details and a lack of standard equipment normally found on most cars.

NISSAN SENTRA

CHASSIS FAILURE

At first glance, many thought that the Sentra SE-R Spec V with its 175-hp engine, sporty suspension, six-speed gearbox and 17-inch wheels was going to wreak havoc with the opposition. Quite the contrary, it was havoc that befell this small Nissan. It placed fourth, just ahead of the Honda Civic and the Ford Focus which are more modestly powered and further handicapped by their tires and suspension.

The cause of this semi-failure is easy to pinpoint. The car's chassis does not have the qualities needed in order to take full advantage of all this power and of all that rubber on the track. These limitations were especially highlighted during the slalom and our tester had quite a handful when forcing through the successive changes of direction. The rigid rear axle could explain this behavior. The designers of this Nissan probably developed the car on a road course where the car could take a set in the corner and generate better side grip, thus allowing it to take full advantage of its power. Its second best lap times on the race track seem to lend weight to this theory.

Like the Mazda MP3, the Sentra is fitted with several performance components which belong to the tuning accessory world. In addition to the obligatory rear spoiler, the brushed aluminum gearshift knob and the contrasting tones of the instrument cluster, one must add the seat-covers in a red based cloth with semi-sheer black band offering a pleasant and sharp contrast to the eye. One point worth mentioning is that, not only are the red-on-black instruments difficult to read, but it is impossible to know whether one's speed is 60 miles an hour or not as the numbering jumps from 50 to 70. It's up to the driver to decide where the speed limit is.

The Sentra SE-R seems to be the product of a strange mixture of a family sedan coupled with an aggressive engine and drivetrain, the most powerful that happened to be on hand. It doesn't just develop 175 hp, it has the temperament of a racing engine with a rev limiter that brutally cuts off the engine at 6500 rpm. And I really mean brutal interruption. Furthermore, although some have appreciated the short throw of the 6-gear shifter, many have also criticized its lack of feeling. It's almost like a video game: click, up a gear; click, next gear.

According to Nissan's press releases, the SE-R Spec V is ready for the racetrack. They should also have added that a roll cage would be needed, as not only would it improve safety, it would give the chassis the badly needed torsional rigidity it lacks. There is more: test results show that Volkswagen engineers have designed a torsion-bar rear suspension that is more efficient than the Sentra.

The SE-R has an interesting performance, but it lacks the design balance and structural integrity that the three cars ahead of it in the rankings possess.

PRO

An outstanding fiery nature which will please enthusiasts who don't like compromise.

CON

Once inside, one thinks that this is a car designed before the age of ergonomics. On the road, the torque steer reminds us of the Saab Viggen.

HONDA CIVIC

HATCHBACK, PLEASE

Several Honda managers were upset when confronted with comments from the specialized press about the new-generation Civic, that it had become more family-oriented, softer and not as performance-driven as before. This test confirmed what we already knew: the current Civic is designed more for comfort and quietness than for performance, which is just about average.

To the carmaker's credit, one must admit that Honda has managed to remain competitive in price and that gas mileage has improved despite the increase in power and cubic capacity. In brief, if you drive in everyday traffic with your 127-hp Civic Coupe, you will be satisfied both by its performance and reliability.

In fact, the problem is not necessarily that Honda is drawing back from performance, it's just that other carmakers have decided to improve the performance of their standard models instead of leaving it to the aftermarket, where the buyer would do it himself at the performance shop.

However, as we have decided in the course of this test to compare each carmaker's best efforts in a given category, Honda seems to lag behind. Things will definitely change for Honda in the spring of 2002 when they bring out the SiR, a 160-hp European-styled hatchback.

If the present Si seems a little slow, it would only require a few improvements to the suspension, wider tires or a few more horses to completely transform this model. This was confirmed when we tested a car that had been modified in this manner. That Civic had the best times in the slalom, and even then, it was powered by a turbo of dubious efficiency. The potential is there and it's up to the owners to modify the car with the numerous parts and accessories which are available on the market.

Honda still keeps the fighting spirit alive in this category, as they have developed and produced a vehicle whose chassis and suspension will accept increased power, suspension improvements and wider tires, and deliver drastically improved performance when these changes are properly selected and installed. This approach has brought a small fortune to the parts and accessories shops in the United States, and Canada, where thousands of young enthusiasts have invested all their savings to improve their Civics.

Unfortunately for Honda, other carmakers have decided to tone up their standard vehicles with factory improvements just for this market segment. The Mazda MP3 and the Nissan Sentra SE-R are obvious examples. I am certain that an ordinary Protegé would not do as well as the Civic in the slalom. The rules of the game have changed and Honda is now well aware of it, hence the new SiR.

If you want to add "Sport" to your Honda Civic, the obvious thing to do is to stop by your performance shop and have it modified according to your tastes and needs. This is quite a popular practice, to the point that some dealers have opened a sports accessory department. Until the SiR comes along, you can invest the money saved on its purchase to improve your present Si.

PRO

Its reliability and sound design will compensate for its lack of performance. The more you drive the car, the better you appreciate it.

CON

Where is the Honda Civic of yesteryear? It has become a family car. It has become anonymous. Quick, a hatchback!

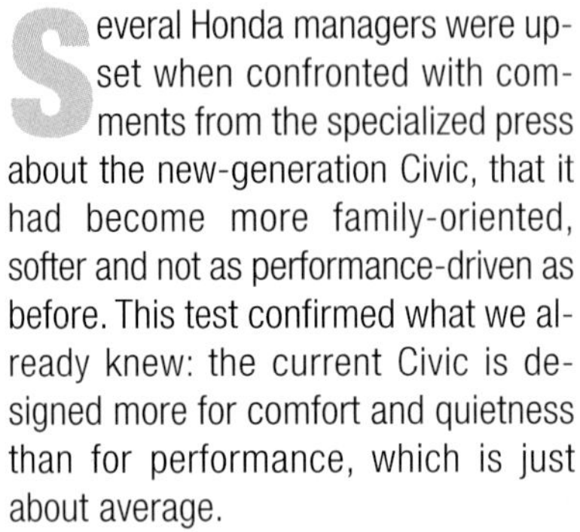

FORD FOCUS

A MISUNDERSTOOD BARGAIN

When Ford unveiled the Focus on the North American market, many were amazed that the company had dared to include a three-door hatchback in their line-up. In North America, this type of design is not very popular, particularly in the United States, and many had thought that Ford would have done better to leave it to the European market. Trying to attract young drivers, Ford marketing managers have fitted the ZX3 with a 130-hp engine, alloy wheels and sport seats. They wanted to market a car which was as enjoyable to drive as it was competitively priced.

The problem with this line of action is that the Ford dealership network is mostly centered on the sale of commonplace generic models. The dealers treated the ZX3 as just another "small econo box," not bothering to reach out to a market that had been faithful for decades to the Volkswagen Golf and Honda Civic. Ford is also guilty of not having developed a sporting image for that model, aimed specifically at those young drivers. The wagon is practical, the sedan is good value, but the ZX3 should not be put in the same mold. In Europe, the approach was quite different and the successful participation of the ZX3 in the high-profile World Rally Championship immediately provided the image of a car worth acquiring and modifying.

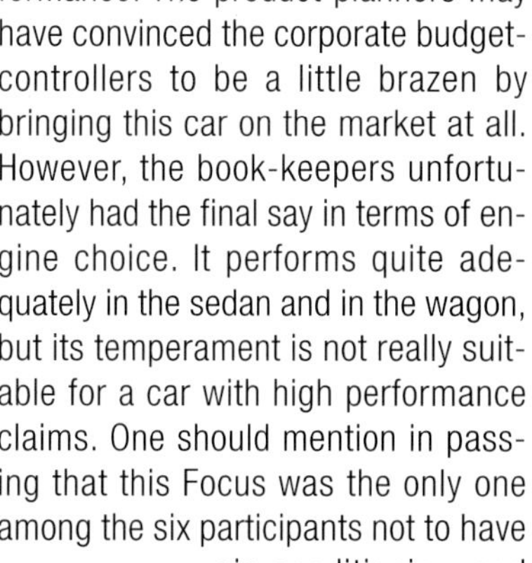

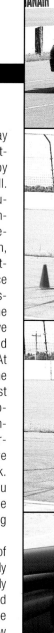

PRO

Very pleasant, the Focus. It is a good choice for someone with a limited budget. The Focus seems to revive the spirit of the 1984 Golf GTI.

CON

It has potential. But it does not show it, and the price tag is too high for a car with such limited standard equipment.

As it is, the ZX3 has an excellent chassis and sound road behavior. The engine, however, lacks responsiveness and power, and was largely responsible for the car's back-of-the-pack performance. The product planners may have convinced the corporate budget-controllers to be a little brazen by bringing this car on the market at all. However, the book-keepers unfortunately had the final say in terms of engine choice. It performs quite adequately in the sedan and in the wagon, but its temperament is not really suitable for a car with high performance claims. One should mention in passing that this Focus was the only one among the six participants not to have air conditioning and power windows. At Ford, it seems that the credo is ''youth must suffer in order to appreciate creature comforts later on''. Furthermore, the car we test-drove was black. On a very hot day, you can imagine that the lack of air conditioning was very noticeable.

Yet, the absence of this accessory probably would have been quickly forgotten if this car had been given better tires. Whereas the leaders of this group had 17-inch low profile tires, the Focus only had 15-inch equipment, as had the Civic.

To give this Focus an equal chance, it needs different rims and wider, high performance tires. That alone would probably have knocked off a second on the slalom time, and would have improved the steering precision while reducing braking distances by a few metres.

There again, Ford will have the answer in the coming months, with the introduction of a hatchback Focus with more muscle, prepared by the SVT division.

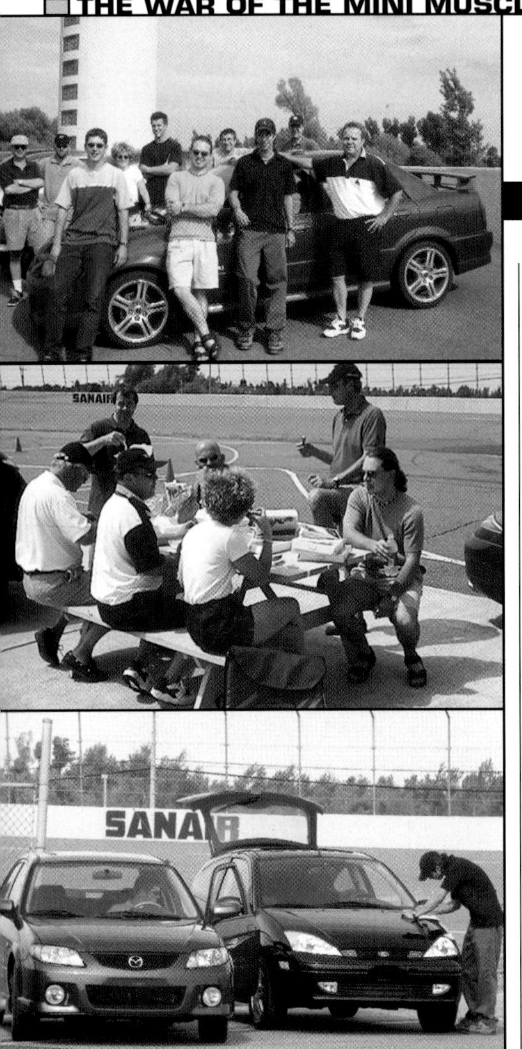

CONCLUSION

SOMETHING FOR EVERYONE

The most expensive and best-equipped car won the match, but the cause and effect relation may not really be there. Indeed, a more economical version of the GTI with a 1.8T 180-hp engine would have done a lot better and is a noticeably lower priced item. One should not be obsessed by its well-equipped appointments, and don't forget that this is in fact an extremely well balanced car with an exceptional chassis.

Although the Mazda MP3 was second overall, it delivers the best price-quality ratio of the six contestants. It practically has everything going for it, including a very competitive price in view of its equipment. Unfortunately, its engine is a little too timid for a better placing. A few more horses and it would have prevailed. Actually, in terms of sound proofing, it does better than the Sentra SE-R Spec V which itself does rather well in this area. The latter is handicapped by a chassis which most certainly was not designed for that kind of performance. Even though it did not perform well at all in the slalom test, this car will be enjoyed by the sport enthusiast because of the power of its engine and its 6-gear racing-type gearbox.

The New Beetle confounded the critics. In spite of its easygoing looks and an overall design which is more convivial than sporting, it did very well in each comparison slot. The fastest on the track, with best engine responsiveness, it brings together a joy of life and the availability of an aggressive driving style. It proved to be the most pleasant surprise of this test.

The Honda Civic and Ford Focus finished last but should not be disregarded. Priced below $20,000, these are very good cars for everyday use. Moreover, the quality of their chassis is such that they open themselves to performance-enhancing modifications. Actually, you will find outlined in the back pages tips on what can be done to improve the performance of these two cars.

Specifications

Specifications	Ford Focus	Honda Civic Si	Mazda MP3	Nissan Sentra SE-R Spec V	Volkswagen Golf GTI	Volkswagen New Beetle
• Wheelbase	103.1 in	103.1 in	102.8 in	99.6 in	98.8 in	98.8 in
• Length	165.7 in	174.4 in	175.2 in	177.6 in	163.4 in	161 in
• Width	66.9 in	67.3 in	66.9 in	67.3 in	68.1 in	67.7 in
• Height	56.3 in	56.7 in	55.5 in	55.5 in	56.7 in	59.1 in
• Weight	2403 lb (1090 kg)	2557 lb (1160 kg)	2632 lb (1194 kg)	2743 lb (1244 kg)	2811 lb (1275 kg)	2866 lb (1300 kg)
• Transmission	manual	manual	manual	manual	manual	manual
• Number of gears	5	5	5	5	5	5
• Engine	4L	4L	4L	4L	V6	4L
• Displacement	2.0-liter	1.6-liter	2.0-liter	2.5-liter	2.8-liter	1.8-liter turbo
• Horsepower	130 hp	127 hp	140 hp	175 hp	174 hp	150 hp
• Front suspension	independent	independent	independent	independent	independent	independent
• Rear suspension	independent	independent	independent	independent	semi-independent	semi-independent
• Front brakes	disc	disc	disc	disc	disc	disc
• Rear brakes	disc	drum	disc	disc	disc	disc
• ABS	yes	yes	yes	yes	yes	yes
• Tires	P195/60R15	P185/65R15	P205/45R17	P215/45Z17	P225/45R17	P225/45R17
• Steering	rack-and-pinion	rack-and-pinion	rack-and-pinion	rack-and-pinion	rack-and-pinion	rack-and-pinion
• Turning circle	35.8 feet (10.9 m)	34 feet (10.4 m)	34 feet (10.4 m)	39.4 feet (12 m)	39 feet (11.9 m)	32.8 feet (10 m)
• Air bags	front / side	front / side	front	front / side	front / side / head	front / side / head
• Fuel tank	13 gallons	13 gallons	13 gallons	19 gallons	15 gallons	15 gallons
• Trunk	12.4 cu. ft	12.9 cu. ft	12.9 cu. ft	11.6 cu. ft	11.9 cu. ft	10.6 cu. ft
• Acceleration 0-60 mph	9.9 sec.	8.7 sec.	9.2 sec.	7.3 sec.	7.1 sec.	8.06 sec.
• Maximum speed	115mph (185 km/h)	122 mph (195 km/h)	122 mph (195 km/h)	115 mph (185 km/h)	137 mph (220 km/h)	115 mph (185 km/h)
• Fuel consumption	29 mpg	33 mpg	27 mpg	24 mpg	23 mpg	29 mpg
	8 L/100 km	7.2 L/100 km	8.7 L/100 km	9.8 L/100 km	10.4 L/100 km	8.2 L/100 km
• Price ($CDN / $US)	17,955 / 14,810	19,000 / n.a.	23,795 / 19,000	21,498 / 17,500	31,295 / 23,450	29,995 / 22,995

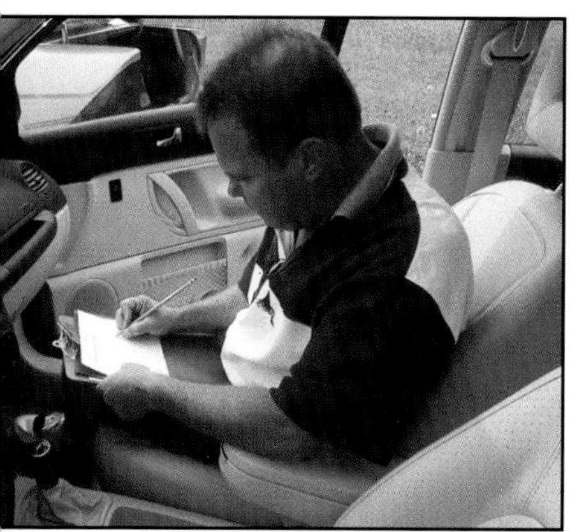

This comparison test allowed us to define three main trends in the present market. The more luxurious models, such as the Golf and the New Beetle, cost-conscious sedans changed into sports machines, such as the MP3 and the Sentra, and finally the Civic and the Focus, which are "ordinary" cars which can be successfully modified. Whatever trend you wish to follow at the time of purchase is up to you. I can only hope that our impressions, the timed performance results and the evaluations of our testing staff will help you to make a better choice.

Denis Duquet

Muscle Made to Measure

As one can see from the comparison test results, both the Honda Civic and the Ford Focus kind of bit the dust. The source of their rather poor showing is easy to understand. They had to con-

Evaluation Sheet

		Ford Focus	Honda Civic Si	Mazda MP3	Nissan Sentra SE-R Spec V	VW Golf GTI	VW New Beetle
Esthetics							
• Exterior	10	7.5	7.6	7.8	7.9	8.0	8.1
• Interior	10	7.0	7.1	8.3	7.6	8.4	7.8
• Ext. finish	10	7.1	8.1	8.9	7.9	8.5	8.4
• Int. finish	10	7.4	7.9	8.5	7.3	7.7	7.0
	40 pts	**29.0**	**30.7**	**33.5**	**30.7**	**32.6**	**31.3**
Accessories							
• Number and practicality	10	6.1	7.8	7.2	7.9	8.6	8.1
• Storage spaces	10	7.0	6.0	7.6	6.8	7.4	7.6
• Instruments/Controls	10	6.6	7.7	9.0	7.5	8.3	7.9
• Ventilation/Heating	10	7.1	7.9	8.1	7.7	9.3	8.6
	40 pts	**26.8**	**29.4**	**31.9**	**29.9**	**33.6**	**32.2**
Body							
• Front access/space	15	12.2	12.5	12.0	13.1	12.5	13.0
• Rear access/space	15	11.1	10.4	12.0	13.4	11.2	8.5
• Trunk: access & volume	5	3.4	4.2	3.7	3.8	3.3	2.1
• Mechanical system access	5	4.0	2.5	3.5	4.0	1.5	1.5
	40 pts	**30.7**	**29.6**	**31.2**	**34.3**	**28.5**	**25.1**
Comfort							
• Suspension	10	8.4	7.4	8.9	7.6	8.8	8.4
• Noise level	10	7.5	7.1	6.9	7.2	8.3	8.2
• Seats	10	8.6	7.0	7.5	7.4	8.1	7.5
• Driving position	10	7.6	7.9	8.5	8.3	8.9	8.1
	40 pts	**32.1**	**29.4**	**31.8**	**30.5**	**34.1**	**32.2**
Engine/Transmission							
• Efficiency	15	12.2	11.5	12.3	13.3	13.6	13.1
• Performance	15	10.3	10.8	11.9	13.9	14.0	13.2
• Gearshift lever	5	3.8	3.5	4.2	4.3	3.6	3.5
• Gearshifting	5	4.0	4.3	4.6	4.2	3.6	3.7
	40 pts	**30.3**	**30.1**	**33.0**	**35.7**	**34.8**	**33.5**
Handling							
• Road adherence	20	15.2	15.8	18.8	16.6	17.7	17.4
• Steering	20	17.7	15.9	17.0	17.2	18.6	16.8
• Brakes	10	6.7	7.1	8.0	7.8	8.2	8.8
	50 pts	**39.6**	**38.8**	**43.8**	**41.6**	**44.5**	**43.0**
Safety							
• Airbags	15	10.0	10.0	10.0	10.0	15.0	15.0
• Visibility	10	8.0	7.4	7.5	7.1	7.3	6.4
• Sideview mirrors	5	3.8	4.0	4.2	4.1	4.2	3.8
	30 pts	**21.8**	**21.4**	**21.7**	**21.2**	**26.5**	**25.2**
Timed Performance							
• Passing performance	10	6.0	6.0	6.0	7.0	8.0	10.0
• Acceleration	20	14.0	16.0	15.0	18.0	20.0	17.0
• Braking	20	15.0	18.0	16.0	15.0	17.0	20.0
• Slalom	10	6.0	6.0	8.0	6.0	10.0	7.0
• Lap	10	6.0	6.0	7.0	8.0	6.0	10.0
	70 pts	**47.0**	**52.0**	**52.0**	**54.0**	**61.0**	**64.0**
Other criteria							
• Baggage space	10	9.0	10.0	10.0	8.0	7.0	6.0
• Test drivers' choice	30	24.0	25.0	28.0	27.0	30.0	26.0
• Price	10	10.0	10.0	8.0	6.0	5.0	6.0
	50 pts	**43.0**	**45.0**	**46.0**	**41.0**	**42.0**	**38.0**
Grand Total	**400 pts**	**300.3**	**306.4**	**324.9**	**318.9**	**337.6**	**324.5**
RANKING		**6**	**5**	**2**	**4**	**1**	**3**

tend with the more powerful engines of their rivals and factory installed modifications to enhance their performance. We have gone a long way from the do-it-yourself performance add-on.

Yet this tradition is not a thing of the past, far from it. It has flourished to such an extent that the manufacturers have decided to join the bandwagon and produce their own brand of bolt-on performance models, such as the Mazda MP3 and the Nissan Sentra SE-R Spec V. We invited two special guests to our comparison test, so that you could have an idea of what these modified economy cars can do. The five-speed Ford Focus ZX3 with a base price of $CDN17,700 ($US 11,115). After modifying the bodywork, the suspension, the exhaust system, the air filter and the tires, the car went through the slalom test a half-second faster. That brought the ticket price to $CDN 27,000 ($US 16,950). The engine remained unchanged. However, a Vortex supercharger can be bolted on the engine and, with a modified chip, this brings the power up to 180 hp, which should shave another second off the slalom time. However, all his will lighten your wallet by $CDN 32,845 ($US 20,625), car included.

The Honda Civic had not only been fitted with the same modifications as the Ford, but it had been completely re-sprayed with a custom paint. Please see the list of modifications. The 1.7-liter Honda engine was fitted with a Garrett turbo, raising power to 170 hp. With the lowered suspension, the extra power and the wide low-profile tires, the Honda won best slalom time of the day, ousting the Golf by 0.24 seconds. At what price all that extra power and performance? $CDN 10,000 ($US 6,300) to $CDN 12,000 ($US 7,525) more, parts and labor included, to be added to the $CDN 19,000 ($US 11,925) base price of the Si Coupe.

All in all, performance is something you have to pay for. However, choosing your own performance accessories will help you personalize your car according to your taste and wishes. Of course, as long as you listen to expert advice.

Denis Duquet

These are two examples of cars that have been aesthetically and mechanically modified. You can follow these examples according to your own budget. Of course, you can let the manufacturer do the job, which is more convenient perhaps, but lacks the personal touch.

FORD FOCUS ZX3

- Double Windset front and rear spoilers
- Hella headlamps
- Technique suspension lowered by 1 inch
- Vibran strut brackets
- Enkei 17x7 aluminum rims
- P205/40ZR17 Toyo tires
- Vibran 2 1/4 muffler
- Volant air filter

A Vortex supercharger will increase the power to 180 hp

HONDA CIVIC COUPE

- Wing West spoiler and wind ducting parts
- Neuspeed lowered springs
- 17-inch alloy wheels
- P215/45ZR7 Toyo tires
- High performance shock absorbers from the 2002 Acura RSX
- Hawks HP+ carbon brakes
- DC Sport Exhaust system
- DC Sport front and rear strut tower crossbars
- Garrett T25 turbo

SURPRISE, SURPRISE

Looking only at performance and roadholding, the results of this comparison test were surprising, as would be a Minardi victory in a Formula 1 Grand Prix. That a car like the Volkswagen New Beetle 1.8T should reach first place in timed laps around a track and then third place in the slalom constitutes an affront that will be difficult to accept for all the macho machines which were on the starting line. For Volkswagen, who has always wanted to give a more masculine image to its reinvented Beetle, this is indeed an exploit which should further its cause in the face of buyers who are sometimes sceptical about its sports performance.

However, rejoicing is probably a little less intense when the German carmaker realizes that the car who effectively gave birth to these mini muscle cars, the GTI, was in fact bested by rivals that were less powerful. In spite of its 174 hp, it dropped to fourth place on the racetrack part of the test. More noticeably, a Mazda MP3 with 34 hp less was half a second faster. And talk about surprise! What about this stunning Madza whose engine is smaller than a sub-woofer and which did not seem to us particularly expressive to start with. But this MP3 has the best chassis of all those econo-sports. Charles-André Bilodeau, our young and talented official slalom driver, sang its praises: "Very well tuned suspension, precise steering, great stability, it's only slightly lacking in power". On the track, this car inspires great confidence, reveals neutral behavior when puhed in corners and is without body roll. I thought it was by far the easiest one to drive, to push to the limit, in spite of tires that were hard and noisy because of flat spots caused by the absence of ABS. Second in the slalom and third on the track, just a shade behind the Nissan Sentra SE-R, the MP3 gave an astonishing performance.

AN AWKWARD GTI

Much as the Mazda was easy to drive, the Volskwagen GTI is a real handful. The VR6 engine overwhelms the front suspension and the soft suspension settings do not help matters. The understeer is pronounced and if one adds a too-vague gearbox, one has to admit that this car is not at ease on the racetrack. The VR6 did a little better in the slalom, loosing by a narrow margin to the surprising MP3. Credit should be given to its torque, which pulls it hard coming out of corners, its 17-inch wheels and, once it has taken a set in a corner, the suspension behaves rather well. Judging by the performances of the New Beetle 1.8T, it is probable that a GTI 1.8T would probably have done better. Yet there again, the magnificent overall balance of the New Beetle is difficult to beat. Roadholding, braking, power, everything combines to produce lap times that one would not even suspect.

SEDUCTION AND DECEPTION

One expected marvelous things from the latest Nissan Sentra SE-R which had seduced quite a few participants in this comparison road test. With its 180 hp and all its aerodynamic appointments, it seemed that it could blow away all its rivals. However, in the slalom, it had to make do with a fourth place which, according to Charles-André, was due to enormous understeer and reluctance of the chassis to slide the back around, in order to square the car and use that power to really accelerate out of the curves. It also gives an impression of awkwardness. The power is there, but the chassis doesn't follow. In the beginning the gearbox linkage feels like a gadget; but one gets used to it and starts to enjoy it with practice. Under full power, during acceleration, the torque steer reminds one of the Saab Viggen, something which I would rather have missed.

THE LATECOMERS

In spite of much less power than average and 15-inch tires that were not up to the task, the Honda Civic Si and the Ford Focus ZX3 performed well, even though they had to make do with a fifth and sixth place, both on the track and in the slalom. These two cars are relatively easy to drive and the chassis and suspension are easy to improve upon using over-the-counter accessories. As they are the cheapest in the group, the lovers of high-performance will be able to modify them without having to break their piggy banks.

As you can see for yourselves, this comparison test was full of surprises and without doubt will become a matter for discussion, if not criticism, among interested perspective buyers.

Jacques Duval

Timed Performances

Slalom	
1 VW Golf GTI VR6	**35.39 sec.**
2 Mazda MP3	**35.66 sec.**
3 VW New Beetle 1.8T	**36.15 sec.**
4 Nissan Sentra SE-R Spec V	**36.22 sec.**
5 Honda Civic Si	**36.55 sec.**
6 Ford Focus ZX3	**36.59 sec.**

Lap times	
1 VW New Beetle 1.8T	**47.72 sec.**
2 Nissan Sentra SE-R Spec V	**48.14 sec.**
3 Mazda MP3	**48.23 sec.**
4 VW Golf GTI VR6	**48.88 sec.**
5 Honda Civic Si	**50.20 sec.**
6 Ford Focus ZX3	**50.73 sec.**

Tires:

VW Golf GTI VR6/VW New Beetle 1.8T:
Michelin Pilot P225/45R17

Nissan Sentra SE-R Spec V:
Continental P215/45ZR17

Mazda MP3:
Dunlop SP Sport: P205/45ZR17

Honda Civic Si:
Firestone FR 690: P185/65R15

Ford Focus ZX3:
Goodyear Eagle RSA: P195/60R15

RESPONSE: from 80 to 120 km/h in 4th gear (50 to 75 mph)	
1 VW New Beetle 1.8T	**8.2 sec.**
2 VW Golf GTI VR6	**8.5 sec.**
3 Nissan Sentra SE-R Spec V	**8.7 sec.**
4 Mazda MP3	**10 sec.**
5 Honda Civic Si	**11.5 sec.**
6 Ford Focus ZX3	**11.8 sec.**

CIRCLE THE WAGONS!

● BY DENIS DUQUET

The last time the *Auto Guide* conducted a wagon comparison test was 20 years ago, in 1982. The showdown took place at the Sanair racetrack, one hour east of Montreal, Que., and the contestants were the Chevrolet Cavalier, Dodge Aries and Mercury Lynx. With the advent of the minivan in the early Eighties, the station wagon had all but vanished from the market. Now, however, wagons – like convertibles – are back with a vengeance. As more and more people decide that minivans are too cumbersome, and sport-utility vehicles too gas-consuming and unpleasant to drive in general, a wagon, with its tailgate and baggage hold clearly more generous than a sedan's trunk, represents an attractive compromise, especially in the compact-car category.

Nowadays, the line between work and play is often blurred as more people use their personal vehicles to transport all kinds of stuff. They prefer compact cars, which are easier to drive in city traffic, consume less fuel and are generally more affordable. Needless to say, automakers caught on to the trend quickly. In the next few months, Pontiac and Toyota will introduce their new models, Vibe and Matrix, respectively. Mazda currently enjoys a good measure of success with its new Protegé5, while the Ford Focus has become the wagon to drive for many people. Even Volkswagen has decided to enter the fray with the Jetta wagon, due in Spring 2002.

Although the Pontiac Vibe and Toyota Matrix will not be available for several months, it was high time for the Auto Guide team to go back to Sanair for another compact wagon comparison test. The lineup was as follows: Chrysler PT Cruiser, Daewoo Nubira, Ford Focus, Mazda Protegé5, Subaru Impreza, Suzuki Esteem and Volkswagen Jetta.

Since the Jetta hasn't yet made it to Canada, we tested a model intended for the U.S. market. Identifying the cars is another fun exercise. Of the seven, the Mazda Protegé5 was clearly the group favorite. While we found the Focus and Jetta to be genuine wagons, the Protegé5 is a compromise between a wagon and a 5-door hatchback. Ditto the Subaru Impreza, whose roundish tail end encroaches on the cargo space. The retro-styled PT Cruiser is harder to classify: it can certainly pass muster as a 5-door sedan, mini-minivan, or truncated wagon. The Nubira and Esteem, although unambiguously wagons in their own right, belong in a more economical category.

Our comparison test focussed more on practicality rather than driving pleasure. Yet, as our test drivers concluded, several of the tested models were not only practical, they were actually a lot of fun to drive – so much so that they might give any same-class compact sedan a run for its money. Which ones, you ask? Read on, and you'll find out.

VOLKSWAGEN JETTA
Surprise Guest

We kept the Jetta wagon as a pleasant surprise for the test drivers. In fact, since the Jetta wasn't even available in Canada at test time, Volkswagen provided the Auto Guide with a version intended for the U.S market. Equipped with a VR6 engine, leather seats and a fairly complete range of equipment, the surprise guest dominated the field in practically every category, especially handling and storage space. With the rear backrest folded down, the Jetta could hold 25 cardboard-boxes, sharing first place with the Ford Focus. With the backrest in place, it came second with 12 boxes, behind the Focus, which could accommodate 14.

"Oh, but that's because the test Jetta was fitted with the more powerful VR6 engine and was generally better equipped than the other test cars," some of you might protest. That's true enough, but if you removed several accessories, and factored in the estimated difference in performance between the VR6 and the standard 2.0-liter engine, the Jetta would have still come out ahead, perhaps by a smaller margin, but its title wouldn't have been at stake.

The Jetta's high ranking is easy to understand. Adorned with a stylishly elegant silhouette, beating even the Mazda Protegé5 – the test drivers' overall favorite – in this department, the car also offers generous cabin space and first-rate seats, not to mention the most efficient suspension system. It barely surpasses the Protegé5 in terms of handling, however, and lags behind with its less-than-crisp gearshift linkage. Incidentally, the Jetta's 174-hp VR6 engine isn't as well adapted to everyday driving as the 180-hp 1.8-liter 4-cylinder Turbo engine under the hood of many other 2002 Volkswagens.

Despite its many good qualities and nearly dominant position in the comparison test, the Jetta wasn't our test drivers' favorite. That honor was reserved for the Mazda Protegé5, which is more affordable and seemed more "user-friendly" in their collective opinion. Still, the Jetta clearly sparkled with its directional stability, precise steering and effortless cornering capabilities.

These qualities are all the more remarkable when you remember that the car in question is a station wagon, capable of transporting significantly more baggage than a sedan of the same class. Then you can add to the mix the more generous warranty that Volkswagen accords its 2002 models. Let's hope that Volkswagen reliability – not always stellar – will also make a big leap forward in 2002.

What they said:

▲ PRO

"I loved driving this car. It has everything: exemplary and quiet handling, comfort, etc."

▼ CON

"Granted, the Jetta has a lot going for it. But the rear seats are strictly reserved for miniature occupants. Reliability, too, is suspect."

MAZDA PROTEGÉ5

Queen of Hearts

All our test drivers succumbed to the Protegé5's overall charm: there's its unique silhouette and fabulous interior on the one hand, and then add in the variety of its standard equipment on the other. "A fine example of Mazda's know-how," commented one driver. All agreed wholeheartedly that the Japanese automaker made exactly the right decision in bringing this hatchback to North America. The market has certainly responded enthusiastically, as demonstrated by the overwhelming number of Protegé5s currently crowding the highways and byways coast to coast.

Mazda's success is hardly surprising, what with its highly competitive price in return for such magnificent equipment. But the car doesn't compare favorably with bona fide station wagons when it comes to the question of storage space. With the rear backrest folded down, the Ford Focus can easily gobble up 25 boxes, as opposed to 20 for the Protegé5. Reset the backrest, and the Focus boasts twice as much room – 14 boxes versus seven! Proof enough that for Mazda buyers, style ranks higher than storage capacity – an intriguing factor, when you remember that the Protegé5 is a station wagon.

Yet another factor that helps to explain the Protegé5's missing out on first place – although second is not bad – is its performance. Although the 2.0-liter 4-cylinder engine cranks out a respectable 130 horsepower, acceleration and passing performance are only average, belying the car's sporty looks. Another 20 hp would have given the car enough ammunition to confront the Volkswagen Jetta and Subaru Impreza head on. As things turned out, the Mazda had to concede a lot of points to both the others in terms of performance.

Like the Jetta, the Protegé5 demonstrated that practicality and driving pleasure don't have to be mutually exclusive. Despite its somewhat less than peppy engine, the car was a lot of fun to drive, tackling sharp corners with aplomb and handling itself nimbly in busy city traffic. Big cars, get out of the way! The only sour note here is the Protegé5's rear visibility, severely hampered by a tiny rear window.

It's obvious that the Protegé5's commercial success will encourage other automakers to follow suit, developing models that combine the advantages of both hatchback and station wagon. The Pontiac Vibe and Toyota Matrix are cases in point. Faced with this new assault, Mazda will have little choice but to up the ante – in other words, to boost the future Protegé5's horsepower while keeping its price range in check. The current model is by no means perfect, but its highly competitive price more than compensates for any flaws. It wouldn't surprise me in the least if Mazda decided to go the "MP3" way with the Protegé5 next year.

What they said:

▲ PRO

"The Protegé5 is far and away my favorite: it's fun to drive, boasts a complete range of equipment and an excellent sticker price. And oh, what a killer look. No argument there."

▼ CON

"Gorgeous car, but noisy cabin, and less than punchy performance. Too bad!"

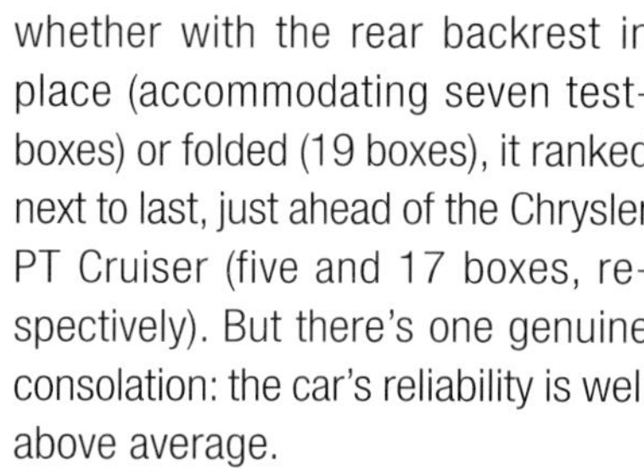

SUBARU IMPREZA

More Bang for the Buck

The Impreza wagon is definitely a serious contender for the championship title, boasting 165 horsepower and all-wheel drive, one of the finest in the business. Its low sticker price is another robust selling point, potentially representing the best quality-performance/price ratio.

Despite its self-appointed station wagon status, however, the Impreza looks more like a hatchback, given a roundish tail end that was clearly designed for style rather than practicality. Even so, it failed to impress our test drivers, who put it way down in fifth place for style. The cockpit fared better, jumping two notches to third place. Oddly, the quality of finish was felt to be barely average on the outside, and way above average inside. As for other criteria, the Impreza invariably ranked third, behind the Volkswagen Jetta and Mazda Protegé5. On the other hand, it did considerably better in terms of acceleration and passing performance, and held on to first place in the braking department.

The Impreza's overall third-place ranking is certainly well-deserved. While the test drivers appreciated its mechanical efficiency, they weren't terribly impressed with its visual presentation, finding it too austere inside and out. Once again, the Jetta and Protegé5 both fared better than the Subaru on this score. The Jetta by virtue of its pure, clean lines, and the Protegé5, as a consequence of its unequaled charm.

Third place, however, doesn't mean the Impreza should be dismissed outright. If you're looking for a car that can take you anywhere, regardless of road conditions, the Impreza is what you need. And don't forget that it can be ordered in the pricier Outback version, which comes with more robust tires and has higher ground clearance. Besides there's also the Impreza WRX, fitted with a whopping 227-hp turbocharged engine for the sports-minded city driver.

But let's get back to the TL test model, the most economical version of the Impreza line. Performance is first-rate, and driving it was great fun. Still, it leaves a lot to be desired as a station wagon. Its storage capacity is one of the lowest in the group. In fact, whether with the rear backrest in place (accommodating seven testboxes) or folded (19 boxes), it ranked next to last, just ahead of the Chrysler PT Cruiser (five and 17 boxes, respectively). But there's one genuine consolation: the car's reliability is well above average.

In the final analysis, therefore, despite its limited storage space, the Impreza has a great deal going for it: all-wheel drive, competitive price, rigid platform, and Subaru reliability. Overall third place isn't so bad after all. Frankly, how important is style anyway, when the car can transport you safely wherever it is that you want to go?

What they said:

▲ PRO

"All-wheel drive makes all the difference, even on dry road surfaces. And it's fun to drive, to boot."

▼ CON

"Despite its obvious qualities as regards performance, the car looks dull, especially next to the Protegé5."

FORD FOCUS
The Most Practical

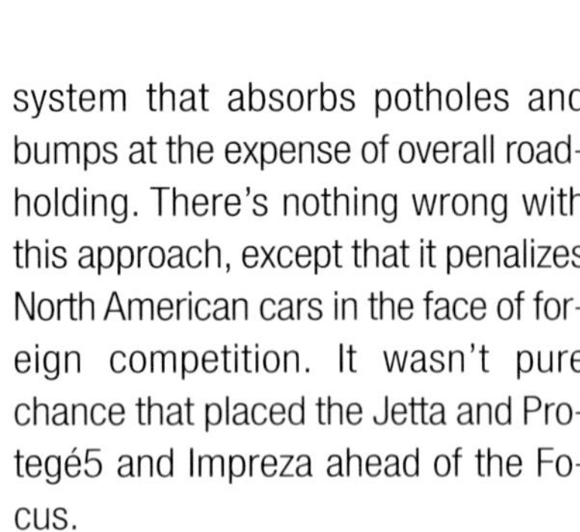

If you're looking for an economical station wagon, with generous storage capacity, the Ford Focus is the one for you. In fact, it led the approval ratings with our group of contestants, accommodating the most test-boxes in its baggage hold, backrest up or down. Its height is simply perfect for a station wagon. And the Focus offers even more storage space than the Volvo V70 when the backrest is in place.

The deal gets sweeter. Even if you order all the options, you'll still come out ahead, price-wise. Are you surprised that the car is so popular? Popular too is its silhouette, among the most catching in the test group. The dashboard is ergonomically sound, if the layout is a tad unusual. The front seats are comfortable and provide superb back support. Still it's not all hunky-dory, and there's definitely room for improvement. Take the non-adjustable steering wheel, for example, which irritated several test drivers. The cost savings it represented was so insignificant that it was hard to understand. Ford could easily have come up with something more useful and agreeable. The quality of finish and materials used, too, is average at best, and it proves detrimental to the overall effect of an otherwise remarkable car.

With 130 horsepower, the Focus was the Mazda Protegé5's equal, in terms of performance. It ranked ahead of the Suzuki Esteem and Daewoo Nubira, but came a distant fourth behind the Volkswagen Jetta, Subaru Impreza, and Chrysler PT Cruiser. As with the Mazda, performance was respectable, but dull. While the Mazda redeemed itself with its ravishing looks, the Focus played the functional card, finishing first in terms of ingress and egress – front and back – baggage hold and mechanical system access. Ironically, the Focus doesn't have as many storage as some of its competitors.

The car acquits itself capably enough on the road, even though its high stance makes it more vulnerable to side winds. Only when you compare it with the other cars does the Focus reveal a number of relative weaknesses: suspension isn't quite as efficient, steering not so precise and handling not as sharp.

North American automakers design their cars with one eye on comfort, in other words, with a suspension system that absorbs potholes and bumps at the expense of overall roadholding. There's nothing wrong with this approach, except that it penalizes North American cars in the face of foreign competition. It wasn't pure chance that placed the Jetta and Protegé5 and Impreza ahead of the Focus.

Despite these reservations, the Focus is good value. It beat the Chrysler PT Cruiser hands down because it corresponded better to true station wagon criteria.

What they said:

▲ PRO

"Nice lines! What's more, it's quiet, comfortable and has tons of storage space. I also appreciated the brakes."

▼ CON

"The Focus would have won a few extra points, if it hadn't been for its poor-quality finish and non-adjustable steering wheel."

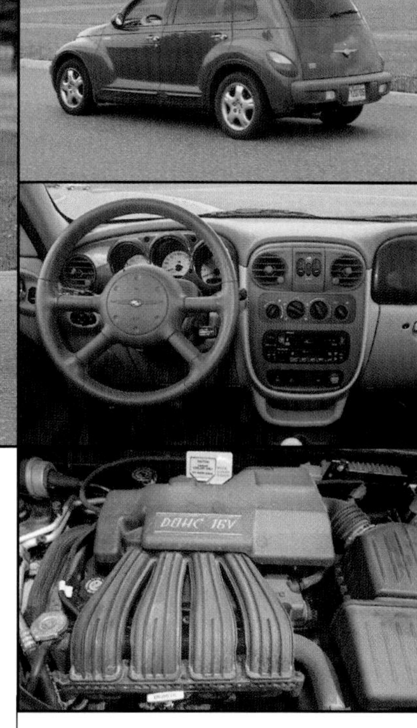

CHRYSLER PT CRUISER
The Wild Card

I'm convinced that many of you will be shocked to discover that the PT Cruiser – a favorite with buyers since its launch in fall 2000 and proclaimed "Car of the Year" by many publications and automobile associations – came as far back as fifth in our compact wagon comparison test. That's mainly because this versatile vehicle was difficult to classify – it's neither a station wagon nor a minivan in the proper sense of those terms. Given its high stance and the configuration of its trunk, the PT Cruiser does share some affinities with bona fide wagons and hatchbacks, a fact that explains its participation in our comparison test.

Despite its imposing stance – with its raised nose and truncated tail end – the PT Cruiser is relatively small. In fact, it turned out to be the shortest – and highest – of the seven contestants. Once the rear backrest is in place, it can accommodate only five test-boxes, two fewer than the Mazda Protegé5 and the Subaru Impreza, the two hatchbacks in our test. Even the Daewoo Nubira did better in this department, handling six more boxes with ease. Things failed to improve even with the backrest folded down – the PT Cruiser still brought up the rear. Its cargo capacity is fair enough for a car, but too small for a station wagon of its class. On the other hand, its low trunk opening and big tailgate facilitate loading and unloading.

One of the criticisms that kept cropping up in almost all our test-drivers' notes involved the uncomfortable front seats – they're especially hard on your testers thighs. Several complained that the PT Cruiser's 150-hp engine had trouble pulling its 3111-lb mass (1411 kg). The Jetta wagon is heavier, but it also has a more powerful engine to propel the extra weight. Opinions varied as to the cockpit's visual presentation: some drivers admired, others absolutely detested, the dashboard's painted panels and the air vents' unusual design.

The PT Cruiser's last-place finish in our comparison test means only that it doesn't stack up favorably with bona fide station wagons or hatchbacks. Be that as it may, the car is a remarkable vehicle in its own right, versatile, fun to drive and acquits itself quite respectably on the road. Besides, who can resist that retro-styled charm?

What they said:

▲ PRO

"Yet another excellent coup from Chrysler. Handling is good and steering precise. A roomy car, given its modest dimensions."

▼ CON

"The interior's1950s look is a bit overdone. Too much for me, at any rate. And the car's more minivan than station wagon."

SUZUKI ESTEEM

Slow but Steady

The Suzuki Esteem has been on the market for a number of years. It's commonly considered to be a subcompact, but given its dimensions and a 122-hp engine, we thought it could go head to head with other compact station wagons, hence its presence in our comparison test.

One of Suzuki's major problems is its apparent inability to keep up with design trends. Its automobiles, acceptable as they may be from a mechanical standpoint, generally look out of date, and unappealing as a result. In fact, one of our test drivers commented that the Esteem's interior reminded him of Japanese cars from 15 years ago. Given the sticker price, is it any wonder that there aren't that many Esteems on our highways?

Slightly smaller than several of the other contestants, the Esteem was nevertheless able to accommodate an impressive number of test boxes – 12 with the backrest in place, the same as the Volkswagen Jetta, and two fewer than the Ford Focus, the champ in this department. With the backrest folded down, it gobbled up another 11 boxes, finishing third. The pleasant surprise here, said the test drivers, was that you didn't have the impression that you were driving a smaller car at all.

One of the Esteem's weakest points is it does'nt feel up to date. The car has been on the world market since 1994, and was revamped in 1998. It was originally equipped with a puffing little 95-hp 1.6-liter engine that, fortunately, was upgraded to a 122-hp 1.8-liter engine in 2000, at least in the wagon version. At last the car no longer brings up the rear in its category, although its manual transmission and the shift lever gate need improvement. I should add at this point that the test car seemed to have been upgraded on that score.

The Esteem came sixth in our comparison test, lagging behind in almost every category: acceleration, braking, driving pleasure, quality of finish, to name only a few. Still, the ranking is more a reflection of the fierce competition that currently prevails in the market rather than the Esteem's individual merits, which are fine. Handling is honest, and the car's upgraded engine is more powerful than ever. What's more, a replacement for the Esteem has already been unveiled in the European market, and should be available in North America early next year. In the meantime, all the Esteem has going for it is acceptable cargo capacity and a decent engine, if a tad too greedy on fuel.

What they said:

▲ PRO

"Adequate handling, braking up to snuff, average driving position. Relatively fun to drive."

▼ CON

"Who would buy a Suzuki? It feels like a musty Japanese car of the mid 1980s. Well, maybe as a second car."

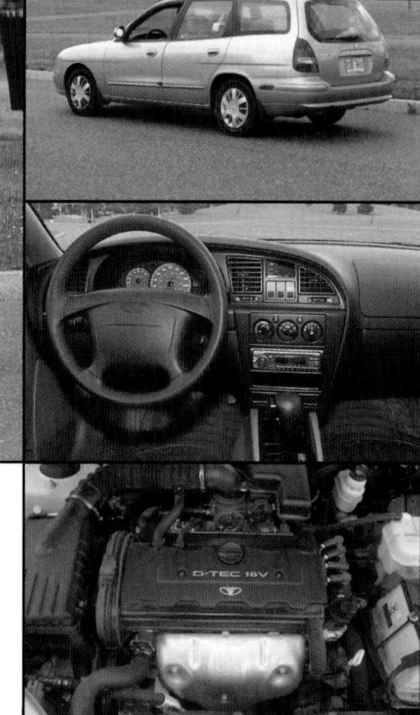

DAEWOO NUBIRA

Wanted: A Buyer

At the time of writing, the future of Daewoo was uncertain. It was in this context that we tested the Daewoo Nubira wagon. The company's precarious future, combined with the fact that it lacks the resources to carry out a number of automobile projects of its own, contributed to the car's last-place finish in our comparison test.

It's not that the Nubira possessed no qualities, it's just that it simply was unable to measure up to the competition. The car ranked dead last in terms of steering and braking. As for handling, it barely managed to beat out the Suzuki Esteem, by 0.1 point, for next-to-last place. Not even the fact that the Nubira was designed by none other than the celebrated Giorgietto Giugiaro seemed to impress our team of test drivers, who put it back in last place for looks. After all, even a genius can make the occasional mistake. In fact, even though the Nubira's silhouette was reasonably elegant, the end result was just too austere and the car paled by comparison when placed next to the competition.

In the past, Daewoo cars were judged to be average in terms of interior and exterior finish. This time around, the Nubira received very low marks on that score, a situation that begs the question: Perhaps the Daewoo employees, perturbed by their company's misfortunes, were doing their job with less enthusiasm than before? But I should also point out that Daewoo provided us with the car only a few hours before the test, and it was entirely possible that preparations hadn't been carried out according to company standards. The confusion we experienced as we took delivery of the Nubira did not inspire confidence either, especially if that sort of thing represented standard practice at all Daewoo dealerships.

In terms of cargo capacity, the Nubira did reasonably well, finishing third, behind the Ford Focus and the Volkswagen Jetta. What's more, it was ranked among the most economical of the test group. Still the Nubira will need to be completely and thoroughly improved in every category: handling, engine efficiency and sound insulation, while maintaining its current price level. Until that happens, the Nubira – barely average and bland – won't stand a chance in the fiercely competitive North American market.

The car's appeal is clearly limited to buyers who need to transport a large amount of baggage without burning too much fuel, or those optimistic enough to believe in Daewoo's ability to mount a comeback.

What they said:

▲ PRO

"It does everything a station wagon is supposed to do. What's more, the price is competitive, horsepower adequate, and cargo capacity is above average."

▼ CON

"Not only is the car dead boring, it's got a terrible radio and a noisy engine. The driving position, too, is bad."

CONCLUSION

Three Categories of Finalists

As the figures indicate, the Volkswagen Jetta is the big winner in every category of the *Auto Guide* compact wagon comparison test. Befitting today's trend in automaking based on surveys and focus groups, "category" in our test context refers to three wagon sub-groups: 1) bona fide station wagons – namely the Ford Focus, Daewoo Nubira, Suzuki Esteem and Volkswagen Jetta; 2) hatchbacks – the Mazda Protegé5 and Subaru Impreza and 3) the hybrid Chrysler PT Cruiser, a group of one.

Our panel unanimously agreed that even if the test Jetta had been fitted with a less powerful engine and more modestly equipped, it would still have won the prize. The German car comfortably accommodated the greatest number of test boxes, exhibited the best road manners and was the most fun to drive. In the bona fide station wagon category, it beat the Focus hands down. The Focus was just as spacious, but fell behind in terms of performance, handling and overall comfort. Ford's cost-saving measures certainly didn't help matters either.

In its turn, though, the Focus finished ahead of the Suzuki Esteem and Daewoo Nubira, in that order. Both are normally considered to belong in a lower category, and between the pair, the Esteem has the edge over the Nubira, despite its higher sticker price.

The Mazda Protegé5 and Subaru Impreza are sold as station wagons and that's the way most consumers think about them. In actual fact, however, they're really hatchbacks, with a longer-than-average tail end – a configuration that lends them a sportier look. What's more, the way they handle makes them more like driving a car than a station wagon, and they don't provide as much cargo space either. The Impreza, with its 165-hp engine, all-wheel drive and youthful allure, represents one of the best values around. Nevertheless, it had to concede a couple points to the Mazda Protegé5, sporting a silhouette and an elaborate cockpit that were so striking they compensated for the car's less-than-stellar motoring performance. In fact, all our test drivers succumbed to the Mazda's dynamic looks, inside and out.

Finally, there's the Chrysler PT Cruiser – a compromise vehicle in every respect. Some team members admired its 1950s retro lines, others intensely disliked them. Still, it's a practical enough car, which can be either used as a mini-minivan or a station wagon, whatever the case may be. It's solid, well assembled and acquits itself quite respectably on the road. But the engine is a tad too average, and the front seats don't suit everyone's posture, or posterior. Still, the car has its staunch defenders.

Because of date conflicts and other logistical considerations, we weren't able to include the all-new 5-door Kia Rio in the test. That will have to wait until next time. And since the Pontiac Vibe and Toyota Matrix will make their first appearance next summer, you can be sure that we won't wait another 20 years before organizing the next wagon showdown.

Denis Duquet

Specifications	Chrysler PT Cruiser	Suzuki Esteem	Ford Focus	Subaru Impreza	Daewoo Nubira	Mazda Protegé5	Volkswagen Jetta
• Wheelbase	103.1 in	97.6 in	102.8 in	99.2 in	101.2 in	102.8 in	98.8 in
• Length	168.9 in	172 in	178 in	173.4 in	179.1 in	170.5 in	174 in
• Width	66.9 in	66.5 in	66.9 in	67.3 in	66.9 in	66.9 in	68.1 in
• Height	63 in	55.9 in	57.1 in	58.3 in	57.9 in	55.9 in	57.9 in
• Weight	3133 lb (1421 kg)	2370 lb (1075 kg)	2612 lb (1185 kg)	3045 lb (1381 kg)	2535 lb (1150 kg)	2714 lb (1231 kg)	3333 lb (1512 kg)
• Transmission	manual	manual	automatic	automatic	automatic	manual	automatic
• Number of gears	5	5	4	4	4	5	4
• Engine	4L	4L	4L	4H	4L	4L	V6
• Displacement	2.4-liter	1.8-liter	2.0-liter	2.5-liter	2.0-liter	2.0-liter	2.8-liter
• Horsepower	150 hp	122 hp	130 hp	165 hp	129 hp	130 hp	174 hp
• Front suspension	ind.	ind.	ind.	ind.	ind.	ind.	ind.
• Rear suspension	rigid	ind.	ind.	ind.	semi-ind.	ind.	ind.
• Front brakes	disc	disc	disc	disc	disc	disc	disc
• Rear brakes	disc	drum	drum	disc	drum	disc	disc
• ABS	no	yes	no	yes	no	yes	yes
• Tires	P205/55R16	P185/60R14	P195/60R15	P195/65R15	P195/55R15	P195/50R16	P205/55R16
• Steering	rack-and-pinion	rack-and-pinion	rack-and-pinion	rack-and-pinion	rack-and-pinion	rack-and-pinion	rack-and-pinion
• Turning circle	40 feet	32 feet	36 feet	33 feet	35 feet	34 feet	36 feet
• Air bags	front/side	front	front/side (opt)	front	front	front	front/side
• Fuel tank	15 gallons	13.5 gallons	13 gallons	16 gallons	14 gallons	14.5 gallons	14.5 gallons
• Trunk	19/64 cu. ft	24 cu. ft	12.4/42.6 cu. ft	12.9/45.2 cu. ft	19.4/29.7 cu. ft	20/24 cu. ft	16.2/51.9 cu. ft
• Acceleration 0-60 mph	10 sec.	10.7 sec.	10.3 sec.	9.7 sec.	12.5 sec.	10.4 sec.	9.1 sec.
• Maximum speed	109 mph (175 km/h)	103 mph (165 km/h)	112 mph (180 km/h)	115 mph (185 km/h)	112 mph (180 km/h)	122 mph (195 km/h)	122 mph (195 km/h)
• Fuel consumption	21 mpg (11L/100km)	26 mpg (8.9 L/100 km)	25 mpg (9.3 L/100 km)	22 mpg (10.8 L/100 km)	21 mpg (11.2 L/100 km)	24 mpg (9.6 L/100 km)	20 mpg (11.7 L/100 km)
• Price ($CDN / $US)	24,000-29,000 / 16,500	18,000-21,000 / 13,700-17,100	19,000-22,000 / 18,800-16,400	23,000-26,000 / 18,000-24,000	18,000 - 21,000 / 12,000-15,600	19,995 / 15,000	25,000-35,000 / 21,450-25,950

A "BOXING" MATCH

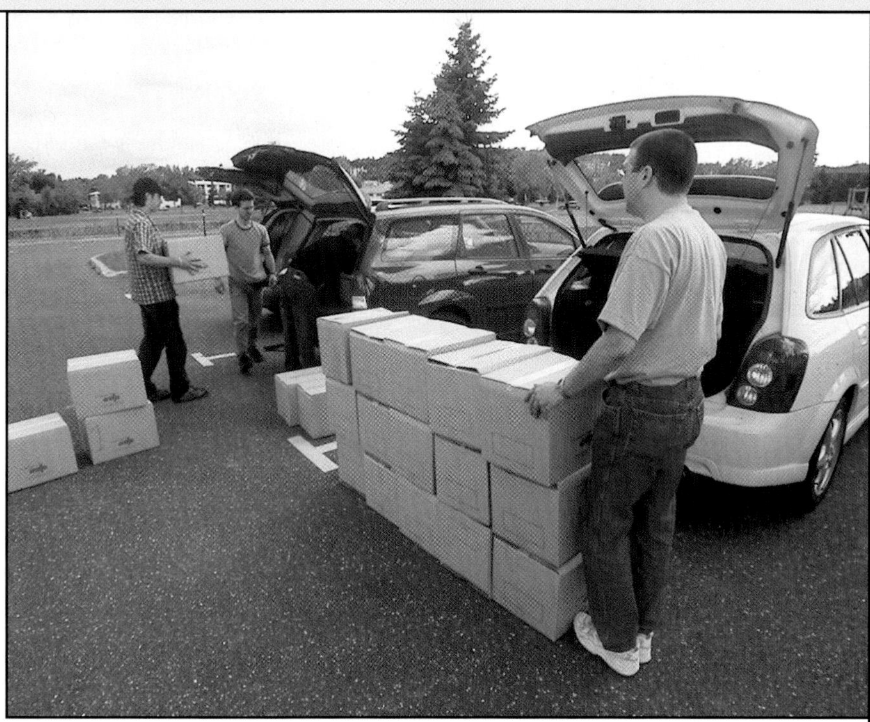

The whole point of owning a station wagon is that it allows the driver to transport more baggage than a sedan thanks to its tailgate and extended tail end. What's more, since a wagon roof is also longer, you can install racks farther apart from each other than on a sedan, to hold longer or more cumbersome items.

As you may have suspected, the actual carrying capacity doesn't always equal the calculated available storage volume. Often, the wheel wells, the trunk's height and even its shape will dictate the size and number of items you can carry. To evaluate the cargo space of each car, we took some boxes used for shipping the *Auto Guide* and loaded as many as we could.

The operation was done in two stages: first with the rear backrest in place, then folded down. As the following results indicate, the Focus is the champ in the first instance, while the PT Cruiser brings up the rear. Once the backrest is folded down, the Focus shares first place with the Volkswagen Jetta, while the Daewoo Nubira is third.

For many buyers, these results are more important than the car's handling or performance. You have to esta-

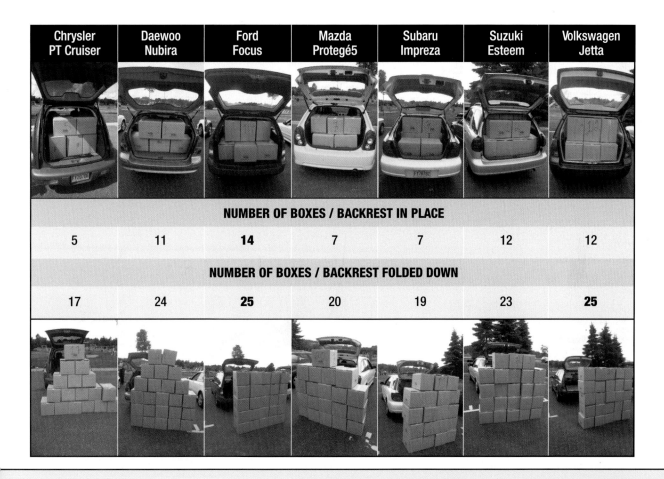

Chrysler PT Cruiser	Daewoo Nubira	Ford Focus	Mazda Protegé5	Subaru Impreza	Suzuki Esteem	Volkswagen Jetta
NUMBER OF BOXES / BACKREST IN PLACE						
5	11	**14**	7	7	12	12
NUMBER OF BOXES / BACKREST FOLDED DOWN						
17	24	**25**	20	19	23	**25**

Evaluation Sheet

		Chrysler PT Cruiser	Suzuki Esteem	Ford Focus	Subaru Impreza	Daewoo Nubira	Mazda Protegé5	Volks. Jetta
Esthetics								
• Exterior	10	8.1	7.3	8.6	7.8	6.3	9.0	9.6
• Interior	10	7.2	6.6	7.3	8.0	5.7	9.0	9.0
• Exterior finish	10	7.6	6.8	7.4	7.7	5.8	8.6	9.3
• Interior finish	10	7.0	6.1	6.9	8.0	5.6	8.8	9.0
	40 pts	**29.9**	**26.8**	**30.2**	**31.5**	**23.4**	**35.4**	**36.9**
Accessories								
• Number and practicality	10	7.7	5.8	6.8	7.0	6.9	8.3	9.0
• Storage spaces	10	8.3	5.0	7.0	6.9	7.1	7.0	8.3
• Instruments/Controls	10	7.9	6.2	7.2	7.2	6.5	8.6	8.5
• Ventilation/Heating	10	7.8	7.7	8.0	8.5	7.5	8.0	9.0
	40 pts	**31.7**	**24.7**	**29.0**	**29.6**	**28.0**	**31.9**	**34.8**
Body								
• Front access/space	15	12.7	10.6	12.4	11.8	12.1	11.4	13.1
• Rear access/space	15	13.5	10.0	12.0	10.4	11.6	12.0	11.1
• Trunk: access & volume	5	3.5	3.6	4.6	4.6	4.3	3.2	4.6
• Mechanical system access	5	1.5	4.0	2.5	4.5	2.5	2.5	2.0
	40 pts	**31.2**	**28.2**	**31.5**	**31.3**	**30.5**	**29.1**	**30.8**
Comfort								
• Suspension	10	7.9	6.0	7.1	8.4	6.6	8.1	8.7
• Noise level	10	7.0	6.6	6.9	7.9	6.2	7.0	8.2
• Seats	10	6.6	6.3	7.3	7.6	6.0	8.4	9.2
• Driving position	10	7.7	6.8	7.5	8.0	7.1	8.6	8.8
	40 pts	**29.2**	**25.7**	**28.8**	**31.9**	**25.9**	**32.1**	**34.9**
Engine/Transmission								
• Efficiency	15	12.5	1.3	12.4	14.3	10.1	13.2	14.1
• Performance	15	12.1	10.5	11.3	12.6	9.1	12.3	13.7
• Gearshift lever	5	3.1	3.5	3.8	4.5	3.7	4.1	4.2
• Gearshifting	5	3.7	3.4	3.6	4.7	3.3	4.4	4.0
	40 pts	**31.4**	**28.7**	**31.1**	**36.1**	**26.2**	**34.0**	**36.0**
Handling								
• Road adherence	20	16.2	13.6	15.3	18.0	13.7	18.5	18.8
• Steering	20	14.7	13.8	15.8	17.9	13.5	18.8	18.5
• Brakes	10	8.3	7.0	7.5	8.6	6.0	8.3	8.8
	50 pts	**39.2**	**34.4**	**38.6**	**44.5**	**33.2**	**45.6**	**46.1**
Safety								
• Airbags	15	15.0	10.0	10.0	10.0	10.0	10.0	15.0
• Visibility	10	6.7	8.1	8.3	8.0	8.3	8.2	8.6
• Sideview mirrors	5	3.5	4.1	3.9	4.0	4.1	3.8	3.7
	30 pts	**25.2**	**22.2**	**22.2**	**22.0**	**22.4**	**22.0**	**27.3**
Timed Performance								
• Passing performance	10	6.0	5.0	8.0	8.0	6.0	7.0	10.0
• Acceleration	20	15.0	13.0	17.0	18.0	14.0	16.0	20.0
• Braking	20	17.0	17.0	20.0	20.0	16.0	16.0	18.0
	50 pts	**38.0**	**35.0**	**45.0**	**46.0**	**36.0**	**39.0**	**48.0**
Other criteria								
• Baggage space	30	21.0	27.0	30.0	23.0	27.0	24.0	29.0
• Test drivers' choice	40	34.0	33.0	35.0	36.0	32.0	40.0	38.0
• Price	10	6.0	9.0	7.0	8.0	10.0	9.0	3.0
	80 pts	**61.0**	**69.0**	**72.0**	**67.0**	**69.0**	**73.0**	**70.0**
Grand Total	**400 pts**	**316.8**	**294.7**	**328.4**	**339.9**	**294.6**	**342.1**	**364.8**
RANKING		**5**	**6**	**4**	**3**	**7**	**2**	**1**

PORSCHE BOXSTER VERSUS SUBARU IMPREZA WRX

BY JACQUES DUVAL PHOTOS: MICHEL FYEN-GAGNON

Pitting the Porsche Boxster, a.k.a. the king of the roadsters, against the impressive Subaru Impreza WRX, the champion of all-wheel drive, may seem as farfetched an idea as organizing a boxing match between the heavyweight champ and featherweight titleholder. But that's the kind of thing that adds a dash of spice to life, even if you suspect that the outcome is a foregone conclusion. And so the more I thought about the idea, the more people found it an intriguing proposition.

Clearly everyone – with the obvious exception of the Boxster drivers – hoped that the humble Subaru would teach the high and mighty Porsche a lesson or two. Indeed, crazy as it may sound, the WRX actually had the edge, if you compare their respective technical specs: 227 horsepower versus 217 for the Boxster, and four-wheel drive versus two-wheel drive. As it turned out, however, the meeting wasn't as lopsided as we all imagined.

And so what at first might have seemed like a screwball notion promised to be a day filled with unexpected developments. Apart from anticipating the fun of comparing apples with oranges, the point of the exercise was to highlight the WRX's "virtues." If the irresistible, $60,000 Porsche Boxster is beyond your means, you can always settle for the $35,000 WRX, and without compromising your taste for performance all that much. The Impreza WRX Turbo may also be just the ticket for those who lust after the German roadster, but who in reality need a four-door sedan to accommodate their young families. That's the basis of this comparison match. Come to think of it, it's not such a goofy idea after all.

Stopwatch test

Side by side at the starting line we have a basic Boxster equipped with a 217-hp 2.7-liter flat-6 engine, and an all-wheel-drive Impreza WRX sedan, fitted with a 227-hp 2.0-liter flat-4 engine. Both come with a 5-speed manual gearbox.

Unlike our regular comparison tests, this one is mainly focussed on evaluating performance. In other words, we'll award the most points to such areas as acceleration, road-holding and braking – the characteristics that make a sports car fun to drive. To set us apart from our competitors, the tests are designed to assess engine efficiency through as complete a performance spectrum as possible, including slalom and circuit-lap tests, both of which will be timed with a stopwatch.

Unbeatable Subaru

Everything went in the Subaru's favor as it scooted off during the quarter-mile event. While the Boxster was dragging its feet either because it was deprived of traction control, or in spite of it, the WRX charged so far ahead that the roadster never managed to catch up. After five separate tries, the Boxster finally conceded defeat, thereby confirming its inability to make up for a nearly 9-tenths-of-a-second deficit during the 0-60 mph shootout. In fact, both the 35-60 mph and 50-75 mph events produced the same results. It wasn't until the 0-0.6 mile event that the Boxster finally left the Subaru behind – 27.1 seconds at 123 mph (198 km/h) versus 28.5 seconds at 118 mph (190km/h) – by resorting to its superior aerodynamic capability that comes into play starting at 100 mph (160 km/h). Strictly in acceleration terms, the Subaru was decidedly ahead, by a full 12 points.

The gap narrows

But straightaway performance is not the prerogative of a sports car and so the Japanese sedan soon began giving ground to the German roadster, especially in terms of braking. The Subaru's tires were mostly at fault here, so was its heavier weight and the less efficient distribution of unsprung mass. Simulating an emergency stop at 60 mph, the Porsche came to a complete halt at 120 feet, compared with 129 feet for the Subaru. In all fairness, 129 feet isn't a bad result, far from it, especially when you keep in mind that the Subaru was pitted against the mighty Porsche, a car

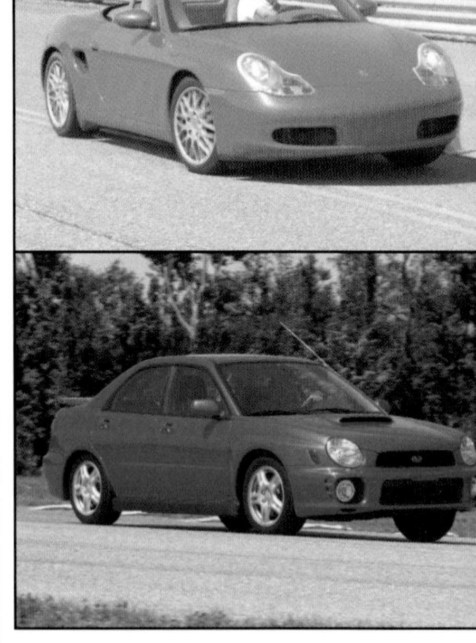

renowned for its brake-force excellence. On the other hand, a few laps at Sanair, followed by the slalom event, were enough to demonstrate that the Subaru's brakes were seriously deficient in the endurance department. The Japanese sedan badly needed vented disc brakes in the rear, or more powerful brakes at the very least. About the slalom event, one test driver wrote the following: "[The Subaru's] excellent chassis and powertrain permit excellent stopwatch results, but the brakes and the 16-inch tires tend to overheat quickly, and performance suffers as a result." To which another driver added these words: "To my pleasant surprise, this Subaru smartly combines performance with versatility. Unfortunately, its brakes quickly deteriorate after a few emergency stops."

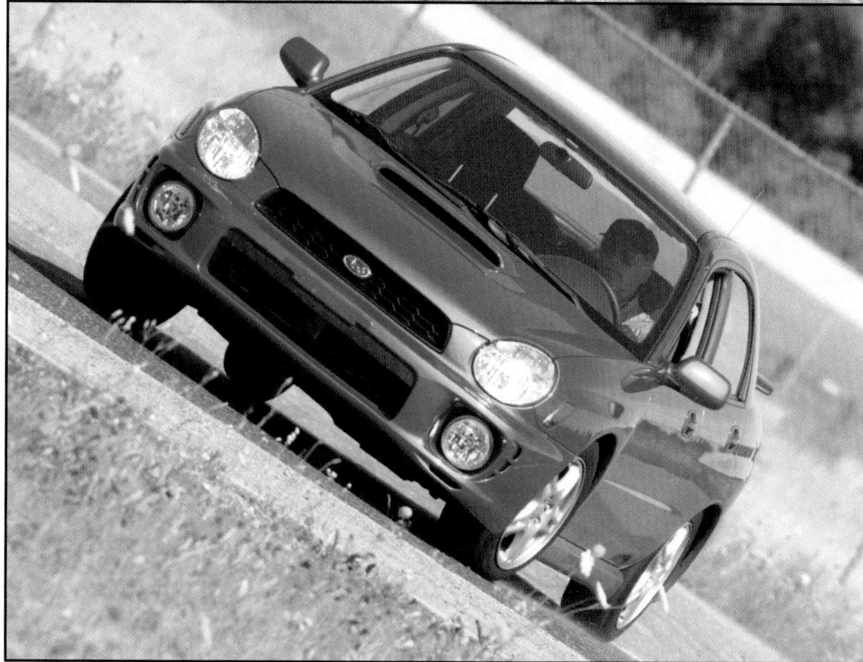

Rain? No problem

In terms of handling, the Porsche scored 10 points over the WRX, so that they now stood neck and neck. Despite the Subaru's all-wheel-drive system, after just one turn on the racing circuit I quickly realized that it was anything but a sports car. Since I drove it after the Boxster, the contrast seemed all the more blatant. Body roll made its presence felt right away and understeer was highly pronounced. On the other hand, had the test been carried out in the rain, the WRX, thanks to traction control, would have made minced meat of the Boxster.

Unlike the Porsche, whose super-precise steering allows you to negotiate turns as nonchalantly as if you were a Grand Prix veteran, the Subaru is tougher to keep on course. In the Sanair's notoriously fast S turn (over 100 mph), weight transfer was virtually imperceptible in the German roadster, while the Japanese sedan felt as if it were going to capsize at any moment. It took everything out of you just to maintain balance. Suffice it to say that the WRX makes you work hard if you want good stopwatch results, while the Boxster proves to be superbly nimble, inspiring absolute confidence – with or without traction control. Fortunately, this electronically-controlled system only kicks in as a last resort, letting the sport-minded driver take the car to its highest level. Incidentally, by deactivating the system, I managed to score one second faster.

In the final analysis, it was due to its achievements on the straightaway that the WRX managed to show such impressive stopwatch results. It conceded a mere second to the Porsche (64.07 second versus 63.04). I should point out here that the Subaru's best circuit-lap time was the equal of the all-powerful 300-hp Porsche 911 Turbo 3.3, which we tested on the same racing circuit in 1985. Not bad for a Japanese subcompact.

Engine efficiency

In terms of engine and transmission, the Porsche scored 44.75, and the Subaru, 43.5 – a virtual tie. Had there been an engine-sound category, the Porsche would have won hands down. But both flat-cylinder engines are equally efficient. The WRX's turbo can take credit for the

Results

	Subaru Impreza WRX	Porsche Boxster
ACCELERATION		
• 37.5-62.5 mph (60-100 km/h)	5.55 sec.	5.45 sec.
• 50-75 mph (80-120 km/h)	7.4 sec.	8.3 sec.
• 0-60 mph	6.14 sec.	6.99 sec.
• ¼ mile	14.6 s / 91 mph (146 km/h)	15.7s / 87 mph (140 km/h)
• 0-0.6 mile • (0-1000 meters)	28.5 s / 118 mph (190 km/h)	27.1 s / 123 mph (198 km/h)
BRAKING • 60-0 mph	129 feet (39.3 m)	120 feet (36.6 m)
SLALOM • 1st test	22.63 sec.	21.32 sec.
• 2nd test	22.32 sec.	20.97 sec.
• 3nd test	21.99 sec.	20.55 sec.
TRACK LAP TIME • 1st	1'05 97 sec.	1'04 50 sec.
• 2nd	1'04 07 sec.	1'03 04 sec.

car's slightly superior performance, but the Porsche's transmission boasts a better gear-ratio spread, making it more agreeable to handle.

A question of comfort

Acquiring a sports car is tantamount to kissing comfort goodbye – in any shape or form. Of course, that's an aspect that Porsche buyers rarely consider – that is, until they get fed up with subjecting their posteriors to each and every pothole and bump in the road. As far as suspension is concerned, our drivers preferred the Subaru because it was able to soak up shocks and jolts more smoothly. But I must also point out that the Porsche would have fared far worse in this department had it been fitted with the optional 18-inch tires. As it turned out, its 17-inch tires offered a good compromise between comfort and roadholding ability. Thanks to its excellent bucket seats, the WRX got an extra quarter-point, finishing ahead of the Boxster in the comfort department – by 1.25 points.

Judging by the mediocre radio that comes with the Boxster, no doubt Porsche assumes that engine sound is

"One of the year's most impressive cars, brilliant on both scores: concept and execution." The mere fact that the WRX can compare itself with the Porsche Boxster in the first place without looking ridiculous proves that all the driver needs to hear. At Subaru, the exact opposite is the case. Engine sound is on the dull side, but the radio and 6-CD changer are impressive, at least for neophytes like us. At the same time, the Japanese sedan received bad marks for failing to include a turbo-boost pressure indicator.

Taste and budget

There's no accounting for taste, as the familiar saying goes. And that's why our drivers didn't seem particularly bothered by the Boxster's sad and "plastified" interior. No matter, they still preferred the Porsche over the Subaru. Denis Duquet wrote: "Its rather modest origins are revealed by the quality of finish as well as the materials used." The dashboard, among other features, seems to want to dazzle you, but instead, looks and feels cheesy. "The presentation is not commensurate with the asking price," another driver remarked.

Honor intact

In the final analysis, thanks to its more affordable price, the Subaru Impreza WRX dramatically redeemed itself, finishing with a respectable overall score, especially when you consider what a formidable adversary it took on – the Porsche Boxster, no less. As Denis Duquet wrote in his notebook,

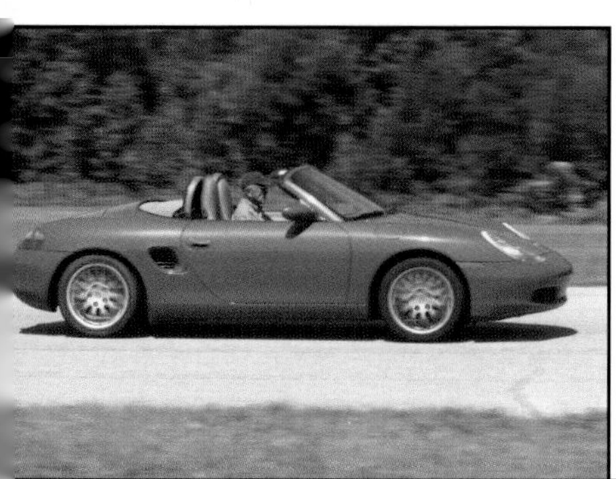

Evaluation Sheet

		Subaru Impreza WRX	Porsche Boxster
Esthetics			
• Exterior	15	9.25	12.75
• Interior	10	6.75	7
	25 pts	**16**	**19.75**
Accessories			
• Radio	10	8.25	6.25
• Climate control	10	7.25	7.50
• Instruments/Controls	20	14.75	16.25
	40 pts	**30.25**	**30**
Comfort			
• Suspension	20	17	15
• Noise level	10	7.25	7.75
• Seats/Driving position	10	7.75	7.50
	40 pts	**32**	**30.25**
Engine/Transmission			
• Efficiency	15	12.5	12.50
• Performance	20	17.25	16.50
• Gearshift lever	10	7	7.75
• Gear shifting	10	6.75	8
	55 pts	**43.5**	**44.75**
Handling			
• Roadholding	50	40.25	44.75
• Steering	20	15.75	18
• Brakes/Endurance	20	14.25	18
	90 pts	**70.25**	**80.75**
PERFORMANCE			
Passing Power			
• 37.5 – 62.5 mph (60-100 km/h)	10	8	10
• 50 – 75 mph (80-120 km/h)	10	10	8
Acceleration			
• 0-60 mph	20	10	8
• ¼ mile	10	10	8
Braking 60-0 mph	10	8	10
Slalom	20	8	10
Track lap time	20	18	20
	100 pts	**72**	**74**
Other			
• Test-drivers' choice	25	19.5	25
• Price	25	25	16
	50 pts	**44.5**	**41**
Grand Total	**400 pts**	**308.5**	**320.5**

it does belong in a class of its own. The king of the roadsters hasn't been dethroned, but the champion of all-wheel drive has certainly obliged it to look over its shoulder to see who's hot on its heels. Furthermore, come wintertime, the Kaiser will be found wanting.

Jacques Duval

PORSCHE BOXSTER

What they said...

The car was designed for sporty driving, and it delivered the goods. It's far and away one of the most fun cars to drive, whether on a racing circuit, highway or even in city traffic. If Porsche could find a way of improving its reliability, it would be great.

Clearly, the Boxster demands that its driver be professionally trained, and then some.

Purebred that it is, the Boxster behaves like a go-kart in a slalom. Without traction control, the rear becomes more unstable, so you have to try and tame it. If not, it'll spin out of control.

SUBARU IMPREZA WRX

What they said...

The Subaru is too much like a speed-shop kind of car. I'd be willing to remortgage my house to buy the Porsche, and if my bank manager said uh-uh, *then I'd probably opt for a WRX wagon, because it's both sporty and practical. That's what the Saab Viggen tried to do, and we all know what happened.*

The Subaru has more than meets the eye, helping us forget the fact that it has two doors in the rear!

Despite its uncommon talents, this car leaves me cold. It feels too "homemade" for my taste – not a very harmonious whole.

Specifications

	Subaru Impreza WRX	Porsche Boxster
• Price ($CDN / $US)	34,995 / 24,520	59,900 / 42,865
• Wheelbase	99.4 in	95.1 in.
• Length	173.4 in	169.9 in.
• Weight	3084 lb (1399 kg)	2778 lb (1260 kg)
• Trunk	11 cu.ft	9.2 cu.ft
• Fuel tank	16 gallons	17 gallons
• Engine	4H 2.0-liter Turbo	6H 2.7-liter
• Horsepower	227 hp at 6000 rpm	217 hp at 6500 rpm
• Torque	217lb-ft at 4000 rpm	192 lb-ft at 4500 rpm
• Transmission	5-speed manual	5-speed manual
• Suspension (front)	double-wishbone	MacPherson strut
• Suspension (rear)	trailing arms and twin parallel links	MacPherson strut with trailing arms
• Brakes	disc ABS	disc ABS
• Steering	rack-and-pinion	rack-and-pinion
• Turning circle	34 feet	36 feet
• Tires (front / rear)	P205/55R16	P205/50ZR17 / P255/40ZR17
• Maximum speed	140 mph (225 km/h)	155 mph (250 km/h)

Photos: Michel Fyen-Gagnon, FYENGAGNON@LR.CGOCABLE.CA

5 SEDANS, 20 DRIVING WHEELS

• **BY DENIS DUQUET** PHOTOS: MICHEL FYEN-GAGNON

Some of you may remember the AMC Eagle, the first modern four-wheel drive automobile. Since its introduction in the early 1980s, it created a brand-new market for a car manufacturer that was going through difficult times. Yet, you only had to drive it to realize that it was in fact a Jeep Cherokee masquerading as a sedan. Components were basic, and the model contributed more to oil company profits than to its manufacturer. Chrysler bought AMC soon after.

Yet, times have really changed and all-wheel drive sedans have evolved considerably. The introduction of the Audi Quattro at about the same time really upset the apple cart. For the first time, a car offered an efficient all-wheel drive system and the road manners of a sports car. The stuff of legends, and an altogether new vehicle category was created: the luxury all-wheel drive sedan. Audi kept the niche to itself for quite a while, as other manufacturers were slow to jump on the bandwagon.

At the beginning of the new millennium, the number of cars in this category has substantially increased. Actually, the Audi A4 has just been redesigned for 2002 and then there is Jaguar, with its brand-new X-Type, only available with an all-wheel drive system. The arrival of these two contenders was a great opportunity to try them out in head-to-head confrontation. But one could not forget the BMW Xi of the 3 Series, introduced in 2001, which marked a return to the rear-wheel-drive category by BMW. Although less popular, one could not leave out the Volkswagen Passat 4Motion, which deserves to be in this group because of its price and its all-wheel drive feature.

We decided to invite a fifth car to join this uncommon confrontation. Although the Subaru Legacy Outback is more often associated with life in the great outdoors than to sporty driving, the new Legacy Outback sedan with its 6-cylinder engine rating over 200 hp did make it a rather interesting contender, despite its mixed mission on-road and off-road tires and a higher than average center of gravity.

So this was the group of five all-wheel drive sedans priced at over $40,000 that we assembled at the racetrack for a competitive test drive. The test included a slalom section, timed laps and general driving along local roads. The skid-pad area was particularly useful for evaluating the quality of the all-wheel drive systems.

This type of vehicle is generally preferred by drivers who like a car with better than average sporting characteristics, offering the kind of peace of mind that only four-wheel drive vehicles can bring to winter driving. This test helped demonstrate that all-wheel drive also contributes to the overall balance of a car and its sports car performance.

AUDI A4

New, improved and dominant

With a comfortable lead over the BMW Xi, the new Audi A4 confirms that the improvements went beyond a simple facelift or interior redesign. The suspension was also modified, improving its on-road performance. The A4 dominated the other contenders in lap times, slalom times and acceleration. In addition, the all-wheel drive systems in this Quattro showed exemplary effectiveness during our skid-pad test.

▲ PRO:

In spite of road going performance that has not improved very much over the older model, it still is the best in its class. This proves that the other manufacturers haven't caught up yet.

▼ CON:

In spite of its undeniable qualities, it is far from perfect. For example, changing gears takes too much effort, and it is too easy to miss a shift.

Admittedly, this sedan was the most powerful of the lot with its 220-hp 3.0-liter V6, and both the chassis and suspension worked hand-in-hand to transmit all this power to the road. Powerful cars are often less than agile on the slalom course, or sometimes hard to control through high-speed curves on a racetrack. However, if there is a fault to find with the road manners of the A4, it would be the brakes, which perform below expectations. In fact, after just a few laps, the brake pads caught fire. It was spectacular, but a little nerve-wracking. However, once the fire was under control, the car's braking performance returned to normal, or nearly.

The A4, everyone's favorite, easily dominated the "Tester's Choice" category. This clear victory is largely explained by its ease of driving, well above the majority of the cars tested. Given the high standards of the contenders, this is no small feat for Audi engineers. In the words of one of the testers, "Now, that's a car!" Besides, he was no different from the other drivers who all left the Audi with smiles on their faces. It's simply that one could really push this car out there on the track and have fun with it, its road behavior is so predictable and easy to control. However, most of the testers did not really appreciate the rather overbearing aspect of its dynamic stability control, which almost seemed to bring the car to a stop in order to get it back in a straight line.

This excellent road cruiser got rather mixed reactions concerning its redesigned rear-end which emphasizes its kinship with the A6. The pure lines of the previous model were rejected and replaced by a more bulbous rear, adding heaviness to its look. Nobody actually hated them, some liked them, while others preferred not to comment. The cockpit was easily considered the most elegant, practical, and topflight of the lot. Although the rear legroom is not as great as you'll find on some other models, access to the rear seats is generally straightforward.

Faultless workmanship, elegance and agility, this Audi A4 has the distinct advantage of offering one of the best all-wheel drive systems along with the Subaru. It clearly deserves first place outright.

BMW 325Xi

Engine limitations

▲ PRO:

Every time you drive a BMW, it is obvious that this carmaker appeals to the needs of the sporting driver. A 330Xi would have overwhelmed the A4.

▼ CON:

I was seduced by the 330Xi and disappointed by the 325X1. The engine is quite simply not up to par, which translates into rather mediocre responsiveness. I also noticed understeer, and the brakes are a little sluggish.

During the winter of 2001, some of *The Auto Guide* crew tested the new BMW 330Xi and praised it lavishly. Jacques Duval and Alain Raymond were particularly enthusiastic about driving this sedan which marks BMW's return to the all-wheel drive category. Unfortunately, its prohibitive price of over $60,000 kept it out of our road test match. We had to make do with its smaller-engined sister, the 325Xi, which was given the task of representing the Munich manufacturer during our road test get-together. Let it be said that those who tested the 330Xi and then drove the 325Xi felt that the Audi A4 would not have finished first so easily if the 330Xi had participated in the comparison test. It's unbelievable what a difference 38 hp can make, every other characteristic being relatively similar on both cars. Not only is the 325Xi not as much fun to drive as its big sister, but this lack of horsepower turned out to be a real handicap during the slalom and on the racetrack. But we must add that our test car was fitted with tires which were below standard. This did result in much sliding and loud protest noises.

Overall, this BMW is well balanced and particularity well equipped for everyday driving. The gearbox was the most pleasant to use and the most precise. The gear ratio steps were almost perfect. However, its all-wheel drive transmission did not do so well on the skid-pad: the system did seem to work intermittently at certain times and the transfer of power from the rear to the front was sometimes slow. On the track, cars with torque sent predominantly to the rear wheels generally seemed to behave in a neutral fashion in corners, with no tendency toward over- or understeer. Cars with predominantly front-wheel drive had a definite tendency to understeer when pushed in corners. However, it was then easier to slide the rear end around than with the basically rear-wheel drive BMW.

The 2.5-liter inline-6 engine, which was the least powerful of all cars tested, defended itself bravely and gave a more than reasonable performance considering its size.

From an aesthetic and practical standpoint, this car was not considered particularly attractive. Most of the comments pertaining to its lines referred to it as being almost on the wrong side of fashionable. And one should add that the dashboard should be modernized fairly soon if it is to avoid looking dated. It is quite obvious that the racy lines and the attractive layout of the Audi A4's appointments did not make the other contenders look their best.

This second place attests to the quality the car's chassis and its overall balanced characteristics. However, BMW should not wait too long before updating the exterior and the interior of the car, otherwise it will take on a slight retro look which may not please the die-hard fans of this German make. Finally, the all-wheel drive transmission could do with some improvements.

VOLKSWAGEN PASSAT

Econo looks, spirited performance

▲ PRO

It lacks a bit of glamor, but I admire the efficiency of this car and its conservative looks. It takes a Volkswagen owner to appreciate the family's elder sister.

▼ CON

The suspension was a little too soft for my liking. As for low-end power, it just wasn't there. And the brakes, although they lack bite, at least didn't dare give up altogether.

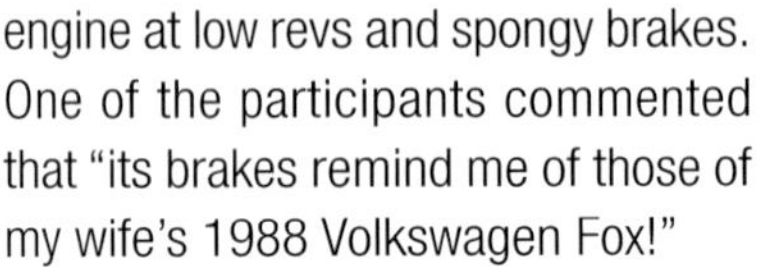

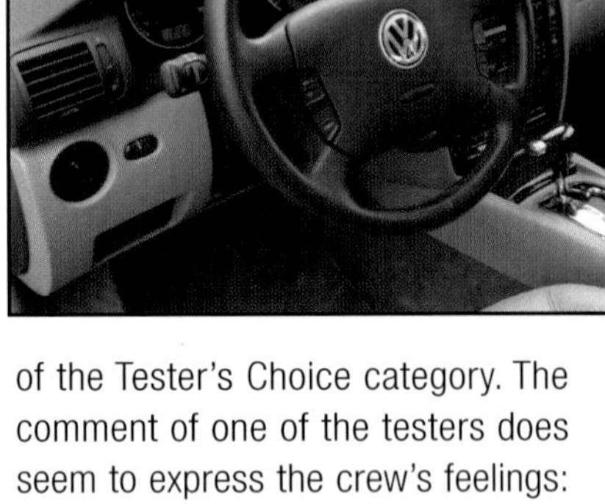

It's been several years now since Volkswagen management competed in market segments that it could not traditionally call its own. A $45,000 Volkswagen would have been unthinkable five years ago; however, it is now a fact, namely this Passat, a contender in this AWD category. Besides, this model is not immediately perceived as a luxury car. In fact, we had quite forgotten about it! Were it not for a miracle, and the perseverance of the company's representatives, this sedan would not have found itself at the starting line.

As is the case with many cars from Wolfsburg, the dynamic qualities of this Passat 4Motion were exemplary and it took second place behind the A4 in lap times and the slalom. However, its engine was not the liveliest and the acceleration times put it next to last. Moreover, the Passat required the longest distance before coming to a halt during braking tests. One should note, however, that it arrived at the last minute and was fitted with tires and brake pads that had seen better days. Nevertheless, the prestigious Volkswagen performed predictably well on the road. However, noise levels could be greatly improved in comparison with the four other sedans in this road test.

Among the negative points, one can't overlook a soft suspension, lazy steering response, an unresponsive engine at low revs and spongy brakes. One of the participants commented that "its brakes remind me of those of my wife's 1988 Volkswagen Fox!"

In spite of a few drawbacks, this Passat 4Motion performed credibly during the time-trials. Later on, its all-wheel traction with a Torsen central differential gave a good account of itself on the skid-pad. The torque distribution was well managed and it was easy to keep control of the car for long periods of time while circling at high speed.

Despite all these qualities, the Passat fell a little short of the other participants because of its overall looks, more functional than luxurious, and a cockpit where the dashboard does not compare favorably with the others. Moreover, the noise levels leave a lot to be desired. Its rather plebeian look drove it to the tail end of the Tester's Choice category. The comment of one of the testers does seem to express the crew's feelings: "In fact, despite its good road handling and performance, the Passat gives an impression of being just an ordinary car. I would never spend $43,000 on that!"

There, you have it. Priced $7000 to $8000 less, the Passat would be a real find. At this price, the potential buyer can choose other alternatives, more interesting and more prestigious. Its overall looks, both inside and outside, are really too bland to encourage people to pay such a heavy price.

SUBARU LEGACY OUTBACK H6

From the forest trail to the racetrack

▲ PRO

The mechanical components are excellent, and in spite of the tires and the "four-wheel drive" ground clearance, its road-holding is a welcome surprise. So are the brakes. And its responsiveness awards it championship status in this category.

▼ CON

I am under the impression that this was a car designed for the mid-scale slot, and that luxury items were bolted on so it could make the high-end class.

When the Subaru Outback appeared on the racetrack, quite a few wondered what this road and track hybrid was doing in a comparison test with a bunch of well-bred Europeans.

However, the claims of this Japanese machine are not as farfetched as you might imagine. First of all, priced at just over $40,000 it falls well within our parameters. Moreover, its 212-hp flat-6 was the second most powerful of the test. Finally, the all-wheel drive system of this Subaru is considered to be one of the best on the market. In the skid-pad tests, the Legacy gave the best performance.

So much for the positive side. We were, however, a little hesitant in comparing this hybrid with true-blue sedans. With two inches more ground clearance and mixed mission on-road and off-road tires, it didn't seem to augur well, particularly in the slalom.

However, the Legacy did perform well in this area. Not only was it not outclassed, but it was head of the class in terms of responsiveness and placed second in terms of acceleration. Although the others in the slalom and in lap times were ahead of the Subaru, differences were minimal.

It did not fare so well when the time came to evaluate its looks. Its lines are not unpleasant, however, they seem too generic to win points over the opposition. The overall design of the cockpit did not go down too well with our testers either. Here are a few comments which seem to size up the situation. "Inside, everything is well laid out, but it still feels artificial. One gets the impression that there is leather, because in this price category, there should be leather. In a nutshell, it seems like an average cockpit with various luxury appointments tagged on." This tester hit the nail on the head, as this Legacy is priced far more reasonably in its 4-cylinder guise. Fitting the H6 engine under the hood encouraged the marketing managers to lay it on a bit thick in terms of presentation, in order to justify its list price. But it is difficult to find fault with the MacIntosh sound system – no relation to the computer – which produces an impressive sound, and also adds a few thousand dollars to the sticker price.

If this test had been run in a sea of mud and on rough tracks, the Outback would have probably finished first. On the racetrack and the open road, it took fourth place, handicapped by its specialized nature. It is the ideal car for those of us with a more conservative driving style, who prefer a softer suspension and riding comfort akin to American sedans. Moreover, this all-wheel drive system has become an institution in its own right. It's up to you to determine whether or not you like its looks. Many think Subaru should ask an Italian designer to restyle the bodywork and interior so that the car's road-going qualities can be better appreciated.

JAGUAR X-TYPE

Welcome to the group

▲ PRO

This car is just as pleasant to watch as it is to drive. On the road, it feels at ease with its rivals. Comfort is excellent, and its traditional luxury is almost overwhelming.

▼ CON

It's on small details that it fell short. No in-car CD changer, restricted rear legroom, performance somewhat lacking.

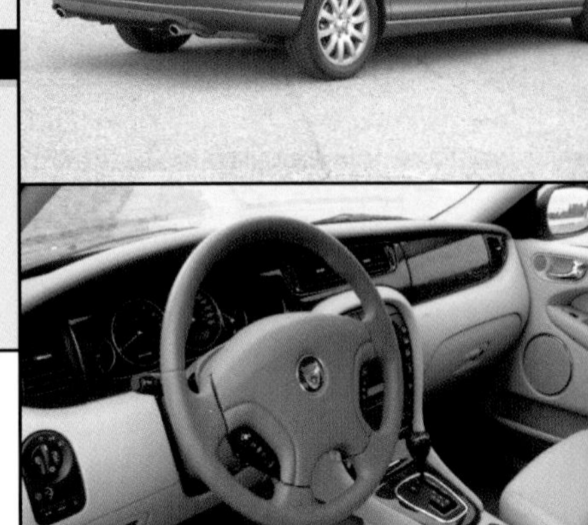

For the first time in its history, the British manufacturer has taken an interest in mid-level sedans. This Coventry-based automaker has taken advantage of its association with Ford and added the Jaguar touch to a Ford Mondeo platform. And don't blame it for its more modest origins. The new Mondeo's roadholding and driving qualities have been much discussed in the European press. With such quality components, one can build a genuine Jaguar.

The stylists managed to keep the attractive Jaguar look, as the X-Type won top honors for its overall appearance. It reminds us of the retro lines of the S-type, while incorporating more modern components, as the X-Type is marketed toward a younger clientele. However, the cockpit did not please everyone. Of course, the leather – unavoidable in cars of this make – and the walnut-like appointments are present, but the quality of the workmanship is closer to a Ford than a Jaguar. Actually, here is a comment which is self-explanatory: "The workmanship and the quality of the materials are not up to par. In some ways, it looks a little cheap." One should also mention that putting the CD changer in the trunk is a little old hat, as practically all the other recent models now feature in-dash 6-CD changer.

The fundamental quality of this car raised some eyebrows. The cigar lighter refused to work and the instrument lighting failed at the end of the day. Briefly, this elegant Briton needs to be improved in this area, otherwise the old horror stories about the Jaguar's lack of reliability will return to haunt the manufacturer.

However, the real Achilles' heel of this car is the engine. The small 195-hp 2.5-liter V6 engine is particularly hard pressed. The car was last in 0-60 mph acceleration tests and only managed to get ahead of the Subaru in the slalom with a fourth place in lap times. This V6 is poorly served by a lazy transmission which hesitates before changing gears and sometimes refuses to change down when power is really needed. This doesn't add to driving enjoyment. Actually, like the other cars of this make, it's an elegant automobile made for boulevards and its road behavior is slanted more toward comfort than performance. It is, however, certain that the 230-hp 3-liter V6 engine would have given the X-Type a better showing in the slalom and on the racetrack, therefore giving it a better ranking.

In the meantime, we all welcome Jaguar to the luxury intermediates, one of the most competitive categories.

CONCLUSION

COME RAIN OR SNOW

This all-wheel drive quintet proves that it's possible to combine sport-like performance and efficient winter traction without the need for these large SUV's. Some of our contenders offer more comfort than the others, while some offer a less gentrified approach, yet all are very fine road-going cars and all have acceptable sporting characteristics. All you need to do is determine the blend of sportiness and comfort you require.

That's the reason why the Audi A4 took the honors. This car is the only one to combine luxury, comfort and roadholding performance with an all-wheel drive. The others follow in decreasing order, depending on their weaknesses on the road or on the racetrack. The BMW 325Xi is a car with great breeding but its engine lacks power and the all-wheel drive transmission was the most ineffective on the skid-pad. You can increase performance by choosing the 330Xi but there is a commensurate increase in price.

The Volkswagen Passat is the most modest, with a price tag of about $40,000, due largely to its all-wheel drive transmission. It explains the more conservative looks and the feeling our testers had that they were driving a somewhat less luxurious car. However, the qualities of its chassis and the 4Motion system made it hang on to third place, ahead of the Subaru Legacy Outback by just a few points.

This was indeed an interesting hybrid, which surprised many by its engine performance and during testing

in categories where normally it would not be expected to perform, such as the slalom and lap times on the racetrack. In spite of its raised suspension and its average tires, it gave a good account of itself. Its on-road, off-road nature, and its comfortable suspension should be of interest to people who often drive on unpaved roads.

The Jaguar X-Type has more character than the others. It had to stay within the tradition of the make and offer a cockpit equipped with leather-clad luxury and wood trim. Its less powerful engine and relatively soft suspension took away points, while the all-wheel transmission was above average. This is a car which did not perform up to expectations, and our testers were disappointed by its Ford-like finish in certain areas.

One thing is certain, the engineers in most of these companies managed to develop all-wheel transmissions which perform well and are efficient. It is important to stress that an all-wheel drive car, which normally provides above average performance on snow and ice in winter, must also be able to offer better roadholding when driven at high speed or when cornering, and that is precisely what these five contenders have revealed both on the track and in the slalom. They can hold their own against the best two-wheel drive cars. For many, they represent an ideal compromise to face winter without having to suffer any drawbacks in terms of driving enjoyment.

Finally, one should mention that the new Volvo S60 AWD should theoretically have participated in this match but the company was unable to supply us with a test car, given the time pressures. Something which the other manufacturers managed to do. Perhaps Volvo preferred to be absent, rather than having to face a comparison test with the best in that category.

FIRE HAZARD

"Your car's on fire... Your car's on fire! Quick, a fire extinguisher!" I was making a pit stop, back from a few spins on the track, testing the road manners of the new Audi A4, and some of my crew were on the verge of panic. Highly visible flames were shooting out of the offside front wheel. Had I hit on the Audi's weak spot or was that just to be expected from extreme braking ?

On this particular racetrack, you have to brake hard, twice in short order from 100 mph, which puts a very real strain on the pads. A little later, the extreme conditions of this test were brought home to me when the BMW 325Xi's front left wheel sprouted flames, though to a lesser extent. Why the left front wheel you may ask? Well I haven't the slightest idea, however these would-be blazes were a new one on me. There lies clear proof that in our profession, we are often playing with fire!

First place
Audi A4 V6:
66.7 s

This being said, the latest A4 model from Audi could claim full honors with the best time on this relatively small racetrack, and in spite of a somewhat sparing use of the brakes. Credit this success to the 220-horsepower engine which at high speed really does take off. The gearbox ratios are well spaced and allow full use of the engine's power, but it is not the easiest to deal with. It is easy to reach the wrong gear and the lever could be a little more precise. As I have mentioned before, this 6-speed manual gearbox is not a good match for the V-6.The A-4 offers good solid cornering, either with or without the Dynamic Stability Control (DSC). With the system off, cornering is more lively with a tad of oversteer, and is easily controlled.

Second place
Volkswagen Passat 4Motion: 67.2 s

Specifications	Audi A4	BMW 325Xi	Jaguar X-Type	Subaru Legacy H6	VW Passat 4Motion
• Wheelbase	104.3 in	107.1 in	106.7 in	104.3 in	106.3 in
• Length	179.1 in	176 in	183.9 in	184.3 in	183.9 in
• Width	56.3 in	56.3 in	54.7 in	58.3 in	57.5 in
• Height	143 cm	143 cm	139 cm	148 cm	146 cm
• Weight	3406 lb (1545 kg)	3047 lb (1382 kg)	3428 lb (1555 kg)	3439lb (1560 kg)	3532 lb (1602 kg)
• Transmission	Manual	Manual	Automatic	Automatic	Automatic
• No. of gear ratios	6	5	5	4	5
• Engine	V6	6L	V6	H6	V6
• Displacement	3.0-liter	2.5-liter	2.5-liter	3.0-liter	2.8-liter
• Horsepower	220 hp	184 hp	194 hp	212 hp	190 hp
• Front suspension	independent	independent	independent	independent	independent
• Rear suspension	independent	independent	independent	independent	independent
• Front brakes	discs	discs	discs	discs	discs
• Rear brakes	discs	discs	discs	discs	discs
• ABS	yes	yes	yes	yes	yes
• Tires	P235/457R17	P205/55R16	P205/55VR16	P225/60R16	P195/65R15
• Steering	rack-and-pinion	rack-and-pinion	rack-and-pinion	rack-and-pinion	rack-and-pinion
• Turning circle	36.4 feet	35.8feet	35.4 feet	36.7 feet	37.4 feet
• Air bags	front, side, head	front, side, head	front, side, head	front, side	front, side, head
• Fuel tank	17.5 gallons	16.7 gallons	15.9 gallons	17 gallons	16.4 gallons
• Trunk	15.7 cu. ft	15.5 cu. ft	17.1 cu. ft	12.4 cu. ft	16.8 cu. ft.
• Acceleration (0-60 mph)	8.2 seconds	8.2 seconds	10.8 seconds	8.8 seconds	9.3 seconds
• Maximum speed	129 mph (208 km/h)	128 mph (206 km/h)	149 mph (240 km/h)	130 mph (210km/h)	130 mph (210 km/h)
• Fuel consumption	22.9 mpg 10.25 L/100 km)	19.4 mpg 12.1 L/100 km)	18.6 mpg (12.6 L/100 km)	18.3 mpg (12.8 L/100 km)	18.8 mpg (12.5 L/100 km)
• Price ($CDN / $US)	49,195 / 30,900	41,050 / 25,775	45,950 / 28,850	44,590 / 28,000	43,495 / 27,375

Although with a smaller cubic capacity, minus 30 hp and a Tiptronic automatic transmission, the Passat takes full advantage of its well-balanced approach. With the exception of the Subaru, it is the most softly sprung of the group and at high speed it really lifts up over the bumps. The brakes also suffered from the track runs and the thousands of clicks on the odometer and they reached the red zone wear point. Its track times are surprising, not to say outstanding, proof that the Passat deserves to be up there with its more prestigious rivals.

Third place

BMW 325Xi:

68.3 s

This BMW had everything going against it and seemed earmarked for last place in track performance: indecisive braking, a sluggish engine with unexciting performance on the open road. While the 330Xi had been

Timed Performance

	0-60 mph	60-0 mph
❶ Audi A4	7.9 s	122 feet
❷ BMW 325Xi	8.5 s	137 feet
❸ Jaguar X-Type	10.7 s	117 feet
❹ Subaru Legacy H6	8.5 s	137 feet
❺ VW Passat	9.8 s	139 feet

Slalom

❶ Audi A4	23.97 sec
❷ BMW 325Xi	24.5 sec
❸ Jaguar X-Type	24.8 sec
❹ Subaru Legacy H6	25.9 sec
❺ VW Passat	24.10 sec

Lap

❶ Audi A4	1.06.7 min
❷ BMW 325Xi	1.08.32 min
❸ Jaguar X-Type	1.10.17 min
❹ Subaru Legacy H6	1.10.27 min
❺ VW Passat	1.07.2 min

N.B. Times for the 4Motion are those listed for the VW Passat. The 2RM version completed the slalom in 24.3 seconds.

Evaluation Sheet

		Audi A4	BMW 325Xi	Jaguar X-Type	Subaru Legacy H6	VW Passat 4Motion
Aesthetics						
• Exterior	10	8.0	8.0	8.1	6.5	7.4
• Interior	10	8.6	7.0	7.4	7.0	7.5
• Ext. finish	10	8.8	8.5	7.0	7.6	8.3
• Int. finish	10	9.1	7.5	7.3	7.7	7.8
	40 pts	**34.5**	**31.0**	**29.8**	**28.8**	**31.0**
Accessories						
• Number and practicality	10	9.0	8.1	7.4	8.7	8.2
• Storage space	10	9.0	7.8	8.7	8.2	8.1
• Instruments/controls	10	9.2	8.3	7.7	7.6	8.4
• Ventilation/heating	10	9.3	8.9	8.4	8.5	9.0
	40 pts	**36.5**	**33.1**	**32.2**	**33.0**	**33.7**
Body						
• Front access/space	15	14.6	12.6	12.7	13.1	13.6
• Rear access/space	15	12.2	11.2	10.5	12.5	11.4
• Trunk: access and volume	5	4.3	3.4	3.7	4.3	4.4
• Mechanical system access	5	3.5	3.0	3.2	4.5	3.0
	40 pts	**34.6**	**30.2**	**30.1**	**34.4**	**32.4**
Comfort						
• Suspension	10	8.8	8.3	7.9	8.0	7.6
• Noise level	10	9.2	8.5	7.5	7.9	7.3
• Seats	10	8.7	7.8	7.9	7.6	7.6
• Driving position	10	9.0	9.1	8.2	8.4	9.2
	40 pts	**35.7**	**33.7**	**31.5**	**31.9**	**31.7**
Engine/Transmission						
• Efficiency	15	13.2	12.4	12.0	12.5	12.6
• Performance	15	13.0	11.9	11.0	12.4	11.6
• Gearshift lever	5	4.5	4.6	3.4	4.5	3.8
• Shiftgate	5	4.5	4.7	3.3	3.4	4.0
	40 pts	**35.2**	**33.6**	**29.7**	**32.8**	**32.0**
Handling						
• Road adherence	20	18.0	17.1	15.6	15.0	15.6
• Steering	10	9.2	9.1	8.5	8.4	8.6
• Brakes	10	7.1	7.6	7.0	8.5	6.2
	40 pts	**34.3**	**33.8**	**31.1**	**31.9**	**30.4**
Safety						
• Air bags	15	15.0	15.0	15.0	10.0	15.0
• Visibility	10	8.0	8.5	8.0	8.8	8.8
• Sideview mirrors	5	4.5	4.7	4.4	4.3	4.6
	30 pts	**27.5**	**28.2**	**27.4**	**23.1**	**28.4**
Timed Performance						
• Passing power	10	8.0	7.0	7.0	10.0	8.0
• Acceleration	10	10.0	8.0	7.0	8.0	7.0
• Braking	10	8.0	7.0	10.0	7.0	7.0
• Slalom	10	10.0	8.0	8.0	7.0	8.0
• Laps	10	10.0	7.0	6.0	6.0	8.0
	50 pts	**46.0**	**37.0**	**38.0**	**38.0**	**38,0**
Other criteria						
• Baggage space	30	28.0	27.0	30.0	27.0	28.0
• Test drivers' choice	40	40.0	38.0	37.0	37.0	36.0
• Price	10	6.0	10.0	7.0	8.0	7.0
	80 pts	**74.0**	**75.0**	**74.0**	**72.0**	**71.0**
Grand Total	**400 pts**	**358.3**	335.6	323.8	325.9	328.6
RANKING		**1**	**2**	**5**	**4**	**3**

a wild and enchanting experience (Road Tests & Reports) the 325 makes me want for more, especially at the beginning of a standing start. However, a bimmer is a bimmer and this easygoing driving style can be deceptive. Its high performance breeding was quite distinctive and prominent in the group. Precision steering that gives you position control on a dime and a smooth manual gearbox are amongst its prime assets. The 330 version would have blown away the opposition, but it was outside the price range we had set for this comparison test.

Fourth place

Jaguar X-Type:

70.1 s

There again, the price barrier excluded the 3.0-liter model and with the 194 hp of the 2.5-liter engine, the small Jag could not face the opposition with the same composure. The car takes too long to power its way out of the curves, which implies a fair amount of body roll. Obviously, Jaguar went for comfort with this model and only the 3.0-liter X-Type with the more massive tires and the stiffer suspension of the Sports package would bring it on a par with its rivals. Switching off the DSC control (Dynamic Stability Control) increases the risk of a spin, more so than in the other models. Having less work, the brakes on the other hand fared quite well in spite of several track runs pushing the envelope.

Fifth place

Subaru Legacy H6 3.0 VDC:

70.27 s

Before you jump to the conclusion that the Subaru Outback H6 should not be part of this elite group, compare its track times with the X-type Jaguar. I must admit though that I did not expect such fast times when I went out on the track. First it really leans out on the curve and when it has found its grip, the impression is that the engine refuses to commit fully, as if the VDC traction control were still locked on. With a high center of gravity, and tires designed for anything except a racetrack, our strong-hearted H6 revealed minimal grip during high-speed curves. A Legacy GT would probably have served Subaru better, however the manufacturer's representatives insisted on including it in this all-wheel drive comparison test.

It is interesting to note that the slalom times and the track times provide the same ranking for the competitors...of course the driving impressions are the same, fire hazards notwithstanding.

Jacques Duval

ALL SEASON TIRES VERSUS SNOW TIRES

The Best Snow Tires

BY JACQUES DUVAL

North Americans love compromise and quick-fix solutions. In every area, we try to make life a little easier, sometimes at the expense of personal safety. The automobile is part and parcel of this supposed quality of life.

That being the case, why not design tires for all seasons and all kinds of weather instead of forcing motorists to alternate between summer and winter tires every year? And that is exactly what happened, although the results were not necessarily what you would have expected. All-weather tires will never be anything but a compromise solution and can never replace good snow tires. Some European markets are completely oblivious of their very existence because no one has even mentioned the idea.

Even government agencies have become aware of how mediocre these tires really are. The Quebec government, for example, commissioned comparison testing in order to obtain scientific data concerning the different ways these two types of tires actually perform.

New proof

Almost all new cars sold on our continent are equipped with all-weather tires. Several motorists have questioned the performance of these tires and whether they would be adequate on snow and ice. Would it make more sense to replace them with winter tires? The answer to that question is an unequivocal yes. And this is not an answer given lightly, as the Quebec Minister of Transport has asked the Quebec Industrial Research Center (CRIQ) to conduct a series of tests in order to evaluate scientifically the performance of all-weather tires and winter tires on compact cars, trucks and sport-utility vehicles. The test results conveyed simple and direct findings. The report concludes: "The test carried out by the CRIQ are conclusive. They demonstrate that in general winter tires perform better than all-weather tires. Based on the experiments conducted one must conclude that winter tires provide better braking performance than all-weather tires, a central feature of road safety."

Not wanting to overwhelm you with statistics, suffice it to say that these tests have clearly demonstrated that braking distances were improved from between 16.6% to 25.1% on hard-packed snow with the use of winter tires. Acceleration tests indicated that acceleration times from 0-35 mph were reduced by about 11.1% for a 4-wheel-drive vehicle and 40.1% for a small van. Although results vary from one vehicle to another and from one tire brand to another, the tests are conclusive.

The following grid shows some partial test results. Two other series of tests were carried out on various surfaces. These confirm the results that were conducted on the snow and compacted ice.

What and how to choose

Faced with a whole slew of tire brands and models, it's hard not to be confused. But clearly, not matter what brand or model chosen, four snow tires are better than four all-weather tires for winter driving. This doesn't mean that you should choose blindly or allow price to be the determining factor. Depending on the vehicle, some winter tires perform better than others. However, a tire's effectiveness will vary according to the surface and weather conditions. It's therefore worthwhile taking advantage of specialist advice. Here are a few points to take into account:

- Get advice from an outlet that offers several brands or from an establishment whose staff has received some form of technical training. If the technical advisor doesn't inquire about the type of car you drive, or the usual road conditions or other relevant information, then leave.
- Don't be influenced solely by price when making your selection.
- Don't discard studded tires. In some areas, they're practically indispensable. Actually, the demand for these tires is on the rise. However, their use is subject to regulation, and they're only allowed at certain times of the year. Some states and provinces forbid their use.
- If you have two winter tires that are partially worn and two new winter tires, install the new tires at the back if your car is a front-wheel drive. Otherwise, there is the risk of a spin.

Information grid

In order to help you choose, here is a summary of test results provided by some European and American specialists in eight different categories. These results are based on information gathered from thousands of road users in North America.

These results are provided for information only. The performance of some products may vary from one car to another as well as actual weather conditions, road surface and ambient temperature. It's up to you to choose the most effective tires for the conditions you most frequently encounter.

Road conditions

Road surface composed of 1 to 2 inches of compacted snow and ice, about minus 20 degrees C, over a tarmac base.

Braking from 35-0 mph (50-0 km/h)

- Sub-compact: Braking distance reduced by 38 feet (11.6 m): 22.8% less
- SUV 4X4: Braking distance reduced by 23.3 feet (7.1 m): 16.6% less
- Minivan: Braking distance reduced by 42 feet (12.8 m): 25.1% less

Acceleration 0-35 mph (0-50 km/h)

- Sub-compact: Distance reduced by 60 feet (18.3 m): 23.7% less
- SUV 4X4: Increase of 16 feet (4.6 m): 11.1% more
- Minivan: Distance reduced by 147 feet (44.9 m): 40.1% less

Swerving at 18 or 25 mph (30 or 40 km/h)

- Sub-compact: Increase of 0.13 g: 37.8% improvement
- SUV 4X4: Increase of 0.03 g: 8.5% improvement
- Minivan: Increase of 0.05 g: 15.2% improvement

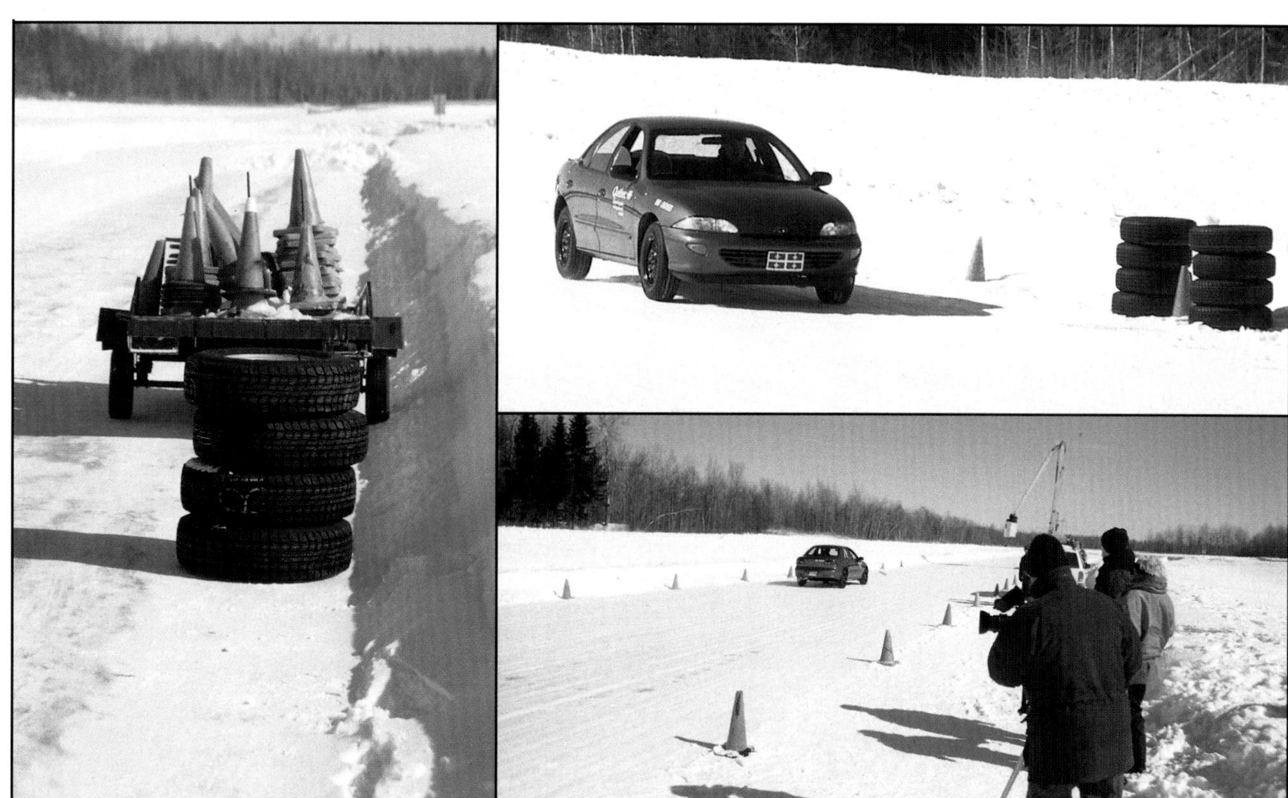

Evaluation Sheet

Brand name	Model	Adherence Dry	Adherence Wet	Adherence Snow	Stability Turning	Response Steering	Comfort	Noise level	Wear	Ranking
Bridgestone	Blizzak LM-22	8.3	8.7	8.9	7.7	7.8	8.0	7.5	7.1	***
Goodyear	Ultra Grip	8.3	8.6	8.5	7.8	7.6	8.0	8.0	7.2	***
Pirelli	Winter 210 Asimmetrico	7.8	8.0	7.9	7.9	7.9	8.7	8.2	7.3	***
Dunlop	Winter Sport M2	8.0	8.3	9.0	7.6	7.7	8.0	7.6	7.5	***
Vredestein	Snowtrac	7.5	7.0	7.4	7.8	7.3	8.3	7.8	8.0	***
Maloya	Cresta	7.4	7.1	7.6	7.3	7.1	8.2	7.9	7.7	***
Toyo	G-02	7.6	7.7	8.5	8.0	7.0	8.0	7.9	8.1	**
Michelin	Pilot Alpin	7.9	8.5	8.6	7.4	7.5	8.2	7.6	7.9	**
Pirelli	Winter Ice Asimmetrico	6.8	7.4	8.8	7.6	7.0	8.0	8.0	7.0	**
Michelin	Artic Alpin	7.6	7.9	8.7	6.9	7.1	7.6	6.7	7.0	**
Goodyear	Ultra Grip Ice	7.5	7.7	8.7	6.8	7.2	7.8	7.0	7.0	**
Uniroyal	Tiger Paw	7.4	6.9	7.6	6.9	7.1	7.0	6.6	6.9	**
Firestone	WinterFire	7.9	7.6	9.1	6.4	6.6	7.9	7.1	7.1	**
Bridgestone	Blizzak MZ-02	7.3	7.5	8.4	6.7	6.7	7.5	6.8	6.7	**
Bridgestone	Blizzak WS-50	6.9	7.5	9.6	6.0	5.9	7.5	6.6	6.2	**
BFGoodrich	Winter Salom	7.1	7.6	8.5	7.5	6.5	8.0	7.0	6.0	**
Goodyear	F32	6.9	7.3	9.1	8.0	6.8	7.0	5.8	6.5	**
Dunlop	Graspic HS-1	6.4	7.6	9.3	5.8	5.7	7.3	7.2	6.0	**
Gislaved	Eurofrost	6.5	6.8	9.3	6.5	5.6	7.3	6.7	6.8	**
Dunlop	Graspic-DS 1	6.4	7.5	8.4	5.2	5.1	7.2	6.8	6.2	*
Cooper	Weather-Master XGR	6.5	7.3	6.8	6.0	6.0	6.3	6.0	6.5	*

A love letter to the Mini

● BY ALAIN RAYMOND

Let's play: What music best defines the Sixties? What fashion? What car? If you cite the Beatles, the miniskirt, and for the last question, either the Beetle, Thunderbird, Porsche 911, Mustang or Corvette – whichever happened to be relevant to your own Sixties' experience – you're right on the mark. But chances are a small minority might choose the Mini, and they, too, have a point. Because if ever there was a car that transformed the entire automotive world during the last 50 years, by virtue of its unprecedented architecture and engineering philosophy, it's none other than the humble Mini.

On the eve of its first ever redesign, not to mention the fact that 2002 has been proclaimed "the Year of the MINI," it seems only fitting to recapitulate the history of that extraordinary car. Under what circumstances did it come into being? And what exactly was it that turned it into a cult-car? Also, what shape will this most memorable minicar take as it embarks on its second career?

THE SUEZ CANAL CRISIS

As the saying goes, "history accounts for a great many things," including automobiles. Barely 11 years after the end of World War II, Europe – still under reconstruction – was poised on the edge of yet another potentially disastrous crisis: the closing of the vital Suez Canal – the continent's key oil-supply route from the Middle East. The crisis prompted governments – and automakers – to search, with various degrees of success, for solutions to this dangerous dependency.

In Great Britain, the British Motor Corporation (BMC) – the country's largest automaker – seized the unexpected opportunity to spearhead an economy-car project long championed by Sir Alec Issigonis, an engineer renowned for his innovative ideas. At the same time, BMC hoped that the new car would help slow down the meteoric rise of a certain popular "people's car" – the Volkswagen.

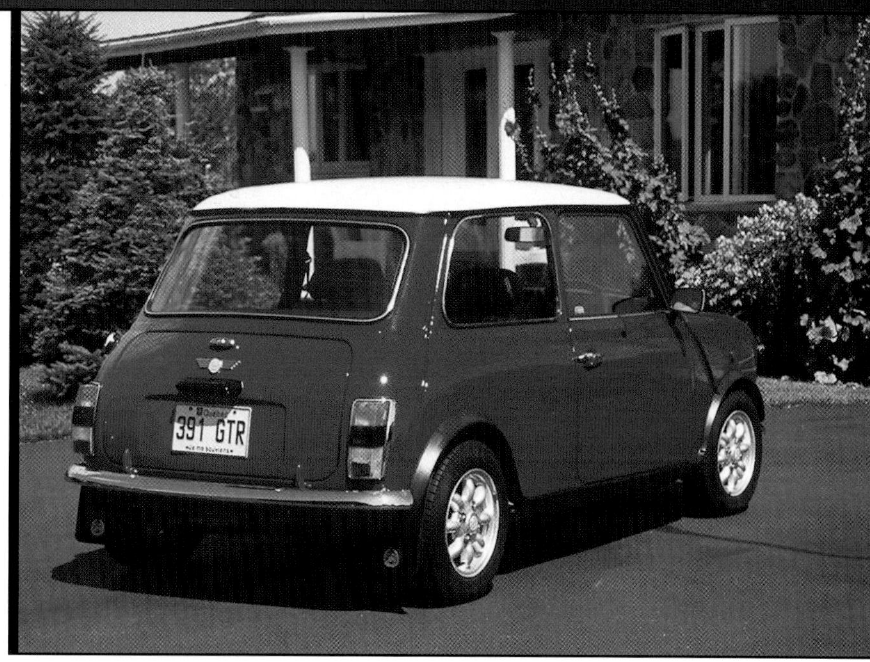

Born in Smyrna, Turkey, of a Greek father – a naturalized British subject – and a Bavarian mother, Issigonis was educated in England where he eventually settled, working as an automotive engineer. It was to him that the world owed the Morris Minor which became the first British car to sell more than a million units while it was in production, between 1948 and 1971. And this, despite its conservative design. Facing new market demands that reflected the looming oil shortage and the steadily restricted urban space, Issigonis set himself an ambitious goal: to build a minimalist car, roughly 120 inches long (3m), capable of seating four passengers with luggage, with a speed as high as 60 mph (100 km/h), and good fuel mileage – about 37 mpg (6 liters per 100 km).

CHALLENGING "ENGINE-IN-THE-REAR" ARCHITECTURE

At that period, Europe's three best-selling cars were the Renault Dauphine, Fiat 600 and Volkswagen ("Beetle" in North America). All three carried their respective engines in the rear, and none met any of Issigonis' four objectives.

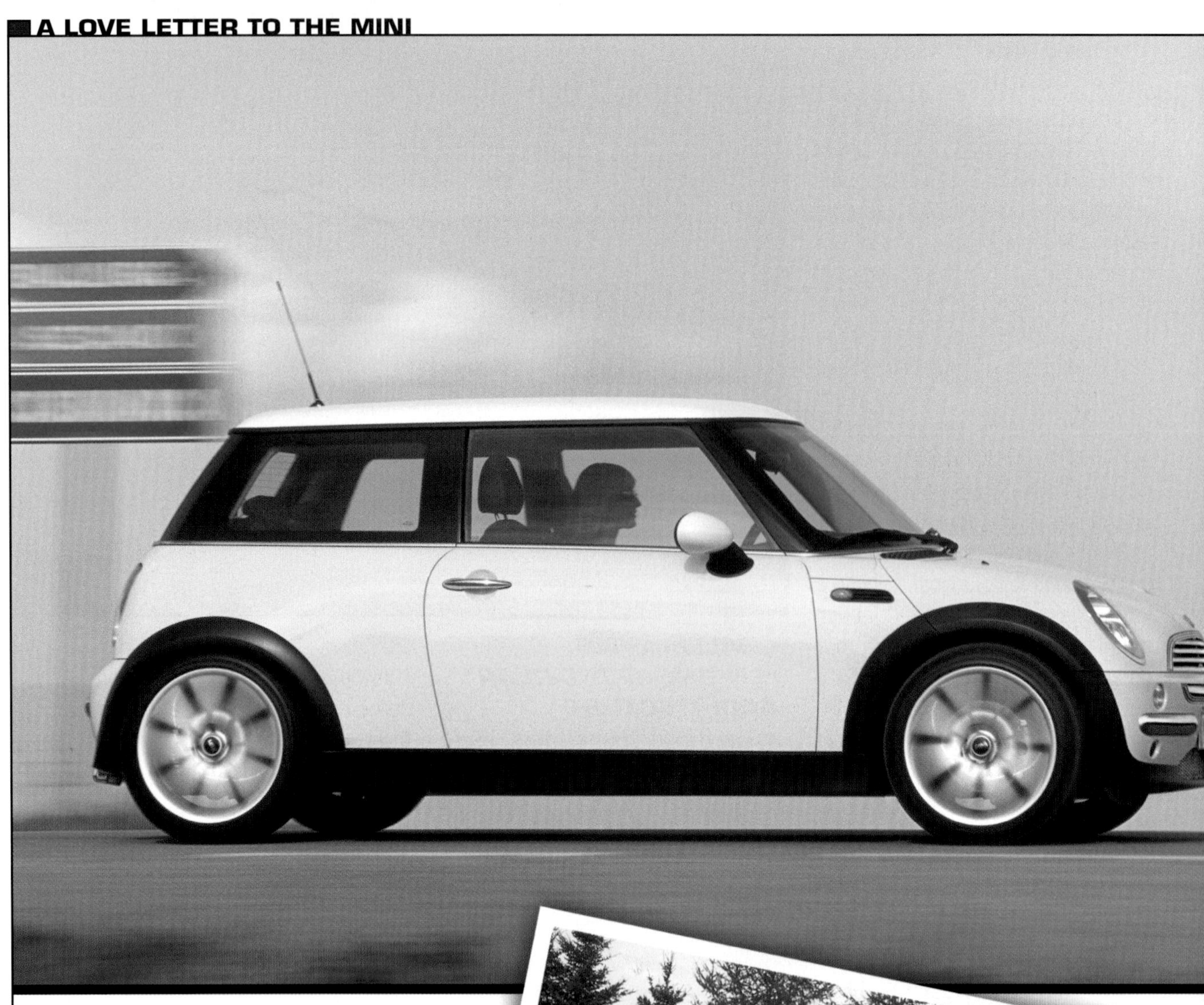

In March 1957, the nine-strong Issigonis team set to work, building prototypes. By October – a mere 220 days later – two of the prototypes were ready for the road! A remarkable feat, given the fact that all the team had to work with was their design board and a simple slide rule. Not even a computer, never mind any other ultramodern gadgets.

In September 1959, the Austin Seven 850 and the Morris Mini Minor (both BMC marques) were unveiled at the London Auto Show. The car's wheelbase was 78.7 inches and overall length was 120 inches. Its miniature 10-inch wheels were mounted at the far corners of the car and its 850-cc 4-cylinder engine was installed transversely in front. And that's how it was that the Mini swept aside 50 years of traditional automaking. Never before had so many technical innovations been included in one car. Issigonis won his bet, not to mention BMC.

Public response at the London Auto Show was enthusiastic. However, the true significance and scope of the Mini's innovative breakthrough became apparent only after the road-test results were published. In addition to its capability of transporting four adults at 60 mph and excellent

fuel mileage (37 mpg), the Mini handled superbly and was a pleasure to drive. Within a few short years, the Mini managed to steal the thunder from all other prominent rear-wheel drive cars, whether they were German, French, Italian or British.

SIR ALEC'S TRIUMPH

For other European automakers, the name Mini was now synonymous with "bludgeon blow," "slap in the face" or "end of an era." Even the venerable Beetle couldn't begin to take it on, its mechanicals having lagged behind damagingly during the mid-Sixties. With the exception of North America, where the "German bug" became a veritable social phenomenon, signaling the beginning of the end of the Big Three automakers' domination.

And as if commercial success were not enough, BMC commissioned John Cooper, another British automotive genius – pioneer of the mid-engine F1 – to "boost" the Mini further, just as Amédée Gordini did for Renault and Carlo Abarth for Fiat. Cooper increased the Mini's cubic capacity to 997 cc and added front disc brakes. Then came the 1100-cc version, followed by the ultimate Mini, the Cooper S with 1275 cc.

Both the Cooper and Cooper S performed so well that not even the Porsche 911 could beat them, finishing behind not once, not twice, but three times at the Monte Carlo Rallye, between 1964 and 1967. In fact, had the French failed to disqualify the winning Mini on a technicality – an obscure incident involving headlights during a race – the Cooper would have won the "Monty" four times!

All in all, the domination was complete. To this day, fans of the Mont-Tremblant, Que., racing circuit still marvel at the way the funky and nimble Minis went head to head against their much bigger and more powerful American V8 rivals all through the Sixties.

Since North Americans don't share the same automotive constraints as Europeans, interest in the Mini soon waned and by 1980, it had become only a blurred memory. Its technical legacy, however, lived on. Models with transversal engine and front-wheel drive began to crop up – Ford Escort, Honda Civic, Chrysler K-Cars, including some that not even Sir Alec Issigonis could have dreamed of, like the Ford Taurus, the humongous Cadillac DeVille and the Chrysler minivans.

Despite the Mini's worldwide success, BMC's fortunes gradually faltered. In 1968 it was absorbed by British Leyland (BL), which had been nationalized three years earlier. BL turned into the Rover Group in 1986, which was then bought by BMW in 1994. Unable to revive the "sinking ship," BMW discarded the ineffectual Rover Group, keeping the Mini marque and its Oxford plant.

Sir Alec Issigonis died in 1988 at the age of 82, but the Mini continued to be produced until October 2000. In 41 years, 5.3 million units were sold, about 10,000 of which were shipped to North America.

STARS AND CROWNS

Throughout its 41-year career, and despite its manufacturer's frequent ups and downs, the Mini reached a kind of milestone that rendered it all the more attractive to BMW. In addition to its success on the racing circuit, the Mini's appeal extended to include scores of celebrities – the Beatles, the Rolling Stones, a bevy of movie stars and even members of the British royal family. Imagine! All these beautiful people drove a Mini! Forever linked to the Sixties' pop cul-

ture, the Mini became a kind of fashion accessory, at least in Europe, and eventually acceded to the rank of cult-car. Such a golden opportunity didn't escape the eagle eyes of BMW management, and they promptly seized it, though they don't normally make small, front-wheel drive cars.

MINI IS DEAD. LONG LIVE THE MINI!

In October 2000, the last Mini rolled off the production line in Oxford, England. But dry your tears, because Sir Alec's baby – the most famous British car of all time – will be back next year, completely revamped and baptized MINI (note the capital letters). The fresh concept was finalized by Rover designers toward the end of the 90s, only to be delayed by the new owner, BMW, who wanted to make certain that the entire project would meet its corporate quality and styling standards. The new MINI, it turned out, was still built in England, although part of the car had been designed in Germany by a multinational team. The engine, for example, was Brazilian, though built in collaboration with American engineers!

AN AFFAIR TO REMEMBER

"It's impossible to create a cult," declares Gert Hildebrand, MINI's chief designer. But if you can get your hands on a cult object, reproduce it while making sure you preserve its "soul," and distribute it to a "well-prepared" public, now that's an affair to remember. In fact, to survive in the current culture of mega-mergers, BMW knows it needs to get involved in every segment of the market, from minicars to luxury "flagships." With the MINI at the low end of the lineup, BMW's 3, 4, and 5 Series in the middle, and Rolls Royce at the top, the Bavarian automaker's autonomy seems more secure, though by no means guaranteed.

Relying on this strategy, and the obligation not to compromise the "cult" image as its guidelines, BMW set to work recreating the MINI. Its first objective: styling must be based on the same "genes," so as to evoke the same kind of emotional appeal.

The second objective: to create a thoroughly modern car, endowed with the most up-to-date technologies and making the experience of driving the car as much fun as humanly possible.

BMW bases its marketing strategy for the MINI on its long-established image of a spiritedly independent automaker offering "refined cars for pure driving pleasure" – high-end, but not exclusive, cars that reflect European refinement and a dash of vitality sometimes lacking in other luxury but "sterile" marques. All in all, cars that appeal both to young, upward mobile professionals and an older, still "young-at-heart" clientele, "financially comfortable and susceptible to the finer things in life."

And that's exactly MINI's niche: professionals – young, self-confident and mostly single – particularly those in the creative arts (advertising, Internet, television, motion pictures, etc.). Female customers are also targeted, especially those under 35 who are firmly plugged into the "virtual" world. Another targeted group includes families with more than one car, and obviously those nostalgic for both the Mini and the Sixties, yearning to relive their 20s.

If these demographic profiles seem a far cry from those that inspired Alec Issigonis and BMC back in 1959, they're meant to be. Gone forever is the cheap, economical minicar aimed at frugal European drivers during an oil-shortage crisis. MINI, cult-car classic, cultivates much more ambitious ambitions. As its new name, spelled out in capital letters, seems to indicate, the MINI has grown up, becoming bigger and wearing leather. Air conditioned and teeming with electronic gadgets, it's gone designer-conscious and looks unabashedly trendy. It even "talks the talk" and gets its own "lifestyle" magazine, *MINIInternational*, published in Anvers, Belgium, a mecca for fashion and the arts.

BMW went through all this rigmarole just to persuade us that MINI is more than just a car, it's an accessory, a reflection of your own personality, or, in the words of chief designer Hildebrand, an "art object." It's a subtle way of warning you that the car is not cheap. To own a MINI Cooper, you need to break your bank account! What's more, BMW plans to ship only 20,000 Coopers and Coopers S to North America for the first year (out of a total production of 100,000). Compared with the 10,000 units shipped over last century, that's a big improvement. Since I've already had a chance to "taste" it and judging by the baby-boomers' passion for nostalgia, I'm willing to bet that the waiting list will be a long one.

But you'll have to see and experience MINI for yourself. For a preview, however, check out the *Auto Guide's* Road Tests and Analyses section. You'll find our account of 48 hours spent with MINI Cooper, along the peaks and valleys of that gorgeous Italian region: the landscape of Umbria. An unforgettable journey.

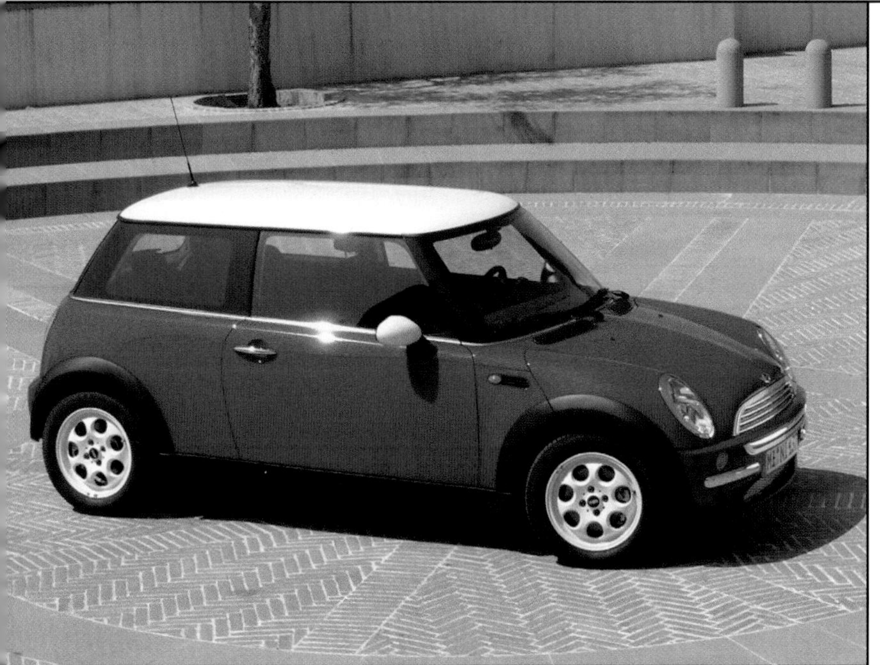

MINI'S SIX SECRETS

The Mini teemed with countless technical features that have genuinely transformed the automotive world as we know it today. Below are the six main features:

Dimensions:

- Only 120 inches long (305 cm), yet it can accommodate four adults plus their luggage.

Suspension:

- At a time when rigid axle and leaf springs were the norm, the Mini boasts entirely independent suspensions with rubber discs instead of springs so as to miniaturize suspension components for maximum cabin space, especially in the rear.

Front-wheel drive:

- In 1959, regardless of engine location (front or rear), rear-wheel drive was the order of the day, even for small cars. By adopting front-wheel drive, the Mini eliminated the propeller shaft, the tunnel that houses it and the rear axle, thus allowing for a flat floor and more cabin space.

Wheels:

- Unprecedented 10-inch wheels that don't encroach on cabin space and trunk space.

Engine:

- For the first time ever, the engine is placed transversely, reducing more than half the normal length of the hood.

Gearbox:

- Traditionally screwed onto one end of the engine, the gearbox lengthened the powerplant and took up considerable space under the floor. In the Mini, it is mounted below the engine, in the oil pan, freeing up much space.

To gauge the impact of the "Mini formula," you need only lift the hood of any car today, from the New Beetle (oh, yes) to the Cadillac Eldorado. Imitation, as they say, is the sincerest form of flattery.

Technical Specifications	1975 Mini 1000	2003 Mini Cooper
• Price ($CDN / $US)	2,875 / n.a.	est. 25,000 / 15,700
• Type	2-door sedan front wheel drive transversal engine	3-door hatchback front wheel drive transversal engine
• Engine	4L 1.0-liter	4 L 1.6-liter
• Horsepower	42 hp at 4950 rpm	115 hp at 6000 rpm
• Torque	52 lb-ft at 2700 rpm	110 lb-ft at 4500 rpm
• Tramission	4-speed manual	5-speed manual
• Brakes front/rear	drum	disc ABS
• Steering	rack-and-pinion	rack-and-pinion, electro-hydraulic assist
• Turning circle	27.9 feet	35 feet
• Suspension front/rear	hydrolastic independent wheels	independent helicoidal springs
• Wheelbase	80.2 in (203.6 cm)	97.1 in (246.7 cm)
• Length	120.1 in (305 cm)	142.8 in (362.6 cm)
• Width	55.5 in (141 cm)	66.5 in (168.8 cm)
• Height	53.1 in (135 cm)	55.6 in (141.3 cm)
• Weight	1461 lb (662.8 kg)	2315 lb (1050 kg)
• Fuel tank	6.6 gallons (25 liter)	13.2 gallons (50 liter)
• Warranty	12 months/12.500 miles (20 000 km)	n.a.
ACCELERATION:		
• 0-60 mph (100 km/h)	18.2 sec.	9.2 sec.**
• Maximum speed	77mph (123.9 km/h)	124 mph (200 km/h)
• Fuel consumption	37 mpg (6.4 L/100 km)	35 mph (6.7 L/100 km)**

(* Source: *1976 Auto Guide*)
(** Data supplied by the automaker)

Jerry Dupuis' Mini Cooper overtakes Jacques Duval's Renault 1093 over an ice-covered track in the early 1960s.

MINI MEMORIES

THE $8.50 CAR

BY JACQUES DUVAL

My head is abuzz with memories as I think back to the early Sixties, the tumultuous era that produced the beloved Mini. In the first place, the car didn't start out with that name, at least not here in Quebec. It was known as the Austin 850, the number referring to its cubic capacity. Its manufacturer, British Motor Corporation (BMC), was then a major player in the industry and could afford to market its cars under two distinct brand names: Austin and Morris. When carrying the Morris badge, the little Austin 850 (sold in England as the Austin Seven) was soon dubbed Mini Minor, a name that was to make it famous.

Anyway, the Mini was what I wanted to buy for my wife. First of all, because it cost only $1295 (oh, yes) and also because there was a special promotion in progress at L.N. Messier, a large store on Mont-Royal Avenue in Montreal. The store had come up with a unique idea, using the Mini's numerical appellation – the 850 – as a basis for its proposed purchase plan. The customer was required to hand over an $8.50 downpayment, and make subsequent weekly installments of $8.50 each until the car was finally paid off. Needless to say, the Minis flew off the "shelves" as fast as they could "make" them. The sales bonanza turned out to be a disaster for the store, however. People bought their cars in May or June, enjoyed driving them during the summer months and then returned them before the terms were up. Most got away with paying less than $100 each and by the fall the store was flooded with hundreds of used and heavily depreciated cars. With neither expertise nor staff to deal with the situation, the store was obliged to swallow monumental losses.

Go-kart scene

Personally, I continued to pay my installments, because I was head over heels in love with the car, leaving my wife – the Mini's theoretical owner – to make do with my own car (a Vauxhall Cresta, if memory serves).

At the time, the streets were crowded almost exclusively with big, cumbersome American cars that sailed along rather like boats on wheels. My favorite pastime was to dodge in and out of traffic in my cute little Mini, and park it wherever I pleased, in spots that were way too tight for most cars. The Mini was quite literally my personal toy, indulging my every whim and fancy.

In fact, this agile "dodging" ability was probably what made it so successful as a racing car.

The Mini's glorious racing career began with the Cooper and Cooper S versions, for which the Mini's original 37 horsepower was doubled, or even tripled. Despite their tiny 10-inch wheels, the Coopers rode like genuine go-karts and managed splendidly next to much bigger cars. Their "gutsiness" earned them legions of young followers at the then "green" Mont-Tremblant circuit. I enjoyed nothing more than watching the way those cute little numbers dominated the competition, not only in their own category, but also the likes of Mustangs and Camaros, cars commonly perceived as invincible. Especially nimble at cornering and with shorter braking distances, the Minis managed to leave speedier and more powerful rivals ridiculously far behind. Nothing could stop them – neither rain, nor snow, as demonstrated by one of their most resounding victories, at the 1969 Grand Prix du Carnaval de Québec.

There, on Quebec City's fabled Plains of Abraham, not even a Porsche 911 could stop John Powell's Mini Cooper S, which went on to win the race. It was a sight to behold – Powell receiving the trophy from the hands of Her Serene Highness, Princess Grace of Monaco, who couldn't quite mask her surprise at seeing a humble little British number beat out cars of much nobler lineage.

The 1976 Auto Guide

Curiously enough, the Mini's only road test for the *Auto Guide* appeared way back in 1976. By that time, the car was called Austin Mini 1000. At $2875, its price had more than doubled, although it was still cheaper than a Honda Civic ($3071), or a Renault 5 ($3895). And the Porsche 911 then cost a princely $18,500.

Physically, the Mini 1000 hadn't changed much, except for its bumpers and engine, which had been increased to a 1.0 liter. It was still as much fun, though its flaws seemed more pronounced next to its contemporary rivals. Seats were notoriously uncomfortable, the trunk outrageously small and the engine as noisy as a bulldozer. While it hardly surpassed 42 horsepower and its 0-60 mph sprint took longer than 18 seconds, the Mini was still lots of fun to drive. I concluded my personal impressions in 1976 as follows: "All British Leyland needs to undertake is a couple of modifications in order to make the Mini a shade more refined, and ready to start a second career." It took 26 years before that wish was fulfilled, by the Mini's new adopted parents – BMW.

Jacques Duval at the start of a winter rallye in 1958.

FERRARI FESTIVAL

In Mont-Tremblant, Que.

From Fiorano to the Laurentians

Heaven on Wheels

BY JACQUES DUVAL PHOTOS: MICHEL FYEN-GAGNON

To celebrate its 30th anniversary in 1996, the *Auto Guide* traveled to Italy for an extra special assignment: testing the three Ferrari models then in production on their home turf, the Fiorano test track, located a few steps from the Ferrari factory itself in Maranello. Needless to say, it was a memorable event and it will remain a highlight in the history of the *Guide*. I would have liked to repeat the experience in time for our 35th anniversary in 2001, but the project fell through for a number of reasons. On the other hand, the one-year delay gave us the opportunity not only to organize a repeat of our 1996 Ferrari Festival, but also to combine it with the reopening of the Circuit Mont-Tremblant – rebuilt in accordance with modern safety standards as set by the Fédération Internationale de l'Automobile (FIA).

Throughout the Festival weekend held at Mont-Tremblant, courtesy of Ferrari Quebec, I was able to drive – with no special constraints or restrictions – the entire Ferrari line: the 456 GTA, 550 Maranello, 360 Modena and, the 4th candle on the cake, the 550 Barchetta Pininfarina. It was a dream reunion.

New and improved circuit

I'd like to begin with a few words about the Circuit Mont-Tremblant. There are three reasons for doing so. Nestled high in Quebec's Laurentian mountains, the circuit has a rich and colorful past. During its heyday from 1964 to 1970, it hosted its fair share of the who's who of automobile racing, from drivers like Jackie Stewart and

Photos: Michel Fyen-Gagnon, FYENGAGNON@LR.CGOCABLE.CA

Bruce McLaren to Americans Mario Andretti and Bobby Unser. The Tremblant racing circuit also did its part in introducing an entire generation of Canadians – men like the great Gilles Villeneuve and others – to the exhilarating sport of automobile racing. Finally, between 1967 and 1973, the Circuit was a favorite venue for the Auto Guide's road-testing activities. That's where I accumulated thousands upon thousands of laps at the wheel of a variety of automobiles, representing such diverse marques as the Dodge Charger Daytona, Lamborghini Miura and Ferrari Daytona, to name but a precious few.

Come to think of it, I road-tested practically all Ferrari's street-legal models of that time – the divine 275 GTB among them – at the Circuit. For that reason, this year's rendezvous with the entire Ferrari line at Tremblant was a fitting homecoming.

The aging circuit had been dying a slow death when a consortium of international investors finally stepped in to give it a new lease on life. Although the basic track layout stays more or less the same, the racing surface itself has been fully repaved and considerably widened. Run-off areas, too, have been widened, making it safer for drivers if they fall off the track, and the notorious back straight hump – the scene of so many sudden "takeoffs" – has been flattened. The one spot that has been changed beyond recognition is the track's signature Namerow Corner (named after a deceased Quebec race driver). Drivers must now dive hard into a blind right, immediately after cresting the rise that preceded the old corner. No more room to see the corner from the top of the rise, brake and set up the car, just a blind dive to the right. Because the change of direction through Namerow is greater, the old flat-out left sweeper leading past the pits has turned into a real, slower corner. You now have to drive it, instead of looking at the gauges or waving to your friends. Only a few familiarization laps are required to show that lap times have dropped by four to five seconds, and to confirm that the notoriously fast and difficult Turn 1 will still separate the men from the boys. In other words, it remains the tough old track that it always was.

Passport to heaven

When I arrived at Circuit Mont-Tremblant that Thursday morning, the promised Ferraris – all three of them – were waiting for me, along with our photographer, Michel Fyen-Gagnon. Michael Nye, President of Ferrari Quebec, was also on hand with the car keys: a blue 456M GTA with automatic transmission, a 550 Maranello, also blue, but with a 6-speed manual, and finally, a gleaming red 360 Modena, complete with the fabulous F1 semi-automatic gearbox. There, lined up smartly in front of me was almost a million dollars worth of rare jewels and more than 1300 horses, all set to take part in this unusual motor derby. A yellow 550 Barchetta was to join the trio later, running the already astronomical bill still higher.

The 456M GTA

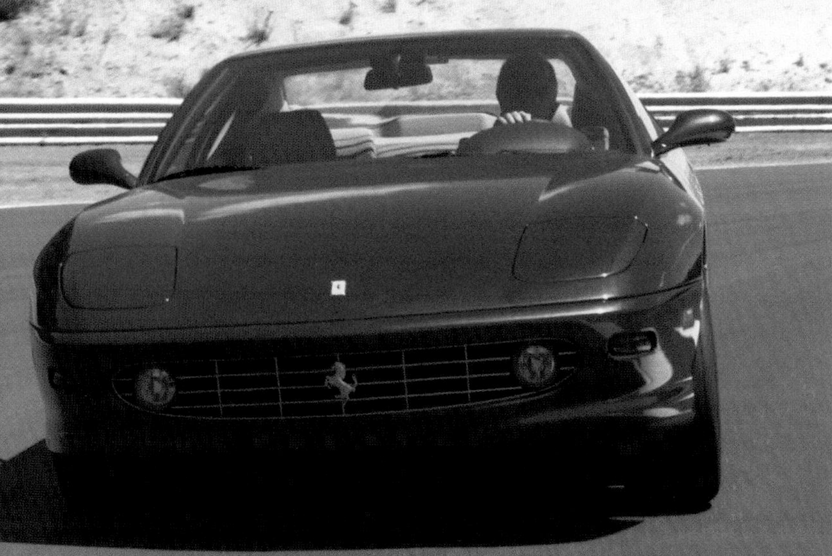

First-class *cabin*

Let's be frank: the Ferrari 456 is not a race car, least of all the GTA automatic version. It's a Grand Touring (GT) car, in the most precise sense of the term. I've written elsewhere in this guidebook about its merits and the positive impressions I had about it following a road test. On a racetrack, the 456's significant weight is much in evidence and the brakes are probably the clearest indication that this model was not designed for jostling through tight turns like a Miata. You'll know straight away that it was intended for loftier pursuits.

The mere fact that the majority of 456s are sold with a 4-speed automatic transmission demonstrates its emphasis on passenger comfort. If the car deserves a criticism, it may be the fact that it is not available with a 5-speed gearbox, something slightly worthier of its name than the

SPECS
456M GTA

Price	$CDN 357,000
Wheelbase	102.4 in
Length	187.4 in
Width	75.6 in
Height	51.2 in
Weight	3726lb (1690kg)
Trunk	11.2 cu.ft
Fuel tank	24 gallons
Engine	V12 5.5-liter
Horsepower(hp/rpm)	442/6 250
Torque (lb-ft/rpm)	398/4 500
Transmission	4-speed automatic
Disc brake diameter	13/12.2 in (330/310 mm)
Suspension	independent
Steering	rack-and-pinion
Turning circle	n.a.
Tires / fr.	P255/45ZR17
Tires / r.	P285/40ZR17

PERFORMANCE

0-60 mph	5.7 s
0-0.60 mile	23.3 s
Braking 60-0	(39.8 m)
Straightaway speed	122 mph (195 km/h)
Maximum speed	186 mph (300 km/h)
Fuel economy (liters/100km)	13 mpg (18 liters)

current gearbox made by – heaven forbid – General Motors.

But don't imagine that this 456 is some sort of antique, incapable of handling a twisty road. Because the opposite is the case. After all, it was behind the wheel of this Ferrari that I set out to navigate the new Circuit Mont-Tremblant. At 125 mph (200 km/h), I thought I would never slow down at the end of a long straightaway, but the brakes – even though I had to push hard on the pedal – certainly didn't let me down. I was also able to get the car back on course without too much effort after a major sideways moment in the Esses (see photos). With the suspension set at "Sport" mode, body roll was significantly reduced, although the car still displayed its initial understeer.

The GTA's 5.5-liter V12 engine remains its most precious asset. It's remarkably supple, and its horsepower seems infinite, accompanied by that exquisite, deep and distinctive Ferrari sound. With 442 hp, the hefty GTA – all 3900 lbs of it (1770 kg) – charged effortlessly ahead and, even though it wasn't in its natural habitat, handled itself quite respectably. An ordinary drive along the highway is all it takes to appreciate what the 456 can offer: first-class, luxury travel at the speed of sound.

The 550 Maranello

A long way from the **Testarossa**

Driving the 550 Maranello after the 456 is like stepping off a Boeing 747 and getting into a jet fighter. If you think an automatic gearbox looks out of place in a sports car like the 456, it would be even more so in the 550 Maranello. Named for the little town that the Italian automaker has called home for more than half a century, this grand-touring coupe is unimaginably fast. After I exited the pit, for example, the car accelerated so swiftly that I almost overshot Corner 1. Anyway, it felt either like a time bomb, a rocket or an intercontinental ballistic missile – take your pick. And the 485 hp cranked out by its 5.5-liter V12 will come in handy to help you get out of the hairy situations you will undoubtedly encounter. Thus, at the top of the little hill leading into Corner 1, the rear axle's slight loss of grip – caused by the sudden loss

SPECS
550 Maranello

Price ($CDN / $US)	329,295 / 206,775
Wheelbase	98.4 in
Length	179.1 in
Width	76 in
Height	50.4 in
Weight	3726 lb(1690 kg)
Trunk	6.5 cu.ft
Fuel tank	30 gallons
Engine	V12 5.5-liter
Horsepower(hp/rpm)	485/7 000
Torque (lb-ft/rpm)	419/5 000
Transmission	6-speed manual
Disc brake diameter	13 in (330 mm)
Suspension	independent
Steering	rack-and-pinion
Turning circle	38 feet
Tires / fr.	P255/40ZR18
Tires / r.	P295/35ZR18

PERFORMANCE

0-60 mph	4.2 s
0-0.60 mile	22.9 s
Braking (60-0 mph)	122 feet (37.2 m)
Straightaway speed	127 mph (205 km/h)
Maximum speed	199 (320 km/h)
Fuel economy (liters/100km)	13 mpg (18.5 liters)

of weight – was quickly corrected thanks to a judicious application of power to the rear wheels.

Of course, the car oversteered like any self-respecting sports car does, but in the 550 Maranello's case, the hyper-responsive steering allowed you to make all the necessary adjustments to prevent the car from spinning out. The normal cornering technique – dive from the outside to the apex, then squeeze power and let the car drift out at the exit, all the way to the outside edge of the track – works to perfection. Replacing the Testarossa, the 550 Maranello is considerably smoother and more civilized. Even though the clutch still feels firm, it has been lightened considerably compared with the one I drove at Fiorano 6 years earlier.

After three laps, the 550 began to signal that it was as heavy as the 456, and as I entered the "Carousel," the brakes started to overheat. I didn't worry too much about it because that usually happens with ultra-fast cars, when the brakes – discs and calipers – don't have enough time to cool down after hard application. Anyway, the problem was easily fixed and I'll return to that point later.

I slowed down a little but it wasn't long before I was back on the pace again. The car felt so easy to drive it acted like a drug. After all, it's a Ferrari – a marque that is synonymous with race-car excellence.

On the road, the 550 is a model of civility, never once hinting at its racetrack exploits. The driving position is impeccable and the seats, though firm, are perfectly comfortable. The massive metal pedals take some getting used to, and the shift lever – housed in its metal sculpted gate – demands a strong physical effort, but not enough to make you long for an automatic transmission.

Roads in the Mont-Tremblant area are notoriously bad, but the very stiff 550 Maranello chassis took them all in stride, proving to be considerably more comfortable than the Porsche 911 Turbo. Admittedly, it doesn't have a lot of storage place, the trunk is tiny and rear visibility is almost non-existent. But these details seem all but irrelevant when you consider the car's versatile capabilities, both as a touring and racing car.

The 360 Modena F1

Beyond **reality**

Last year, a quick test of the 360 Modena F1 – the most popular and affordable of the Ferraris – left me a little puzzled. Having driven it exclusively in city traffic, I couldn't really enjoy its Formula-One type transmission, derived from those that Ferrari pioneered for its race cars.

Mounted behind and on each side of the steering column are spoon-shaped paddles that allow the driver to shift the 6 speeds of this unique transmission, either up (right) or down (left). You can also switch to automatic mode by activating a button located on the center console. The mechanism is by no means complicated in itself, but let's just say it's a tad awkward at the beginning.

For everyday driving, this transmission is the pits. In sport driving, however, it's a totally different ballgame, making the

SPECS
360 Modena F1

Price ($CDN / $US)	237,000 / 148,825
Wheelbase	102.4 in
Length	176 in
Width	75.6 in
Height	47.6 in
Weight	2844lb (1290kg)
Trunk	4.2 cu.ft
Fuel tank	22 gallons
Engine	V8 3.6-liter
Horsepower(hp/rpm)	400/8 500
Torque (lb-ft/rpm)	275/4 750
Transmission	6-sp. Sequential automatic
Disc brake diameter	13/13 in (330/330 mm)
Suspension	independent
Steering	rack-and-pinion
Turning circle	35 feet
Tires / fr.	P215/45ZR18
Tires / r.	P275/40ZR18

PERFORMANCE

0-60 mph	4.5 s
0-0.60 mile	22.9 s
Braking (60-0 mph)	119 feet (36.4 m)
Straightaway speed	130 mph (210 km/h)
Maximum speed	183 mph (295 km/h)
Fuel economy (liters/100km)	14 mpg (17 liters)

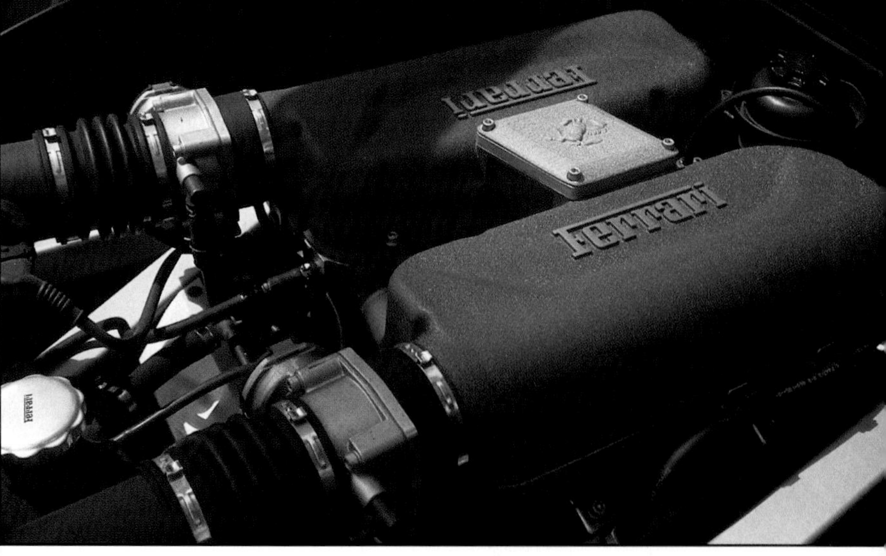

Modena the easiest-to-drive production car ever. Sporting a middle-mounted V8 with 400 ponies under the rear glass engine cover and an all-aluminum body, reducing its total weight to less than 2900 lbs (1300 kg) in the process, the 360 behaves as nimbly on a circuit as any race car out there. Its protruding front wings made it easy to position the car in the corners, much like my old Porsche 904 GTS, but with a lot more power.

People often comment about the magical sound that the Ferrari V12 engine emits, but this V8 is also capable of producing gorgeous decibels, with distinctive high notes as the gearbox upshifts sharply at peak revs (8500 rpm). Needless to say, the F1-like gearbox is totally in its element at moments like these, performing to near perfection. The sound wafting into the cockpit is sheer delight.

Unlike the 456 which slightly understeered on turning, or the 550 with its initial slight oversteer, the Modena stayed absolutely neutral, a model of stability and balance. Braking remained solid, too, after five or six laps.

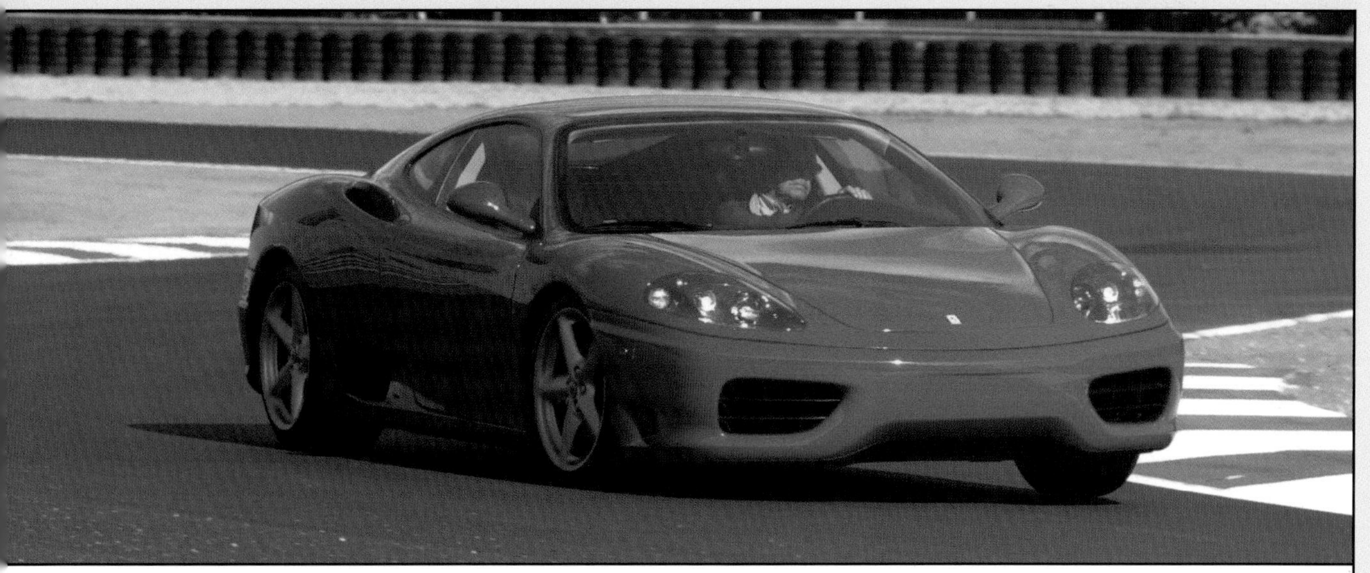

Brutal awakening

Driving back to the city in the 360 F1 was a different kettle of fish, however. I felt like a novice who had just got his driver's licence and still hadn't a clue about how to coordinate the clutch and the gearshift lever. With the gearbox set in "sequential" mode, the car jerked when changing gears. So unless you're driving on a deserted road, it is better to leave the transmission in "full automatic" mode.

Having forgotten to reset the suspension from "sport" back to "normal," I was pleasantly surprised to find how comfortable the ride was. As with other Ferraris, both the seats and driving position are beyond reproach. What's more, the front seats are spacious and there's ample shoulder room. On the other hand, 3/4 rear visibility is virtually nonexistent. That's probably the reason why the reverse gear comes with a "beep," as if to warn pedestrians to get out of the way.

The interior is not as refined as the 456's, but finish is markedly improved over the earlier models. At one point, driving at 130mph (210 km/h) on the main straight at the Circuit, I wanted to keep on going since the speedometer needle still had room to move up – the dial is graduated to 212 mph (340 km/h) – but I couldn't do it because the road ran out. So I settled for the rapturous sound of the 3.6-liter V8 as it revved up to 8500 rpm, letting myself be transported to a surreal realm where time is measured in fractions of a second.

The 550 Barchetta

Ferrari

A bonus

Initially, the all-new 550 Barchetta Pininfarina was not supposed to be a participant in our Ferrari Festival. After all, this Spider version of the Maranello is a limited-edition model worth a dizzying $400,000. But I struck gold that day, when the owner of the first Barchetta in Quebec (who insists on remaining anonymous) was kind enough to let me use his car to show off the new Circuit to my friend Luigi Chinetti, Jr., whose father was the first Ferrari importer in North America. Luigi had raced at Tremblant during the 1960s and his Ferrari 275 SP had

SPECS

550 Barchetta

Price ($CDN / $US)	400,000 / 251,175
Wheelbase	98.4 in
Length	179.1 in
Width	76 in
Height	49.6 in
Weight	3902lb (1770kg)
Trunk	6.5 cu.ft
Fuel tank	30 gallons
Engine	V12 5.5-liter
Horsepower(hp/rpm)	485/7 000
Torque (lb-ft/rpm)	419/5 000
Transmission	6-speed manual
Disc brake diameter	12.6 in (320 mm)
Suspension	independent
Steering	rack-and-pinion
Turning circle	38 feet
Tires / fr.	P255/40ZR18
Tires / r.	P295/35ZR18

PERFORMANCE

0-60 mph	4.2 s
0-0.60 mile	22.9 s
Braking (60-0 mph)	122 feet (37.2 m)
Straightaway speed	127 mph (205 km/h)
Maximum speed	186 (300 km/h)
Fuel economy (liters/100km)	13 mpg (18.5 liters)

actually been badly damaged in a fire caused by another car that had burst into flames on the track.

The owner of several collector's Ferraris, the younger Chinetti was a guest at Tremblant during our "Festival" and I was asked to show him the new track aboard the Barchetta, which had only 400 miles (630 km) on its odometer, as I later discovered.

The upshot was that I was able to drive the Barchetta as fast as I could without its owner batting an eyelid. Despite its slightly heavier weight, the roadster proved to be as nimble as the coupe, if not nimbler. The 550 was fitted with special brakes (optional), and I never once felt the need to brake earlier than normal at the end of the main straightaway. Even with a passenger on board, I suspect that the Barchetta was a second or two faster than the coupe.

Even without a rigid top, the chassis felt incredibly solid, a quality that I also noted when we later went for a spin over the rough local roads. But let's get back to the racetrack. Thanks to its big Bridgestone Pole Position S02 tires, the roadster stuck to the road like a bug to your windshield, making you want to drive even faster. And that's one of the major attributes of all Ferraris – they inspire unlimited confidence – the reason no doubt why my passenger remained absolutely calm and unruffled as I sprinted around the Circuit's 2.65-miles (4.5 km).

This second Ferrari Festival probably didn't carry quite the same cachet as the first, held at the exotic Fiorano track – where the great Michael Schumacher, for one, tests his F1 entries. But I received immense pleasure from it all the same, because of my past association with the Circuit Mont-Tremblant and the prospect and possibility of driving such effortlessly smooth and exciting cars as Ferraris – with no angry pedestrian complaining about squealing tires. I hope I have succeeded in sharing this pleasure with my readers.

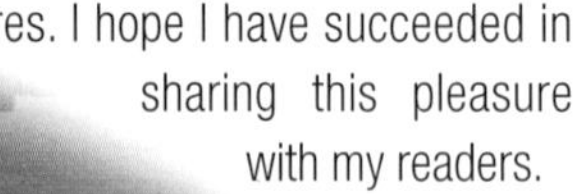

Behind the wheel of a 550 Barchetta, Jacques Duval shows off the new Mont-Tremblant racetrack to Luigi Chinetti.

6 MERCEDES ON THE LOOSE

AMG INVASION IN SHANNONVILLE

● **BY JACQUES DUVAL** PHOTOGRAPHS: MICHEL FYEN-GAGNON

I've seen lots of mosquitoes before – alive, buzzing about when it's hot and sticky, or dead, their squashed bodies sticking to human skin, or encrusted on a car's front grille or thereabouts. But the strange sight of dead mosquitoes glued to the doors of a Mercedes was a new experience for me, saying a great deal about its driver, or rather his unorthodox driving style. The man I'm talking about is Bernd Schneider, former F1 driver and twice winner of the German Touring Car Championship (DTM). In three so-called "hot laps," here in Shannonville, Québec, this skid artist treated us to a spectacular demonstration of his fabulous skills, expertly handling a powerful Mercedes coupe – a CLK55 AMG, equipped with a 349-hp V8 – through a series of daredevil, "acrobatic" maneuvers.

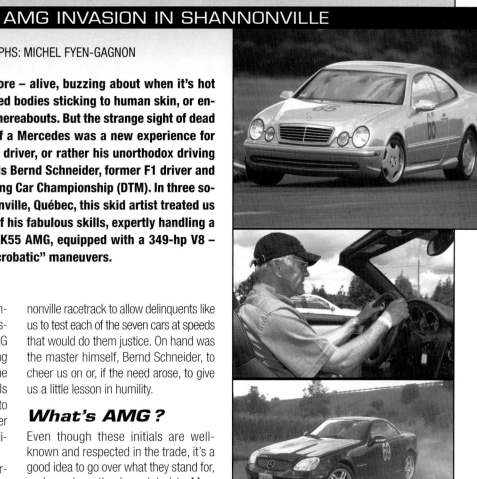

That was the highlight of an entire day I spent studying and assessing Mercedes-Benz's AMG line. Our local speed limits being what they are, road-testing the six AMG-modified Mercedes models (seven, if you include the ML55) proved to be tricky business –you'd end up either totally frustrated, or having your driver's licence confiscated.

To get around this problem, the German firm came up with the ingenious idea of organizing an AMG day at the Shannonville racetrack to allow delinquents like us to test each of the seven cars at speeds that would do them justice. On hand was the master himself, Bernd Schneider, to cheer us on or, if the need arose, to give us a little lesson in humility.

What's AMG?

Even though these initials are well-known and respected in the trade, it's a good idea to go over what they stand for, and see how they're related to Mercedes-Benz. Today, many automakers have at their disposal a special division responsible for developing high-performance versions of their products. BMW, for example, boasts Motorsport, and Ford has SVO (Special Vehicle Operation) – both in-house divisions.

AMG, on the other hand, began as an independent company, hired by Mercedes to upgrade its road-version engines for competition purposes. The initials were chosen in honor of the company's founders – Hans Werner Aufrecht, a former employee at Daimler-Benz, and Eberhard Melcher – who set up shop in an old millhouse at Burgstall, Germany in 1968. The letter G stands for Grossaspach, Aufrecht's hometown.

One of AMG's first contracts was the Mercedes 300 SEL equipped with a 428-hp 6.9-liter engine. In 1971, it came first in its category at the 24 Hours of Spa, an endurance race for touring cars. In addition to tuning cars for various races around the world, AMG catered to a small group of preferred clients, offering them still more powerful versions of different AMG-tuned models. Occasionally the consulting firm, now relocated in Affalterbach, a mere stone's throw from the Mercedes plant, even made custom-ordered automobiles for OPEC bigwigs.

From racetrack to Main Street

In 1988 AMG's fortunes took a quantum leap when Mercedes called on the firm to tune its cars for the German Touring Car Championship (DTM), a collaboration that eventually led to the creation of an AMG tuning division at Mercedes itself in 1990. Three years later, the company and its 400 employees delivered its first completed project – the C36, 5000 units of which were produced. The C36 was soon followed by the E50, with sales of 2000 units.

AMG reached another milestone in 1997, completing a racing prototype – the CLK GTR – in a record 128 days. The prototype went on to win two consecutive FIA world championships in GT class, in 1997 and 1998. Since then, needless to say, Mercedes-AMG has never looked back. The combination has proven to be well-matched and profitable as demonstrated by their sales figures for the year 2000: 11,500 AMG-modified cars were sold, along with 28,000 AMG accessory packages and 34,000 AMG wheels. Incidentally, you can personalize virtually any Mercedes-Benz model with AMG accessories, ranging from wheels to body panels.

Clients as test drivers

Two years ago, the CLK55 was designated Formula-I's official safety car. "That's the special edition," said marketing director Mario Sptizner. Only a handful of units were produced, one of which was bought by the owner of Cirque du Soleil. The same Herr Sptizner told me that AMG boasted the best group of test drivers in the world at its disposal – namely, its own clients. "No one else is better placed to critique our products and motivate us to improve on them," he said, adding, "After all, it's the fanatics who take the trouble to pay close attention to the tiniest detail, and that's what helps us grow." You should have seen how enthusiastic Sptizner was as he proudly displayed the upcoming SL55 AMG, which he said will be equipped with a new Japanese-made *Kompressor*.

AMG SL55

CLK55

Of the seven AMG models on hand at Shannonville, the CLK55 coupe is the best-known and most coveted model. It's equipped with a 5-speed driver-adaptive automatic transmission, as was the case with all the cars tested on that occasion. On the road, the engine was a little slow in responding, at least whenever the car's stability control system (ESP) was engaged. Once the system was deactivated, however, along came the inevitable "smoke show" – torque alone, for example, was a thundering 376 lb-ft. That said, ESP actually helped the car to accelerate from 0-60 mph in a respectable 5.3 seconds. Passing performance, too, is excellent thanks to the monstrous torque – just floor the accelerator at roughly 37 mph and you'll see why. But like it or not, ESP and sport-driving are not really compatible, and believe me, even the great Bernd Schneider turned it off while he was executing his "hot laps." Although the CLK55 doesn't stick to the road as firmly as the M3, it feels a lot more comfortable, thanks to its 17-inch tires.

On the racetrack, the CLK55 was far and away the most stable of the entire AMG line that we tested. While it tends to skid easily, you can just as easily steer through the skid – all the while using the accelerator – so as to get the car back on its track. And although I wasn't terribly impressed with the brakes when I drove the car on the road, the racetrack proved to be a more charitable venue, since I was able to complete lap after lap without the brakes overheating unduly.

As for the rest, all you need to know is that the rear seats may cost you a few good friends if you make them sit there for long journeys. And while we're on the subject, the power-assist front seats – once they've been collapsed – take an inordinate length of time to put back in their original positions. Just so you know – it might not be a good idea to take any passengers on your next outing. Other than that, this fast and gorgeous Mercedes perfectly embodies the definition of a grand-touring car, whether on the straightaway or twisting road.

SLK32

20,000 rpm for the SLK32

Don't be alarmed, those revs refer to the supercharger's cooling fan, not the engine! With a weight-to-power ratio of only 9.41 lbs per hp (4.27 kg), this AMG-modified Mercedes is fast, outrageously fast. Just think about it, there's almost twice as much power (349 hp) than in the original version, which has only 191 hp. With 332 lb-ft of torque, 300 of which is available at 2300 rpm, the SLK32 is the fastest of the whole AMG line, though it's not necessarily the most fun to drive. Behind the wheel, you get the distinct feeling that it belongs to an earlier generation. In fact, the original concept goes back to 1996, while all the others, except the E Class, are more recent.

Suspension proves to be stiff, rather than firm, while engine noise is overwhelming, if not downright embarrassing. This little coupe-convertible is not as refined as the other AMG-modified cars. I much prefer the standard SLK320, whose 215 hp is quite sufficient. Naturally, the car's smaller size makes it easier to handle and is nimbler on the racetrack, but despite its oversized ventilated discs –13.2 inches (334 mm) in diameter in front, and 11.8 inches (300 mm) in rear – braking doesn't equal its performance. And yet the SLK32 is the lightest car of the lot.

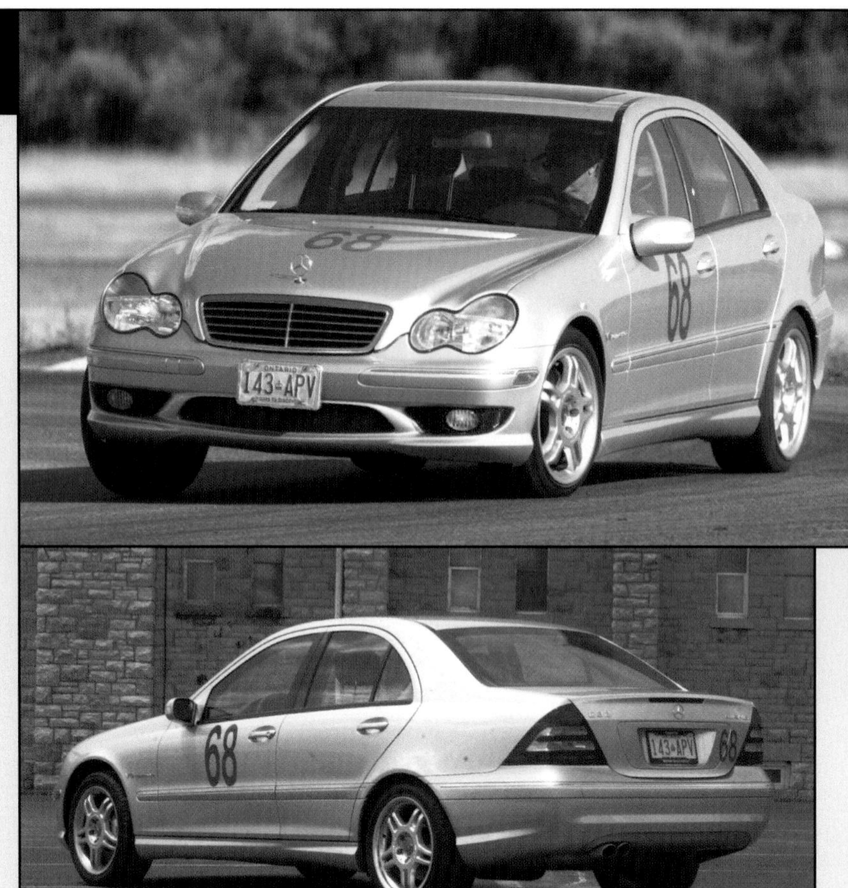

Fabulous C32

But the car that truly stole my heart in Shannonville was the new 5-seat C32 AMG, no question about it. It's a bona-fide sport sedan, luxurious, fast, oozing self-confidence and a sheer delight to drive. Equipped with the same supercharged *Kompressor* V6 engine as the SLK32, and paired to an AMG-programmed Speedshift 5-speed automatic transmission. Under heavy braking, for example, the box automatically downshifts and selects the most appropriate gear to handle the situation. And if you hold the gear lever to the left – in other words, at manual mode or Speedshift – again the box will automatically select the best ratio for maximum acceleration. This so-called intelligent transmission maintains a constant gear ratio during cornering to prevent any upshift at mid-corner, which could destabilize the car. Compared with a conventional automatic transmission, Speedshift permits faster gear changes, by as much as 35%.

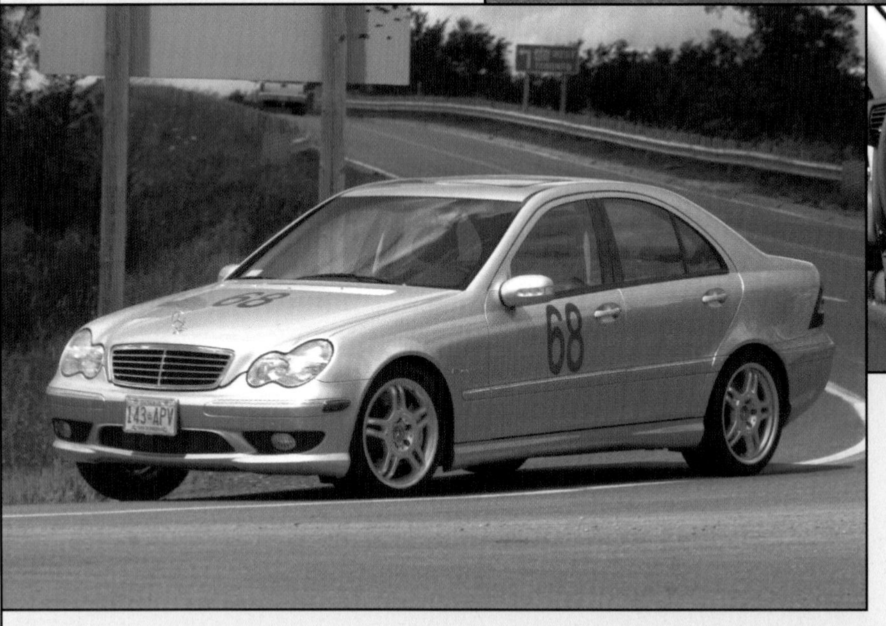

The C32 AMG also gets its own suspension, with made-to-measure stabilizer bars and gas-pressurized shock absorbers. It sports wider vented disc brakes with 4-piston calipers (2 in the back), as well as 17-inch wheels decked out in robust tires – 225/45R in front and 225/40R in rear.

Careful attention was devoted to the interior as well: leather sport seats and a smart instrument cluster. Despite somewhat vague steering, this C32AMG is sporty and easy to maneuver. Handling is on the neutral side. While it may not measure up to the M3 in performance terms, the C32 leads by a country mile in everyday driving conditions, proving to be more civilized and comfortable.

CL55

Top-of-the-line

The most expensive and refined of Mercedes, the CL coupe has reached a level of perfection so rarefied that there's very little room for improvement. Apart from horsepower, which was boosted to 349 from 306, the AMG-modified version isn't all that different from the standard version, whose road-test results are described elsewhere in this guidebook. Incidentally, the CL600's V12 engine offers an extra 14 hp, over and above that of the AMG engine.

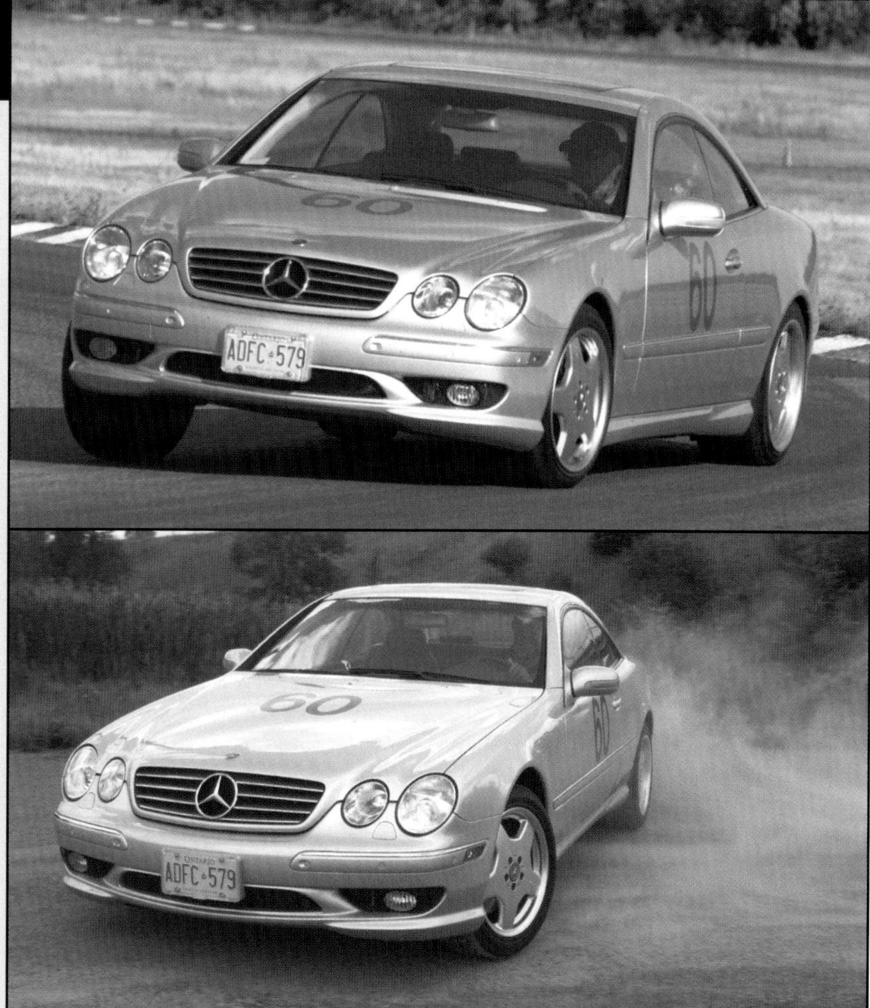

Last year, the CL55 AMG replaced the CLK55 as Formula One's official safety car, an honor that it will likely relinquish in 2002 in favor of the new SL55 AMG. Be that as it may, the CL55 AMG's signature characteristic remains its active suspension system, known as Active Body Control (ABC), which minimizes body roll during cornering and prevents diving movements caused by acceleration or braking. In fast driving conditions, the unique ABC system also reduces body movements by an astounding 60%.

Despite its indisputable virtues, the car has a heavy feel, especially when you brake, or even accelerate. In fact, it takes just under 6 seconds to go from 0-60 mph. On the racetrack, handling is less reassuring than other models: the car is a little too supple to drive even the least bit sportily, and steering transmits each and every bump and pothole. But on the road the CL coupe shines, proving to be close to perfection.

S55

Sport Limousine

Somehow, I imagined the S55 – the limousine of the Mercedes S Class – to be cut from the same mold as the CL coupe. But once I became accustomed to its tendency to understeer on the Shannonville racetrack, this was the car in which I felt most comfortable. And heaven only knows a racetrack is not the S55's natural habitat, even though it gets the same accoutrements as the CL coupe, such as the sophisticated ABC suspension system, modern V8 engine and 18-inch tires, to name only the obvious.

As you may have guessed, performance is virtually a carbon copy of the CL coupe's. In fact, I'd be really surprised if that wasn't the case, since the S55 was based on the sedan. But I'd hesitate calling it a sport sedan, given its imposing size. In my book, it feels more like a limousine for "the rich and in a hurry."

E55

AMG's very own

Of all the AMG models tested at Shannonville, I've no hesitation in announcing that the E55 was the leanest, meanest and most macho. A hot rod among its companion. I couldn't quite put my finger on it, but I found that the racetrack and the E55 were a perfect fit. For a car of its weight, it proved to be incredibly easy to drive. Pushed to the limit, it handled the resulting skids elegantly on all four wheels, exhibiting perfect neutrality – as befits a racing car blessed with unsurpassed unsprung-mass distribution.

Doubtless the E55's secret is the fact that it was the only model fitted with an AMG-handcrafted powertrain. As it happened, final assembly was carried out at AMG's own shops in Affalterbach, an hour's drive northeast of Sindelfingen, home of Mercedes-Benz. Once the basic chassis had been put together, it was shipped to AMG to be fitted with a 5.5-liter V8 engine, transmission and suspension. The final result is a gem of a machine – beautifully integrated and reassuringly solid. That said, I'll happily pass on the 18-inch tires. They're fabulous on a racetrack, but not quite as charitable over the ubiquitous bumps and potholes in our roads.

All good things must come to an end and after an entire day spent behind the wheels of various AMG models, testing them on the racetrack and on the road, I'd say that Mercedes has traveled a long way from the austere and rigorous company I came to know from visits made early in my career. With the backing of the self-proclaimed "made-for-passion" AMG, the German automaker has succeeded splendidly in revitalizing its image. Its three-point star – whether perched on F1 one-seaters or super-sports models – has never shone so brilliantly.

Technical Specs	CLK55	SLK32	C32	CL55	S55	E55
• Price (CDN / $US)	107,500 / 67,500	76,900 / 48,300	65,900 / 41,400	148,900 / 93,500	140,500 / 88,225	101,600 / 63,800
• Type	4-seat coupe	2-seat roadster	5-seat sedan	2 + 2 coupe	5-seat sedan	5-seat sedan
• Weight	3483 lb (1580 kg)	3219 lb (1460 kg)	3538 lb (1605 kg)	4112 lb (1865 kg)	4189 lb (1900 kg)	3781 lb (1715 kg)
• Front suspension	Independent double wishbone, Bilstein shocks	Independent double wishbone 3-link axle	McPherson struts, anti-dive control	Independent 4-link with triangular lower control arms	Independent 4-link with triangular lower control arms	Independent double wishbone with triangular lower control arms
• Rear suspension	Multi-link axle Bilstein shocks	Multi-link axle Gas-pressurized shocks	Multi-link axle Gas-pressurized shocks	Multi-link axle ABC active suspension	Multi-link axle ABC active suspension	Multi-link axle Bilstein shocks
• Brakes front/rear	Vented disc brakes AMG	Vented disc brakes AMG	Vented disc brakes AMG	Vented disc brakes AMG	Vented disc brakes AMG	Vented disc brakes AMG
• Tires front/rear	P225/45ZR17 P245/40ZR17	P225/45ZR17 P245/40ZR17	P225/45ZR17 P245/40ZR17	P245/45ZR18 P275/40ZR18	P245/45ZR18 P275/40ZR18	P245/45ZR18 P275/40ZR18
• Engine	5.5 liter 24-valve SOHC V8	3.2-liter Turbo V6	3.2-liter Turbo V6	5.5 liter 24-valve SOHC V8	5.5 liter 24-valve SOHC V8	5.5 liter 24-valve SOHC V8
• Transmission	5-speed automatic with TouchShift	5-speed automatic with TouchShift and SpeedShift	5-speed automatic with TouchShift and SpeedShift	5-speed automatic with TouchShift	5-speed automatic with TouchShift	5-speed automatic with TouchShift
• Horsepower	342 hp at 5500 rpm	349 hp at 6100 rpm	349 hp at 6100 rpm	349 hp at 5500 rpm	349 hp at 5500 rpm	349 hp at 5500 rpm
• Torque	376 lb-ft at 3000 rpm	332 lb-ft at 4400 rpm	332 lb-ft at 4400 rpm	391 lb-ft at 3150 - 4500 rpm	391 lb-ft at 3150 - 4500 rpm	391 lb-ft at 3150 - 4500 rpm
• Acceleration 0-60 mph (0-100 k/h)	5.1 seconds	5 seconds	5.1 seconds	5.9 seconds	5.9 seconds	5.8 seconds
• Maximum speed	155 mph (250 km/h) electronically limited	155 mph (250 km/h) electronically limited	155 mph (250 km/h) electronically limited	155 mph (250 km/h) electronically limited	155 mph (250 km/h) electronically limited	155 mph (250 km/h) electronically limited

The Hidden Face of Mercedes-Benz

In spite of all the efforts of the German marque to be seen as a diversfied brand, the name Mercedes-Benz is still linked with prestigious and expensive cars. When I drove around, first in a Smart and then in a small A Class sedan, people generally had no idea that these were Mercedes products. It was hard to believe their exclamations of surprise when I explained to them that these models, if they were sold in North America would cost probably between $12,000 and $20,000. In fact, Mercedes, from now on, is active in all market segments and if the North American market ever shows an interest in the Smart or the A Class then these cars would be imported to our shores.

SMART: The Answer to Traffic Jams

It would take a particularly jaded individual to see the Smart drive by without giving it a second glance. Its unusual look, tiny size and the flashy colors of this two-seater, an urban vehicle at heart, can't help but be noticed. All it

pedal: it is a sequential control system and you only need to push the gear lever forwards or backwards to change gear. You can also rely on the automatic transmission. Its mechanism is rather notchy and sometimes unpleasant, but one cannot have everything.

Perhaps slightly delinquent but immensely practical in town, the Smart feels much more at ease in this environment than in the countryside or on the highway.

The Smart may not be considered a real car in the eyes of many, but everyone or almost everyone simply adores it. All it takes is to mention the word Mercedes-Benz or a price of approximately $12,000 to notice that it would indeed have quite a following if the government consented to soften the regulations, which at the moment, bar the Smart from its North American visa.

takes is to park it facing a sidewalk, occupying a space just big enough for a motorcycle, to notice people smiling at you and giving you the thumbs up. On top of having a very peculiar look, the Smart barely pollutes and is quite happy to drive around on a few drops of gas, which translates into an average of 60 mpg (5 l/100) with its 54-hp 3-cylinder engine. Its length being equal to the width of an ordinary car, is there a need to admit that one can really have fun playing in traffic jams? This strange-wheeled vehicle was off to a shaky start in Europe where it has been on the market for three years.

The product of a joint venture between Mercedes-Benz and Nicolas Hayek, the inventor of Swatch wrist watches, its look was definitely attractive but its road behavior left very much to be desired. However, Mercedes took the bull by the horns and modified this mini mini-car in several ways, including addressing its cornering stability. It now no longer wants to roll on its side, and thanks to a high powered advertising campaign and a lower price tag, the Smart is beginning to recruit a whole bunch of new buyers.

Given the high price of gas, it is worth asking oneself the following question: is the Smart suitable in North America? Its tiny size is in fact quite alarming when one knows that it will have to share the road with giants such as the Ford Expedition or the Chevrolet Tahoe, but surely it is no more dangerous than riding a motorcycle or worse, a bicycle.

At the Wheel

But what is there to expect from a Smart? First, the cockpit is a surprise, its unusual dashboard and its pastel shades are amazing. It is even roomy and its equipment belongs to a luxury car: electric windows and central locking, ignition lock, air conditioning, air bags, radio cassette player, etc. The comfort from the bucket seats compensate for the firmness of the suspension, and given its urban role, the Smart handles itself extremely well. The ABS, the traction control and the stability control provide state of the art technology.

Set transversely in the back, the small 54 hp 599 cm^3 3-cylinder turbo bursts into life when turning the ignition key on the floor. The power is more than enough for the 1588 lbs (720 kg) of this micro car and provides genuine acceleration with a top speed of 90 mph (140 km/h) that no one will really want to attain, given the sound level at high speed, and a rather indecisive trajectory. The gearbox sports six gears without a clutch

A Class Prestige at a Low Price

It is more than likely that the Mercedes-Benz sub-compact, the A Class will eventually sail across the Atlantic to be marketed in North America. It might be interesting to note that this car, a direct rival to the Volkswagen Golf, provoked the ire of the lord and master of Volkswagen, Dr. Ferdinand Piëch. "If Mercedes wants to play on our turf, we shall play on theirs," he is quoted as saying when the A Class appeared in 1998. And that is why Volkswagen will soon be unveiling an upscale motor car to challenge the Mercedes S Class.

Meanwhile, back at the ranch, the firm from Stuttgart will remodel this car before exporting it to either the United States or Canada. The car which was lent to me for testing was a A Class Elegance equipped with a 4-cylinder 1.9-liter engine with 125 hp. With only a mass of about 2200 lbs (1000 kg), the acceleration time is excellent (8.7 seconds from 0 to 60 mph) with mileage around 30 mpg (7.5 l/100 km).

Danger

However, as much as the Smart is amusing, the tiny Mercedes (it is only 11' 10" long) does reveal some rather annoying features. Its soft long legged suspension, for example, reminds one of the old Citroëns. The chassis is set rather high and creates a lot of body roll which is probably more annoying than dangerous since Mercedes proceeded to a gigantic recall once this car had failed the emergency swerve test established by a Swedish magazine, designed to test the stability of a vehicle during a rapid lane change. During this test the A Class had simply over-turned, to the annoyance of the Mercedes engineers. The problem has now been rectified.

On the other hand, the clutchless transmission is easy to use. During braking, the car begins to undulate in a disquieting manner. Worse, I nearly had a crash while braking slightly with my left foot as I was exiting out of a highway. The brake assist system, which is standard equipment on most Mercedes vehicles, is designed to sense an emergency situation and in turn increases the braking effort. Apparently this system measures the time it takes to go from the accelerator to the brake pedal. If the driver does this quickly enough as during an emergency, the emergency brake assist kicks in. In my case, the small A Class braked so hard and with such deceleration that I was slammed forward. I got out of it with a bruised shoulder but if a car had been behind me, it is certain that it never would have had the time to stop. In conclusion, the A Class is not quite at the same level as other Mercedes models and it would be wise to wait for the second generation version before exporting it to North America.

Jacques Duval

Technical Specs

	SMART	MERCEDES BENZ A CLASS
• Type	2-seater, front-wheel drive	4-seat sedan, front-wheel drive
• Price (in France)	approx. $12,000	approx. $20,000
• Wheelbase/length	71.2 in / 98.4 in	95.2 in /140.9 in
• Weight	1588 lbs (720 kg)	2414 lbs (1095 kg)
• Engine	6.0-liter 3-cylinder Turbo	1.9-liter 4-cylinder
• Power	54 hp	125 hp
• Transmission	6-speed semi-automatic	5-speed semi-automatic
• Acceleration 0-60 mph	15.2 s	8.7 s
• Maximum speed	87 mph (140 km/h)	124 mph (198 km/h)
• Fuel consumption	41 mpg (5.5 L/100 km)	30 mpg (7.5 L/100 km)

PROTOTYPES

AUDI AVANTISSIMO ▶

This concept luxury wagon is in most of its essentials an Avant version of the Audi A8. Using Audi's exclusive aluminum space frame body construction (ASF), engineers were able to maintain an exceptionally light weight for a vehicle of its size. The tailgate is controlled by an electro-hydraulic system that opens and closes it.

◀ AUDI AVANTISSIMO

Thanks to all-wheel drive and a 4.2-liter twin-turbo V8 engine rating 430 hp, the Avantissimo can handle any and all driving conditions. With four-wheel air springs, comfort and roadholding are virtually guaranteed. Ground clearance is adjustable.

▲ AUDI STEPPENWOLF

For the time being, Audi claims that the Steppenwolf is just a concept vehicle. But there's no smoke without fire, and Audi doesn't usually build vehicles like this without plans for eventua producing it. The Steppenwolf is the logical evolution of the Auc Allroad, and would be a worthy response to the Porsche Cayenr

AUDI AVANTISSIMO ▲

Despite its considerable minivan dimensions – 199 inches (506 cm) long and 75 inches (191 cm) wide – this unique Audi displays precision handling and exceptional agility. Sports performance, in other words.

AUDI STEPPENWOLF

With its 3.2-liter V6 engine developing 225 horsepower, this all-terrain coupe scoots from 0-60mph in less than 8 seconds. Top speed is 140 mph (230 km/h). But the highlight is the height-adjustable air suspension that permits a maximum ground clearance of 8.6 inches (22 cm).

BERTONE FILO

Famous for highly stylized and innovative cars, Bertone lives up to its reputation with the Filo, an elegant monospace concept based on the Opel Zafira platform. The vehicle's systems are operated electronically, using the drive-by-wire technology developed by SKF and Nokia.

BERTONE FILO

The Filo's masterstroke is the electronic-control module, handling functions like acceleration, steering, brakes, audio system, climate control, navigation system, cell phone, etc. The result is a sparse dashboard and pedal-free floor space.

BERTONE FILO

Thanks to drive-by-wire technology, Bertone designers were able to create a more spacious, user-friendly and comfortable cockpit. Freed from the traditional constraints such as the steering column, pedals and various controls, driver and passengers can now enjoy more cabin space in both front and rear. Like many prototypes, the Filo sports "suicide doors" at the back.

BMW X COUPE

This is one of the year's most controversial concept cars. The X coupe's shape is disturbing-looking at best. Still, it's the heir apparent to the X Roadster – a good example of BMW 's new styling direction.

▲ BMW X COUPE

This wild prototype is based on the chassis of the BMW X5 off-roader, and powered by a turbodiesel engine: a 3.5 in-line 6-cylinder producing 184 hp and 332 lb-ft of torque. Its 5-speed automatic transmission is controlled by buttons on the steering wheel. Finally, like the X5, the X coupe has all-wheel drive and boasts all the expected electronic driving aids.

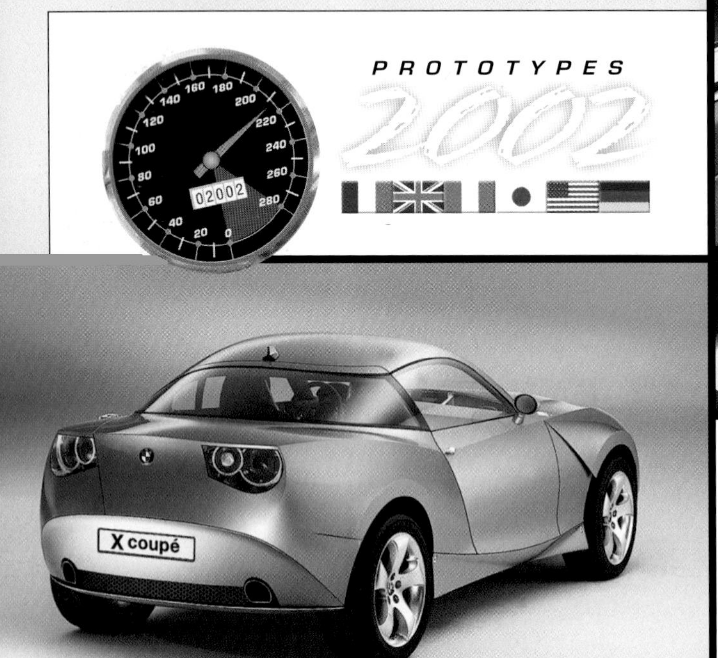

▲ BMW X COUPE

Not a 2+2 seater, but rather a 1+3 where the driver is given more space and a higher-than-average driving position.

BUICK BENGAL ▶

Buick has shoved aside all its sedans-turned-hatchbacks and minivans – the Lacrosse, for one – to showcase the Bengal, a hot-looking convertible aimed at young buyers. The name Bengal, in fact, was chosen in honor of Tiger Woods.

▲ BUICK BENGAL

This 2-seater roadster is powered by a V6 engine working through the front wheels. An ingenious retractable tonneau cover reveals space for either 2 extra passengers and/or cargo. The Bengal boasts voice-activated controls and flat-panel speakers.

▲ CADILLAC VIZON

This amazingly roomy hybrid vehicle inherits its looks from the boxy silhouette of the Cadillac Evoq. It sports a unique DVD player with built-in screen. The various electronically-controlled safety features, too, are one of a kind.

▲ CHEVROLET BORREGO

The "bow-tie" folks at Chevrolet hope to attract younger buyers with Borrego, a half truck/half sporty car created at GM's Los Angeles design studio. A reconfigurable mid-car gate allows seating for two extra passengers or cargo space.

▲ CADILLAC VIZON

Road handling is taken care of by a Stabilitrak traction system. Naturally, the Vizon is powered by a version of the famous 4.6-liter Northstar engine.

▲ CHEVROLET BORREGO

This unique Chevrolet features a 2.5-liter flat-4 engine producing 250 hp and an all-wheel-drive system provided by GM's new partner Subaru. It also carries an air compressor and a pressurized water tank. It's a hybrid in more ways than one.

▲ CHRYSLER CROSSFIRE

Unlike most concept cars that are designed strictly for show, the Crossfire can be driven at high speeds. Powered by a 2.7-liter V6 engine with 275 hp, it gets from 0-60 mph in 5.9 seconds. This elegant Chrysler was slated for production on a limited scale, like the Dodge Viper. However, given DaimlerChrysler's current financial situation, that hardly seems likely.

◀ CHRYSLER CROSSFIRE

In the company's own words, the Crossfire "combines European proportions with American character." The model's long hood gives a hint of the car's power and rear-wheel drive. The dividing strip down the center of the windshield seems like a throwback in time, sharply contrasting with the contemporary all-aluminum frame and carbon-fiber body.

DODGE POWERBOX

North American automakers want to continue selling SUVs by the millions. But because these vehicles are not exactly environmentally friendly, the latest Detroit trend is to make them cleaner and more fuel-efficient. The Powerbox is one of the results, sporting a hybrid powertrain.

DODGE POWERBOX

This is the "lift-tail Combogate." Depending on the cargo, you can either lift the tailgate, or use it as a swinging gate.

DODGE POWERBOX

Thanks to its V6 engine that runs on compressed natural gas with an assist from an electric motor, this big Dodge off-roader performs so well it's thought to hide a colossal V8 under the hood. But fuel consumption is lowered by 60% and emissions are virtually zero. Moreover, the machine charges forward from 0-60 mph in about 7 seconds.

DODGE SUPER HEMI

Designers of this big retro-style sedan wanted to pay homage to the North American hard-top sedans of the 1950s. Too bad the Hemi looks more like a caricature of the genre than a tribute.

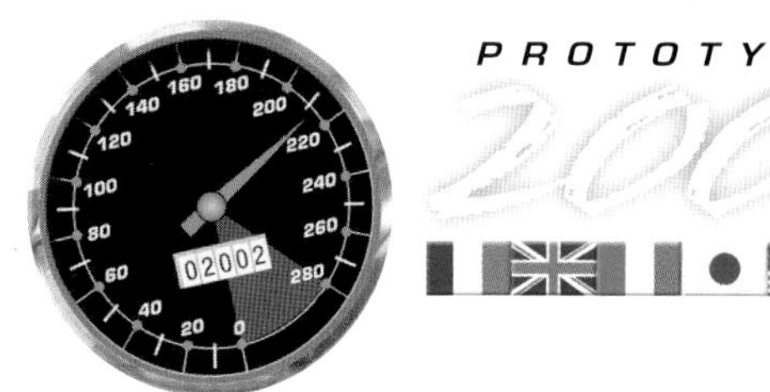

DODGE SUPER HEMI ▲

The Dodge Super Hemi is powered by a 5.7-liter V8 engine with hemispherical combustion chambers. Its 353 horsepower ensures a top speed of 155 mph (248 km/h). Worth noting are the super-sophisticated Infotronic system, developed in collaboration with Sun Microsystems, and the Sirius satellite transponder.

DODGE VIPER C3 ▶

This is neither a prototype nor a concept car, but the 2003 edition of the powerful Dodge Viper. It sports a more contemporary silhouette that looks as spectacular as always – and boasts yet more engine power. We're talking 505/500/500, that is, 505 cubic inches, 500 hp and 500 lb-ft of torque!

◀ DODGE VIPER C3

The Dodge Viper Chapter 3's impressive 8.3-liter V10 engine's job is to propel the 19-inch rear wheels via a 6-speed manual gearbox. In addition to breathtaking performance, the roadster feels more civilized than before, thanks to a more comfortable cockpit and a newly-designed dash. Worth noting: the speedometer indicates a top speed of 220 *miles* per hour.

EDONIS ▶

The Edonis is one of the year's best surprises. Oddly enough, it was unveiled in almost complete anonymity on New Year's Day, 2001 by the Italian consulting firm B. Engineering of Modena. Under the guidance of Jean-Marc Borel, the company plans to produce only 21 of these super racers – one for each century. The Edonis was developed in collaboration with Michelin, which provided the Pax System tires.

▲ EDONIS

This 2-seat coupe demonstrates all the characteristics of an outstanding high-performance car. Powered by a 3.8-liter V12 twin-turbo engine producing 500 hp, it can reach a top speed of 225 mph (360 km/h) and charge forward from 0-60 mph in less than 4 seconds.

▲ FORD EX CONCEPT

The Ford Ex Concept is the most extreme of Ford's "No Boundaries" SUVs, and looks rather like a stylish dune buggy. As is the rule for its category, the Ford Ex features composite body sections on a tubular frame, and the engine is moved to the rear. But hang on for dear life, we're talking V8 with 375 hp!

FORD EXPLORER SPORTSMAN CONCEPT ▶

This is the ideal vehicle for the fly-fishing crowd, according to the folks at Ford. Too bad the Explorer 2002, from which this concept vehicle is derived, doesn't sport the same bold looks. Worth noting are the detachable roof rack, well thought-out storage space, and a 4.6-liter V8 engine generating 240 hp.

◀ FORD FORTY-NINE

J Mays, Ford's vice president of design, is quite frank about it. As its name suggests, the retro-style Forty-Nine concept was modeled after the original 1949 Ford, which was wildly popular in postwar America – one of the milestones marking the start of the baby-boom generation.

FORD FORTY-NINE ▶

Despite its retro-style silhouette, the Forty-Nine's mechanicals are very up-to-date: the car is based on the new Thunderbird's platform. It sports a 3.9-liter V8 engine all decked out in chrome – fitting for a neo hot-rod

HISPANO SUIZA – MAZEL ▲

The K8 is an all-wheel-drive, luxury 4-seat sedan. It has a 4.2-liter V8 engine with 360 hp, coupled to a 6-speed transmission.

HISPANO SUIZA – MAZEL ▶

A Spanish engineering firm called Mazel is planning to revive this legendary marque. Hispano-Suiza dominated the automotive world in the years preceding World War II. Mazel's first effort was the creation the HS21 coupe, unveiled at the Geneva Motor Show last year. The Hispano-Suiza K8 is their second, shown earlier this year.

◀ HONDA MODEL X

Designers of the Honda Model X were inspired by the first X Games, held in San Diego in 1998, and featuring aggressive in-line skating, bicycle stunts, skateboarding, speed-climbing and other such events. The Model X – a crossbreed between an SUV and a mini truck – was conceived with a young sporty crowd in mind.

HONDA MODEL X ▶

Honda points out that this concept vehicle is aimed at young buyers – active and mostly male. It features a next-generation 4-cylinder i-VTEC engine, driving through the front wheels. The 2-liter unit produces just under 200 hp and is coupled to a 5-speed manual transmission. And of course, you can surf the net without getting out of the car.

HYUNDAI HCDV ▶

The HCD6 was styled at Hyundai's HACTI design studio in Fountain Valley, California. In addition to carbon-fiber bumpers and an integrated roll bar in the center, this concept car is further distinguished by dramatic-looking side air-intakes.

The body is painted using the Mysteria system supplied by Dupont.

◀ HYUNDAI HCDV

Hyundai must be very proud of the HCD6's 2.7 V6 engine with 215 hp, judging from the see-through engine cover. Display dials are arranged in a concave dial section. Eighteen-inch Zero Pressure tires eliminate the need for a spare.

INFINITI FX45 ▶

This concept vehicle was dubbed "bionic cheetah" by the Infiniti design team itself. It's the company's attempt to convince customers to stay with the marque rather than turn to, say, the Nissan Z cars. Some variant of this prototype has an excellent chance of being produced one day.

INFINITI FX45 ▲

Styled in Japan, the Infinity FX45 is an all-wheel-drive sport coupe. Moreover, it's based on the mythical Nissan Skyline platform, one of the sportiest cars on the Japanese market.

▲ INFINITI FX45

Engineers really pulled out all the stops on this one. The FX45 is propelled by a 4.5-liter V8 engine – the same that powers the Q45 – which should produce in excess of 300 hp. Like many prototypes, the FX45 is fitted with 20-inch tires to fill up the wheels' arches and provide a striking visual impact.

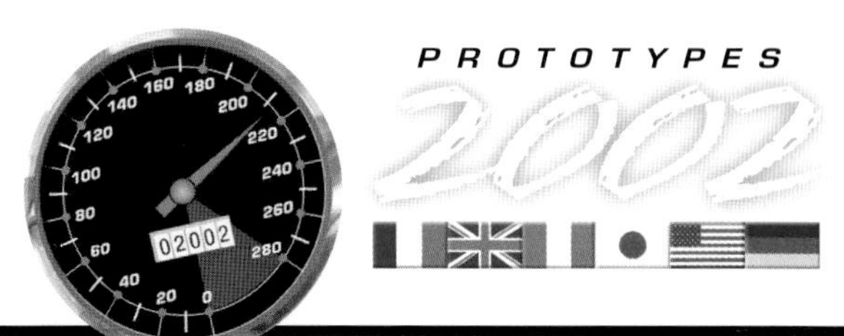

ITALDESIGN ▲
ASTON MARTIN 20/20

The Italian auto designer Giorgietto Giugiaro has long intended to make various structural elements part of the visual impact of his designs. Here, he applies this approach to the Aston Martin 20/20.

▲ ITALDESIGN
ASTON MARTIN 20/20

The Aston Martin 20/20 is based on the DB7's platform. Its 6.0-liter V12 engine produces 500 hp, and is mated to a 6-speed manual transmission.

◄ ITALDESIGN
ASTON MARTIN 20/20

Aston Martin management contributed generously to the creation of the 20/20, providing mechanical elements as well as technical assistance. This is hardly surprising, since Ulrich Bez, Aston Martin's chief executive, is Giorgietto Giugiaro's long-time buddy.

ITALDESIGN ►
MASERATI SPIDER CORSA

This "racing" version of the Maserati roadster was styled at Giorgietto Giugiaro's Italdesign studio. It's considered a prelude to a single model racing series organized for the super rich and friends of the studio. A good retro concept. Wanted: Sponsors to fund the racing series and the car.

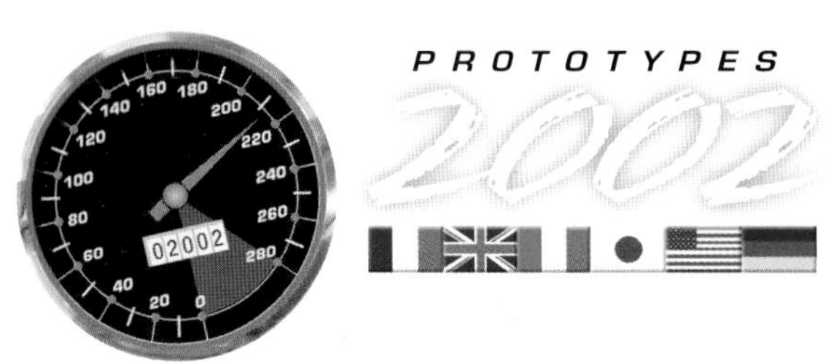

▲ ITALDESIGN TOUAREG

To mark the 80th birthday of the celebrated photographer Helmut Newton, Giorgietto Giugiaro produced a "road" version of the Touareg prototype for Mitsubishi. It was unveiled last year at the Turin Auto Show. This Mitsubishi Montero certainly sports unusual looks. It's powered by a 5.4-liter Chevrolet V8 engine, rated at 280 hp.

JAGUAR F-TYPE ▲

The F-Type will be the lower-priced model of the SK line. Its silhouette is based on the legendary E-Type. It will likely be fitted with a supercharged V6.

JAGUAR F-TYPE ▶

Jaguar unveiled this elegant roadster at the Detroit Auto Show back in 2000. Feedback was so overwhelmingly positive that the following year, the company announced it was going to mass-produce it.

◀ JAGUAR R-COUPE

Unveiled at the Frankfurt Auto Show this year, the Jaguar R-Coupe concept embodies the Coventry-based company's new design philosophy. According to design director Ian Callum, the time has come to consider automobile design in a "fresh and forward-thinking way." The cockpit still features luxurious wood and leather trim, but the overall retro look is gone.

JAGUAR R-COUPE

The R-Coupe's wheelbase is the same as the Jaguar X-Type sedan's; ditto its 4.0-liter V8 engine and rear-wheel drive system. But its dimensions and general features put it in the same class as the Mercedes CL. Judging from Jaguar's current design trends, the XJ8 sedan's replacement, planned for late 2002, could very well feature many of the R-Coupe's styling elements.

JEEP WILLYS

For years, Jeep designers have maintained a conservative approach. Now, chief designer Trevor Creed and his team decided to "marry 21st-century technology with 20th-century tradition," starting with the Willys. This concept vehicle is propelled by a supercharged version of the1.6-liter 4-cylinder Tritech engine developing 160 hp.

JEEP WILLYS

Sporting a tubular aluminum chassis and composite body, the Jeep Willys is fitted with 22-inch wheels for good ground clearance and the same suspension system as the Jeep Liberty. Naturally, the signature Jeep grille stays put in its accustomed place.

KAZ

The humongous KAZ is propelled by eight electric engines. Sporting eight wheels, six of which steer, this road version of the "Sheikansen" reaches a top speed of 187 mph (300 km/h), with a quarter-mile time of 14.5 seconds.

KAZ ▶

Sometimes, it takes a group effort to produce a disaster. Take KAZ, the environmentally-friendly concept vehicle developed by Professor Hiroshi Shimizu, of the University of Keio, Japan, and styled by the famous Italian design studio I.DE.A. Unfortunately, KAZ – which stands for "Keio Advanced Zero-Emission" – amounts to little more than a monstrosity on wheels.

◀ LAND ROVER DEFENDER TOMB RAIDER

Given SUV's current popularity, it's not surprising to see one of them figure prominently in the popular adventure movie "Tomb Raider" – a spin-off of the video game of the same name. The movie stars Angelina Jolie – playing the heroine, Lara Croft – behind the wheel of a unique version of the Land Rover Defender, specially built by Land Rover and Paramount Pictures.

LAND ROVER DEFENDER TOMB RAIDER ▶

The Defender "Tomb Raider" is based on the Defender minivan, and fitted with a 4.0-liter V8 gasoline engine producing 184 hp. The body is painted Bonatti grey with aluminum fenders. This special-edition Defender is equipped with a winch, auxiliary head-lights mounted on reinforcement bars and an expedition-tool box.

◀ MAZDA RX-8

The Mazda RX-8 is the next step in the evolution of the RX-Evolv concept, presented at the Tokyo Auto Show in October 1999. Sporting four "freestyle" doors, four comfortable seats and the RENESIS rotary engine, the RX-8 is bound to generate a market buzz. Its central-forward engine location results in ideal 50/50 weight distribution and virtually guarantees excellent road handling

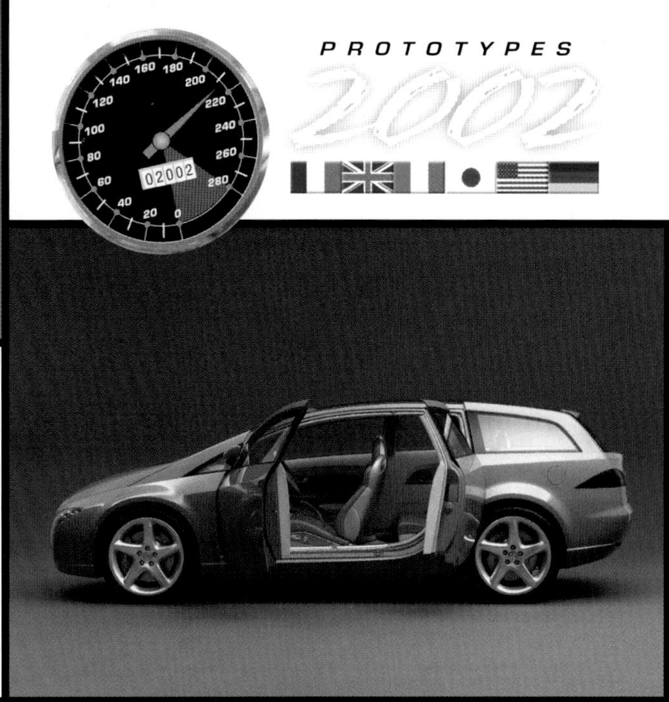

MAZDA SPORT TOURER ▲

The MX Sport Tourer is powered by a unique hybrid drive system consisting of a 2.0-liter S-VT gasoline engine and an electric motor. On highways and rugged terrain, the S-VT is used in four-wheel-drive mode. In the city, the driver can switch to the Zero-emission rear-wheel-drive electric motor mode, good for speeds between 25 and 30 mph (40 to 50 km/h). Batteries are recharged by an internal combustion engine and by kinetic energy generated by the braking system.

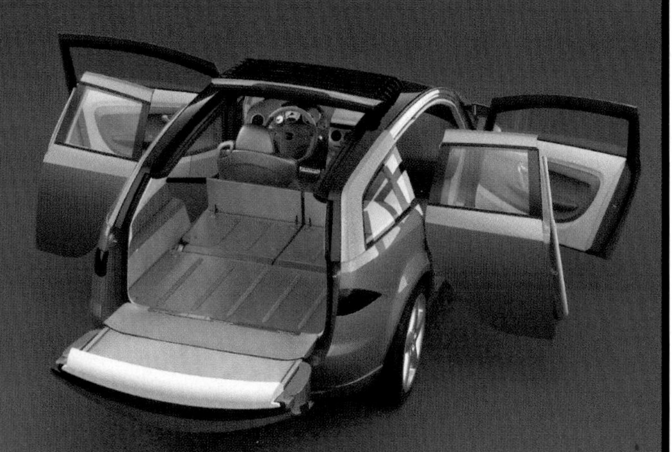

▲ MAZDA SPORT TOURER

The MX Sport Tourer features "freestyle" doors – borrowed from the RX-8 model – with no center pillar for easy access to the rear seats; a sports-car cockpit and a practical cargo area, not to mention a structure that retracts the roof, thus transforming the vehicle into a pseudo-minivan.

◀ MAZDA SPORT TOURER

The rear hatch glass can be lowered and the rear seats stored away electrically to leave a flat floor and increase cargo space to 44 cubic feet. The rear hatch glass can be raised or lowered for easier access to the cargo area.

NISSAN ALPHA-T ▲

Nissan's design studio dreamed up this monstrosity to stimulate public interest and declare its intention to mass-produce a full-size, V8-powered truck in North America. Mission accomplished: the unforgettable alpha-T is actually considered by many as the Pontiac Aztek of big trucks.

▲ NISSAN ALPHA-T

This odd-shaped full-size Nissan truck features "butterfly" doors, a power-operated slide-out cargo box floor, and is fitted with a 4.5-liter V8 engine generating more than 300 hp. It will be assembled at a North American plant and will hit the market in two years or so.

▲ NISSAN CHAPPO

This tentative-looking cube is still a work-in-progress that Nissan hopes will appeal to the next generation of buyers. Nissan will need all the luck it can get. This motorized whatchamacallit is bound to be poohed-poohed by the target customer group who will have developed more sophisticated tastes.

NISSAN MM.E ▲

Remarkably compact and driver-friendly, the MM.e concept offers leading edge technology at the same time – such is the challenge that the Nissan Design team assigned to itself. Unveiled for the first time at the 2001 Frankfurt Auto Show, the MM.e embodies Nissan's "second coming." It will be marketed as the new-generation Micra.

NISSAN MM.E ▶

The instrument panel is located in front of the driver and takes the form of a liquid-crystal display screen. The little console behind the two-spoke steering wheel houses the tachometer and digital speedometer, flanked by a fuel gauge on one side and a water thermometer on the other. For easy identification, controls for the headlights and wipers/washer fluid are covered with an orange-colored acrylic material, ditto the alloy CVT gearbox shifter.

◀ OLDSMOBILE 04

This unusual Oldsmobile concept car was unveiled many weeks after the division itself was closed down. Hats off to them!

OLDSMOBILE 04 ▲

Once again, Oldsmobile designers looked to Europe in order to find inspiration for this convertible. In fact, the platform is borrowed from Opel. The dash – consisting of liquid crystal displays – can be reconfigured to show the information the driver wants, while the flexible Targa top can be set up according to need and climatic conditions.

▲ OPEL XTREME GULLWING

To build up public enthusiasm and confidence in the Xtreme Gullwing, Opel borrowed the platform and drivetrain from the modified Opel Astra racing cars, as entered in the German Touring Car Championship.

◀ OPEL XTREME GULLWING

Opel has been trying hard to rejuvenate its old-fashioned image on the European market. This concept car, called Xtreme Gullwing, was unveiled at the Geneva Auto Show. It caused quite a buzz, and it's easy to see why. Who could resist that spectacular orange silhouette, complete with a 500-hp engine?

PEUGEOT CAMÉLEO ▲

To get public feedback regarding the yet-to-be unveiled 307 wagon, Peugeot's design team created the Caméleo. This wagon concept car, turned "pick-up truck" for the occasion, demonstrates the versatility of the initial configuration.

▲ PEUGEOT CAMÉLEO

This Peugeot is proof of SUV influence on European automakers. However, chances are slim that this semi-SUV will be mass-produced. The station wagon version will be available in the near future.

PININFARINA OSÉE ▶

For the first time ever, Pininfarina developed a concept car from mechanical components provided by Citroën. To build this 3-seat coupe with a central engine, designers looked to the older Citroën DS and SM – both considered design paragons of their time – for inspiration.

◀ PININFARINA OSÉE

Like all self-respecting Citroëns, the Pininfarina Osée boasts hydroactive suspension, which helps the car achieve a low drag coefficient. The engine – a 3.0-liter V6 producing 194 hp – is centrally mounted and coupled to a 5-speed sequential gearbox.

PININFARINA OSÉE ▶

The driver's seat is in the center, with the passengers on either side, slightly further back. The steering wheel, seats, and pedals are adjustable. The instruments, naturally, are centrally mounted.

PONTIAC REV ▼

Rumors in Detroit have it that this Pontiac will be mass-produced in a few years. For this concept car, engineers combined the power and handling of a Firebird with off-road driving capabilities of an all-terrain vehicle.

▲ PONTIAC REV

The Pontiac REV is an all-wheel-drive propelled by a 3.0-liter V6 engine producing 245 hp. The extremely low rear door facilitates cargo loading. The headlights are designed to respond to steering inputs and thus provide optimal light on the road, just like the mythical Citroën SM.

▲ PORSCHE CARRERA GT

Launched at the Paris Auto Show in spring 2000, the Carrera GT is Porsche's most spectacular model – boasting its very own frame – the first one since the advent of the GT1, which debuted in 1997. Production of this mid-engine sports car will be limited and the price will be approximately $500,000. This time around, the Stuttgart automaker promises that its model will meet North American safety and emission requirements.

◄ PORSCHE CARRERA GT

The Carrera GT is propelled by a 5.5-liter V10 rating 550 hp. It scoots from 0-60 mph in 4 seconds and maximum speed is 203 mph (325 km/h). Tires are P265/30ZR19 in front and P335/30ZR20 in the rear.

RENAULT TALISMAN ►

The Talisman completes Renault's troika of unconventional and super-luxury cars, the first two being the Avantime and Vel Satis. Its exotic body design, especially for a high-end car, is only a foretaste of what awaits inside.

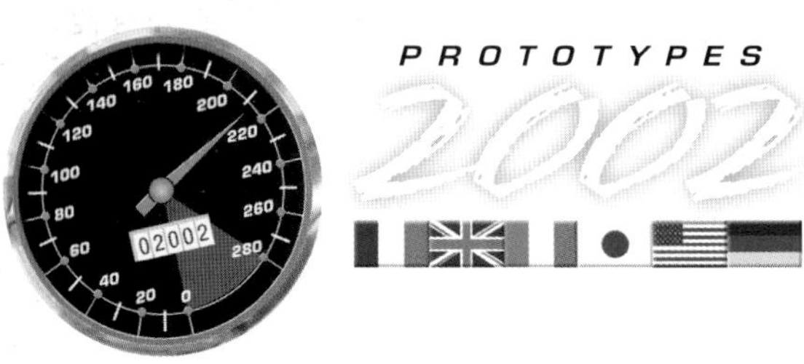

RENAULT TALISMAN ▶

This futuristic rear-wheel-drive Renault is powered by a Nissan-made engine, a 4.5-liter V8 rating 340 hp paired to a 5-speed automatic gearbox.

RENAULT TALISMAN ▲

The dashboard is attached to the front body panel by slender metal beams. It's designed to move in tandem with the pedal system to accommodate the driver's changing positions, since the carbon-structure seats are not adjustable. Through the steering wheel, you can spot four round liquid-crystal gauges.

▲ RENAULT TALISMAN

Access is a snap, through the wide gull-wing doors – measuring as much as 97 inches (2.45 m) – that open and close electro-hydraulically. Like the Avantime, there's no center (B) pillar.

.

◀ RENAULT VEL SATIS

Renault chose the Vel Satis to replace its luxury sedan Safrane. Although it resembles a concept car, this enigmatic-looking sedan will be sold as-is in Europe. With this top-of-the-line 5-door hatchback, the French automaker hopes to reinvent luxury cars. Renault's avant-garde styling cues will filter down to its Avantime and Espace, which the French automaker hopes will be worthy alternatives for customers in search of luxury and exclusivity.

▲ RINSPEED ADVANTIGE

This Swiss automotive specialty firm often comes up with wacky, certainly unusual, car designs. A 24 hours of Le Mans racer look-alike, the Rinspeed Advantige is nevertheless a virtually zero-emission prototype.

▲ RENAULT VEL SATIS

Thanks to the Nissan-Renault partnership, the Vel Satis is fitted with Nissan's 3.5-liter V6 engine with variable cam timing, producing 235 hp. A turbocharged diesel 3.0-liter option is also available. Both engines are coupled to a Pro-Active 5-speed automatic transmission.

▲ RINSPEED ADVANTIGE

This elegant and environmentally-friendly car runs on biofuel made from kitchen and garden waste. Its 1.8-liter, 4-cylinder engine produces 120 hp. It moves from 0-60 mph in 6 seconds and can reach a top speed of 128 mph (205 km/h).

SAAB X9 ▲

With the arrival of Michael Mauer – of Mercedes SLK fame – as head of design at Saab, many in the automotive world believed that the Swedish automaker would unveil a new roadster at the Frankfurt Auto Show. Instead, Mauer surprised everyone with the Saab X9, a hybrid car that reflects both Saab styling tradition and the shape of things to come.

◀ SAAB X9

The Saab X9 is at once a coupe, roadster, wagon and pick-up truck. The top and tailgate can open wide, and the telescopic cabin floor protrudes slightly from the rear end.

SAAB X9 ▶

The Saab X9 is more than just a versatile vehicle. Powered by a 3.0-liter V6 engine rating 300 hp, this prototype could very well propel the Swedish automaker into the forefront of luxury cars.

◀ SAAB X9

Saab indicates that the X9 concept will be mass-produced, albeit in a more toned-down version. It might even replace the 1960s-era Sonnet, whose career proved to be all too brief. Chances are good that the production model will retain many of the X9's interesting features. The tailgate, for example, is not attached to the rooftop.

SUZUKI GSX-R/4 ▶

Suzuki resorted to its legendary motorcycle know-how to design this spectacular concept car. Its 175-hp 1.3-liter 4-cylinder was based on the engine of the fantastic Suzuki Hayabusa, currently the fastest production motorcycle.

SUZUKI GSX-R/4 ▲

This miniature car – 140 inches (355 cm) long and 39.7 inches (101 cm) wide – uses center-mounted shock absorbers, just like F1 race cars. It features an all-aluminum tubular frame and composite body panels.

▲ VOLKSWAGEN MICROBUS

After the New Beetle, Volkswagen proceeded to redesign the Microbus, which reached cult status during the hippie1960s. The new version was designed in California, and its "biosphere" green color is fittingly up-to-date.

VOLKSWAGEN MICROBUS ▲

Will the Microbus be mass-produced? Only Wolfsburg management knows for sure. Since the Microbus is fitted with an EuroVan chassis and a 3.2-liter V6 engine, mass-production wouldn't be difficult. The cockpit will be entirely revised, but hopefully not the excellent silhouette.

▲ VOLVO ACC

This is a prototype of Volvo's future all-terrain vehicle. The Adventure Concept Car (ACC) is by no means the definitive production model, due out in two years. This robust and comfortable 4-seater is used as a market tester and is built on the X-Country's platform.

◀ VOLVO SCC

This Volvo wagon ensures absolute safety. The see-through A pillar provides better driver visibility while all occupants are protected by 4-point seatbelts. The rear seats can be lifted so children and small-size adults can properly adjust their seatbelts. Rearward-facing cameras replace rearview mirrors.

VOLVO SCC ▶

The Volvo Safety Concept Car (SCC) is considered by many to be one of the year's most impressive from every viewpoint: style, functionality and safety.

0
20
40
60
80
100
120
140
160
180
200
220
240
260
280
02002

Pickup Trucks

- CHEVROLET
- DODGE
- FORD
- HUMMER
- MAZDA
- NISSAN
- TOYOTA

CHEVROLET SILVERADO GMC SIERRA

GMC **SIERRA DENALI**

Exceptional in Every Category

General Motors has pulled off the impossible in its bid to regild its trademark in almost all pickup categories. Ironically, it was by taking on Ford's quasi-impregnable F-series that GM achieved its best success for years. In the process, its engineers have developed a chassis that has become the industry standard; and more often than not, its engines take the nod over the competition in both power and fuel economy, though not always reflecting leading-edge technology.

This feat is all the more remarkable given the importance of the truck market in North America and the ferocious competition it spawns. Light-duty trucks have been the best-selling models for years, proving exceptionally profitable for their makers. The stake has been amplified in the past few years when more and more individuals and families adopt them as touring cars. This slice of the market represents more than 25% of overall sales, pushing the major automakers to increase pickup comfort and improve roadholding capability, even in the Heavy-Duty (HD) category.

Rejuvenation process

After being outstripped by Ford and Dodge in the truck category, General Motors has reversed the situation with its new HD series, by retaining the multi-section modular frame – the 1500 series's main asset – as well as the interior layout, generally considered to be as comfortable as a regular automobile. Engines, too, have been suitably upgraded to ensure GM's supremacy in terms of payload and towing capacity. For those who want their pickup to shoot ahead even when heavily loaded, there's the 8.1-liter V8, producing 340 horsepower and 455 lb-ft of torque. Another choice is the all-new 6.6-liter V8 Duramax turbodiesel, co-developed with Isuzu, offering 300 hp and a more than respectable 520 lb-ft of torque.

Sturdy stuff

Like the 8.1-liter gasoline engine, the turbodiesel is available with the ZF 6-speed manual transmission, or the Allison 5-speed automatic. If your needs are more modest, the 300 hp Vortec 6000 may be the answer. It comes with a 5-speed manual or a 4-speed automatic.

Towing capabilities, too, have been boosted: tag-along capacity is 58,500 lbs (26,500 kg), while "gooseneck" (fifth

▲ PROS

• Impressive engines • Efficient transmission • Comfortable seats • Large payload capacity • Well-sorted suspension

▼ CONS

• Heavy fuel consumption (gasoline engine) • Some roughness in lower gears (automatic transmission) • High price • Specialized use

wheel) capacity is now up to 77, 000 lbs (35,000 kg). Impressive!

Smooth drive

Despite gargantuan engines and springs capable of carrying heavy loads, GM's HD pickups provide the same comfort and driveability as the 1500 series models. Braking power and front-rear distribution are adequate, an important factor in a light-duty truck. It allows the driver to brake without concern, even when the truck is heavily loaded or hauling a trailer. What's more, all Silverado and Sierra models boast the Allison automatic transmission with a "hauling" mode that prevents untimely upshifts or downshifts. It also downshifts on steep hills in order to ensure better control of the vehicle and prevent excessive wear and tear on the brakes. But watch out for the transmission, which did jerk on some occasions, especially when moving from first to second gear.

What about other models?

If their novelty makes HD models prominent this year, they shouldn't overshadow other 1500 series models, which are much better adapted for use as a car – although with dimensions as cumbersome as their more powerful siblings, they are better suited to rural conditions than the city. Furthermore, whether fitted with gasoline or turbodiesel engines, all 1500 series light-duty trucks consume considerably more fuel than a sedan, even one with a big engine.

Roadholding capabilities of the Chevrolet Silverado and GMC Sierra are identical in all models, the only difference being a firmer suspension for HDs, although the latter prove amazingly comfortable for their category. Directional stability is good overall and cornering behavior is acceptable. But intrepid drivers should keep an eye out for the chronic understeer to avoid nasty surprises. Never forget that these are light-duty trucks: as such they don't have the same kind of agility as a sedan or even a sport-utility vehicle.

Overall, the pickup's road manners are excellent while their driveability is heightened by comfortable seats, good sound insulation and one of the best dashboards in any truck, large or small.

Denis Duquet

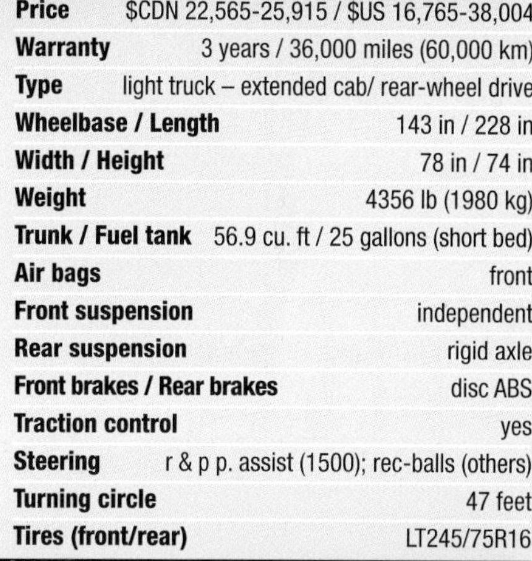

SPECIFICATIONS	LT
Price	$CDN 22,565-25,915 / $US 16,765-38,004
Warranty	3 years / 36,000 miles (60,000 km)
Type	light truck – extended cab/ rear-wheel drive
Wheelbase / Length	143 in / 228 in
Width / Height	78 in / 74 in
Weight	4356 lb (1980 kg)
Trunk / Fuel tank	56.9 cu. ft / 25 gallons (short bed)
Air bags	front
Front suspension	independent
Rear suspension	rigid axle
Front brakes / Rear brakes	disc ABS
Traction control	yes
Steering	r & p p. assist (1500); rec-balls (others)
Turning circle	47 feet
Tires (front/rear)	LT245/75R16

PERFORMANCE	
Engine	V8 4.8-liter
Transmission	4-speed automatic
Horsepower	270 hp at 5200 rpm
Torque	285 lb-ft at 4000 rpm
Other engines	V6 4.3-l 200 hp; V8 5.3-l 285 hp; V8 6-l 300 hp HD class; V8 6-l 300 hp; V8 8.1-l 340 hp; V8 6.6-l turbodiesel 300 hp
Other transmission	5-speed manual; 6-speed manual
Acceleration (0-60 mph)	9.8 s; 10.6 s (V6)
Maximum speed	112mph (180 km/h)
Braking (60-0 mph)	145 feet (44.2 m)
Fuel consumption	16.9 mpg (13.4L/100 km/h)

COMPETITION

• Dodge Ram • Ford F150 • Toyota Tundra

NEW FOR 2002

• Sierra Denali to be replaced in 2003
• Chrome bumpers • Sunshade with extension

RATING	(out of 5 stars)
Driveability	★★★½
Comfort	★★★★
Reliability	★★★★
Roominess	★★★★
Winter driving rating	★★★½
Safety	★★★½
Resale value	★★★★½

CHEVROLET S-10 GMC SONOMA

GMC **SONOMA**

Multiple Choices

Despite the ever-increasing popularity of pickup trucks, compact models have not evolved at the same pace as their bigger, costlier and "thirstier" cousins. Given the current volatility concerning supply-and-demand at gas pumps, why isn't this particular market segment doing any better?

The answer is a simple one. Full-size pickups are a more profitable line for manufacturers, and they also happen to be what the market is clamoring for. When it comes to the world of trucks, the bigger and more powerful the better. That's why Toyota brought out the Tundra, while Nissan, the compact-pickup innovator, announced that it will develop a full-size model for the North American market within the next few years. For the time being at least, fuel prices don't seem to be a serious factor.

And so the general public's love affair with bigger models like the Chevrolet Silverado and GMC Sierra all but overshadows the compact-model market. It's a quiet sector of the automobile economy, therefore, regularly bringing out carry-over models year after year.

This year's S-10 and Sonoma, for instance, are little changed. The only modifications worth mentioning are a new, cleaner-looking front fascia and chromed horizontal bar grille. As far as the rest goes, it involves the various configurations which are offered. For example, extended-cab models now come with a standard third door, while those with regular cab and extended box have been discontinued – yet another indication that the vehicle was designed more for family purposes rather than commercial use.

Forgotten generation

In fact, it was to satisfy market demands that GM Canada decided to bring out the Crew-cab model, launched last year in the United States. It will be available exclusively in a 4X4 version. This part-time all-wheel drive system is controlled by a button located on the upper part of the dashboard.

Not bad at all

Although the last design dates back to 1994, these two pickup models still look as fresh as they ever did, noticeably similar to the Silverado and Sierra, both

▲ PROS

- Insta-trac system • Crew-cab model
- Numerous options • Practical dashboard
- V6 engine

▼ CONS

- Average passive safety • So-so tires • 2.2-liter engine • Uncomfortable jump seats (3-door model)
- Ineffective rear suspension

of which underwent major makeovers in 1999. The extended-cab model is the most successful of all, its long box in the rear contributing significantly to the overall balance.

The cockpit has been refined over the years. Its dashboard beats the Dodge Dakota's or Ford Ranger's hands down, both in terms of functionality and style. The front seats offer little lateral support – read, little comfort on twisty roads. The Crew-cab model offers a comfortable rear bench, with considerably more legroom than the Nissan Frontier, whose own record is abysmal in this area.

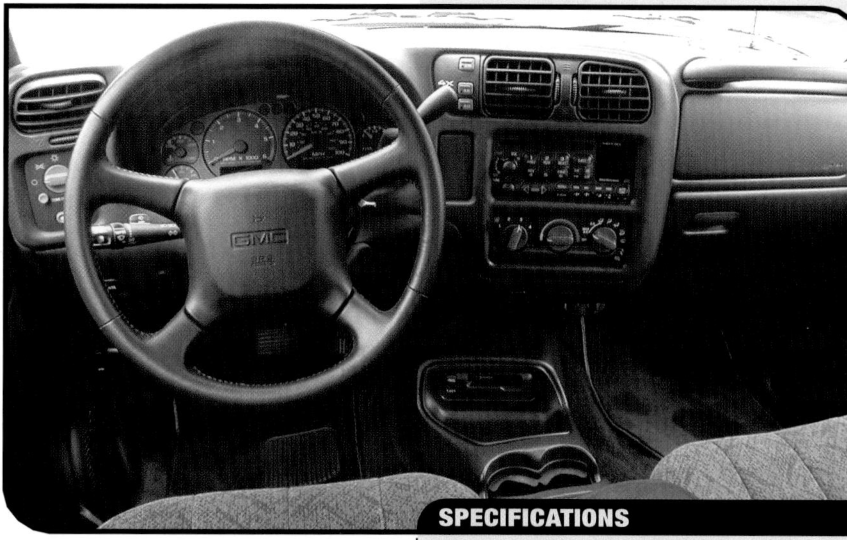

Quiet and powerful

The standard 2.2-liter 120-hp engine is not much help, unless you plan to transport nothing but empty boxes. Best of all is the 4.3-liter Vortec, which generates 190 hp in the 4x4 versions, and 180 hp in the 4X2. Four-speed manual transmission is standard on all models, while the 4-speed automatic is optional.

The cabin is comfortable and the quality of sound insulation is better than average. Road behavior is predictable, steering is precise for a pickup truck, and directional stability gets a passing grade. Understeer is pronounced on entry into corners, going to pronounced oversteer on exit. On the other hand, beware of rough roads if you drive unloaded. The rear axle tends to "dance around" on bumpy roads, which may cause the truck to swerve now and then. For city driving, the truck's elevated driving position and large exterior mirrors are definite assets. While the S-10/Sonoma isn't exactly agile, it still compares very favorably with its Nissan and Toyota counterparts, both of which leave a lot to be desired in this area.

Due to be replaced in the near future, the S-10/Sonoma are still viable compact-pickup choices, in terms of technical specs, styling and handling, not to mention an inexhaustible list of options which will help you personalize your very own machine.

Denis Duquet

SPECIFICATIONS

Price	$CDN 17,060-24,775 / $US 13,434-17,079
Warranty	3 years / 36,000 miles (60,000 km)
Type	compact pickup / 4X4
Wheelbase / Length	122.8 in / 206.3 in
Width / Height	67.7 in / 62.6 in
Weight	3219 lb. (1460 kg)
Trunk / Fuel tank	39.7 cu.ft / 18 gallons
Air bags	front
Front suspension	independent
Rear suspension	rigid axle
Front brakes / Rear brakes	disc / drum ABS
Traction control	no
Steering	recirculating balls, power assist
Turning circle	43 feet
Tires (front/rear)	P235/70R15

PERFORMANCE

Engine	V6 4.3 liter
Transmission	5-speed manual
Horsepower	190 hp at 4400 rpm
Torque	250 lb-ft at 2800 rpm
Other engines	4L 2.2 liter 120 hp V6 4.3 liter 180 hp (4X2)
Other transmission	4-speed automatic
Acceleration (0-60 mph)	11.3 s; 9.4 s (V6)
Maximum speed	109 mph (175 km/h)
Braking (60-0 mph)	146 feet (44.6 m)
Fuel consumption	22 mpg (10.3 L/100 km)

COMPETITION

• Ford Ranger • Mazda B Series
• Toyota Tacoma

NEW FOR 2002

• Crew cab model offered in Canada • Long-box model discontinued • New front fascia • Revised grille

RATING (out of 5 stars)

Driveability	★★★
Comfort	★★★½
Reliability	★★★½
Roominess	★★½
Winter driving rating	★★★
Safety	★★★
Resale value	★★★½

DODGE DAKOTA

DODGE **DAKOTA**

Champion of Compromise

Over the years, pickup trucks have become steadily trendier and attracted new fans to the category. After all, it looks cool to drive a pickup truck. People might think you're heading off to your country place, your hunting or fishing lodge, or else transporting equipment to an equestrian center or some exclusive, extreme-sport club. But more seriously, folks, if pickup trucks have indeed become so popular, it's because they're amazingly versatile, especially for active do-it-yourselfers.

Unfortunately, it's often a tricky business choosing a truck that perfectly meets all your expectations because, like military supplies, they're either too small or too big. If you're faced with this dilemma, the Dodge Dakota might be just what you're looking for. It's 12 inches (31 cm) shorter than the Chevrolet Silverado, but longer than the Ford Ranger when configured the same way. What's more, the Dakota can be fitted with a choice of engines: a 120 hp 4-cylinder, a 3.9-liter V6, the 235 hp Next-Generation 4.7-liter Magnum® V8, or a thundering 5.9-liter V8, the most powerful of all. Thus equipped, no job is too big or too small for this champion of compromise.

Worthy solution

Given its self-appointed position between two categories, the Dakota comes with an exhaustive list of options, aimed at covering all the possible bases. For example, if you're looking for a mid-size pickup with good gas mileage simply for grocery shopping and transporting an oversized bundle from time to time, the Dakota's regular-cab model, powered by the 4-cylinder engine paired to a 5-speed manual gearbox, would be a logical choice.

Best of the lineup

On the other hand, if you need to tow a heavy trailer on a regular basis, opt instead for the 5.9-liter V8 version. Trust me, its engine power is far above average, and so is fuel consumption. But beware, its 4-speed automatic gearbox is not exactly a model of smoothness.

In my considered opinion, the best of the lineup is the Dodge Dakota Quad Cab, fitted with a 4.7-liter overhead-camshaft V8 engine and its own, exclusive 4-speed automatic transmission.

▲ PROS

- Comfortable cockpit • Engine options
- Excellent cargo capacity • Interesting dimensions • Quad Cab version

▼ CONS

- Dull dashboard . Finish needs work
- Guzzler 5.9-liter V8 • Poor fuel economy
- Unresponsive rear axle (without payload)

The difference between this gearbox and that in the 5.9-liter V8 version is night-and-day. On the other hand, if genuine trucking is your thing, you can always order a manual transmission with any engine, except the 5.9-liter V8. By the way, the Quad Cab's standard 3.9-liter V6's performance is quite decent, but its fuel consumption is similar to that of the 4.7-liter V8 – so, more food for thought.

As befits its champion-of-compromise image, the Quad Cab constitutes a worthy intermediate solution. Instead of access panels – as is often the case with bigger pickup models like the Toyota Tundra – Dodge engineers chose a four-door design for the Quad Cab, providing surprisingly comfortable rear seats as a result. In fact, this model is so well executed that it offers significantly ampler legroom than even the latest Ram Quad Cab.

Yes, but...

On the highway, the moderately-sized Dodge Dakota displays predictable handling characteristics. It's also relatively nimble in city traffic and easy to park, even though it's bigger than a compact-size pickup truck. The front seats provide little lateral support but are comfortable nonetheless. The cabin is well appointed and feels convivial; but the dashboard, while functional, is not much to look at. At least the instruments and controls are clearly identified and easy to read. What's more, in the 4X4 version, you can switch smoothly from one mode to the other simply by turning a button.

In the last analysis, though, this so-called champion of compromise doesn't always perform consistently. The suspension, for instance, is too stiff, and the rear axle tends to bounce on rough surfaces. Finally, despite the electronic braking force distribution, braking in wet weather – and especially when there's no payload – is still an iffy thing to do. But despite these limitations, the Dodge Dakota remains an ideal pickup truck option for most buyers.

Denis Duquet

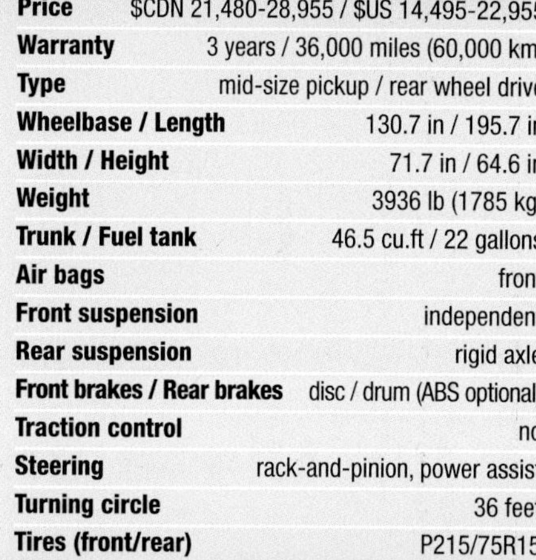

SPECIFICATIONS	
Price	$CDN 21,480-28,955 / $US 14,495-22,955
Warranty	3 years / 36,000 miles (60,000 km)
Type	mid-size pickup / rear wheel drive
Wheelbase / Length	130.7 in / 195.7 in
Width / Height	71.7 in / 64.6 in
Weight	3936 lb (1785 kg)
Trunk / Fuel tank	46.5 cu.ft / 22 gallons
Air bags	front
Front suspension	independent
Rear suspension	rigid axle
Front brakes / Rear brakes	disc / drum (ABS optional)
Traction control	no
Steering	rack-and-pinion, power assist
Turning circle	36 feet
Tires (front/rear)	P215/75R15

PERFORMANCE	
Engine	V6 3.9-liter
Transmission	4-speed automatic
Horsepower	175 hp at 4800 rpm
Torque	225 lb-ft at 3200 rpm
Other engines	4L 2.5-liter 120 hp; V8 4.7-liter 235 hp; V8 5.9-liter 250 hp
Other transmission	5-speed manual
Acceleration (0-60 mph)	9.6 s; 8.4 s (V8 4.7-liter)
Maximum speed	109 mph (175 km/h)
Braking (60-0 mph)	150 feet (45.7 m)
Fuel consumption	17.7 mpg (12.8 L/100 km)

COMPETITION

- Ford F-150 Crew Cab • Nissan Frontier 4-doors
- Toyota Tundra

NEW FOR 2002

- 17-inch wheels on some models
- Additional equipment with various versions

RATING	**(out of 5 stars)**
Driveability	★★★★
Comfort	★★★★
Reliability	★★★½
Roominess	★★★½
Winter driving rating	★★★
Safety	★★★½
Resale value	★★★★

DODGE RAM

DODGE **RAM SPORT**

Up Close and Personal

The arrival of the "new-wave" Dodge Ram in 1994 shook up the truck world in no uncertain terms. Its aggressive silhouette – inspired by the much larger Class-8 trucks – was eye-catching enough to attract a new legion of buyers who wouldn't have otherwise discovered its qualities. After seven years, the Ram has been revamped for 2002, although at first glance the updated design looks practically the same as the previous generation.

At closer range, however, you'll notice that the new silhouette is more refined. The sculpted front fenders have been retained, but their shape is more studied, now flush with the cargo bed's sides. The dual-lamp headlights are new, as are the Ram's signature grilles – three of them, without a doubt a first in the industry. The SLT has a chrome grille shell with a gray honeycomb center and imposing chrome crosshairs. The SLT Plus uses the same grille, except for its body-colored shell. And finally, the Sport model is adorned with a body-colored grille, with a chrome billet-bar center.

The cockpit has a more subdued appearance. But here again, you must look carefully before you can detect anything different, like the all-new instrument panel featuring white gauges, and the audio/climate control unit at the center of the dashboard. The new Ram also has adjustable pedals and a side-impact curtain airbag.

But it's the Quad Cab, or 4-door version, that offers the most changes: the rear bench, for instance, has a 60/40 split to accommodate a steel panel that can serve as a flat-load floor, with additional storage space underneath. On the other hand, the rear seats are not as spacious as those of its rival, the Ford Super Crew, despite the fact that Dodge engineers took two inches (5 cm) from the cargo bed to enlarge the cabin.

Worth a second look

The regular-cab model boasts, behind the front seats, a space large enough to house a storage tray and several other bulky items. In the debit column are the uneven floor on the passenger side, which restricts footroom and the cheap-feeling texture of the leather seats.

▲ PROS

- Adjustable pedals • Improved front suspension
- Cleaner shape • Inflatable side panels
- Well laid-out storage space

▼ CONS

- Old-style 5.9-liter V8 and its automatic gearbox
- Poor use of rear space (Quad Cab) • Front floor too high • Cheesy leather texture

Multiple choices

The new Ram also gets a new chassis, with hydroformed frame rails, new rack-and-pinion steering, independent front suspension (4X4 model), as well as four-wheel disc brakes (all models).

In addition to the 5.9-liter V8, the Ram can be fitted with a choice of two all-new engines: the 3.7-liter V6 with 235 horsepower, and the 4.7-liter V8 that replaces the old 5.2-liter V8. Incidentally, this same 4.7-liter engine also powers the Grand Cherokee. Both the V6 and V8 come with a manual gearbox as standard equipment, although you can pair them with the new 45RFE automatic transmission. Finally, the Sport model comes with massive 20-inch polished cast-aluminum wheels.

The Chrysler people promised us the world in terms of driving pleasure. And their confident prediction is partially right since the new Ram clearly proves to be a better integrated vehicle. Steering is more precise and braking more progressive, even though ABS is still an optional feature.

Of the three engines, the 5.9-liter V8 delivers the most impressive acceleration, but its transmission is jerky and gear changes tend to occur at the most inopportune moment. The 4.7-liter V8 and the V6 fare better, thanks to the 45RFE automatic gearbox, which does its job remarkably well. Although noisy, the V6 proves to be a viable option. After all, it produces an impressive 235 horsepower, only 20 fewer than the 4.7-liter V8.

More refined, and endowed with a hydroformed – read, more rigid – chassis, the new Dodge Ram is a competent workhorse, and fun to drive. It's currently ranked between the Chevrolet Silverado and the Toyota Tundra.

Denis Duquet

SPECIFICATIONS

Price	$CDN 23,255-30,365 / $US 16,000-29,480
Warranty	3 years / 36,000 miles (60,000 km)
Type	mid-size pickup / rear wheel drive
Wheelbase / Length	140.6 in / 227.6 in
Width / Height	79.4 in / 74.4 in
Weight	4883 lb (2215 kg)
Trunk / Fuel tank	70.0 cu. ft / 35 gallons
Air bags	front, head
Front suspension	independent
Rear suspension	rigid axle
Front brakes / Rear brakes	disc ABS
Traction control	no
Steering	rack-and-pinion, power assist
Turning circle	46 feet
Tires (front/rear)	P245/70R17 (P275/55R20 Sport)

PERFORMANCE

Engine	V8 5.9-liter
Transmission	4-speed automatic
Horsepower	245 hp at 4000 rpm
Torque	335 lb-ft at 3200 rpm
Other engines	V6 3.7-liter 215 hp; V8 4.7-liter 235 hp
Other transmission	5-speed manual (V8 5.9-liter)
Acceleration (0-60 mph)	9.8 sec.
Maximum speed	112 mph (180 km/h)
Braking (60-0 mph)	148 feet (45.2 m)
Fuel consumption	14.5 mpg (15.6 L/100 km)

COMPETITION

• Chevrolet Silverado/GMC Sierra • Ford F-150 • Toyota Tundra

NEW FOR 2002

• Adjustable pedals • Curtain airbag • New hydroformed chassis • New engines (V8 4.7, V6 3.7)

RATING (out of 5 stars)

Driveability	★★★★
Comfort	★★★½
Reliability	★★★★★
Roominess	★★★★
Winter driving rating	★★★
Safety	★★★½
Resale value	★★★★

FORD F-150/SVT LIGHTNING

FORD **F-150**

Play Time

Despite the ever increasing price of fuel, the light-duty truck market remains stable. Not only did new companies proliferate, spurring the demand for commercial vehicles, but so did the number of individuals who've been buying trucks for personal use.

This is the fastest-growing segment of the market, inciting manufacturers to adapt their commercial vehicles to more regular use, making them increasingly comfortable and versatile, and equipping them with more sophisticated suspension systems. The situation also encourages automakers to extend their various lists of options and even to design more marginal models. Among the latter, we find the SVT Lightning, a sport version of the F-150. It boasts a regular cabin and performance is on a par with many a sport coupe.

Whoa, Jim!

This one-of-a-kind light-duty truck was developed by Ford's Special Vehicle Team (SVT). The idea was to transform a production vehicle into – yes, that's right – a high-performance car. The effort sounds all the more preposterous when you remember that the vehicle in question is the most popular light-duty truck on the market.

As befits a self-respecting sports vehicle, the Lightning is powered by a muscular engine, a supercharged version of Ford's 5.4-liter Triton V8 engine, producing a whopping 380 horsepower and 450 lb-ft of torque. That said, the results of the first test-drive, in 2000, reveal a less than impressive acceleration (0-60 mph in 6.2 seconds). I must add that at the time, the engine only had 360 hp. With an extra 20 hp since last year and a shorter final drive ratio, the truck charges forward from 0-60 mph in 5.8 seconds. Curiously, despite such velocity, acceleration is very linear and you don't get the impression it actually goes that fast… at least until you get pulled over by a policeman for speeding.

Diversity

Straight-line acceleration is one thing, but changing direction with aplomb is another. The Lightning's rear suspension sits 2 inches (5 cm) lower than standard, a little less so in the front. Thanks to Bilstein monotube shocks and Goodyear P295/45ZR18 tires, the Lightning stays in good contact with the road.

The Lightning is not much of a "work truck," but just step on the accelerator

▲ PROS

• Robust engine • Good variety of models • Predictable road handling • Complete set of accessories • Comfortable cabin

▼ CONS

• Nondescript dashboard • High fuel consumption • High price • Harsh, unresponsive rear suspension • Large size

along a twisty road and it will make your hair stand on end. Despite a higher-than-average center of gravity, the tires and the modified suspension help this truck stick to the road like a sports car. Steering always feels a little vague, the seats lack lateral support and the rear suspension has a hard time handling bumps; still, driving it is quite an experience. It's the most powerful sports truck on the market, exceeding the power output of both the GMC Sierra C3 and the Dodge Dakota R/T by around 10 horsepower.

But seriously...

Admittedly, the Lightning is the result of an exercise in futility. But Ford's F-series consists mainly of practical models, such as the SuperDuty, generally reserved for construction professionals and owners of big trailers. Worth noting among this fleet is the F-150 SuperCrew – perfect for anyone looking for a truck capable of transporting mid-sized loads, but with a sedan-like cabin for four adults. The SuperCrew is not as versatile as the Chevrolet Avalanche, however, which boasts a collapsible cabin wall, making it easy to transport cumbersome objects without having to leave the tailgate open.

Despite all the above, the SuperCrew remains a viable choice. That is, if you don't mind its large dimensions – a handicap in city traffic – its big gas-guzzling V8 engine and its rather firm suspension. What's more, the solid rear axle, controlled by leaf springs, is no match for its rivals, who use a more sophisticated coil-sprung rear end. Naturally, the SuperCrew also comes in 4X4.

Also, keep in mind that the simplest standard cab model – also the most modestly equipped – sells more vehicles than any other member of the F-150 family. You can also order it with a 5-speed manual transmission, which is more fun to use. Like its owner, it's more often at work than at play.

Denis Duquet

SPECIFICATIONS	SVT LIGHTNING
Price	$CDN 22,730-34,125 / $US 17,810-34,910
Warranty	3 years / 36,000 miles (60,000 km)
Type	2-door light truck / rear wheel drive
Wheelbase / Length	120 in / 208 in
Width / Height	79 in / 71 in
Weight	4674 lb (2120 kg)
Trunk / Fuel tank	short box / 25 gallons
Air bags	front
Front suspension	independent
Rear suspension	rigid axle
Front brakes / Rear brakes	disc ABS
Traction control	no
Steering	recirculating balls; power assist
Turning circle	40 feet
Tires (front/rear)	P295/45ZR18

PERFORMANCE	
Engine	V8 4.6 liter
Transmission	4-speed automatic
Horsepower	380 hp at 4750 rpm
Torque	450 lb-ft at 3250 rpm
Other engines	V6 4.2 liter 202 hp; V8 4.6 liter 220 hp; V8 5.4 liter 260 hp
Other transmission	5-speed manual
Acceleration (0-60 mph)	8.1 sec
Maximum speed	142 mph (228 km/h)
Braking (60-0 mph)	130 feet (39.7 m)
Fuel consumption	14.6 mpg (15.5 L/100 km)

COMPETITION

- Dodge Ram R/T • GMC Sierra Denali

NEW FOR 2002

- New accessory package
- Fuel-cap warning indicator

RATING	(out of 5 stars)
Driveability	★★★★
Comfort	★★★
Reliability	★★★★
Roominess	★★★
Winter driving rating	★★
Safety	★★★★
Resale value	★★★★

AMG HUMMER

AMG **HUMMER**

The Best Is Yet to Come

Even though the US Army Humvees contributed to the Coalition victory over Iraq during the Gulf War, the AMG Hummer – from which the Humvees were derived – lost its own battle. Not only did AM General's contract with the US Army expire, but now the automaker's days are numbered. In the meantime, we have to endure the current Hummer model for a while longer, because its replacement models, designed exclusively for civilian use, are still in the works. That's the bad news.

Now on to the good news: the Hummer will be replaced by more civilized vehicles to be produced in collaboration with General Motors, which has acquired the rights to use the Hummer name around the world. But take it easy! There's no danger that GM will ruin the Hummer. The company certainly has its shortcomings, but it can't possibly produce anything more mechanically primitive or unreliable than the existing Hummer. GM's first order of the day will be to assist AM General develop and produce two replacement models, the H1 and H2. Both will retain the old Hummer's off-road capabilities, but will be given a new, more attractive exterior, a refined cockpit, stronger powertrain and better overall reliability. The H1 will be the same size as the current model, while the H2's dimensions will be more sensible because it's based on the platform of the Chevrolet Silverado and GMC Sierra. In all probability, the H2 will also be offered as a sport-utility truck (SUT), along the lines of the Chevrolet Avalanche. Like the latter, the H2 SUT will be fitted with a cargo bed and a detachable cabin wall.

Poor soldiers!

Today's Hummer sells for more than $120,000 (US $ 90,000), but don't let that fool you into expecting a comfortable ride. Despite AMG's best efforts, results are decidedly disappointing. While this juggernaut is a tried and true all-terrain vehicle in the purest sense, it's also one of the most uncomfortable machines that has ever existed. Pity the poor soldiers who has to travel in the military version of the Hummer. Its austere, bare cabin actually looks scary.

Rough ride

Once again, we chose to test-drive the civilian version. The doorsill is so elevated that you have to lift up your leg quite high to reach over it. The driver's seat is of the bucket variety, ridiculously minuscule and

▲ PROS

- Sophisticated all-wheel drive • Robust frame
- Choice of models • Guaranteed impact
- Impressive potential

▼ CONS

- Hopeless maneuverability • Oversize vehicle • Primitive cockpit • Worrisome reliability

HUMMER **H2**

stuck between the B pillar and the huge center console that houses the driving shaft going to the rear wheels. To ensure maximum ground clearance, the powertrain is placed very high in the frame, seriously encroaching on the cabin space.

The center console is fabricated from a subpar, nondescript synthetic material and stands as high as the dashboard. And the designer of the dashboard must have been told to ignore ergonomics, because the various controls, display panels and assorted storage bins are scattered about in no clear order. Moreover, the instruments look as if they'd been borrowed from a school bus or a tractor. The transmission and transfer-case levers at least are both placed within easy reach of the driver, ditto the climate control, which is mounted to one side of the center console. Display panels are easy to read and the switches for fuel tank and tire-pressure gauge are sensibly located to the right of the steering wheel.

If it's intimacy you want in the Hummer, forget it. The four seats (including the driver's) are placed far apart, each pushed up against its respective door. And you might as well forget about admiring the landscape while driving, because visibility is limited, made worse by a vertical beam in the middle of the windshield.

It's unfortunate that the Hummer can't provide a panoramic view as it poops along, because it's incredibly slow. The big 6.5-liter turbodiesel V8 sorely needs extra horsepower to lug that 7169-lb mass with any semblance of speed. But its impressive torque comes in handy when off-roading. And it's precisely in this situation – where muddy trails replace the paved road – that the Hummer proudly displays its advantages: all-wheel drive as well as individually gear-driven wheels. With options such as low-range and individually inflatable/deflatable tires for better traction, this military-inspired vehicle can truly go anywhere, providing the track is wide enough and the driver knows what he's doing.

No doubt about it, the Hummer is an exceptional all-terrain vehicle in certain circumstances, but too often its dimensions and weight are more of a handicap than an asset.

Denis Duquet

HUMMER **H2**

SPECIFICATIONS

Price	$CDN 121,250 / $US 76,862-95,404
Warranty	3 years / 36,000 miles (60,000 km)
Type	Wagon / all wheel drive
Wheelbase / Length	130 in / 184.6 in
Width / Height	86.6 in / 75 in
Weight	7169 lb (3252 kg)
Trunk / Fuel tank	n.a. / 25 gal. + 17 gal. reserve
Air bags	no
Front suspension	independent
Rear suspension	independent
Front brakes / Rear brakes	disc ABS
Traction control	no
Steering	recirculating-balls, variable assist
Turning circle	27 feet
Tires (front/rear)	P37X12.50R16.5

PERFORMANCE

Engine	V8 turbodiesel 6.5 liter
Transmission	4-speed automatic
Horsepower	195 hp at 3400 rpm
Torque	430 lb-ft at 1800 rpm
Other engines	none
Other transmission	none
Acceleration (0-60 mph)	19.6 sec
Maximum speed	84 mph (135 km/h)
Braking (60-0 mph)	154 feet (47 m)
Fuel consumption	12.6 mpg (18 L/100 km)

COMPETITION

- None

NEW FOR 2002

No major change

RATING (out of 5 stars)

Driveability	★★
Comfort	★★
Reliability	★★
Roominess	★★
Winter driving rating	★★★★★
Safety	★★★★½
Resale value	★★★½

MAZDA B SERIES FORD RANGER

MAZDA **B4000**

Utility Twins

In the automotive world, it's not uncommon for two different models from two different manufacturers to share a similar platform in order to reduce costs and optimize production. Neither is it strange to find two different brands sharing the same model while slightly modifying its appearance and characteristics. The subject of our interest here involves an even more intimate relationship, as the Ranger pickup truck and the Mazda B Series are practically identical twins.

Which immediately prompts the burning question: Why should you choose one particular brand over another? Surveys commissioned by Mazda concluded that a majority of buyers refused to do business with a North-American car dealer. A question of perception, and perhaps memories of some unpleasant past experience drove these potential buyers to choose a Japanese make.

Considerations of reliability are not an issue here, as the Mazda truck shares the same mechanical components as the Ranger. Fortunately, this vehicle is also one of the most reliable on the market, and it has been for several years. On the other hand, Mazda has a definite advantage in terms of service.

Refinement and strength

But whatever manufacturer you select, you can't go wrong, as both have produced reliable, efficient and durable trucks. Even though they seem like twins on the mechanical side, there are some differences in terms of look. The Mazda version has a more elegant allure. A few modifications to the silhouette, the cab, the front grille with the Mazda badge and, more important, a more convivial interior, all contributc to greater charisma from the Mazda truck. Ford's color schemes seem to have been chosen by a retired funeral home director who also happened to be color-blind. Another point for Mazda.

Work and pleasure

Both at Ford and Mazda it's the king cab version that's the most popular. It usually comes equipped with almost all the accessory options in the catalog. You may even order an in-dash 6-CD changer, following the lead of many other luxury cars. Rear seating access is through access panels located on either side of the cab.

▲ PROS

• Excellent workmanship • 5-speed automatic gearbox • Solid construction • User friendly four-wheel drive controls • Well appointed cockpit

▼ CONS

• Climate control needs work • Stiff rear suspension • Thirsty V6 engine • Uncomfortable rear half-seats

You first have to open the door before opening the rear panel. Although called rear seating, the space behind the bucket seats is usually used as storage space with two swing seats used as (very) temporary accommodation.

The 4.0-liter overhead cam V6, first introduced on this vehicle last year, produces 205 hp and it's a definite improvement over the 4.0-liter overhead valve V6 it replaced, which was not only less powerful, but was also known to vibrate rather unpleasantly through some engine speeds. The 3.0-liter V6 is a compromise solution, favored only by those who want a V6 and don't have too much to carry. The new 4-cylinder engine introduced last year is an interesting choice and provides good gas mileage when coupled with a 5-speed manual gearbox.

Despite their luxurious accessories, trucks serve a practical purpose and their relatively firm suspension does not always take kindly to bumpy roads. The rear axle has a tendency to hop and if you don't want to slide off your seat, you will have to hang on to something. Otherwise, the body and chassis are solid. Roadholding is predictable on a good surface, however it deteriorates at the same rate as the quality of the road surface.

The Ranger does manage a different look than the Mazda. Moreover the Edge model is a Ford exclusive, aimed at a younger clientele. Unfortunately, like most of the new Ford products, with the exception of the Thunderbird, Ford stylists seem to be stuck in a very conservative rut. A little more aggressiveness might just be the ticket. But it's difficult to argue with success, as the Ranger is still the most popular model in its class.

Despite everything, these trucks manage to fulfill various personal transportation needs as well as an above average carrying capacity; all this in a machine that has gained in sophistication and reliability over the years.

Denis Duquet

SPECIFICATIONS	**B4000**
Price	$CDN 15,995-25,590 / $US 12,595-24,695
Warranty	3 years / 36,000 miles (60,000 km)
Type	compact pickup truck / 4X4
Wheelbase / Length	130 in / 201.6 in
Width / Height	69.3 in / 64.6 in
Weight	3572 lb (1620 kg)
Trunk / Fuel tank	37.3 cu. ft / 20 gallons
Air bags	front
Front suspension	independent
Rear suspension	rigid axle
Front brakes / Rear brakes	disc ABS / drum ABS
Traction control	no
Steering	rack-and-pinion, power assist
Turning circle	40 feet
Tires (front/rear)	P225/70R15

PERFORMANCE	
Engine	V6 4.0-liter
Transmission	5-speed automatic
Horsepower	210 hp at 5250 rpm
Torque	240 lb-ft at 3250 rpm
Other engines	V6 3.0-liter 150 hp; 4L 2.3-liter 134 hp
Other transmission	5-speed manual; 4-speed automatic
Acceleration (0-60 mph)	10.5 sec
Maximum speed	110 mph (175 km/h)
Braking (60-0 mph)	141 feet (43 m)
Fuel consumption	16.3 mpg (13.9 L/100 km)

COMPETITION

• Chevrolet S-10 • GMC Sonoma • Ford Ranger • Toyota Tacoma • Nissan Frontier • Dodge Dakota

NEW FOR 2002

No major change

RATING	**(out of 5 stars)**
Driveability	★★★
Comfort	★★★
Reliability	★★★★
Roominess	★★★
Winter driving rating	★★
Safety	★★★
Resale value	★★★★

FORD **RANGER**

NISSAN FRONTIER

NISSAN **FRONTIER**

Step by Step

Nissan must get a kick out of developing its Frontier pickup truck one step at a time. After the number-two Japanese automaker spent what seemed like an eternity revamping its legendary Hardbody model, the Frontier model was finally unveiled in 1998.

And even then, the quasi retro-styled Frontier started its official career with a meager 124-hp 4-cylinder engine. Despite Nissan's numerous explanations for the delayed development of the Frontier's V6, the general assumption heard around the automotive industry was simply that the company was suffering from a lack of funds to develop the new engine.

As Nissan's fortunes improved, thanks to a merger with Renault in 1999, engineers hastened to make the Frontier as competitive as possible. One concrete step forward was achieved when the multi-seat cabin version was unveiled in 1999, a first for this category. Unfortunately, the exterior of this new version looked as if it belonged in another era and the dashboard was horrid. What's more, the much anticipated 3.3-liter V6 engine didn't live up to expectations, producing too little horsepower even to compete with other models on the market, let alone pose a real threat. The engine was also rough and noisy, and got steadily noisier as you went up the rev range.

Last year, the body was extensively revised, particularly the front end. A new grille now sat prettily above an imposing bumper, incorporating an air scoop in the center and flanked by clear-lens fog lamps. There was also a roof rack, similar to that used on the Nissan Xterra, which conferred an aggressive and modern look on the truck. The interior looked just as dramatic with a stylish center module. But on closer inspection, you'll discover that the changes are minor at best, amounting to little more than a new color for the plastic materials, newly designed control buttons and a number of black-on-white display dials. Still, the overall visual effect represented more than the sum of all the changes.

Piece meal

Last but not least was the inclusion of an Eaton compressor in the 3.3-liter V6 atmospheric engine, increasing horsepower to 210, a tacit admission that the engine lacked power in its original, atmospheric version. Once again, Nissan engineers had

▲ PROS

• Excellent finish • 4-door cab • Guaranteed reliability • High-quality material • Wide choice of bodies

▼ CONS

• Barely adequate handling • Obsolete chassis • Regular cab too small • Rough V6 engine • Suspension needs work

favored torque and reliability over power and driving pleasure, much to the chagrin of those many buyers who use the Frontier essentially as a touring vehicle. While the increased engine power was enthusiastically welcomed, the whistling sound that pervaded the cabin as you accelerated was downright annoying.

Dakota's equal?

For 2002, Nissan introduced a 4-door extended cab version, by 18 inches (46 cm). The model's overall length is now 211 inches (536 cm), 8.2 inches longer than the Dodge Dakota. Still, you shouldn't overload the Frontier's cargo bed, in case the engine runs "out of steam." The Dakota with an even longer cargo bed (by a couple of inches) is better suited to towing heavy cargo, because it can be fitted with a choice of two V8 engines, capable of developing 230 hp and 250 hp respectively. Even though its frame was reinforced to compensate for the extended wheelbase (by 15 inches), I can't help wondering whether the Frontier's overall sturdiness will be affected by the extended cab. After all, it was initially developed as a compact pickup truck, rather than a midsize variety.

Be that as it may, the Frontier's new dimensions add to its versatility. It has certainly come a long way from its debut as an economical alternative pickup truck, available in countless versions. Over the years, Nissan has come to imitate other automakers.

Despite all these transformations, the Frontier is still handicapped by a suspension system that allows too much sideways skipping by the wheels and needs to be revised and much improved. More work, please.

Denis Duquet

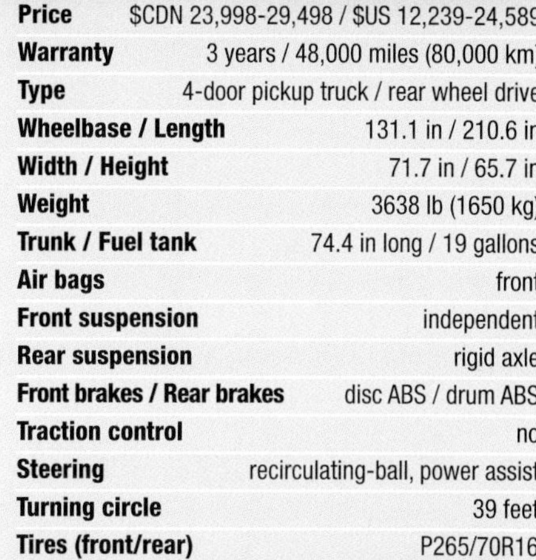

SPECIFICATIONS	
Price	$CDN 23,998-29,498 / $US 12,239-24,589
Warranty	3 years / 48,000 miles (80,000 km)
Type	4-door pickup truck / rear wheel drive
Wheelbase / Length	131.1 in / 210.6 in
Width / Height	71.7 in / 65.7 in
Weight	3638 lb (1650 kg)
Trunk / Fuel tank	74.4 in long / 19 gallons
Air bags	front
Front suspension	independent
Rear suspension	rigid axle
Front brakes / Rear brakes	disc ABS / drum ABS
Traction control	no
Steering	recirculating-ball, power assist
Turning circle	39 feet
Tires (front/rear)	P265/70R16

PERFORMANCE	
Engine	V6 3.3-liter
Transmission	5-speed manual
Horsepower	170 hp at 4800 rpm
Torque	200 lb-ft at 2800 rpm
Other engines	V6 3.3-liter turbocharged 210 hp; 4L 2.4-liter 143 hp
Other transmission	4-speed automatic
Acceleration (0-60 mph)	11.2 s (V6 170 hp); 10.2 s (V6 210 hp)
Maximum speed	109 mph (175 km/h)
Braking (60-0 mph)	134 feet (41.3 m)
Fuel consumption	16.4 mpg (13.8 L/100 km)

COMPETITION

• Chevrolet S-10/GMC Sonoma • Ford Ranger • Mazda B-Series • Toyota Tacoma

NEW FOR 2002

• Emergency brake pedal • Multi-seat cabin (extended) • New dashboard

RATING	(out of 5 stars)
Driveability	★★★½
Comfort	★★★½
Reliability	★★★★½
Roominess	★★★½
Winter driving rating	★★★
Safety	★★★½
Resale value	★★★

TOYOTA TACOMA

TOYOTA **TACOMA**

Fashion Rules

Toyota vehicles generally have a subdued and sober look, a fact of life that has garnered the automaker the reputation of being a bastion of conservatism. And yet, there's nothing remotely conservative about Toyota's technical know-how, or the sheer variety of its products. The Tacoma pickup truck reflects the company's efforts to keep up with current trends.

Toyota pickup trucks are popular in the United States, especially on the West Coast. In a region where buyers tend to keep their vehicles for as long as possible, the durability and reliability of Toyota trucks – not to mention their up-to-date styling and concept – are major assets. The four-door Tacoma Xtracab has proved to be so popular that Toyota decided to develop a companion truck – the four-door Doublecab, Nissan Frontier-style. The Regular Cab model, on the other hand, is no longer available in Canada – again, a decision dictated by market considerations.

Like its rival, the Nissan Frontier, the Tacoma benefited from a number of styling revisions last year. Ignoring the current trend for bodywork characterized by flat lines and shapes, Toyota stylists opted instead for horizontally sculpted body panels combined with enlarged wheel wells. The result confers an overall aggressive, off-road look. The front "whale-smile" fascia, on the other hand, appears more like a caricature than a serious design gesture. And let's not spend too much time lingering over the cabin. It is impeccably finished, although the general presentation is on the dull side.

What they want

I remember a survey that was conducted some time ago among American high-school students. Almost unanimously, they revealed that the vehicle of their dreams was a Toyota 4X4 pickup truck. Although there hasn't been a similar survey taken recently, no one can convince me that the 2002 Tacoma Double Cab and its 190-hp 3.4-liter V6 engine won't constitute another dream vehicle for those youngsters. Realizing that most buyers who opt for four-wheel drive do so more on account of a vehicle's looks rather than for its practical vocation, Toyota came up with the idea for the Pre Runner model. It has a suspension

Sturdy as ever

▲ PROS

- Choice of models • Comfortable seats
- Guaranteed reliability • Modern design
- Quality build

▼ CONS

- Extra-firm suspension • High sticker price
- 2.4-liter engine • Vague steering

system similar to that used in 4X4 models, but the Pre Runner is in fact a rear-wheel drive vehicle. Does that sound illogical? You bet, but that's what the buyers want. So I rest my case.

But let's get back to our Doublecab model. Although the rear seats are narrower than the Toyota Tundra's, they're more comfortable, offering adequate leg- and headroom. The front seats are just as comfortable, but they're on the low side and so the driving position suffers as a result. And don't imagine for a moment that the Xtracab model will allow you to transport passengers on its tiny foldable seats. Because you'll be sorely disappointed. Like all other extended-cab pickup trucks, the Tacoma's rear cabin is better suited to baggage than human beings.

Of the two engines offered with the four-wheel drive model – the 150-hp 2.7-liter inline 4 and the 190-hp 3.4-liter V6 – the latter is clearly your best bet. It's both ultra-smooth and Toyota-durable. I can't say the same thing about the "lazy," hesitant automatic transmission. The 4X2 model comes with a 2.4-liter four-cylinder engine developing 142 hp. But it's not worth your while, in my opinion, being both anemic and noisy.

Sturdy, well assembled, and available in multiple models, this Toyota pickup disappoints in the handling column. The super-firm suspension can hardly take care of road irregularities while road-holding in general is barely acceptable. Still, Toyota reliability and durability, as well as the vehicle's excellent resale value should compensate for these shortcomings.

Denis Duquet

SPECIFICATIONS

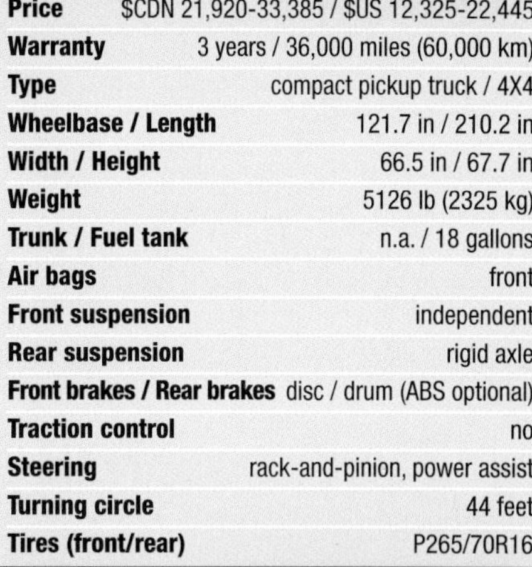

Price	$CDN 21,920-33,385 / $US 12,325-22,445
Warranty	3 years / 36,000 miles (60,000 km)
Type	compact pickup truck / 4X4
Wheelbase / Length	121.7 in / 210.2 in
Width / Height	66.5 in / 67.7 in
Weight	5126 lb (2325 kg)
Trunk / Fuel tank	n.a. / 18 gallons
Air bags	front
Front suspension	independent
Rear suspension	rigid axle
Front brakes / Rear brakes	disc / drum (ABS optional)
Traction control	no
Steering	rack-and-pinion, power assist
Turning circle	44 feet
Tires (front/rear)	P265/70R16

PERFORMANCE

Engine	V6 3.4-liter
Transmission	4-speed automatic
Horsepower	190 hp at 4800 rpm
Torque	220 lb-ft at 3600 rpm
Other engines	4L 2.7-liter 150 hp ; 4L 2.4-liter 142 hp (4X2)
Other transmission	5-speed manual
Acceleration (0-60 mph)	11.2 sec
Maximum speed	103 mph (165 km/h)
Braking (60-0 mph)	150 feet (45.6 m)
Fuel consumption	16.7 mpg (13.6 L/100 km)

COMPETITION

• Chevrolet S-10 • Ford Ranger • Mazda B Series • Nissan Frontier

NEW FOR 2002

No major change

RATING (out of 5 stars)

Driveability	★★★
Comfort	★★★½
Reliability	★★★★★
Roominess	★★★★
Winter driving rating	★★★½
Safety	★★★½
Resale value	★★★★

TOYOTA TUNDRA

TOYOTA **TUNDRA**

Almost full-size

Failure, as the saying goes, is part of learning, and Toyota has certainly learned its lessons from the T100 fiasco. Anxious to enter the North American full-size pickup truck market, the premier Japanese automaker came up with the "half-man, half-beast" T100. The creature fell short of the company's expectations, to put it as politely as possible.

It's now up to the bigger and more powerful Tundra to remedy the situation. Even in this case, Toyota engineers can hardly be accused of succumbing to North America's prevailing "bigger is better" mentality. Next to the Chevrolet Silverado, Dodge Ram and Ford F-150, Toyota's "big" Tundra looks decidedly puny. Narrower and lower, it "feels" rather like a Dodge Dakota, which is ranked a notch below the so-called Detroit trio.

And that's precisely why the Tundra should appeal to all those buyers for whom bigger is not necessarily better, or to the folks who swear only by Toyota's legendary reliability, to say nothing of its vehicles' renowned longevity. On the other hand, it's not a good idea to take the whole family on long, leisurely trips, lest you alienate the rear passengers of your 4-door Access-cab Tundra forever. Not only is the rear bench the most uncomfortable in the entire industry, but it's also tricky to get into.

By contrast, the front seats are comfortable and the driving position is absolutely irreproachable. The dashboard, on the other hand, could have been more appealingly designed – Toyota designers have certainly demonstrated their creativity in the past, namely with the Highlander and the RAV4. Now it seems as if they had deliberately adopted a sterile, no-nonsense look this time around, no doubt in keeping with the Tundra's practical nature.

Smooth as silk

If you were to put a blindfolded passenger in different pickup trucks and then conduct a comparison test on bad roads, the Tundra would probably win hands down. Not only does the rear suspension seamlessly soak up all the bumps and potholes, but the Toyota pickup is eerily quiet and its muscular 4.7-liter V8 DOHC engine with 245 horsepower proves to be

▲ PROS

- Comfortable suspension • Guaranteed reliability
- Impressive sound insulation • Reasonable dimensions • Super-quiet V8 engine

▼ CONS

- Brakes need work • Narrow cabin
- Nondescript silhouette
- Uncomfortable rear seats

smoothness incarnate – frankly, the best in its category.

Still, things aren't all that rosy in the Tundra kingdom. The truck is actually saddled with a number of flaws that may discourage at least some buyers. It's fine for everyday driving, but if you should change lanes abruptly or make any similar emergency maneuver, the Tundra will lean over dramatically and exhibit severe understeer. Even the brakes, while effective enough under normal circumstances, don't exactly deliver the goods in an emergency setting. The rear disc brakes certainly help, but things can get pretty hairy.

The Tundra's fuel economy is a tad higher than the Chevrolet Silverado, even though the latter is powered by a 5.3-liter V8 engine which gives it an extra 40 horsepower. Of course, a 3.4-liter 190-hp V6 is also available, and might be just the ticket if all you need to do is haul your groceries back home and maybe the occasional cumbersome but lightweight item. For heavier-duty tasks, though, stick with the V8. And to economize on gas, you may want to opt for the 5-speed manual transmission.

All in all, the Tundra has a lot going for it. It's superbly assembled – as are all Toyotas – quiet, comfortable, and handles respectably in city traffic. It's an excellent choice for buyers who don't necessarily depend on their pickup to make a living. The only drawback here is that, unlike its Detroit rivals, Toyota's biggest pickup truck doesn't come with a wide range of styles, engines and other such permutations.

Denis Duquet

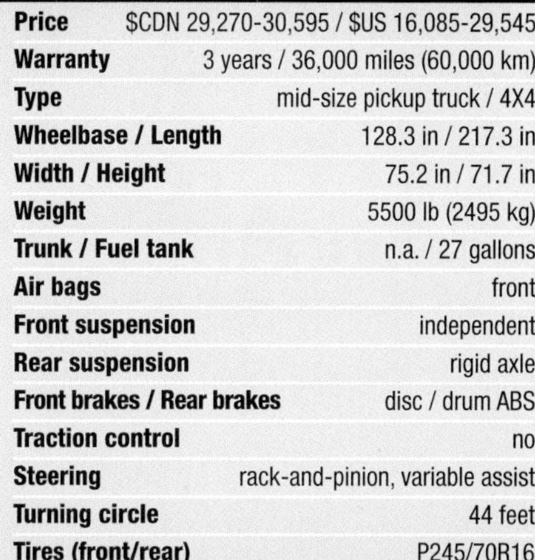

SPECIFICATIONS	
Price	$CDN 29,270-30,595 / $US 16,085-29,545
Warranty	3 years / 36,000 miles (60,000 km)
Type	mid-size pickup truck / 4X4
Wheelbase / Length	128.3 in / 217.3 in
Width / Height	75.2 in / 71.7 in
Weight	5500 lb (2495 kg)
Trunk / Fuel tank	n.a. / 27 gallons
Air bags	front
Front suspension	independent
Rear suspension	rigid axle
Front brakes / Rear brakes	disc / drum ABS
Traction control	no
Steering	rack-and-pinion, variable assist
Turning circle	44 feet
Tires (front/rear)	P245/70R16

PERFORMANCE	
Engine	V8 4.7 liter
Transmission	4-speed automatic
Horsepower	245 hp at 4600 rpm
Torque	320 lb-ft at 3400 rpm
Other engines	V6 3.4-liter 190 hp
Other transmission	5-speed manual
Acceleration (0-60 mph)	10.9 sec
Maximum speed	109 mph (175 km/h)
Braking (60-0 mph)	132 feet (40.3 m)
Fuel consumption	20.4 mpg (11.9 L/100 km)

COMPETITION

- Chevrolet Silverado / GMC Sierra • Dodge Dakota
- Dodge Ram • Ford F-150

NEW FOR 2002

- No major change

RATING	(out of 5 stars)
Driveability	★★★½
Comfort	★★★★½
Reliability	★★★½
Roominess	★★★
Winter driving rating	★★★★
Safety	★★★½
Resale value	★★★½

0
20
40
60
80
100
120
140
160
180
200
220
240
260
280
02002

Exotic Sports Cars

- ACURA
- ASTON MARTIN
- BMW
- FERRARI
- LAMBORGHINI
- MASERATI
- MERCEDES-BENZ
- PORSCHE

ACURA NSX-T

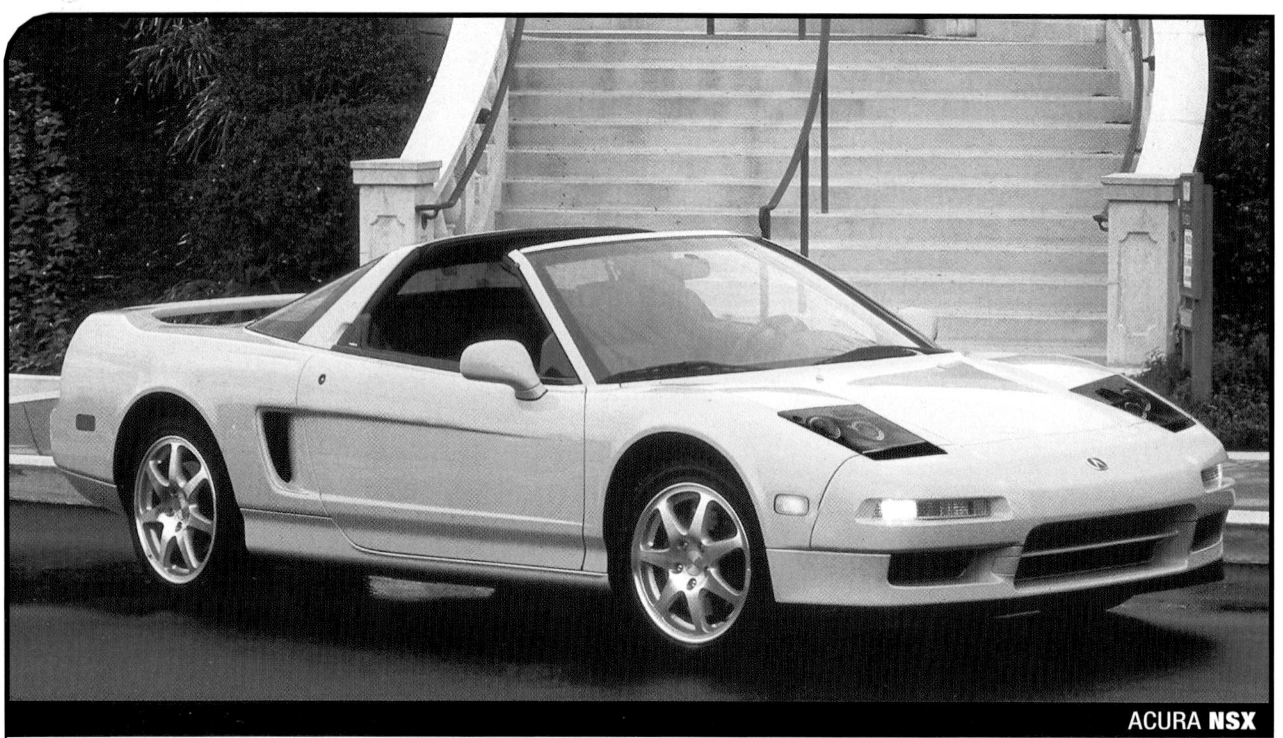

ACURA **NSX**

Waiting Impatiently

By now everyone will have read or heard about the new engine that at least in principle the Acura NSX should get. A V8 was first mentioned, then a V10 or V12. Later, there was talk of a power increase for the current V6. The most persistent rumor, however, involved the "future" V8 that will eventually grace the Acura RL. Then that, too, fell through when it was announced the 2002 Acura RL would retain its 6-cylinder engine. Like the RL, the 2002 NSX-T remains unchanged, pending a redesign, scheduled for 2003 or 2004... according to the latest buzz.

This sort of speculation also says something about the car buffs' impatience with the apparently sluggish evolution of this supercar. The NSX was the first car ever sold in North America (1991) with a variable cam profile (VTEC) engine. If that doesn't impress you, how about the fact that the NSX was the first production car anywhere to be made almost entirely of aluminum, and that a gentleman called Ayrton Senna – who knew perhaps only too well how to extract the best out of its frame – contributed to its development. Any one other than Senna would have demanded more power.

Super powertrain

Unanimously praised by the technical press corps when it first arrived on the scene – and for good reason – the NSX has always enjoyed a delightfully just-right feel, in a category where cars are most often touted for sheer engine power rather than overall balance. Its 3.2-liter 290-hp V6 engine with titanium connecting rods catapults you from 0-60 mph in just over 5 seconds, and will make your hair stand on end when it hits 8000 rpm. In addition to variable valve profile and timing, the engine features a variable-volume induction system as well as six ignition coils. This superb powertrain is paired to a perfectly spaced 6-speed manual transmission, a model of smoothness and precision if I ever saw one. A sequential-type 4-speed automatic gearbox is also available, but only with the old 3.0-liter engine that develops 252 hp. And when you realize that the Acura 3.2 TL S-Type sedan provides 260 hp, it makes you wonder what that extra $100,000 is for.

Aficionados on hold

▲ PROS

• Exemplary handling • High-level performance (manual) • Quality of assembly and build • Sturdy drivetrain • User-friendly

▼ CONS

• Austere interior • Dated exterior • High price • Performance/price ratio • Poor engine power (automatic)

Refined, but aging

The car's centrally mounted engine results in an excellent front/rear weight balance (42/58) which in turns favors high-speed handling. In this regard, the NSX is further aided by a sport-tuned all-aluminum independent suspension. But that doesn't necessarily mean that comfort has been sacrificed in the process. Slipping into the NSX's cockpit is as free and easy as getting behind the wheel of an Accord. The electrically power-assisted steering is highly responsive, as are the brakes with four-channel ABS, delivering excellent stopping distances. When pushed, the NSX is user-friendly, proving to be more forgiving of your mistakes than other fast-and-furious supercars. Some purists might find fault with its "civilized" manners, but I can't help but admire its remarkable mechanical resilience and the ease with which it lets you control it.

But – and this is entirely subjective – I must admit I find its silhouette a little antiquated. The interior, too, looks boring. But the NSX redeems itself with the Targa top (which unfortunately reduces chassis stiffness), with its calmly sensible ergonomics, and the luxury accessories such as leather seats, automatic climate control and Bose audio system – the least Acura can provide for a car in this high price range.

And here we put a finger on one of the factors that may be responsible for the NSX's semi-commercial flop: its $141,000 sticker price. That's a substantial amount of money for a car that, unlike a Porsche or a Ferrari, has no inherited prestige. Furthermore, while Acura proceeds with changes at a snail's space (the last major refinements took place in 1997), the competition forges ahead much faster. Corvette models, for example, offer superior performance for less than half the price of an NSX. A new engine would have renewed interest for this sports car, but, if the current rumors are to be believed, NSX aficionados will have to wait a while longer – until the next redesign.

Jean-Georges Laliberté

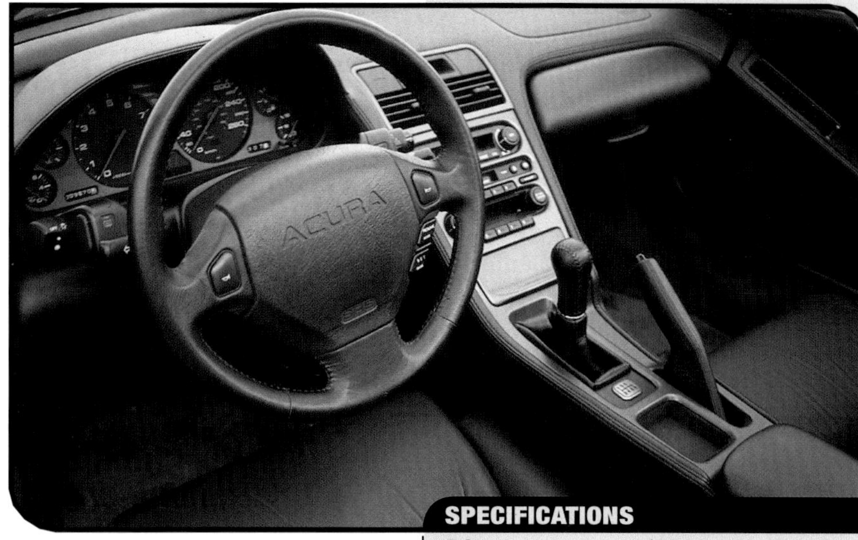

SPECIFICATIONS

Price	$CDN 141,000 / $US 88,845
Warranty	3 years / 36,000 miles (60,000 km)
Type	2-seat coupe / rear wheel drive, mid-engine
Wheelbase / Length	99.6 in / 174.2 in
Width / Height	71.3 in / 46.1 in
Weight	3164 lb (1435 kg)
Trunk / Fuel tank	5.4 cu.ft / 19 gallons
Air bags	front
Front suspension	independent, d. wishbone (alum.)
Rear suspension	independent, d. wishbone (alum.)
Front brakes / Rear brakes	disc ABS
Traction control	yes
Steering	rack-and-pinion, variable assist
Turning circle	38 feet
Tires (front/rear)	P215/45ZR16 / P245/40ZR17

PERFORMANCE

Engine	V6 3.2-liter 24-valve VTEC
Transmission	6-speed manual
Horsepower	290 hp at 7100 rpm
Torque	224 lb-ft at 5500 rpm
Other engines	V6 3.0-liter 252 hp
Other transmission	4-speed automatic (sequential)
Acceleration (0-60 mph)	5.2 sec
Maximum speed	171 mph (275 km/h)
Braking (60-0 mph)	118 feet (36 m)
Fuel consumption	17.2 mpg (13.2 L/100 km)

COMPETITION

• Chevrolet Corvette • Dodge Viper • Ferrari 360 Modena • Jaguar XKR • Porsche 911

NEW FOR 2002

No major change

RATING	**(out of 5 stars)**
Driveability	★★★★½
Comfort	★★★
Reliability	★★★★
Roominess	★★
Winter driving rating	★★
Safety	★★★
Resale value	★★★

ASTON MARTIN VANQUISH

ASTON MARTIN **VANQUISH**

Green Gold

Leading automobile designers will tell you that they have a soft spot for Aston Martin. And when asked to name their favorite model, they'll almost invariably point to the DB7. As a matter of fact, you'll be hard pressed to come up with anything more appealing although, with the advent of the BMW Z8, opinions are slightly more divided as to which is the world's finest supercar. Still, none of this seems to matter much, since it was none other than the DB7 – launched in 1997 – that single-handedly brought the prestigious British automaker back from the brink. What's more, Aston Martin now appears to be well on its way to profitability.

The last-chance DB7 was joined two years later by the DB7 Vantage, which quickly became the company's flagship vehicle. Powered by a superb V12 engine, the Vantage was literally Aston Martin's entry ticket back into the select supercar group which is now led by Ferrari. The dye is cast. It's a new beginning.

Next came the Vanquish, brimming with even grander ambitions – nothing less than a modern-day "British Gold Rush." Its role is not just to shatter the competition, but to surpass it. That's a tall order to be sure, but at the creative pace that Aston Martin proceeds, every aspiration – however far-fetched – is encouraged, and the sky's the limit.

Test bed

Now part of the Ford Motor Company, Aston Martin has become the American automaker's rolling test bed of cutting-edge technology destined for future productions. The Vanquish is the first model developed under Ford's tutelage, incorporating all the latest design and space-age construction techniques.

The best is yet to come

And that's precisely what it takes to convince the most famous of secret agents, James Bond, who had succumbed to BMW's charms in the recent years, to resume his derring-do behind the wheel of an Aston Martin. And not just any old model, mind you, but the Vanquish V12 itself. Lucky dog! As if squiring the most beautiful women in the world around weren't enough, he has to have the most exciting car, too.

Spontaneous performance

The Vanquish's V12 is an updated version of the DB7's engine – much lighter and pack-

▲ PROS

- Bewitching transmission • Exhilarating performance • Driving pleasure
- Dynamic silhouette

▼ CONS

- Bargain-basement controls • Inflated price • Steering wheel needs revision
- Weighty machine

ing even more horsepower. Paired to one of the finest sequential gearboxes anywhere, it displays its true colors at very low rpms indeed, which accounts for the car's responsive, not to say exhilarating, performance.

After all, Aston Martin engineers claim that practically 80% of the V12's maximum torque is available at 1500 rpm. So no dead sport, thank you, on upshifts – a sharp contrast with the Ferrari, whose 5.9-liter V12 engine favors high revs.

The Vanquish, on the other hand, is incisive and spontaneous – a genuine supercar, no doubt about it. Its drive-by-wire electronic accelerator responds to your slightest request and reactions are peppy without being brutal, despite the breath-taking 460 ponies under the hood. For the young and the restless, the Vanquish offers a Formula-One environment, in the shape of a semi-automatic gearbox and a red-engine starter button. Two F1-style paddles (up on the right, down on the left) are mounted behind the steering wheel to facilitate lightning-swift gear changes. If such controls sounded like simple gadgetry in the past, they're all true now, and wondrously effective.

Start the engine and an indescribable sound ensues, simply magical. On the road, the Vanquish feels firmer than its little sister, the DB7, and so much the better. Despite its significant weight – 4040 lbs (1835 kg) – the car is surprisingly agile on twisting roads. Its stiffer body and chassis is reassuring, tempting you to drive it to the limit.

Braking, also highly perfected, consists of Brembo ventilated disc brakes with ABS.

Other features include 19-inch alloy wheels and custom-developed Yokohama tires.

Diversified lineup

Aston Martin is well on its way to profitability, but it's not there yet, not by a long shot. The DB7 (Vantage/Vantage Volante) is just a beginning, a foundation on which much remains to be built. The company has already announced that a third car, more affordable this time, is currently on the drawing board. Targeting the Porsche 911 and Ferrari 360 Modena, the new Aston will take its cue from Jaguar, notably its V8 engine, which will be developed at Cosworth, another Ford entity.

Eclipsed today by Ferrari, the British firm has every intention of reclaiming its rightful place, at least for as long, and as far, as Ford allows it to go.

Louis Butcher

SPECIFICATIONS	
Price	$CDN 375,000 / $US 237,000
Warranty	3 years /36,000 miles (60,000 km)
Type	2-seat coupe or 2+2/rear wheel drive
Wheelbase / Length	105.9 in / 183.9 in
Width / Height	67.7 in / 44.9 in
Weight	4045 lb (1835 kg)
Trunk / Fuel tank	n.a. / 21 gallons
Air bags	front and side
Front suspension	independent
Rear suspension	independent
Front brakes / Rear brakes	disc
Traction control	yes
Steering	rack-and-pinion, power assist
Turning circle	42 feet
Tires (front/rear)	P255/40 ZR19 / P285/40ZR19

PERFORMANCE	
Engine	V12 6.0-liter 48 valve
Transmission	6-speed semi-automatic (sequential)
Horsepower	460 hp at 6500 rpm
Torque	400 lb-ft at 5000 rpm
Other engines	none
Other transmission	none
Acceleration (0-60 mph)	4.8 sec
Maximum speed	190 mph (305 km/h)
Braking (60-0 mph)	n.a.
Fuel consumption	10.8 mpg (21 L/100 km)

COMPETITION

- Ferrari 550 Maranello

NEW FOR 2002

- New model

RATING	(out of 5 stars)
Driveability	★★★★★
Comfort	★★★★
Reliability	★★★★★
Roominess	★★★½
Winter driving rating	★★½
Safety	★★★★
Resale value	★★★★★

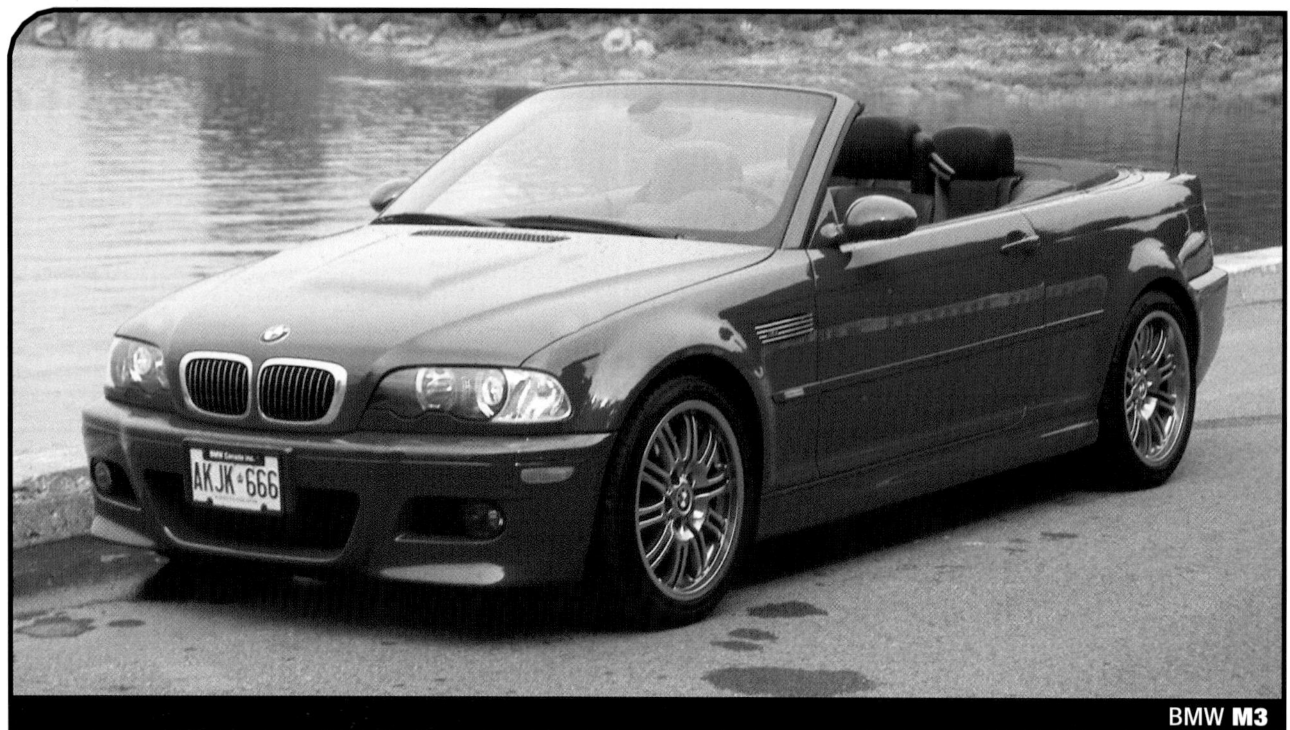

BMW **M3**

When Dream Meets Reality?

What a thrill, you'll say, to have the chance to drive two of the world's most desirable high-performance cars – BMW M3's convertible and coupe – back to back over two weeks. It was a dream assignment all right, except that the dream was severely disturbed by the harsh reality of chronically bad roads and speed limits – every conceivable obstacle was present to diminish the kind of performance this dynamic duo is capable of. That said, should we all succumb to the lure of the M3?

After a two-year absence from the BMW catalog, the M3 – the Motorsports version of the 3 Series – is back at the top of the Bavarian automaker's bread-and-butter lineup. More than ever before, the coupe and convertible stand out in a crowd of less ambitious 3 Series models.

Gorgeous decor

BMW's distinctive signature is all over the machine: the aluminum hood with its center bulge to accommodate the larger engine, front bumper incorporating a spoiler with large air intakes, four polished stainless-steel exhausts, side grilles to let warm air escape and, of course, the large low-profile tires gripping the 18-inch alloy wheels. The tricolor M3 emblems are everywhere – on the stylish aluminum doorsills, huge footrest, gear lever and speedometer. Even the steering wheel – which, incidentally, is thicker than the Coupe Ci 330's – is leather-wrapped in thread carrying the colors of BMW Motorsports!

Impressive specs

Capital M all the way!

No matter how stylish the exterior, however, it cannot overshadow BMW's achievements as the world's purveyor of ultra-high performance sports-car engines, and in this area, its F1 records speak volumes. BMW's expertise is incontestable, what with the kind of engines whose crankshafts can spin at 18,000 rpm, and with pistons mean speed of 80 feet (25 m) per second – just like the V10 powering Ralf Schumacher's and Juan Pablo Montoya's Williams

▲ PROS

- Exciting engine • Incredible road handling
- Super precise steering • Well-built convertible
- Complete standard equipment

▼ CONS

- Elongated gear lever track • Noisy differential
- Steep price • Uncomfortable on rough roads
- Unpleasant city driving

race cars – under its belt. If you need more proof, check out the 3.2-liter inline 6 powering the latest M3s. As always, BMW engineers favor atmospheric, high-rpm engines over turbocharged varieties to increase horsepower. Aside from its whopping 333 hp developed at 8000 rpm, the M3 engine gets individual butterfly valves for each of its six cylinders, infinitely variable-timing control on both intake and exhaust camshafts (VANOS), as well as an electronically controlled accelerator.

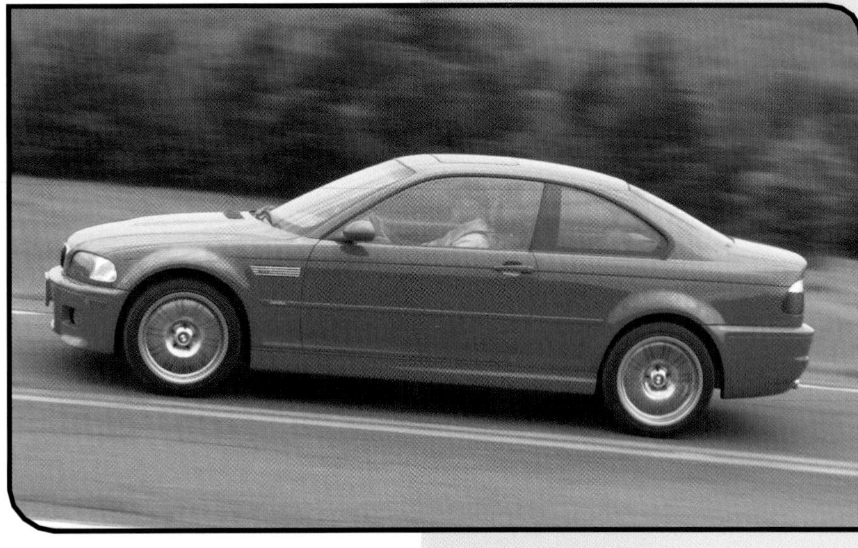

Power is managed exclusively by a 6-speed manual transmission, the only one available, assisted by an imposing array of electronic features, ranging from Variable M locking Differential to Dynamic Stability Control III (DSC). Finally, the M3 benefits from optimized components – lower unsprung weight, a wider track front and rear, and a quartet of oversized, ventilated disc brakes. In short, the stage is now set for an extraordinary driving experience.

Exceptional convertible

As far as high-performance cars are concerned, coupes generally do better than convertibles. In the M3's case, however, the convertible – though slightly handicapped by its extra 365 lbs – performed so splendidly that it came close to eclipsing the coupe. In fact, it was the best convertible I've ever driven. Its sound insulation was outstanding, even at speeds as high as 155 mph (250 km/h). You can drive over 75 mph (120 km/h) and carry on a normal conversation without raising your voice. With the soft top in place (the mechanism is disarmingly simple, involving the use of a mere button), wind noise is practically non-existent. What's more, even though you feel every bump and pothole in the road, they have no effect whatsoever on the body's rigidity. Like the coupe, the convertible is as solid as a bank

vault, and free from all extraneous noise, however faint, as well as from torsion-induced squeaks that are the lot of most high-performance cars.

Still smoking...

The engine is enormously impressive, thanks not only to its exceptional power-per-liter, but also by virtue of its unmistakable sports-car sound. Acceleration is swift if you use lots of wheelspin or let the traction control system do its thing. What's more, it won't cut out the engine completely, as often happens with other traction control systems. The convertible shot from 0-60 mph in 5.8 seconds, just three-tenths of a second behind the coupe – not exactly an impressive performance, but that's the fault of the gearbox, whose lever track is much too long for a sports car. Furthermore, in both M3 test models, excessive free play in the differential made city driving tricky, not to mention the annoying whining sound it produced. Adding insult to injury, the accelerator was hardly progressive, taking much away from driving pleasure.

Strong constitution

Roadholding, on the other hand, is fabulous. Both M3s seem ready to take on any supercar either on a tight, twisty race track. It's your choice! Handling is completely neutral, and, guided by super precise and quick steering, the BMWs negotiate curves as smoothly as a good Munich beer slips down your throat. No hint of under- or oversteering. Body roll? Never heard of it. Alas, their 18-inch tires, combined with a rather stiff suspension, are another story. You require a strong lower back to ride in these cars. It's so unpleasant that it takes away all the driving fun. At least the brakes – though criticized by the world press – will fare better in North America, where speed limits are much lower than in Europe.

A quick glance inside the car shows that the coupe is a genuine 4-seater, whereas the convertible offers pseudo-rear seats. The coupe's trunk, too, is more generous, although in the convertible, the space reserved for storing the soft top can double as cargo space. Included in both M3s are sport seats with optional adjustable seat back width, providing excellent lateral support, a tachometer with diodes to show engine temperature, and a speedometer indicating a top speed of 185 mph (300 km/h). It's a pity such prowess cannot be fully exploited in North America.

A winning combination

If the M3 feels a little too cramped for your taste, check out the BMW M5 – a 5-seat sport sedan based on the 5 Series model. It's as nimble on twisting roads as the M3, although it's more spacious and offers a smoother ride on rough surfaces. Powered by a robust 5.0-liter V8, with 400 hp and 368 lb-ft of torque, the M5 is arguably one of the most balanced high-performance cars in the world. It boasts all the technical sophistication you'll find in an M3, and a vast range of standard features. Come to think of it, the M5 really offers the best of both worlds: performance as spirited as the Z8 combined with the comfort of a great sedan – that's as close to a winning combination as ever existed.

Jacques Duval

SPECIFICATIONS

Price	$CDN 73,500-105,500 / $US 46,045-70,045
Warranty	4 years / 48,000 miles (80,000 km)
Type	4-seat coupe; convertible / rear wheel drive
Wheelbase / Length	107.5 in / 176.8 in
Width / Height	70.1 in./53.9 in.; 53.5in.
Weight	3415 lb (1549 kg); 3781 lb (1715 kg)
Trunk / Fuel tank	14.5 cu.ft; 9.2 cu.ft / 17 gallons
Air bags	front, side and head
Front suspension	independent
Rear suspension	independent
Front brakes / Rear brakes	vented disc ABS
Traction control	yes
Steering	rack-and-pinion, power assist
Turning circle	36 feet
Tires (front/rear)	P255/40ZR18

PERFORMANCE

Engine	6L 3.2-liter
Transmission	6-speed manual
Horsepower	333 hp at 7900 rpm
Torque	262 lb-ft at 4900 rpm
Other engines	none
Other transmission	none
Acceleration (0-60 mph)	5.5 sec; 5.8 sec (convert.)
Maximum speed	155 mph (250 km/h) (electronically limited)
Braking (60-0 mph)	124 feet (37.8 m)
Fuel consumption	18.6 mpg (12.2 L/100 km)

COMPETITION

• Audi S4 • Mercedes-Benz CLK55

NEW FOR 2002

• New model

RATING (out of 5 stars)

Driveability	★★★★
Comfort	★★½
Reliability	★★★★★
Roominess	★★★
Winter driving rating	★★½
Safety	★★★★
Resale value	★★★★½

BMW Z8

BMW **Z8**

The Ultimate Roadster

The BMW Z8, unlike even a Ferrari or a Porsche, is first and foremost a car for the connoisseur; in other words, much more than something you buy simply to impress your friends and neighbors. Launched last year, this limited-edition automobile is BMW's ultimate roadster – a jewel in the crown of a carmaker universally renowned for creating unsurpassed driving pleasure.

Rather than revisiting my own driving impressions, reported in last year's *Auto Guide*, I thought it might be more interesting to hear the comments of a car fanatic who has also fallen under the Z8's spell. I'm talking about Richard Petit, president of KébecSon – a Montreal-based hi-fi audio company – and the happy owner of a Z8. Indeed, who better to tell us about this fabulous roadster, which is regarded by many as an instant classic? In addition to his grey Z8, Petit also owns a Z1, BMW's first modern-era roadster, launched 13 years ago. Petit loves the finer things in life, which explains his attraction to the Z8.

But let's give the floor to Petit.

JD: What do you find most appealing about the Z8?

RP: Many things really. First of all, I've had my Z1 for 12 years, and it's never given me any problems, only satisfaction. I'm also impressed by the Z8's architecture and the quality of its construction. The mere fact that you can see the hood while you're driving is extremely gratifying, and that's a detail that other automakers often neglect in favor of aerodynamics. The Z8's interior is also very seductive, especially at night. Lighting is both ingenious and discreet. Brilliant, in fact. Details like these make this BMW irresistible, at least to me.

Just ask the driver

What Petit likes best

JD: Does the Z8 meet all your expectations?

RP: Absolutely, and then some. Engine power is phenomenal. You know, performance wasn't that high on my list of priorities when I decided to buy the Z8, but there's so much power, 400 horses, and it's hard to resist!

JD: What do you like about the Z8?

RP: First and foremost, its split personality. It's excellent both as a touring car and sports car. The body is also incredibly rigid for a convertible, which for me is a huge asset, because I hate rattles. What I find

▲ PROS

- Dazzling performance • Exceptional handling
- Exquisite design • Impressive comfort
- Superb engine

▼ CONS

- Astronomical price • Narrow trunk
- Plastic rear window • Wind noise

most extraordinary is the effort that BMW engineers have put into building something that's both an art object and also a car you can appreciate in any number of different ways. I've had a lot of dream cars in the past, Ferrari, Porsche, you name it – but none was ever this easy to drive. The first five minutes behind the wheel of the Z8 are probably less exhilarating than in a Ferrari, but I always feel better afterward. Finally, I like the Z8's understated look. It attracts far less attention than other cars of its ilk, and for me that's a big plus.

What Petit likes a little less

JD: If you had your druthers, what changes would you make? In other words, is there anything about the Z8 that you don't like?

RP: As you mentioned in last year's *Auto Guide*, I find the fact that there's no defogger for the rear window, and that the window itself is made of plastic, is unacceptable for a car of this class and price range. And since BMW is usually so "bang on" about its wheels, I'd suggest that the Z8 could use more stylized ones. That's about it. But all told, the Z8 is simply a fantastic car. It embodies the best of what has defined automobiles in the past, and some of the outstanding elements of what's yet to come.

Z8 revisited

A brief test drive of the BWM Z8 enabled me to relive the same sensations I felt last year when it was first unveiled. As always, the car proved to be unbelievably docile in city traffic, no matter how congested. And the minute the road was clear, its 5.0-liter V8 propelled it forward enthusiastically, taking less than 5 seconds to go from 0-60 mph, and a mere 16 seconds to reach 120 mph.

Braking is just as powerful. At 60 mph, it can stop dead in 2.5 seconds. Other electronic aids like traction control keep you under control in case you get carried away and decide to explore that extraordinary engine power to the full. If you deactivate the traction control feature, you'll find the driving pleasure going up another notch. But don't forget to turn it back on.

As I wrote last year, the BMW Z8 combines the raw power of a Dodge Viper with the good manners of a Porsche 911. It's an irresistible combination. Just ask Richard Petit.

Jacques Duval

SPECIFICATIONS

Price	$CDN 195,000 / $US 128,645
Warranty	4 years / 48,000 miles (80,000 km)
Type	2-seat roadster / rear wheel drive
Wheelbase / Length	114.2 in /173.4 in
Width / Height	72 in / 52 in
Weight	3494 lb (1585 kg)
Trunk / Fuel tank	7.2 cu. ft / 19 gallons
Air bags	front and side
Front suspension	independent
Rear suspension	independent
Front brakes / Rear brakes	disc ABS
Traction control	yes
Steering	rack-and-pinion, variable assist
Turning circle	39 feet
Tires (front/rear)	P245/45ZR18 / P275/40ZR18

PERFORMANCE

Engine	V8 5.0-liter
Transmission	6-speed manual
Horsepower	400 hp at 6600 rpm
Torque	369 lb-ft at 3800 rpm
Other engines	none
Other transmission	none
Acceleration (0-60 mph)	4.9 sec
Maximum speed	155mph (250 km/h)
Braking (60-0 mph)	123 feet (37.5 m)
Fuel consumption	15.6 mpg (14.5 L/100 km)

COMPETITION

• Aston Martin Volante • Ferrari 360 Modena Spyder • Porsche 911 Turbo

NEW FOR 2002

No major change

RATING (out of 5 stars)

Driveability	★★★★
Comfort	★★★★
Reliability	★★★★
Roominess	★★
Winter driving rating	★★★
Safety	★★★★
Resale value	★★★★★

FERRARI 456M GT

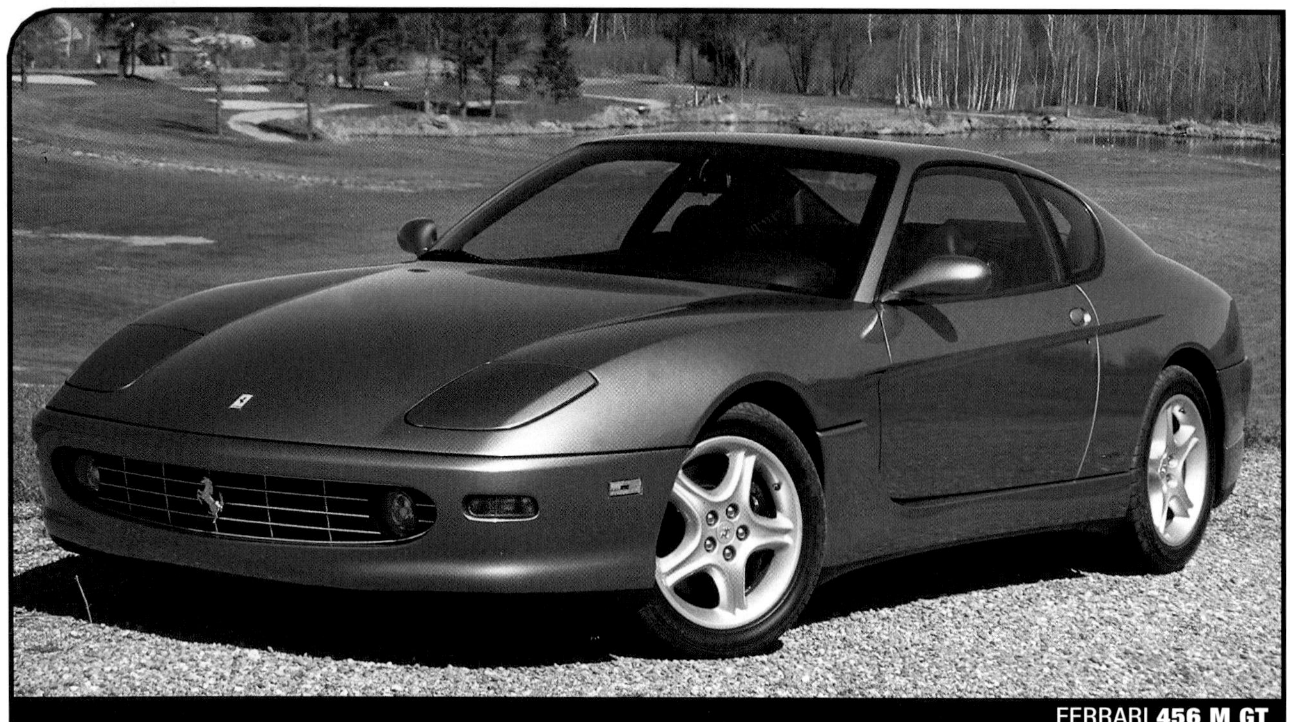

FERRARI 456 M GT

The Stuff of Champions

A small metal plate on the right-hand side of the dashboard reads "Campioni del mondo 2000," a reminder that I'm behind the wheel of an exceptional car. Of all the automakers on the planet, Ferrari alone can proudly display such an honor, because it's the only name in Formula 1 racing that manufactures every single part for its own race cars, from chassis to engine. It's safe to assume that sooner or later, such expertise will trickle down to the assembly line in Maranello, Italy, where thousands of Ferrari sports cars are manufactured each year and sold to a global elite at staggering prices.

Since there's only room at the top for one, and that spot is currently occupied by Michael Schumacher, the rest of us humble drivers will have to settle for second best – and that's the thrill of test-driving one of these missiles on four wheels. My test model was the priciest production Ferrari, the 456M GT, which some snobs describe as the most "bourgeois" of the Ferrari line. Certainly, it doesn't have the flashy looks of a 360 Modena or the explosive performance of a 550 Maranello – the other two models that are listed in the prestigious Italian firm's catalog. On the other hand, the late Enzo Ferrari founder of the Ferrari dynasty, would have agreed that of all the models, the 456M GT is the most faithful to the traditional Ferrari image, reminiscent of those Grand Touring cars endowed with a front V12 engine and a 2+2 body, preferably painted bright red. Mine (alas, for only a few exciting hours) was pewter, a color which enhances the car's classic look still further. The 456M GT is the least "selfish" of the three production Ferraris, boasting two rear seats, and it is the model that best lends itself to daily driving use.

Una bella machina

A vibrant 442 hp

Some people think wrongly I hasten to add, that Ferrari epitomizes the very finest in automobile manufactury, from every viewpoint. I'll admit that the marque is known mainly for its interesting mechanics and irresistible bodywork. It doesn't really matter that Ferrari's assembly-line standards are not as rigorous as those of a German carmaker, or that some of its components lack a degree of refinement. What's important for the Italian firm is engine power – the more the better – com-

▲ PROS

• Exceptional engine • Explosive performances • High-level handling • Easy to drive

▼ CONS

• Stiff stickshift • Ergonomics need work • Prohibitive price • Firm commands • No spare tire

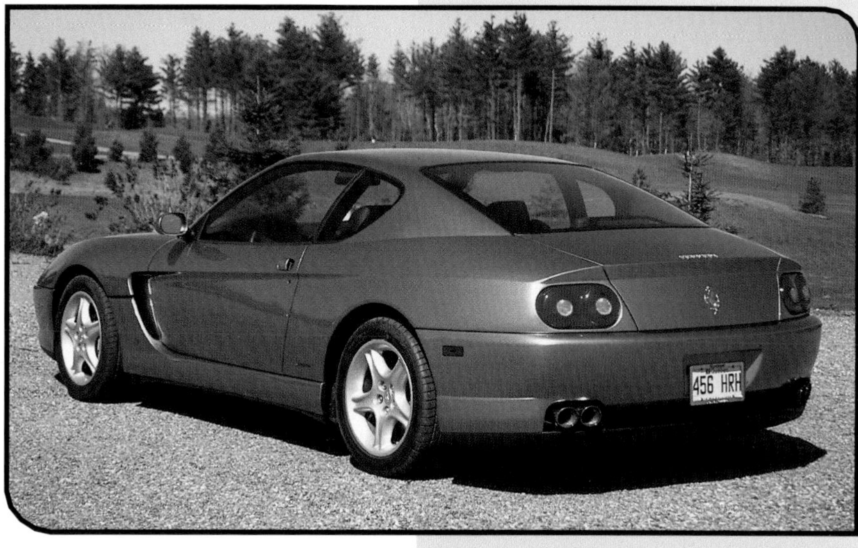

bined with that distinctive, exquisite sonority, and a sleek designer body. The 456M, like most Ferraris, was styled by the prestigious Pininfarina studio. Its 5.5-liter 4-overhead-cam engine with 48 valves produces a vibrant 442 horsepower.

Most 456Ms are fitted with automatic transmission which explains the model's "civilized manners." My test car was a nice exception to the rule, sporting a 6-speed manual gearbox. The stickshift, topped with a brushed-aluminum knob, confers a distinguished air to the otherwise banal interior, except for the aforementioned metal plate and a speedometer showing a maximum speed of 210 mph (340 km/h).

Staggering price

With a $351,000 price tag (US $ 225,000), it's natural to feel nervous taking the car out for a spin, for fear some idiot will bump into you on your first sortie. But once you've overcome that sense of apprehension, you'll be amazed how docile the beast actually is.

While you fully expect a Ferrari to be the epitome of a purebred species – stubborn and difficult to tame – the road models do "calm down" after a while. The "concrete-like" clutch will soften, the engine will become less sharp and the steering wheel less "agitated." And soon, your fear of engine stall will fade away. The only aspect that will never change is the distinctively ferocious Ferrari sound.

But this sort of "civility" doesn't guarantee smoothness. Even though the car is amazingly easy to drive, the manual transmission requires a certain deftness to handle properly. The stickshift is firm, so make sure you manipulate it with precision through the notches within the little metal grid that acts as a guide. Make a slight error and you'll be treated to some harsh grinding noises.

The engine is remarkably adaptive, enabling you to cruise at low speeds without having to worry about the rpms. Whether the needle hovers at 1000 or 7000 rpm, the V12 has no trouble adjusting. In 2nd gear, the car leaps past 60 mph in roughly 5 seconds. If you were in Germany, you could just keep going like that until you reach top speed, to see how the speed-sensitive spoiler, integrated in the rear bumper, will adjust itself. I amused myself by tailgating a

FERRARI **456 M GT**

powerful motocycle whose incredulous rider couldn't help looking back to see what kind of car could stick to him like that.

From racetrack to road

Despite its fairly large size (roughly the same as the 5-Series BMW) and a couple of extra pounds that its all-aluminum body and carbon-fiber hood couldn't quite shed, the biggest of the Ferraris is so nimble it feels more compact than it really is – maybe it's the slim and quasi-invisible nose that gives off that impression. But one thing is certain, the 456M is not as intimidating as I had thought.

Having driven it at high speeds on Ferrari's private circuit at Fiorano, I can say that the 456's rather neutral road behavior exhibits excellent front/rear weight distribution balance, thanks in partly to the fact that the gearbox is mounted on the rear axle. And after test-driving the car over bumpy roads, I can report that its level of comfort is more than adequate, probably superior to that of the Porsche 911. The only discomfort I felt as I hit one pothole after another stemmed from my anger at having to subject this gem of a car to such appalling road conditions. If you have the good fortune to drive a Ferrari, I hope you'll have the good sense to choose better roads.

Wake-up call

If we must judge the measure of a Ferrari by the quality of its finish and interior, then it won't get very high marks. Unlike most luxury cars, the 456M GT doesn't really attach a great deal of importance to the level of sophistication or the number of extra accessories. But at least the car has superb English-leather seats that provide an excellent driving position, in addition to a well-appointed, driver-oriented instrument panel. One of the things I like most in a Ferrari is its Fiam compressed-air horn, an ever-present feature since time immemorial. Its clear and vibrant sound is just the perfect thing to "wake

■ STANDARD EQUIPMENT

- Climate control • Power seats
- Radio with CD • Power windows and mirrors

■ OPTIONAL EQUIPMENT

- Automatic transmission • Ferrari badges
- Color brake calipers

up" Sunday drivers on the road.

The rather snug rear seats must have been made to alleviate the driver's guilt feelings for not taking his kids out for a Ferrari ride from time to time. The trunk is large enough to store two golf bags – today's standard test for this type of car.

The 456M is, first and foremost, a Grand-Touring car – superbly bodied and endowed with mechanics based on the technology and experience that Ferrari has accumulated during its 50 years of building race cars, winning nine F1 world titles in the process. Ferrari remains the only F1 marque to build its cars from start to finish, an aspect the company deservedly brags about when launching its road models.

Jacques Duval

SPECIFICATIONS

Price	$CDN 351,000 / $US 225,000
Warranty	2 years / unlimited mileage
Type	coupe 2+2 / rear wheel drive
Wheelbase / Length	102 in / 187.5 in
Width / Height	76 in / 51 in
Weight	3726 lb (1690 kg)
Trunk / Fuel tank	n.a. / 29 gallons
Air bags	front and side
Front suspension	independent
Rear suspension	independent
Front brakes / Rear brakes	vented disc, ABS
Traction control	yes
Steering	rack-and-pinion, power assist
Turning circle	n.a.
Tires (front/rear)	P255/45ZR17; P285/40ZR17

PERFORMANCE

Engine	V12 5.5 liter
Transmission	6-speed manual
Horsepower	442 hp at 6250 rpm
Torque	398 lb-ft at 4500 rpm
Other engines	none
Other transmission	4-speed automatic
Acceleration (0-60 mph)	5.2 sec
Maximum speed	186 mph (300 km/h)
Braking (60-0 mph)	n.a.
Fuel consumption	12 mpg (18L/100 km)

COMPETITION

- Aston Martin Vanquish • BMW Z8
- Porsche 911 Turbo

NEW FOR 2002

No major change

RATING (out of 5 stars)

Driveability	★★★★½
Comfort	★★★½
Reliability	★★★½
Roominess	★★★½
Winter driving rating	★★
Safety	★★★★
Resale value	★★★★★

LAMBORGHINI MURCIELAGO

LAMBORGHINI **MURCIELAGO**

Legendary Bull

In an attempt to claim its rightful place at the top of the supercars, Lamborghini, if you'll pardon the phrase, decided to take the bull by the horns. Unveiled in the middle of the night on the volcanic slopes of Mt. Etna in Sicily, the successor to the fiery Diablo has taken the name Murciélago. It's the name of a legendary bull known for its courage and tenacity in the Spanish arenas of Cordoba over a century ago. The name may not seem very commercial, but, what about the car?

The Murcielago is faithful to the styling concepts of its illustrious predecessors and has kept the gull-wing doors. Somehow, its overall lines are more refined, and the bodywork has fewer openings and indentations than before. Apart from two immense air scoops at the front, the wing and hood surface is smoother-flowing and enhances the aerodynamic shape of the car. The back and the flanks of the Murcielago reveal some family traits with large side vents to assist in brake and engine cooling. The top air scoops are lowered or raised automatically according to the engine's needs.

Under Audi rule

This is the first Lamborghini produced with the help of Audi (who took over this Italian make two years ago) and relies heavily on an 550-hp 6.2-liter V12 (85 more than the Maranello Ferrari) which it delivers at 7500 rpm, with 480 lb-ft of torque at 5500 rpm Given such specifications, even the new Aston Martin Vanquish is outdone in terms of sheer power and torque.

Is it necessary to mention that such heavy artillery is more prevalent on the racetrack, and until now could only be found in racing cars? You be the judge: 0-60 mph in 3.8 seconds and a top speed of 206 mph. Can anyone do better? No one it seems for the moment, as the McLaren GT F1 (3.3 seconds and 232 mph) is no longer in production.

0-60, 3.8 seconds

Harnessing this phenomenal power, the new Murciélago has kept the all-wheel drive system of the Diablo with its central viscous coupler. And just not to take any chances, a stability control system has been added. There is also a new six-speed manual gearbox.

The lowering of the centrally mounted engine means that the car's center of

▲ PROS

Insufficient data

▼ CONS

Insufficient data

gravity has also moved down. This was made possible by the use of a dry sump lubrication system for the engine, whereby the oil is housed in a separate tank rather than in the sump under the engine.

The interior design shows the influence of Audi, which has acquired a reputation for excellence in cockpit and dashboard design. There, the Murciélago has gone beyond the cobbled-together look of the past and the overall impression is that of interior space easier to live with on a daily basis than the Diablo. The price of this new model is not disclosed for the moment but it is known that the production target is set at 400 a year.

Jacques Duval

SPECIFICATIONS

Price	n.a.
Warranty	n.a.
Type	2-seat coupe / four wheel drive
Wheelbase / Length	104.9 in / 180.3 in
Width / Height	80.5 in / 44.7 in
Weight	3638 lb (1650 kg)
Trunk / Fuel tank	n.a. / 26.5 gallons
Air bags	front and side
Front suspension	independent (adaptive)
Rear suspension	independent
Front brakes / Rear brakes	disc ABS
Traction control	yes
Steering	rack-and-pinion, power assist
Turning circle	41 feet
Tires (front/rear)	2P45/35ZR18 / P335/30ZR18

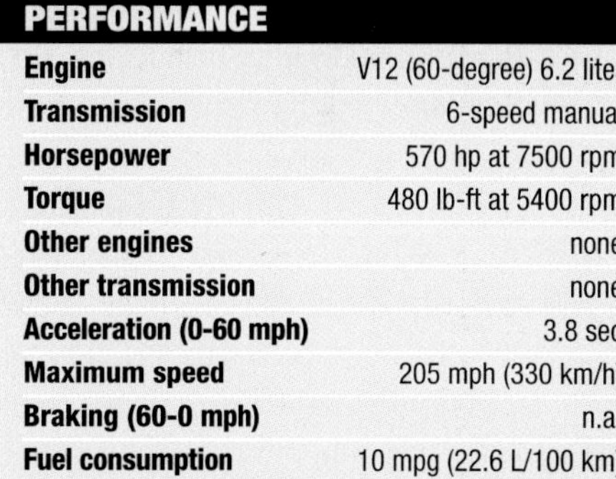

PERFORMANCE

Engine	V12 (60-degree) 6.2 liter
Transmission	6-speed manual
Horsepower	570 hp at 7500 rpm
Torque	480 lb-ft at 5400 rpm
Other engines	none
Other transmission	none
Acceleration (0-60 mph)	3.8 sec
Maximum speed	205 mph (330 km/h)
Braking (60-0 mph)	n.a.
Fuel consumption	10 mpg (22.6 L/100 km)

COMPETITION

• Ferrari 550 Maranello • Aston Martin Vanquish
• Porsche 911 GT2

NEW FOR 2002

• New model

RATING (out of 5 stars)

Driveability	N.A.
Comfort	
Reliability	
Roominess	
Winter driving rating	
Safety	
Resale value	

MASERATI **SPYDER**

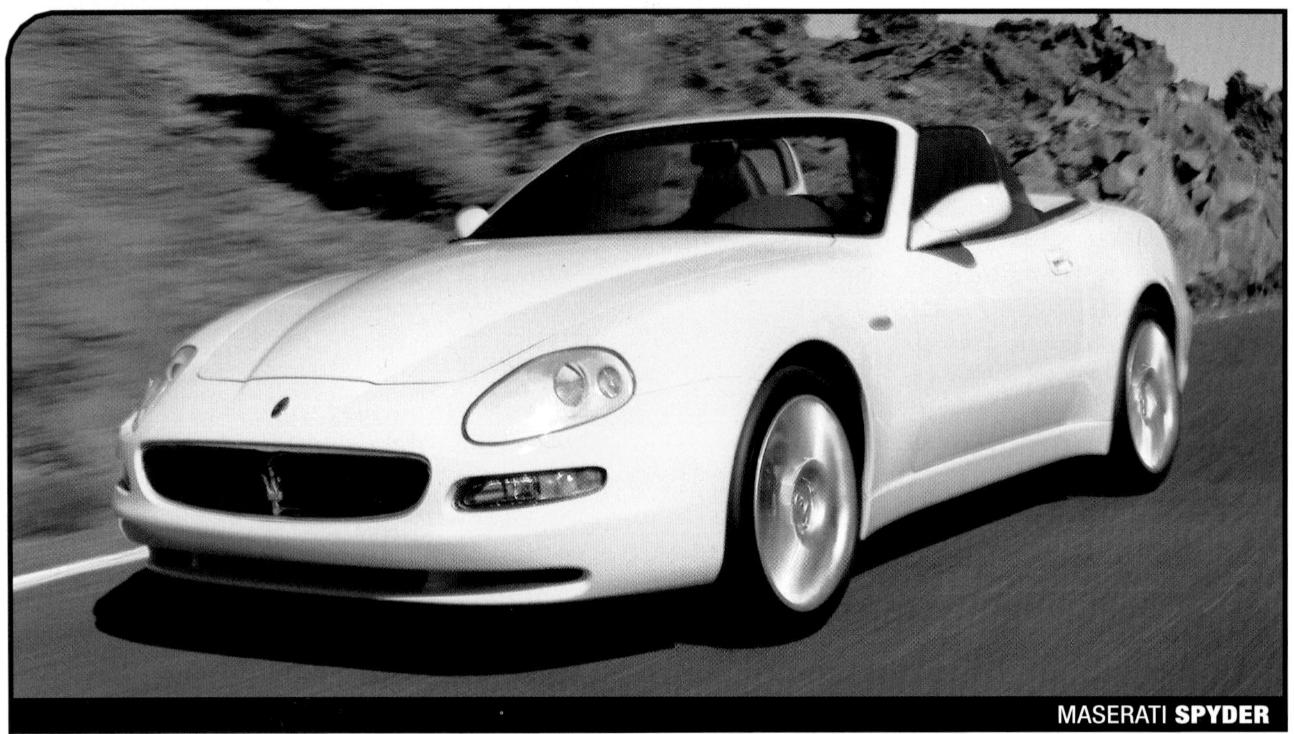

MASERATI **SPYDER**

New Beginning

After a decade-long absence, the Italian sports-car manufacturer Maserati is returning to the North American market with its most recent model – the Spyder.

Maserati has been through tough times in recent years, attracting a good deal of negative press in the process. Now that the unhappy De Tomaso era is finally over and done with, the company hopes to rediscover its past glory. The arrival of the 3200 GT coupe, launched with great pomp and circumstance at the Paris Auto Show in 1998, confirms Maserati's determination.

The ailing company was bought by Fiat in 1993 and brought under the Ferrari umbrella four years later. The task of rebuilding Maserati was a painful and costly business, involving a drastic restructuring plan that effectively shut down the Maserati plant for six months. The cost of just laying out the groundwork for a new company, for example, was a cool $20 million (US).

And by the time Maserati was up and running again – in other words, the entire infrastructure set in place – Ferrari is thought to have injected a massive US$ 350 million.

The future is a V8

At long last, Ferrari's dogged efforts are starting to bear fruit, in the form of the 3200 GT line. Maserati can now look forward with some equanimity. Its future is riding on the new Spyder.

This 2+2 convertible was designed by Giorgetto Giugiaro, who also developed the 3200 GT coupe. There is obviously some resemblance between the two models, but the Spyder is distinguished by its frame shortened by 9 inches (22 cm).

Bye-bye, twin-turbo !

Under the hood, which again features the signature Maserati oval shape, lies a normally-aspirated 4.2-liter V8 engine. Maserati has finally abandoned the infamous twin-turbo – its trademark for 20 years and the main cause of its business problems.

Some of you may remember the twin-turbo coupe, built between 1981 and 1987, at a time when Maserati was owned by an Argentinean industrialist named Alejandro De Tomaso. A powerful motor, to be sure, but as fragile as a Lada engine.

▲ PROS

- **Modern drivetrain • Precise steering**
- **Robust stereo system • Sporty handling**
- **Unique silhouette**

▼ CONS

- **Body noise • Limited use • No trunk**
- **Poor visibility • Stiff suspension**

Then there was a joint venture with Chrysler, which turned out to be another flop. It gave rise to the Maserati TC cabriolet, which was little more than a disguised LeBaron bearing a stratospheric price tag. Talk about a shaky past. But luckily, Fiat managed to move beyond this sorry episode.

There is now a V8 engine in Maserati's future. This lighter engine, 44 lbs (20 kg) less than the twin-turbo and more responsive, is the beating heart of the new Spyder – rating 390 hp and delivering a top speed of 178 mph (285 km/h). Maserati will most likely drop the V12, a Ferrari trademark, from its catalog in favor of the new V8, which is Maserati-designed and produced from start to finish.

Better weight distribution

The Spyder offers yet another important innovation, this time involving the location of the 6-speed manual transmission. While the gearbox on the 3200 GT was mounted behind the engine, the Spyder's gearbox is located in front of the rear differential. This unusual configuration – these days at least – allows for much better weight distribution (53/47). The gearbox's power shifting mode will be controlled from the steering wheel thanks to the Magneti Marelli device dubbed *Cambiocorsa* (Italian for racing gearbox) by Maserati.

Six months after the Spyder launch, scheduled for spring 2002, a hardtop version will be introduced.

Maserati's forecasts are optimistic. The Italian manufacturer intends to sell 600 Spyders in Europe and three times as many in the United States, its most lucrative market. The two models will be unveiled at the Detroit Auto Show in January 2002.

Louis Butcher

SPECIFICATIONS

Price	$CDN 140,000 (est.) / $US 89,000 (est.)
Warranty	n.a.
Type	convertible / rear wheel drive
Wheelbase / Length	96.1 in / 169.3 in
Width / Height	71.7 in / 51.2 in
Weight	3792 lb (1720 kg)
Trunk / Fuel tank	n.a.
Air bags	front and side
Front suspension	independent
Rear suspension	independent
Front brakes / Rear brakes	disc/disc
Traction control	yes
Steering	rack-and-pinion, power assist
Turning circle	n.a.
Tires (front/rear)	P235/40Z18/P265/35Z18

PERFORMANCE

Engine	V8 4.2-liter
Transmission	6-speed manual
Horsepower	390 hp at 7000 rpm
Torque	n.a.
Other engines	none
Other transmission	none
Acceleration (0-60 mph)	5.1 sec
Maximum speed	176 mph (283 km/h)
Braking (60-0 mph)	n.a.
Fuel consumption	12 mpg (18.9 L/100 km)

COMPETITION

- Jaguar XK8 • Mercedes-Benz CL and SL
- Porsche 911

NEW FOR 2002

- New model

RATING (out of 5 stars)

Driveability	★★★★
Comfort	★★★★
Reliability	New model
Roominess	★★★★
Winter driving rating	★★★
Safety	★★★★
Resale value	New model

MERCEDES-BENZ CL

MERCEDES-BENZ **CL500**

Of *Gran Turismo* and High Tech

Like all self-respecting prestigious marques, Mercedes-Benz has its carefully guarded traditions. Its opulent CL coupes – those universal symbols of passion and achievement – proudly carry the torch, with unequalled refinement and GT-class performance.

The latest generation of the luxury CL coupe line – first introduced two years ago – epitomizes Mercedes-Benz's "passage to the XXIst century," to use the company's own words. The rather self-congratulatory tone of the statement is neither pretentious nor exaggerated, given the plush overall feel of the new CL coupe. Its audacious design reveals a happy marriage between the classic and the modern. But the CL coupe is more than just a pretty face, boasting a drag coefficient of 0.28 – an aerodynamic feat worth noting, given the car's dimensions.

The interior matches this achievement, with a wealth of standard equipment smartly set off against fine leather and wood trim. Considering the sticker price that's $125,000 and change for an entry-level copy, that's the least a buyer should expect. The interior bears an eerie resemblance to that of the S Class, with 4 genuine seats as opposed to the competition's usual 2 "pseudo" rear seats. At the center of the dash is the COMAND display, which manages the telephone, stereo system and satellite navigation system (GPS).

Three models, three engines

While its predecessors abandoned all sporty ambitions, the current CL generation brags about its more "inspired" driving. Shorter (by 2.8 inches) and seriously slimmer, this 2-door "limo" is elegance itself, in stark contrast to its predecessor's stodgy figure.

In a class by itself

The CL500 has lost a total of 500 lbs (226 kg), by using aluminum and other composite materials. It is fitted with a 5.0-liter V8 engine producing 302 horsepower, as opposed to the monstrous 6-liter V12 that powers the CL600, increasing its weight back by 435 lbs (197 kg). This increase, however, is compensated by superior power, all 362 hp's worth, against 306 hp for the CL500 51 motor.

Between the two models is the CL55 AMG, the designated Formula-One "safety car." Customized by the tuner AMG itself, the CL55 AMG boasts even more elabo-

▲ PROS

- Driving pleasure • Impressive active suspension
- Incomparable elegance • Spacious cabin
- Supreme refinement

▼ CONS

- Cumbersome dimensions • Excessive driving assistance • Stiff price

rate standard equipment, distinctive interior and exterior, more powerful brakes (with larger disks and calipers),18-inch alloy wheels, low-profile high-performance tires. And look under the hood for the best part: a hand-built 5.5-liter V8 producing 349 horsepower, which, at the slightest touch on the pedal, pins you to your seat.

But don't underestimate the CL600, which can be further enhanced by the Sport Package, also AMG-made, which includes a front spoiler, rear spoiler as well as 18-inch wheels and high-performance tires.

Hi-tech alphabet soup

Like their predecessors, these huge coupes are based on the S Class sedan platform. In addition to embodying the finest of all Mercedes-Benz lines, they boast total command of technology. Active Body Control (ABC), a high-performance active suspension system, is the latest addition to the panoply of driving-aid systems such as traction control, antilock brakes (ABS), panic-braking assistance (BAS), stability control (ESP), and, last but not least, the satellite navigation system (GPS) – standard on all CL models. In short, a veritable hi-tech alphabet soup.

The active suspension system reduces body roll and pitch during acceleration, braking or cornering. Built with hydraulic, electronic and mechanical components, it was designed to reduce body roll by 68%, but a button on the dashboard offers the driver two options: "normal" and "sport." If he opts for the latter, body roll is down 95%.

But to say that our CL500 test model was a sports car is a stretch. Although it demonstrated much more pep than its predecessor, understeer was perceptible during cornering. If you pushed hard enough, though, a battery of electronic aids will immediately kick in to correct matters. While some drivers may appreciate such efficiency, purists may not.

Unlike true GT-class cars such as the Ferrari 456M GT, Maserati 3200GT or Aston-Martin DB7 Vantage, Mercedes's flagship comes solely with automatic transmission – as was the case with the Jaguar SK8, although the latter has since turned into a GT. Luxurywise, the CL coupe is a worthy rival of the Bentley Continental, which costs twice, even three times as much... which is to say that the CL is pretty much in a class by itself.

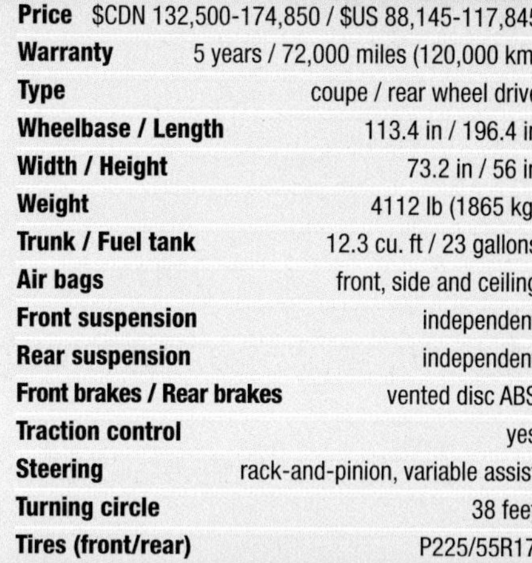

SPECIFICATIONS	
Price	$CDN 132,500-174,850 / $US 88,145-117,845
Warranty	5 years / 72,000 miles (120,000 km)
Type	coupe / rear wheel drive
Wheelbase / Length	113.4 in / 196.4 in
Width / Height	73.2 in / 56 in
Weight	4112 lb (1865 kg)
Trunk / Fuel tank	12.3 cu. ft / 23 gallons
Air bags	front, side and ceiling
Front suspension	independent
Rear suspension	independent
Front brakes / Rear brakes	vented disc ABS
Traction control	yes
Steering	rack-and-pinion, variable assist
Turning circle	38 feet
Tires (front/rear)	P225/55R17

PERFORMANCE	
Engine	V8 5-liter
Transmission	5-speed automatic
Horsepower	302 hp at 5500 rpm
Torque	339 lb-ft at 2700 – 4250 rpm
Other engines	V8 5.5-liter 349 hp; V12 6-liter 362 hp
Other transmission	none
Acceleration (0-60 mph)	6.5 sec
Maximum speed	155 mph (250 km/h)
Braking (60-0 mph)	119 feet (36.2 m)
Fuel consumption	16.8 mpg (13.5 L/100 km)

COMPETITION

• Bentley Continental • Jaguar XK8

NEW FOR 2002

• Distronic system

RATING	(out of 5 stars)
Driveability	★★★★
Comfort	★★★★★
Reliability	★★★★
Roominess	★★★½
Winter driving rating	★★★
Safety	★★★★★
Resale value	★★★★½

MERCEDES-BENZ SL

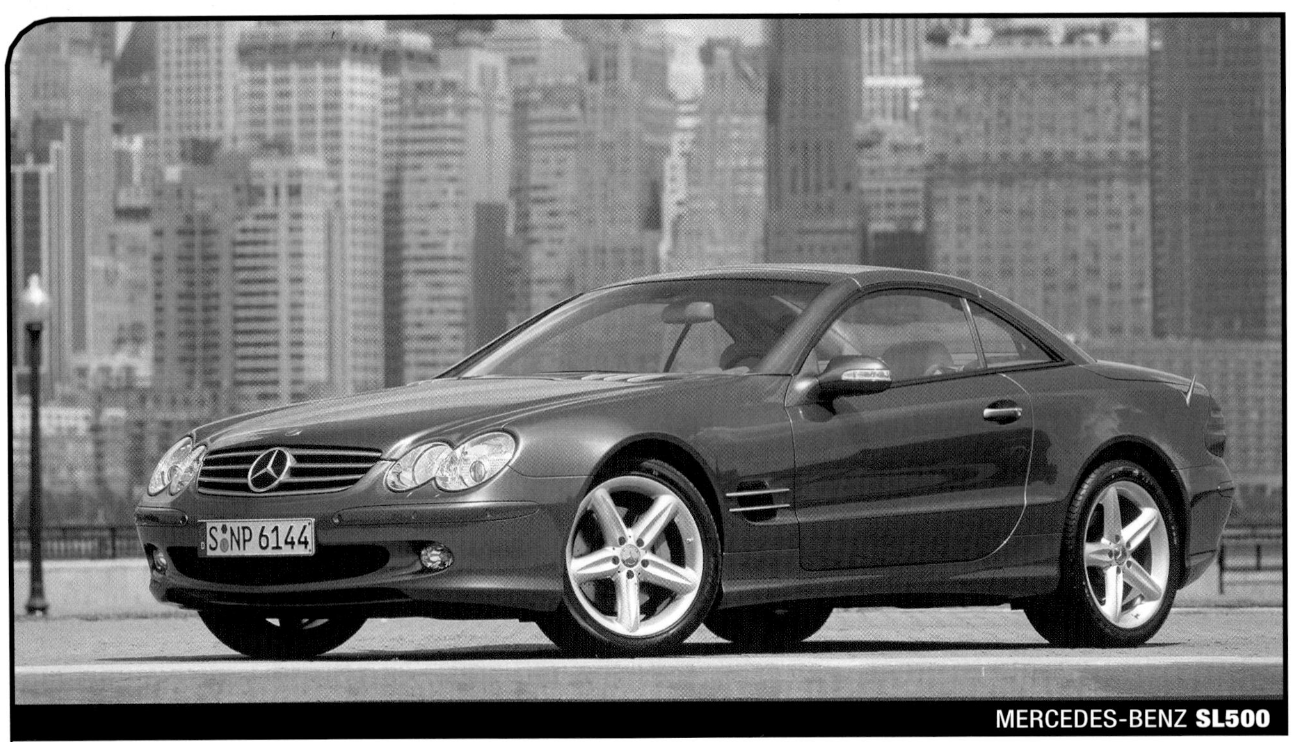

MERCEDES-BENZ **SL500**

Reinvented Dream

"A cabriolet named Desire," I wrote a few years ago about the legendary Mercedes-Benz SL500. In fact, few other cars can make you daydream more than this luxury roadster, considered by many – the celebrated vocalist Lionel Ritchie among them – to be the all-time ultimate in sports-car chic. On July 31, 2001, Mercedes-Benz reinvented that dream, unveiling the fifth-generation SL at the Deichtorhallen exhibition hall in Hamburg, Germany.

There, before a 600-strong international automotive press corps, the new SL made its grand entrance amid much fanfare, preceded by Lionel Ritchie and his partner-in-song, Juliette, belting out the car's special theme song, "The One."

But no amount of fanfare could steal the thunder from the SL's stunning design, mixing stylistic details taken from the first-generation SL300, launched in 1954, and from current, more aerodynamic Mercedes models. As a result, the new SL's drag coefficient is an enviable 0.29, more than nine percent lower than was the case in the previous-generation SL.

In case you're wondering why Mercedes went in so much trouble just to unveil a new model, it's because this sort of event doesn't happen everyday as far as the German automaker is concerned. Thanks to their almost timeless design, Mercedes-Benz automobiles generally enjoy remarkable longevity.

A brief history

The SL series got its start in 1954, with the legendary "gullwing" coupe. By 1957, the coupe had turned into a roadster and remained that way until 1963 when it was retired. The 1400 coupes and 1858 roadsters that came off the production lines during this period are today collector's items, worth hundreds of thousands of dollars.

New benchmark

The second-generation series (SL230 to 280), which made a big splash with its then-controversial pagoda-shaped retractable hardtop, lasted from 1963 to 1971. The third generation (SL280 to 560) proved to be the most popular and lasted the longest, spanning nearly 20 years, from 1971 to 1989. Finally, the fourth

▲ PROS

- Insufficient data

▼ CONS

- Insufficient data

generation was set to celebrate its 12th anniversary when Mercedes decided to take it out of production in favor of the latest generation.

From coupe to roadster in 16 seconds

The latest SL looks positively dignified and, like its predecessors, has been designed to last for many years to come. The silhouette is, in fact, a spectacularly harmonious combination of elements "borrowed" from various Mercedes models. The front wings and side air inlets, for example, are reminiscent of the SLR prototype, the radiator grille was taken from the CL coupe and the "four-eyed" headlights from the C Class. Most remarkable of all is the folding hardtop – "donated" by the SLK roadster – which engineers managed to integrate without adding even an extra ounce to the car, despite the different mechanisms needed to operate the roof. On the contrary, the latest SL is 115 lbs (52 kg) lighter than its predecessor, thanks to the use of aluminum for the hood, front wings, doors and trunk lid, to name just a few. The hood alone is 33 lbs (15 kg) lighter than the steel variety, which was the case in the past.

At the push of a button, the "vario-roof" – to use Mercedes' lingo – can be opened or closed within 16 seconds, turning a roadster into a comfortable coupe and vice versa. Trunk space is a generous 8.3 cubic feet (235 liters) when the vario-roof is open, and 11.2 cubic feet (317 liters) when it is closed.

A few months after the new SL500's arrival in North America, scheduled for March 2002, owners will have the option of fitting their coupe-roadster with an all-glass version of the vario-roof.

MERCEDES-BENZ **SL55 AMG**

World premiere

Needless to say, the new SL Class features the whole range of technologies developed by Mercedes over the past few years. Better still, it showcases another world first: the Sensotronic Brake Control (SBC), an electro-hydraulic system aimed at optimizing braking force in emergency situations by reducing the stopping dis-

tance (by three percent in this case). If the driver switches his foot quickly from the accelerator to the brake pedal, SBC recognizes the early signs of an emergency and reacts automatically. With the help of the high-pressure reservoir, SBC raises the pressure in the brake lines and instantaneously positions the pads onto the brake discs, which can then spring into action with full strength as soon as the brake pedal is depressed.

SBC also offers high levels of safety when braking through corners. While conventional braking systems apply the same brake pressure on the outer and inner wheels of a given axle when cornering, SBC – with its variable brake force distribution feature – allows the brake force to be divided laterally according to the demands of the situation.

SBC's quick intervention was made possible thanks to something called "by-wire" technology, which communicates the driver's commands electronically, rather than mechanically or hydraulically, as has been the case traditionally. Although "by-wire" technology has been used in Formula-One cars in the past few years, the Mercedes SL Class is the first production car to benefit from it.

Like the CL coupe, the SL also features what Mercedes calls Active Body Control (ABC), an active suspension system that reduces body roll and pitching to a minimum while cornering or braking. The car's technical specs include many other letters of the alphabet such as ABS (Anti-lock Braking System), ESP (Electronic Stability Program) and ASC (Acceleration Skid Control).

Under the hood is the familiar 5.0-liter 24-valve V8 with 306 horsepower, the same that powers several other Benzes. Paired to a 5-speed automatic transmission that can be shifted manually, the V8 delivers a respectable 0-60 mph time of 6.3 seconds. If you expect more than that,

you'll have to wait for the SL55 AMG version, which is on its way.

Comfort and safety

The SL coupe/roadster carries a full share of equipment and accessories. The interior is less austere than in the past, plush with fine wood, leather and aluminum trim. Buyers can choose from two types of leather, four high-quality trims and five interior colors. Main instruments sport the classic chronometer design, evoking images of the sports cars of yore. The automatic climate control continues this theme, featuring eye-pleasing aluminum rings around its control buttons.

Nor has comfort and safety been neglected. The car's so-called "integral" seats incorporate every conceivable feature such as seatbelt tensioners and belt force limiters. Last but not least, the SL introduces new head-thorax airbags in the doors for optimum side-impact protection.

The SL further boasts two batteries that supply power for the many electronic systems, as well as an electronic remote-control key for the vario-roof. Quite frankly, I can never praise the SL500 enough, and it's hard to fault Mercedes-Benz for peppering its press kit with such superlatives as: "stylistically scintillating and technically sophisticated sports car," "the most rigorous concept for any 21st-century sports car," "comfort and sportiveness without compromise," "successful combination of tradition and modernity," "the badge SL remains the mark of an automobile that embodies perfect technology."

In short, the fifth-generation SL is filled with promises. Given Mercedes' reputation, chances are good that those promises will be kept.

Jacques Duval

SPECIFICATIONS	
Price	$CDN 116,500-169,000 / $US 84,445-129,595
Warranty	4 years / 48,000 miles (80,000 km)
Type	2-seat coupe-roadster / rear wheel drive
Wheelbase / Length	100.8 in / 178.5 in
Width / Height	71.5 in / n.a.
Weight	4067 lb (1845 kg)
Trunk / Fuel tank	8.3 to 11.2 cu.ft / 21 gallons
Air bags	front, side, head and thorax
Front suspension	independent
Rear suspension	independent
Front brakes / Rear brakes	vented disc, ABS + SBC
Traction control	yes
Steering	rack-and-pinion, variable assist
Turning circle	36 feet
Tires (front/rear)	P255/45R17

PERFORMANCE	
Engine	V8 5.0-liter
Transmission	5-speed automatic
Horsepower	306 hp at 5600 rpm
Torque	339 lb-ft at 2700 – 4200 rpm
Other engines	none
Other transmission	none
Acceleration (0-60 mph)	6.3 sec
Maximum speed	155 mph (250 km/h)
Braking (60-0 mph)	n.a.
Fuel consumption	17.9 mpg (12.7 L/100 km)

COMPETITION

• Jaguar XK8 • Lexus SC 430

NEW FOR 2002

• New model • SL55 AMG version

RATING	(out of 5 stars)
Driveability	★★★★★
Comfort	★★★★★
Reliability	★★★★★
Roominess	★★★
Winter driving rating	★★★★★
Safety	★★★★
Resale value	★★★★½

PORSCHE 911 TURBO

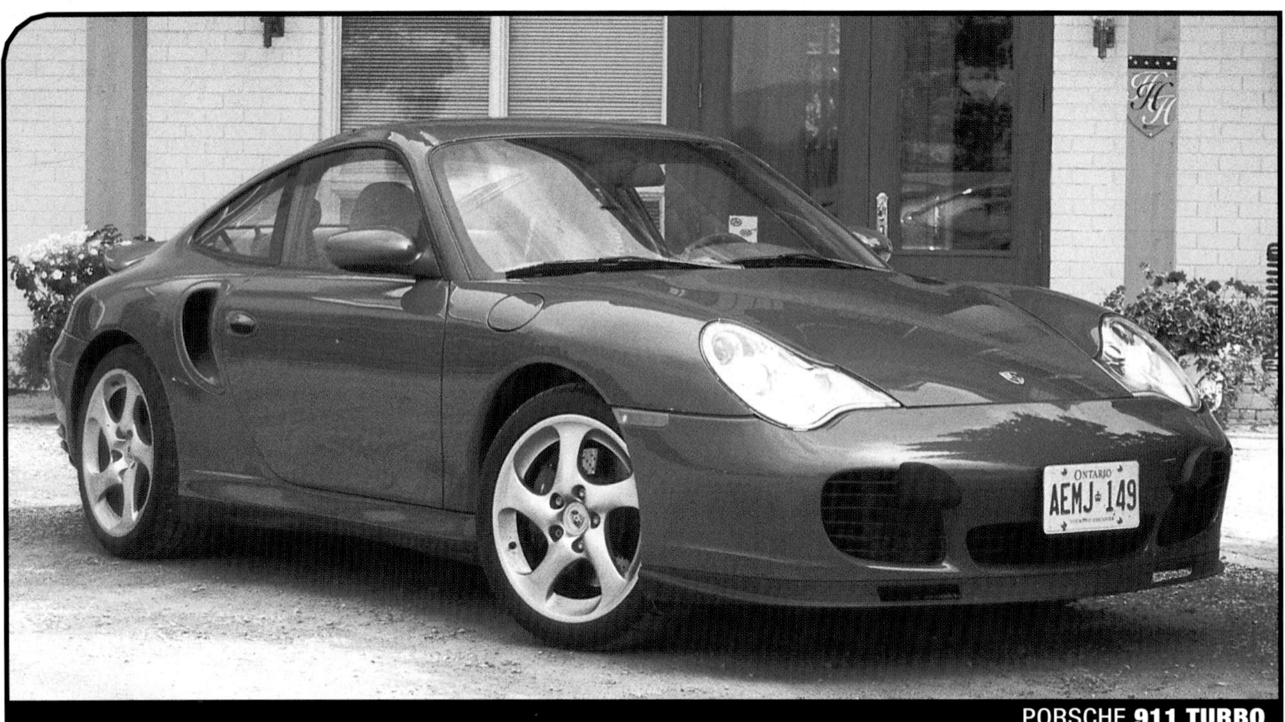

PORSCHE **911 TURBO**

The Laureate

Winner of the *Auto Guide*'s comparison test last year ("World Summit"), which pitted it against the BMW Z8 and the Jaguar XKR, the Porsche 911 Turbo is the quasi-undisputed queen of high-performance automobiles. I say "quasi" because the *Auto Guide* wasn't able to compare it head-to-head with the Ferrari 360 Modena. A grand showdown between these two "road warriors" would certainly have revealed some interesting statistics.

In the meantime, it's safe to assume that the Porsche 911 Turbo would defeat its Italian rival handily in terms of braking, but engine-wise, both cars are neck and neck. As for the weight/power ratio, the 360 enjoys a slight edge: 7 lbs (3.2 kg) per horsepower, as against 8 lbs (3.6 kg) for the 911. In real life, however, these two powerful sprinters are very comparable.

But sheer engine power isn't always the ultimate measurement of a sports car. Handling is equally important. In a drag race, I would probably put my money on the Ferrari, on the strength of its central engine position and the relative ease with which it can be driven at high speed. To get good stopwatch results from the Porsche, you need an accomplished and experienced driver, someone who's totally familiar with the behavior of its rear-mounted engine. Thanks to all-wheel drive and the ultrasophisticated Porsche Stability Management system (PSM), the 911 Turbo is more "convivial", but it's still tricky to drive if you're not used to its ways.

Advantage: engine

The 911 owes its overflowing energy to a 420 hp 3.6-liter flat-6 engine, with twin turbos and intercoolers to boot. Response time is a tad slow, which can be a good thing, because the engine will be less likely to stall on normal take-offs from standstill.

Civilized performance

The standard 6-speed manual gearbox is a delight. But I can't say I like the optional Tiptronic S transmission. It's not a disaster, far from it, but it scales down the driving fun a notch or two.

Braking, however, is extraordinary, owing to the oversized discs – 13 inches (330 mm) in front and 11 inches (280 mm) in back. Perfectly ventilated, they dissipate heat effectively, and are thus conducive to sport driving. In case you find the standard brakes not up to your personal standards, you may want to consider the optional ceramic composite

▲ PROS

- Dizzying performance • Easier to drive
- Excellent sound insulation • Innovative brakes
- Reassuring road manners

▼ CONS

- Cheap-looking dashboard • Little trunk space
- Noisy tires • Poor shock absorbers
- Superfluous Tiptronic

brake discs, which are said to reduce the unsprung weight by 44 lbs (20 kg). They're also more durable, lasting up to 187,500 miles (300,000 km).

Glued to the road

With huge low-profile 18-inch tires, all-wheel drive and a rather firm suspension, the 911 Turbo is virtually glued to the road. Even when the car is driven at the limit, understeer is barely discernible, and the rear end gets only slightly out of line. On the other hand, at the slightest sign of instability, PSM automatically kicks in to correct the situation. What's more Porsche's traction control system doesn't affect the driving pleasure in the least, as is often the case with less sophisticated systems.

But on bad roads you're bound to experience a certain degree of discomfort. My test model exhibited some body noises, which was a pity since the car was otherwise remarkably well sound-insulated. Even at high speeds, you can easily carry on a proper conversation without so much as raising your voice.

Dull dashboard

Slightly restyled for 2002, the normally-aspirated 911 now sports a "turbo" look, designed essentially to differentiate the 911 from the Boxster, Porsche's entry-level model. However, the automaker has done nothing to appease those critics who've been bashing the 911 Turbo's cheap-looking dashboard for years. As a result, despite the car's substantially higher price, buyers have to shell out a good deal more if they want to "personalize" the car's interior, plus the fact that they have to contend with the absence of an in-dash glove compartment and the tiny trunk.

I had the opportunity to drive three 911 Turbos last year. Each time I was mightily impressed by the car's active safety features. This may sound surprising, especially when you realize that there's more to a car that can hit a top speed of over 185 mph (300 km/h). But you've got to drive it at least once, if only to appreciate what a joy it can be when speed and safety complement each other perfectly.

Jacques Duval

SPECIFICATIONS

Price	$CDN 168,400 / $US 111,765
Warranty	4 years/ 48,000 miles (80,000 km)
Type	2+2 coupe / all wheel drive
Wheelbase / Length	92.5 in / 175.6 in
Width / Height	70.4 in / 51.2 in
Weight	3395 lb (1540 kg)
Trunk / Fuel tank	4.6 cu.ft / 24 gallons
Air bags	front and side
Front suspension	independent
Rear suspension	independent
Front brakes / Rear brakes	vented disc ABS
Traction control	yes
Steering	rack-and-pinion, power assist
Turning circle	37 feet
Tires (front/rear)	P225/40ZR18 / P295/30ZR18

PERFORMANCE

Engine	3.6-liter biturbo 6H
Transmission	6-speed manual
Horsepower	420 hp at 6000 rpm
Torque	414 lb-ft at 2700 rpm
Other engines	none
Other transmission	5-speed Tiptronic
Acceleration (0-60 mph)	4.2 sec
Maximum speed	190 mph (305 km/h)
Braking (60-0 mph)	126 feet (38.4 m)
Fuel consumption	17.6 mpg (12.9 L/100 km)

COMPETITION

- BMW Z8 • Ferrari 360 Modena • Aston Martin DB7
- Jaguar XKR Silverstone

NEW FOR 2002

No major change

RATING (out of 5 stars)

Driveability	★★★★★
Comfort	★★
Reliability	★★★★
Roominess	★★½
Winter driving rating	★★★½
Safety	★★★★
Resale value	★★★★½

0
20
40
60
80
100
120
140
160
180
200
220
240
260
280
02002

Road Tests & Analyses

- ACURA
- AUDI
- BMW
- BUICK
- CADILLAC
- CHEVROLET
- CHRYSLER
- DAEWOO
- DODGE
- FORD
- HONDA
- HYUNDAI
- INFINITI
- JAGUAR
- JEEP
- KIA
- LAND ROVER
- LEXUS
- LINCOLN
- MAZDA
- MERCEDES-BENZ
- MERCURY
- MINI
- NISSAN
- OLDSMOBILE
- PONTIAC
- PORSCHE
- SAAB
- SATURN
- SUBARU
- SUZUKI
- TOYOTA
- VOLKSWAGEN
- VOLVO

ACURA 1.7 EL (not available in the U.S.)

ACURA 1.7 EL

"Luxury" in Name Only...

No doubt early readers of the *Auto Guide* (the first edition was published in 1967) will remember cars like the Meteor Rideau 500 or the Pontiac Parisienne. Those models, like many others, were in fact American cars built under different names for the Canadian market. The Meteor, for example, was a carbon copy of any generic Ford automobile to which a couple of features were added and a new, preferably Canadian-sounding, name given. The current Acura 1.7 EL shares the same principle; it, too, is sold only in Canada.

In fact, this bottom-of-the-line Acura is a humble Honda Civic, restyled and renamed. The idea is to provide Acura dealerships with an affordable, entry-level luxury model so as to create a little buzz in their showrooms.

That said, does the Acura 1.7 El (built in the same Ontario plant as the Honda), really offer anything more than its prestigious badge, or is it simply a dolled-up Civic? To find out, we test-drove it over 600 miles last winter.

Poor sound insulation

This is far from being a bad car, but I can't see how anyone can justify spending the extra money, rather than sticking with the Honda Civic. Call it whatever you like, the EL simply can't deny its kinship with the Civic. It's no luxury car.

Take the sound insulation. The 1.7 EL is no better than its economy-class cousin. Road noises were so loud I thought one of the doors was not properly shut. The ergonomics, too, are bad. Command buttons for various features are scattered about, making them awkward to reach. The button controlling the heated seats, for example, is under the dashboard, right in front of the center console, while the driver has to lean forward to reach the command buttons for the sunroof, the cruise control and the rearview mirrors – all located to the left of the steering wheel.

So dream on!

Test-driving in winter revealed a few assembly problems. In cold weather, friction between the leather, plastic and vinyl – materials used for the interior – caused squeaking sounds that I found hard to accept in a so-called "luxury car." The interior's look, on the other hand, is absolutely first class. Honda (er... Acura) certainly paid special attention to the seats, which are super comfortable. The driver is also treated to a center arm-

▲ PROS

- Quality build • Good standard equipment
- Excellent engine/transmission
- Comfortable seats • Decent fuel economy

▼ CONS

- Bad sound insulation • Poor ergonomics
- Body noises in winter • Narrow rear seats
- Not available in the U.S.

rest, and the passengers to much-appreciated grab handles. Storage space is good and visibility excellent.

Elbow to elbow

It's the Acura EL's lack of space, especially in the back, that painfully reminds us of the Civic. To start with, the narrow doors make entry difficult and there's not much headroom. We're in a subcompact model for sure. Curiously, the trunk is almost as spacious as that of the Honda Accord, which is a much larger car.

Compared with its predecessor, the 1.6 EL, this Acura fares slightly better, mechanically speaking. Torque has been boosted from 107 to 114 lb-ft. The 127-hp 4-cylinder VTEC-E is no more powerful than necessary, though the attraction here is the moderate fuel consumption, about 32 mpg. The engine performs pleasantly enough, whether with automatic transmission or the 5-speed manual that came with our 1.7 EL Premium test model (there's also a Touring model which is less expensive). Driving response is remarkably smooth, especially if compared with the Chrysler PT Cruiser, the focus of the *Auto Guide*'s current in-depth test-drive.

Equipped with ordinary tires, however, this low-end Acura is no miracle worker when it comes to roadholding. It's merely adequate. Winter driving is another story. Since cold weather firms up the suspension, the car's overall comfort is affected.

Mind you, it's not as bad as the Honda Insight (see test) but it's a problem nonetheless, and should be taken into account. As with all Hondas or Acuras (except perhaps the S2000), steering is too light which may not please everyone. Safety features, on the other hand, are commendable: in addition to the four-wheel disc brakes with ABS, the standard Acura 1.7 EL comes with front and side airbags.

It will take a lot more than just leather and wood-patterned trim to turn this econo car into a mini-limousine. The Acura 1.7 EL simply hasn't got the right kind of engine or suspension, nor can it perform up to its self-proclaimed "luxury car" status. It's not a bad car, let me emphasize, but it certainly doesn't belong in "Business Class."

Jacques Duval

SPECIFICATIONS	Premium
Price	$CDN 21,500-23,500
Warranty	3 years / 36,000 miles (60,000 km)
Type	sedan /front wheel drive
Wheelbase / Length	103 in / 176.7 in
Width / Height	67.5 in / 56.7 in
Weight	2584 lb (1172 kg)
Trunk / Fuel tank	12.9 cu. ft / 13 gallons
Air bags	front and side
Front suspension	independent
Rear suspension	independent
Front brakes / Rear brakes	disc ABS
Traction control	no
Steering	rack-and-pinion, power assist
Turning circle	34 feet
Tires (front/rear)	P185/65R15
PERFORMANCE	
Engine	4L, 1.7 SOHC 16-valve VTEC-E
Transmission	5-speed manual
Horsepower	127 hp at 6300 rpm
Torque	114 lb-ft at 4800 rpm
Other engines	none
Other transmission	4-speed automatic
Acceleration (0-60 mph)	9 sec
Maximum speed	122 mph (195 km/h)
Braking (60-0 mph)	137 feet (41.7 m)
Fuel consumption	32.4 mpg (7 L/100 km)

COMPETITION

- Chrysler Sebring • Daewoo Leganza
- Hyundai Sonata • Toyota Corolla • VW Jetta

NEW FOR 2002

- Enhanced ride & handling • Variable intermittent
- Wipers standard on all models

RATING	(out of 5 stars)
Driveability	★★★½
Comfort	★★★½
Reliability	★★★★★
Roominess	★★★
Winter driving rating	★★½
Safety	★★★★
Resale value	★★★★½

ACURA 3.5 RL

ACURA 3.5 RL

One Last Round

In last year's *Auto Guide,* we wrote that Acura was on the verge of retiring its top-of-the-line sedan, the 3.5 RL. However, without fanfare, the 2002 model arrived last May at various dealerships across the country. All eyes are now on the Integra's replacement, the RSX, so we'll have to be satisfied with a slightly touched up version of the big 3.5 RL sedan for one more year.

The minute you step on the accelerator, the mighty Acura responds lethargically. Clearly, the V6's 225 hp (15 more hp than in 2001) can adequately propel that almost 4000-lb mass (1800 kg), but cannot provide the kind of performance worthy of this type of car. My stopwatch confirmed the observation, registering a 0-60 mph time of 9.2 seconds. The test car was brand new, so it may have been possible to achieve a better time later on, but I don't believe the feeling of sluggishness will disappear. What's more, the automatic gearbox doesn't exactly enhance acceleration because unlike other more up-to-date transmissions, it lacks a 5th gear, and downshifting lacks flexibility. As for fuel consumption, the heavy car will force you to pay a visit to your favorite gas-pump attendant often, and he'll point out that it requires super unleaded. Despite its unresponsiveness, the V6 Acura's ride is flexibility and silence personified, and that aspect should appeal to Sunday drivers.

Classics galore

The middle-of-the-road powertrain suits the Acura's classic lines to a tee, lines that confer a totally nondescript allure to the car. From the rear, this Acura looks like an S-Class Mercedes-Benz; from the front, you'd say it's an Acura CL, and from the side, well, I don't know – for heaven's sake, Acura, do something worthy of this Integra replacement. Take a trip to Italy; copy Chrysler – do anything at all, just so you can set yourself apart, and get out of that rut you're in!

Stay tuned

The classic lines reach deep inside the cockpit, but at least here, they work. The dashboard is neatly arrayed, instruments and controls are easy to read and reach, high-quality leather, camphor wood trim, all contribute to a feeling of

▲ PROS

• Excellent sound insulation • Good directional stability • Guaranteed reliability • Well-appointed and comfortable cabin • Strong dealerships

▼ CONS

• CD player in trunk • End-of-line model
• Heavy weight • High fuel consumption
• Non-descript styling • Poor performance

luxury and serenity. Also worth a mention is the nifty Bose sound system. But there's no CD player to be found. That's strange, since the radio sports a button that reads CD/TAPE. So where is that CD player? In the console? No. Maybe the glove compartment. Wrong again, it's ...let's see... in the trunk. Frustrating, to say the least! And to think that even the little Ford Focus offers an in-dash 6-CD changer. You'd think Acura did this on purpose to discourage you from buying an RL. And while we're at it, better tell them that the radio and cruise controls mounted on the steering wheel don't illuminate at night.

Or maybe we should just forget about the CD player and tune in to a good classical music station ("classic" and "classical" seem to crop up a lot here), to settle our nerves. At least, we've got power seats and power steering for a good driving position. Hey, it's nicely elevated and the view is terrific, despite the long hoodline. Folks sitting in the back get the same treatment. Why the front passenger's seat is not height-adjustable as well is beyond me.

Wait till next year

On the road, the Acura 3.5 RL has excellent sound insulation. It's easy to drive, handles itself admirably and the well-tuned suspension, featuring wider tires for 2002, takes care of the bumps and potholes with panache. Even on twisty roads, the Acura turns effortlessly, despite its hefty size. No problem on that score. Obviously, in tight turns, with 60% of its weight at the front, understeer rears its ugly head and, if pushed, the anti-skid control will kick in. Braking is adequate, no complaint there, but it would be nice to include panic braking assist in the next reincarnation, if only to keep up with the competition.

After traveling almost 400 miles aboard this large Acura, I can safely conclude that there is some catching up to do both in terms of powertrain and equipment, if the carmaker wants to remain competitive. If you want a name you can trust, full-service dealerships and classic automobiles, then the 3.5 RL may be the car for you. If not, wait until next year.

Alain Raymond

SPECIFICATIONS	
Price	$CDN 54,000 / $US 43,630
Warranty	3 years / 36,000 miles (60,000 km)
Type	sedan / front wheel drive
Wheelbase / Length	115 in / 197 in
Width / Height	72 in / 54 in
Weight	3898 lb (1768 kg)
Trunk / Fuel tank	14.8 cu. ft / 18 gallons
Air bags	front and side
Front suspension	independent, double wishbone
Rear suspension	independent, double wishbone
Front brakes / Rear brakes	disc ABS
Traction control	yes
Steering	rack-and-pinion, variable assist
Turning circle	39 feet
Tires (front/rear)	P225/55R16 94V

PERFORMANCE	
Engine	V6 3.5 liter 24-valve DOHC
Transmission	4-speed automatic
Horsepower	225 hp at 5200 rpm
Torque	231 lb-ft at 2800 rpm
Other engines	none
Other transmission	none
Acceleration (0-60 mph)	9.2 sec
Maximum speed	140 mph (225 km/h)
Braking (60-0 mph)	135 feet (41 m)
Fuel consumption	16.8 mpg (13.5 L/100 km)

COMPETITION

• Audi A6 • BMW 528 • Lexus GS 300 • Lincoln LS • Millenia • M-B E320 • Seville • Volvo S80

NEW FOR 2002

• More powerful engine • Bigger tires • Firmed-up suspension

RATING	(out of 5 stars)
Driveability	★★★
Comfort	★★★½
Reliability	★★★★½
Roominess	★★★★
Winter driving rating	★★★★
Safety	★★★★
Resale value	★★★

ACURA MDX

ACURA **MDX**

A Worthy Champ

Acura's first real incursion into the highly competitive sport-utility vehicle (SUV) market has not gone unnoticed. Hailed by the media as a resounding success story, the MDX went on to win the 2001 *Auto Guide*'s "Best in Class" award, *Motor Trend's* "Truck of the Year" and the prestigious "North American Truck of the Year."

Such an honor roll should seal the MDX's high standing and there's no need to read on, right? Not exactly. There's always the reverse of the medal, however prestigious. Besides, there's no such thing as a perfect car in this ordinary world. That said, what can I tell you about the Acura MDX?

Priced under $50,000, this SUV has been responsible for the serious dent in sales of the Lexus RX300 which, since it arrived 3 years ago, was the only luxury SUV model to be regarded as more "car" than "truck." The MDX's trump card is its spacious interior, for both occupants and luggage. It's close to 9 inches longer and 6 inches wider than the RX300, and that's a big difference. The MDX owes this advantage to its kinship with the Honda Odyssey minivan that shares its platform and assembly line in Alliston, Ontario.

Frugal consumer

The same affiliation entitles the MDX to a 4-wheel independent suspension that does wonders for overall comfort, and a 240-hp 3.5-liter V6, the same engine as the CL coupe. Coupled with a 5-speed automatic transmission, the V6 is one of the MDX's nice surprises. Despite the substantial weight, performance is quite adequate. But the V6's most attractive feature is its unbelievably reasonable fuel economy.

This Acura has an imposing physique, with dimensions comparable to the Explorer, and superior to the Jeep Grand Cherokee. Yet, its consumption is a mere 18 mpg, way lower than the competition.

And the last shall be first

I test-drove in winter, and the MDX proved exceptionally nimble on snowy roads. No matter how fast I swerved and turned, the car refused to skid. Instead it offered me a reassuring sense of security. Traction was all the more remarkable thanks to the Variable Torque Management (VTM) system which automatically transfers engine torque to the rear wheels at up to 18 mph as driving conditions become rougher. To engage this electronically-con-

▲ PROS

• Excellent engine • Above average overall comfort • Spacious and multi-functional cockpit • Reasonable fuel economy • Efficient all-wheel-drive

▼ CONS

• Hard-to-use third-row seats • Wind noise • Dirt-prone rear window • No skidplate underneath the car

trolled system, place the gear shift lever at 1-2 and press the VTM-4Lock button on the dashboard. During acceleration, 52% of engine power goes to the rear wheels, and as all-wheel-drive kicks in, the MDX gradually switches to front-wheel drive. This also explains the SUV's low fuel consumption.

On a paved road, the MDX performed just as admirably, though it felt too much like a truck for my liking. But that's a small price to pay for an 8-inch ground clearance. Directional stability was excellent, braking and steering adequate, although wind noise was evident at highway speed. In such conditions, the engine did not appear eager to work very hard and even the gentlest hill reduced speed by several mph. Also, in bad weather, the rear window got dirty incredibly fast and you need an ample supply of washer fluid to keep it clean. Too bad the rear windshield wiper can't be set in intermittent mode. Another negative point is the size of the back headrests, which impair rear visibility, although they can be removed and stowed away on the floor.

Warm Interior

The MDX's interior is extremely attractive and is no doubt what attracts the buyer's attention at first. The dashboard is tastefully designed. The center console has two levels: the lower part is big enough to hold CDs, and atop the dashboard is a screen displaying readouts from the onboard computer, the compass and a tachometer-like device indicating instant fuel consumption, which I found confusing. Seats are well-designed and access here is easier than in most other 4X4s, including the Mazda Tribute. Every current luxury accessory is present, and exquisitely finished.

The second-row seat is subdivided and features folding seatbacks and is designed for three adults, although the passenger in the middle will feel squished. Still it's better than the third-row benchseat, almost hidden in the floor way in the back, fit only for boneless kids. However, thumbs up to Acura for the user-friendly doorlocks.

These good points amply compensate for the little irritants in the minds of those who have chosen the Acura MDX as SUV of the Year. I'm among them and my in-depth test-drive confirmed my initial choice.

Jacques Duval

SPECIFICATIONS	
Price	$CDN 47,000 / $US 34,850
Warranty	3 years / 36,000 miles (60,000 km)
Type	sport-utility 7-seat / all wheel drive
Wheelbase / Length	106.3 in / 188.6 in
Width / Height	76.8 in / 71.2 in
Weight	4392 lb (1992 kg)
Trunk / Fuel tank	14.8 – 49.6 cu. ft / 19 gallons
Air bags	front and side
Front suspension	independent
Rear suspension	independent
Front brakes / Rear brakes	disc ABS
Traction control	no
Steering	rack-and-pinion, power assist
Turning circle	46 feet
Tires (front/rear)	P235/65R17

PERFORMANCE	
Engine	V6 3.5 liter VTEC
Transmission	5-speed automatic
Horsepower	240 hp at 5300 rpm
Torque	245 lb-ft at 3000-5000 rpm
Other engines	none
Other transmission	none
Acceleration (0-60 mph)	8.8 sec
Maximum speed	122 mph (195 km/h)
Braking (60-0 mph)	134 feet (42.4 m)
Fuel consumption	17.7 mpg (12.8 L/100 km)

COMPETITION

• Audi Allroad Quattro • BMW X3 • Infiniti QX4 • Jeep Liberty • Lexus RX 300 • M-B ML320

NEW FOR 2002

• Intermittent rear wiper • Latch system in 2nd-row seating • Enhanced sound insulation

RATING	(out of 5 stars)
Driveability	★★★★
Comfort	★★★½
Reliability	★★★★
Roominess	★★★★
Winter driving rating	★★★★½
Safety	★★★★
Resale value	★★★★

ACURA RSX

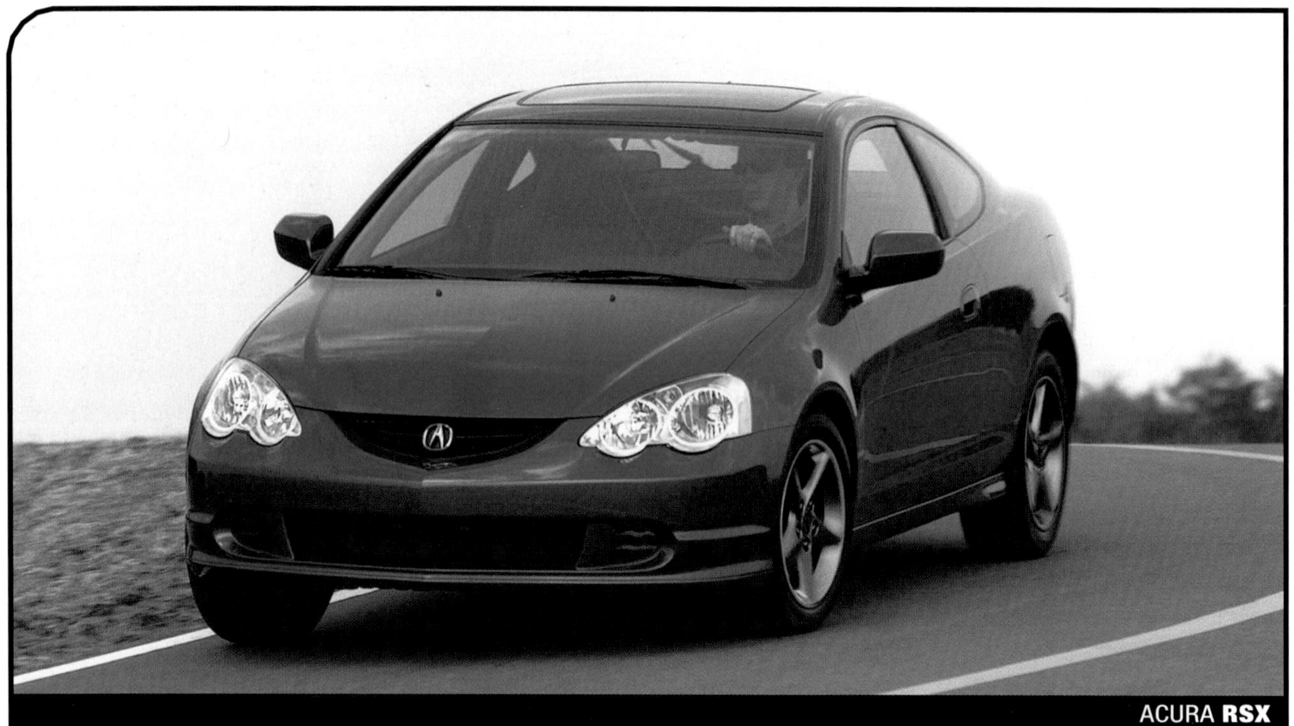

ACURA **RSX**

Split Personality

The wildly popular Acura Integra was "retired" a few months ago, much to the regret of its countless admirers. Oddly enough, it was its immense success that ensured its demise. According to the marketing types at Acura, the car became so popular that people began referring to it simply as Integra, forgetting it was really an Acura. Its replacement – a four-seat sport coupe called Acura RSX – comes in three trim levels: base, Premium and Type S. Whether it will measure up to its legendary predecessor remains to be seen.

The Acura RSX, especially the Type S, is without a doubt one of the two most exciting cars on the market today – the other being the Impreza WRX, Subaru's high-performance all-wheel drive sedan. The stage is now set for a fierce rivalry between the pair, despite their very different "architecture."

High-tech engines

Both the base and Premium models of the Acura RSX are powered by a 2.0-liter 16-valve 4-cylinder engine equipped with the new i-VTEC system, a technology developed exclusively for Acura and Honda. For the uninitiated, i-VTEC stands for "intelligent-Variable Valve Timing and Lift Electronic Control," allowing infinite variability in valve timing and lift to achieve maximum engine performance and minimum emissions. What's more, the system is combined with VTC (Variable Time Control), ensuring a variable control of ignition timing. Despite such sophisticated technology, the base-model engine came up short during my test-drive through the Rockies, near Banff, AB, where, admittedly, the rarefied air didn't help matters.

Well-rounded

Power-wise, the RSX Type S is far superior since its engine, also a 2.0-liter, is fitted with an even more efficient version of the i-VTEC system, borrowed from the NSX. Its extra 40 horsepower is enough to take care of the main shortcoming in the RSX's base model. We're now talking about 200 hp generated at 7400 rpm and transferred to the front wheels via a 6-speed manual

▲ PROS

- Responsive engine • Fun manual gearbox
- Excellent handling • Quality interior
- Comfortable seats

▼ CONS

- Disappointing 160-hp engine • Bad ¾ visibility in the rear • Poor sound insulation
- High cargo sill • No grab handle

gearbox, only available with this model. The 160 hp versions of the RSX are either fitted with a 5-speed manual or automatic (with Sequential SportShift) box. The base model, incidentally, doesn't come with ABS.

If the performance of the Type S reminds you of the Honda S2000 roadster, it's because both share practically the same mechanical technology, down to the crankshaft and connecting rods. Other notable RSX characteristics include the 11.8-inch front brakes (as opposed to the standard 10.3-inch), a firmed-up suspension system with control-link struts in front and double wishbones in back, and 16-inch wheels. For the rest, all RSX models sport a more rigid chassis, where torsional rigidity was increased by 35% and resistance to torsion by 116%.

Smart-looking cockpit

On the inside, the comfortable leather sport seats, the Bose Music System with in-dash 6-CD changer, and various other amenities help the Type S stand out from the crowd. Incidentally, all RSXs are equipped with automatic climate control, front and side airbags, power windows and mirrors. Although the coupe's lines lack originality, considerable attention has been given to the presentation of the dashboard. The instrument pod looks classy in its perforated imitation suede cover, and the display panels, attractively set off against a silvery background, are easy to read. The three-spoke steering wheel comes leather-wrapped, and the climate-control buttons sport a smart stopwatch-look. At night, the soft amber glow emanating from the dash confers a soothing and elegant atmosphere. But I'm surprised there's no grab handle for the front-seat passenger. He or she has to scramble as best they can every time the driver decides to speed up and find out how the car handles on twisting roads.

Sluggish 160 hp

The first 200 miles into my test-drive of the 5-speed Acura RSX Premium weren't terribly exciting. Frankly, the 160-hp engine

ACURA **RSX**

lacked real punch during acceleration – even when I downshifted to 4th gear to pass another car. It's a pity because the model has got everything you could ever want in a car. With only 2.6 turns lock-to-lock, the steering wheel was lightning swift. The short shift lever was also a pleasure to handle. But the car's so-so road manners were an annoying reminder of its lethargic engine. No matter how hard I stepped on the accelerator, nothing happened. Overtaking, especially at high altitudes, was a lost cause, unless I got ready well ahead of time.

I suppose this kind of horsepower would be adequate in a regular subcompact. But we're talking about RSX here, albeit the base model, and at the price charged, you have the right to expect more than a mere little sport coupe. It looks great, but leaves a lot to be desired. At the very least, the base model should be fitted with the Type S engine – its 40 extra horses would have made all the difference.

Type S – almost an S2000

For all intents and purposes, the RSX Type S is an S2000, cleverly disguised as a 2+2 coupe. Naturally, with 40 hp fewer, it doesn't leap forward like the Honda roadster, but provides an exciting driving experience nonetheless. To find the power, though, you need to work at the shift lever, keeping between 6000 to 8000 rpm. But there's no doubt you'll love it, especially the superb 6-speed manual box, which feels more like a playful toy than something you have to work at as if it were a chore. Moreover, behind its sporty behavior, the Type S proves to be well suited to the kind of stop-and-go performance that's so common in city traffic.

All in all, this RSX is a fine vehicle both for daily and sporty driving, accompanied by the sharp, reassuring sound

■ STANDARD EQUIPMENT

• Automatic climate control • Anti-theft system • Heated mirror • 6-speaker stereo system

■ OPTIONAL EQUIPMENT

• Bose Stereo (Type S) • Leather trim (Premium and Type S) • 6-speed transmission (Type S)

of an engine brimming with endless reserves of rpms. I wonder though why Acura engineers decided to space out the gearbox's upper ratios the way they did. In 4th gear, for example, you reach 115 mph at 8000 rpm, then 140 mph in 5th at the same revs, while the 6th gear is virtually an overdrive designed to reduce fuel consumption. Tighter gear ratios would have enhanced acceleration, an area where the Type S underperforms. Admittedly, the high altitudes in the Rocky Mountains didn't help matters, but the 7.9 seconds it took to go from 0-60 mph weren't record-breaking material either.

Front-wheel drive? What's that?
The car's road behavior is impressive, making us forget that we're dealing with front-wheel drive – without a doubt, its greatest achievement. Understeer is barely noticeable, there's no torque effect in the steering wheel, and road handling is almost neutral despite the presence of the kind of tires designed more for overall comfort than adherence on twisting roads. That much said, bumps and potholes don't pass unnoticed despite well-padded bucket seats that, incidentally, provide an impeccable driving position.

And since nothing is ever perfect, let me say, first of all, that all RSX coupes suffer from poor sound insulation – a common problem with most Acura/Honda models – and it's particularly acute on the highway. Noise level was further exacerbated by a whistling sound emanating from the sunroof, at least in the two cars I tested. Secondly, 3/4 visibility is practically non-existent in the rear, due to a wide blind spot. And finally, the rear seats are useful only for kids – of the pint-sized, quiet variety, I hasten to add. Access to the generously sized luggage compartment (17.8 cubic feet) is hindered by a way-too-high cargo sill.

If the split personality demonstrated by these sporty new Acuras appeals to many customers, others may balk at the fact that they're offered in only one bodystyle. In this department, the Integra line was more complete – another reason to mourn its passing.

Jacques Duval

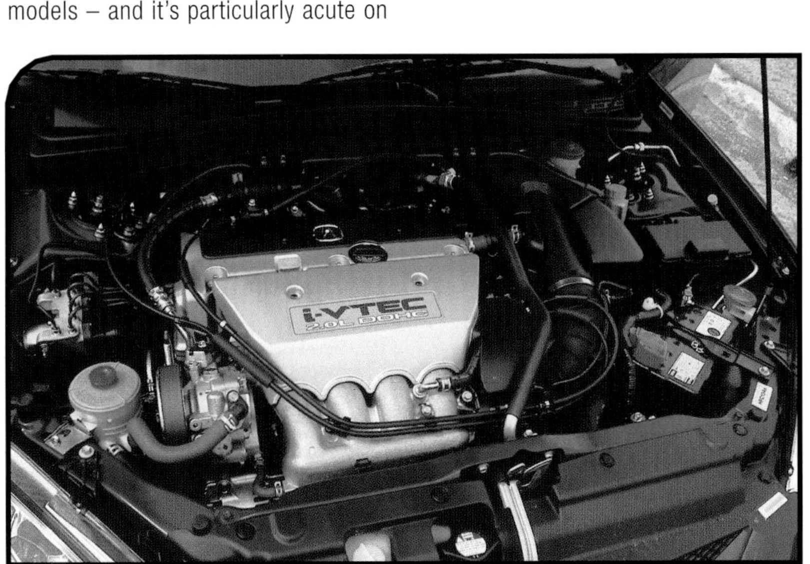

SPECIFICATIONS	Type S
Price	$CDN 24,000-31,000 / $US 19,950-23,650
Warranty	3 years / 36,000 miles (60,000 km)
Type	coupe / front wheel drive
Wheelbase / Length	101 in / 172 in
Width / Height	68 in / 55 in
Weight	2701 lb (1225 kg)
Trunk / Fuel tank	17.8 cu. ft / 13 gallons
Air bags	front and side
Front suspension	independent
Rear suspension	independent
Front brakes / Rear brakes	disc ABS
Traction control	no
Steering	rack-and-pinion, variable assist
Turning circle	37 feet
Tires (front/rear)	P205/55R16

PERFORMANCE	
Engine	4L 2 liter
Transmission	6-speed manual
Horsepower	200 hp at 7400 rpm
Torque	142 lb-ft at 6000 rpm
Other engines	4L 2 liter 160 hp
Other transmission	5-speed auto; 5 speed manual (160 hp)
Acceleration (0-60 mph)	7.9 sec (9.8 sec, 160 hp auto)
Maximum speed	143 mph (230 km/h)
Braking (60-0 mph)	137.1 feet (41.8 m)
Fuel consumption	23.9 mpg (9.5 L/100 km)

COMPETITION

- Celica GTS • Focus ZX3 • Impreza WRX
- Protegé MP3 • Sentra SER

NEW FOR 2002

- New model

RATING	(out of 5 stars)
Driveability	★★★★
Comfort	★★★½
Reliability	New model
Roominess	★★★½
Winter driving rating	★★★
Safety	★★★★
Resale value	New model

ACURA TL ACURA CL

ACURA **TL TYPE S**

Mind the Doors!

Hailed as the best automobile for price/quality ratio, this year's Acura TL sedan boasts a facelift and a more substantial engine borrowed from its quasi-twin, the CL Type S coupe. However, I can't help wonder whether the sedan isn't really a four-door version of the coupe. Or, perhaps the coupe is a sedan with two doors? Confusing? You bet! But anything's possible, judging from the astounding number of models coming off the same platform.

Before getting down to the nitty-gritty of the sedan's high-performance version, let's take a look at the coupe. Once highly desirable, sports coupes have fallen on hard times. No one seems much interested in two-door models anymore. And Acura doesn't help matters with its CL Type S coupe. Despite the more powerful VTEC engine, it looks and feels more like an amputated sedan than a sports coupe. Worse, the model is saddled with a rather stiff suspension and an excessive turning circle, not to mention body rattlles – all no-nos for any car, but unacceptable in one with a price tag reflecting its Grand Touring status. To make a comeback, the sports-coupe market will need models like the old Fiat 124, for example, which was wildly popular in the late 1960s, or the current Peugeot 406 coupe, unavailable in North America. Too bad!

Super engine

Getting back to the Acura CL, there are no problems with the engine. This 3.2-liter V6 works smoothly and effectively with the 5-speed automatic transmission and pleasing SportShift mode. In either manual or automatic mode, the 260 horsepower engine propels the car from 0-60 mph in 7.2 seconds, emitting a honeyed basso-profundo rumble. Another plus is the torque-sensing steering gear. But if the big 17-inch tires are terrific for directional stability, they're a nuisance for the turning radius. You really have to "wiggle" the car back and forth when you park or try to get out of a tight parking spot. The car's overall comfort, too, is badly affected by the stiff tires. Test-driving our Acura CL coupe in winter, the tires often felt like concrete.

Think engine!

The interior boasts excellent features, including generous, comfortably contoured seats, power-adjustable driver's seat, perfect front visibility thanks to the panoramic windshield, and an easy-to-read instrument cluster set against a light-colored background.

▲ PROS

- Superb engine • Excellent performance
- Comfortable seats • Good visibility
- Nice interior (sedans)

▼ CONS

- Abrupt suspension • Turning circle too wide
- 4-season tires • No manual transmission
- Unpleasant xenon headlights

The rear, however, is so cramped it might as well have been designed for kids. Headroom is seriously lacking. Worse, the power-adjustable backs of the front seats take forever to clear access to the rear.

Styling changes – The TL Type S

So why not consider the 4-door TL Type S sedan, which now boasts the same engine as the coupe. And what an engine! Just imagine what you'd get by combining the chassis of an Audi A6 or A4 with the Acura V6 VTEC engine. Like the coupe, the sedan has a firmed-up suspension along with a system intended to ensure the car's stability under all driving conditions. The tires are upgraded from 16 to 17 inches; alas, they are of the 4-season variety and therefore incompatible with sport driving, not to mention their adverse effects on initial retardation when measuring braking distances (from 60 mph).

Styling revisions to all TL 2002s are restricted to a slightly redesigned front end, which now sports standard integrated fog lamps, and new taillights in back.

As with the CL coupe, the engine could use a more suitable chassis, providing both overall comfort and better roadholding. The suspension also leaves something to be desired. Driving on a bad road can be a bone-rattling experience. And if you corner closer to the limit, the car tends toward excessive roll, and the tires can't compensate for untimely oversteering.

Both Acuras (CL and TL) come with an excellent automatic transmission with manual-shifting mode. The latter option would get more use if the gear shift selector was more straightforward. But I must tell you how little I appreciate the high-intensity discharge xenon headlights, standard in the TL Type S. Their intense illumination lacks progressivity and the illumination cuts off so abruptly it makes it look as if you're facing a wall. Mind you, the TL is not the only deluxe automobile to use these so-called high-tech headlights. I've been driving a Porsche 911 for three years, and I'm still not used to its lightbeams.

That said, the regular Acura TL is still the best there is for price/quality ratio. The Coupe and the Type S try hard to jazz things up, but no cigars.

Jacques Duval

ACURA **CL**

SPECIFICATIONS	**Type S**
Price	$CDN 37,000-41,000 / $US 29,360-31,710
Warranty	3 years / 36,000 miles (60,000 km)
Type	5-seat sedan / front wheel drive
Wheelbase / Length	108.1 in / 192.5 in
Width / Height	70.7 in / 53.7 in
Weight	3558 lb (1614 kg)
Trunk / Fuel tank	14.3 cu. ft / 17 gallons
Air bags	front and side
Front suspension	independent
Rear suspension	independent
Front brakes / Rear brakes	disc ABS
Traction control	yes
Steering	rack-and-pinion, variable assist
Turning circle	39 feet
Tires (front/rear)	P215/50R17

PERFORMANCE	
Engine	V6 3.2 liter
Transmission	5-speed automatic
Horsepower	260 hp at 6100 rpm
Torque	232 lb-ft at 3500-5500 rpm
Other engines	V6 3.2 liter, 225 hp (TL)
Other transmission	none
Acceleration (0-60 mph)	7.2 sec
Maximum speed	143 mph (230 km/h)
Braking (60-0 mph)	153 feet (46.5 m)
Fuel consumption	18.9 mpg (12 L/100 km)

COMPETITION

• Infiniti I35 • Lexus ES 300 • Oldsmobile Aurora • Saab 93 • Volkswagen Passat GLX • Volvo S60

NEW FOR 2002

• Type S 260 hp version • Styling touch-ups • Standard fog lamps • New 6 CD changer

RATING	**(out of 5 stars)**
Driveability	★★★½
Comfort	★★★
Reliability	★★★★★
Roominess	★★★★
Winter driving rating	★★★½
Safety	★★★★
Resale value	★★★★

AUDI A4/S4

AUDI **A4**

An Awfully Risky Proposition

Updating the Audi A4 turned out to be a tricky business, given the car's successful run to date and the important role it has played in reviving Audi's fortunes in North America. In fact, replacing a popular car model is often the most difficult challenge facing any automaker. The Ford Motor Company understands the problem all too well, having failed with the revamped Taurus. The car went from being an exquisite original model to just one among many, dragging its sales down with it. The question now is: Will the new A4 meet the same fate?

Until now, the acquisition of an Audi A4 quattro constituted both a love affair and a marriage of convenience. Not only was this German sedan exquisitely attired, but it was also a formidable performer, especially on slippery surfaces, thanks to the quattro all-wheel drive. Will the 2002 version retain all these seductive qualities? I'm afraid not. The all-wheel-drive system is still there, but the new A4 has lost some of its irresistible allure. The front end hasn't strayed too far from the previous model and looks fine, but the totally redesigned rear deck – incorporating details borrowed from the A6 – isn't quite right. So thank goodness the new model scores high marks in several other respects.

What's new?

Buyers of the new all-wheel-drive A4 can choose between two engines: an all-new 220-hp 3.0-liter V6, the same that powers the Audi A6; or last year's turbocharged 1.8-liter 4-cylinder – with 170 horsepower, up from 150.

Standard with the V6 is a 6-speed manual gearbox. Surprisingly, the two cylinder banks in this version are still arranged at a 90-degree angle, even though a 60-degree arrangement was found to cause less vibration. Nevertheless, Audi engineers deliberately chose to retain the wider angle so they could incorporate various engine components inside the V opening. In turn, the more compact engine allowed for – among other advantages – a lower hoodline, enhancing the car's overall aerodynamics. Other innovations include balance shafts, which make sure that the engine stays vibration-free throughout its rev range, and an

Marriage of convenience

▲ PROS

- Avant-garde Multitronic transmission
- Excellent comfort • Increased cabin space
- More powerful V6 engine • Solid road manners

▼ CONS

- Average performance • Dull design • Ill-adapted 6-speed manual gearbox • Multitronic offered only in front-wheel-drive version

aluminum engine block cast according to a process developed by Cosworth Technology, the British engineering firm renowned for its Formula-One engines. Incidentally, Cosworth is currently owned by the Volkswagen group.

Audi also hopes to double sales of the other all-wheel-drive A4 version – the 170-hp 1.8 T (for turbo). This engine can be coupled either to a 5-speed manual gearbox, or a Tiptronic transmission with Sport mode that allows you to delay gearshifting for better acceleration.

Come next spring, buyers of the front-wheel-drive A4 can opt for Multitronic, a new continuously variable transmission (CVT) that proves to be as effective as a manual gearbox, in terms both of acceleration and fuel economy.

The chassis, too, has undergone several changes. The body is 45% stiffer, the tracks are wider, and the larger brakes now boast a hydraulic brake assist system, which, as its name suggests, assists "the driver in emergency braking situations by automatically increasing braking pressure." Suspension, too, has been radically modified. Both the quattro and front-wheel-drive versions of the A4 now sport a fully independent trapezoidal-link rear suspension which, like the front suspension, consists of light-alloy components.

More cabin space

The A4's dimensions have all been increased in order to provide more cabin space. Legroom in the rear, for instance, benefits from an extra two inches (4.3 cm). Like the new A6, noise level in the new A4 has been reduced by 3 decibels thanks to double door joints and thicker glass. Equipment-wise, there's Telematics by OnStar (a technology developed by General Motors), which provides a whole range of services – anything from sending for help in emergency situations to making reservations at

your favorite eatery. The 2002 A4 also boasts a state-of-the-art 10-speaker audio system developed by Bose, one of the best in the industry.

En route

In the final analysis, it was the 4-cylinder 1.8 T with the 5-speed manual gearbox

that best corresponded to my personal definition of a sport sedan. Needless to say, it was the most fun to drive and also one of the least expensive of all the test models provided at the time of the A4 launch. The engine proved to be remarkably quiet and dynamic, and I'm not in the least surprised that a leading car magazine voted it one of the world's 10 best engines. Acceleration wasn't exactly dramatic, and I had to downshift often just to maintain a steady pace on hilly roads. Still, the manual gearbox was so easy to manipulate that it grew on me in no time.

Equipped with the Sport package, which included 17-inch wheels and a lowered (by roughly one inch) suspension, this A4 negotiated turns effortlessly. Understeer was barely noticeable.

On the other hand, the V6 version – without the Sport package – didn't handle "spirited" driving quite as well. The driving position seemed higher and as I suspected, the regular suspension (as opposed to sport suspension) "robbed" the car of some of the handling ability I'd enjoyed in the 1.8 T. Adding insult to injury, though, there was no compensating extra comfort. My test drives took place in Vermont, where the rough and bumpy roads were a perfect venue to test the car's body rigidity. It passed the exam with flying colors, and no rattles were heard. Steering faithfully transmitted road feel. Absolutely no torque effect on that score.

Disguised Passat

The only fault anyone will find with this entry-level Audi is its obvious "kinship" with the Volkswagen Passat. But the link is less apparent in the plushier, high-end models. Except for the cheesy imitation carbon-fiber (in lieu of wood) trim on the dashboard, the 1.8 T's interior is reasonably engaging. Make a note of the three-spoke steering wheel, aluminum-rimmed instruments, shift knob, and a glove compartment so big you could stow away any troublesome passenger.

In models with manual transmission, the very comfortable elbow rest has to be dispensed with because it blocks access to the gear lever. In the rear, the new A4 kept its promise of more legroom, which had been ruthlessly limited in the 2001 model. The rear bench can comfortably seat two adults. But the drive shaft tunnel seriously hampers the middle seat from accommodating a third passenger. The trunk is narrow, but exceptionally deep, so no complaint there.

Multitronic or 6-speed?

A spin in the front-wheel drive A4 allowed me to reassess the Multitronic progressive automatic transmission (see article on the A6). Its main advantage is providing an infinite number of transmission ratios so as to obtain optimum power on demand, and as such, it acquitted itself well enough to impress many test drivers. But I found its initial response time a tad slow, a minor problem that Audi engineers are well aware of. Nonetheless, Multitronic (or Tiptronic, as it's called in the quattro versions) is by far preferable to the 6-speed manual gearbox, which proved to be utterly ill-suited to the 3.0-liter V6 engine. It was so stiff it made city driving particularly trying. The V6 engine was a little more vigorous that the old 2.7-liter, but still seemed sluggish at low rpms.

The A4 is no longer the only car that can ride in sand and snow. Its competition has multiplied over the years, and now includes BMW (325 Xi), Jaguar (X-Type), Volvo (S60), Volkswagen (Passat 4Motion) and even Subaru (Legacy GT). In this company, Audi required no less than a master stroke to keep its revamped model in the lead in its category. The new A4 is certainly a good car, but I wouldn't go quite so far as calling it exceptional – a nuance that will spell success or failure in future.

Jacques Duval

SPECIFICATIONS	**A4 1.8T**
Price	$CDN 37,225-57,200 / $US 25,090-41,050
Warranty	4 years/ 48,000 miles (80,000 km)
Type	5-seat sedan / all wheel drive
Wheelbase / Length	104.3 in / 179 in
Width / Height	69.5 in / 56.2 in
Weight	3406 lb (1545 kg)
Trunk / Fuel tank	15.7 cu. ft / 17 gallons
Air bags	front, side, and head
Front suspension	independent
Rear suspension	independent
Front brakes / Rear brakes	disc ABS
Traction control	yes
Steering	rack-and-pinion, variable assist
Turning circle	36 feet
Tires (front/rear)	P235/45R17 (optional)

PERFORMANCE	
Engine	4L 1.8-liter turbo
Transmission	5-speed manual
Horsepower	170 hp at 5900 rpm
Torque	166 lb-ft at 1950-5000 rpm
Other engines	V6 3.0-liter 220 hp
Other transmission	5-speed automatic Multitronic
Acceleration (0-60 mph)	9.8 sec; 8.2 sec (V6)
Maximum speed	129 mph (208 km/h)
Braking (60-0 mph)	124 feet (37.8 m)
Fuel consumption	23.1 mpg (9.8L/100 km)

COMPETITION

- BMW 3 Series • Jaguar X-Type • Lexus IS 300
- Mercedes-Benz C Class • VW Passat • Volvo S60

NEW FOR 2002

- New model

RATING	**(out of 5 stars)**
Driveability	★★★★
Comfort	★★★★
Reliability	★★★★★
Roominess	★★★½
Winter driving rating	★★★★½
Safety	★★★★
Resale value	★★★★★

AUDI A6/S6

AUDI **S6 AVANT QUATTRO**

An Extraordinary Breakthrough

Audi finally has found an answer to the question posed by the *Auto Guide* seven years ago. "Is there an engine under the hood?" we asked politely in 1995, puzzled by the A6's lethargic 2.7-liter V6. This year, the company has adopted an all-new powertrain, consisting chiefly of a 3.0-liter 220-hp engine, combined with a new automatic transmission (front-wheel-drive models), as well as a number of other mechanical refinements for its automotive lineup – the A6 base model, 2.7 T, 4.2 V8, and the recently unveiled S6.

Audi's press release touting a "new chapter in the success story of the A6" sounds perhaps a shade presumptuous. But it's reasonable to claim that the current model is discernibly different from its immediate predecessor, though you will have to look further than the tip of your nose!

While styling changes seem minor at best, the technical modifications are positively significant, in particular the V6 engine with five valves per cylinder, and the unique Multitronic automatic transmission. Twice before, Audi's own engineers attempted – unsuccessfully – to invigorate the sluggish V6, but despite its much ballyhooed 200 horsepower, the inadequate torque continued to prove annoying to its drivers.

For its 2002 models, the company offers a new 3.0-liter engine with an aluminum block. According to Audi, "the new and old engines share only one basic concept: the arrangement of the cylinder banks at an angle of 90 degrees." Although the extra power appears unexceptional, performance has been significantly improved and optimized, thanks in large measure to the Continuously Variable Transmission (CVT), in other words, the Multitronic transmission system. So hats off to Audi for overcoming all the drawbacks inherent in this type of transmission, its use, up to this point, having been limited to smaller engines. The secret, says the company, lies in a link-plate chain made entirely from steel, instead of the Van Dorn link belt heretofore used on CVTs.

A step forward

Performance plus

Without venturing too deeply into impenetrable technical discourse, let's see how Multitronic works: While conventional

▲ PROS

• Accrued power • Improved steering wheel feel • Predictable safe handling • Refined interior • Revolutionary transmission • Steadier steering

▼ CONS

• Engine still "timid" • Multitronic not available on Quattro • Occasional rattling • Tight front seats

gearboxes transmit torque via five or six sets of pinion or planetary gears, Audi's progressive system permits a theoretically infinite number of transmission ratios. In other words, Multitronic features a range of continuously variable ratios, virtually ensuring that the engine can operate under optimal conditions at all times – a far cry from the conventional automatic gearbox with a staging of four or five set ratios as we're commonly used to.

The transmission's central component is called the variator, a device resembling a V-belt that links two axially adjustable sets of pulley halves. And instead of a conventional torque converter, Audi has developed a multi-plate clutch running in an oilbath. Audi's Multitronic is the first system of its kind to use magnesium for the transmission casing, reducing the weight by roughly 15 lbs (7 kg).

Audi assures us that this new transmission is completely reliable and delivers the kind of performance associated with a manual gearbox, both in terms of acceleration and fuel economy.

The only problem is that this superb Multitronic technology will not be available on models with Quattro all-wheel drive, but is reserved exclusively for front-wheel drive Audis.

Invisible to the eye

Among the 2002 sedan and Avant wagon models' other notable characteristics are the Tiptronic sporty shift mode selector button, a 10-lb reduction in unsprung weight, modified springs and shock absorbers, and a more powerful brake assist system. There are also new door seals, thicker glass in the side windows and a wiper system designed to reduce wind noise – three elements that reduce overall noise by two decibels.

In addition, both the sedan and Avant wagon get a new double radiator grille, new headlights with clear-glass covers (high-intensity xenon Plus headlights are optional) as well as aluminum trim around the dashboard.

Technological breakthrough

Driving the new Audi A6 in Ingolstadt, Germany, I felt distinctly privileged for the chance to experience first-hand an extraordinary technological breakthrough. Behind the wheel of a front-wheel drive model, equipped with Multitronic, everything was cool... until I pressed the

accelerator all the way down to get past an old geezer on the road. At once, the tachometer needle shot up, acceleration reached its maximum level and just stayed there, instead of diminishing as is usually the case with conventional transmissions while upshifting. I couldn't for the life of me discern any sign of gear changes. Audi's sales team should definitely warn their customers about Multitronic's special behavior, lest they start getting complaints about the car's "stuck-in-gear" transmission.

All in all, ratio variation (I almost wrote gearshifting) was virtually indiscernible and the ride was as smooth as silk. As a bonus, Multitronic responds more quickly than conventional automatic transmissions, as if compensating for the meager increase in horsepower provided by the new Audi engine. Actually, if the 2002 A6 sprints from 0-60 mph 1.3 seconds faster than its predecessor, at least half the gain is due to the new transmission. Its 8-second acceleration time still doesn't compare favorably with the competition, but the A6 teems with a host of other qualities instead – a trendy appearance, highly refined interior, plush comfort and sound, if not sporty, ride quality.

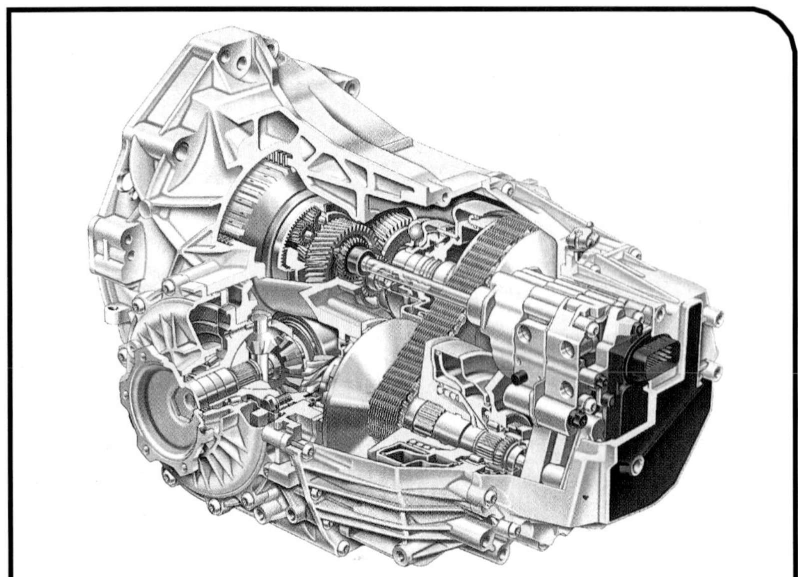

48 variations, including the S6

The Audi A6 has unquestionably the greatest number of models – 48 on the European market, once all engine options have been taken into account. Up until now, North Americans who wanted something more powerful than the base 220-hp version, could opt for

■ STANDARD EQUIPMENT

• Dual zone climate control • Radio with 6CD player • 6-speed manual transmission

■ OPTIONAL EQUIPMENT

•Rear seat airbags • Heated rear seats • Sunroof / Leather package • Nav system

the 2.7 T with its bi-turbo 250-hp engine – the sportiest and most desirable. This year, Audi has added the much-anticipated S6 to its North American lineup, powered by a new version of its 4.2-liter V8 engine. I wasn't terribly impressed with the original, which was designed more for luxury than for driving pleasure.

However, with its 17-inch alloy wheels, lowered suspension and stabilizers and a V8 engine capable of generating 340 hp and 310 lb-ft of torque, the S6 should turn out to be a valuable ally for the S8 (see following pages).

As for the entry-level A6, it's a pity that the revolutionary Multitronic transmission is limited to front-wheel drive models, because, for most buyers, Audi and Quattro are virtually indistinguishable.

Jacques Duval

SPECIFICATIONS	3.0 front wheel
Price	$CDN 54,335-88,500 / $US 34,950-49,950
Warranty	4 years / 48,000 miles (80,000 km)
Type	5-seat sedan / front wheel drive
Wheelbase / Length	108.7 in / 192 in
Width / Height	71.3 in / 57.2 in
Weight	3516 lb (1595 kg)
Trunk / Fuel tank	19.5 cu. ft / 19 gallons
Air bags	front and side (4)
Front suspension	independent
Rear suspension	independent
Front brakes / Rear brakes	disc ABS + brake assist
Traction control	yes
Steering	rack-and-pinion, variable assist
Turning circle	38 feet
Tires (front/rear)	P205/55R16

PERFORMANCE	
Engine	V6 3-liter
Transmission	Automatic, continously variable (CVT)
Horsepower	220 hp at 6300 rpm
Torque	221 lb-ft at 3200 rpm
Other engines	bi-turbo V6 250 hp; 4.2 V8 300 or 340 hp (S6)
Other transmission	5-speed Tiptronic
Acceleration (0-60 mph)	8 sec
Maximum speed	130 mph (210 km/h) (limited)
Braking (60-0 mph)	121 feet (36.8 m)
Fuel consumption	17.5 mpg (13 L/100 km)

COMPETITION

• BMW 530i • Jaguar S-Type • Lexus GS 430
• M-Benz E320 • Volvo S80 • VW Passat W8

NEW FOR 2002

• CVT trans. • New V6 • More powerful front brakes
• OnStar Option • Tiptronic with sporty shift program

RATING	(out of 5 stars)
Driveability	★★★½
Comfort	★★★★½
Reliability	★★★★★
Roominess	★★★½
Winter driving rating	★★★★½
Safety	★★★★★
Resale value	★★★½

AUDI A8 AUDI S8

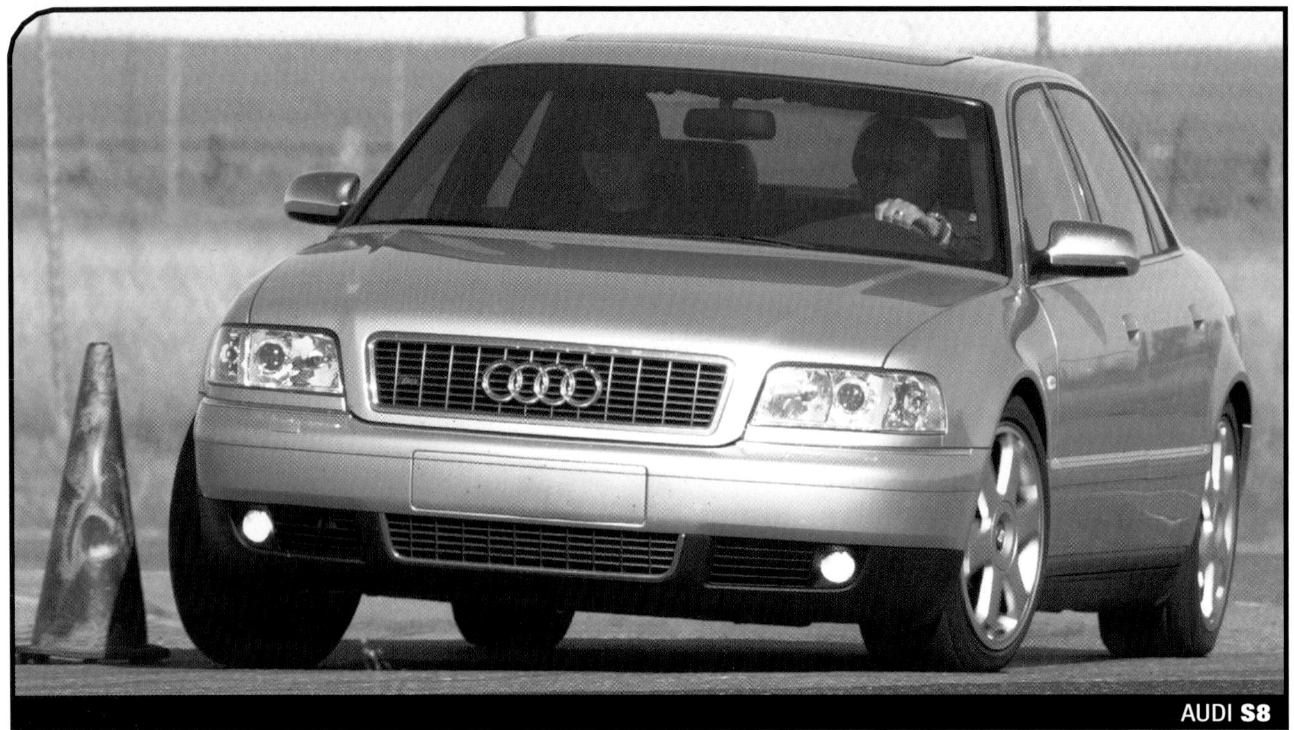
AUDI S8

False Modesty

***The Auto Guide* has already had many nice things to say about the Audi A8, considered by many to be one of the finest cars in the world. This year, just before the remodeling that the A8 badly needed in order to reassert itself, this upscale sedan from the German car manufacturer got a big sister: the S8.**

The S8 keeps its cards close to its vest and many a better known car can make the mistake of underestimating its performance. Already fast, the Audi S8 has 50 more hp than the A8 version. It unleashes 360 hp from the 4.2 V8 engine, which functions admirably with a Tiptronic 5-gear transmission twin control system (steering wheel and shift lever).

Mechanically, the S8 also benefits from Brembo brakes with four pistons, aluminum brake calipers and, of course, four ventilated discs.

Aluminum and Quattro

The difference between the S8 and a normal A8 is rather discreet and a quick glance at the bodywork won't help you tell them apart. The only visible signs are limited to the aluminum casings for the fender mirrors, the double exhaust pipe, the forged alloy 18-inch Avus wheels and some discreet insignia front and rear. Inside, the driver of an S8 gets, among other things, leather seats with a central Alcantara strip (cloth resembling brushed leather), a beautiful three-spoke steering wheel and very sophisticated inside appointments that rely on dark wood panels.

The S8 shares the A8's unflashy lines. However, this is well compensated for on the road, where it revels in its natural element, revealing a remarkable efficiency which proves beyond doubt that speed is not the only advantage of high-performance cars. The Quattro all-wheel drive is especially appreciated on slippery surfaces, while the aluminum bodywork of all A8/S8 models has dramatically proven its collision resistance after numerous tests.

Behind the wheel, you get an immediate impression of tremendous safety, largely due to a suspension that has been meticulously designed and developed. It is definitely on the firm side; however, the car does not have the slightest tendency to hop over bumps in the road, as is often the case with several other sport-performance cars. Under these driving conditions, I would even go so far as to say that it

▲ PROS

- All-wheel drive • Brilliant roadholding
- Exceptional safety • Full set of accessories
- High performance

▼ CONS

- Annoying central pillar • Exorbitant price
- Firm seats • Slow engine response
- Wide turning circle

seems less skittish than a Mercedes E55 or even a Porsche 911.

Without the DSC (Dynamic Stability Control), roadholding is neutral with some slight oversteer when pushed to the limit. With the system activated, the car does not lose its spirited nature, as the anti-skid system only interferes when the absolute limit of adhesion is reached. The rigidity of the structure is quite exceptional and contributes significantly to the S8's excellent road manners. The car glides over worst road surfaces without the slightest noise from the bodywork. The firmness of the chassis has no effect on riding comfort.

A few laps around the track, however, makes you realize that the brakes have trouble bearing the extreme demands imposed upon them on a twisty racetrack. This loss of efficiency is quite normal, however, in a car that is both heavy and capable of reaching very high speeds between corners.

The engine shows no reluctance to unleash its full power; however, it does hesitate a little when full power is applied quickly and the transmission also reveals a slightly sluggish response. Adding a Sport mode to the Tiptronic transmission in 2002 should solve the problem. Finally, the steering is always extremely pleasant, on condition that its rather wide turning circle be tolerated.

Master cuddling

Inside, luxury is foremost with an abundance of accessories, including a sliding roof with photo-electric cells triggering ventilation when the cockpit temperature goes above a set temperature. Although extremely pleasant and well designed, the stiff front seats can become uncomfortable over time. Let's also note the excessive width of the central (B) pillar, which sometimes completely obscures lateral visibility. Safety is very well looked after, as the A8/S8 are equipped with eight air bags, two of which are located in the front backrests to protect the rear passengers. And the rear passengers are extremely well treated as legroom is particularly generous and the benchseat is heated.

The Audi A8/S8 may not look striking. However, they are destined for connoisseurs who know how to appreciate them for what they are – that is, extraordinary driving machines.

Jacques Duval

SPECIFICATIONS	**S8**
Price	$CDN 86,500-102,000 / $US 62,750-73,050
Warranty	4 years / 48,000 miles (80,000 km)
Type	5-seat sedan / all wheel drive
Wheelbase / Length	113.4 in / 198.2 in
Width / Height	79 in / 55.8 in
Weight	4067 lb (1845 kg)
Trunk / Fuel tank	17.6 cu. ft / 24 gallons
Air bags	front, side, front-rear and head
Front suspension	independent
Rear suspension	independent
Front brakes / Rear brakes	disc ABS and EBD
Traction control	no
Steering	rack-and-pinion, variable assist
Turning circle	40 feet (12.25 m)
Tires (front/rear)	P245/45ZR18

PERFORMANCE	
Engine	V8 4.2 liter
Transmission	5-speed Tiptronic
Horsepower	360 hp at 7000 rpm
Torque	317 lb-ft at 3400 rpm
Other engines	V 8 4.2 liter 310 hp
Other transmission	none
Acceleration (0-60 mph)	6.2 sec
Maximum speed	155 mph (250 km/h)
Braking (60-0 mph)	118 feet (35.9 m)
Fuel consumption	15.1 mpg (15 L/100 km)

COMPETITION

• BMW M5 • Infiniti Q45 • Lexus GS 430
• Mercedes-Benz E55

NEW FOR 2002

• In-dash 6-CD changer • 18-inch alloy wheels (A8)
• Optional tire pressure gauge • Tiptronic

RATING	**(out of 5 stars)**
Driveability	★★★★½
Comfort	★★★★
Reliability	★★★★
Roominess	★★★★
Winter driving rating	★★★★½
Safety	★★★★★
Resale value	★★★½

AUDI ALLROAD QUATTRO

AUDI **ALLROAD QUATTRO**

Not Just a Wagon in High Heels

Although the Audi Allroad borrowed its bodywork and many mechanical components from the wagon on which it was modeled, this sport-ute Audi – put together to counter the Mercedes ML and BMW X5 – has almost everything in its armory to combat its rivals on equal terms.

According to Audi, the Allroad represents "the best of both worlds": that is, it includes the best features of a luxury car combined with the muscle of a sport ute. This is quite true. However, comparing it directly to either one of the "two worlds" doesn't work to its advantage. The Allroad is neither a luxury sedan nor a four-wheel drive utility vehicle as we imagine them, but a combination of the two with all that implies in terms of compromise. As a result, steering – tuned for handling the rough-and-tumble rigors of off-road driving – proves disconcertingly light on the straightaway. With a suspension designed to be equally at home on hairpin bends or in deep ruts, the Audi Allroad's road manners clearly can't rival a luxury sedan's.

Twin-turbo V6 or V8?

Once you've acknowledged these small sacrifices, this car is sheer delight. The 250-hp twin-turbo V6 engine, working closely with the 5-speed Tiptronic transmission, eliminates once and for all the Audi wagon's number-one bugaboo: its shortness of breath. Despite a slight delay during acceleration (caused by turbo lag), the Allroad sprints from 0-60 mph in 7.7 seconds. Of course, this 2.7-liter V6 lacks the responsiveness or the clear-cut power of a V8. In fact, Audi is about to offer the 300-hp V8 – the same engine that powers the current Audi A6 4.2 – as an option. In the meantime, all 2002 models offer an in-dash 6 CD changer, brushed-aluminium interior fixtures and newly styled taillights.

Judicious compromise

On the technical side, the pneumatic suspension with variable height is easier to adjust, while the Tiptronic transmission now has a Sport mode which delays shifting to a higher rev range in order to increase response times.

Despite the pneumatic suspension that automatically lowers the chassis around 75 mph (120 km/h), fuel consumption is high – 16 mpg (14 liters per 100 km) – due to the car's weight (nearly two tons) and the integral Quattro drivetrain. While roadholding is satisfactory, overall comfort is irreproachable. The Audi Allroad is

▲ PROS

• Good off-road driving • Great creature comforts • Reliability • Strong, confidence-inspiring perform… • Variable-height suspension • Very well-equipped

▼ CONS

• 4X4 without the look • Light steering • Poor gas mileage • Turbo lag

superlatively smooth, leaving all other SUVs far behind. Braking is also impressive, even if you have to make a few steering corrections during an emergency stop.

The small rattles that marred some Audis in the past were not discernible in my test model, but I must add that it was practically a new car. A small off-road expedition allowed some experimenting with the Allroad's variable-height suspension. The ground clearance goes from 5.6 inches (14.2 cm) to 8.2 inches (20.8 cm), allowing the car to go over rocks and stumps which might otherwise have damaged its bottom, even though that's already protected by a sheet of stainless steel. Thanks to the special tires, whose ribs and design are particularly well suited for off-road conditions, the Allroad will be hot on the tracks of the great majority of sport utes when off-roading. Incidentally, while the Goodyear tires sport a particularly attractive design, I doubt if they'd work efficiently in deep snow.

Comfort zone

Like in all the Audis, the Allroad interior resembles an attractive spread in a glossy architectural magazine. At night, however, the host of reddish warning lights on the controls is a nuisance, as some are reflected in the left-hand side mirror. Luxury lurks at every corner: for example, the heated steering wheel, adjustable in height and reach, the trip computer and the dual-zone heating system. In off-road mode, you'll appreciate the fold-away exterior mirrors, which make life easier in tight spots – and, of course, the GPS navigation system, which keep you from losing your way. Like all A6 station wagons, the rear seats are spacious, storage bins are numerous and practical. What's more, you can even add a third-row bench in the space reserved for cargo, large enough to accommodate two children.

Luxurious, comfortable, and boasting an impressive line of active and passive safety features, not to mention its trademark Quattro all-wheel drive, the Audi Allroad should appeal to those SUV drivers who have grown weary of being knocked around in traditional 4X4s, those dangerous, off-putting and generally unpleasant-to-drive gas-guzzlers.

Jacques Duval

SPECIFICATIONS	
Price	$CDN 58,800-59,900 / $US 42,450
Warranty	3 years / 48,000 miles (80,000 km)
Type	Wagon / all wheel drive
Wheelbase / Length	108.7 in / 189.4 in
Width / Height	76 in / 60.2 in
Weight	4233 lb (1920 kg)
Trunk / Fuel tank	16.1 cu. ft / 19 gallons
Air bags	front, side and ceiling (optional)
Front suspension	independent
Rear suspension	independent
Front brakes / Rear brakes	vented disc ABS
Traction control	yes
Steering	rack-and-pinion, variable assist
Turning circle	38 ft
Tires (front/rear)	P225/55R17W

PERFORMANCE	
Engine	V6 2.7-liter turbo
Transmission	Tiptronic 5-speed automatic
Horsepower	250 hp at 5800 rpm
Torque	258 lb-ft at 1850 rpm
Other engines	none
Other transmission	6-speed manual
Acceleration (0-60 mph)	7.7 sec
Maximum speed	130 mph (209 km/h)
Braking (60-0 mph)	130 ft (39.7 m)
Fuel consumption	16.3 mpg (13.9 L/100 km)

COMPETITION

• Volvo V70 XC

NEW FOR 2002

• 6-CD changer • Redesigned taillights • Tiptronic with sport mode • Minor revisions in cabin

RATING	**(out of 5 stars)**
Driveability	★★★½
Comfort	★★★★
Reliability	★★★★
Roominess	★★★½
Winter driving rating	★★★★½
Safety	★★★★★
Resale value	★★★½

AUDI TT ROADSTER

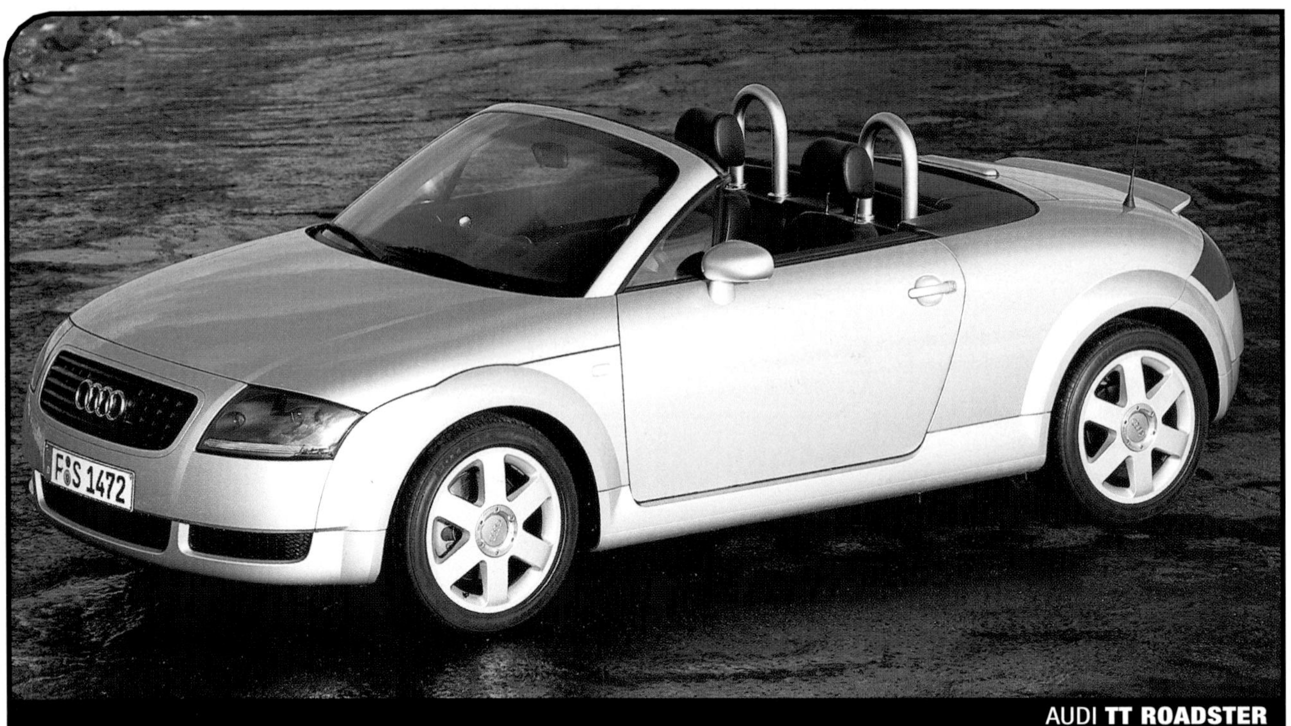

AUDI **TT ROADSTER**

How to Be Seen, and Seen Again

Many carmakers still try to attract those few people who are thinking about buying a vehicle of limited use such as a roadster. The Audi TT Roadster is living proof that they'll go to enormous pains to seduce this small group of potential customers. How does one rationalize the purchase of so impractical a two-seater? That's easy, you can't!

What one first notices about this car is that even when parked by the sidewalk, people enjoy gawking at it. The style is astounding, "revolutionary," despite the years that have gone by since it first appeared in an environment which traditionally is reluctant to follow anyone's lead. The impression is that the makeup of these lines has something organic about it, which triggers smiles and winks wherever it goes. If there ever was a blemish to this picture, I think it lies with the roofline that is at odds with the overall design of the TT. Once the roof is up, its massive lines overwhelm the whole car. From the inside, this oppressive mass could soon become a nightmare for the claustrophobic.

The interior finish, however, is pleasant. In my opinion, the workmanship and the ergonomics set a new benchmark against which all the carmakers who insist on the precision and quality of their products will be judged. The seats show a much-appreciated balance between comfort and support. The choice of materials and colors is harmonious and the design of the instrument cluster does not interfere with its legibility. Optional is a brown stitched leather border similar to the material used in baseball mitts. Personally, my taste is more conservative, but I must admit that the overall effect is outstanding.

Disappointing

Due to the cockpit's small size, one has the impression that the driver's legroom is insufficient, yet the possibilities of numerous adjustments lead to a snug fit. There are some rattles, however, and there is an impression of confinement. The controls used in normal driving are easy to access, although the power roof controls and door locks are difficult to reach. There is a general lack of space for the controls as well as for the pas-

▲ PROS

- Revolutionary lines
- All-wheel drive
- Comfortable driving position

▼ CONS

- Practically non-existent trunk
- Body rattles • Massive roof design
- Engine power difficult to muster

sengers. The brushed aluminum on the air vent openings, the pedals, the retractable lid of the radio and a few other cleverly chosen pieces of equipment give this roadster the look and breeding of a collector's car but mass produced.

Forces unleashed

After having appraised the exterior, one would expect commensurate performance. Our expectations were unfulfilled, as the alleged 225 horses were very difficult to find. Below 3500 rpm, nothing much happens. Beyond that, there is a burst of energy that heralds a full gallop, however it vanishes, and just whets our appetite for more. Intermediate gearing which is too long, excessive weight propelled by the relatively small engine, as well as an all-wheel drive, all combine and lead to our disappointment with throttle response, along with not helping performance. However, everything seems to even out, give or take a little body roll, when the first curves are encountered and the car's composure returns.

The Audi TT Roadster is an example to be followed in terms of its revolutionary lines and the quality of its materials. It is less impressive in terms of performance. This is of no great consequence as most buyers reason that their decision to purchase is based on love at first sight, and is not influenced by technical specifications. You can be sure that if creating an impression is what you wish for, wherever you go with a TT Roadster, people will stare.

Mathieu Bouthillette

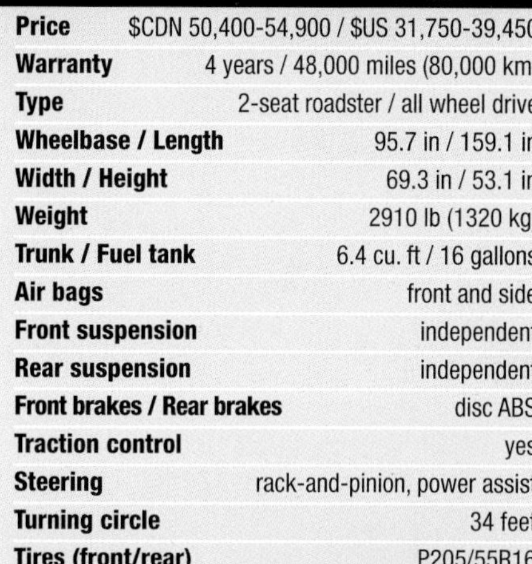

SPECIFICATIONS	**Roadster**
Price	$CDN 50,400-54,900 / $US 31,750-39,450
Warranty	4 years / 48,000 miles (80,000 km)
Type	2-seat roadster / all wheel drive
Wheelbase / Length	95.7 in / 159.1 in
Width / Height	69.3 in / 53.1 in
Weight	2910 lb (1320 kg)
Trunk / Fuel tank	6.4 cu. ft / 16 gallons
Air bags	front and side
Front suspension	independent
Rear suspension	independent
Front brakes / Rear brakes	disc ABS
Traction control	yes
Steering	rack-and-pinion, power assist
Turning circle	34 feet
Tires (front/rear)	P205/55R16

PERFORMANCE	
Engine	4L 1.8-liter turbo 20 valves
Transmission	6-speed manual
Horsepower	225 hp at 5900 rpm
Torque	207 lb-ft at 2200 - 5500 rpm
Other engines	4L 1.8-liter turbo 180 hp
Other transmission	5-speed manual
Acceleration (0-60 mph)	7 sec; 8.2 sec (180 hp)
Maximum speed	143 mph (225 hp) (230 km/h)
Braking (60-0 mph)	103 feet (31.3 m)
Fuel consumption	20.6 mpg (11 L/100 km)

COMPETITION

- BMW Z3 • Honda S2000 • Mercedes-Benz SLK
- Porsche Boxster

NEW FOR 2002

- Homelink system optional • Blue soft top 3
- Standard CD player

RATING	**(out of 5 stars)**
Driveability	★★★
Comfort	★★★
Reliability	★★★★
Roominess	★★
Winter driving rating	★★½
Safety	★★★★
Resale value	★★★

BMW 3 SERIES

BMW **325iT**

Choices Galore

Trying to figure out the permutations and combinations of BMW's 3 Series is no picnic – there are some 15 versions, using 4 body styles and just as many engine types. An embarrassment of riches, if you ask me. For 2002, BMW has added a Touring wagon to the current crop of sedans, coupes and convertibles. The latest newcomer is powered by a 2.5-liter engine, and delivered with your choice of rear- or all-wheel drive (325it, Xit). The four engine types are the 2.2-liter (320i sedan), 2.5-liter (325), 3.0-liter (330) and 3.2-liter (M3).

This article will focus mainly on the 330Xi sedan, since the M3 coupe and convertible are already featured in the "Great Sports Cars" section. Incidentally, the letter X in 330Xi – as well as in 325Xi and Xit – denotes BMW's new four-wheel drive option. Thus equipped, the 330Xi sedan can now climb snowy hills as confidently as the Audi A4, rather than watch the Audi A4 leave it embarrassingly behind as has so often happened in the past.

In fact, BMW has taken the bull by the horns. Tired of seeing Audi racking up sales simply because BMW rear-wheel drivers supposedly couldn't perform adequately in harsh winter conditions, the Bavarian automaker decided to equip its 325 and 330 with all-wheel drive. And not just any old AWD, mind you, but the highly sophisticated system borrowed from the X5, BMW's own 4X4. That alone will turn the 3 Series into formidable winter performers, not to mention ABS, traction control and a superb dynamic stability control system (DSC).

The 330Xi was indeed amazing. No matter how strenuously we twisted and turned on icy surfaces, we never once lost control of the car. Only after deactivating the DSC, did we finally manage to make the car spin.

Pleasure retained

Even with two extra driving wheels, this BMW has lost none of its legendary driving pleasure. With the engine placed slightly behind the front axle, the car drives like an ordinary, rear-wheel-drive BMW, whereas with the Audi A4, you instinctively know you're dealing first and foremost with front-wheel drive, complete with rather pronounced understeer.

▲ PROS

• Dynamic Stability Control (DSC) • Excellent handling • Moderate fuel consumption • Phenomenal winter capabilities • Superb engine

▼ CONS

• Clutch not progressive enough • Noisy all-wheel drive • Tight rear seats • Too many costly options

By combining driving pleasure with AWD, the 330Xi has finally caught up with its Audi rival – but in many other respects, it's already way ahead. Its 3.0-liter inline 6 with 225 hp, for example, is clearly more vigorous than the A4's 3.0-liter V6, or the 1.8-liter turbo engine. Bursting with so much power and torque, the BMW engine is also a delight at high rpm, emitting a basso profundo rumble that's so soothing to the ears. With a 5-speed manual gearbox, it handles like a genuine sports car. Braking is highly effective and the rack-and-pinion steering unfailingly precise. Despite the 17-inch tires, the ride is smooth and comfortable.

But the 330Xi is a small car, so the seats are on the tight side, especially in the rear. The trunk, too, is narrow and smallish, but with fold-down seats, the problem is partly solved. Ski lovers will be happy to learn that the car comes outfitted with a special pouch in which to carry the boards, so the interior won't get soiled.

On the highway, the car was relatively noisy. I couldn't tell whether it was because of the all-wheel drive, or the Pirelli snow tires, or a combination of the two. But the growling was insistent and could be annoying in the long run.

Watch those options!

The interior feels nice, with excellent seats, variable-assist power steering, easy-to-read instruments and exquisite finish. But I must point out that the test car was overequipped, and the excessive option list can bring the bill up to about $60,300, for a car with a base price of $45,000. Frankly, all you need to shell out is an extra $3100 for all-wheel drive, and that will take care of all your problems. If you want a satellite navigation system, it will set you back $3900. The Premium package (leather finish, power seat, Harmon Kardon stereo system) means another $5000. With a couple more accessories, you'll soon be looking at $60,300. For this amount, however, you might as well consider the superior Audi A6, or even a BMW 5 Series model.

With the 330Xi, BMW should be able to entice those buyers who deserted it for Audi and the A4 to return. The 330Xi does cost slightly more, but as they say, it's more than just a pretty bauble.

Jacques Duval

330 Xi

SPECIFICATIONS	**330 Xi**
Price	$CDN 34,500-62,900 / $US 27,635-43,045
Warranty	4 years / 48,000 miles (80,000 km)
Type	5-seat sedan / all wheel drive
Wheelbase / Length	107.3 in / 176 in
Width / Height	68.5 in / 55.7 in
Weight	3516 lb (1595 kg)
Trunk / Fuel tank	15.5 cu.ft / 17 gallons
Air bags	front, side fr/r (head optional)
Front suspension	independent
Rear suspension	independent
Front brakes / Rear brakes	disc ABS
Traction control	yes
Steering	rack-and-pinion, variable assist
Turning circle	36 feet
Tires (front/rear)	P225/45ZR17

PERFORMANCE	
Engine	6L 3.0-liter
Transmission	5-speed manual
Horsepower	225 hp at 5900 rpm
Torque	214 lb-ft at 3500 rpm
Other engines	6L 2.2 (168 hp); 2.5 (184 hp); 3.2 (333 hp)
Other transmission	5-speed automatic
Acceleration (0-60 mph)	7 sec
Maximum speed	128 mph (206 km/h)
Braking (60-0 mph)	115 feet (35 m)
Fuel consumption	20.8 mpg (10.9 L/100 km)

COMPETITION

• Audi A4 • Jaguar X-Type • Mercedes-Benz C320 • Saab 9⁵ • Volvo S60 AWD

NEW FOR 2002

• New colors • New interior features • Station wagon • Steptronic

RATING	**(out of 5 stars)**
Driveability	★★★★
Comfort	★★★½
Reliability	★★★★
Roominess	★★★
Winter driving rating	★★★★
Safety	★★★★½
Resale value	★★★★

BMW 5 SERIES

BMW **M5**

Pleasure to the Power of 5

Most luxury cars are not sports cars. And most sports cars are not luxurious. The BMW 5 Series are amongst the rare cars who really manage to bring together harmoniously luxury and sport characteristics. And if you really want to embarrass a Corvette or a Porsche 911, try the M5 version. You will not be disappointed.

If life is spoiling you, and you feel jaded, you need some real driving fun; do yourself a favour and buy a BMW 5 Series. Six years after its last revamping, the 5 Series is still seductive. Roomier than the popular "small" sedans of the 3 Series and far more distinguished, the BMW 5 Series will introduce you to real driving pleasure. They are solid, they are solidly built, they are reassuring, and with a selection of two different models and a choice of four engines, there is enough there to satisfy any taste and – on the condition that they are reasonably thickly lined – there is one to satisfy any wallet.

Doubling your pleasure

When one realizes that the engine power available goes from 184 to 400 HP, one must also realize that the chassis is designed with serious performance in mind. The rigidity of the whole platform and the high quality of the suspension systems incorporating aluminium parts permit this doubling of power with what is essentially the same chassis while preserving its exceptional agility and balance for a 1,700 kg (3,700 lbs) machine.

BMW offers this large selection of power options through four different engines, two of which are in-line 3.0-6-cylinder (2.5 litre, 184 HP and 3 litre, 225 HP) which also power the 3 Series models, a 4.0 litre V8 (282 HP) and another 5.0-litre V8 (400 HP) which propel the magical M5 at breathtaking speeds. The price tag obviously revs up with the power rating, however, if you are rather indifferent to power, the 6-cylinder models are quite a viable option. Responsive, robust, with satisfactory performance, the 2.5 litre and its big brother the 3 litre will allow you to savour a BMW without necessarily having to mortgage the house.

Still a benchmark

The fact remains however that the V8 of the 540i is a mechanical marvel which fits the sedan like a glove. The terrific torque guarantees quick responsiveness whatever the gear you selected in the 6

▲ PROS

- Distinguished look • Rigid frame • riding comfort
- Choice of engines • Excellent roadholding
- Upscale performance (540i and M5)

▼ CONS

- Complexity of some controls • Restricted access to the trunk • High price (540i and M5)
- Models close to retirement

much higher speed. On the highway, at speeds that command respect, it's like riding on an air cushion. I kid you not.

M for Mamma Mia!

There is nothing better than to test an M5 to the full other than a real racetrack. First, a few laps around the track to get used to the beast, then gradually increase the tempo. First observation: the track is too short to take full advantage of the 400 HP V8. You have barely finished with a curve when the next one is on top of you. Acceleration is simply out of this world: I counted five seconds to go from50 mph (80 km/h) to 75 mph (120 km/h) in fourth gear ... and 0 to 63 mph takes 5.5 seconds. As to the brakes, it takes 112 feet (34 m) to get the 1,700-kg mass from 60-0 mph (100 km/h). Can anyone do better? Finally, road holding: on entry into a corner, the M5 is neutral, then moves to gradual understeer, and one must lift off the accelerator just slightly to get the back of the car to come around. Obviously, the various electronic aides work their magic as needed, but even without them it was impossible for me to get the back to slide. One must admit that the Michelin Pilot Sport tires on 18-inch rims are determined to keep their reputation.

Thus, for $104,250, you can go for a nice leisurely drive with the family on some country road or "burn rubber" on a racing track, at the wheel of a sedan which bears no comparison. Apart from the financial strain, you will have to sacrifice a little bit of creature comfort and pretend to ignore the vibrations which somehow reach the cockpit (the 35 profile of the tires are the cause), without forgetting to limit the size of your luggage, as the trunk won't open enough to get high items in. You had better hope that you won't need the spare tire, as you will only find in the trunk a kit that just re-pressurises your flat tire. To compensate, BMW has a low pressure warming light that will give you a fair warning before you run out of air.

The ultimate sports sedan, the M5 is just not for anybody, and quite frankly I am not quite sure whether it is something that we can handle. Our road network, our driving habits and the speed limits, do not lend themselves to this type of vehicle. We could only end up frustrated. It's too bad.

SPECIFICATIONS	**M5**
Price	$CDN 55,200-105,500 / $US 36,045-70,045
Warranty	years / 48,000 miles (80,000 km)
Type	sedan / rear wheel drive
Wheelbase / Length	111.4 in / 188.2 in
Width / Height	70.9 in / 56.7 in
Weight	4023 lb (1825 kg)
Trunk / Fuel tank	16.2 cu. ft / 19 gallons
Air bags	front, side and head
Front suspension	independent
Rear suspension	independent
Front brakes / Rear brakes	disc
Traction control	yes
Steering	rack-and-pinion, power assist
Turning circle	48 feet
Tires (front/rear)	P245/40ZR18 / P275/35ZR18

PERFORMANCE	
Engine	V8 5-liter 32 valves
Transmission	6-speed manual
Horsepower	400 hp at 6600 rpm
Torque	368 lb-ft at 3800 rpm
Other engines	6L 2.5-liter 184 hp; 3.0-liter 225 hp; V8 4.4-liter 282 hp
Other transmission	5-speed automatic (except M5)
Acceleration (0-60 mph)	5.5 sec
Maximum speed	155 mph (250 km/h)
Braking (60-0 mph)	112 feet (34 m)
Fuel consumption	13.3 mpg (17 L/100 km)

COMPETITION

- Mercedes-Benz E55 AMG

NEW FOR 2002

No major change

RATING	**(out of 5 stars)**
Driveability	★★★★
Comfort	★½
Reliability	★★★
Roominess	★
Winter driving rating	★★
Safety	★★½
Resale value	★★★★½

BMW 7 SERIES

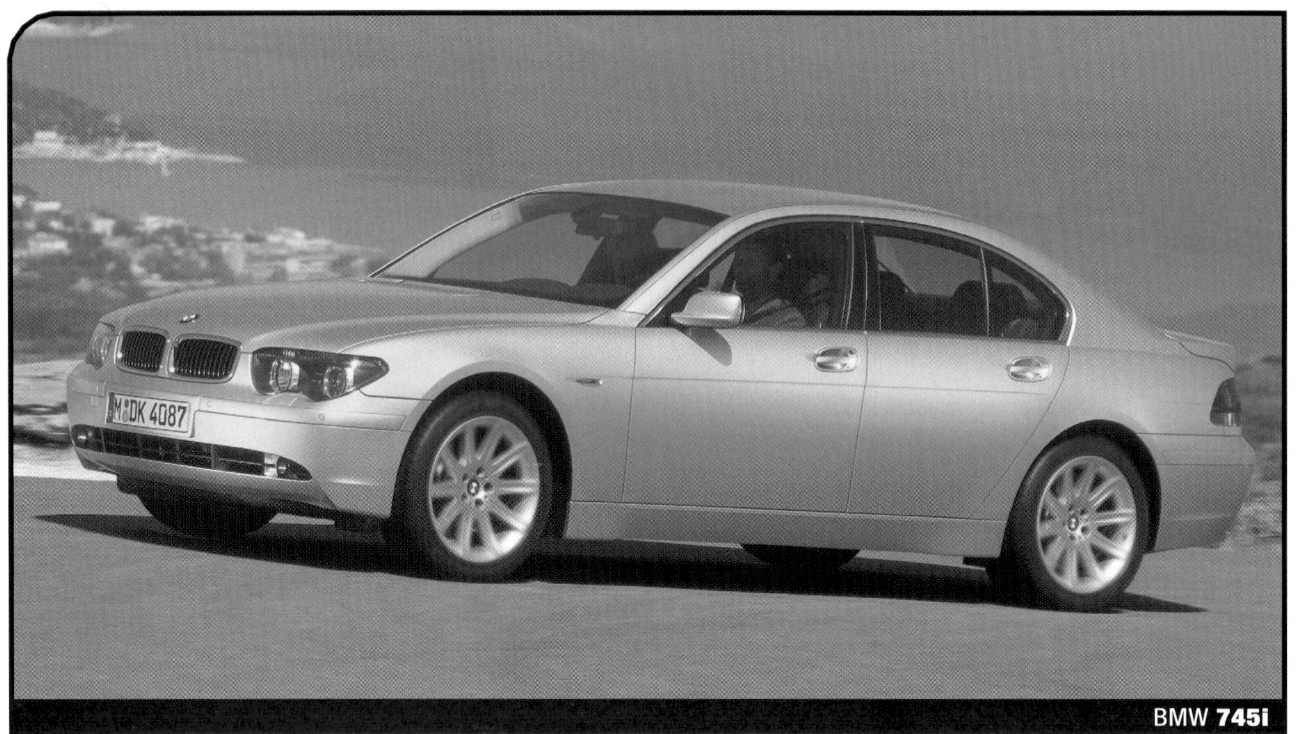

BMW **745i**

The car of the future, today

Until this year, BMW seemed to have thrown in the towel with its prestige 7 Series sedan. Outclassed, not to say humiliated by Mercedes-Benz and its superb S Class, the Munich carmaker seemed to be indifferent to its old time rival's success. Practically untouched for eight years, the 740 was showing signs of age, particularly as the models introduced in 1994 had been updated rather timidly. For 2002, the Bavarian brand has sounded the charge with "the upscale motor car of tomorrow." What is this all about?

First, it is quite clear that BMW intends to hoist the new 7 Series at the top of the luxury car pyramid. This is at least what one is led to believe while reading the 56 pages describing the future 745i which will only arrive at the BMW dealer showrooms in January 2002.

The first 6-speed automatic transmission

This German carmaker has spared no effort to create a car which, through state-of-the-art technology and new equipment, should catch up with if not overtake its rivals. Although the new engine has the same cubic capacity as the previous one, the 4.4-liter V8 has acquired an extra 49 hp. Its 333 hp, variable cam timing systems (called Double Vanos), variable camshaft profiles (Valvetronic) and for the first time, an infinitely variable-length intake manifold. These new technologies have not only allowed greater power and responsiveness from the engine, but have improved gas mileage by 14%.

Transmission of all this power is left to the first 6-speed automatic box ever fitted to a production car anywhere. This compact high efficiency gearbox comes with shift-by-wire technology (no mechanical linkage), controlled from a steering wheel selector and, when in manual mode (Steptronic), with small stalks under the steering wheel.

Upstage Mercedes?

It seems promising but only experience will tell whether these innovations are as extraordinary as alleged. One thing is for certain. BMW is determined to preserve the sporting characteristics of its grand luxury limousine as acceleration time from 0 to 60 is indicated at 6.3 seconds. Maximum speed is limited according to German law to 156 mph (250 km/h).

There is no doubt that the new 7 Series will be a very strong performer on the high-

▲ PROS

- Not test-driven (available January 2002)

▼ CONS

- Not available

way. Yet, BMW promises a car which will be equally at ease on the back roads. All-aluminum suspension with continuously variable shock absorbers and, as an option, pneumatic rear springs with automatic self-leveling, work to further strengthen the already good roadholding qualities of the 745i.

Learning to drive again?

Where BMW does not hesitate to renovate radically, it is with a new system which could redefine the way we drive a car. Called iDrive, this concept referred to as intelligent could theoretically handle up to 700 different functions. It eliminates the need for an ignition key and the gear shifter. The few necessary elements involved in basic driving are centered on the steering wheel and the occasional functions are then controlled from the center of the dashboard. Other functions such as air conditioning, the audio system, the cell phone and the GPS navigation system are controlled by a knob on the center console. On top of that, the driver can select the information he wants to have displayed on the dashboard screen. One only has to mention that this BMW has 123 servomotors to understand the complexity and possible risks that something may go wrong.

Given the average age of potential buyers of the 7 Series, one wonders if this clientele will adapt to such revolutionary changes in its driving habits. One thing is certain, quite a few may hesitate before shelling out $100,000 for a car that brings together so much new untested technology.

Even passive safety systems have been redefined. Thus, the lateral air curtains are synchronized with the rear air bags (which are optional) in order to protect from head injuries both in the front and in the back. Moreover, reactive headrests come forward automatically to protect against the famous whiplash effect in case of a rear collision. Finally, front passengers will benefit from air bags protecting their knees. BMW has also managed to upstage Mercedes by fitting the latest 7 Series with a sensor system (ISIS) which senses and reacts at a very high speed to detect imminent collisions and put all the active security systems on alert.

For once, BMW seems determined to take the high ground in this prestigious automobile category.

Jacques Duval

SPECIFICATIONS	**745i**
Price	n.a.
Warranty	4 years/48,000 miles (80,000 km)
Type	5-seat sedan / rear wheel drive
Wheelbase / Length	117.7 in / 198.0 in
Width / Height	74.8 in / 58.7 in
Weight	4123 lb (1870 kg)
Trunk / Fuel tank	17.7 cu.ft / 23 gallons
Air bags	front, side fr/r, knees and head
Front suspension	independent
Rear suspension	independent
Front brakes / Rear brakes	disc ABS
Traction control	yes
Steering	rack-and-pinion, variable assist
Turning circle	n.a.
Tires (front/rear)	P245/55R17

PERFORMANCE	
Engine	V8 4.4-liter
Transmission	6-speed automatic
Horsepower	333 hp at 6100 rpm
Torque	332 lb-ft at 3600 rpm
Other engines	none
Other transmission	none
Acceleration (0-60 mph)	6.3 sec
Maximum speed	156 mph (250 km/h)
Braking (60-0 mph)	n.a.
Fuel consumption	18.6 mpg (12.2 L/100 km)

COMPETITION

• Audi A8 • Infiniti Q45 • Jaguar Vanden Plas
• Lexus LS430 • Mercedes-Benz S Class

NEW FOR 2002

• New model

RATING	**(out of 5 stars)**
Driveability	Not available
Comfort	
Reliability	
Roominess	
Winter driving rating	
Safety	
Resale value	

BMW X5

BMW **X5**

Mission Accomplished

Last year, BMW launched its first 4X4, christened the X5. Knowing that its customers never venture off the beaten path, the Munich firm applied its familiar theme of "pure driving pleasure," endowing the X5 with car-like qualities, rather than following the off-road approach. The result is convincing, even eloquent.

Still, it was a gamble. BMW's reputation has been the stuff of legend, but whether its automotive approach would lend itself to the specialized characteristics of sport-utilities was another story. Skeptics abounded in the press room.

The Bavarian carmaker prefers the term "Sport Activity Vehicle" (SAV) to designate its 4X4. If the word "sport" figures indiscriminately in automobile parlance, its use in this context is entirely appropriate, given the awesome capabilities of the X5 – an all-terrain vehicle that's not quite what it seems, according to BMW. The X5's chosen playground is the paved road, the off-road rough stuff is for others. There, you've been warned.

And that's exactly what BMW had in mind when it built the X5: Optimizing the machine's road-handling capabilities. To achieve its objective, it settled on a robust unibody, and fitted it with a sophisticated four-wheel independent suspension borrowed from the 7-series sedans. The front suspension features double-articulated MacPherson struts, expressly designed for the X5, while the rear consists of a multi-link configuration. Automatic air suspension is also available, as standard equipment or option, depending on the version.

Now on to the all-important part. The X5 comes in two versions, and the main difference between them is found under the hood: one is fitted with a 3-liter in-line 6-cylinder engine, the other, a 4.4-liter V8.

With 225 hp, the in-line 6 has no trouble pulling the heavy carcass of this SAV. The manual transmission obviously does a better job, but the automatic is far from shabby, allowing a 0-60 mph time of just under 9 seconds.

Driving pleasure personified

When it comes to torque and acceleration, however, the V8 leaves the in-line 6 in the dust. Despite its refined and elegant appearance, the V8-equipped X5 growls like the muscle cars of yore, and scoots like one, too.

This mixing of genres is all the more impressive because, unlike muscle cars, the

▲ PROS

• Good styling • Spacious and comfortable cockpit • Excellent engines • Sporty handling • Powerful brakes

▼ CONS

• Limited off-road capabilities • High fuel consumption (V8) • Technical limitations • Expensive options • Uneven after-sales service

X5's ability extends beyond the straight-ahead highway. The BMW touch makes all the difference, in the fluid way its vehicles handle themselves on the road. In this regard, the X5 stands out from the crowd, and no matter what SUV detractors like me may suspect, the fact is, BMW's first 4X4 lives up to its distinguished family name.

Like all vehicles bearing the BMW seal, the X5 carries itself with aplomb, regardless of road conditions. It's exceptionally nimble, thanks to all-wheel drive and, blessed with highly precise steering and ultra-powerful brakes, it has already surged ahead of the competition. No other SUV can claim such smooth and well-balanced road behavior, such control over body roll. To say that the X5 is the Formula 1 of 4X4s is getting a bit carried away. But, really, we're talking about the BMW of 4X4s here. That about sums it all up.

Gorgeous, but not perfect

When you move in the highest circles, appearance is as important as content. In such a rarefied atmosphere, the knives may not exactly be out, but you can feel their presence. In any case, it's better to arouse envy than suffer fools, and the X5 does just that. Exquisitely "turned out," it's caused quite a stir everywhere it's gone. Let's not beat around the bush: The X5 is without the shadow of a doubt the best-looking SUV on the market.

The interior features typically BMW stuff, from the dashboard, steering wheel and controls to the soft-hued, lush cockpit. It's as comfortable as it is spacious and the rear seats make the X5's number-1 rival – the Mercedes-Benz M Class (ML320 and 430) – blush with envy. Not only is there more legroom, but the seats are much more comfortable, elegantly sculpted and better padded. Ergonomics are simply perfect, offering nifty nooks and crannies as well as ample overall storage space. The trunk is cavernous and easy to reach.

The only discordant note is the X5's list of expensive option packages, for which there's no good reason, considering the vehicle's steep sticker price. Also, some of the electronic accessories didn't even function properly at the time of our test drives. I might add that some BMW dealers aren't exactly adept at after-sales service. So think hard and exercise caution when the time comes to acquire such a luxury item. Because that's what the X5 is – a luxury item.

SPECIFICATIONS	3.0i
Price	$CDN 56,800-68,800 / $US 39,470-49,970
Warranty	4 years / 48,000 miles (80,000 km)
Type	sport-utility / all wheel drive
Wheelbase / Length	111 in / 184 in
Width / Height	74 in / 67 in
Weight	4519 lb (2050 kg)
Trunk / Fuel tank	16.1 cu. ft / 25 gallons
Air bags	front, side and head
Front suspension	independent
Rear suspension	independent
Front brakes / Rear brakes	vented disc ABS / disc ABS
Traction control	yes
Steering	rack-and-pinion; variable assist
Turning circle	40 feet
Tires (front/rear)	P235/65R17

PERFORMANCE	
Engine	6L 3-liter
Transmission	5-speed automatic
Horsepower	225 hp at 5900 rpm
Torque	214 lb-ft at 3500 rpm
Other engines	V8 4.4-liter 282 hp
Other transmission	5-speed manual
Acceleration (0-60 mph)	7.6 sec
Maximum speed	128 mph (206 km/h) (limited)
Braking (60-0 mph)	128 feet (38.9 m)
Fuel consumption	16.1 mpg (14.1 L/100 km)

COMPETITION

• Acura MDX • Infiniti QX4 • Lexus LX 470 • Mercedes-Benz M Class • Porsche Cayenne

NEW FOR 2002

No major change

RATING	(out of 5 stars)
Driveability	★★★½
Comfort	★★★½
Reliability	★★★
Roominess	★★★★
Winter driving rating	★★★★½
Safety	★★★★
Resale value	★★★★

BMW Z3

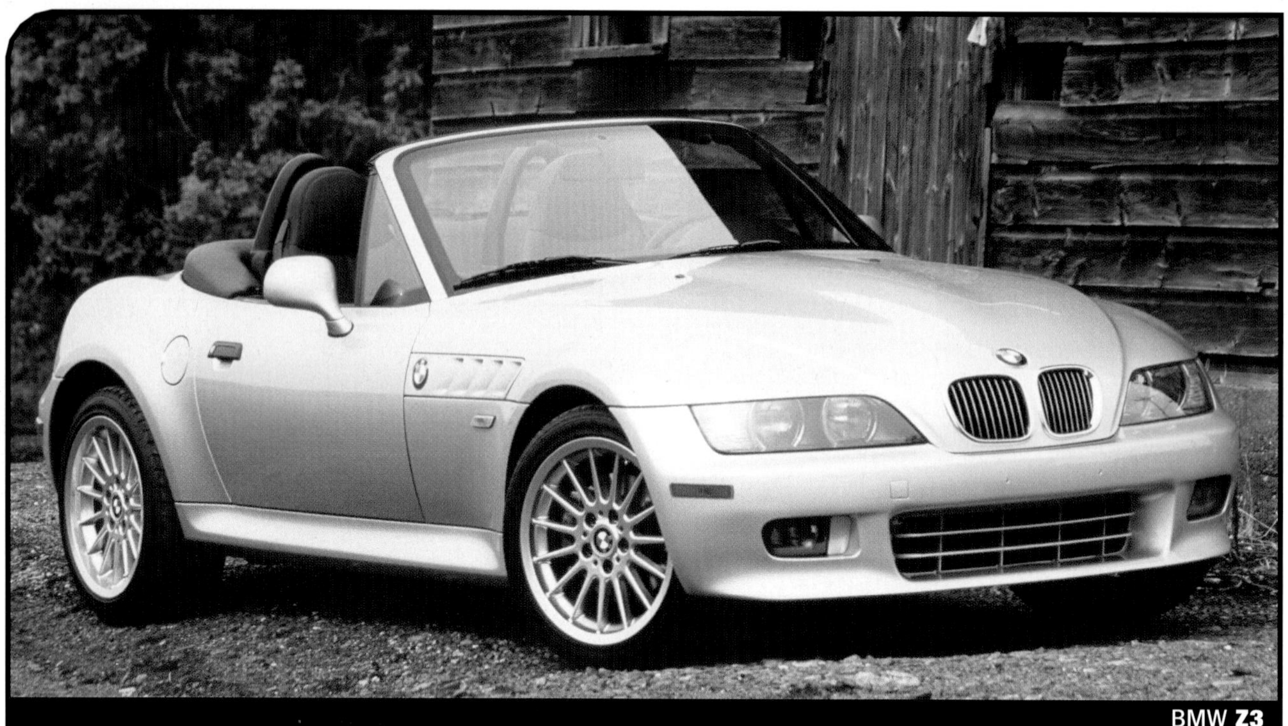

BMW **Z3**

Z3's Metamorphosis

In my considered opinion, BMWs are generally very fine cars which offer genuine driving pleasure. I emphasize the word "generally" as there is one model, just one, that I cannot stand: the Z3. Ungraceful, bulbous lines, unbalanced shape bordering on distaste – quite frankly, an ugly coupe. But beware, replies the enthusiast: the car is very popular! And they're right.

As soon as it came out in 1996, the Z3 roadster attracted a lot of comments. On the one hand, to decry the far too easy-going 138-hp 4-cylinder and on the other hand (and more so) to question this shape ... which is of course questionable! It is interesting to note that on this subject opinions are generally dramatically opposed to each other: one simply adores it or detests it. Since then, in the course of a first metamorphosis, the Z3 roadster acquired cylinders (two exactly), and quite a few horses, and then it grew a roof to receive the name Z3 coupe, then it paid a visit to the "M" performance shop (BMW Motorsport) to change itself into a ballistic missile.

Meanwhile, back on Earth

Mechanically speaking, the last few models of the first generation Z3 offer a 2.5-liter 6-cylinder (184 hp) and a 3.0-liter (225 hp) which replaces the older 2.8-liter of a previous vintage. The 5-speed manual gearbox is ready for service: if you are not interested in sporty driving, you can always choose the 5-speed automatic gearbox. Between these two engines, it is obviously the 3.0-liter which is the most satisfying. Responsive, supersmooth, it delivers ample low range torque with a beautiful sound, this in-line 6 propels the 2860 lbs (1300 kg) roadster with disconcerting ease and pushes it from 0 to 60 mph (100 km/h) in less than 6.5 seconds. More impressive still, the four large disc brakes with the enormous tires on the 17-inch rims bring this machine to a halt in 120 feet (36 m) and a bit, from 60 mph.

Soon to be replaced

So much for numbers and pedigree. When it comes to movement, the Z3 has inherited numerous parts from the present day sedans of the 3 Series, except for the rear suspension which comes from a 3 Series of the previous generation, which may explain the slight skittishness of the rear axle when pressed vigorously. Fortunately, the standard track control system kicks in

▲ PROS

• Spirited performance (3.0 liter) • Better reliability • Excellent brakes • Real driving pleasure

▼ CONS

• Controversial lines • Plastic soft top window • Small trunk • Soon to be retired

to correct driver excesses. Same thing with the anti-skid and anti-locking control devices, which allow you, should you wish it, to drive the roadster all year-round without too many complications as long as you use winter tires, of course. Let us mention that the Z3 coupe, which reminds us of the boxy-shaped wagons of the 1960s, is obviously a better option for the rigors of winter and offers to boot far better cargo space. As far as looks are concerned, one either likes or dislikes, according to taste. Be that as it may, the Z3 coupe is no longer in the Canadian catalog, probably because of disappointing sales.

As far as equipment is concerned, and in view of the price tag, the Z3 has all the essentials: air conditioning, electric windows, heated wing mirrors, CD player, power seats, four air bags. As far as performance is concerned, the 3.0-liter is the one to have if you want to do more than doodle around. But BMW will make you pay for it ... $9000.

New generation Z3 on the way

Yes indeed, the first generation Z3 will soon be retired before the new roadster – with the controversial new lines of the X coupe presented by BMW at the Detroit Auto Show in January 2001 – replaces it. Longer and wider, the future Z3 roadster is roomier and has more cargo space (a must for golfers). The power operated soft top will have a glass window and will be stored under the rigid top in the manner of the Porsche Boxster. Two inverted U-frames inspired by the magical Z8 protect the passenger's and driver's heads. As for the power plant, nothing official for the moment, but we can bet that the 3.0-liter 6-cylinder will be available. The coupe is not in the production plans as of now. As for an eventual magical M model, one will probably have to move to the United States in order to get one of these futuristic rockets on wheels because, according to the planners at BMW, Canada does not seem a likely place for that kind of machinery. Our roads, perhaps?

Alain Raymond

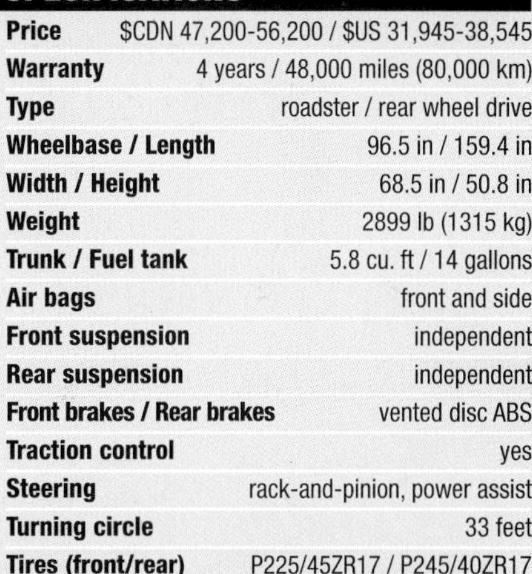

SPECIFICATIONS

Price	$CDN 47,200-56,200 / $US 31,945-38,545
Warranty	4 years / 48,000 miles (80,000 km)
Type	roadster / rear wheel drive
Wheelbase / Length	96.5 in / 159.4 in
Width / Height	68.5 in / 50.8 in
Weight	2899 lb (1315 kg)
Trunk / Fuel tank	5.8 cu. ft / 14 gallons
Air bags	front and side
Front suspension	independent
Rear suspension	independent
Front brakes / Rear brakes	vented disc ABS
Traction control	yes
Steering	rack-and-pinion, power assist
Turning circle	33 feet
Tires (front/rear)	P225/45ZR17 / P245/40ZR17

PERFORMANCE

Engine	6L 3.0-liter
Transmission	5-speed manual
Horsepower	225 hp at 5500 rpm
Torque	214 lb-ft at 3500 rpm
Other engines	6L 2.5-liter 184 hp
Other transmission	5-speed automatic
Acceleration (0-60 mph)	6.5 sec
Maximum speed	128 mph (206 km/h)
Braking (60-0 mph)	119 ft (36.2 m)
Fuel consumption	20.3 mpg (11.2 L/100 km)

COMPETITION

• Audi TT Roadster • Honda S2000
• Mercedes-Benz SLK • Porsche Boxster

NEW FOR 2002

• New model expected in 2002

RATING	**(out of 5 stars)**
Driveability	★★★★
Comfort	★★★½
Reliability	★★★½
Roominess	★★
Winter driving rating	★★
Safety	★★★
Resale value	★★★½

BUICK CENTURY BUICK REGAL OLDSMOBILE INTRIGUE

BUICK **CENTURY**

1887 – 2002 R.I.P.

It was in 1887 that Ransom Eli Olds built the first "Oldsmobile" – a three-wheeled, steam-powered vehicle. A hundred and fifteen years later, at the dawn of the 21st century, General Motors has finally decided to pull the plug on the oldest American automobile marque. Herewith, a farewell Oldsmobile test drive – as a tribute from the *Auto Guide*.

If you're puzzled by GM's decision to abandon the Oldsmobile, remember that business managers and accountants have their own special reasons, which aren't always fathomable to ordinary folks like you and me. Rather than complaining about them, let's just enjoy one last spin in the Oldsmobile Intrigue – one of the more popular General Motors sedans.

An Audi TT it's not, but the Intrigue looks smart enough all the same, oozing understated charm with its bona fide classic lines. The snout is pure Oldsmobile, especially the elongated headlights and lower twin air intakes that replace the central grille.

Middle-class charm

Needless to say, such grace and discretion are also present inside the cabin. The instrument panel extends all the way to the center console, which houses the CD/stereo, heating and climate-control systems. Controls are well indicated and within easy reach – those mounted on the steering wheel are even illuminated at night. All are discreet, well thought out and efficient. On the other hand, the finish and the quality of the materials used leave a great deal to be desired.

Other pluses include the conveniently placed elbow rests, in-dash ignition key, OnStar vehicle assistance system, rear bench with fold-down individual backrests, power exterior mirrors (though not heated) and a good-sized catch-all net in the trunk. In the debit column are the so-so rear seats and the lack of side-impact airbags and of adjustable pedals (standard on its rival, the Ford Taurus). Incidentally, as is the case in the Taurus, the difference in height between the accelerator and brake pedal is disconcertingly pronounced. And watch out for those wide, slippery leather seats, especially when you're cornering. You'd better hang on tight to the steering wheel for support, even though that's not its primary job. But it just goes to show, the Intrigue wasn't built for twisting and turning. So, buyers beware!

Farewell Olds

▲ PROS

• Airy and comfortable cockpit • Harmonious lines • Reliability on the rise • Vigorous and efficient engine

▼ CONS

• Condemned marque • Front seats lacking support • So-so driving pleasure • Sub-par finish

These complaints don't mean handling is bad, however. Far from it. Both understeer and body roll are under control even though the front of the car carries much more than half (64%) its total weight. When braking, you will never forget that you're working on a 3500-lb mass, and on top of that, the brake pedal is a tad too stiff, and steering is heavy. On the other hand, the standard four-wheel disc brakes with ABS are powerful. Traction control is optional.

Fantastic V6

Power is supplied by the excellent 3.5-liter DOHC V6, paired to a highly responsive 4-speed automatic gearbox. Thanks to 230 lb-ft of torque, it takes a mere 6.5 seconds to go from 50 to 75 mph (80 to 120 km/h) – leaving the Ford Taurus in the dust. For 2002, GM is offering a 5-year or 62,500-mile (100,000 km) warranty, in order to clear its Intrigue inventory.

Despite all the foregoing qualities – good acceleration, excellent road manners, powerful brakes, above-average overall comfort – I can't say that the Intrigue is fun to drive. There's something lacking, and I can't quite put my finger on it: maybe it's the steering, which I find a tad uncommunicative, or is it the "not quite there" suspension? Too much weight in the front? Or the inadequate front seats? Or could it be simply a question of image: the image of a carmaker who hasn't quite succeeded in ... reshaping its image?

Buick cousins to the rescue?

Will the Buick Century and Regal – which share the Intrigue's platform – pick up where the latter has left off? Time will tell. In the meantime, neither measures up to the Oldsmobile. The Century, the homelier of the pair, will no doubt appeal to buyers who have grown weary of those huge 1970s sedans. It's quiet, spongy (seats and suspension), and acquits itself reasonably well – that is, on smooth surfaces and at low speeds. The less homely Regal (I was going to say "sportier") will not feel quite so lethargic if you opt for the boosted, 240-hp version of the V6, but I must warn you that for all those extra horses, it doesn't perform any better than the Century.

All in all, if you insist on buying a GM car no matter what, the Intrigue is your best bet. So hurry, before they're all gone.

Alain Raymond

OLDSMOBILE **INTRIGUE**

SPECIFICATIONS	GLS
Price	$CDN 25,325-33,680 / $US 20,630-27,245
Warranty	5 years / 60,000 miles (100,000 km)
Type	sedan / front wheel drive
Wheelbase / Length	109 in / 195.9 in
Width / Height	73.6 in / 56.7 in
Weight	3435 lb (1558 kg)
Trunk / Fuel tank	16.3 cu. ft / 18 gallons
Air bags	front
Front suspension	independent
Rear suspension	independent
Front brakes / Rear brakes	disc ABS
Traction control	yes
Steering	rack-and-pinion, power assist
Turning circle	40 feet
Tires (front/rear)	P225/60R16

PERFORMANCE	
Engine	V6 3.5-liter
Transmission	4-speed automatic
Horsepower	215 hp at 5600 rpm
Torque	230 lb-ft at 4400 rpm
Other engines	none
Other transmission	none
Acceleration (0-60 mph)	8.3 sec
Maximum speed	109 mph (175 km/h)
Braking (60-0 mph)	145 feet (44.2 m)
Fuel consumption	19.1 mpg (11.9 L/100 km)

COMPETITION

• Acura TL • Chevrolet Impala • Chrysler Intrepid • Ford Taurus • Honda Accord V6 • Nissan Maxima

NEW FOR 2002

• 5-year / 60,000 miles (100,000 km) warranty
• New colors • New radios

RATING	(out of 5 stars)
Driveability	★★★
Comfort	★★★½
Reliability	★★★½
Roominess	★★★★
Winter driving rating	★★★½
Safety	★★★½
Resale value	★★

BUICK PARK AVENUE BUICK PARK AVENUE ULTRA

BUICK **PARK AVENUE**

Adrift in a Sea of "Hot Babes"

I remember my aunt's wedding as if it were yesterday. It was in the early 1950s, and because I was only a kid the event seemed as dull as dishwater — until one of my uncles drove up in a big Buick, amid oohs and aahs from the assembled company. *Uncle Ed's got a Buick! Isn't that swell! What luxury! And what a machine!*

Fast forward to the same scene today. You're at a family gathering and Uncle Jerry shows up in a Park Avenue Ultra. Do you suppose somebody's going to get all excited, or whisper to his or her tablemate that Uncle Jerry drives a Park Avenue? Fat chance! The name no longer carries the same cachet, Ultra version or not.

Out of popular favor today, the Buick division continues to produce full-sized sedans which hold less and less appeal, because they all lack a certain quality – you know, that exotic aura that gets people enthused. And so, little by little, those sedans slid into obscurity. That's really too bad, because a closer look at the Park Avenue, for example, will reveal plenty. In short, it doesn't have to be envious of those big-ticket Japanese cars in its category, which look even blander and probably don't ride as well either.

Lost generation

In 1996, the Park Avenue was given a few minor touch-ups – Buick's idea of "rejuvenating" its glorious lines of yesteryear. With their customer-satisfaction index high in their minds, Buick management chose to err on the side of caution and play the continuity card. The Park Avenue still looks elegant, but its lines seem more and more old-fashioned when placed beside competitors which are generally given a makeover every three years. It's true that Buick's customers are conservative, but surely that doesn't mean the division can't use some imagination.

A hidden gem

The cockpit is more modern since the 1970s-style dashboard was replaced. Unfortunately, commands are far apart and you need long arms to reach the audio and climate controls located at the far-right end. In addition, the steering wheel looks as though it has been borrowed from a low-end Korean car, ditto the stiff gearshift mounted on the steering column. On the other hand, the finish and

▲ PROS

- Adequate equipment • Competitive price
- Fine roadholding • Good performance
- Reliable mechanicals

▼ CONS

- Body roll at turns • Cumbersome dimensions
- Ergonomics need work • Front seats lack support • Nondescript exterior

the quality of material and assembly are first rate. The cabin is roomy enough but could be even better, considering the car's exterior dimensions.

Buick takes its customer-pampering vocation seriously, offering excellent cabin sound insulation, comfortable front seats and a good-size rear bench. But once again, the bucket seats have minimal lateral support, and so are not conducive to sporty driving. But don't count the Park Avenue out just yet – with the Grand Touring package, this Buick can be as sporty and quick as the better performers from the imported bunch.

Exemplary road manners

Many people decry the 3.8-liter V6 engine, saying it's too old-fashioned. But although it dates back many moons, the third-generation version does its job quite well, thank you. The normally-aspirated version, with 205 hp, is just about at its limit, though acceleration is peppy enough. Unfortunately, the old-fashioned pushrod and rocker valve actuation system becomes unhappy at higher rpms and the engine "runs out of steam" as the tachometer needle moves up. For everyday driving, though, the Park Avenue handles nicely, and its fuel economy is modest, given its large size. The Ultra is fitted with a supercharged version of the 3.8-liter, producing 240 horses. This time around, engine breathing is excellent and you can charge ahead from 0-60 mph in slightly less than 9 seconds. Acceleration is such that you can go from 37 to 75 mph in less than 5 seconds. Wow!

Though big, the Park Avenue's road manners are remarkable, whether on the highway or any twisting back-country road. Detractors or not, the magnetic-variable-effort power steering is precise while providing too little feedback; the chassis is satisfactorily rigid and the suspension well tuned. Braking, too, is powerful. You'd be surprised to discover that this sizeable machine is more than capable of obliging your temptation to drive it like a sports car!

It's too bad that Buick's reputation isn't higher than its current level. Is it a lack of means or imagination?

Denis Duquet

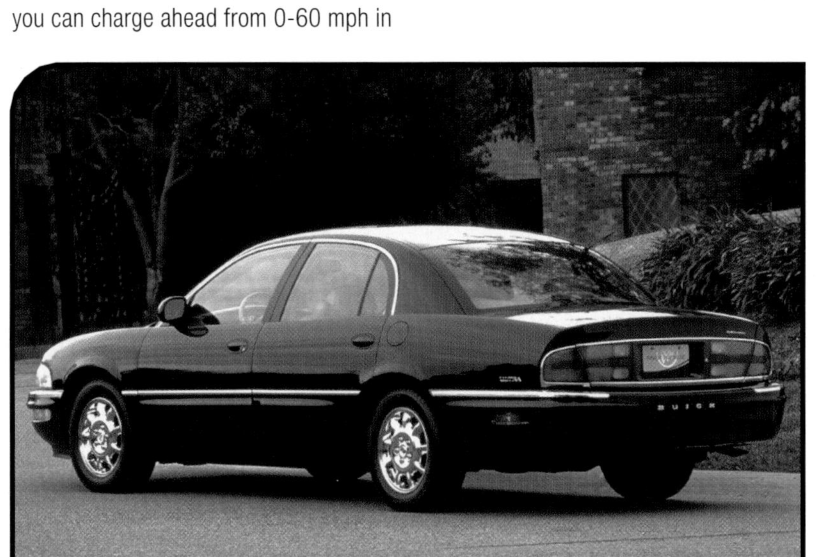

SPECIFICATIONS	
Price	$CDN 43,700-48,820 / $US 33,850-38,360
Warranty	3 years / 36,000 miles (60,000 km)
Type	sedan / front wheel drive
Wheelbase / Length	113.8 in / 206.7 in
Width / Height	74.8 in / 58.3 in
Weight	3946 lb (1790 kg)
Trunk / Fuel tank	19.1 cu. ft / 19 gallons
Air bags	front and side
Front suspension	independent
Rear suspension	independent
Front brakes / Rear brakes	vented disc ABS
Traction control	yes
Steering	rack-and-pinion, variable assist
Turning circle	40 feet
Tires (front/rear)	P225/60R16

PERFORMANCE	
Engine	V6 3.8 liter
Transmission	4-speed automatic
Horsepower	205 hp at 5200 rpm
Torque	230 lb-pi at 4000 rpm
Other engines	V6 3.8 liter supercharged 240 hp
Other transmission	none
Acceleration (0-60 mph)	9.1 s ; 10.6 s
Maximum speed	106 mph (170 km)
Braking (60-0 mph)	140 feet (42.8 m)
Fuel consumption	17.7 mpg ; 16.7 mpg (Ultra) (12.8; 13.6 L/100 km)

COMPETITION

• Acura RL • Cadillac DeVille • Chrysler 300 M • Infiniti Q45 • Lincoln Continental

NEW FOR 2002

• Armrest/standard rear storage • New trim for dashboard and doors • Redesigned center console

RATING	(out of 5 stars)
Driveability	★★★
Comfort	★★★★
Reliability	★★★★
Roominess	★★★★
Winter driving rating	★★★½
Safety	★★★★
Resale value	★★★★½

BUICK RENDEZVOUS PONTIAC AZTEK

BUICK **RENDEZVOUS**

Advantage Buick

Many will wonder why General Motors "returned to the scene of the crime" with a vehicle based on the Pontiac Aztek, one of the industry's biggest flops a year ago. But, rather than "stoning" GM in public, let's give it credit for boldness and determination. After all, Pontiac's setback was mostly to do with its looks, which were too different to suit the majority of buyers.

Ironically, style is precisely what the new Buick RendezVous is noted for. Even though its exterior has yet to win universal approval, I'm sure you'll agree that it looks much nicer than the Aztek. Its front end and profile, for example, are more in keeping with today's approach. The rear fascia, however, still looks ordinary. Designers tried hard to disguise the vehicle's height, but couldn't quite shake that minivan shape.

The cockpit is also well executed, with an elegant dashboard whose instrument displays, set against a silvery background, confer a classic and appropriate touch. But flow-directing adjustments for the ventilation outlets need rethinking, as does the location of other outlets. A few people will also find fault with the patterns on the fabric seat coverings. But these are minor details; all in all, the RendezVous is a nice car. What's more, it gives you the option of third-row seating, which Buick claims can comfortably accommodate any two adults. On the other hand, legroom and ventilation in the rear are barely adequate. Visibility, too, is limited owing to the huge C pillar and the minuscule rear window. Fortunately, the third seat can be folded flat. When it's deployed, there's practically no room for luggage.

Worth a mention is the fact that, to accommodate third-row seating, engineers had to opt for an independent rear suspension on the front- and all-wheel drive models that, in addition to ensuring excellent roadholding, allows the third seat to fold down flat and doesn't intrude on trunk space.

Looking better

Balance, please

Despite a relatively low cockpit floor, the RendezVous offers a minivan-style driving position. Combined with a rather high center of gravity, this should discourage any temptation to sports-drive the RendezVous. Incidentally, the front-

▲ PROS

• Buick more elegant • Tried and true engine • Spaciousness • Independent suspension standard on Buick • Optional AWD

▼ CONS

• Controversial styling (Aztek) • Pronounced understeer (Aztek TA) • Lacks power • Average rear ventilation • Some less-than-useful accessories

drive Aztek, with its auto-leveling rear suspension, will cause serious understeer if the driver pushes the car too hard in corners. In addition, the car is sensitive to lateral wind.

Having tested the front-drive RendezVous, we can say that the independent rear suspension makes all the difference. The shocks and springs are also better calibrated than the Aztek's. And the use of monotube shocks provides better control and extra comfort.

Both the Buick and Pontiac continue to be fitted with the 3.4-liter 185hp V6 engine, coupled to the 4T-55 E 4-speed automatic transmission. But I suspect the 185 hp might prove inadequate when the vehicle is fully loaded and traveling on an uneven road.

The Versatrak all-wheel-drive system is used on both vehicles. Its response time is quicker than any visco-coupling mechanism, and torque distribution to the wheels with the most traction is also more precise. But keep in mind that this system is essentially designed for variable road conditions, not the Rubicon Trail.The RendezVous offers a better quality/price ratio than the Aztek, and both its interior and exterior have a more conventional look. Incidentally, before Pontiac decided to lower its price, the Buick was less expensive.

The Aztek is nothing much to write home about, unless you're drawn to its bolder, more futurist style. Ditto for the cockpit, which looks decidedly hipper with the plethora of textures and a dashboard that belongs to a video game. In the rear, the Pontiac boasts a convenient split tailgate: a flip-up rear window and a lower swing-gate. And for party guys and gals, there's the 10-speaker stereo system designed to project the sound through the rear opening. Other than that, the Aztek offers accessories that differ greatly from the Buick's. The latter, I find, are more interesting.

The choice is yours. Go for the RendezVous, and you'll find yourself in the same league as Tiger Woods, or go for the Aztek and you'll keep company with the rainbow-haired windsurfing dude down the street.

Denis Duquet

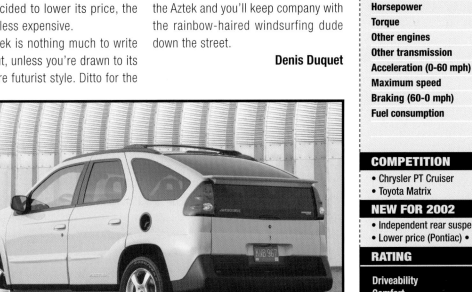

PONTIAC **AZTEK**

SPECIFICATIONS

Price	$CDN 30,995-40,095 / $US 25,499-28,022
Warranty	3 years / 36,000 miles (60,000 km)
Type	hybrid / all wheel drive
Wheelbase / Length	112 in / 187 in
Width / Height	73 in / 69 in
Weight	3781 lb (1715 kg)
Trunk / Fuel tank	45.4 cu. ft / 18 gallons
Air bags	front and side
Front suspension	independent
Rear suspension	independent
Front brakes / Rear brakes	disc ABS
Traction control	yes (front drive only)
Steering	rack-and-pinion, power assist
Turning circle	36 feet
Tires (front/rear)	P215/70R16

PERFORMANCE

Engine	V6 3.4 liter
Transmission	4-speed automatic
Horsepower	185 hp at 5200 rpm
Torque	210 lb-ft at 4000 rpm
Other engines	none
Other transmission	none
Acceleration (0-60 mph)	12.3 sec
Maximum speed	118 mph (190 km/h)
Braking (60-0 mph)	140 feet (42.6 m)
Fuel consumption	18 mpg (12.6 L/100 km)

COMPETITION

- Chrysler PT Cruiser
- Toyota Matrix

NEW FOR 2002

- Independent rear suspension standard (Buick)
- Lower price (Pontiac) • 3rd seat optional (Buick)

RATING (out of 5 stars)

Driveability	★★★½
Comfort	★★★★
Reliability	★★★
Roominess	★★★★
Winter driving rating	★★★★
Safety	★★★★½
Resale value	★★½

CADILLAC CATERA CADILLAC CTS

CADILLAC **CTS**

Wait Till Next Year!

The 2002 Catera shows off nothing new, simply because the model will be discontinued. In the meantime, it's still listed in the Cadillac catalog, pending its replacement, which is slated to arrive in early 2002 as the 2003 model. According to Cadillac, the second-generation Catera will be an entirely new car, assembled in North America to boot, with features guaranteed to meet the needs and desires of its intended customers.

Until then, the 2001 Cateras will be available in various dealership showrooms until stocks are depleted. It's not a bad car, far from it, and even worth buying, especially if it's offered at a discounted, end-of-line price. And you can count on the car lasting many years. The Catera was based on the Opel Omega and built in Germany. As I said, it's a decent enough car, but on the other hand, it holds very limited appeal for sport-oriented customers – the targeted audience. "Caddy Junior" promised to be sporty. In my humble opinion, it's nimble at best.

Many people complain about its dull silhouette, saying it looks more like a Saturn than a Cadillac. For one thing, the cockpit has nothing in common with other Cadillacs, especially its unappealing color scheme. But the single greatest weakness of this American-flavored European car has always been its 3.0-liter V6 engine. Not because the mechanicals are too fragile, but because they never quite match North American driving conditions.

In fact, the solid engine is compact and up-to-date, boasting 24 valves and double overhead camshafts. But its 200 horsepower proves to be too modest. It sounds good on paper, only its delivery is not always linear. So if you want some punch during acceleration, you have to resort to the gearbox's sport mode. In addition to normal, sport and winter modes, the 4-speed automatic transmission includes an adaptive logic so that you can tailor shift-patterns to suit your own driving style. Rounding out the Catera's technical specs are four-wheel brakes with ABS and traction control.

The best is yet to come

The same V6, that is now powering the Saturn LS, is certainly a good choice for the latter. But it needs a few more horses to justify its presence in a so-called deluxe car like the Catera. The extra power would have made better use of

▲ PROS

- Sophisticated platform • Exemplary handling
- Precise steering • User-friendly dashboard
- Comfortable seats

▼ CONS

- 2001 model • Nondescript silhouette
- Sport mode button on stickshift • Poor resale value • Cupholders too easily deployed

the chassis which is second to none when compared to other German-made car frames. With its MacPherson strut front suspension, multi-link rear suspension with automatic load leveling, and recirculating-ball steering, the Catera has the same drive-train as many highly-prized German cars. Moreover, the front suspension boasts hydraulic control-arm bushings that, among other things, assure precise steering as well as good feedback from the road.

Finally, the Catera has the distinction of being the first rear-wheel drive Cadillac – a forerunner, in other words, despite its lackluster beginnings – since the majority of new Cadillacs will be of the rear-wheel drive variety.

Fine touring car

If the Catera's low price appeals to you, then go ahead and buy one. Its "dull" silhouette will turn into an asset, because it will "age" well, stylewise. The cockpit is roomy for a car of this category and can accommodate the largest of passengers. The dashboard is elegant and well balanced, if a tad banal, no doubt influenced by a global marketing approach.

What's most interesting about the car, however, is its overall roadholding capabilities. Handling is exemplary, especially on the highway and at high speeds, when the V6 engine seems to thrive. On twisting roads, the Catera certainly delivers the goods, demonstrating once again that rear-wheel-drive sport sedans are far and away the most fun to drive. Steering is precise and road feedback excellent. Good news also about the brakes, which prove time and again to be heat-resistant despite constant braking at high speed. And if you add the Sport Package, which includes heavy-duty suspension and 17-inch tires, you'll get even better roadholding, though I doubt if it will help soften the suspension on bumpy roads.

This "European" Cadillac has had only limited success, due to its absence of panache and a general level of performance that is not commensurate with its sticker price. Let's hope that the next model will do better.

Denis Duquet

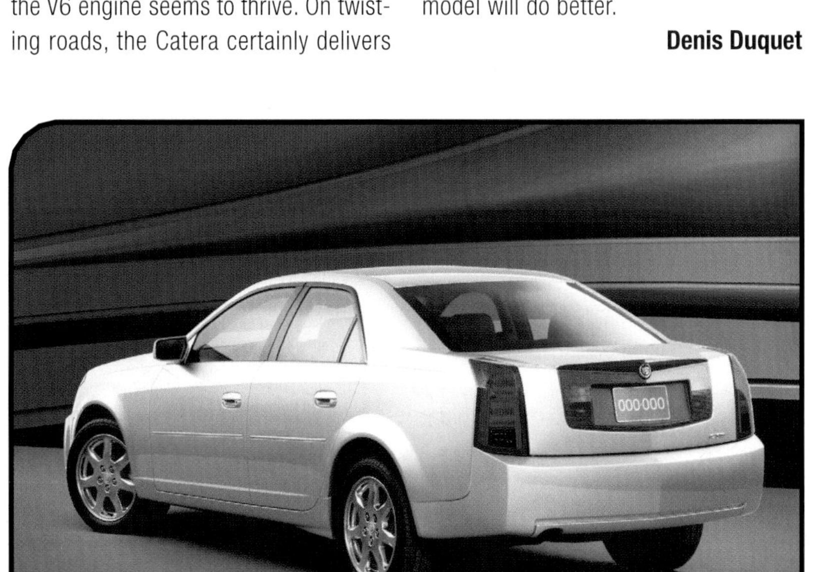

SPECIFICATIONS	
Price	$CDN 42,485-44,790 / $US 31,945
Warranty	4 years / 48,000 miles (80,000 km)
Type	sedan / rear wheel drive
Wheelbase / Length	107.5 in / 194 in
Width / Height	70 in / 56 in
Weight	3770 lb (1710 kg)
Trunk / Fuel tank	14.5 cu. ft / 16 gallons
Air bags	front and side
Front suspension	independent
Rear suspension	Independent
Front brakes / Rear brakes	disc ABS
Traction control	yes
Steering	rec. balls, power assist
Turning circle	33 feet
Tires (front/rear)	P225/55R16

PERFORMANCE	
Engine	V6 3 liter 24-valve
Transmission	4-speed automatic
Horsepower	200 hp at 6 000 rpm
Torque	192 lb-ft at 3 600 rpm
Other engines	none
Other transmission	none
Acceleration (0-60 mph)	9.2 sec
Maximum speed	127 mph (205 km/h)
Braking (60-0 mph)	126 feet (38.5 m)
Fuel consumption	18.1 mpg (12.5 L/100 km)

COMPETITION

• Acura 3.2 TL • Audi A4 • BMW 330Ci • Infiniti I35 • Lincoln LS • Lexus ES 300 • Millenia • M-B C280

NEW FOR 2002

• Clearance of 2001 models in inventory
• 2002 model n.a.

RATING	**(out of 5 stars)**
Driveability	★★★½
Comfort	★★★★
Reliability	★★★½
Roominess	★★★★
Winter driving rating	★★★½
Safety	★★★★
Resale value	★★½

CADILLAC DEVILLE

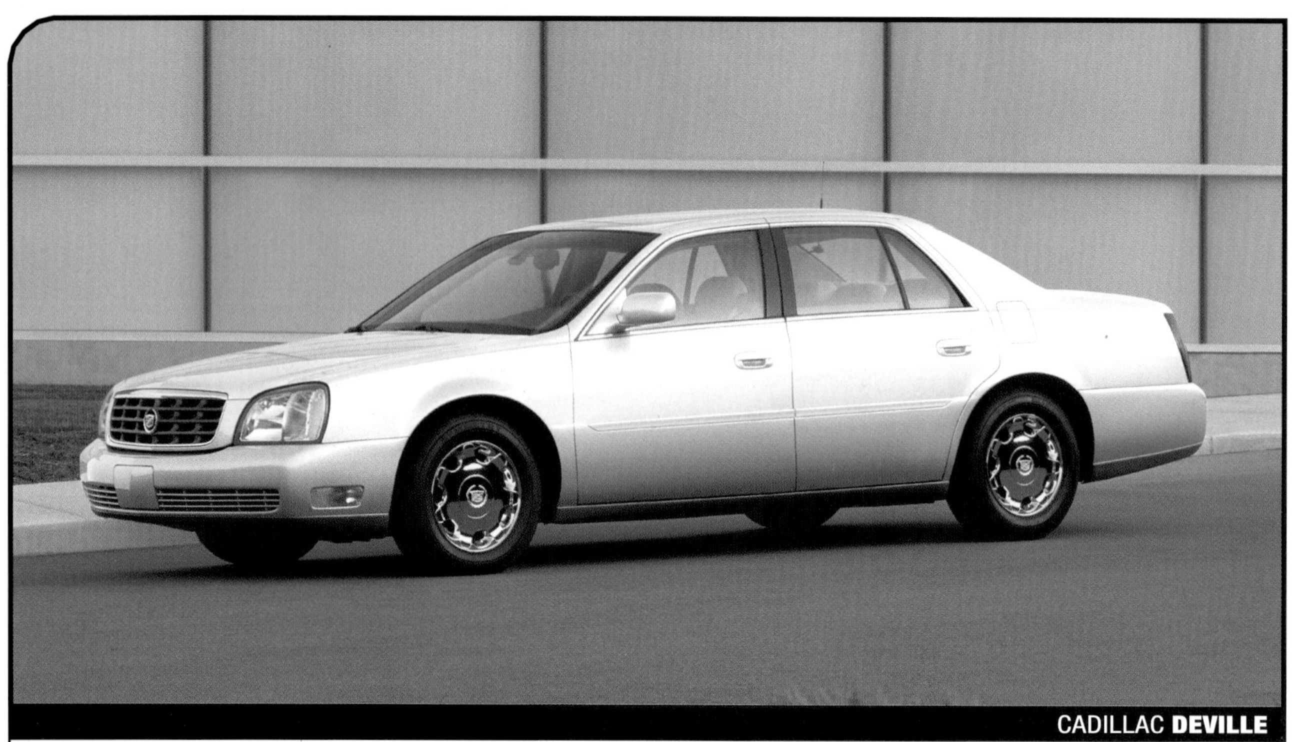

CADILLAC **DEVILLE**

Welcome Back, Caddy!

Let's face it. What normal human being would want to be caught dead behind the wheel of a Cadillac? Even though the Seville and the Catera have clearly demonstrated that Cadillac is no longer synonymous with stodginess, GM's prestigious division continues to be dogged by the comparison. Thoroughly revised last year, the Cadillac DeVille confirms that the marque is well on its way to reinforcing its new, younger image.

The 2002 DeVille comes in three trim levels: DeVille, DeVille High Luxury Sedan (DHS) and DeVille Touring Sedan (DTS). DHS is considered to be the ritziest, and DTS the sportiest. All three versions are powered by the finest engine ever designed by GM: the 4.6-liter V8 Northstar. The base model and DHS get 275 hp, enough to face the competition head on. The DTS receives 300 hp, catapulting Cadillac into the lead in its category.

It's no surprise that the DTS – weighing upwards of 4000 lbs (1843 kg) – leaps forward from 0-60 mph in just over 7 seconds. Power is there and so is torque. And when the time comes for passing a vehicle, the DeVille doesn't waste time either: mudge the accelerator and presto, it's done. What a babe!

This Northstar engine oozes sportiness. And there's a bonus. At the slightest signal from the accelerator, it emits a muted growl that's pure music. Great for the old adrenaline. Still, it's a quiet engine all in all and it suits the automatic transmission beautifully. Accelerating through the gears is swift, yet smooth as silk.

What I find most impressive is the way the engine handles torque effect, practically reducing it to zero. And since the DeVille, unlike its imported rivals, is front-wheel drive, skeptics expected the worst, what with 300 hp at its disposal. Well, they were wrong. Torque effect is barely discernible, even under hard acceleration. But watch out for the steering wheel's reactions when you drive on rough roads. This engine power doesn't always sit comfortably in the front wheels.

Move over, Lexus!

On winding roads, the DTS' exemplary handling will confound the same skeptics, while handily defusing the popular prejudices aimed at American full-size luxury sedans. It's true that with the earlier DeVilles we would have gone through half a dozen body rolls while negotiating curves at high speeds. With the DTS, the most we'll need to worry about is a little squealing of the tires.

▲ PROS

• Competitive price • Impressive road manners • Spacious and plush cockpit • Superb engine

▼ CONS

• Cumbersome dimensions • Dubious Night Vision system • Excessive turning circle • Poor support for front seats • Unproven reliability

One of the DTS' virtues is its Continuously Variable Road-Sensing Suspension (CVRSS). It works marvels on curves, ensuring excellent directional stability and an extraordinarily smooth and comfortable ride. The car simply never wavers abruptly: body rolls are superbly controlled, ditto the weight distribution. Bumps and potholes, too, are expertly absorbed. And wait 'till you try the brakes capable of immobilizing this huge mass promptly.

Another improvement is the responsiveness to steering inputs, which no longer gives the impression of swimming in molasses. Not only is the power assist well dispensed, but you can feel the assist decrease as the speed increases. Watch out for the wide turning circle, though.

No dinosaur

Frankly speaking, this sedan is no beauty; but mercifully it bears no resemblance to the hideous dinosaur it replaces. The interior is well executed: the dashboard is clearly laid out and easy to consult, enhanced by electro-luminescent gauges. The quality of finish – not always a strong point at Cadillac – has noticeably improved.

Rear seats are spacious – no surprise in a car like the DeVille. But the front bucket seats sorely lack adequate lateral and back support. The leather upholstery makes you slide back and forth, so that you're constantly trying to sit up and find a comfortable position. Standard equipment includes the OnStar satellite navigation system, trip computer capable of displaying no less than 50 different messages, a hi-fi stereo system and heated seats for all passengers.

The DHS and DTS can be equipped with the infrared Night Vision system, which enables you to detect obstacles (objects, people, animals) beyond the range of the headlights. This accessory speaks volumes about the DeVille's impressive list of active- and passive-safety features. And the DeVille price range is highly competitive. Our test model – a DTS equipped with several such luxurious options, including the Night Vision system – costs a good $10,000 less than a Lexus LS 430. But Japanese cars are renowned for their legendary reliability, whereas Cadillacs, while steadily improving, have yet to prove their mettle. Time alone will tell.

SPECIFICATIONS	DTS
Price	$CDN 52,555-63,575 / $US 41,665-47,237
Warranty	4 years / 48,000 miles (80,000 km)
Type	sedan / front wheel drive
Wheelbase / Length	115.4 in / 207.1 in
Width / Height	74.4 in / 56.7 in
Weight	4045 lb (1835 kg)
Trunk / Fuel tank	19.1 cu. ft / 17 gallons
Air bags	front and side
Front suspension	independent
Rear suspension	independent
Front brakes / Rear brakes	disc ABS
Traction control	yes
Steering	rack-and-pinion, variable assist
Turning circle	41 feet
Tires (front/rear)	P235/55R17
PERFORMANCE	
Engine	V8 4.6 liter
Transmission	4-speed automatic
Horsepower	300 hp at 6000 rpm
Torque	295 lb-ft at 4400 rpm
Other engines	V8 4.6 liter 275 hp
Other transmission	none
Acceleration (0-60 mph)	7.1 sec
Maximum speed	130 mph (210 km/h) (limited)
Braking (60-0 mph)	134 feet (40.7 m)
Fuel consumption	16.5 mpg (13.7 L/100 km)

COMPETITION

- Acura 3.5 RL • Infiniti Q45
- Lexus LS 430 • Lincoln Town Car

NEW FOR 2002

- Standard rear airbags • Revamped shocks
- DVD navigation system

RATING	(out of 5 stars)
Driveability	★★★½
Comfort	★★★★★
Reliability	★★★½
Roominess	★★★★★
Winter driving rating	★★★½
Safety	★★★★½
Resale value	★★

CADILLAC **ELDORADO**

Heading Down the Highway

It's all been confirmed, by GM itself no less. The antiquated Cadillac Eldorado has entered its last production year. They've been announcing this "good" news year after year, only to be contradicted each time by the return of the big coupe. Now, though, it's finally official. In fact the Cadillac team has even concocted a "Special Edition" to mark the current model's final curtain call.

"Special Edition," indeed: different wheels, carbon fiber accessories, an exhaust system with a special sonority, a vintage year plaque and the proverbial "exclusive" flaming red color. Detroit has been trotting out this clichéd – though tried-and-true – formula since time immemorial, and it never fails to grab the attention of, if I may use the expression, "collectors." In all fairness, the Eldorado holds its own capably at very high speeds whether on the highway or through the twists and turns of a snaking canyon in California.

But, unless you're thoroughly addicted to the Eldorado's somewhat "far-out" lines, no one should shed a tear for this moribund model, so named to honor a golden dream that, in the end, enriched a mere handful of colonial adventurers. I also doubt that this big coupe ever made much money for Cadillac, given its lackluster sales in the past few years.

Ungainly image

Among the more plausible explanations for this consumer disaffection is the fact that luxury coupes hold absolutely no appeal these days, having been totally supplanted by the newer and sexier roadsters. One also has to admit that whoever designed the Cadillac Eldorado in the first place, totally missed the boat. The car's design has stuck out like a sore thumb ever since its debut in the early 1990s. Worse, once you've managed to open its heavy, super-long door to get behind the wheel, you're confronted with an utterly nondescript dashboard. But take heart, the rear can comfortably accommodate two fully-grown adults.

So long Eldorado!

More luxurious than sporty, and despite the kind of outline that is more appropriate for a funeral procession than

▲ PROS

- Comfortable seats • Impressive performance
- Northstar engine • Sophisticated suspension
- Spacious cockpit

▼ CONS

- Last model • "Special edition"
- Magnetic power steering
- Ungainly silhouette • Unpopular category

a car rally, the Eldorado is an impressive machine nonetheless, fitted with a powerful Northstar 4.6-liter V8 engine, Continuously Variable Road-Sensing Suspension (CVRSS) and Stabilitrak system. Beneath that ungainly, big-American-car image there lies a fantastic touring car.

It's a pity we live in a world where "image is everything." And the image projected by the Eldorado is such that many people would rather walk for miles in a drenching rain than be caught behind the wheel of this nondescript, tacky-looking Caddy.

Crystal ball

The Eldorado will head down the highway in 2002 and will most probably be replaced by the high-performance XLR, a super luxurious roadster beside which the Eldorado looks like a poor relation.

It's all speculation at this point, of course, but most observers of the automotive scene firmly believe that the XLR will replace the Eldorado once the last 2002 model rolls off the production line. Based on the Corvette platform, but propelled by the legendary Northstar engine, this newcomer carries high expectations, one of which will be to make Cadillac a major player in the sports-car arena. Another factor: the division recently adopted a new program aimed at participating in the "24 Hours of Le Mans" race in 2002. This time, it will be easier to buy into Cadillac's sporty image.

If all goes according to plan, the Evoq will be marketed as a top-of-the-line roadster, and only 5000 units will be produced annually. And, of course, they want to make it the Cadillac of sports roadsters.

Denis Duquet

CADILLAC **XLR**

SPECIFICATIONS	
Price	$CDN 57,450 / $US 41,156-44,731
Warranty	4 years / 48,000 miles (80,000 km)
Type	coupe / front wheel drivet
Wheelbase / Length	107.9 in / 200.4 in
Width / Height	75.6 in / 53.5 in
Weight	3880 lb (1760 kg)
Trunk / Fuel tank	15.4 cu. ft / 19 gallons
Air bags	front
Front suspension	independent
Rear suspension	independent
Front brakes / Rear brakes	disc ABS
Traction control	yes
Steering	rack-and-pinion, variable assist
Turning circle	40 feet
Tires (front/rear)	P235/60R16

PERFORMANCE	
Engine	V8 4.6 liter
Transmission	4-speed automatic
Horsepower	300 hp at 6000 rpm
Torque	295 lb-ft at 4400 rpm
Other engines	none
Other transmission	none
Acceleration (0-60 mph)	7.7 sec
Maximum speed	149 mph
Braking (60-0 mph)	137 feet (41.9 m)
Fuel consumption	18.4 mpg (12.3 L/100 km)

COMPETITION

None

NEW FOR 2002

• Last year • "Special edition"

RATING	(out of 5 stars)
Driveability	★★★
Comfort	★★★★½
Reliability	★★★★
Roominess	★★★★
Winter driving rating	★★★½
Safety	★★★
Resale value	★★

CADILLAC ESCALADE

CADILLAC **ESCALADE**

The Cadillac of SUVs

Better late than never! The top brass at Cadillac must have breathed a sigh of relief when the 2002 Escalades were finally shipped to dealership showrooms in spring 2001. This time around, the vehicle is competitive and endowed with the distinctive Cadillac features.

After years of ignoring the luxury sport-utility phenomenon, the folks at Cadillac finally decided to get into the act. A new platform had to be built, but in the meantime, they had to make do with the Yukon Denali to which they hastily added the Cadillac touch – a Caddy crest, leather seats, a last-minute grille – and the job was done.

Fortunately, this makeshift situation lasted only a few months, long enough to signal Cadillac's intentions to potential buyers and snatch a few sales away from the highly popular Lincoln Navigator. The 2001 model was finally retired – and none too soon. The 2002 version is well worth the wait because it has now become the benchmark for big all-terrain vehicles in terms of performance, comfort and handling.

More than just a modified truck

Although the Escalade borrowed its platform from the Yukon Denali – itself derived from the Chevrolet Silverado /GMC Sierra light trucks – it would be wrong to assume that the Cadillac is simply a modified version of these vehicles with a couple of extra accessories thrown in. In fact, the Escalade sets itself apart with a computer-controlled suspension system that constantly modifies the shocks' firmness to suit vehicle speed, road conditions and body roll. Secondly, it's fitted with the standard StabiliTrak, one of the most efficient and sophisticated stability-enhancing systems offered in North America. With Stabilitrak, lateral slides are automatically corrected by a combination of selective application of each brake and reduction in engine torque.

The tops

And speaking of engines, Cadillac engineers pulled out all the stops and fitted the Escalade with the high-compression Vortec 6000 V8. With a whopping 345 horsepower, you can imagine the powerful acceleration this brute is capable of. With very little effort, we made 0-60 mph in less than 10 seconds. Not bad for a 5800-lb juggernaut (2635 kg). And for those of you who are interested, towing capacity is 8500 lbs (3856 kg).

▲ PROS

• Sophisticated chassis • Interesting presentation • Comfortable seats • High-performance engine • Comfortable suspension

▼ CONS

• Steep price • High fuel consumption • Cumbersome dimensions • Controversial silhouette • Impractical running boards

Standard features also include 4-speed automatic transmission with Tow/Haul mode.

Guaranteed impact

Cadillac has never exactly been known as a styling icon. With its imposing grille, oversized headlights and squarish front wings, however, the Escalade really does stand out, and seems to appeal to – or at least impress – a lot of people, since many kept looking our way to admire the test model.

The cockpit is not only spacious, but very comfortable. The front seats lack depth and the integrated seatbelts tend to over-retract. But those are minor details. The dashboard looks like the Yukon Denali's, except for the various dials which are smartly trimmed with brushed aluminum. The analog clock mounted on the center console adds a deluxe feeling to the overall interior.

The second-row bench is comfortable enough, except for the middle section, which is hard on the back. The third row can accommodate 2 adults, but you need to be agile to get in there.

To climb into the cockpit, you have to step on the running board and hang on to the steering wheel. Once inside though, you'll enjoy the excellent driving position. On the road, the Escalade responds to the slightest pressure on the accelerator. This colossus proves amazingly docile. Moreover, you don't get the impression of being behind the wheel of such an imposing vehicle. Despite larger than usual rearview mirrors, the Ultrasonic Rear Parking Assist feature was greatly appreciated during our test drive.

The computer-controlled road-sensing suspension performs brilliantly, much better than Lincoln Navigator's. And, by the way, the latter's handling capabilities pale beside the Escalade. Steering could be a little more precise, body roll less obvious and cornering smoother. But all in all, the Escalade does a remarkable job in its category.

People normally use the expression "the Cadillac of..." to indicate the exceptional quality of a product. This time, it's the Escalade's turn to be labeled "the Cadillac of SUVs."

Denis Duquet

SPECIFICATIONS

Price	$CDN 65,900-72,700 / $US 49,990
Warranty	4 years / 48,000 miles (80,000 km)
Type	luxury sport-utility / all wheel drive
Wheelbase / Length	116 in / 199 in
Width / Height	79 in / 74 in
Weight	4758 lb (2158 kg)
Trunk / Fuel tank	63.6 or 108.2 cu. ft / 26 gallons
Air bags	front
Front suspension	independent
Rear suspension	rigid axle
Front brakes / Rear brakes	disc ABS
Traction control	yes
Steering	recirculating-balls, variable assist
Turning circle	39 feet
Tires (front/rear)	P265/70R17

PERFORMANCE

Engine	V8 6 liter
Transmission	4-speed automatic
Horsepower	345 hp at 5200 rpm
Torque	380 lb-ft at 4000 rpm
Other engines	none
Other transmission	none
Acceleration (0-60 mph)	8.7 sec
Maximum speed	109 mph (175 km/h)
Braking (60-0 mph)	161 feet (49 m)
Fuel consumption	14.2 mpg (15.9 L/100 km)

COMPETITION

- Lexus LX 470 • Lincoln Navigator
- Land Rover Range Rover

NEW FOR 2002

- New model

RATING	**(out of 5 stars)**
Driveability	★★★
Comfort	★★★★
Reliability	★★★
Roominess	★★★★
Winter driving rating	★★★★★
Safety	★★★★½
Resale value	★★★½

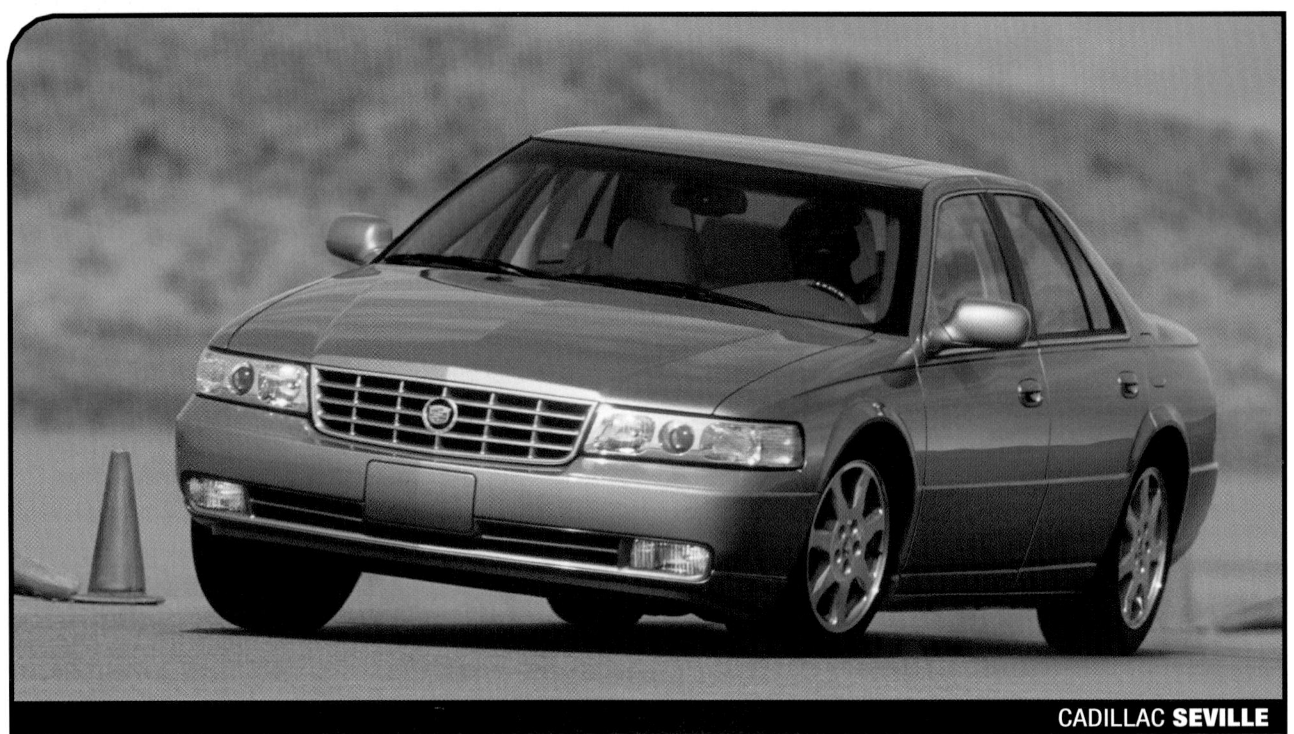

CADILLAC **SEVILLE**

At the Crossroads

In business terms, profitability always prevails over everything else. This time around, it's the Oldsmobile division that's getting the chop, GM's top brass having decided there was no point in relaunching a marque that has suffered too many lean years.

In the meantime, as Oldsmobile models slowly recede into the sunset, the Seville remains one of Cadillac's cornerstones. Granted, the DeVille is the most widely sold Cadillac sedan, but the Seville is considered the sportiest. In fact, if you're one of those enthusiasts who swear only by American-made luxury cars, the Seville figures among the precious few, viable choices you've got, in terms of performance and road handling.

GM's G-platform probably doesn't mean much to the general public, but ask people in the industry and they'll tell you it's one of the most successful automobile platforms in existence. Originally built for the Oldsmobile Aurora, it was subsequently modified for various Cadillac sedans. The Seville, for instance, is derived from the G-platform. Its chassis, made of hydroformed parts, is thus suitably rigid and light; ditto the front and rear subframes of the sophisticated Continuously-Variable Road-Sensing Suspension (CVRSS). Throw in the Northstar 4.6-liter V8 engine, with 300 or 270 horsepower depending on the model, and you've got yourself quite a machine.

Past prestige

Indeed, the Seville is one of the most interesting American-made cars to drive. The quality of the acceleration and cornering is such that it will be able to take on its imported rivals with ease. Still fans of European and Japanese cars are unimpressed with its nondescript curvy silhouette and traditional cockpit. As far as they're concerned, the dashboard is too spartan, and they even find fault with the V8 engine sound. It's true that the Seville's styling verges on the boring side. Add to this list the so-so tires, as well as the slope and the thickness of the A pillar, which blocks most of the driver's visibility. And not everybody likes the Magnasteer II steering assist, either.

Superbly luxurious

Despite these negative notes, the Seville STS – with its 300-hp engine, sportier suspension and 17-inch tires – is

▲ PROS

- Adequate performance • Comfortable front seats
- Complete equipment • Northstar engine
- Sound roadholding

▼ CONS

- Inadequate tires • Negative image
- Overassisted steering • So-so rear seats
- Thick A pillar

a superbly luxurious sport sedan worthy of its name. Whether Cadillac can muster up its past prestige to attract buyers to the Seville remains to be seen.

Tragic destiny

The first-generation Aurora was supposed to have been Oldsmobile's flagship car. The division was in financial trouble and they wanted a "cult-model" to reverse its fortunes. Sporting a modern chassis and fitted with a 4.0-liter V8 engine derived from Cadillac's Northstar, the Aurora was finally launched in 1995, after many delays and false starts. Unfortunately, it just never took off. The failure was blamed on its badly-sorted suspension and odd shape.

Completely redesigned in 2001, the Aurora now exhibits a more European silhouette, a standard 3.5-liter V6 engine and far superior standard equipment. At last, it seemed well on its way to achieving some measure of success; that is, until GM suddenly announced that it was pulling the plug on Oldsmobile.

Although its days are now counted, the Aurora remains an interesting sedan, boasting the most even-handed road manners of all full-size GM sedans. The Seville acquits itself very well, but to me the Aurora feels more agile. Next to European cars, its silhouette is nothing much to write home about; still, it looks better than those bland Acura and Infiniti models.

If you're amazed by the whopping 250 horsepower of the 4.0-liter V8 engine, capable of propelling the car from 0-60 mph in a mere 8 seconds, the standard V6 isn't that far behind. After all, it generates only 35 fewer horses.

On the other hand, the Aurora, like the Cadillac Seville, should have been fitted with a 5-speed automatic transmission. The final product could have been so much more refined. Its current 4-speed automatic gearbox was the benchmark not so long ago, but the competition usually fares better in this regard.

Both sedans are almost there, almost "world class." If only they were blessed with a few more details, they could have been leaders in their class. So close, yet so far apart.

Denis Duquet

OLDSMOBILE **AURORA**

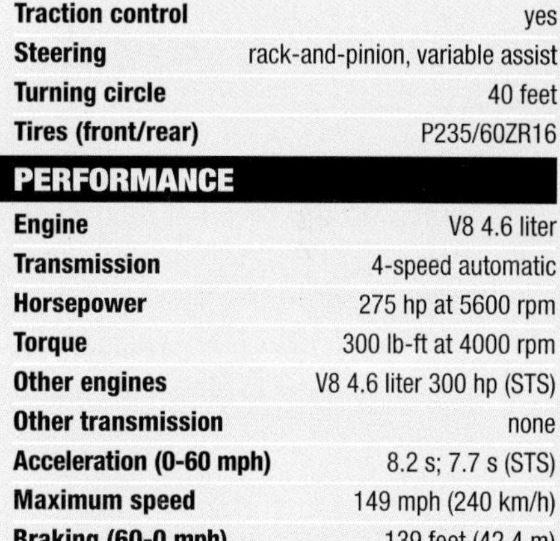

SPECIFICATIONS	**SLS**
Price	$CDN 59,450-67,015 / $US 31,289-48,965
Warranty	4 years / 48,000 miles (80,000 km)
Type	sedan / front wheel drive
Wheelbase / Length	112.2 in / 200.8 in
Width / Height	74.8 in / 55.5 in
Weight	3968 lb (1800 kg)
Trunk / Fuel tank	15.7 cu. ft / 19 gallons
Air bags	front and side
Front suspension	yes
Rear suspension	independent
Front brakes / Rear brakes	disc ABS
Traction control	yes
Steering	rack-and-pinion, variable assist
Turning circle	40 feet
Tires (front/rear)	P235/60ZR16

PERFORMANCE	
Engine	V8 4.6 liter
Transmission	4-speed automatic
Horsepower	275 hp at 5600 rpm
Torque	300 lb-ft at 4000 rpm
Other engines	V8 4.6 liter 300 hp (STS)
Other transmission	none
Acceleration (0-60 mph)	8.2 s; 7.7 s (STS)
Maximum speed	149 mph (240 km/h)
Braking (60-0 mph)	139 feet (42.4 m)
Fuel consumption	18.7 mpg (12.1 L/100 km)

COMPETITION

• Audi A6 • BMW 540 • Jaguar S-Type V8 • Lexus GS 430 • Mercedes-Benz E430 • Volvo S80 T6

NEW FOR 2002

• DVD Navigation system • New badge • Magneride suspension (STS) • Parking radar (standard)

RATING	**(out of 5 stars)**
Driveability	4
Comfort	4
Reliability	3.5
Roominess	4
Winter driving rating	3.5
Safety	4
Resale value	3.5

CHEVROLET ASTRO GMC SAFARI

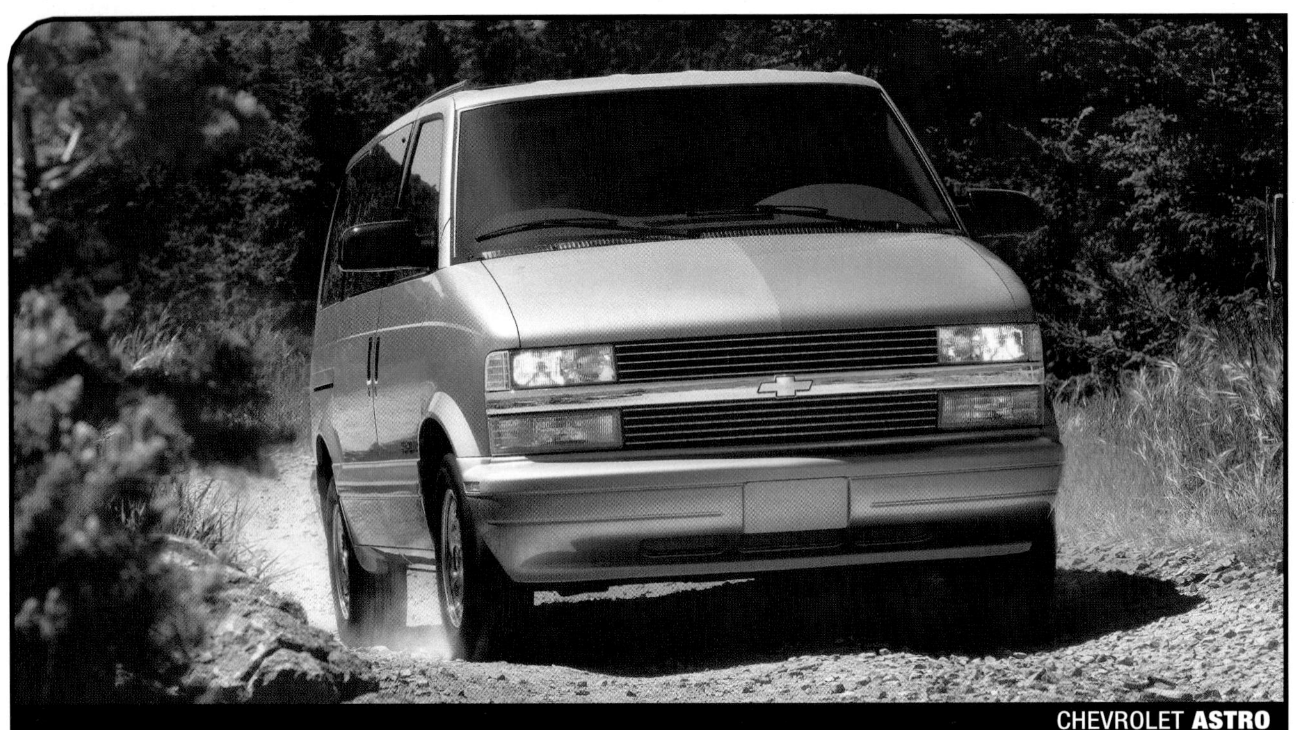

CHEVROLET **ASTRO**

Old-Timers

This famous duo recently celebrated their 17th anniversary in the marketplace. That's no mean feat considering the initial setbacks because the company originally misjudged the direction of the market. Conceived as GM's answer to the wildly successful Chrysler Magicwagon, both the Astro and Safari failed miserably as commercial vehicles, but managed to hang on, eventually carving out their own specialized market niche.

At the time, GM and Ford were convinced that front-wheel-drive minivans were merely a passing trend, representing 25% of the market at best. Engineers therefore fitted both the Astro and Safari with a longitudinal engine linked to a rear differential and a chassis derived from the S-10 light-duty truck. The idea was to produce a sturdy commercial vehicle, capable of meeting the needs of small entrepreneurs, who theoretically accounted for 75% of its market. This also explains the rear swing-gate, which was favored in commercial vehicles, to replace the proverbial tailgate.

Today, 17 years later, both vehicles are still on the road. Over the years, GM engineers worked to refine and adapt them to suit the needs of a different class of customer: the family. Buyers can now order a rear opening consisting of a upper window and lower swing-gates. Rear visibility has been greatly improved, and the rear door features such amenities as electric de-icer and windshield wipers, while providing easy access to the luggage area. An astute compromise indeed.

The dashboard, too, has been refined over time. Since the engine encroaches on the cabin, designers found a way to anchor the console and the storage tray to the dashboard without taking up too much space. The overall presentation doesn't look too truck-like, and controls for the radio and climate control are within easy reach. What's more, their oversized buttons are clearly identified in large letters and easy to manipulate.

Practical relics

Unfortunately, the space used up by the wheel wells severely limits footroom for front-cabin occupants. The front seats are not exactly comfortable, either. Two rear benches – each with three detachable seats – are standard equipment. In the more luxurious LT trim, these benches are fitted with individual adjustable reclining backrests. But, removable though these benches are, you need plenty of muscle to take them out. Finally, in warm weather, ventilation is poor

▲ PROS

- Optional all-wheel drive • Robust V6 engine
- 5500-lb towing capacity (2500 kg) • Easy to park
- Reasonable fuel consumption

▼ CONS

- High center of gravity • Brute silhouette
- Limited footroom • Ventilation needs work
- Endangered species

in the back, where occupants get only occasional bursts of fresh air from the front-cabin air conditioner, happily standard equipment on all models. Let me assure you, it's well worth the extra money to pay for the optional front-and-rear air conditioner, unless you buy the LT, in which case it comes as standard equipment.

Solid mechanicals

At the time of their launch in 1985, the Astro and Safari were both fitted with a 4.3-liter V6 carburetor engine. That goes to show the age of this type of vehicle. A year later, it was fitted with fuel injection; then in 1996, with sequential fuel injection. Over the years, a computer-controlled 4-speed automatic gearbox was added. And so, on a steady basis, the mechanicals have been refined. The body, too, has gone through a number of modifications, to make it more solid. One feature remains: the vehicle's only sliding door is always on the right-hand side, and power doors are out of the question.

Driving either of these minivans is hardly the thrill of a lifetime, but the result can be satisfying given their roots. Sitting high up, left foot curled over your right leg, you have to cling hard to the steering wheel when turning to compensate for the soft seat. The lack of foot-room gets harder to put up with as the hours go by. Fortunately, the Vortec 4300 engine performs satisfactorily as its 190 horsepower ably takes command of every rpm range managed by the gearbox. Cornering behavior is adequate but you must keep the vehicle's high center of gravity in mind at all times. Directional stability is good on the open road, although a strong side wind tends to make the vehicle weave slightly. In this situation, the all-wheel-drive trim is more reassuring, and a better buy. In the city, despite its boxy shape, this docile minivan is easy to drive. The fair-sized rearview mirrors are helpful and parking is easy thanks to a very tight turning circle.

So, unless you decide to go for "pure driving pleasure" in a more modern vehicle, these old timers are good bets, even offering optional all-wheel drive. Besides, their towing capacity of almost 5500 lbs (2500 kg) is bound to appeal to quite a few customers.

Denis Duquet

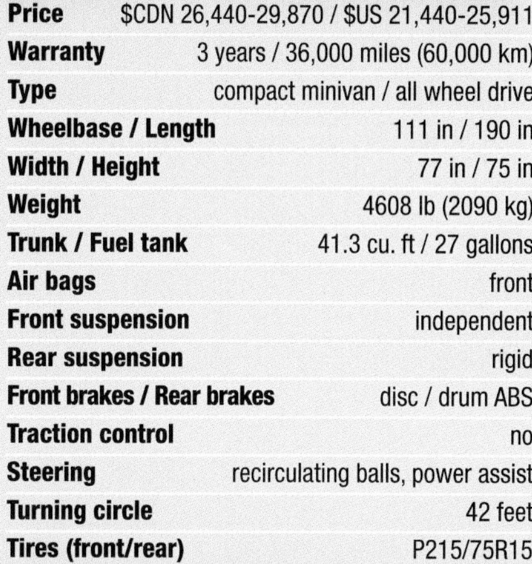

SPECIFICATIONS	
Price	$CDN 26,440-29,870 / $US 21,440-25,911
Warranty	3 years / 36,000 miles (60,000 km)
Type	compact minivan / all wheel drive
Wheelbase / Length	111 in / 190 in
Width / Height	77 in / 75 in
Weight	4608 lb (2090 kg)
Trunk / Fuel tank	41.3 cu. ft / 27 gallons
Air bags	front
Front suspension	independent
Rear suspension	rigid
Front brakes / Rear brakes	disc / drum ABS
Traction control	no
Steering	recirculating balls, power assist
Turning circle	42 feet
Tires (front/rear)	P215/75R15

PERFORMANCE	
Engine	V6 4.3-liter
Transmission	4-speed automatic
Horsepower	190 hp at 4400 rpm
Torque	250 lb-ft at 2800 rpm
Other engines	none
Other transmission	none
Acceleration (0-60 mph)	11.9 sec
Maximum speed	112 mph (180 km/h)
Braking (60-0 mph)	145 feet (44.2 m)
Fuel consumption	16.9 mpg (13.4 L/100 km)

COMPETITION

• Dodge Caravan • Ford Windstar

NEW FOR 2002

• Multi-Port V6 engine

RATING	(out of 5 stars)
Driveability	★★★
Comfort	★★★
Reliability	★★★
Roominess	★★★★
Winter driving rating	★★★½
Safety	★★★
Resale value	★★★

CHEVROLET AVALANCHE CADILLAC ESCALADE EXT

CHEVROLET **AVALANCHE**

A Hybrid to End All Hybrids

Time was when cars were just touring vehicles, trucks were utility vehicles and 4X4s, off-roaders. The distinction between the categories was crystal clear and automakers didn't try mixing them up, let alone turning a pickup truck into a sport-utility vehicle, or a car into an off-roader. Today, however, "automotive hybridizing" is a common phenomenon the world over, as demonstrated by the kind of vehicles crowding highways and byways anywhere. This phenomenon is most obvious in the utility-vehicle market. Some pickup trucks, for instance, are equipped with luxury-car cabins and SUV-style all-wheel drive. On the other hand, all-terrain vehicles – once austere and rough-and-ready looking – now ride like passenger cars.

The Chevrolet Avalanche was developed out of this whirlwind of mutations and category crossing. It's the mutant of mutants – a hybrid to end all hybrids – with a versatility that transcends every category. Chevrolet dubbed it the "Ultimate Utility Vehicle," and it's hard to imagine how the automaker could have come up with a better description.

While the Avalanche is basically a Chevrolet Suburban with a cargo box, the Suburban itself is a sport-utility vehicle built on the platform of the Chevrolet Silverado pickup truck, sharing the Silverado's chassis as well as many components of its drivetrain. Talk about coming full circle!

Obviously, the Suburban's chassis was duly modified to suit its SUV vocation. It also enjoys a cushier and quieter cabin as well as a more comfortable suspension than the base pickup.

Abracadabra!

Ultra versatile

It's easy enough to convert a vehicle from one category to another, but there's no guarantee that the vehicle thus converted will be as effective as a clean-sheet approach would have been. Avalanche engineers have reason to be proud of their one-of-a-kind end product: a Suburban sport-utility vehicle whose tail end was sliced off and converted into a cargo box. The secret is something that Chevrolet calls "Midgate," a middle tailgate consisting of an upper, removable glass window and a lower fold-down

▲ PROS

- **Appealing concept • Midgate system**
- **Side-panel storage compartments**
- **Sound handling • Unequaled versatility**

▼ CONS

- **Overdone bodystyle • Cumbersome size**
- **Heavy cargo cover • High price • Over-the-top North Face version**

door separating the cabin and the cargo box. You want fresh air in the cabin? Just remove the glass – by unlatching two handles – and slide it into a sleeve inset in the fold-down door. Some spoil-sports will point out that the Ford Sport Trak offers the same feature, except with power assist. But look at it this way, the lower part of the Ford tailgate cannot be folded down like the Avalanche's.

To make the entire Midgate "disappear," remove and stow the glass inside the fold-down door, then flip it forward into the cabin. As you do this, you will also flip the split-folding rear bench seat forward, thereby extending the 63-inch (160 cm) cargo box to 97.6 inches (248 cm) – long enough to hold those cumbersome plywood sheets. At the back of the Avalanche, there's another tailgate – a standard-issue pickup truck variety – made of PRO-TEC, a synthetic material that's both light and durable.

And that's not all. The cargo bed – made of steel and plastic-lined – is covered by a removable three-panel plastic tonneau cover weighing 275 lbs (125 kg). Like the rear tailgate, this cover is lockable, and can be stowed on board, in a pouch hung along one of the cargo area side panels. But I doubt if most drivers will bother with the pouch at all – except, perhaps, under special circumstances.

Furthermore, the cargo bed's side panels boast lockable storage compart-

CADILLAC **ESCALADE EXT**

CHEVROLET AVALANCHE/CADILLAC ESCALADE EXT

ments with drain holes that can double as ice-coolers. Also worth mentioning is an ignition key that can be used for all locks. The remote control key, on the other hand, can only activate the door locks. The rear bumper features another nifty idea: indented steps at each end where you can place the tip of your foot for better grip as you pull on the handle.

Believe me, all this is only a brief preview. Like a versatile Swiss Army knife, the Avalanche can be used in so many ways, able to cope with any driving circumstances.

Surprise, surprise

Generally speaking, all-purpose vehicles look more impressive in showrooms than on the road. Happily for General Motors, the well-executed, inventive Avalanche is the exception to that rule.

Some people may not be impressed by the exterior – with its overdone body cladding and outsized bumpers. But the cabin is a copycat of the Suburban – practical, ergonomically sound and user-friendly. The central air vent could have been placed a little closer to the driver and the way the CD player is mounted on the center console looks as if it arrived as an afterthought. At least it's easy to reach. Passengers in the back have nothing to complain about: the split-folding bench is perfectly comfortable and space abounds.

What impresses me most is the Avalanche's better than average handling, utterly unaffected by all the permutations and combinations. You can drive along any secondary road without having to worry about slowing down for corners. On the wide-open road, the suspension is comfortable and there's absolutely no wind noise. In fact, you're up to 100 mph in no time at all. So keep an eye on the speedometer.

The Avalanche's dimensions are equivalent to those of a full-size pickup truck, with all the implications for city driving. When parking, for instance, make sure you take account of the Avalanche's height, so as not to damage other cars. On the other hand, its relatively narrow turning circle certainly helps matters.

And if you open the Midgate in order to accommodate a 4X4 ATV or motorbike, or what have you, cabin comfort will barely be affected by such things as exterior noise, wind or reduced chassis rigidity. And regardless of the configuration you adopt, the Avalanche – powered by a capable 285 hp 5.3-liter V8 engine coupled to a most compatible 4L60-E 4-speed automatic transmission – behaves predictably, just like the Suburban. What's more, you have the option of getting the excellent Auto-Trac all-wheel drive system, which will allow you to switch from 2HI to Auto 4WD, 4HI, 4LO or Neutral.

For once, GM came up with an intriguing concept and one that works wonders.

■ STANDARD EQUIPMENT

• Air conditioning • MidGate system • ABS four-wheel disks • Variable power steering with all-wheel drive • Rigid top • Cruise control • Power windows

■ OPTIONAL EQUIPMENT

• 4 x 4 system • Leather seats • Running board • Bils shock-absorbers • North Star model • Luggage rack • Electric power sliding roof

What about Cadillac?

Cadillac missed out on the initial luxury sport-utility boom because of its late entry into the field. This time around, the division made sure not to make the same mistake twice by announcing the arrival of the Escalade EXT, the "Caddy" version of the Chevrolet model, way ahead of its launch, scheduled for later in the year.

Like the base Escalade, the EXT is derived from an existing model, but "done up" as befits a genuine Cadillac. The front end is essentially the same as the standard model, while the interior bristles with luxurious leather and wood trim, more comfortable seats, in-dash wood appliqués and leather-wrapped steering wheel. The EXT also differs from the Chevrolet Escalade by its 345-hp 6.0-liter V8 engine, the Stabiliti Trak system and Ultrasonic Rear Parking Assist.

In addition to lending its Midgate technology to Cadillac, Chevrolet also offers other variants of its model. A heavy-duty model, equipped with a more powerful engine, is also available and you can order the North Face special edition, equipped with a unique leather interior, exclusive exterior color and, of course, a collection of North Face brand bags.

In a nutshell, GM believes they have launched a pre-emptive strike over the competition with the Avalanche and its Midgate system. A rarity for GM, and they intend to take advantage of it all.

Denis Duquet

SPECIFICATIONS

Price	$CDN 42,505-46,680 / $US 30,965-49,990
Warranty	17,0793 years / 36,000 miles (60,000 km)
Type	hybrid pickup truck / all wheel drive
Wheelbase / Length	129.9 in / 221.7 in
Width / Height	79.6 in / 73.6 in
Weight	5677 lb (2575 kg)
Trunk / Fuel tank	63 to 97.2 in / 31 gallons
Air bags	front and side
Front suspension	independent
Rear suspension	rigid axle
Front brakes / Rear brakes	disc ABS
Traction control	yes
Steering	recirculating-ball, power assist
Turning circle	46 feet
Tires (front/rear)	P265/70R16

PERFORMANCE

Engine	V8 5.3-liter
Transmission	4-speed automatic
Horsepower	285 hp at 5200 rpm
Torque	325 lb-ft at 4000 rpm
Other engines	V8 6.0-liter 345 hp
Other transmission	none
Acceleration (0-60 mph)	11. 9 sec
Maximum speed	112 mph (180 km/h)
Braking (60-0 mph)	157 feet (47.8 m)
Fuel consumption	14.8 mpg (15.3 L/100 km)

COMPETITION

- Ford Super Crew

NEW FOR 2002

- New model • Cadillac version (345 hp)

RATING (out of 5 stars)

Driveability	★★★★
Comfort	★★★
Reliability	New model
Roominess	★★★★
Winter driving rating	★★★★
Safety	★★★★
Resale value	New model

CHEVROLET BLAZER GMC JIMMY

CHEVROLET **BLAZER**

In Transit...

With the thundering arrival of the new Chevy TrailBlazer, GMC Envoy and Oldsmobile Bravada, some of us were convinced that the Blazer and Jimmy would disappear overnight. Well, not quite yet. In all probability, the duo will be replaced or withdrawn from the market, but not before 2003. So, if you're one of those who pine for the good old days, there's still time to enjoy these two classics.

While their exterior has evolved over the years, the duo's boxy shape and other fittings are still fairly recognizable. Say all you want about GM fans' attraction to the slightly retro lines, the fact is these sentimental customers are about to disappear. What with the likes of TrailBlazer, Envoy and Bravada currently muscling in on the market, all vehicles whose styling and mechanicals are far more up-to-the-minute. But the veterans can't be dismissed outright. At least not yet. Take the dashboard, for instance. It looks contemporary and has excellent ergonomics. Ditto for the quality of the material used, especially the textured plastic.

In the minus column, though, is the subpar finish of the cockpit. GM has made great strides in this area, but our test model was still marred by badly aligned plastic parts and some assembly flaws that are frankly unacceptable in a 2002 vehicle. This is more apparent in the cheaper models, which lack the leather trim they badly need to enhance their looks.

The rear seat, too, leaves much to be desired. I wonder what GM engineers were thinking when they designed the ridiculously low bench. Any normal-sized person would have to sit with his head between his legs. And pity whoever has to sit between the two sections of the folding backrest. He'll need to contort his body constantly trying to find a comfortable position.

Waiting for the end

Time was when sport-utilities were almost exclusively utilitarian and hardly ever sporty-looking. They were actually light-duty trucks transformed into big station wagons and adapted for city driving. They sported a drivetrain specially designed for off-road driving, and as robust a suspension as possible, at the expense of the vehicle's overall comfort. Naturally, a solid axle rear suspension maintained in place by leaf springs was standard. And everyone deliberately adjusted the steering mechanism to provide excessive

▲ PROS

- AutoTrak system • Comfortable suspension
- Improving reliability • Robust engine
- Well-appointed dashboard

▼ CONS

- End-of-line model • Imprecise steering at center
- Uncomfortable rear seat
- Uneven finish • Useless 2-door model

movement in the straight-ahead position to decrease the chance of an injury caused by kickback in the steering wheel if you accidentally hit a rock or a stump.

Even though tangible mechanical improvements have transformed the Blazer and Jimmy over the years, a few basic components are still present. The engine is still the 4.3-liter 190 hp V6, coupled to a 5-speed manual gearbox for the two-door model, or a 4-speed automatic in the 4-door. Wishful thinkers can always pretend that the two-door version with manual transmission is more sports car than sport-ute This may be partly true, but don't get excited and try driving it that way. This manual transmission was designed for a truck, and the wide steps between its gear ratio have absolutely nothing to do with a sports car's. Moreover, it takes forever to engage the clutch.

Comfortable, but...

You need only drive the new TrailBlazer and Envoy to realize how firmly the Blazer and Jimmy are from another era. That said, their highly competitive price, combined with the irrational affection of die-hard GM fans, will guarantee decent sales figures. Fortunately, the Touring suspension is offered as standard equipment. That's the best you can get for normal use, not to mention the most comfortable on highways as well as on bumpy or rough roads, common in many regions of North America.

On the highway, strangely enough, the Blazer and Jimmy's road manners prove to be most interesting. Despite the solid rear axle and leaf springs, results weren't all that bad. Steering is vague at center, but you get used to it. Engine noise sounds more industrial than sporty and the 190 hp only kicks in at high RPMs. But the machine is reliable and somewhat fuel efficient. On curving roads, body roll is pronounced and you should always keep its high center of gravity in mind, and exercise caution.

These 4X4's are average both on and off-road. Two drive systems are offered: AutoTrak, intended for city and highway drivers, and the on-demand transfer case system, for off-road enthusiasts.

There are better vehicles on the market, but these two veterans are offered at competitive prices through a vast dealer network.

Denis Duquet

SPECIFICATIONS	LT
Price	$CDN 28,455-34,585 / $US 19,770-29,860
Warranty	3 years / 36,000 miles (60,000 km)
Type	sport-utility 4 doors / all wheel drive
Wheelbase / Length	107 in / 183 in
Width / Height	68 in / 64 in
Weight	4045 lb (1835 kg)
Trunk / Fuel tank	37.3 or 74.1 cu. ft / 18 gallons
Air bags	front
Front suspension	independent
Rear suspension	rigid axle
Front brakes / Rear brakes	disc ABS
Traction control	no
Steering	recirculating balls, variable assist
Turning circle	43 feet
Tires (front/rear)	P235/70R15

PERFORMANCE	
Engine	V6 4.3-liter
Transmission	4-speed automatic
Horsepower	190 hp at 4400 rpm
Torque	250 lb-ft at 2800 rpm
Other engines	none
Other transmission	manual 5-speed (2-door)
Acceleration (0-60 mph)	10.7 sec
Maximum speed	103 mph (165 km/h) (limited)
Braking (60-0 mph)	131 feet (40 m)
Fuel consumption	15.5 mpg (14.6 L/100 km)

COMPETITION

• Ford Explorer • Jeep Grand Cherokee
• Nissan Pathfinder • Toyota 4Runner

NEW FOR 2002

• Monochrome paint (Blazer) • New grille

RATING	(out of 5 stars)
Driveability	★★★
Comfort	★★★★
Reliability	★★★
Roominess	★★★
Winter driving rating	★★★★
Safety	★★★
Resale value	★★½

CHEVROLET CAMARO PONTIAC FIREBIRD

CHEVROLET **CAMARO SS**

The Last Hurrah

Note to collectors: The Chevrolet Camaro SS and the Pontiac Firebird Firehawk will make their final appearance this year. The 2002 model marks the end of the line for these coupes, direct descendants of the muscle cars of the 1970s. We were invited by SLP Engineering Inc., of LaSalle, Que. – GM's official "tuner" – to test drive the ultimate edition of this SLP-tuned duo. Here's our special report.

Let me confess right off the bat my aversion to "brutes," I prefer the virtues of "finesse" and nimbleness in automobile matters. But I must also admit that I've come to love these two moribund sisters. Visually speaking, the Firehawk brings a smile to my face, while the Camaro – in her red outfit and black top – exudes endless charm. Her fluid lines, fine nose and tapered hoodline remind me of the very first Camaros – before the bulges-and-fake-muscles period. Today, these are collectors' items, and they make us yearn for those fabulous 1970s muscle cars. It's unfortunate that GM – or Ford and Chrysler for that matter – chose not to retain and refine their charm further without going over the top.

A whopping 345 horsepower

That said, let's leave nostalgia aside and study the latest editions of the Camaro SS / Firebird Firehawk duo, both of which have been "spiced up" by SLP Engineering. For 2002, in addition to the refined mechanics, the Camaro, with SLP options, gets a new grille and new alloy wheels fitted with imposing BF Goodrich G-Force 17-inch tires; while the Firehawk inherits a new composite hood with functional air scoops, as well as a new Firehawk front fascia badge.

Strong sensations

Under the hood, the all-aluminum 5.7-liter LS1 V8 – same as the Corvette – was boosted to 345 hp from 325 thanks to a modified air-induction and exhaust system. The suspension option features the 1LE kit – Bilstein shocks, Auburn differential and G-Force tires (Camaro) or Firestone Firehawk tires (Firebird). Let me add that these tire brands are recommended only if you plan to use the car on a race track occasionally.

Thus fitted, both are capable of explosive performances. With 345 hp, and matching torque to support the car's

▲ PROS

- Superb engine • 6-speed transmission
- Excellent handling on smooth surfaces
- Excellent power/price ratio • Collector's item

▼ CONS

- Restricted interior space • Exaggerated styling
- Uncomfortable suspension
- Brakes need work

3590 lbs (1630 kg), the slightest touch on the right pedal will propel the car as though it were a space shuttle, accompanied by the gorgeous deep-throated gargle of its eight unbridled cylinders. The stopwatch confirmed this sensation, clocking a 0-60 mph time of 5.2 seconds. The G-Force tires, when they are at the proper operating temperature, exhibited remarkable traction on the little slalom circuit made available to us. Bear in mind that the Camaro doesn't like tight turns. To ward off untimely understeer, you have to slow down properly before entering a turn, even if it means resorting to first gear to get back up to speed on the straightaway. The brakes are reasonably effective, but they are not quite on a par with the powertrain when it comes to sport driving. They require, among other things, a firmer pedal.

Predictable behavior

On the road, the two coupes exhibit the same characteristic: a curt suspension that can't really handle bad roads (notorious in Michigan), but is fine on smooth surfaces. Visibility is limited due to the low driving position and the long hoodline. Footroom is so bad in the front that an *Auto Guide* journalist dubbed the GM coupe "the only one-seater on the market." Despite the narrow cockpit, the driver – or more aptly, pilot – will appreciate the contoured Sport seat, which hugs your body shape snugly and provides excellent support. Unfortunately, those gorgeous seats are available only on the Firehawk, which explains Pontiac's greater popularity, or so they claim. And to think I prefer the Camaro...

Thanks to a 6-speed manual transmission – not always easy to manipulate – and the gigantic torque generated by that awesome GM V8, both the Camaro and Firebird cruise at 60 mph at 1400 rpm and fuel consumption is 18 mpg. But don't get excited, these are not Honda Civics, and the minute you hit the city, consumption will jump to 12 mpg.

If you are single; if your passenger has very small feet; if you lust after strong sensations and can tame a 345-hp machine; if you've got another car for winter driving; and if you don't mind being called a dinosaur, treat yourself to the last "pony car" from GM. The power/price ratio is unbeatable.

Alain Raymond

PONTIAC **FIREBIRD FIREHAWK**

SPECIFICATIONS	**SS**
Price	$CDN 26,995-46,590 / $US 17,880-31,790
Warranty	3 years / 36,000 miles (60,000 km)
Type	coupe 2+2 / rear wheel drive
Wheelbase / Length	101 in / 194 in
Width / Height	74 in / 52 in
Weight	3593 lb (1630 kg)
Trunk / Fuel tank	7.6 cu. ft / 17 gallons
Air bags	front and side
Front suspension	independent
Rear suspension	rigid axle
Front brakes / Rear brakes	disc
Traction control	yes
Steering	rack-and-pinion; power assist
Turning circle	38 feet
Tires (front/rear)	P275/40ZR17

PERFORMANCE	
Engine	V8 5.7-liter
Transmission	6-speed manual
Horsepower	345 hp at 5200 rpm
Torque	345 lb-ft at 4400 rpm
Other engines	V6 3.8-liter 200 hp; V8 5.7-liter 305 hp
Other transmission	4-speed automatic; 5-speed manual
Acceleration (0-60 mph)	5.2 s; 6.6 s (305 hp)
Maximum speed	162 mph (260 km/h)
Braking (60-0 mph)	131 feet (40 m)
Fuel consumption	12 mpg (18.9 L/100 km)

COMPETITION

- Ford Mustang

NEW FOR 2002

- G-Force tires (option)

RATING	**(out of 5 stars)**
Driveability	★★★½
Comfort	★★½
Reliability	★★½
Roominess	★★
Winter driving rating	★★
Safety	★★★½
Resale value	★

CHEVROLET CAVALIER PONTIAC SUNFIRE

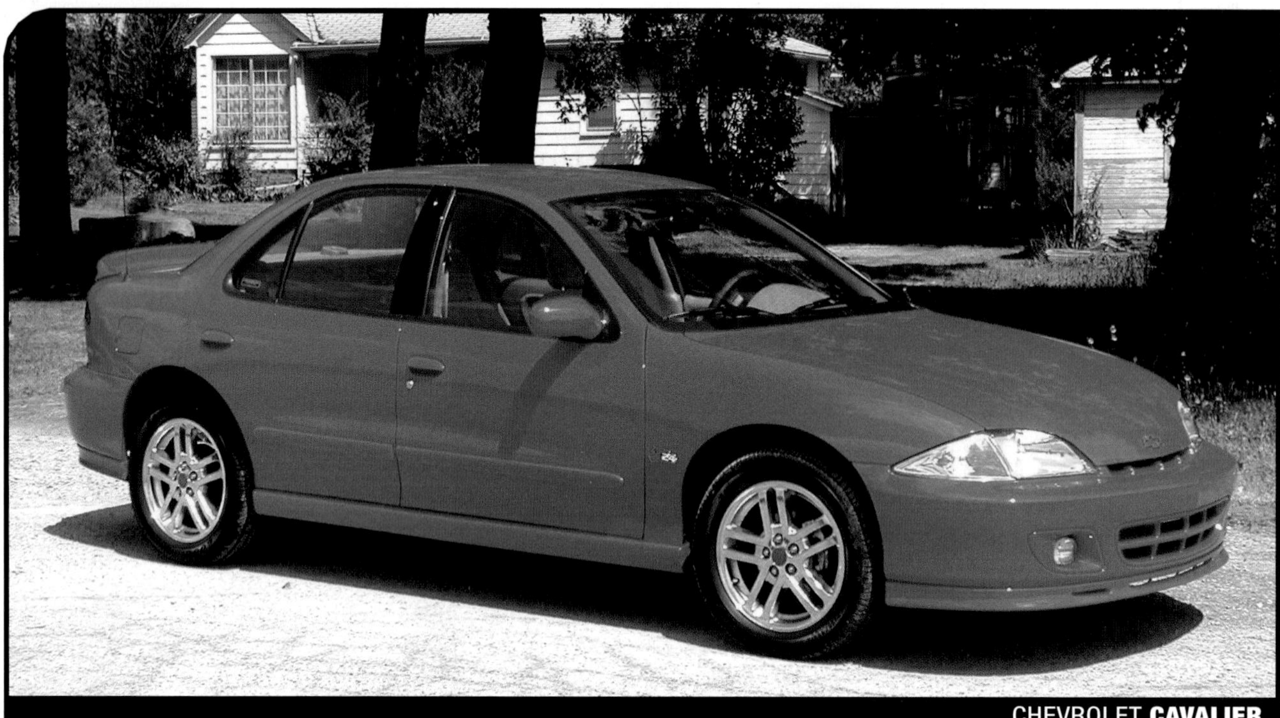

CHEVROLET **CAVALIER**

Please Be Patient!

Surrounded by enthusiastic journalists at the New York Auto Show, Ron Zarella, GM's president of North American operations, was asked about his company's plans to improve its position in the compact and subcompact market. The question was raised in light of the success of the Ford Focus, currently the world's best-selling car. Zarella shrugged his shoulders and admitted that it was going to take at least a few more years before the current Chevrolet Cavalier and Pontiac Sunfire models could be updated or eventually replaced.

Then, speaking quite candidly, he added: "We're devoting most of our energies to developing new light trucks and SUVs, because that's where the money is. The Cavalier and Sunfire will just have to wait." And who can blame him really? Especially when you consider the fact that both models continue to be ranked among the most popular cars on North American roads.

Introduced in 1981 as 1982 models, Cavalier and Sunfire only underwent major make-overs 13 years later, in 1995. If this trend continues, the next redesign will not happen before the year 2008!

Fortunately, in 2000, both the exterior and dashboard of the Cavalier and Sunfire were modified to obtain a more contemporary look. Although these were minor changes, they were good enough to help both models stand up well to the competition. As a matter of fact, it's hard to find fault with the quality of their ergonomics and dashboards. Controls are easy to reach and instrument displays are generously sized, and therefore easy to read. Sunfire has the edge, but in my opinion both cars look fine.

Nothing is ever perfect, mind you, and the pair's principal flaw is the poor-quality plastic used in the cockpit, the number of parts that don't even fit well together, and the hideous fabric seat coverings that look as if the material had been purchased at a clearance warehouse. Frankly, this sort of gaffe is inexcusable. Worth noting, however, is the fact that the fabric and upholstery were treated with "Scotchgard" protector. These cars have been around for ages and GM could quite easily have upgraded the cockpit, which already benefits from the models' spacious cabin both front and rear.

Sunfire has the edge

The engineers face an even more daunting task. They must maintain the mechanicals

▲ PROS

• 2.4-liter engine • Roominess • Efficient transmissions • Irreproachable ergonomics • Average comfort

▼ CONS

• Disappointing reliability • Poor finish • Rough 2.2-liter engine • Weak resale value • Mediocre tires

to make sure that the Cavalier and Sunfire can keep up with the competition, which is semi-transformed every five years. Too often, though, GM engineers continue to recycle their mechanical components over and over, despite the fact that these same components were originally chosen for reasons of economy.

The standard engine is a 2.5-liter 4-cylinder with pushrod-actuated overhead valves, upgraded from the 2.2-liter engine that came with the first Cavalier way back in 1981. Even Pontiac rejected it at the time, opting instead for a 1.8-liter SOHC engine. On the other hand, the car is fitted with a modern and efficient 5-speed manual transmission made by the German company Getrag. Despite its ancient configuration, the noisy and torquey engine copes well with the 4-speed automatic transmission.

But without a doubt both compacts fare better when fitted with the modern 2.4-liter DOHC engine whose 150 hp puts them at the head of their class. The Ford Focus, for example, only has a 130 hp engine, while the Neon boasts 132 horses.

City slickers

The team responsible for the Cavalier and Sunfire are never shy about admitting that their mission was to come up with a car that carries itself with dash and elegance, with a spacious cockpit, a decent-sized trunk and a drivetrain that is easy to build and maintain.

They managed to achieve all of the above. But they did so without too much consideration for driveability, performance, attention to detail and execution.

As a result, handling is mediocre on all models of these two car families, with excessive body roll while cornering, vague steering response and a spongy brake pedal. All this isn't so bad, but if you're a sport driver, then you're guaranteed to fall asleep at the wheel. And only the rudimentary ABS brakes will wake you up: the mechanism is overly sensitive and very noisy.

What the Cavalier and the Sunfire have going for them are their looks, a most complete range of standard equipment, inexpensive spare parts, an extensive network of dealers across the country and favorable financing terms. If you want more, then you'll have to look elsewhere.

Denis Duquet

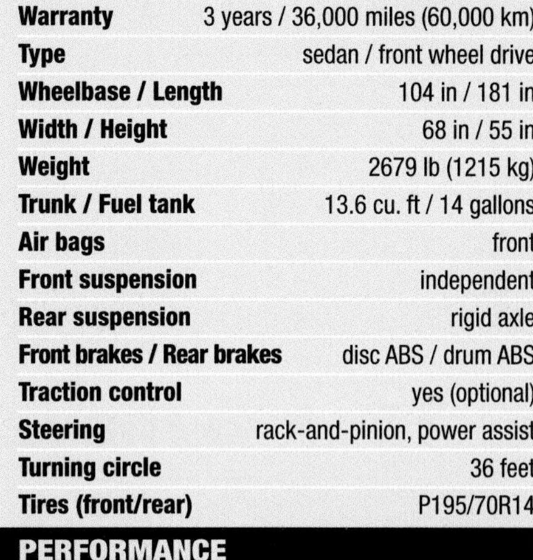

SPECIFICATIONS	**LS**
Price	$CDN 15,100-22,975 / $US 13,800-17,065
Warranty	3 years / 36,000 miles (60,000 km)
Type	sedan / front wheel drive
Wheelbase / Length	104 in / 181 in
Width / Height	68 in / 55 in
Weight	2679 lb (1215 kg)
Trunk / Fuel tank	13.6 cu. ft / 14 gallons
Air bags	front
Front suspension	independent
Rear suspension	rigid axle
Front brakes / Rear brakes	disc ABS / drum ABS
Traction control	yes (optional)
Steering	rack-and-pinion, power assist
Turning circle	36 feet
Tires (front/rear)	P195/70R14

PERFORMANCE	
Engine	4L 2.4-liter
Transmission	4-speed automatic
Horsepower	150 hp at 5600 rpm
Torque	155 lb-ft at 4400 rpm
Other engines	4L 2.5 liter 115 hp
Other transmission	5-speed manual
Acceleration (0-60 mph)	12.4 s ; 9.1 s (Z24 man.)
Maximum speed	99 mpg (160 km/h)
Braking (60-0 mph)	143 feet (43.5 m)
Fuel consumption	32.3 mpg (7 L/100 km)

COMPETITION

• Chrysler Neon • Daewoo Nubira • Ford Focus • Honda Civic • Hyundai Elantra • Kia Spectra

NEW FOR 2002

No major change

RATING	**(out of 5 stars)**
Driveability	★★
Comfort	★★★
Reliability	★★
Roominess	★★★½
Winter driving rating	★★★½
Safety	★★★
Resale value	★★

PONTIAC **SUNFIRE**

CHEVROLET CORVETTE

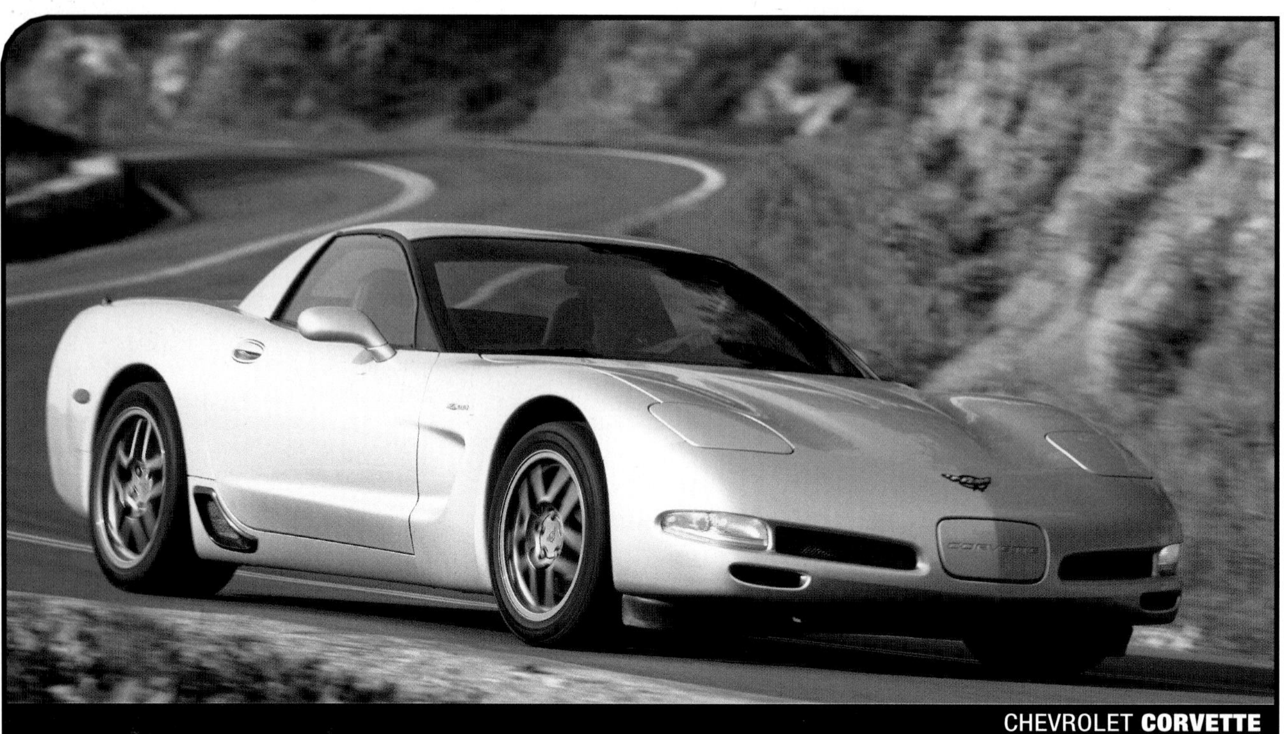

CHEVROLET **CORVETTE**

True Believers!

Sooner or later, inflation will finally remove the Corvette's most redeeming feature – its excellent price/performance ratio. As recently as last year, the *Auto Guide* touted America's premier production-line sports car as the one with the most reasonably priced horses on the market. Well, the horses are still there, and in ever-increasing numbers. Unfortunately, their cost is galloping along at the same pace. Today, a Z06 costs as much as the competition.

But the true believers will declare that nothing can rival a Corvette and I understand their feelings! The Dodge Viper, for example, which costs a whole lot more, is literally unbearable in a daily commute, while the Boxsters S, M3, SLK 32 or any other European sports cars for that matter, will never tempt the diehards away from Corvette showrooms. Those well-bred Europeans cost just as much as their American cousin, but what they're all missing is Corvette's twin hallmarks – energy and insolence.

With that digression out of the way, what's the scoop on the 2002 model? The big news, of course, concerns the arrival of a new Z06 version, which the *Auto Guide* road-tested last year. Its LS V8 engine gets an extra 20 horses (for a total of 405), equaling the old LT5 V8 engine that propelled the Corvette ZR1. This gain in horsepower was due to new, lighter hollow stem valves, a revised camshaft and a low-restriction air cleaner design. At the same time, the car was fitted with a new and larger aluminum front stabilizer bar and a stiffer rear leaf spring. Its rear shock valving, too, was modified and finally the alloy wheels, though seemingly the same as before, were actually made of cast aluminum, reducing the weight of the unsprung masses. Inside the cockpit, a standard Head-Up Display projects the various instruments and gauges digitally onto the windshield, allowing the driver to keep his or her eyes on the road.

Two engines, three versions

The most agile Corvette – the Z06 – is only available with a hard top. If you want a convertible or a coupe, you'll have to settle for a 5.7-liter V8 engine with 350 horsepower, which can be paired either to a 4-speed automatic transmission or a 6-speed manual. The Z06, on the other hand, comes with a manual gearbox only. All 2002 Corvettes come equipped with the Second-Genera-

▲ PROS

• Construction quality on the rise • Decent trunk (hard top) • Explosive performance • Remarkable roadholding • Unbeatable brakes

▼ CONS

• Dubious comfort • No spare tire • Large turning circle • Rising price • Unstable on rough roads

tion Active Handling, featuring rear-brake stability control. It also works in tandem with the traction control feature, assisting the driver in maintaining control over excessive wheelspin. The traction control feature can be switched off manually as needed.

Serious performance

These days, European sports-car drivers can no longer afford to turn up their noses at the Corvette, least of all the Z06. It's quite capable of taking on any supercar, not just on the straightaway, but on twisting roads as well, so long as the surface is smooth. The Corvette is highly allergic to potholes and bumps in the road, which give it a bad case of nerves, not to mention affecting its directional stability and causing it to lose balance. Overall comfort has been gradually improved, and the car's leather seats are excellent, although I suspect your rheumatic grandmother may have a hard time coping with all the jolts and jerks. What can I say, the suspension is simply incapable of absorbing them.

Bumps in the road!

The Z06's engine generates so much power and torque that it can readily be paired with practically any long-ratioed gearbox. In 6th gear, for example, its impressive V8 only revs up to 2000 rpm, which means that at the maximum 6500 rpm, you can theoretically reach a whopping 245 mph (390 km/h)! I'd be happy driving at 177 mph (285 km/h), simply because at top speed, the Corvette is incapable of handling the slightest bump in the road – something I experienced firsthand on a test circuit in Montreal North a couple of years ago. Incidentally, the speedometer can be adjusted to display the speed either in miles or kilometers. Also, the manual transmission gear lever is stiff, requiring so much effort that it might reactivate your tendinitis!

If power abounds aboard the Corvette, it has braking force to match, boasting the shortest stopping distance in the annals of the *Auto Guide* – a mere 114 feet (34.7 meters)!

Although the Z06 is the best of the Corvettes, many drivers will be just as happy behind the wheel of the coupe or convertible versions, powered by the LS1 engine. These models have also been improved over the years and Corvette first-timers will find the performance spectacular, whichever model they drive.

Jacques Duval

SPECIFICATIONS	**Z06 405**
Price	$CDN 62,400-70,780 / $US 40,925-48,700
Warranty	3 years / 36,000 miles (60,000 km)
Type	hardtop two-seater / rear wheel drive
Wheelbase / Length	104.9 in / 179.7 in
Width / Height	73.6 in / 47.6 in
Weight	3117 lb (1414 kg)
Trunk / Fuel tank	13.3 cu. ft / 19 gallons
Air bags	front
Front suspension	independent
Rear suspension	independent
Front brakes / Rear brakes	disc ABS
Traction control	yes
Steering	rack-and-pinion, variable assist
Turning circle	40 feet
Tires (front/rear)	P265/40ZR17 / P295/35ZR18

PERFORMANCE	
Engine	V8 5.7-liter
Transmission	6-speed manual
Horsepower	405 hp at 6000 rpm
Torque	400 lb-ft at 4800 rpm
Other engines	V8 5.7-liter 350 hp
Other transmission	4-speed automatic
Acceleration (0-60 mph)	4.5 s; 5.6 s (350 hp)
Maximum speed	177 mph (285 km/h)
Braking (60-0 mph)	114 feet (34.7 m)
Fuel consumption	17.7 mpg (12.8 L/100 km)

COMPETITION

- Acura NSX-T • Dodge Viper • Jaguar XKR
- Lexus SC 430 • Porsche Carrera

NEW FOR 2002

- 405 hp engine • In-dash CD player
- Upgraded suspensions

RATING	**(out of 5 stars)**
Driveability	★★★★½
Comfort	★★★
Reliability	★★★½
Roominess	★★★
Winter driving rating	★
Safety	★★★★
Resale value	★★★★

CHEVROLET IMPALA CHEVROLET MONTE CARLO

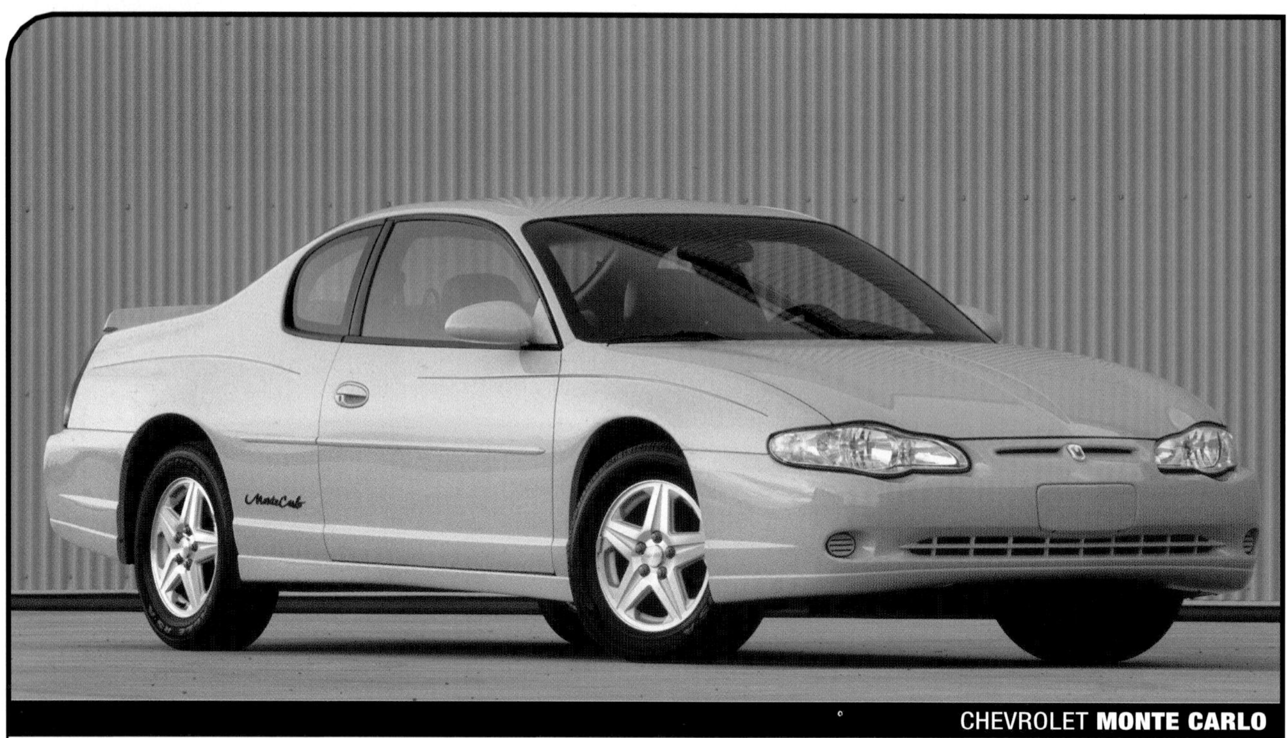

CHEVROLET **MONTE CARLO**

Near or Far-Sighted?

Recently, General Motors has been mounting an all-out campaign to attract well-known automobile designers – those universally recognized for their work in a variety of consumer markets. You need only glance at the Chevrolet Impala and Monte Carlo – a four-door sedan and a sport coupe, respectively – to understand the reason for these recruiting efforts.

No doubt both cars have their particular qualities, but both are saddled with utterly nondescript silhouettes. The Impala looks as if it had been designed for near-sighted buyers who need look at it close up to see the nifty details, while the Monte Carlo seems to be intended for the far-sighted, because it looks a lot nicer from a distance.

Competent and well rounded

From the front and side, the Impala looks decent enough, but the rear end is a disaster, what with those bold, totally out-of-place round taillights. Thank goodness for the Sport trim package, which offers more subdued taillights and five-spoke alloy wheels.

The cabin is spacious and reasonably elegant, with a darker-hued, classier dashboard than is usually the case in a Chevy. This year, the Sport package comes with a ceiling light in quasi carbon fiber and a newly styled instrument cluster. Adults of all sizes can fit comfortably in both the front and rear seats. But while the front seats provide adequate lateral support, the rear seats are too low to be really comfortable, especially on long trips.

Controversial silhouette notwithstanding, the Impala boasts one of the best chassis in its category. The platform is rigid, the fully independent suspension well tuned, and steering precise. Despite its "big American car" appearance, this Chevy corners effortlessly and its 3.8-liter V6 engine responds even to the slightest demand from the accelerator – a responsiveness that also makes it perfect for city driving. That's probably the reason why it's so popular with taxi drivers and the police force. The standard 3.4-liter V6 isn't bad either, except that it runs out of steam more quickly.

NYPD / NASCAR

▲ PROS

- Comfortable cabin • Decent finish
- Powerful brakes • Reliable powertrain
- Sound road manners

▼ CONS

- Body roll on turns • Wide girth
- Nondescript exterior • Rear seats too low
- 3.4-liter engine needs work

All in all, the Impala is a well-rounded car, pleasant enough to drive, but hampered by what most buyers perceive as an off-putting exterior.

Disappointing

Wildly popular during the 1970s, the Monte Carlo made a comeback two years ago – one of the rare, big, mid-size sport coupes on the market. Even though it shares its platform with the Impala, the Monte Carlo is very much its own car, in terms both of looks and road manners.

Styling-wise, this sport coupe has no equal, and that's not necessarily a compliment. Designed as a basis for the NASCAR racer – where aerodynamics takes precedence over aesthetics – the Monte Carlo obviously looks more eloquent on the racing circuit than in city traffic, where it sticks out markedly with its roundish, oddly shaped taillights.

According to Chevrolet, however, most buyers appreciate the way it looks. So much the better for them, but I beg to differ. The mediocre cockpit doesn't help either. The plastic finish, for instance, looks even cheesier than in the Impala.

If all you want is a big coupe with average handling and performance, the Monte Carlo won't disappoint you. On the other hand, if you're a true-blue sporty driver, don't expect too much! Despite its sporty looks – especially the SS model – the Monte Carlo's performance is average at best. Powered by a 3.4-liter V6 with 180 horsepower, it takes more than 9 seconds to scoot from 0-60 mph. The only redeeming note here is the car's excellent fuel economy.

Frankly, the Monte Carlo deserves the 4.0-liter V8 engine that currently powers the Oldsmobile Aurora, coupled with a 5-speed manual gearbox. Only then will it be worthy of its sport coupe vocation. Otherwise, don't delude yourself about its sporty qualities.

Denis Duquet

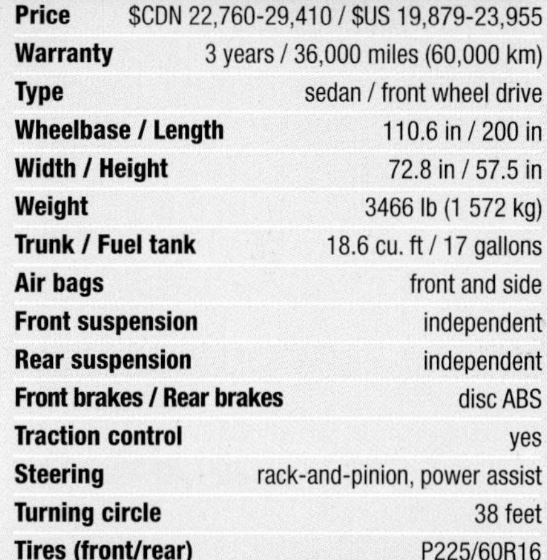

SPECIFICATIONS	
Price	$CDN 22,760-29,410 / $US 19,879-23,955
Warranty	3 years / 36,000 miles (60,000 km)
Type	sedan / front wheel drive
Wheelbase / Length	110.6 in / 200 in
Width / Height	72.8 in / 57.5 in
Weight	3466 lb (1 572 kg)
Trunk / Fuel tank	18.6 cu. ft / 17 gallons
Air bags	front and side
Front suspension	independent
Rear suspension	independent
Front brakes / Rear brakes	disc ABS
Traction control	yes
Steering	rack-and-pinion, power assist
Turning circle	38 feet
Tires (front/rear)	P225/60R16

PERFORMANCE	
Engine	V6 3.8-liter
Transmission	4-speed automatic
Horsepower	200 hp at 5200 rpm
Torque	225 lb-ft at 4000 rpm
Other engines	V6 3.4-liter 180 hp
Other transmission	none
Acceleration (0-60 mph)	9.6 sec
Maximum speed	118 mph (190 km/h)
Braking (60-0 mph)	136 feet (41.6 m)
Fuel consumption	18 mpg (12.6 L/100 km)

COMPETITION

- Chrysler Intrepid • Ford Taurus • Mercury Grand Marquis • Toyota Avalon

NEW FOR 2002

- Dual front temperature controls • New colors
- Sport trim package

RATING	(out of 5 stars)
Driveability	★★★
Comfort	★★★★
Reliability	★★★★
Roominess	★★★★
Winter driving rating	★★★½
Safety	★★★★
Resale value	★★★

CHEVROLET **IMPALA**

CHEVROLET MALIBU OLDSMOBILE ALERO

CHEVROLET **MALIBU**

The Laws of Reason

If you were to ask test drivers taking part in a comparison test to choose between the Chevrolet Malibu and the Oldsmobile Alero, the Alero will clearly be the hands-down winner, even after a short test drive. Not only is its exterior more refined, but it outstrips the Malibu in terms of handling and driving pleasure. What's more, it comes in both sedan and coupe versions.

In a nutshell, then, this Oldsmobile has all the road qualities needed to interest those people who are looking for a car that's both practical and pleasant to drive. Among its attractive features are precise steering, excellent cornering ability and a cabin comparable to that of many Japanese cars. On the other hand, the suspension is overly firm and can become an annoyance on bumpy roads.

Still, the 150-hp 2.4-liter 4-cylinder DOHC engine allows you to relax and enjoy the drive, especially when it's coupled to the Getrag 5-speed manual transmission. But this engine has always been noisy when you accelerate and an overly heavy clutch pedal makes driving in the city uncomfortable. For many drivers, the 170-hp 3.4-liter V6 paired to a 4-speed automatic transmission is the more logical choice.

Unfortunately, all this information is rather beside the point, as the Oldsmobile division is about to disappear – probably by mid-decade at the latest. The Alero is destined to become an orphan in the near future.

Malibu: the wise choice

If the mission of the Alero designers was to develop a car capable of taking on its Japanese competitors head to head, the Malibu team's goal was to offer an excellent quality/performance/price ratio. In other words, it's the ideal sedan for the average North American family in search of a car that combines the qualities of "nice design, good quality and low price."

This explains a compromise characteristic of this mid-size sedan. The Malibu is not the kind of car designed to make you fall head over heels in love as soon as you spot one in the showroom. You have to be more interested in its complete range of equipment, no-problem drivetrain and acceptable design.

Let's have some fun trying to find out if this solidly built Chevrolet deserves the label "nice design, good quality and low price." The

▲ PROS

• Complete equipment • Excellent audio system • Good acceleration (V6) • Large trunk • Roominess

▼ CONS

• Average tires • Body roll in corners • Little driving pleasure • Nondescript design • Subpar materials

Malibu just barely passes muster in the "nice design" department. Its masses are well balanced, the distribution of the various elements is adequate and it doesn't disgrace itself when it comes down to styling. It's just this kind of sobriety that will allow the car to age "gracefully," aesthetically speaking. From a practical viewpoint, the cabin is close to being completely stripped while some materials seem to have been selected strictly for commercial use. The dashboard is straightforward and unflashy, everything is within reach and controls are easy to use. The audio system also gets high marks, offering excellent sound for a car in this price range. The front seats, on the other hand, are average, providing inadequate lateral support and are upholstered with material that may displease finicky types. The back seats have excellent legroom and the 60/40 backrest can be flipped forward, adding to the car's versatility.

The Malibu therefore deserves average marks in styling terms. To meet the "good quality" criteria, engineers used tried and true mechanical components. The 3.1-liter V6 is certainly not new, but its reliability has been demonstrated beyond question, ditto the 4-speed automatic transmission. Also worth noting is the independent rear suspension and standard brakes with ABS.

No problems when you get behind the wheel and take this Chevy out for a spin. In the plus column are its quiet ride, directional stability, neutral behavior while cornering and the engine's adequate performance. On the other hand, if you push the car the least bit hard, it will exhibit serious understeer, the tires will squeal and the vehicle becomes unstable. Both engines work well enough, although they could be more efficient. In a nutshell, the Malibu is a good family car, so long as you don't try to make it exceed its limits.

Finally, with a sticker price of about $25,000, the Malibu meets the "low price" criterion, boasting a complete range of equipment as well as tried and true mechanical components. And that makes it one of the best deals on the market.

Denis Duquet

OLDSMOBILE **ALERO**

SPECIFICATIONS

Price	$CDN 21,745-27,670 / $US 17,735-22,775
Warranty	3 years / 36,000 miles (60,000 km)
Type	sedan / front wheel drive
Wheelbase / Length	107.1 in / 190.6 in
Width / Height	69.3 in / 56.3 in
Weight	3075 lb (1395 kg)
Trunk / Fuel tank	16.4 cu. ft / 14 gallons
Air bags	front
Front suspension	independent
Rear suspension	independent
Front brakes / Rear brakes	disc ABS / drum ABS
Traction control	no
Steering	rack-and-pinion, power assist
Turning circle	36 feet
Tires (front/rear)	P205/60R15

PERFORMANCE

Engine	V6 3.1-liter
Transmission	4-speed automatic
Horsepower	170 hp at 5200 rpm
Torque	190 lb-ft at 4000 rpm
Other engines	none
Other transmission	none
Acceleration (0-60 mph)	9.6 sec
Maximum speed	106 mph (170 km/h) (electron. lim.)
Braking (60-0 mph)	138 feet (42 m)
Fuel consumption	21.6 mpg (10.5 L/100 km)

COMPETITION

- Accord • Altima • Camry • Leganza
- Mazda 626 • Sebring • Sonata

NEW FOR 2002

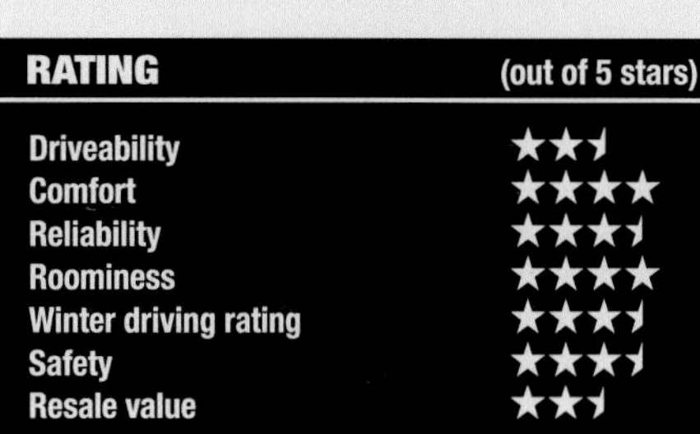

RATING (out of 5 stars)

Driveability	★★½
Comfort	★★★★
Reliability	★★★½
Roominess	★★★★
Winter driving rating	★★★½
Safety	★★★½
Resale value	★★½

CHEVROLET TAHOE CHEVROLET SUBURBAN GMC YUKON/YUKON XL

GMC **YUKON XL DENALI**

The XXL Gang

If you're interested in one these juggernauts and live, say, in the trendy district with quaint streets, think twice. Because it will look totally out of place in narrow thoroughfares and you'll need a sharp eye and remarkable coordination just to park it. Besides, each gas fill up will put you in the poorhouse.

But for someone whose professional or recreational activities require a robust and spacious sport-utility, the Tahoe, Yukon or Suburban may be the perfect solution. True, their squarish shape isn't exactly art-gallery material, and their platform, borrowed from the Silverado and Sierra trucks, precludes all sport-driving. Still, they're robust enough to satisfy the needs of outdoors enthusiasts and specialized workers. Seen in that light, these big vehicles have their redeeming features.

Identical twins

Before taking a closer look, let me point out that the Tahoe and the Yukon are virtually identical, so the following comments apply to both models.

Belonging to the full-size SUV category, the pair's dimensions are more reasonable than the Ford Expedition, which is 5.9 inch (15 cm) longer and about 550 lbs (250 kg) heavier. Even the Toyota Sequoia is longer and heavier than the Tahoe. This doesn't prevent the latter from providing more luggage space, a roomy passenger cabin, even the option of a third-row seat. And unless you have very particular needs, you can transport practically anything in this sport-utility, whose quasi-retro appearance seems to make quite a few folks happy.

The benchmark

Like most GM sport-utilities, the dashboard is a good example of efficient control layout. But I wonder why the cassette player is banished under the dashboard. Was it an afterthought on the part of the designers? The front bucket seats are comfortable and include seatbelts integrated into the seats themselves. The rear seats are not too bad, but the flat backrest and thin upholstery don't exactly encourage you to take long trips. What's more, the relatively narrow door makes it hard to get in and out.

▲ PROS

- Roominess • Comfortable cockpit • Choice of engines • Balanced handling • Reasonable fuel consumption

▼ CONS

- Large size • Finish needs improvement
- Retro lines • Difficult access to third-row seat

The most pleasant surprise is actually driving this colossus. Given its size and technical specs, you'd imagine it would throw you around and scare you silly. But handling is quite honest, as long as you don't confuse this Tahoe with a Corvette. Steering is still a little vague and the rear end tends to slide sideways when turning on rough surfaces. Brakes are powerful and well modulated. On the other hand, many buyers have complained about their lack of durability. The all-wheel drive is less sophisticated than the Toyota Sequoia's, but superior to the Ford Expedition's.

The standard engine, a 4.8-liter 275 hp V8, is sufficient for most situations, easily handling an impressive towing capacity of 8680 lbs (3946 kg). The 4-speed automatic gearbox is another plus. Mechanically identical, the GMC Yukon offers a better appointed interior, and the Denali version, even more luxury.

Big families

Though the Chevy Suburban sports an exterior virtually identical to the Tahoe, it's substantially bigger. In fact, it's 20.5 inches (52 cm) longer than its little brother. This vehicle is intended for big families, needing to transport 7 to 9 passengers with their luggage or to tow a 8600-lb (3900-kg) trailer.

This is not a vehicle for everyone. Unless you feel claustrophobic and wish to drive something with a cockpit as huge as a ballroom, you don't really need it.

Once a conveyance for road-maintenance and construction workers, the Suburban has been refined over the years. Like the Tahoe, it's amazingly nimble and provides excellent comfort on long trips. Its handling is such that you can negotiate sharp curves with little effort.

Whatever V8 you've got under the hood, the gas is going to cost you big time. Be that as it may, the engines of these two sturdy vehicles guzzle less than the competition in general, giving the edge to General Motors.

Any way you look at it, these SUVs are awesome. It wouldn't be a bad idea for GM to send a couple of truck guys over to its car division.

Denis Duquet

SPECIFICATIONS

Price	$CDN 41,695-60,850 / $US 25,671-40,454
Warranty	3 years / 36,000 miles (60,000 km)
Type	sport-utility 6 / 8 seats / all wheel drive
Wheelbase / Length	116 in / 199 in
Width / Height	79 in /77 in
Weight	5426 lb (2461 kg)
Trunk / Fuel tank	16.3 cu. ft / 26 gallons
Air bags	front and side
Front suspension	independent
Rear suspension	rigid
Front brakes / Rear brakes	disc ABS
Traction control	yes
Steering	recirculating balls, power assist
Turning circle	38 feet
Tires (front/rear)	P265/70R17

PERFORMANCE

Engine	V8 6-liter
Transmission	4-speed automatic
Horsepower	320 hp at 5000 rpm
Torque	365 lb-ft at 4000 rpm
Other engines	V8 4.8-liter 275 hp - V8 5.3-liter 285 hp V8 8.1 liter 240 hp (Suburban and XL)
Other transmission	none
Acceleration (0-60 mph)	9.4 sec
Maximum speed	109 mph (175 km/h)
Braking (60-0 mph)	153 feet (46.6 m)
Fuel consumption	15.3 mpg (14.8 L/100 km)

COMPETITION

- Ford Expedition/Lincoln Navigator
- Toyota Sequoia

NEW FOR 2002

- Certain models discontinued • Standard tailgate
- Standard HomeLink

RATING (out of 5 stars)

Driveability	★★★½
Comfort	★★★★
Reliability	★★★★
Roominess	★★★★★
Winter driving rating	★★★★
Safety	★★★★★
Resale value	★★★½

CHEVROLET TRAILBLAZER GMC ENVOY OLDS. BRAVADA

GMC **ENVOY**

No Longer Old-Fashioned!

For years, General Motors countered the competition's forays into the sport-utility market by coming up with technical refinements and styling revisions for models that in some cases dated back to the 1970s. The savings must have pleased the bean counters, but customers didn't see things the same way, and sales continued to drop over the years despite the public's strong and constantly growing demand for SUVs.

Convinced that a counter-attack with leading-edge technology was in order, the big shots at GM have finally given the green light for developing a new troika of bigger and more technologically-advanced vehicles – fit to do battle with the category's leaders. GM's first order of the day is to increase the size of the replacement models for the Chevy Blazer, GMC Jimmy and Oldsmobile Bravada. Although their dimensions have always been considered just fine, Americans seem to want bigger and bigger vehicles. The new models, therefore, are 7.1 inches (19 cm) longer, 6.7 inches (17 cm) wider and 7.1 inches (19 cm) taller. The extra inches may not sound like a whole lot, but they add loads of extra comfort to all three models, especially in the rear – much more legroom and infinitely more comfortable seats. In addition, by tipping the backrest forward, the headrests fold down automatically, eliminating the annoying need to find storage space for them.

An in-line 6

In addition to an up-to-the minute, bigger body, the new SUVs are fitted with brand new mechanicals. The engineers retained the independent chassis, maintaining the vehicles' heavy-duty off-road capabilities and therefore increasing their chance for long-term survival in the marketplace. The chassis has been stiffened by 25%, allowing the use of more supple springs and shocks and, in turn, adding to the vehicles' overall comfort and handling.

Three's a crowd

This happy state of affairs can also be attributed to the multi-link rigid-axle rear suspension, whose leaf springs have been replaced with coils. The front suspension is also new, sporting dual A-arms to ensure both car-like comfort and off-road toughness. Incidentally, this

▲ PROS

• Impressive engine • Rigid platform
• Good handling • Powerful brakes
• Rear seat easy to fold

▼ CONS

• Perilous start (see text) • Large size
• Untested engine • Bravada bound to be discontinued • Disappointing finish

suspension nearly caused a disaster last April, when a break in the lower arm of the front suspension was discovered in thousands of units already in circulation. GM promptly recalled the vehicles, replaced the defective arm and added reinforcement to all existing and future models. Let's hope that this is an isolated case and is not an indication of poor overall reliability and mechanical integrity.

Things might have been much worse. The general recall could have been prompted by the new 4.2-liter in-line 6-cylinder engine, the first of its kind ever to be developed by GM since 1963 (it's not to be confused with the ancient and sturdy "in-line 6" of the old days). In addition to its all-aluminum cylinder block and head, this "six" features dual overhead camshafts, 4 valves per cylinder and coil-on-plug ignition. In addition, the vehicle's electronic motor control system is the most sophisticated currently in use at GM.

With 270 horsepower, this engine is the most powerful 6-cylinder ever offered in a sport-utility, surpassing even all V8 engines in the same category. Both the Ford Explorer and Jeep Liberty feature 210 hp V6 engines.

GM engineers chose an in-line engine, partly because of its smoothness – there's almost no vibration – and partly because it's much cheaper to produce than a Vee engine which requires twice as many camshafts and traction parts. All the savings thus realized could be invested in an even more sophisticated engine for future customers.

It's possible to order the two-wheel drive version of the TrailBlazer or Envoy. But the Autotrac system is optional. A simple command button placed on the dashboard allows you to go from "2Hi" – or two-wheel drive – to "4Auto," "4Hi" or "4Lo" and, of course, to neutral.

This system is of the passive variety. In "4Auto," rear-wheel drive is maintained until road conditions warrant a change. In "4Hi," power is distributed 50/50 between the front and rear wheels. On the other hand, the Smartrak system on the Oldsmobile Bravada is an all-wheel drive system that automatically transfers torque to the wheels with the best traction.

CHEV. TRAILBLAZER/GMC ENVOY/OLDS. BRAVADA

CHEVROLET **TRAILBLAZER**

Since all the vehicles share the same platform and mechanicals, is there really a difference between them? We test-drove the models and here's what we discovered.

Chevrolet TrailBlazer: practicality

The Chevy predictably retains the same grille as the Silverado and Avalanche trucks, a feature that suits this GM division's tough image. However, its rear fascia looks more elegant than the other two models' – the taillights and back-up lights make all the difference. Unlike the Blazer that it replaces – the cockpit has a smoother finish, the dashboard is neater, more stylized and as practical as ever. Unfortunately, the designers couldn't resist cutting corners – old habits die hard – and it shows. Here and there, a few plastic odds and ends don't exactly fit together, producing tacky-looking gaps.

That said, this Chevy has plenty of guts. But what impressed us first and foremost was its healthy road manners. The ride was surprisingly smooth and comfortable especially considering its solid rear axles, even when we hit potholes and bumps on the highway. It's impossible to perceive any rocking motion of the body on the suspension as is the case with a number of Japanese vehicles that try to disguise a rather primitive platform.

It's too bad the TrailBlazer doesn't have the option of "self-leveling" air suspension like the Envoy and Bravada. This would provide yet more comfort and guarantee that the vehicle's attitude is constantly corrected, an important component if you have to pull a trailer or when the luggage compartment is fully loaded.

GMC Envoy: the happy medium

Unlike the Chevy TrailBlazer, which likes to trade on its rough-and-tumble image, the Envoy, with its roundish grille, bulging fenders and bodysides, seems less intimidating, more user friendly. The same can be said of the cockpit: the dashboard is entirely different with its roundish ventilation outlets, woodlike trim and lush leather seats.

The high-performance 6-cylinder engine propels the Envoy from 0-60 mph in 8.2 seconds. Not bad! But consumption is almost 15 mpg (15 liters per 100 km), not too impressive for the category, although it's slightly better than either the Ford V6, the Mazda Tribute or the Ford Escape. The latter even has 70 fewer horses. On the road, corner-handling is good and directional stability beyond reproach, even though steering response is sluggish. Thanks to the air suspension, the Envoy offers a smoother, more comfortable ride than the Trailblazer. Incidentally, starting in 2002 the Envoy will

■ STANDARD EQUIPMENT

• 270 hp 4.2 liter 6-cylinder engine • Automatic gearbox • Power steering • OnStar system • Air conditioning

■ OPTIONAL EQUIPMENT

• DVD player on XL
• Electric Sun roof
• Automatic climate control

add an XL trim level – 16.1 inches (41 cm) longer and 3.1 inches (8 cm) taller – plus third-row seating, more comfortable and easier to access than Ford Explorer's. Moreover, DVD with LCD screen can be ordered for rear passengers in both the standard and extended versions.

Oldsmobile Bravada

There's a certain irony in attending the launch of an all-new Oldsmobile right after the announcement of the division's imminent closure. You don't need a crystal ball to predict that Bravada's career as an Oldsmobile will be short-lived. On the other hand, it wouldn't surprise us to find this model at Saturn, or even Cadillac.

The Bravada differs from the other two models in that it's intended for paved roads, not muddy trails. The suspension, tires, silhouette, grille – similar to the Aurora's – and fairly comprehensive equipment all make this Olds a vehicle intended for the driver who limits his travels to the road, and would be content with the occasional excursion off the beaten track. Moreover, everything in the cockpit points to a sedan rather than a sport-utility.

Many people will feel this is an ideal compromise between big city and cross-country trail. After all, everyone wants an all-terrain vehicle, minus the inconveniences, that is. They like rugged trails even less. Problem is, the Bravada is condemned to disappear in the near, uncertain future.

All three models are sufficiently different in their handling and styling to suit the needs of three distinct customer groups. In addition they all offer impressive performances. Will the build quality and reliability remain high over the coming months? Only time will tell.

Denis Duquet

SPECIFICATIONS

Price	$CDN 34,600-46,455 / $US 25,755-34,767
Warranty	3 years / 36,000 miles (60,000 km)
Type	5-door sport-utility / 4X4
Wheelbase / Length	113 in / 192 in
Width / Height	74 in / 72 in
Weight	4627 lb (2099 kg)
Trunk / Fuel tank	39.8 cu. ft / 18.4 gallons
Air bags	front and side
Front suspension	independent
Rear suspension	rigid
Front brakes / Rear brakes	disc ABS
Traction control	yes (4X2)
Steering	rack-and-pinion, power assist
Turning circle	36 feet
Tires (front/rear)	P245/70R16

PERFORMANCE

Engine	6L 4.2-liter
Transmission	4-speed automatic
Horsepower	270 hp at 6000 rpm
Torque	275 lb-ft at 3600 rpm
Other engines	none
Other transmission	none
Acceleration (0-60 mph)	9.1 sec
Maximum speed	118 mph (190 km/h)
Braking (60-0 mph)	131 feet (40 m)
Fuel consumption	14.6 mpg (15.5 L/100 km)

COMPETITION

• Ford Explorer • Jeep Grand Cherokee • M-B ML320 • Nissan Pathfinder • Toyota 4Runner

COMPETITION

• New model • Inline 6-cyl engine • Air suspension (Envoy, Bravada) • New hydroformed frame

RATING (out of 5 stars)

Driveability	★★★½
Comfort	★★★½
Reliability	New model
Roominess	★★★½
Winter driving rating	★★★★
Safety	★★★★½
Resale value	New model

CHEVROLET VENTURE

PONTIAC MONTANA
OLDS SILHOUETTE

PONTIAC **MONTANA**

Performance Before Style

"What an ugly-looking thing!" exclaimed my companion as I wheeled out the MontanaVision for a road test. And to think that the Pontiac division takes pride in its ability to design spunky minivans!

Often, that means gratuitously complicated lines, an appearance made even more unwieldy by artifices of all sorts. This time around, the creative outburst has been partially tempered by Pontiac's need to share the Montana's body structure with two other GM minivans: the Chevrolet Venture and Oldsmobile Silhouette. Chevrolet, as you know, belongs more to the "stripped" school of design, while Oldsmobile tries its best, as always, to pass off its Silhouette as a car.

That said, the verdict is the same for the whole trio: all are perceived by the public as looking more practical than stylish, and that's really a compliment when you remember that all three do reasonably well on the market. And their customer-satisfaction ratings are all above average, which will come as a surprise to many people.

GM was the first automaker to install a liquid-crystal display screen (LCD) and VHS videocassette player in its minivans. This year, the cumbersome VHS has been replaced by the vastly superior hi-fi DVD system, complete with wireless headsets and a larger screen, turning the minivan into a high-tech home entertainment center on wheels in a flash. For rear-seat occupants, long trips are no longer synonymous with boredom and restlessness. Instead, they're great opportunities to watch favorite movies or play that fabulous video game.

Video games on wheels

Practicality above all else

Entertainment aside, the Venture/Montana/Silhouette trio stand out from the crowd with their practical cabin layout and predictable road handling.

The dashboard is the same in all three minivans. It won't win any prizes for good looks, but it's simple and functional. The egg-shaped panel includes a variety of dials, clear and easy to read. On the right-hand side, three air vents hang above the audio and climate controls. Control buttons are a handy size and easily identifiable. But

▲ PROS

• DVD system (optional) • Practical cabin • Predictable handling • Reliable mechanicals • Versa-trak system

▼ CONS

• Anonymous appearance • Average tires • Endangered Oldsmobile model • Slow automatic sliding doors • Chassis needs strengthening between the front seats, where a detachable net basket now sits, which can hold various items for easy retrieval.

The most unique feature of the Honda Odyssey is the way its rear seat can be folded down flush with the floor. It's an ingenious solution, but it allows tire rumbling and other road noise to infiltrate the cabin. In all GM minivans, there's a floor-mounted storage tray in the rear, slightly raised to accommodate the stowable rear bench, making for a perfectly flat floor. The arrangement isn't exactly elegant, but it's eminently practical.

Better assembled, more complete

GM minivans have come a long way. Most of the annoying factors from the early days – mainly relating to poor assembly and quality of finish – have been eliminated, although the body still rattles on occasion. Chief among the new improvements for 2002 is the optional Versa-trak all-wheel drive system. The powerplant is still the reliable 3.4-liter V6 with 185 hp – not exactly exciting, but perfectly suitable.

The front seats are comfortable, but offer little lateral support. The driving position, on the other hand, is better than average, as is the rear 3/4 visibility. In fact, everything about this minivan trio is above average, including handling.

This "average" policy extends to the price range as well. GM minivans are certainly not the most economical, but they're not the most expensive either. So, if you appreciate compromise, here's your chance.

Denis Duquet

OLDSMOBILE **SILHOUETTE**

SPECIFICATIONS

Price	$CDN 27,870-44,135 / $US 21,840-36,420
Warranty	3 years / 36,000 miles (60,000 km)
Type	minivan (extended wheelbase) / traction
Wheelbase / Length	119.7 in ; 201.2 in
Width / Height	72.8 in / 68.1 in
Weight	3880 lb (1760 kg)
Trunk / Fuel tank	24.2; 155.9 cu.ft (no seat)/24 gal
Air bags	front and side
Front suspension	independent
Rear suspension	rigid axle
Front brakes / Rear brakes	disc / drum ABS
Traction control	yes
Steering	rack-and-pinion, power assist
Turning circle	37 feet
Tires (front/rear)	P215/70R15

PERFORMANCE

Engine	V6 3.4-liter
Transmission	4-speed automatic
Horsepower	185 hp at 5200 rpm
Torque	210 lb-ft at 4000 rpm
Other engines	none
Other transmission	none
Acceleration (0-60 mph)	12.6 sec
Maximum speed	112 mph (180 km/h)
Braking (60-0 mph)	141 feet (43.1 m)
Fuel consumption	17.1 mpg (13.2 L/100 km)

COMPETITION

• Chrysler T & C • Ford Windstar • Honda Odyssey • Mazda MPV • Toyota Sienna

NEW FOR 2002

• DVD system • Larger LCD screen • 16-inch wheels on some models • Versa-Trak all-wheel drive

RATING (out of 5 stars)

Driveability	★★★
Comfort	★★★
Reliability	★★★½
Roominess	★★★★
Winter driving rating	★★★
Safety	★★★
Resale value	★★★½

CHRYSLER 300 M

CHRYSLER **300 M**

A Classic in the Making

Classic: A work of enduring excellence. Over the years, many fine cars have entered the annals of automobile history, although not all are considered classics. Beyond the qualities that they doubtless possess, only a precious few embody that indefinable something that indelibly strikes the imagination.

Launched in 1955, Chrysler's 300 series eventually acquired classic status. It was only a matter of time before its prestigious name would be revived. But the 300 series' "second coming" – the 300 M – turned out to be more than a mere exercise in brand marketing by Chrysler, because in the process the carmaker attempted to create an entirely new standard-bearer capable of inspiring future generations of designers.

Elegance and comfort

This year, the LHS has been retired, leaving the 300 M as Chrysler's lone entry in the full-size sport sedan category. The description suits the exterior of this modernized muscle car perfectly, combining elegance and power. I can find only one fault: the raised trunkline, which affects rear visibility.

Inside, the eye is instantly attracted to the clean-looking instrument panel displaying black figures on a white background. The rest of the cockpit is a soft-hued amalgam of chrome, imitation wood and fairly high quality plastic – slightly marred by the presence of that ubiquitous, unmistakable polymer. The Deluxe package comes with genuine walnut trim along with automatic day-night rearview mirror and dual power-assisted exterior mirrors that adjust automatically when backing up.

American Dream

The cabin is spacious. The heated leather-trimmed seats – power adjustable in the front, 60/40 split-folding in the rear – offer excellent passenger comfort. As expected in a car in this type, it's loaded with power everything, from door locks with a speed-sensitive auto-locking feature to the Chrysler Memory System which offers two personalized settings for the driver's power seat adjustments, power exterior mirrors, and radio station presets.

▲ PROS

- Adequate power engine • Competitive price
- Exciting interior and exterior design
- Adequate road handling • Spacious cabin

▼ CONS

- Average quality of materials • Poor rear visibility • Road noise • Vague steering
- Unwieldy size

Touring or sporty

The engine – it made its debut in the Chrysler Prowler – is a 3.5-liter V6, producing 250 hp at 6400 rpm, and 250 lb-ft of torque at 3900 rpm. It runs respectably enough, though not as smoothly as several of the 300 M's Japanese rivals. The 300 M's only gearbox is a 4-speed automatic, with the Autostick feature, providing a manual mode. Performance is adequate under all circumstances, but the 300 M could certainly use a 5-speed manual gearbox – the new standard in this market.

The stylish and sport-oriented 300 M is also beautifully turned out. It can be equipped with an optional handling package, which includes European-tuned suspension and steering, stronger brakes and high-performance Michelin tires. Fitted with these extras, the big sedan is surprisingly agile and easy to handle. These qualities are not as noticeable in the base version of the 300 M, but even there handling is stable and balanced. Though the steering feels vague straight ahead it offers adequate response, and the suspension smoothly absorbs all potholes and bumps while keeping body roll under reasonable control.

Stopping distances are impressively short, thanks to the confidence-inspiring force of the four-wheel disc brakes with ABS. On the debit side, despite an enviable aerodynamic coefficient, the cabin does let through a significant amount of noise, which can become annoying on rough roads, especially if you drive at higher speeds.

In sum, the 300 M may not be tops in any single aspect, and it doesn't compare favorably with its Japanese rivals. Still, its overall qualities and competitive price are hard to beat. In the coming months, Chrysler will unveil its "300 M Special," a new model that is indeed... special – with 18-inch wheels and a bumped-up 255-horsepower engine it will no doubt creep a little bit closer to that elusive "classic" status.

Jean-Georges Laliberté

SPECIFICATIONS

Price	$CDN 39,900-43,305 / $US 29,360
Warranty	3 years / 36,000 miles (60,000 km)
Type	sedan / front wheel drive
Wheelbase / Length	113 in / 197.6 in
Width / Height	74.4 in / 55.9 in
Weight	3627 lb (1645 kg)
Trunk / Fuel tank	16.8 cu. ft / 17 gallons
Air bags	front (side optional)
Front suspension	independent
Rear suspension	independent
Front brakes / Rear brakes	disc ABS
Traction control	yes
Steering	rack-and-pinion, variable assist
Turning circle	38 feet
Tires (front/rear)	P225/55R17

PERFORMANCE

Engine	V6 3.5-liter
Transmission	4-speed automatic
Horsepower	250 hp at 6400 rpm
Torque	250 lb-ft at 3900 rpm
Other engines	none
Other transmission	none
Acceleration (0-60 mph)	8.2 sec
Maximum speed	118 mph (190 km/h)
Braking (60-0 mph)	128 feet (39 m)
Fuel consumption	18.9 mpg (12 L/100 km)

COMPETITION

• Acura TL • Audi A6 • BMW 530 • Lexus ES 300 • Oldsmobile Aurora

NEW FOR 2002

• 300 M Special • 18-inch wheels • Sport suspension • Tire-pressure gauge • New colors

RATING (out of 5 stars)

Driveability	★★★★
Comfort	★★★★
Reliability	★★★
Roominess	★★★★½
Winter driving rating	★★★
Safety	★★★★
Resale value	★★★

CHRYSLER CONCORDE CHRYSLER INTREPID

CHRYSLER **CONCORDE**

Long Live the Difference!

Since their arrival on the market, many people have found it almost impossible to tell the Concorde and the Intrepid apart. Both feature futuristic lines and their road manners are among the best in their class.

It's quite true that they're similar, but only partly so. Although they share the same mechanical components and platform, there's a way to tell them apart through their road behavior and individual character. The Concorde is more of a family sedan than the Intrepid, which is sold in the United States under the Dodge label – a more plebeian make with a sporty orientation.

To highlight their differences, the Concorde was modified in many areas for 2002, placing an emphasis on its more luxurious leanings.

The middle-class family car

This year, as the Chrysler LHS was phased out, the Concorde became Chrysler's official luxury limousine. The 300M is still around, but it has been modified to strengthen its sporty character. Going back to the Concorde, the front and rear are visually closer to the defunct LHS. In fact, the Concorde LXi model is the de facto LHS replacement, while the top-of-the-line Limited model features the LHS dashboard. These changes clearly demonstrate that the LHS didn't exactly wow consumers. In retrospect, it was little more than a stretched Concorde (by an inch or two) with a more complete range of standard equipment.

While the LHS suffered from somewhat vague, subdued road manners, the Concorde LXi proves to be a far more stable performer. Its solid roadholding in corners benefits greatly from its 17-inch wheels. Step up to the Limited, and you'll get a more powerful version of the 3.5-liter V6. It produces 250hp – 16 extra horses than the base version of the same engine. This additional horsepower is particularly noticeable in terms of acceleration and passing power.

Sophisticated sedans

Frankly, with the Concorde Limited now on the scene, no one will mourn the LHS' passing. Come to think of it, the LHS would have passed anyway, already outclassed, as it were, by the 300M.

The sports car

In Canada, the Dodge name is associated with trucks and sport utility vehicles. In the

▲ PROS

- Good roadholding • Impressive roominess
- Intrepid R/T model • Rigid platform
- Up-to-date engines

▼ CONS

- Outsized • Poor rear visibility • High trunk opening • Average resale value
- Wind noise

United States, Dodge is associated with vehicles of a sporting nature, most of which are R/T models. Dodge's participation in the Winston Cup and other NASCAR series, as well as its formidable Viper, further add to the make's sporting image.

While Dodge coupes and sedans are sold in Canada under the Chrysler label, they nonetheless retain their sporting characteristics. The Intrepid R/T, for example, features a specially-tuned suspension, more powerful disc brakes, low-profile 17-inch tires, and the high-efficiency version of the 3.5-liter V6 engine. Curiously, this same engine is claimed to develop 242 hp – 8 fewer horses than that powering the Concorde Limited.

However, there's a noticeable difference in roadholding between these two models. The Intrepid R/T's suspension and the softer rubber of its tires provide grip on the road long after the Concorde's tires have given up. The R/T's steering also offers better feedback, and its brake-pedal feel is definitely superior.

The Intrepid comes in three trim levels. The base SE features a 200-hp 2.7-liter V6. Tick the ES model on your order form and your Intrepid will come with a 234-hp 3.5-liter V6 and16-inch wheels, and finally the R/T, whose specs we've already gone over.

Last year, a long-term road test revealed that the reliability and the workmanship of these cars had been greatly improved. Nothing happened to spoil this 9,000-mile (15,000 km) road test. Given their list price, both Concorde and Intrepid models offer a good quality/price ratio for those of us looking for a large sedan with sensible road manners.

Denis Duquet

SPECIFICATIONS	**Limited**
Price	$CDN 27,210-31,970 / $US 23,135-27,380
Warranty	3 years / 36,000 miles (60,000 km)
Type	sedan / front-wheel drive
Wheelbase / Length	113 in / 207.4 in
Width / Height	74.4 in / 55.9 in
Weight	3568 lb (1618 kg)
Trunk / Fuel tank	18.7 cu. ft / 17 gallons
Air bags	front and side
Front suspension	independent
Rear suspension	independent
Front brakes / Rear brakes	disc ABS
Traction control	yes
Steering	rack-and-pinion, variable assist
Turning circle	38 feet
Tires (front/rear)	P225/55R17

PERFORMANCE	
Engine	V6 3.5-liter
Transmission	4-speed automatic
Horsepower	250 hp at 6400 rpm
Torque	250 lb-ft at 3900 rpm
Other engines	V6 2.7-l 200 hp; V6 3.5-l 234 hp
Other transmission	none
Acceleration (0-60 mph)	8.0 s (Ltd); 8.7 s (3.5-l); 10.2 s (2.7-l)
Maximum speed	130 mph (210 km/h)
Braking (60-0 mph)	129 feet (39.2 m)
Fuel consumption	18 mpg (R/T) ; 22 mpg (SE); 21 mpg (ES 3.2-liter) (12; 10.3; 10.8 L/100 km)

COMPETITION

• Buick LeSabre • Chevrolet Impala • Pontiac Grand Prix • Ford Taurus • Toyota Avalon

NEW FOR 2002

• Exclusive dashboard for the LXi Limited
• Modified front and rear (Concorde)

RATING	**(out of 5 stars)**
Driveability	★★★★
Comfort	★★★★½
Reliability	★★★½
Roominess	★★★★★
Winter driving rating	★★★★
Safety	★★★★
Resale value	★★★

CHRYSLER NEON

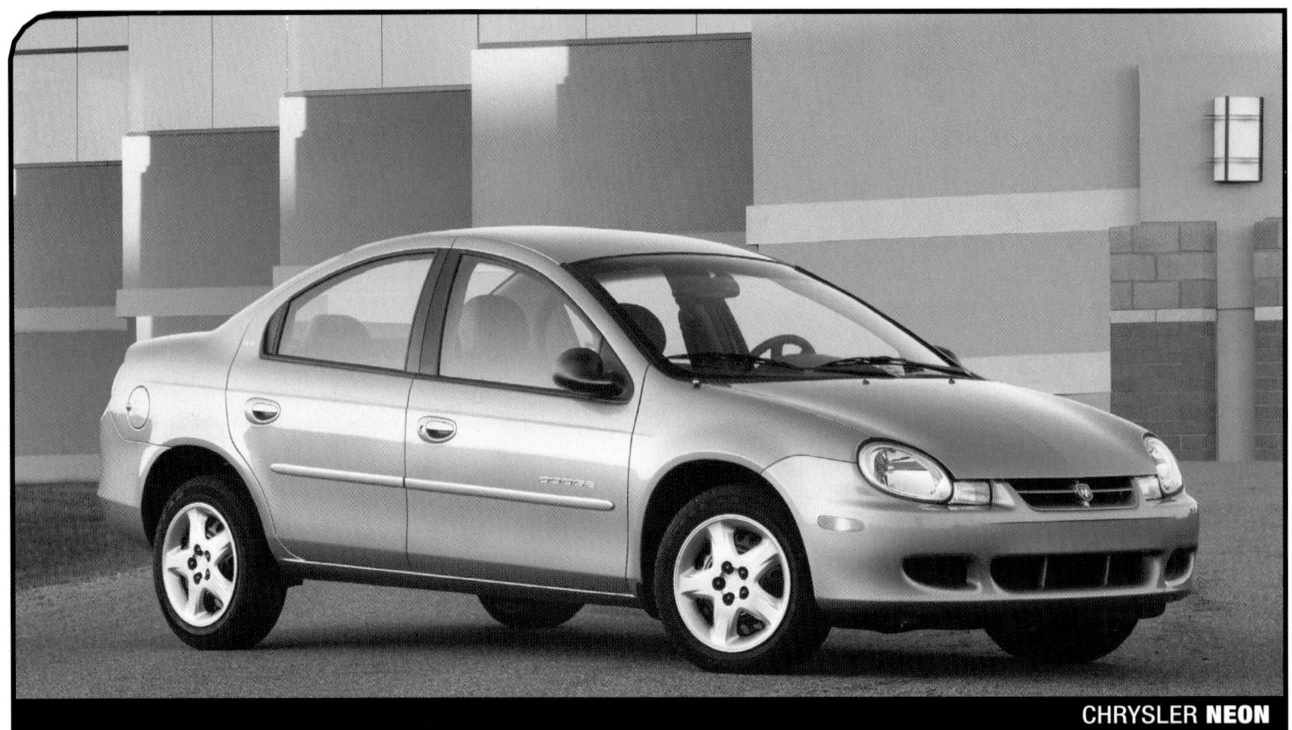

CHRYSLER **NEON**

A Subdued Round of Applause

By the time the second-generation Neon rolled off the assembly line in 2000, DaimlerChrysler engineers had almost eliminated all the flaws that had bedeviled the first-generation model. Handling was now much more predictable, braking more reliable and the cabin markedly more spacious. We road-tested it over a period of several months in 2000, and were impressed.

For some unknown reason, though, the engineers retained the "antique" 3-speed automatic transmission, despite widespread criticism leveled at its excessive noise level and poor fuel economy. This year, the automaker finally gave in and introduced a 4X4 Neon; in other words, a vehicle equipped with a 2.0-liter 4-cylinder engine coupled to a 4-speed gearbox.

This new addition doesn't mean that the Neon has been radically transformed. But one thing has changed, its engine performance, especially acceleration, is now so much smoother as a result. For the first time since its 1995 launch, we can confidently declare that the Neon has finally attained a proper balance. Frankly, this 4-speed concession came none too soon, since the market has been increasingly flooded with 5-speed automatic and continuously variable transmissions. It was absolutely imperative that DaimlerChrysler move into the "modern era."

Multi-purpose sedan

Time was when a North American automobile's exterior was no indication of its interior cabin space, and the two were not always in sync. The Neon, however, is the exact opposite of that situation. While it is neither the longest nor the widest in its category, it can easily accommodate four adults, thanks to the sill extensions. On the other hand, the front seats are on the soft side and provide little lateral support – in other words, they're not terribly comfortable for traveling on twisting roads. And since the car doesn't handle corners very well, that's another reason to stick to the straightaway. The Neon is still a comfortable enough car for taking relatively long trips, especially now that the noise level has been significantly reduced, with the 4-speed automatic transmission.

The right balance

The plastic used in the cabin feels skimpy, but overall finish is fairly decent

▲ PROS

• Adequate cabin space • 4-speed automatic transmission • More complete equipment • Predictable road manners • Well adapted engine

▼ CONS

• Cupholders impractical • Disappointing 150-hp engine • High trunk opening • Poor lateral support (seats) • Uneven finish

and the controls are sensibly arranged. While the Neon hasn't exactly got the makings of a class leader, it's a perfectly acceptable car both for suburbanites – young and not so young – and for traditional family buyers.

Sport version?

In the past year, DaimlerChrysler has added a sport version to the lineup: the Neon R/T (for Road and Track). It comes equipped with a more powerful version of the Neon's 2.0-liter SOHC 16-valve engine (150 horsepower), as well as a lowered suspension, complete with firmer springs and better-quality shock absorbers. Needless to say, also standard are four-wheel disc brakes and 16-inch alloy wheels.

So now you're all set to indulge yourself behind the wheel of this slick sport sedan with its smart rear-deck spoiler. Alas, appearances prove to be deceptive, because in the final analysis the Neon R/T isn't quite the fireball it was cracked up to be. Not that the entire machine is below par, because it isn't. Standard equipment is markedly superior both to the LE and LX versions – there's no argument about that. What seems to hold the car back is the platform, not of quite the same caliber as the firmer sport suspension and low-profile tires, so that a drive on bumpy roads isn't what I would call a picnic. Granted, the 18 extra horses do make a difference, but you have to keep the revs high to feel them working, and even then, it's not as much as you might have expected. Still, the 0-60 mph time is roughly a second shorter than in the regular Neon – no mean feat, if you ask me.

Summing up, the Neon deserves a place on your list of cars for careful consideration, if only for the number of recent developments: a new generation in 2000, a 4-speed automatic transmission this year, and DaimlerChrysler's corporate promise to make the quality of finish and assembly an even higher priority.

Denis Duquet

SPECIFICATIONS	
Price	$CDN 18,505-23,140 / $US 13,205
Warranty	3 years / 36,000 miles (60,000 km)
Type	sedan / front wheel drive
Wheelbase / Length	105.1 in / 174.4 in
Width / Height	67.3 in / 55.9 in
Weight	2566 lb (1164 kg)
Trunk / Fuel tank	13.1 cu. ft / 12 gallons
Air bags	front (side optional)
Front suspension	independent
Rear suspension	independent
Front brakes / Rear brakes	disc / drum
Traction control	no
Steering	rack-and-pinion, power assist
Turning circle	35 feet
Tires (front/rear)	P185/60R15

PERFORMANCE	
Engine	4L 2.0-liter
Transmission	5-speed manual
Horsepower	132-hp at 5600 rpm
Torque	130 lb-ft at 4600 rpm
Other engines	4L 2.0-liter 150-hp
Other transmission	4-speed automatic
Acceleration (0-60 mph)	9.7 sec (man.); 10.3 sec; 8.9 sec (R/T)
Maximum speed	109 mph (175 km/h)
Braking (60-0 mph)	135 feet (41.2 m)
Fuel consumption	26.7 mpg (8.5 L/100 km)

COMPETITION

- Cavalier/Sunfire • Civic • Corolla • Elantra
- Focus • Nubira • Protegé • Spectra

NEW FOR 2002

- 4-speed automatic gearbox • New grille on LE/LX
- New rear spoiler (optional)

RATING	**(out of 5 stars)**
Driveability	★★★½
Comfort	★★★½
Reliability	★★★½
Roominess	★★★½
Winter driving rating	★★★½
Safety	★★★
Resale value	★★★

CHRYSLER PT CRUISER

CHRYSLER **PT CRUISER**

12,000 Miles Later...

The Chrysler PT Cruiser has enjoyed a remarkable debut, considering its first-generation status, audacious styling, and Chrysler's shaky reputation in terms of reliability. It has now completed its first season: was its debut in 2000? with a clean bill of health, as demonstrated throughout the Auto Guide's extended road test, covering a total of more than 12,000 miles (20,000 km).

Skeptical about the much-publicized long-term prospects for this "Car of the Year," we contacted Chrysler and requested a test model for one year in order to find out for ourselves. We'll let you judge the results.

Apart from an early visit to a Chrysler dealership's garage because of defective power windows, our PT never had a reason to go back. Its logbook – where test drivers enter impressions after driving the car – certainly contained critical remarks, but all in all the results exceeded our expectations.

The test model was a turquoise, 2001 Limited Edition PT Cruiser, equipped with a 5-speed manual transmission. The first negative comment we spotted in the logbook no longer applied, however. This was because the PTs built after the one that we were driving had their power-window command switches mounted on the dashboard, rather than on the back of the small center console located between the front seats.

Expanded palette

Before analyzing the various annotations in the logbook, let's go over the differences between the 2002 model and the test model. First of all, those first-generation PT owners can relax and sleep soundly because the new model contains no radical changes. Three trim levels are offered: base, Touring Edition and Limited Edition. Standard features in each version include an armrest for the front passenger, AM/FM/CD, a storage compartment under the front seats and the latest gadget of all – a handle that allows you to open the trunk from the inside. And if you think that the PT looks dull and boring, the 2002 model offers a special paint job decorated with a flame motif as an option. Since the car boasts nothing more "inflamed" than the pallid 2.4-liter 150 hp engine, the spe-

Successful debut

▲ PROS

- **Adequate handling • Comfortable suspension**
- **Multi-purpose vehicle**
- **Reassuring reliability • Roominess**

▼ CONS

- **Anemic engine • Poor rear visibility**
- **High fuel consumption • Stiff signal-light lever**
- **Uncomfortable seats**

cial paint job will make your PT look like the hottest thing in town. Finally, two more colors have been added to the original palette: almond and steel blue.

The verdict

Our extended road test was conducted mainly in winter. Let me tell you that it's downright dangerous to drive the car on snowy roads with the original 4-season tires. Even though our test model had front-wheel drive, the PT Cruiser definitely needs four good winter tires. With its truncated rear end, the car has the same problem as many station wagons: the rear window gets dirty quickly in bad weather, so that the wipers need to work hard if you want to keep visibility even half-way decent.

Even though the 150 hp engine behaved itself respectably, the test drivers all found fault with it. It wasn't peppy enough, they claimed, and fuel consumption was high – 20 mpg (11.8 liters per 100 km) – for its category. On the other hand, many of them appreciated how quiet it was. They also liked the manual gearshift lever, even though finding reverse was hard at times. For those who prefer automatic transmission, by all means order it. The only inconvenience is that it tends to dampen acceleration slightly.

Oddly enough, despite its less than stellar performance, all the drivers agreed that the retro-style PT Cruiser was great fun to drive. The superbly rigid chassis and rattle-free body had much to do with it. Factor in the highly flexible cabin – offering various configuration options – and you've got yourself an immensely practical vehicle.

Painful seats

What bothered most of us about the PT – yours truly among them – was the uncomfortable front seats, which are too high under the thighs for any average-sized driver. So any long trip is sure to cause a twinge of sciatica. For myself, the problem was irritating enough not to consider buying a PT Cruiser, despite its above-average road manners and comfort. That said, in over 12,000 miles, our PT had surmounted the biggest obstacle that loomed in its way – the uncertain reliability associated with the Chrysler name. That alone speaks volumes.

Jacques Duval

PT CRUISER CONVERTIBLE

SPECIFICATIONS	Limited
Price	$CDN 23,650-28,950 / $US 16,500
Warranty	3 years / 36,000 miles (60,000 km)
Type	5-door hatchback / front wheel drive
Wheelbase / Length	103 in / 168.8 in
Width / Height	66.9 in / 63 in
Weight	3111 lb (1411 kg)
Trunk / Fuel tank	19 to 64 cu. ft / 15 gallons
Air bags	front and side (optional)
Front suspension	independent
Rear suspension	rigid axle
Front brakes / Rear brakes	disc / drum (disc optional)
Traction control	yes (optional)
Steering	rack-and-pinion, power assist
Turning circle	36 feet
Tires (front/rear)	P205/55R16

PERFORMANCE	
Engine	4L 2.4-liter
Transmission	5-speed manual
Horsepower	150 hp at 5200 rpm
Torque	162 lb-ft at 4000 rpm
Other engines	none
Other transmission	5-speed automatic
Acceleration (0-60 mph)	9.8 sec
Maximum speed	109 mph (175 km/h)
Braking (60-0 mph)	135 feet (41.2 m)
Fuel consumption	19.2 mpg (11.8 L/100 km)

COMPETITION

- Ford Focus wagon • Mazda Protegé5
- Subaru Impreza Outback • VW Jetta wagon

NEW FOR 2002

- New standard features (see text)
- Two new colors

RATING	(out of 5 stars)
Driveability	★★★½
Comfort	★★★½
Reliability	★★★★
Roominess	★★★★
Winter driving rating	★★★½
Safety	★★★½
Resale value	★★★★

CHRYSLER SEBRING

CHRYSLER **SEBRING**

Three for One

Don't think for a moment that DaimlerChrysler is about to offer three automobiles for the price of one, like some popular eyeglass companies. Well, not quite. What the automaker is actually proposing is a choice of three different vehicles, each bearing the same name – Sebring. While the sedan and the convertible share mechanical components, the coupe is an entirely different car.

The Sebring convertible was introduced in early 2001, a few months after the appearance of the other two cars. The previous version of the Sebring convertible used a hybrid platform borrowed from Mitsubishi. This time around, however, the sedan and convertible are pure Chrysler while the coupe is actually a Mitsubishi Eclipse with a pseudonym.

But let's return to the convertible which is essentially identical to the sedan, most notably the oval grille integrated into the bumpers and a plunging nose. Both models are equipped with standard 2.6-liter V6 engines developing 200 horsepower, coupled to an automatic gearbox. At some point in the not too distant future, you'll be able to order the convertible with a 5-speed manual transmission. In the United States, this same convertible is also offered with a 2.4-liter 4-cylinder engine.

The convertible is hardly a sporty automobile. Still, the lined top has an appealing look, and the car boasts comfort-tuned suspension and two decently comfortable rear seats, not to mention a competitive price. Handling is fine under normal driving conditions, but enthusiastic drivers will quickly discover the chassis' limitations. Which is a pity, because Chrysler engineers could have easily strengthened the platform to reduce twist and deflection under load.

Two solitudes

The Sebring sedan can hold its own, and then some, against any of its Japanese competitors. The new-generation model represents a significant improvement over its predecessor, especially in terms of handling and braking. The front suspension no longer bounces up and down over road irregularities, while the brakes are more progressive and the pedal far less spongy.

▲ PROS

- **Adequate engine • Complete equipment**
- **Elegant silhouette • Sound handling**
- **Spacious cabin**

▼ CONS

- **Autostick control (sedan and convertible)**
- **CD player's location • No manual gearbox with 4-cylinder engine**

Test-driving the sedan on a particularly twisty road, I was impressed by how easy it was to control the car. Body roll was minimal and the seats provided better lateral support than before.

The cabin features gauges set against a white background and in-dash imitation-wood trim, like the Chrysler Intrepid and Concorde. Unfortunately, the CD player and the 12-volt outlet are located so far down that you have to bend over double in order to reach it.

The base Sebring sedan comes with a 2.4-liter 4-cylinder engine with 150 horsepower, paired to a 4-speed automatic transmission. Performance is adequate, but I couldn't help wishing that Chrysler also offered a manual transmission. The other engine being offered is a 2.7-liter V6 with 200 hp. The extra power that it provides is obviously what the car needed.

The coupe comes in two trim levels: the base version gets a 2.4-liter 4-cylinder engine paired to a 4-speed automatic transmission. The next level, however, is an entirely different vehicle, built by Mitsubishi in Normal, Illinois. It comes with a Mitsubishi V6 engine generating 200 hp, like the Sebring sedan, although it emits a much sportier – in other words, more exciting – sound. Two transmissions are available: a 5-speed manual or 4-speed automatic.

Although the cockpit looks a little too "tortured" for my taste, the coupe is still fun to drive, provided you don't get too carried away and imagine it's a genuine sports car. Well assembled and comfortable, it will give the Toyota Camry Solara and Honda Accord Coupe a run for their money.

Denis Duquet

SPECIFICATIONS	
Price	$CDN 23,650-37,505 / $US 18,570-29,540
Warranty	3 years / 36,000 miles (60,000 km)
Type	convertible / front wheel drive
Wheelbase / Length	90.2 in / 193.7 in
Width / Height	70.4 in / 55.1 in
Weight	3309 lb (1501 kg)
Trunk / Fuel tank	11.3 cu. ft (16.2 gallons)
Air bags	front (side optional)
Front suspension	independent
Rear suspension	independent
Front brakes / Rear brakes	disc (ABS optional)
Traction control	no (offered in coupe)
Steering	rack-and-pinion, power assist
Turning circle	36 ft
Tires (front/rear)	P205/65TR15

PERFORMANCE	
Engine	4L 2.4-liter
Transmission	4-speed automatic
Horsepower	150 hp at 5200 rpm
Torque	167 lb-ft at 4000 rpm
Other engines	V6 2.7-liter 200 hp; V6 3.0-liter 200 hp
Other transmission	5-speed manual (coupe)
Acceleration (0-60 mph)	11.4 sec
Maximum speed	130 mph (210 km/h)
Braking (60-0 mph)	137.1 ft (41.8 m)
Fuel consumption	23.9 mpg(9.5 L /100 km)

COMPETITION

• Buick Regal • Ford Taurus • Honda Accord • Toyota Camry

NEW FOR 2002

No major change

RATING	**(out of 5 stars)**
Driveability	★★★★
Comfort	★★★★
Reliability	★★★½
Roominess	★★★½
Winter driving rating	★★★½
Safety	★★★★
Resale value	★★★

DAEWOO LANOS

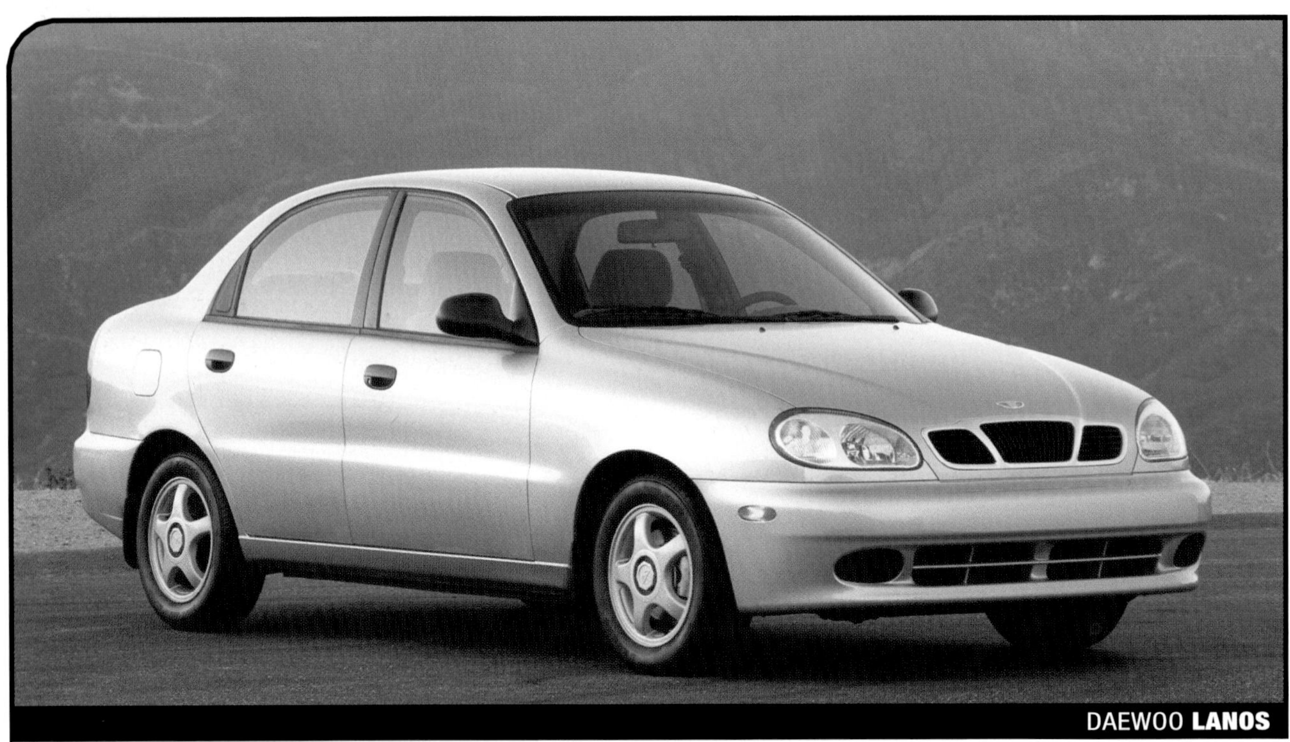

DAEWOO **LANOS**

Let Me Count the Days

At the time we went to press, the Daewoo saga was playing itself out. The latest rumor is that GM and its Italian partner, Fiat, are on the verge of taking over the automobile division of what was once one of Korea's biggest conglomerates, covering every aspect of the country's economy, from civil engineering and automaking to ship building. How all of this attention will affect Daewoo – an automobile empire with plants in 12 countries, and a potential output of 2 million cars – is anyone's guess.

This introduction sums up the current sense of gloom and doom prevailing at Daewoo, and the uncertainty facing its customers. And that's a pity, since the company was off to a fine start, with its first cars making a good impression.

I test-drove both the Lanos 4-door sedan and 3-door hatchback, and found them to be serious, good-value cars.

The sedan is powered by a 1.6-liter 4-cylinder engine with 105 hp, while the hatchback – which bears an eerie resemblance to the Honda Civic – is fitted with a 1.5-liter producing 86 hp. With that kind of horsepower, performance is understandably not one of the hatchback's strong points. In fourth gear, for example, it takes 14 seconds to go from 50 to 75 mph (80 to 120 km/h). So think hard before you even consider passing another vehicle on the road. The sedan fares slightly better, but given low engine torque, it's not a good idea to opt for automatic transmission, especially if you tend to take long trips.

Weak engine power, however, is an advantage in terms of fuel consumption. Here, both models – each weighing less than 2650 lbs (1 200 kg) – do rather well. Another pleasant surprise was the low level of engine noise as we cruised along the highway. Wind noise, however, is another story, betraying the simple aerodynamics of the car's body, which was the brainchild of Giorgietto Giugiaro of ItalDesign.

Uncertain times

Simplicity first

Designed without fuss, the Lanos looks attractive enough, especially the hatchback, which should appeal to younger buyers. The fan-shaped grille that graces all Daewoo cars is a nice touch, a sort of "family crest" that is too often absent from better known marques.

▲ PROS

- Affordable • Adequate equipment
- Good-looking car • Low fuel consumption

▼ CONS

- Carmaker at risk • Radio off-limits
- Torque effect • Poor acceleration

The cockpit, is helpfully and ergonomically simple, where all the principal controls are easy to reach. But I take exception to the size of the radio buttons which are frustratingly tiny. And, adding insult to injury, the radio lights go out as soon as it is turned off. Heaven help you if you find yourself on the highway, fumbling for the light switch or the darkened radio buttons on a dark and stormy night... And while we're on the subject, the cockpit could use a couple more cheerful colors than that dreary "military gray" that makes everything look so austere. Other tones would have given the car a sorely needed touch of cheerfulness.

Inflate your tires!

In the city, both Lanos models thread their way through traffic so easily that you forget about their limited engine power. But when you accelerate into a turn, you may be surprised to feel some torque effect in the steering wheel.

The Lanos' equipment is adequate, especially considering its sticker price: $14,000 (US$ 9100): height-adjustable driver's seat, intermittent windshield wipers (rear window wipers on the 3-door hatchback), 4-speaker AM/FM radio. In the minus column is the stingy window surface covered by the wipers and the lack of interior control for the hatchback's tailgate.

Thanks to its compact size and light weight, the Lanos is easy to drive and proves to be a nimble machine. But its rudimentary suspension and front disc/rear drum brakes betray the "low-tech" state of affairs of Korean automaking. But hey, it rides just fine, and turns and brakes properly.

I'll end my review with an anecdote: When taking possession of the 3-door Lanos, I was a little surprised by its lack of stability on straightaways. Cruising at 60 mph, I had to correct the car's attitude constantly just to maintain its trajectory. *This is annoying, and even dangerous,* I thought, and decided to check the tire pressure at the first opportunity. That was a good idea, because the pressure turned out to be 6 psi short. I fixed the problem and on my next sortie on the highway, all that worrisome wavering was gone so, watch out for the tires, on Daewoo or whatever its next name may be!

Alain Raymond

SPECIFICATIONS	**S**
Price	$CDN 13,100-14,900 / $US 9,659-13,459
Warranty	3 years / 36,000 miles (60,000 km)
Type	hatchback / front wheel drive
Wheelbase / Length	99.2 in / 160.2 in
Width / Height	66.5 in / 56.3 in
Weight	2447 lb (1110 kg)
Trunk / Fuel tank	8.8 cu.ft / 13 gallons
Air bags	front
Front suspension	independent
Rear suspension	rigid axle
Front brakes / Rear brakes	disc, drum
Traction control	no
Steering	rack-and-pinion, power assist
Turning circle	32 feet
Tires (front/rear)	P185/60R14

PERFORMANCE	
Engine	4L 1.5-liter
Transmission	5-speed manual
Horsepower	86 hp at 5800 rpm
Torque	96 lb-ft at 3400 rpm
Other engines	1.6-liter 105 hp (4-door only)
Other transmission	4-speed automatic
Acceleration (0-60 mph)	12 sec
Maximum speed	99 mph (160 km/h)
Braking (60-0 mph)	128 feet (39 m)
Fuel consumption	34.9; 31.4 mpg (6.5; 7.2 L/100 km)

COMPETITION

• Honda Civic • Hyundai Accent • Mazda Protegé • Toyota Echo

NEW FOR 2002

No major change

RATING	**(out of 5 stars)**
Driveability	★★★
Comfort	★★★
Reliability	★★★½
Roominess	★★★½
Winter driving rating	★★★★
Safety	★★★½
Resale value	★★★★

DAEWOO LEGANZA

DAEWOO **LEGANZA**

Style Before Substance

As a latecomer to the automobile industry, Daewoo knew it would have to contend with the skepticism of customers – at least at the outset – and leave nothing to chance. It gave its flagship car a regal name – Leganza – derived from the combination of the Italian words *elegante* (elegant) and *forza* (strength, power). Next, Daewoo recruited Porsche as its technical adviser, while commissioning the prestigious Lotus team to fine tune its suspension. And who better than the legendary Giorgetto Giugiaro, of ItalDesign in Turin, to take charge of styling the Leganza? A promising beginning, if you ask me. Now, let's see if the finished product lives up to these high-powered contributions.

At first glance, the Leganza looks pretty appealing. You won't mistake it for a high-end luxury car, as Daewoo would like you to imagine, but it holds up well enough next to most models in its particular category. Despite the Korean automaker's still shaky financial situation, this year's Leganza was treated to a few improvements, especially the chrome grille and the headlights.

The interior, too, looks flattering at first. But on closer inspection, several irritating features are apparent. Assembly quality, for instance, leaves a lot to be desired. The leather upholstery in the top-of-the-line CDX model doesn't feel as supple as the competition's. And the fake wood trim, designed to confer a luxurious effect, simply looks ridiculous. All in all, Daewoo's latest efforts to impress are just that – major efforts, little substance. Take the dashboard, where every single feature is so excessively curvy or roundish, the whole thing looks contrived.

Quantity at quality's expense

Most dials are simple and easy to use, except the radio buttons, which are so complicated you'll need to take your eyes off the road to operate them. Incidentally, the graphic equalizer seems pointless, looking as if it were there just as a decoration.

The driver's seat is height adjustable, which is a good thing, but the front seats have very little support – a bad thing – especially on long trips. In the rear, leg and head- room is decent, although it could be more comfortable, given the Leganza's dimensions. The trunk has a low, wide

▲ PROS

- Comfortable ride • Flattering appearance
- Predictable handling • Price/equipment ratio
- Spacious trunk

▼ CONS

- Average roominess • Body roll • Noisy engine
- Poor resale value • Unproven reliability

opening and is as spacious as the Toyota Camry's or the Honda Accord's. The rear bench is foldable 60/40.

This Korean-made car is unbeatable, when you think about it in terms of price/equipment ratio. The base model – the SX – offers standard air conditioning, power windows and locks, cruise control, heated outside mirrors and AM/FM//cassette/CD with 6 speakers. And all that for roughly $21,000! For another $4000, you can get the top-of-the-line CDX, which comes with power sunroof, alloy wheels, antilock brakes (ABS) and an even more luxurious interior including heated and power leather seats.

Limited performance

The Leganza is propelled by a 2.2-liter 4-cylinder engine. At cruising speed, it's soft and discreet, but as the tachometer needle inches up, the engine starts to vibrate and howl at the same time. Acceleration is acceptable, though it'll make you pine for a V6, (which, incidentally, will arrive with the 2003 model) and a manual transmission, which would make better use of the 131 horsepower.

The 4-speed automatic transmission works well enough, but gear changes tend to be harsh under hard acceleration. In city traffic, it has trouble adapting to the stop-and-go driving mode.

The MacPherson-strut front suspension and transversal arms in the rear ensure a comfortable ride. But on sharp curves, the tires tend to squeal and body roll is excessive, so go easy on the accelerator when you turn. Braking is adequate and linear, thanks to the standard 4-disc varieties, and the ABS efficient.

All in all, the Leganza is a well-conceived car, reasonably priced considering the extensive standard equipment it offers. But its road manners, while comfortable and predictable, are quickly upset as speed builds. It appeals strictly to customers with limited budgets and whose driving habits require minimal mechanical performance. Given Daewoo's current financial woes, perhaps only a crystal ball-gazer will be able to predict the Leganza's long-term prospects.

Jean-Georges Laliberté

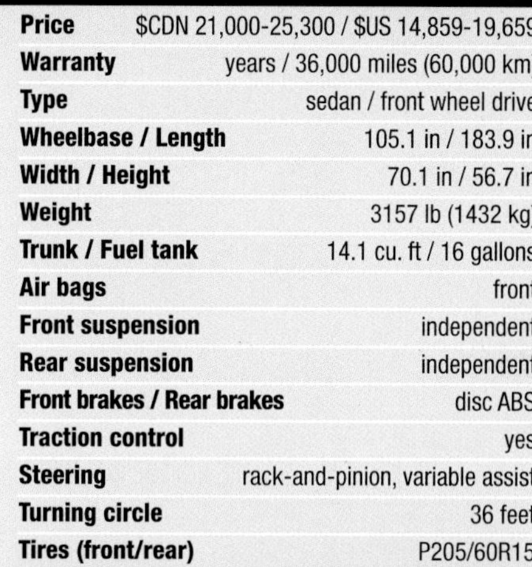

SPECIFICATIONS	CDX
Price	$CDN 21,000-25,300 / $US 14,859-19,659
Warranty	years / 36,000 miles (60,000 km)
Type	sedan / front wheel drive
Wheelbase / Length	105.1 in / 183.9 in
Width / Height	70.1 in / 56.7 in
Weight	3157 lb (1432 kg)
Trunk / Fuel tank	14.1 cu. ft / 16 gallons
Air bags	front
Front suspension	independent
Rear suspension	independent
Front brakes / Rear brakes	disc ABS
Traction control	yes
Steering	rack-and-pinion, variable assist
Turning circle	36 feet
Tires (front/rear)	P205/60R15

PERFORMANCE	
Engine	4L 2.2-liter valving system
Transmission	4-speed automatic
Horsepower	131 hp at 5200 rpm
Torque	148 lb-ft at 2800 rpm
Other engines	none
Other transmission	none
Acceleration (0-60 mph)	10.7 sec
Maximum speed	122 mph (195 km/h)
Braking (60-0 mph)	142 feet (43.4 m)
Fuel consumption	22.6 mpg (10 L/100 km)

COMPETITION

• Accord • Altima • Malibu • Mazda 626 • Sebring • Sonata • Taurus

NEW FOR 2002

• Some styling touch-ups

RATING	(out of 5 stars)
Driveability	★★★
Comfort	★★★½
Reliability	★★★
Roominess	★★★½
Winter driving rating	★★★
Safety	★★★
Resale value	★★

DAEWOO NUBIRA

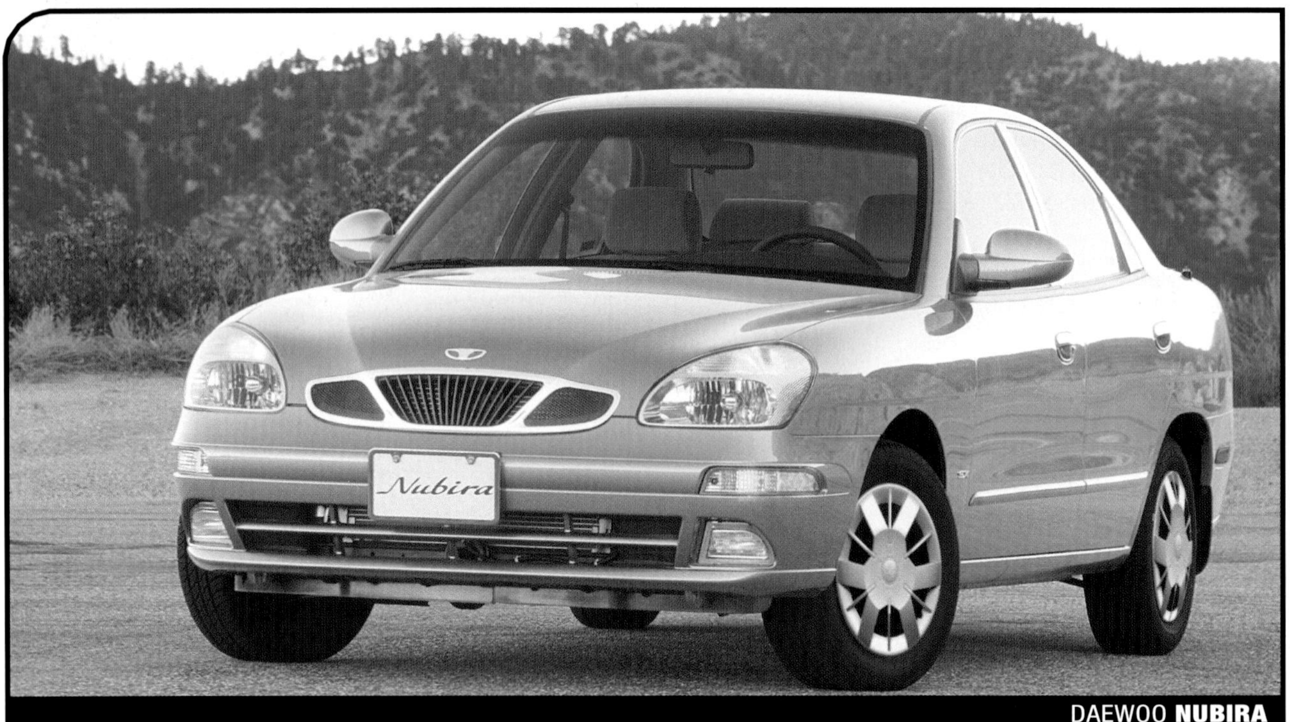

DAEWOO **NUBIRA**

The Corridor of Death

Already the 2000 edition of *The Auto Guide* mentioned the financial tribulations of the large Korean company called Daewoo. Now at death's door, this conglomerate was one of the most important on the face of the earth, until its founder decided to make off with billions of dollars in his luggage. That's right folks, he left with over 20 billion US dollars. No wonder Daewoo has been technically bankrupt these last few months.

In spite of this debacle, the company is being kept alive until either Ford or GM decides to purchase it, or the Korean government nationalizes it. Chances are the name will stay and new products will be developed soon. Not that the current products are inadequate, but they could do with a little rejuvenation.

The proof lies in the results of our comparison test where the Nubira wagon finished last. In spite of some strong points and a very competitive price tag, it could not beat the American, German or Japanese competition. On almost every basis of comparison it was at a disadvantage, sometimes by very little but enough to place it at the bottom of the list. Yet the Nubira was considered acceptable overall when first introduced on the market 24 months ago. Now most of its rivals have been modified, improved or redesigned, but the Nubira has stayed the same. A wealthier manufacturer could probably have improved the road handling with more precise steering or made changes to the suspension that would reduce body roll. The dashboard would probably have been replaced. Finally the engine would be quicker and smoother. The Nubira wagon was modified last year; the styling and a few technical points were changed, but not enough. On top of that, the carmaker persists in fitting a radio with controls so small that a toothpick is needed to operate them.

S.O.S

The present models were introduced in 1997. Six years later, rejuvenation is imperative, especially in this very competitive market.

Before you start thinking we're talking major refit here, it must be emphasized that the car is among the more solidly built in its class, it comes completely equipped and the reliability of

▲ PROS

- Mechanically reliable • Well-equipped
- Roominess • Competitively priced
- Comfortable ride

▼ CONS

- Uncertain future • Dubious resale value • Noisy
- Indifferent tires • Imprecise manual gearbox

this small Korean import is beyond question. A long-term test stretching over several months has demonstrated that the mechanicals are solid if not refined.

Hope for the future

I was in a parking lot the other day, and a Nubira sedan caught my eye, as it had a really nice green paint job, alloy wheels and a rear spoiler. The car can have an attractive look, quite capable of being favorably compared to others as long as it abandons colors such as black, dark blue or even white.

Although not the best in terms of roadholding and performance, the Nubira manages quite well. Unfortunately, other Korean cars keep on improving.

This sedan is roomy but the interior needs work. The cloth covers are drab and the quality of the plastic reminds us that some Korean manufacturers are still behind the Japanese in this area. That becomes more noticeable when the 2.0-liter engine begins to growl and vibrate. The 129 horses are quite noticeable. Too bad the gearbox's lack of precision becomes an annoying nuisance after a few miles. The 4-speed automatic transmission is a little notchy, but at least you can drive through town without having to worry about how the shifter is going to work.

During my trip to Korea a few years ago, someone wanted me to buy a wallet and his main pitch was that it was "almost leather." Well, this Nubira can "almost compete" on par with its rivals. It would not take much to improve its competitive edge.

Denis Duquet

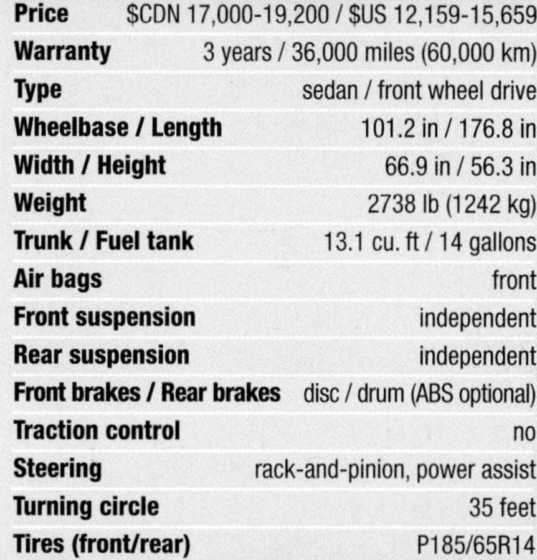

SPECIFICATIONS	
Price	$CDN 17,000-19,200 / $US 12,159-15,659
Warranty	3 years / 36,000 miles (60,000 km)
Type	sedan / front wheel drive
Wheelbase / Length	101.2 in / 176.8 in
Width / Height	66.9 in / 56.3 in
Weight	2738 lb (1242 kg)
Trunk / Fuel tank	13.1 cu. ft / 14 gallons
Air bags	front
Front suspension	independent
Rear suspension	independent
Front brakes / Rear brakes	disc / drum (ABS optional)
Traction control	no
Steering	rack-and-pinion, power assist
Turning circle	35 feet
Tires (front/rear)	P185/65R14

PERFORMANCE	
Engine	4L 2.0-liter
Transmission	5-speed manual
Horsepower	129-hp at 5400 rpm
Torque	136 lb-ft at 4400 rpm
Other engines	none
Other transmission	4-speed automatic
Acceleration (0-60 mph)	9.5 sec; 10.1 sec (auto.)
Maximum speed	118 mph (190 km/h)
Braking (60-0 mph)	145 feet (44.2 m)
Fuel consumption	25.2 mpg (9 L/100 km)

COMPETITION

• Cavalier/Sunfire • Corolla • Elantra • Focus • Neon • Protegé • Sentra • Spectra

NEW FOR 2002

• Minor changes to cabin and body

RATING	(out of 5 stars)
Driveability	★★½
Comfort	★★★
Reliability	★★★½
Roominess	★★★½
Winter driving rating	★★★½
Safety	★★★
Resale value	★

DODGE CARAVAN CHRYSLER TOWN & COUNTRY

DODGE **GRAND CARAVAN**

Refined, But Too Impersonal

Since last year, the Dodge Caravan, Grand Caravan and Chrysler Town & Country are the best thought out and most interesting minivans on the market. Yet the new generation, revised and improved at great cost in 2001, doesn't seem to be making much of an impact on consumers.

This is a little surprising, since these models include a host of features you won't find in the competition's vehicles. Take the power sliding doors, for instance. Not only do you gain cabin space, but the door closes a great deal faster, and the mechanism is automatically disengaged as soon as you pull on the door. DaimlerChrysler remains the only manufacturer to offer a power tailgate. You probably think that's a useless gadget. At least, that was my opinion until I found myself in the back of the vehicle, caught by a torrential downpour and trying to deal with armloads of stuff. Watching the tailgate open as if by magic convinced me of its essential virtue on the spot. For many people, particularly those of small stature, this feature is a godsend.

Other elements in the plus column include the overall refined quality of the cockpit, sound insulation and the ingenious, removable center console. Finally, the dashboard looks less austere than either the Honda Odyssey's or Ford Windstar's – two notorious style offenders.

Most reliable

Also worth noting is the fact that both the Chrysler and Dodge vans can be ordered with the renowned Steyr-Puch all-wheel drive, whose 2002 version has been thoroughly revised, simplified and significantly lightened. In fact, only GM, with its Versatrak system, offers all-wheel drive in this category.

Spice it up a little!

Finally, both the 3.3-liter and 3.8-liter V6s – producing 180 hp and 215 hp respectively – prove adequate, unless you have a special reason to require extra power. Incidentally, because of recent budget cuts, DaimlerChrysler abandoned its plan to develop a 3.5-liter 250 hp V6 engine.

This minivan is the best integrated and best equipped on the market. Yet potential buyers seem more hesitant than ever to buy it. It's true that the dubious reliability of many Dodge and Chrysler prod-

▲ PROS

• Efficient front suspension • Good sound insulation • Multiple storage bins • Power tailgate • Rigid platform

▼ CONS

• Badly located handbrake lever • Confining rear seatbelt • Heavy removable seats • Understated appearance

ucts is a turn-off, but that's not the only reason why people stay away. I suspect that the carmaker was so fixated on fine-tuning the vehicles' mechanicals and features that it didn't pay enough attention to the model's appearance, and customers simply can see that its entire minivan line was being thoroughly revamped.

Always first

And that's a pity, since the road manners of the new models are much improved. The front suspension is as efficient as ever, and there's a lot less bobbing and pitching than in previous models, especially in the front of the vehicle. Those who have driven a pre-2001 Magicwagon know what I'm talking about. In the current model, bumps and potholes are all neatly absorbed. What's more, steering is the most precise in its category. Thanks to the adjustable pedals – new for 2002 – any driver, regardless of height, can find his or her perfect driving conditions. The Chrysler Town & Country features memory settings for the pedals.

Both the Caravan and Chrysler Town & Country offer excellent directional stability, good sound insulation and comfortable seats, making them logical choices for carrying passengers and cargo on long trips. Besides, they boast the best ventilation and climate control systems on the market. Rear passengers are not as spoiled as those up front, what with the seats being placed too close to the preceding row. In addition, the seatbelts are a tad tight for comfort.

Despite undeniable qualities that make it a leader in its category, this minivan sorely lacks personality. By being too eager to refine the vehicle's mechanicals, the automaker neglected its equally important visual appearance.

Denis Duquet

CHRYSLER **TOWN & COUNTRY**

SPECIFICATIONS

Price	$CDN 25,430-50,015 / $US 19,800-38,165
Warranty	3 years / 36,000 miles (60,000 km)
Type	minivan / front wheel drive
Wheelbase / Length	113.4 in / 189 in
Width / Height	78.3 in / 68.9 in
Weight	3909 lb (1773 kg)
Trunk / Fuel tank	15.1 cu. ft; 20 cu. ft (no seat)/20 gal.
Air bags	front and side
Front suspension	independent
Rear suspension	torque bar
Front brakes / Rear brakes	disc ABS
Traction control	yes
Steering	rack-and-pinion, power assist
Turning circle	39 feet
Tires (front/rear)	P235/70R15

PERFORMANCE

Engine	V6 3.3-liter
Transmission	4-speed automatic
Horsepower	180 hp at 5200 rpm
Torque	210 lb-ft at 4000 rpm
Other engines	V6 3.8-liter 215 hp
Other transmission	none
Acceleration (0-60 mph)	10.9 s ; 9.8 s (3.8-liters)
Maximum speed	112 mph (180 km/h)
Braking (60-0 mph)	141 feet (43 m)
Fuel consumption	22.2 mpg (10.2 L/100 km)

COMPETITION

- Chev. Venture/Olds Silhouette/Pont. Montana
- Ford Windstar • Honda Odyssey • Toyota Sienna

NEW FOR 2002

- Adjustable pedals • Standard 3.8-liter V6 engine (Grand Caravan) • Tire-pressure gauge

RATING (out of 5 stars)

Driveability	★★★★
Comfort	★★★★½
Reliability	★★★½
Roominess	★★★★
Winter driving rating	★★★★
Safety	★★★½
Resale value	★★★½

DODGE DURANGO

DODGE **DURANGO**

Simple and Efficient

In the automobile business, as in any other, the simplest solutions are often the most efficient. The Dodge Durango is a case in point. Designers and engineers combined efforts to come up with a practical and robust vehicle, built from existing mechanical components, without encroaching on Jeep territory.

Given the fact that the Dodge division of DaimlerChrysler relies heavily on its light-truck market to boost sales figures, it would have been careless not to capitalize on the current SUV craze. On the other hand, an effort to create a Jeep Grand Cherokee clone would have served no other useful purpose than to jeopardize sales generated by the Jeep division, which specializes in all-terrain vehicles.

The Durango team wanted to build a vehicle capable of towing heavy loads and coping with all kinds of road conditions. They set their sights on the platform of the Dakota, a popular pickup truck at the time. What they needed to do was to transform the cab-and-cargo-bed chassis into an SUV frame, tune the rear suspension accordingly, and modify the exhaust system to reduce its noise level.

When the Durango was unveiled in 1998, it came with three engine options: the 3.9-liter V6 – which turned out to be short-lived, as well as the 5.2-liter and 5.9-liter V8s. Today, the V6 is no longer offered, while the 5.2-liter V8 has been replaced by the 4.7-liter V8, which first powered the Grand Cherokee. With 235 horsepower, this overhead cam engine is more technically up-to-date than the big 5.9-liter whose 10 extra horses can't honestly justify its existence for normal use, or its heavy fuel consumption. The only reason to order the big engine is its 335 lb-ft of torque, which does a better towing job than the 295 lb-ft provided by the 4.7-liter engine. The latter is paired to a new Multispeed 5-speed automatic transmission while the 5.9-liter comes with a 4-speed gearbox, a carryover from the preceding year that may partly be responsible for the high fuel consumption.

The real McCoy

Elegantly macho

It's never easy to come up with a look that's both refined and at the same time

▲ PROS

- Engine options • Good towing capacity
- Optional all-wheel drive • Side safety curtain
- Sturdy design

▼ CONS

- High fuel consumption • Large size • Rear axle unsuited to rough roads • Sound insulation needs work • Third-row seat for kids only

reflects the category's tough-guy image. In my opinion, Durango has pulled it off brilliantly. The front fascia and side moldings are borrowed from the Dakota. With the rear section thoroughly integrated and the raised roofline, the overall appearance looks well balanced and elegantly macho.

The cockpit and dashboard were modified last year – exactly three years after the Durango's first launch, as planned – making the vehicle look less "industrial" and more sophisticated than the original model. The one thing that never changed is the simple mechanism for folding down the third-row seat in order to get a flat cargo floor. The rear bench, incidentally, is totally uncomfortable, but that's the case with most other vehicles in the same category.

Working tool

On the road, handling is predictable, the ride comfortable and steering precise. Whatever you do with the Durango, though, don't try to drive it like a sports car. For a truck-derived sport-utility vehicle, its performance results are adequate, but obviously not as refined as the Chevrolet TrailBlazer's or the GMC Envoy's. On rough roads, handling is truck-like and braking is powerful and progressive. The latter can only get better, thanks to the "progressive effort transfer" to the rear wheels, scheduled for the 2002 model.

Always bear in mind that the Durango was designed as a working tool, with better-than-average comfort, and capable of tackling a wide range of off-road obstacles. Incidentally, all-wheel drive is standard in the R/T model and optional in the other versions, equipped with a part-time system preferred by purists. The R/T also boasts a 250 hp engine, commensurate with its sportier character.

Denis Duquet

SPECIFICATIONS

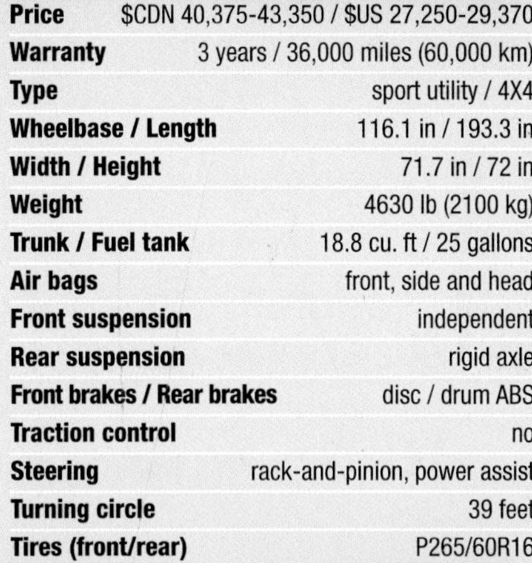

Price	$CDN 40,375-43,350 / $US 27,250-29,370
Warranty	3 years / 36,000 miles (60,000 km)
Type	sport utility / 4X4
Wheelbase / Length	116.1 in / 193.3 in
Width / Height	71.7 in / 72 in
Weight	4630 lb (2100 kg)
Trunk / Fuel tank	18.8 cu. ft / 25 gallons
Air bags	front, side and head
Front suspension	independent
Rear suspension	rigid axle
Front brakes / Rear brakes	disc / drum ABS
Traction control	no
Steering	rack-and-pinion, power assist
Turning circle	39 feet
Tires (front/rear)	P265/60R16

PERFORMANCE

Engine	V8 4.7 liter
Transmission	5-speed automatic
Horsepower	235 hp at 4800 rpm
Torque	295 lb-ft at 3200 rpm
Other engines	V8 5.9 liter 245 hp ; V8 5.9 liter 250 hp (R/T)
Other transmission	4-speed automatic (5.9 liter)
Acceleration (0-60 mph)	8.1 s (250 hp); 9 s (235 hp)
Maximum speed	115 mph (185 km/h)
Braking (60-0 mph)	136 feet (41.6 m)
Fuel consumption	13.8 mpg (16.4 L/100 km)

COMPETITION

- Chevrolet TrailBlazer/GMC Envoy
- Ford Expedition • Toyota Sequoia

NEW FOR 2002

- Side safety curtain • New 16-in alloy wheels
- Multi-speed auto. transmission • DVD system (opt.)

RATING (out of 5 stars)

Driveability	★★★
Comfort	★★★
Reliability	★★★
Roominess	★★★★
Winter driving rating	★★★★
Safety	★★★
Resale value	★★★★½

DODGE VIPER/CHRYSLER PROWLER

DODGE **VIPER**

If Performance Is Your Thing

The two top performance models at Dodge and Chrysler are really at odds in terms of personality. The Viper is, of course, the more powerful of the two, while the Prowler's lines are more retro-looking. The Viper is still a brute with one of the nicest bodies in the business.

I am talking about the coupe of course, as the roadster is not as attractive. It looks fine with the top down, but the hardtop model needs more work in my opinion. But, whatever the model, the cockpit is severely cramped. You have to slide into the driver's seat as you would in a racing car. The thick seats are comfortable, but lateral support is mostly provided by the door and the massive console between the two riders.

Once inside the car, however, it's easy to find a good driving position, thanks to the manually adjustable pedals and the tilt steering wheel. The instrument panel, black on white backing, are easy to read, are centered on the dashboard and angled toward the driver. Among them is the fuel gauge whose needle drops very rapidly when the accelerator is pressed a little too hard. The large rambunctious 8-liter V10 under the hood is not just a powerhouse, it is also very thirsty. Just as it should be, the manual gearbox is the only option. The throw of the shifter is short and the mechanism is precise. Since last year, the brakes have an ABS system, which is a real benefit. Without ABS, the front wheels gleefully lock at will, so that the driver had to constantly modulate the brake pedal. In fact, driving the Viper is rather like riding a whirlwind. Since there's no traction control, a good coordination between the clutch and accelerator is a prerequisite, otherwise, performance may suffer or the car will slide. And despite the massive P335/30ZR18 rear tires, both the 450-hp GT and 460-hp GTS are ready to provide a dragster-style burnout any time you want.

Zap! Pow!

Prowler: the golden dream

This revival of the retro hot rod look from the Chrysler stylists is being mass-produced within U.S. federal safety requirements, without compromising its unique personality. Despite its retro look, the mechanical components are right up-to-date, including the chassis and many suspension components made of aluminum, while some bodywork parts are made of a com-

▲ PROS

- Better braking • Excellent roadholding
- Improving workmanship • Seductive profile
- Surprisingly strong performance

▼ CONS

- Basic comfort • Low fuel mileage
- No footrest • Single-purpose toy
- Tight cockpit

posite material. This rear-wheel drive vehicle has a fully independent 4-wheel suspension with impressive 17-inch wheels at the front and 20-inch wheels at the rear. The 253-hp 3.5-liter DOHC V6 is no blaring V8, but it does go from 0 to 60 mph in 6.5 seconds, thanks to the car's excellent power-to-weight ratio.

When the top is up, you have to slide into the car, even contorting your body to avoid banging your head against the roofline which is very low, in keeping with the car's unique shape. Although watertight, and featuring a glass rear window with electric defogger, this soft-top would upset claustrophobics. The driver's seat is very low, and rear visibility leaves a lot to be desired. Fortunately, the outside rearview mirrors are conveniently located and a decent size.

The vertical center console resembles any other Chrysler's, while the instrument panel spreads out horizontally, with the speedometer smack in the center. The tachometer, bolted to the steering column, enhances the retro effect.

Such an example of styling and technological achievement acquits itself respectably on the road. While it's neutral in high-speed curves thanks to its wide rear tires, the car exhibits some understeer in tight curves at a normal driving speed. The V6 engine is well suited for its chosen task, even though enthusiasts would have preferred a V8 engine.

A cramped cockpit, uncomfortable driving position, ultra-firm suspension – such elements sum up the Prowler. Still, its passionate fans are undeterred. They willingly put up with such a high price just to indulge the opportunity to relive the past in the present tense – that is, with all the modern conveniences.

Denis Duquet

CHRYSLER **PROWLER**

SPECIFICATIONS	**GTS**
Price	$CDN 106,515-110,285 / $US 70,000-73,000
Warranty	3 years / 36,000 miles (60,000 km)
Type	2-seat GT Coupe / rear wheel drive
Wheelbase / Length	96.1 in / 176.8 in
Width / Height	75.6 in / 48.0 in
Weight	3459 lb (1569 kg)
Trunk / Fuel tank	9.2 cu.ft / 19 gallons
Air bags	front
Front suspension	independent
Rear suspension	independent
Front brakes / Rear brakes	vented disc ABS
Traction control	no
Steering	rack-and-pinion, power assist
Turning circle	40 feet
Tires (front/rear)	P275/35ZR18 / P335/30ZR18

PERFORMANCE	
Engine	V10 8.0-liter
Transmission	6-speed manual
Horsepower	460 hp at 5200 rpm
Torque	500 lb-ft at 3700 rpm
Other engines	V10 8.0-liter 450 hp
Other transmission	none
Acceleration (0-60 mph)	4.4 sec
Maximum speed	189 mph (304.6 km/h)
Braking (60-0 mph)	162 feet (without ABS) (49.3 m)
Fuel consumption	12.6 mpg (18 L/100 km)

COMPETITION

• Chevrolet Corvette

NEW FOR 2002

• Last year for current model • New colors

RATING	**(out of 5 stars)**
Driveability	★★★½
Comfort	★
Reliability	★★★
Roominess	★★
Winter driving rating	★★★★★
Safety	★★★
Resale value	★★★★

FORD ESCAPE

FORD **ESCAPE**

The Compromise

Ford likes trucks, great big trucks. While motorists dread the day when they'll have to dole out three or four dollars for every gallon of gas at the pump, you have to ask yourself what Ford management was thinking about when they introduced such heavyweights as the Expedition or worse still, the Excursion. Thankfully, Ford made a wise decision by looking in another direction, where sobriety makes much better sense.

Given its limited experience in the compact all-terrain vehicle market, Ford availed itself of the expertise of Mazda, its Japanese partner, in order to develop an attractive new model, called the Escape.

It's a truck that shares many characteristics with its Mazda relative, the Tribute. In order to distinguish between the two vehicles, Ford made sure to add its own personal stamp to the Escape, making it more, well, trucky.

Surprising comfort

The Escape's compact size belies some great features in the cabin. To start with, it's as spacious as any of its rivals, such as the Subaru Forester or Jeep Liberty. Four adults with luggage will find all the space they need.

The interior does go along with the current Ford look. In fact, the instrument cluster on the Escape uses the same components as the Explorer Sport and Sport Trac models. The white dials are easy to read, pleasant and original.

You also notice that the gearshift lever is mounted on the steering column, just like the good old days. But it's a lever that, once set in "Drive," makes it trickier to reach the radio and ventilation controls.

This set-up, unusual these days, has the advantage of freeing up the center console, for the benefit of additional storage nooks and crannies. A neat idea.

Latecomer

Ford and Mazda appeared on the scene long after the compact all-terrain vehicle craze had started, giving free rein to models such as the Honda CR-V, Toyota RAV4 and Suzuki Vitara, which were already popular.

This late arrival, however, worked to the benefit of the partners, who were able

▲ PROS

- All-wheel-drive drivetrain • Competitive prices
- Off-road ability • Predictable roadholding
- Roomy

▼ CONS

- Awkward gear lever • Excessive fuel consumption
- Low-energy 4-cylinder • No manual gearbox with the V6 • Unexciting cockpit

to study the market and correct some of the start-up errors made by their competitors. Though not perfect, the Escape performs aggressively on the road, attacking curves with relative ease. Steering is precise and an independent rear suspension is a definite advantage, although in terms of roadholding, its sibling, the Tribute, seems to have a slight advantage. On the other hand, the less gentrified Escape boasts better off-road capabilities, as demonstrated by *The Auto Guide*'s compact-SUV comparison test.

The Escape doesn't ride as comfortably as a car, but it doesn't feel like a truck either. Your best bet is the XLT version, despite the steep sticker price and abnormally high fuel consumption. Why? Simply because the 4-cylinder version seems so utterly inadequate, even for everyday tasks.

Road-testing the two versions under similar conditions, I noticed that the 4-cylinder engine was hard-pressed during both acceleration and responsiveness tests. The problem was further exacerbated when the vehicle was fully loaded. Given the Escape's intended use, the V6 is by far a better choice, even though it's noisy, especially when full power is suddenly needed.

The XLT version is the jewel of the Escape model lineup for 2002, featuring a 3.0-liter V6 engine as standard equipment, in-dash 6 CD changer, electrically powered driver's seat and electronic keyless access system.

The Escape and the Tribute, siblings that were separated at birth, obviously share many common features. That's why it's very easy to compare them with each other. If our evaluations have not convinced you, that means the differences between the two are even less noticeable than we thought.

Louis Butcher

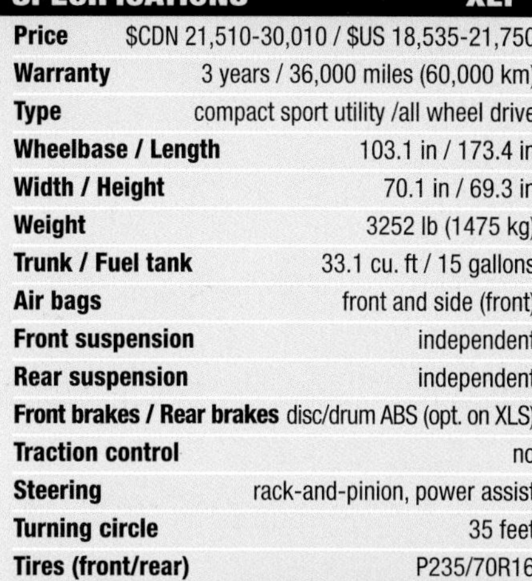

SPECIFICATIONS	**XLT**
Price	$CDN 21,510-30,010 / $US 18,535-21,750
Warranty	3 years / 36,000 miles (60,000 km)
Type	compact sport utility /all wheel drive
Wheelbase / Length	103.1 in / 173.4 in
Width / Height	70.1 in / 69.3 in
Weight	3252 lb (1475 kg)
Trunk / Fuel tank	33.1 cu. ft / 15 gallons
Air bags	front and side (front)
Front suspension	independent
Rear suspension	independent
Front brakes / Rear brakes	disc/drum ABS (opt. on XLS)
Traction control	no
Steering	rack-and-pinion, power assist
Turning circle	35 feet
Tires (front/rear)	P235/70R16

PERFORMANCE	
Engine	V6 3.0-liter Duratec
Transmission	4-speed automatic
Horsepower	201 hp at 5900 rpm
Torque	196 lb-ft at 4700 rpm
Other engines	4L 2.0-liter Zetec 127 hp
Other transmission	5-speed manual
Acceleration (0-60 mph)	11.4 sec; 12.8 sec (4L)
Maximum speed	112.5 mph (180 km/h)
Braking (60-0 mph)	143 feet (43.6 m)
Fuel consumption	17/23 mpg (4L) (13.9 /10.3 L/100 km)

COMPETITION

- Chev. Tracker/Suzuki Vitara, Gr. Vitara
- Honda CR-V • Hyundai SantaFe • Toyota RAV4

NEW FOR 2002

- New colors • Standard power-adjustable driver seat (XLT) • 6-CD changer (XLT) • Keyless entry (XLT)

RATING	**(out of 5 stars)**
Driveability	★★★½
Comfort	★★★½
Reliability	★★★★
Roominess	★★★★
Winter driving rating	★★★★
Safety	★★★½
Resale value	★★★½

FORD EXPEDITION LINCOLN NAVIGATOR

FORD **EXPEDITION**

The Party's Over, or Is It?

At long last it appears that the craze for full-size 4X4s has begun to subside, to the relief of the Friends of the Earth on the one hand, and to the disappointment of the opposing camp – the die-hard, "bigger-is-better" crowd. Still, it doesn't represent the kind of debacle that environmentalists have so eagerly anticipated, though demand for those motorized mastodons seems to have stabilized.

Instead, more and more customers are now turning to hybrid models – more comfortable, less "thirsty" and better adapted to their personal needs. Looking back, did people really need those 7-seat vehicles, propelled by mighty V8 engines that generated payload and towing capacity verging on the industrial? Like it or not, the enthusiasm for SUVs is going to stick around for a long time, but it's the smaller models that are becoming increasingly popular.

Ford's know-how

If sales of the Expedition have slowed down, that's not because the vehicle is short on qualities. Time and again it has proved to be amazingly nimble for a vehicle of its class and its handling is perfectly straightforward. It's not the kind of vehicle you'd take to a race track – its high center of gravity and impressive girth preclude that sort of activity – but those who use the Expedition sensibly will appreciate its cornering capabilities, well-modulated braking force and relatively precise steering.

Two engines are offered. The XLT model gets a 4.6-liter V8 215-horsepower engine. The Eddie Bauer edition, more upscale, comes with a 5.4-liter V8, with an extra 45 hp. That's the engine to go for, because the 4.6-liter is not as powerful and consumes just as much fuel. Both engines are modern and reliable, although their fuel consumption is above average for their category. The Expedition comes with a 4-speed automatic transmission only, and its drivetrain is the adjustable Control Trac system, which can be set in various modes: two-wheel-drive, automatic four-wheel-drive, 4Hi or 4Lo. Auto-leveling air suspension is also available, as an option.

Excess rules, OK?

As I said before, the Expedition is not without appeal, whether in terms of engine power or dynamics. But its sheer size is simply too unwieldy, and the third bench seat can barely accommodate two teenagers. By

▲ PROS

- **Generous cabin space • Practical dashboard**
- **Predictable handling • Renowned reliability**
- **Solid mechanicals**

▼ CONS

- **Average visibility • Body roll • Cumbersome dimensions • High fuel economy • Uncomfortable rear bench**

comparison, the new GMC Denali XL is more manageable and more comfortable.

If Expedition sales decline further, that will be because drivers finally understand the kind of SUV it has always been: a commercial vehicle disguised as a family-oriented means of transportation.

The Lincoln touch

The Navigator's arrival in the marketplace spoiled the fun for other luxury full-size SUVs. Its engineers had a relatively easy job, because the Navigator is little more than a Ford Expedition with a "Lincoln touch," in the form of the "exclusive" 5.4-liter 300-hp V8 Intech engine. For the rest, the Navigator is identical to the Ford, including the 4 disc brakes with ABS. Curiously, however, the Lincoln doesn't brake as reassuringly as the Expedition does.

The reason for this disparity is simple. Since the Navigator's suspension is tuned more for comfort than handling, it's suppler and, as a result, can't control weight transfer as effectively. In fact, everything about the Navigator was conceived in terms of driver and passenger comfort. The front- and middle-row leather bucket seats, for example, are first-rate and provide firm back support. On the other hand, side support leaves something to be desired, as does the third-row bench seat – uncomfortable and tough to get into. A wood and leather-wrapped steering wheel, as well as splashes of wood on the dashboard and center console, contribute to making the Navigator a living-room on wheels, capable of venturing off the beaten path. And if by now your friends and neighbors still can't appreciate how luxurious this all-terrain vehicle is, the imposing Lincoln grille will set the record straight.

Once an automobile category becomes popular, can excess be far behind? This answer is, virtually never. The Lincoln all-terrain Navigator is a prime example of such fashionable excess, as is the Cadillac Escalade and the BMW X5. It's true that a market exists for vehicles in this price range, size and horsepower, but it caters to a tiny segment at best. Despite its comfort and mechanical prowess, the Navigator isn't designed for the big city. Just try driving and parking it, and you'll quickly see what I mean. If you're not convinced, fill it up at the pump and then see if your pocketbook squeaks.

Denis Duquet

LINCOLN **NAVIGATOR**

SPECIFICATIONS	
Price	$CDN 41,255-50,865 / $US 30,855-48,480
Warranty	3 years / 36,000 miles (60,000 km)
Type	sport utility / all wheel drive
Wheelbase / Length	118.9 in / 204.7 in
Width / Height	76.8 in / 78.7 in
Weight	5668 lb (2571 kg)
Trunk / Fuel tank	60.9 to 110.7 cu. ft / 29.9 gallons
Air bags	front, side
Front suspension	independent
Rear suspension	rigid axle
Front brakes / Rear brakes	disc ABS
Traction control	no
Steering	rack-and-pinion, variable assist
Turning circle	40 feet
Tires (front/rear)	P245/75R16

PERFORMANCE	
Engine	V8 4.6-liter
Transmission	4-speed automatic
Horsepower	215 hp at 4400 rpm
Torque	290 lb-ft at 3250 rpm
Other engines	5.4-liter 260 hp; 300 hp (Nav.)
Other transmission	none
Acceleration (0-60 mph)	10.6 sec
Maximum speed	118 mph (190 km/h)
Braking (60-0 mph)	144 feet
Fuel consumption	13.5 mpg (16.8 L/100 km)

COMPETITION

• BMW X5 • Cadillac Escalade • Chevrolet Suburban/ GMC Yukon XL • Chevrolet Tahoe • Lexus LX 470

NEW FOR 2002

• Audio-video system • Black monochrome cockpit (optional on Navigator) • Seatbelt reminder

RATING	(out of 5 stars)
Driveability	★★★
Comfort	★★★½
Reliability	★★★½
Roominess	★★★★
Winter driving rating	★★★★½
Safety	★★★★½
Resale value	★★★

FORD EXPLORER

FORD **EXPLORER**

Refined Mechanics, Dull Lines

Ever since J Mays took over as Ford's chief designer, upper management in Dearborn firmly believes they've got the answer to all their styling issues, given Mays' much ballyhooed credentials. But his reputation may be tarnished by the bland lines of the new Explorer, Ford's number-one seller in its category.

The design team could have used more imagination and boldness when conjuring up this sport-utility vehicle. It's one thing to follow the boss's demand that special attention be given to details so the cockpit looks more like an automobile's, but this shouldn't come at the expense of creativity. You need only park the "new and improved" Explorer next to the old model to see the changes were minor.

On the other hand, I'd be wrong not to mention the ingenious larger rear window that can be flipped open for easier access to the storage area; and the extraordinary feat of making room for third-row seating in the rear. The bench is not removable, but you can collapse the backrest for more cargo room. Come to think of it, since third-row seating is optional, you might decide to forget about it and save some money.

Engineers' coup

Since the Explorer remains the best-selling sport-utility vehicle in its line, Ford may have been tempted to leave things pretty much as they were, save for a few styling touch-ups. But that's not the case: not only has the drivetrain been upgraded, but so has the platform.

Until now, the Explorer was mounted on a separate chassis whose rigid rear axle was attached to leaf springs not unlike your great-grandfather's hay wagon. In order to make room for third-row seating in the rear, engineers were obliged to alter this configuration. The traditional rear axle had to go and the only solution was to develop a brand new independent rear suspension. Thanks to the two half shafts poking through the frame rails and the differential bolted between them, the engineers were able to lay a rear cabin floor a good 7 inches lower than the previous model. Furthermore, to correct the listless front suspension once and for all, engineers replaced the torsion bars with coil

Verdict: false hopes

▲ PROS

- Choice of engines • Improved 4X4 status
- Modern chassis • Multiple airbags
- Smart rear window

▼ CONS

- Boring design • Cumbersome third-row seat
- Heavy fuel consumption
- Useless running boards • High price

springs. The wheelbase was lengthened by 2.6 inches and enclosed-type frame rails were introduced for greater rigidity.

Despite the old Explorer's huge popularity, its engines never made much of an impression. Some lacked power, others vibrated – all were gas guzzlers. This year, two new engines are offered. No doubt the most popular will be the standard 4.0-liter SOHC V6, which generates 210 horsepower and is available with a 5-speed manual transmission. For those who need to haul heavy cargo, there's the 240 hp, 4.6-liter V8, which comes with a 5-speed automatic.

Far more civilized

A vehicle's technical data often raises hopes, only to disappoint later on. The new Explorer's specifications certainly sound promising and makes us look forward to checking out its road manners. Even if few drivers intend to use the vehicle in the woods or on unpaved roads, we still need to know how it behaves off the road.

A few excursions on muddy roads prove that the new Explorer performs better than the previous model, and only slightly better than average. It certainly doesn't measure up to, say, the Grand Cherokee. But I rather like the command button on the dashboard that allows you to switch from "4X4 Auto" to "4X4 High" or "4X4 Low."

On the road, the "new and improved" Explorer's road manners are clearly more sophisticated than its predecessor's. The front no longer jerks aimlessly, the independent rear end smooths out road imperfections and the lateral stability is better when cornering. But let's not forget that the Explorer is an SUV with all the implied driving limitations. Ford admits as much, and this year offers a dual-stage airbag system to prevent injuries in case of rollover. And even though troubling details about the vehicle's Firestone tires have dominated the news in recent months, they are still being offered. However, buyers can always request other brands without having to pay extra.

Although the new Explorer failed to impress us, it has nevertheless improved in terms of driving and roadholding capabilities.

Denis Duquet

SPECIFICATIONS

Price	$CDN 37,370-39,105 / $US 26,500-34,655
Warranty	3 years / 36,000 miles (60,000 km)
Type	sport-utility / all wheel drive
Wheelbase / Length	114 in / 189 in
Width / Height	72 in / 72 in
Weight	4354 lb (1975 kg)
Trunk / Fuel tank	46.6 cu. ft / 22 gallons
Air bags	front and side
Front suspension	independent
Rear suspension	independent
Front brakes / Rear brakes	disc ABS
Traction control	no
Steering	rack-and-pinion, power assist
Turning circle	37 feet
Tires (front/rear)	P255/70R16

PERFORMANCE

Engine	V6 4-liter
Transmission	5-speed automatic
Horsepower	210 hp at 5250 rpm
Torque	250 lb-ft at 4000 rpm
Other engines	V8 4.6-liter 240 hp
Other transmission	5-speed manual (V6)
Acceleration (0-60 mph)	8.9 sec
Maximum speed	118 mph (190 km/h)
Braking (60-0 mph)	122 feet (37.2 m)
Fuel consumption	16.7 mpg (13.6 L/100 km)

COMPETITION

• Chevrolet TrailBlazer/GMC Envoy • Jeep Grand Cherokee • Nissan Pathfinder • Toyota 4Runner

NEW FOR 2002

New model

RATING (out of 5 stars)

Driveability	★★★★
Comfort	★★★★
Reliability	New model
Roominess	★★★★
Winter driving rating	★★★★
Safety	★★★★½
Resale value	★★★½

FORD EXPLORER SPORT EXPLORER SPORT TRAC

FORD **EXPLORER SPORT**

Yes to One, No to the Other

All Ford Explorers are not alike. The independent rear suspension platform of the new 4-door model, for example, is much more refined than that of the 2-door Sport model or the Sport Trac SUV/truck hybrid.

The 2-door version is equipped with the rear rigid-axle platform borrowed from the previous generation. For years, 2-door sport-utilities were the norm rather than the exception. But the recent invasion of the 4-door breed has changed all that. So, to make the Explorer Sport appeal to a younger clientele, designers have given it a positively rugged exterior, complete with an aggressive-looking grille and bulging fenders. Inside, the dashboard has been totally jazzed up and sound insulation greatly improved.

To make the Sport Explorer even more competitive, engineers have fitted it with a SOHC 4.0-liter V6 engine producing 205 horsepower, coupled to a 5-speed automatic gearbox. Manual transmission is optional.

On paper, the Explorer Sport has everything it takes to appeal to a particular class of customer. But reality is a different story. The suspension can't absorb road imperfections effectively, and as a result, driver and passengers are constantly knocked about. This sort of suspension problem was common, even inevitable, on SUVs a few years ago, but it's inexcusable today – the fierce competition among SUVs took care of that. Frankly, you've got to be a babe in the woods or else a Ford die-hard even to consider buying this rattletrap. And as if all the above weren't enough, the front seats are utterly uncomfortable, and access to the rear bench requires the skills of a contortionist. Not even its competitive sticker price will entice me in the Explorer Sport's direction.

Hybrid vehicle

In the world of automobiles and their derivative products, sometimes a mere detail or two is all it takes to make a substantial difference. Although the Sport Trac is fitted with the same powertrain as the Explorer Sport, it is far superior thanks to two pieces of statistical data.

The first figure – 14.5 inches (36 cm) – refers to the length by which the chassis was extended in order to retain the four-door front cab and accommodate a cargo bed. And even though the longer wheelbase adds immeasurably to the comfort level on rough roads, it doesn't affect the

▲ PROS

- Roominess • Strong engine performance
- Composite cargo bed
- Well-appointed dashboard

▼ CONS

- Average tires • Tonneau cover's lock needs work
- High fuel consumption • Useless roof rack
- Uncomfortable driving position

vehicle's road-handling capabilities, because its rigidity was increased by 40%, thanks to the use of gussets, a new tubular crossmembers and thick side rails.

The second stat – 50 inches (124 cm) – refers to the length of the composite cargo bed. This new material, called SMC, won't rust, is shock-resistant and 20% lighter than a steel box.

The Sport Trac has an interesting design, well-proportioned between front and rear. The front cab looks just fine and suits the shorter-than-average cargo bed. Like the Sport model, its cabin is well appointed, with a dashboard just as modern as the new Explorer's. According to some aficionados, the latter is the benchmark in its category, an opinion that yours truly doesn't share.

Grows on you

But we can't always be sure with a hybrid vehicle. Generally speaking, it doesn't work well as a sport-ute, and neither is it a good truck. But the Sport Trac kind of grows on you, because it performs honestly. The rear suspension is firm and doesn't always cope with potholes and bumps effectively, but the extended wheelbase somehow neutralizes most of the jarring and jolting, allowing the initial shock to dissipate rapidly.

The slightly elevated front bucket seats make for a so-so driving position. But the rear proves to be surprisingly spacious, especially with the 70/30 bench that can be folded down entirely or partway. The cargo bed is shorter than an average pickup truck, but you can transport taller items than you could if you were driving a conventional sport-utility. With the Cargo Keeper feature, the cargo bed can be lengthened by a couple of inches. On the other hand, the lockable hard tonneau cover can help or harm matters. The lock is located on the top, making the vehicle vulnerable to water entry, and in winter there's a risk of the lock freezing – something we experienced during our test-drive.

Even though the Sport Trac doesn't boast the ingenious multi-function capabilities of the Chevrolet Avalanche, it's a good combination sport-ute/truck and is much nicer to drive than the 2-door Explorer. Let's just hope Ford will find a way to make its 4.0-liter V6 a little less thirsty.

Denis Duquet

SPECIFICATIONS

Price	$CDN 30,280-32, 330 / $US 21,635-25,280
Warranty	3 years / 36,000 miles (60,000 km)
Type	sport-utility 2 doors / 4X4
Wheelbase / Length	102 in / 181 in
Width / Height	70 in / 68.1 in
Weight	4398 lb (1995 kg)
Trunk / Fuel tank	71.4 cu. ft / 17 gallons
Air bags	front, side opt.
Front suspension	independent
Rear suspension	rigid axle
Front brakes / Rear brakes	disc ABS
Traction control	no
Steering	rack-and-pinion, power assist
Turning circle	43 feet
Tires (front/rear)	P235/75R15

PERFORMANCE

Engine	V6 4.0-liter
Transmission	5-speed manual
Horsepower	205 hp at 5000 rpm
Torque	238 lb-ft at 3000 rpm
Other engines	none
Other transmission	5-speed automatic
Acceleration (0-60 mph)	8.4 sec
Maximum speed	118 mph (190 km/h)
Braking (60-0 mph)	143 feet (43.7 m)
Fuel consumption	17.7 mpg (12.8 L/100 km)

COMPETITION

- Chevrolet Blazer/GMC Jimmy

NEW FOR 2002

- Electronically controlled mirror standard on some models

RATING (out of 5 stars)

Driveability	★★★½
Comfort	★★★
Reliability	★★★★
Roominess	★★★
Winter driving rating	★★★★
Safety	★★★★
Resale value	★★

FORD FOCUS

FORD **FOCUS ZX5**

Improving the Formula

Maybe it's a tough job, but someone's got to do it, and it might as well be Ford. A cute little American-made car, intelligently conceived and executed, fun to drive, and offered at a competitive price. Those who mourned the Ford Escort's passing, particularly the station wagon version, will be happy to discover that Ford has retained the formula, and managed to improve on it, demonstrating that it's actually possible for an American carmaker to compete with its Asian and European counterparts in the subcompact category. The old adage still rings true: if you want something bad enough, you'll find a way to get it.

As befits a Ford subcompact, the Focus wagon has both looks and versatility. More balanced than its sedan "sister," the Focus "break," to use Ford's lingo, seems to have won public approval, judging from the number of units crowding the roads.

Clear instructions

The cockpit, too, scores marks for originality and ergonomics. Granted, not everyone will appreciate the dashboard's "different" design, but no one can reasonably say it lacks originality. Ergonomically speaking, control buttons and knobs are conveniently located and easy to activate, unhampered by cupholders. The dials and indicators are well laid out and easy to read. The driver's seat is height-adjustable. Also worth mentioning is the owner's manual, located in the glove compartment. Instructions describing the car's main features are presented in clear and concise language, accompanied by excellent illustrations. But there's still room for improvement: the steering wheel, for instance, is not adjustable; the brake pedal and accelerator are too far apart (like the Taurus); finally, the car could use an in-dash PRNDL transmission shift indicator and a few storage bins for the rear cabin.

Looks and versatility

Not fast, but not unpleasant

Powered by a 2.0-liter 4-cylinder Zetec engine, the Focus SE wagon boasts 130 horsepower, which is a tad borderline, and 135 lb-ft of torque, which is excellent. It takes more than 10 seconds to move from 0-60 mph, but acceleration is otherwise acceptable, taking 9 seconds

▲ PROS

- Appealing lines • Competitive price
- Good ergonomics • Roominess
- Predictable road manners

▼ CONS

- Average performance • Pedals need work
- Poor reliability • Rear drum brakes

to go from 50 to 75 mph (80 to 120 km/h). All in all, a worthy performance for a city car, not exactly meant for enthusiastic driving. Thanks to a well dampened suspension that efficiently absorbs bumps, the Focus exhibits excellent road manners, with body roll and understeer well controlled.

And the brakes, Mr. Ford?

So far, so good. The Focus rides and turns properly. The same thing can't be said of the brakes. Under normal conditions, all seems to be well, the pedal is pleasingly firm and the car slows down as expected. But try panic braking, and the rear wheels will lock immediately. If you need to turn, and the road is uneven or wet, the car will spin dramatically and the flat spot will show up on the rear tires if the car skids for too long. This is one more piece of evidence that carmakers usually try to allay safety concerns while keeping to outdated technology. In fact, many of today's cars still lack rear disc brakes, whose superiority and efficiency has been proven over and over again for nearly 50 years. The same complaint can be made of ABS, which would have prevented the rear wheels' untimely lock. So, carmakers of the world, listen up. If you're really concerned about safety, stop kowtowing to the bean counters, drop that lame compromise and fit all vehicles with disc brakes and ABS.

Cool profile

Knowing that the majority of Focus buyers are in the 25-35 age group, Ford added another coupe in 2002 – the ZX5, a 5-door version of the ZX3. Scheduled to hit the market at the end of 2001, the ZX5 combines the virtues of a station wagon with the sexy appeal of a coupe – a trendy, but tried-and-true formula, judging from the wildly popular Mazda Protegé5 and other models of the same ilk.

A distinguished 3-door coupe, a classic sedan, a popular station wagon and now, a new 5-door coupe. The lineup is impressive. But there's always an opportunity to go one better: improved reliability is a good goal to start with, and perhaps a true-blue 3-door sport coupe some day?

Alain Raymond

SPECIFICATIONS	SE
Price	$CDN 15,970-21,980 / $US 12,805-16,915
Warranty	3 years / 36,000 miles (60,000 km)
Type	wagon / front wheel drive
Wheelbase / Length	103.1 in / 178.3 in
Width / Height	66.9 in / 58.7 in
Weight	2634 lb (1195 kg)
Trunk / Fuel tank	13.2 to 19.7 cu. ft / 13 gallons
Air bags	front
Front suspension	independent
Rear suspension	independent
Front brakes / Rear brakes	disc / drum
Traction control	no
Steering	rack-and-pinion, power assist
Turning circle	36 feet
Tires (front/rear)	P195/60R15

PERFORMANCE	
Engine	4L 2.0-liter Zetec
Transmission	4-speed automatic
Horsepower	130 hp at 5300 rpm
Torque	135 lb-ft at 4500 rpm
Other engines	4L 2-liter 110 hp
Other transmission	5-speed manual
Acceleration (0-60 mph)	10.2 sec
Maximum speed	115 mph (185 km/h)
Braking (60-0 mph)	138 feet (42 m)
Fuel consumption	26.7 mpg (8.5 L/100 km)

COMPETITION

• Cavalier / Sunfire • Civic • Corolla • Elantra • Golf • Protegé • Sentra • Spectra

NEW FOR 2002

• ZX5 model • Brushed-aluminum trim (ZTS, ZTW and ZX5) • Optional 6-CD changer • Optional sunroof

RATING	(out of 5 stars)
Driveability	★★★½
Comfort	★★★½
Reliability	★★
Roominess	★★★★
Winter driving rating	★★★
Safety	★★★
Resale value	★★★

FORD MUSTANG

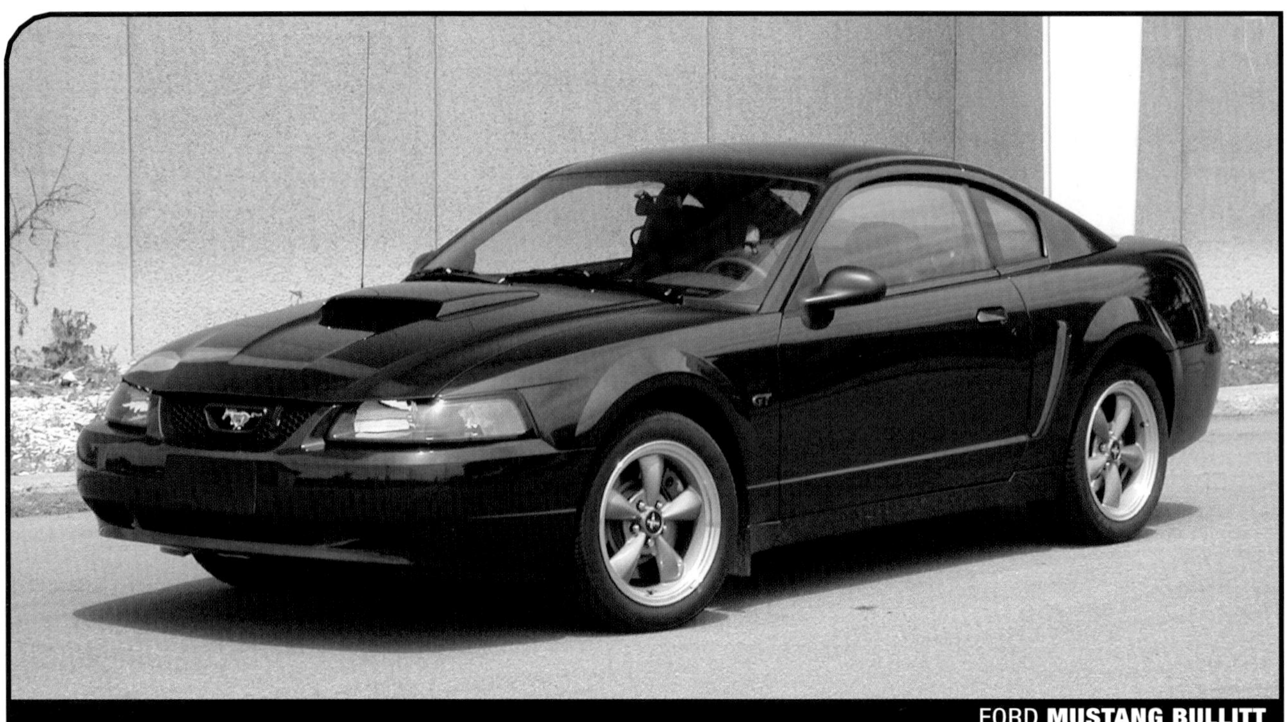

FORD **MUSTANG BULLITT**

The Chase

The Ford Mustang has more or less survived the onslaught of time. Having reached an icon status within the American auto industry, this sports coupe has overcome fashions and trends, and kept a following, which could have found good reason to turn their backs on it. Ford has known for a long time that it did not have to work too hard to keep this model popular. So after nearly forty years, the Mustang is not ready for retirement. Quite the contrary. Those that would have gladly sent it off to car heaven a few years ago witnessed, to their sorrow, the disappearance of the lesser known Probe which was seen by many as an heir apparent.

The 2002 vintage confirms continuity for the Mustang. A few changes however, just to create an interest in the basic model, but overall it remains the same. More discreet, the "basic model" does not offer the powerful V8 of the GT, but it is pleasant to drive and more importantly ... has a far more attractive price.

Film magic

There are the good and the bad. In the film "Bullitt," the bad guys drive a Dodge Charger. Chasing them is the good-guy detective Frank Bullitt driving his dark green 68 Mustang. The film "Bullitt" received no Oscar, yet the chase sequence was an unforgettable delight to all cinema fans. Today, 34 years later, it is still remembered as the most impressive chase scene ever. Without props or special effects, Steve McQueen screams around the streets of San Francisco aboard his Mustang GT 390. And guess what? The good guy won!

The Bullitt GT 2002 is named after the most famous "car chase scene" in the history of cinema. Ford will only build 6,500 exclusive models, 500 being destined to the Canadian market. The car is no more than a "made-up" GT in spite of some features taken from the famous screen car.

An icon

To share the visual impact of the GT 68 model, the Bullitt GT 2002 has wide scoops, 17-inch rims and the suspension has been lowered by about an inch. It also has some features not found on the movie Mustang: a brushed-aluminium fuel filler door and a massive hood scoop that is non-functional. Driving this muscle car

▲ PROS

- Highly responsive and lively V8
- Improved finish • Better manual gearbox
- Exclusive Bullitt model

▼ CONS

- Rigid rear axle • Old-fashioned frame
- Uncomfortable seats • Poor gas mileage (GT & Bullitt)

with a 4.6-liter V8 that has gained 5 hp and 5 lb-ft of torque is fun and an invitation to excess.

The deep-throated rumble and exhaust roar makes the blood boil and the slick 5-speed shifter of the manual gearbox easily chews out the full performance of the V8.

Aging platform

The Bullitt GT has some of the Mustang's shortcomings. The 30-year-old platform needs updating, as riding over a bumpy road will demonstrate. This of course need only apply to those of us who leave the multi-lane highways for neglected country lanes.

A review of the Mustang suspension by Ford is on our yearly wish list. The now old-fashioned rear axle generates road handling that under adverse conditions makes the driver keep his two hands firmly gripping the wheel. Having the ABS as standard equipment would have been better. Safety has a price it seems, as this crucial piece of equipment only comes as an option if you choose the base model. Good news, however, instead of the 15-inch wheels, there are 16-inch wheels for 2002.

The Mustang cockpit has not changed much. A little Ford effort would be greatly appreciated. Uncomfortable seats don't help long drives in the country. It's the same thing every year. The Mustang comes with a new MP3-type sound system which compresses the music signal onto a long-playing CD disc. We should hear more about this new concept developed by Mazda in their Protegé MP3 model in the coming years.

Louis Butcher

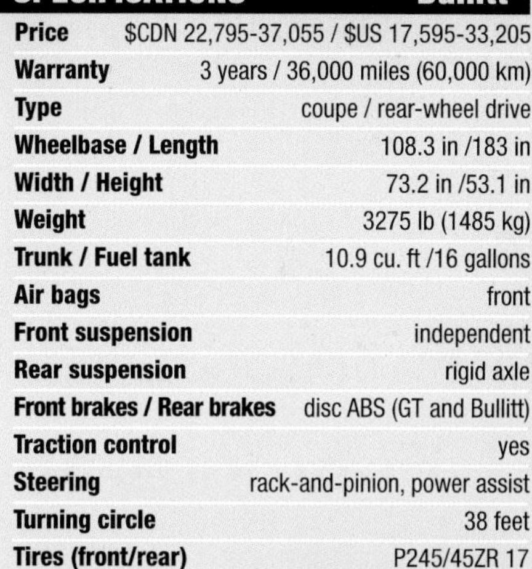

SPECIFICATIONS	Bullitt
Price	$CDN 22,795-37,055 / $US 17,595-33,205
Warranty	3 years / 36,000 miles (60,000 km)
Type	coupe / rear-wheel drive
Wheelbase / Length	108.3 in /183 in
Width / Height	73.2 in /53.1 in
Weight	3275 lb (1485 kg)
Trunk / Fuel tank	10.9 cu. ft /16 gallons
Air bags	front
Front suspension	independent
Rear suspension	rigid axle
Front brakes / Rear brakes	disc ABS (GT and Bullitt)
Traction control	yes
Steering	rack-and-pinion, power assist
Turning circle	38 feet
Tires (front/rear)	P245/45ZR 17

PERFORMANCE	
Engine	V8 4.6-liter (GT and Bullitt)
Transmission	5-speed manual
Horsepower	265-hp at 5000 rpm
Torque	305 lb-ft at 4000 rpm
Other engines	V6 3.8-liter 190-hp; V8 4.6-liter 260-hp (GT)
Other transmission	4-speed automatic
Acceleration (0-60 mph)	5.9 sec (Bullitt)
Maximum speed	112 mph (180 km/h) (limited)
Braking (60-0 mph)	130 feet (39.6 m)
Fuel consumption	13.7 mpg (16.5 L/100 km)

COMPETITION

- Chevrolet Camaro/Pontiac Firebird

NEW FOR 2002

- Standard 16-inch wheels and tires
- New air scoops and hood (V6)

RATING	(out of 5 stars)
Driveability	★★★★
Comfort	★★★
Reliability	★★★
Roominess	★★★
Winter driving rating	★★★½
Safety	★★★
Resale value	★★★½

FORD TAURUS

FORD **TAURUS SEL**

Fabulous Rental Car!

Of the 10 best-selling cars in North America, only one is American made: the Ford Taurus. The rest are Japanese – mostly Honda and Toyota – and you can bet your bottom dollar that they're here to stay. How long Ford can sustain its presence in the annual top-ten list depends on how willing it is to divert some of its attention away from the lucrative, though ephemeral, truck market and concentrate instead on the sedan market.

For the 2000 Taurus model, Ford shed the "bio" look of the vehicle's third generation in favor of more conservative lines, both outside and inside. In fact, the new cockpit looks so painfully conventional it lacks originality. Ergonomics, too, seem dubious.

Bad ergonomics

Judge for yourself: there are 33 buttons on the center control panel! Yes, 33, eight of which are for climate control and the audio system alone. You can't get more redundant than that. Instead, had the designers retained three buttons from the previous model, they could have done without a dozen of those plastic ones and simplified the driver's job at the same time. Obviously, ergonomics play a crucial active-safety role, because nothing distracts the driver more than trying to figure out complicated commands on the dashboard.

Other ergonomic flaws: the steering wheel spokes are such that you can't rest your hands at the 9 and 3 o'clock positions; the cruise control buttons don't illuminate at night; and most incredible of all, the accelerator and the brake pedal are so far apart that you have to lift up your foot all the way before you can apply the brakes. Not to worry, though, airbags abound in this Ford!

Simply wheels

On the other hand, these same foot pedals are the only ones that are power-adjustable in this car category. With power steering, power foot pedals and power seat, you're guaranteed a good driving position, no matter what size you are. Other selling points are the comfortable front seats and spacious rear cabin. A perfect car indeed for traveling reps or vacationing families.

▲ PROS

- Satisfactory engine • Good road manners
- Roominess • Power adjustable pedals
- Competitive price

▼ CONS

- Poor ergonomics • Brakes need work
- Average assembly quality
- Not much fun to drive

Great engine, but watch out for the brakes!

On the road, the Taurus conducts itself reasonably well with its 3.0-liter V6 engine with 200 hp. Vigorous and adaptive, this modern 24-valve V6 is coupled to a satisfactory automatic gearbox. Acceleration is straightforward, overtaking is not a problem (50-75 mph in 7.2 seconds) and fuel consumption is reasonable for a car of its size.

All in all, handling is excellent. Both body roll and understeer are properly controlled, and the suspension well tuned. Had the steering been a little less stiff, we might have even talked about the Ford Taurus in terms of "driving pleasure."

The brakes on our test car were less impressive, however. Each time they were applied the least bit vigorously, the steering wheel vibrated, a sign of warpage in the front discs – not a reassuring sign for a car that had clocked less than 9000 miles (15,000 km). Moreover, the archaic rear drum brakes tend to lock up prematurely, and give the pedal a spongy feeling. It's almost unbelievable – even scandalous – that 50 years after the invention of disc brakes, ancient – make that antique – drums still grace so-called modern cars.

What's more, the car exhibited both wind noise and body rattles, an indication that its assembly quality leaves much to be desired. An interior finish part came loose inside the trunk, and the carpets kept moving back and forth under our feet.

A permanent fixture in commercial car fleets and rental companies, the Taurus is a perfect choice for those who think about cars in terms of wheels, and nothing else.

Alain Raymond

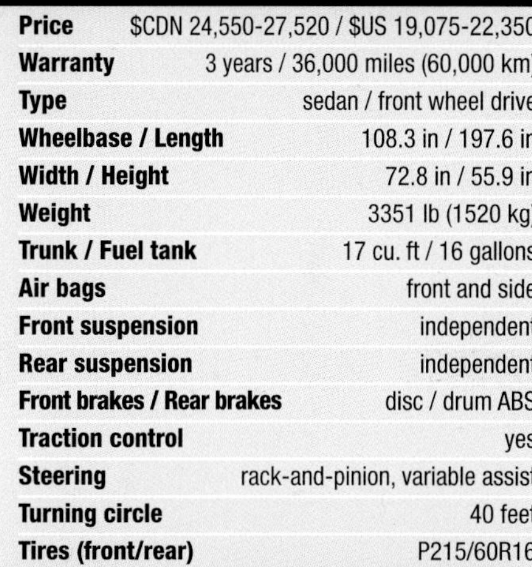

SPECIFICATIONS	**SEL**
Price	$CDN 24,550-27,520 / $US 19,075-22,350
Warranty	3 years / 36,000 miles (60,000 km)
Type	sedan / front wheel drive
Wheelbase / Length	108.3 in / 197.6 in
Width / Height	72.8 in / 55.9 in
Weight	3351 lb (1520 kg)
Trunk / Fuel tank	17 cu. ft / 16 gallons
Air bags	front and side
Front suspension	independent
Rear suspension	independent
Front brakes / Rear brakes	disc / drum ABS
Traction control	yes
Steering	rack-and-pinion, variable assist
Turning circle	40 feet
Tires (front/rear)	P215/60R16

PERFORMANCE	
Engine	V6 3.0-liter
Transmission	4-speed automatic
Horsepower	200 hp at 5750 rpm
Torque	200 lb-ft at 4500 rpm
Other engines	V6 3.0-liter 153 hp
Other transmission	none
Acceleration (0-60 mph)	9.1 sec
Maximum speed	109 mph (175 km/h)
Braking (60-0 mph)	143 feet (43.7 m)
Fuel consumption	19.1 mpg (11.9 L/100 km)

COMPETITION

- Buick Regal/Oldsmobile Intrigue • Chevrolet Impala/ Pontiac Grand Prix • Chrysler Intrepid

NEW FOR 2002

- New colors

RATING	**(out of 5 stars)**
Driveability	★★½
Comfort	★★★½
Reliability	★★½
Roominess	★★★★
Winter driving rating	★★★½
Safety	★★★½
Resale value	★★

FORD THUNDERBIRD

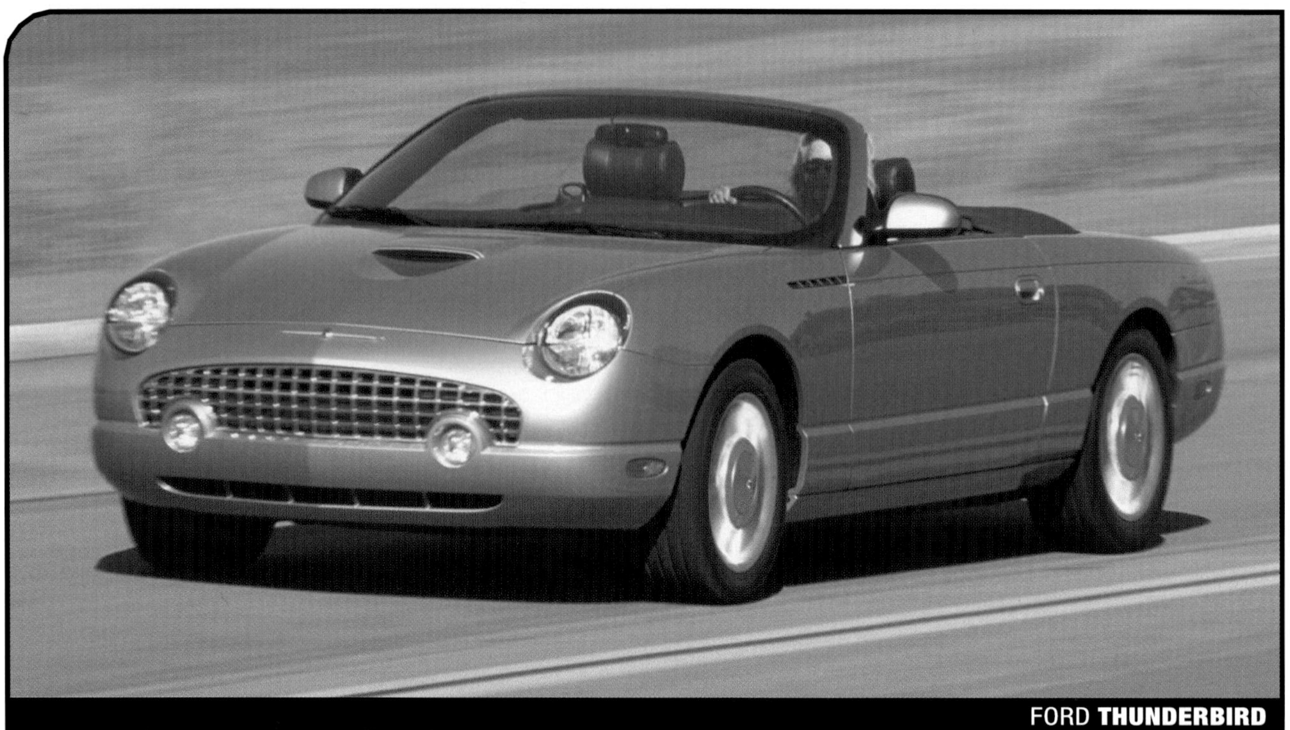

FORD **THUNDERBIRD**

Live for the Moment

The new Thunderbird is the kind of car that inspires you to "live for the moment," to go for a free-spirited spin, singing and whistling as you roll along, and all the while relishing the eager attention that the car will attract.

Yet, this isn't the fall of 1954, when the 1955 Thunderbird – one of America's true cult cars – was unveiled for the first time. The new 2002 Thunderbird has finally rolled off the assembly line, after more than a year of announcements and press leaks. Never in recent history has an automobile been the object of so much media attention and carefully staged events. The prototype was introduced at the Detroit Auto Show in 1999, before making appearances at other major auto shows around the world. Then, in Los Angeles in 2001, Ford revealed the new T-Bird's "five magnificent colors." Even the upscale Neiman-Marcus department store in Dallas, Texas, got into the act, offering a special T-Bird edition in its annual catalog. Needless to say, the special model was sold out within 24 hours.

Finally, at the 2001 Detroit Auto Show, the definitive version of the Thunderbird was unveiled, by none other than singer Ray Charles. Obviously, nobody at Ford seemed to care very much that a visually impaired individual was presenting the car. For those who did wonder, however, let me assure you that, in fact, Mr. Charles wasn't driving – but sitting in the passenger seat.

Memory lane

Since the new Thunderbird is intended to be a tribute to the past, let's take a quick trip down memory lane and revisit something of its history. In 1951, at the Paris Auto Show held in the Grand Palais, Lewis D. Crusoe, then Ford's general manager, and his designer, George Walker, were busy admiring the collection of sporty European cars being unveiled. At one point, Crusoe asked his colleague why Ford wasn't making similar models. Walker nonchalantly replied that such a car was actually in the works back home in Dearborn, Michigan. At the first opportune moment, the designer rushed to the nearest telephone, dialed the Ford headquarters and ordered his assistants

Modern icon

▲ PROS

- Eye-catching lines • Guaranteed impact
- Sound road manners • Watertight top
- Well developed drivetrain

▼ CONS

- Excessive body rattling • Pitching on rough roads
- Roof cover too rigid • Roof too low
- Subpar wiper control

to get the project going. And that's how the Thunderbird began to fly.

The new creation sported a Ferrari-inspired grille, a hood scoop and stylized tailpipes. The elegant roadster was shaped like an inverted wedge with a dramatically streamlined tail end. Only one detail remained: it needed a name. Many were suggested – Detroiter, Beaver and Hep Cat were the front runners. But none made the grade. Frustrated, Crusoe offered to buy a new suit for anyone who could come up with a winner. It was then that a young Ford stylist, Alden "Gib" Giberson, came forward with "Thunderbird." Giberson got his suit – and a legend was born.

Modern times

Fast forward to 2002 and now let's return to the new T-Bird and its five superb colors. Designers have succeeded in blending new and old harmoniously. The latest lines are crisper and smartly complement some of the original key elements like the badge, grille, inverted wedge, hood scoop and "afterburner"-type round headlamps.

The cockpit looks decidedly less retro. The seats are comfortable and offer adequate lateral support. Most controls – borrowed from other Ford cars – are easy to reach, except the plethora of buttons for the radio and climate control, which require a little more attention than necessary. But the worst offender is the turn signal lever which also controls the washer fluid and wipers. Each time I wanted to use the turn signal, I ended up washing the windscreen as well as activating the wipers.

The steering wheel is adjustable for both height and reach, making it easy to find a comfortable driving position and to move around in the cramped cockpit when the top is in place. By the way, the soft top can be folded and put back up in no time at all. On the other hand, not only is the top too rigid, it's also too rudimentary for a car in this price range and takes up too much precious space in the already small trunk. You could also try stowing it behind the bucket seats, if you want to put some luggage in the trunk.

I won't bore you with a lengthy technical discourse because the new Thunderbird

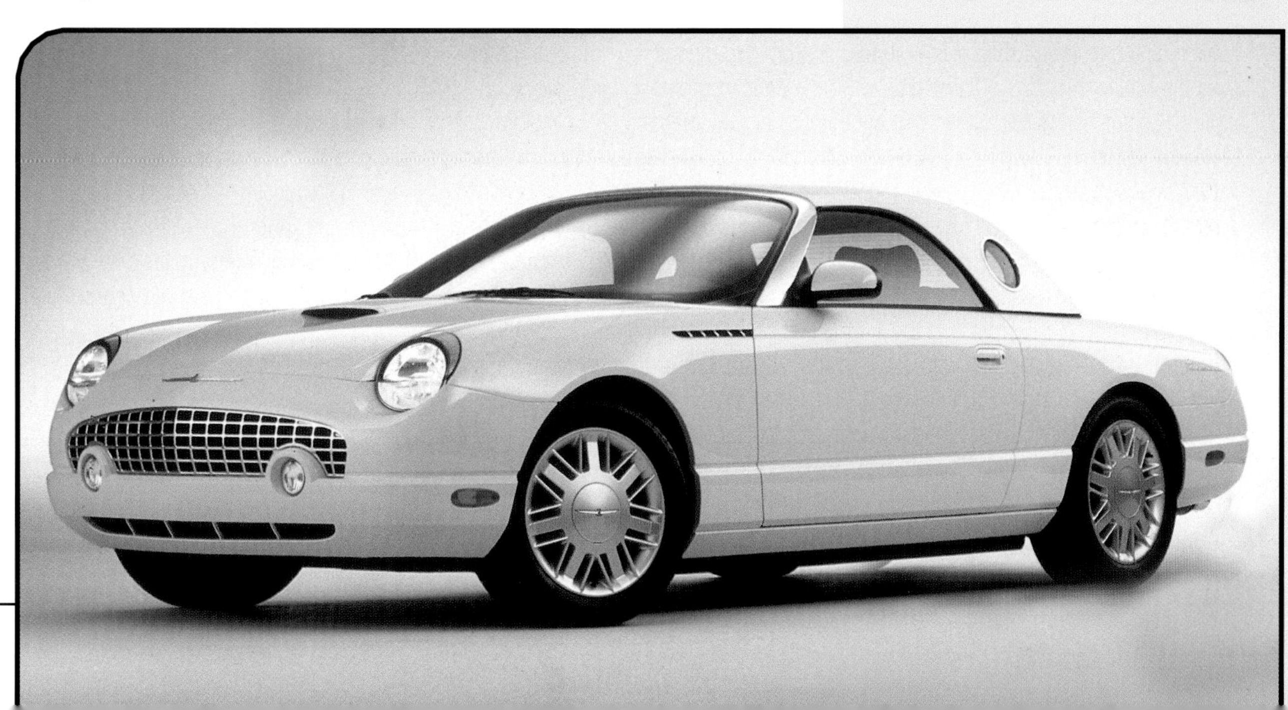

FORD THUNDERBIRD

A Pleasant Surprise

I'll admit that I didn't expect much as I took the wheel of this reincarnated Thunderbird. Cars that finally arrive after a lengthy period of gestation – the T-Bird's first prototype was unveiled at the Detroit Auto Show three years ago – are generally disappointing. Despite a long and difficult "birth," however, the 2002 Thunderbird appears to be surprisingly well adjusted. While some automobile journalists rather dismiss it as a "boulevard cruiser," I think it deserves a more flattering designation.

Despite its two-seater convertible status, the T-Bird is not a bona fide sports car, as its warm, seductive engine rumble would make you believe. If its V8 engine was "borrowed" from the Lincoln LS, it nonetheless boasts a pair of tailpipes that are perfectly adapted to its own roadster nature. Mated to a compatible 5-speed automatic transmission, the engine readily springs into action at the slightest nudge from the accelerator. Its 0-60 mph time of 8.2 seconds won't make it into the record books, but I'm also willing to bet that nobody's going to complain about it either.

Naturally, driving with the top down is infinitely more pleasurable, and the T-Bird obliges with excellent seats and an eye-pleasing and colorful dashboard. This "boulevard cruiser" will never shy away from any country road either, and its road manners, though by no means ideal, are perfectly acceptable. Oddly enough, body roll is conspicuously absent, and the car tends to pitch instead. At high speeds, it's inclined to waver – proof that the T-Bird was built for touring on the good old American turnpikes infested with state police patrols, rather than for scorching down the Autobahn.

On the other hand, comfort is A-one, even on rough surfaces, and the noise level – usually high in convertibles – has been reduced to a bare minimum. In a nutshell, this new Thunderbird has pleasantly surprised me.

Jacques Duval

quite simply a 2-door convertible version of the Lincoln LS. The wheelbase has been shortened by 7 inches (18 cm) and the length by 7.4 inches (19 cm). There's only one engine, a 252-hp 3.9-liter V8 – the same that powers the Lincoln LS and the Jaguar S-Type – coupled to a 4-speed automatic transmission. Naturally, the car is equipped with a four-wheel independent suspension system, four-wheel disc brakes with ABS, and traction control to keep your T-Bird on the straightaway.

More than a salute

Driving this "bird" is more like "living it up" than participating in a Grand Prix race. No doubt this kind of playfulness was subliminally encouraged by the T-Bird's cool silhouette, not to mention the spirit in

■ STANDARD EQUIPMENT

• 3.9-liter V8 engine • 5-speed automatic transmission • Electronically-controlled air conditioning • Automatic soft top • Adjustable steering wheel

■ OPTIONAL EQUIPMENT

• Hard top • Two-tone seats • Fog lamps

which it was conceived. Not that this 2-seater has no road manners or lacks acceleration and braking force. On the contrary, it can scoot from 0-60 mph in a mere 7.9 seconds and its road behavior is exemplary. At normal speeds, it can corner effortlessly and with aplomb, leaving you free to chat with your passenger or else be carried away by your favorite song wafting from the radio or high-quality in-dash 6-CD changer. Even at 75 mph (120 km/h), and with the top down, you can still carry on a conversation without raising your voice. I particularly appreciate the fact that the audio system's volume and mute buttons are mounted on the rim of the steering hub – a nice touch for a convertible, where the noise level is always markedly higher than in regular cars.

Although my test car was not a production model, its body was surprisingly rigid. But there was some rattling emerging from under the dashboard, which I supposed was an indication that the car might have been an early model.

The new Thunderbird is obviously more than just a salute to the past. It's a well built car in every way. Elegant, comfortable, with excellent road manners, it will charm all those nostalgic customers into shelling out $50,000 and more so they can ... take a spin and relax. A hardtop and heated rear glass will set them back another $5000. But at this price, they'll get a porthole window on each side – an authentic 1950s touch.

There's little doubt the Thunderbird is one of the most intriguing cars to roll off the Ford assembly line in a long time. But you'll need to hurry if you want one, because production is limited to just 25,000 cars a year. After all, good things are always in short supply.

Denis Duquet/Jacques Duval

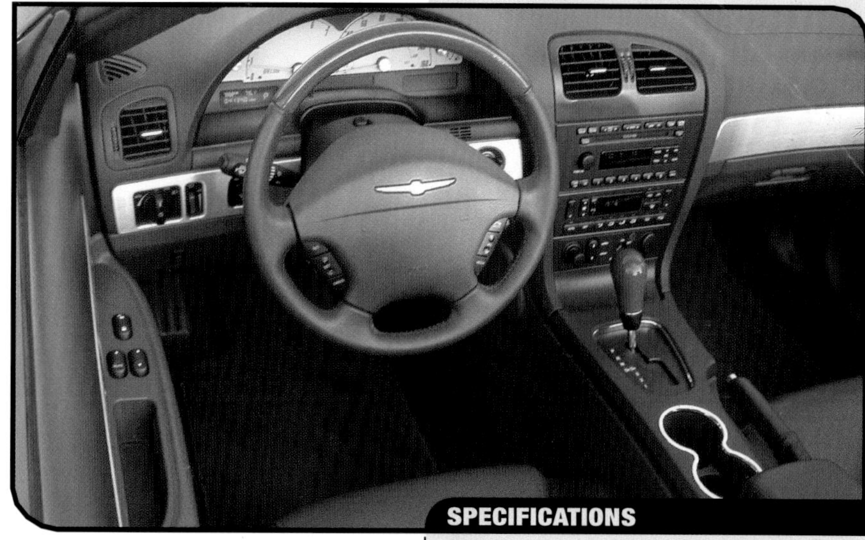

SPECIFICATIONS

Price	$CDN 51,550-56,550 / $US 34,495-38,995
Warranty	3 years / 36,000 miles (60,000 km)
Type	2-seat convertible
Wheelbase / Length	107.1 in / 186.2 in
Width / Height	72 in / 52 in
Weight	3746 lb (1699 kg)
Trunk / Fuel tank	6.7 cu. ft /18 gallons
Air bags	front and side
Front suspension	independent
Rear suspension	independent
Front brakes / Rear brakes	disc ABS
Traction control	yes
Steering	rack-and-pinion, variable assist
Turning circle	37.5 feet
Tires (front/rear)	P235/50VR17

PERFORMANCE

Engine	V8 3.9-liter
Transmission	5-speed automatic
Horsepower	252 hp at 6100 rpm
Torque	267 lb-ft at 4300 rpm
Other engines	none
Other transmission	none
Acceleration (0-60 mph)	7.8 sec
Maximum speed	137 mph (215 km/h)
Braking (60-0 mph)	130 feet (39.6 m)
Fuel consumption	15.6 mpg (14.5 L/100 km)

COMPETITION

• BMW 325Ci • Mercedes-Benz CLK
• Saab 9³ Cabrio • Volvo C70

NEW FOR 2002

• All-new model

RATING (out of 5 stars)

Driveability	★★★★
Comfort	★★★½
Reliability	New model
Roominess	★★
Winter driving rating	★★
Safety	★★★½
Resale value	New model

FORD WINDSTAR

FORD **WINDSTAR**

Family-Style Sport

If the Ford Explorer's recent and well-publicized problems have kept the company's directors awake at night, they can sleep soundly when the time comes to tally up sales figures for the Windstar minivan. In fact, it would be difficult to find a more politically correct vehicle. Not only does it excel in terms of passive-safety features, but its road performance is satisfying and absolutely worry-free.

With the Windstar minivan, there's no need to agonize over what wheelbase – long or short – you want, because there's only one. Its overall length is identical to that of the Honda Odyssey, the market's darling over the past few years. While its 3.8-liter V6 with 200 horsepower isn't the most powerful in the category, it's one of the least polluting of engines, considering its middle-of-the-road fuel economy. The Windstar has come a long way from its troubled beginnings, currently ranking at midpoint in its category in terms of reliability – a happy medium.

If styling ranks high on your list of priorities, then this minivan – hardly a beauty-contest contender – stands little or no chance. But the Sport model provided for our road test looked very smart indeed with its five-spoke alloy wheels, black grille and rear spoiler placed just above the tailgate window. Personally, I doubt whether the spoiler conveys any aerodynamic effect at all, but it certainly adds to the Windstar's visual impact, such as it is.

The Maytag effect

Engineers and designers seem to have been so fixated on the vehicle's overall "politically correct" demeanor, that they wound up with a soulless, strictly utilitarian product. No wonder the Maytag company chose the Windstar as an experimental vehicle to transport its home appliances.

Happy medium

Our test model had none of Maytag's accessories. It was fitted instead with the Family Entertainment System that included a VHS video cassette player, Sony Playstation, cordless headphones and, naturally, a liquid-crystal display screen (LCD). With these gadgets, an entire family can take off on a long trip,

▲ PROS

• Audio-visual system • Complete standard equipment • 5-star passive-safety features • Quality of finish • Reliable engine

▼ CONS

• Borderline roominess • Display gauges need work • High fuel consumption • Slow power sliding doors

reassured for once that the kids will be quiet in the back. What's more, the driver can keep an eye on them, thanks to a large, central rearview mirror.

Happy medium

Everything about the Windstar – its general presentation, styling, handling – is strictly average. The driver sits before a utilitarian dashboard, virtually devoid of anything worth mentioning. And somebody should do something about the display dials, which resemble those paper cutouts that you often see affixed to mock-up accessories in home-renovation trade shows. Also, despite the Windstar's large dimensions, the driver has relatively little legroom.

Our test model was equipped with self-sealing Uniroyal tires and a standard low tire-pressure warning system, that consists of a warning light on the dashboard that illuminates if one or more tires become deflated.

Handling is satisfactory. The 200-hp V6 engine propels the Windstar from 0-60 mph in slightly more than 10 seconds, but it's noisy. Roadholding is problem-free, but also excitement-free. The suspension does its job respectably. On city streets or twisty roads, however, the Windstar isn't as agile as a Dodge Grand Caravan or a Honda Odyssey. Incidentally, the Family Security II option group now includes the electronic traction control system Advance Trac.

The Windstar's reliability has improved noticeably over the years and now ranks midway in its minivan field. What's more, it's offered at an affordable price, yet considered one of the best on the market in terms of passive safety. These elements alone are enough to lure many buyers away from the competition.

Denis Duquet

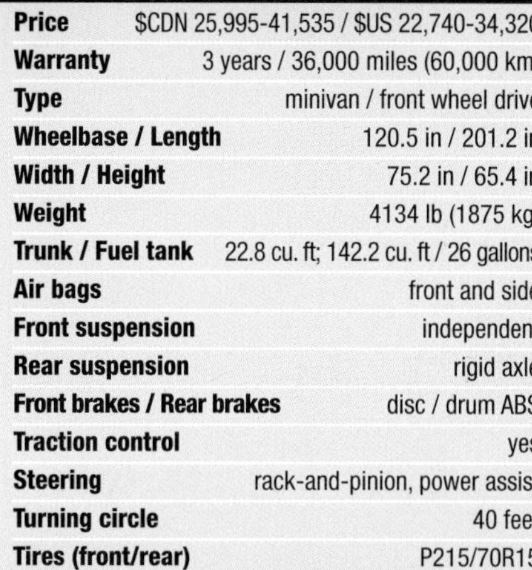

SPECIFICATIONS	**Windstar**
Price	$CDN 25,995-41,535 / $US 22,740-34,320
Warranty	3 years / 36,000 miles (60,000 km)
Type	minivan / front wheel drive
Wheelbase / Length	120.5 in / 201.2 in
Width / Height	75.2 in / 65.4 in
Weight	4134 lb (1875 kg)
Trunk / Fuel tank	22.8 cu. ft; 142.2 cu. ft / 26 gallons
Air bags	front and side
Front suspension	independent
Rear suspension	rigid axle
Front brakes / Rear brakes	disc / drum ABS
Traction control	yes
Steering	rack-and-pinion, power assist
Turning circle	40 feet
Tires (front/rear)	P215/70R15

PERFORMANCE	
Engine	V6 3.8-liter
Transmission	4-speed automatic
Horsepower	200 hp at 4900 rpm
Torque	240 lb-ft at 3600 rpm
Other engines	none
Other transmission	none
Acceleration (0-60 mph)	9.6 sec
Maximum speed	112 mph (180 km/h)
Braking (60-0 mph)	139 feet (42.3 m)
Fuel consumption	18.7 mpg (12.1 L/100 km)

COMPETITION

• Caravan • Mazda MPV • Odyssey • Sienna • Venture/Montana

NEW FOR 2002

• Advance Trac included in Family Security II option group • New option groups

RATING	**(out of 5 stars)**
Driveability	★★★
Comfort	★★★★
Reliability	★★★½
Roominess	★★★★½
Winter driving rating	★★★★
Safety	★★★★★
Resale value	★★★

HONDA ACCORD

HONDA **ACCORD**

Do Rely on Appearances!

The Honda Accord is often accused of becoming too "gentrified" with each generation, moving closer to a boring, soulless car. Not true, yet not quite false. Your choice of model and engine/gearbox combination can make a difference.

The Accord was completely redesigned three years ago, and ever since Honda has made a point of differentiating between the sedan and the coupe, insisting they are separate entities. It's rare that automobile makers go to such lengths to distinguish between two versions of the same model.

If, as they say, appearances are misleading, then the Accord is the exception that confims the rule. In a crowded shopping-center parking lot, the Accord Sedan is certainly the hardest car to pick out – its design is so impersonal it blends into the landscape.

With its slim shape and curved end, the coupe looks much more attractive. But that's hardly a compliment – any car looks better than the Accord Sedan. That said, the coupe's looks are inspired by the so-called *New Edge Design,* a popular American concept. The fact is, unlike the sad-looking sedan, the coupe is actually fun to drive. Let's take a closer look.

Gorgeous mechanics

Rule No 1: To get a feel for any driving sensation there may be in an Accord, you must opt for manual transmission. That's even truer in the case of the Accord Coupe. Trouble is, the V6 doesn't come with manual transmission.

But take heart, the coupe's 4-cylinder VTEC is far from being inadequate. It proved to be as flexible as it was efficient, as we've come to expect of a Honda engine. Even though it starts to come alive at 4000 rpm, it will happily stay in that rev range if you want it to.

Coupe has the edge

But really, to enjoy this superb power source – and "superb" is not too strong here – you need the manual transmission. All the more reason since Honda is a leader in the field.

The 3-liter V6 VTEC, like its 4-cylinder cousin, is eerily silent on the road. At cruising speed, or even higher, you simply don't hear engine noise. But when things are too quiet, watch out! For behind all the silky smoothness and silence there

▲ PROS

• Exceptional reliability • Exemplary manual transmission • Functional cockpit • Refined mechanicals • Sporty driving (coupe)

▼ CONS

• Finish not as sharp • Manual transmission not available with V6 • Nondescript appearance (sedan) • Slow automatic gearbox • Vague steering (V6)

lurks a temper, as witnessed by the car's punchy initial and mid-range acceleration.

The automatic transmission, too, works smoothly, although it could be more assertive. Such listlessness seems common to all Honda models (including Acura) fitted with this type of transmission.

Roadholding is provided through flawless double-wishbone front and rear suspensions, making for a smooth drive and excellent road manners. There's a difference between the sedan and the coupe, however. Without being exactly sporty, the latter offers a more inspired performance. Body roll and understeer are well controlled, and handling inspires confidence.

Curiously, steering response varies according to the type of engine under the hood. With the 4-cylinder, it works beautifully. With the V6, it seems sluggish. Strange.

Familiar territory

No surprises regarding the interior. Honda Accord regulars will find themselves at home: a no-muss, no-fuss presentation, where functionality prevails over designer looks.

What the cabin lacks in originality, it makes up in comfort and ergonomics. The driver's seat is comfortably appointed, controls are simple and easy to reach, while storage space abounds. Here again, the coupe scores high with a user-friendly center console, complete with cupholders and two large all-purpose storage bins.

The coupe's interior, too, looks particularly welcoming, with bucket seats and a lusher interior. In the rear, legroom and headroom are just snug, as expected of any self-respecting coupe. But I've seen much worse in this type of car.

My only complaint is the quality of the finish that, in both test cars, is not as sharp as it has been. Some attribute this to the fact that the cars were assembled in the U.S. – not an implausible theory, although the Accord's overall quality seems unaffected and the car remains a paragon of reliability. Next to such solid assets and a mechanical performance that borders on perfection, one can easily overlook the Accord's lack of charisma, a shortcoming that doesn't quite apply to the coupe.

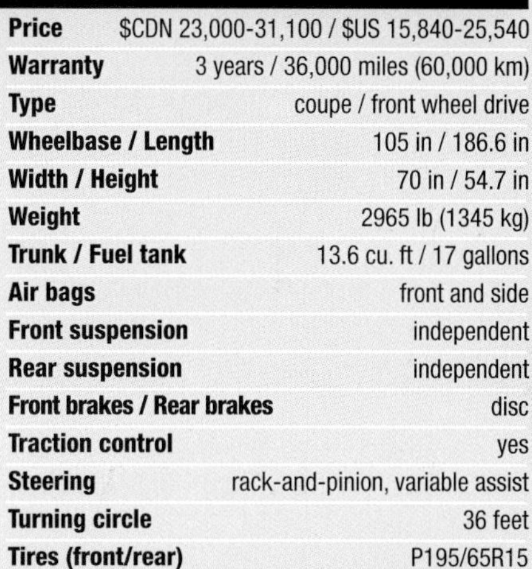

SPECIFICATIONS	LX
Price	$CDN 23,000-31,100 / $US 15,840-25,540
Warranty	3 years / 36,000 miles (60,000 km)
Type	coupe / front wheel drive
Wheelbase / Length	105 in / 186.6 in
Width / Height	70 in / 54.7 in
Weight	2965 lb (1345 kg)
Trunk / Fuel tank	13.6 cu. ft / 17 gallons
Air bags	front and side
Front suspension	independent
Rear suspension	independent
Front brakes / Rear brakes	disc
Traction control	yes
Steering	rack-and-pinion, variable assist
Turning circle	36 feet
Tires (front/rear)	P195/65R15

PERFORMANCE	
Engine	4L 2.3-liter VTEC
Transmission	5-speed manual
Horsepower	150 hp at 5700 rpm
Torque	152 lb-ft at 4900 rpm
Other engines	V6 3-liter 200 hp VTEC; 4L 2.3-liter 139 hp
Other transmission	4-speed automatic
Acceleration (0-60 mph)	9 sec
Maximum speed	130 mph (210 km/h)
Braking (60-0 mph)	128 feet (39 m)
Fuel consumption	22 mpg (10.3 L/100 km)

COMPETITION

• Altima • Camry • Legacy • Malibu • Mazda 626 • Sebring • Saturn LS

NEW FOR 2002

• LX models replaced by Special Edition models
• More complete equipment

RATING	(out of 5 stars)
Driveability	★★★½
Comfort	★★★★
Reliability	★★★★★
Roominess	★★★½
Winter driving rating	★★★½
Safety	★★★★
Resale value	★★★★★

HONDA CIVIC

Honda Raises the Bar

Despite its undeniable air of "gentrification," the new Honda Civic sticks hard and fast to its original philosophy of offering a reliable and practical vehicle to as many customers as it can reach. Redesigned last year for the seventh time since its introduction, the Civic has raised the bar once again in terms of security, comfort, cabin space and economy.

Obviously, bold looks are not what the Honda Civic is all about. Instead, the key idea is harmony, as demonstrated by the smooth integration of the front headlights and the taillights, precisely inserted into the fenders. The body panels are as tightly assembled as any superior, or more expensive, automobile. However, the coupe with its low roofline, slender lines and prominent taillights, looks outstanding.

The interior, too, is meticulously put together, boasting many storage areas. Gathered in a pod, the instruments are easy to read and controls are neatly arranged. The seats are bigger than in earlier models, and thus offer better support. Finally, the driver is treated to an excellent driving position.

Although the Civic's overall length has been shortened by a couple of inches, the cabin contains an extra 3 cubic feet, thanks mainly to ingenious engineering, and the car's added width. The new rear suspension configuration allows for a flatter floor which in turn provides two more inches of legroom for back-seat passenger. Furthermore, the bench can be folded 60/40, adding more space to an already generous-sized trunk. The only negative note here is the trunk's narrow opening, making access difficult.

Nice balance

The Civic comes in two models: two-door coupe and four-door sedan, both of which are available in a variety of trim levels: DX, LX and Si (coupe only). The base DX is pretty bare-boned, where even basic amenities such as central door locks, CD player and climate control are optional. Opt for the middle level LX and you get a tachometer, height-adjustable driver's seat, cruise control, many regular power-assisted amenities and ABS (sedan only). In addition to all this, the Si coupe comes with the more powerful VTEC

▲ PROS

- Excellent overall design • Improved comfort
- Attractive quality/price ratio
- Low consumption • Reliable mechanicals

▼ CONS

- ABS optional in Si model • Spartan DX versions
- Borderline engine power
- So-so tires

engine, 15-inch alloy wheels and a sunroof.

And on the road?

The base 1.6-liter engine has been upgraded to 1.7-liter, slightly lower than the competition. Lighter and more compact, it produces 115 horsepower, up from 106 previously, and 110 lb-ft of torque, up from 103 lb-ft. That's too little and passing power especially is insufficient as you try to overtake another vehicle. In the Si coupe, the VTEC delivers 127 horsepower and 114 lb-ft of torque at 700 fewer rpms than before. These modest increases seem all the more acceptable when you consider the roughly 5% gain in fuel economy.

As always, the engine turns over ever so smoothly and quietly, developing sufficient power under normal driving conditions. At low rpm, both engine options are perceptibly sluggish, although the VTEC asserts itself fairly quickly and is always eager to move up the rpm scale.

Steering is linear and well-tuned, and transmits road feel efficiently. The disc/drum brakes, as well as the ABS, react promptly to every command. This year's model has improved suspension, firmer and more effective, thanks to the increased rigidity of the antiroll bars. Finally, the manual transmission and the nicely linear clutch action are a match made in heaven, and even the clumsiest drivers can shift gears like a true-blue F1 driver.

The car is also noticeably quieter: the wind seems to slip discreetly by, so that noise, vibration and harshness have all been reduced, although not completely.

All in all, the new Honda Civic is quieter and more comfortable, if perhaps a little less agile than before. But it's still right up there as a leader in its class, thoroughly reliable and capable of providing miles of pleasurable, worry-free road travel.

Jean-Georges Laliberté

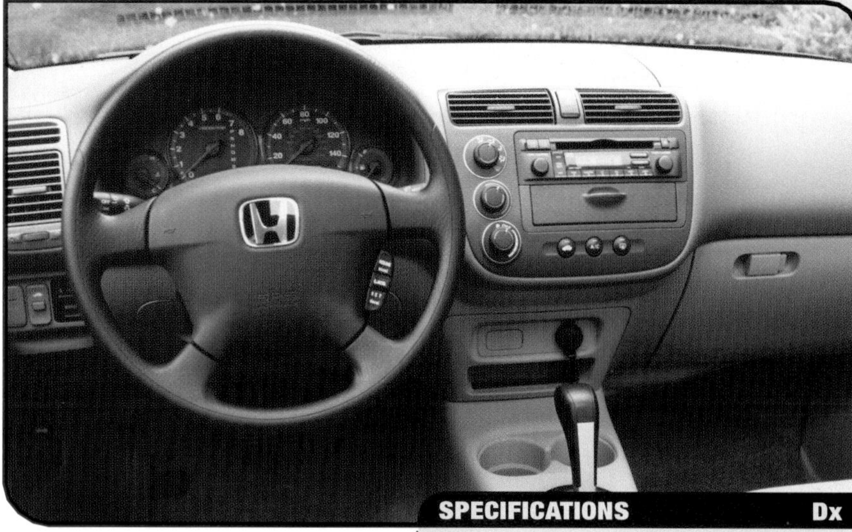

SPECIFICATIONS	**Dx**
Price	$CDN 15,900-19,900 / $US 13,200-17,350
Warranty	3 years / 36,000 miles (60,000 km)
Type	sedan / front wheel drive
Wheelbase / Length	103.1 in / 174.4 in
Width / Height	67.3 in / 56.7 in
Weight	2425 lb (1100 kg)
Trunk / Fuel tank	12.9 cu. ft / 13 gallons
Air bags	front
Front suspension	independent
Rear suspension	independent
Front brakes / Rear brakes	disc / drum (ABS LX Si)
Traction control	no
Steering	rack-and-pinion, variable assist
Turning circle	34 feet
Tires (front/rear)	P185/70R14
PERFORMANCE	
Engine	4L 1.7 liter
Transmission	5-speed manual
Horsepower	115 hp at 6100 rpm
Torque	110 lb-ft at 4500 rpm
Other engines	4L 1.7 liter 127 hp
Other transmission	4-speed automatic
Acceleration (0-60 mph)	9.2 s; 8.7 s (127 hp)
Maximum speed	115 mph (185 km/h)
Braking (60-0 mph)	143 feet (43.5 m)
Fuel consumption	36 mpg (6.3 L/100 km)

COMPETITION

• Daewoo Nubira • Ford Focus • Hyundai Elantra • Mazda Protegé • Nissan Sentra • Toyota Corolla

NEW FOR 2002

• Rear stabilizer bar • 15-inch steel wheels
• New accessories

RATING	**(out of 5 stars)**
Driveability	★★★½
Comfort	★★★½
Reliability	★★★★½
Roominess	★★★½
Winter driving rating	★★★
Safety	★★★½
Resale value	★★★★★

HONDA CR-V

HONDA **CR-V**

A Million and One Reasons

With worldwide sales amounting to more than one million units since it first appeared in January 1997, the Honda CR-V is the undisputed leader in the compact sport-utility category, particularly in the United States and Canada. Quite clearly, customers don't seem to worry about the CR-V's sluggish engine or its all-wheel-drive system, a feature that seems better suited to the paved road than off the beaten track. Instead, they like the CR-V's handling, excellent fuel economy and, of course, Honda's renowned reliability.

Rather than tamper with a winning formula, Honda chose instead to lightly modify the CR-V, correcting old weaknesses and retaining the strong points. While no one will blame Honda for playing it safe, the automaker could certainly have afforded to make more substantial changes.

Something old, something new

The first-generation CR-V's biggest drawback was its meager power output (see the *Auto Guide* SUV comparison test in the first part of this guidebook). Although basically reliable, the 2.0-liter 4-cylinder engine had the bad luck to be noisy and sluggish. Horsepower has been increased from 147 to 160 for the second-generation model, thanks to Honda's newly developed Variable Valve Timing and Lift Electronic Control system (iVTEC). Also playing a key role are the Variable Timing Control (VTC) and similar engine refinements. It would probably have been just as easy for engineers to give the CR-V a V6 engine, since much of the competition now comes equipped with V6 power. As things turned out, however, Honda decided to reserve the V6 for a larger model based on the Acura MDX, itself a descendant of the Odyssey minivan.

Customer rules

In any case, the 13 extra horses were enough to improve the CR-V's acceleration and passing power, as well as reduce engine noise. Cabin noise, too, has been significantly lowered. And while the interior space has slightly increased, there is less front legroom, especially on the passenger side. The front seats, on the other hand, are broader and more comfortable. The rear seats can slide forward and back, allowing more legroom for their occupants:

▲ PROS

• Better sound insulation • Ingenious manual brake lever • More comfortable seats • More powerful engine

▼ CONS

• Cheap seat coverings • Design practically unchanged • Limited legroom (front cabin) • Right-hand side tailgate hinges

Both transmissions have been revised – the manual box gets shorter throws while the automatic is smoother and now boasts a Grade Logic Control system. Finally, the CR-V's new platform offers more torsional and bending rigidity, improving ride quality and crash safety in the process. What remains unchanged is the CR-V's Real Time 4WD system, a set of hydraulic pumps that automatically transfer torque to the rear wheels if there's a loss of traction at the front.

Macho in black

The new CR-V's exterior reflects the same "evolutionary" approach as the drivetrain. The overall lines remain more or less unchanged, although the front end got a few alterations – particularly the bumper, which is now slightly raised in the center to accommodate an imposing air scoop. The entire unit is made of macho-looking black plastic. And speaking of black plastic, a strip of this material runs along the windshield all the way to the rear on each side of the roof. Finally, the two-part tailgate has been replaced by a single-piece element with hinges on the right hand side. The rear glass window opens individually.

Inside the cabin, the dashboard design is less austere with a vertical center console incorporating the audio system in its upper part and the three oversized, user-friendly climate control buttons in the lower. The ingenious hand brake lever is located at the left.

On the road, both driver and passengers will discover a livelier vehicle, with better sound insulation and a suspension that expertly absorbs every bump or pothole. What's more, steering is so precise that cornering is a snap. All things considered, I'd say that handling and driving pleasure have increased by 25%. Be that as it may, the "new and improved" CR-V still would have failed to dominate *The Auto Guide* comparison test.

Denis Duquet

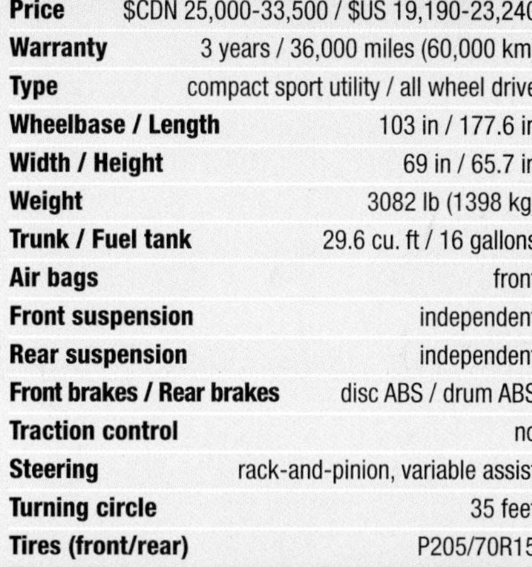

SPECIFICATIONS

Price	$CDN 25,000-33,500 / $US 19,190-23,240
Warranty	3 years / 36,000 miles (60,000 km)
Type	compact sport utility / all wheel drive
Wheelbase / Length	103 in / 177.6 in
Width / Height	69 in / 65.7 in
Weight	3082 lb (1398 kg)
Trunk / Fuel tank	29.6 cu. ft / 16 gallons
Air bags	front
Front suspension	independent
Rear suspension	independent
Front brakes / Rear brakes	disc ABS / drum ABS
Traction control	no
Steering	rack-and-pinion, variable assist
Turning circle	35 feet
Tires (front/rear)	P205/70R15

PERFORMANCE

Engine	4L 2.0 liter
Transmission	4-speed automatic
Horsepower	146 hp at 6200 rpm
Torque	133 lb-ft at 4300 rpm
Other engines	none
Other transmission	5-speed manual
Acceleration (0-60 mph)	10.7 sec
Maximum speed	109 mph (175 km/h)
Braking (60-0 mph)	143 feet (43.6 m)
Fuel consumption	19 mpg (11.8 L/100 km)

COMPETITION

- Escape/Tribute • Forester • RAV4 • SantaFe • Tracker/Vitara •

NEW FOR 2002

- Some minor modifications

RATING	**(out of 5 stars)**
Driveability	★★★½
Comfort	★★★½
Reliability	★★★★
Roominess	★★★½
Winter driving rating	★★★★½
Safety	★★★★
Resale value	★★★★

HONDA INSIGHT

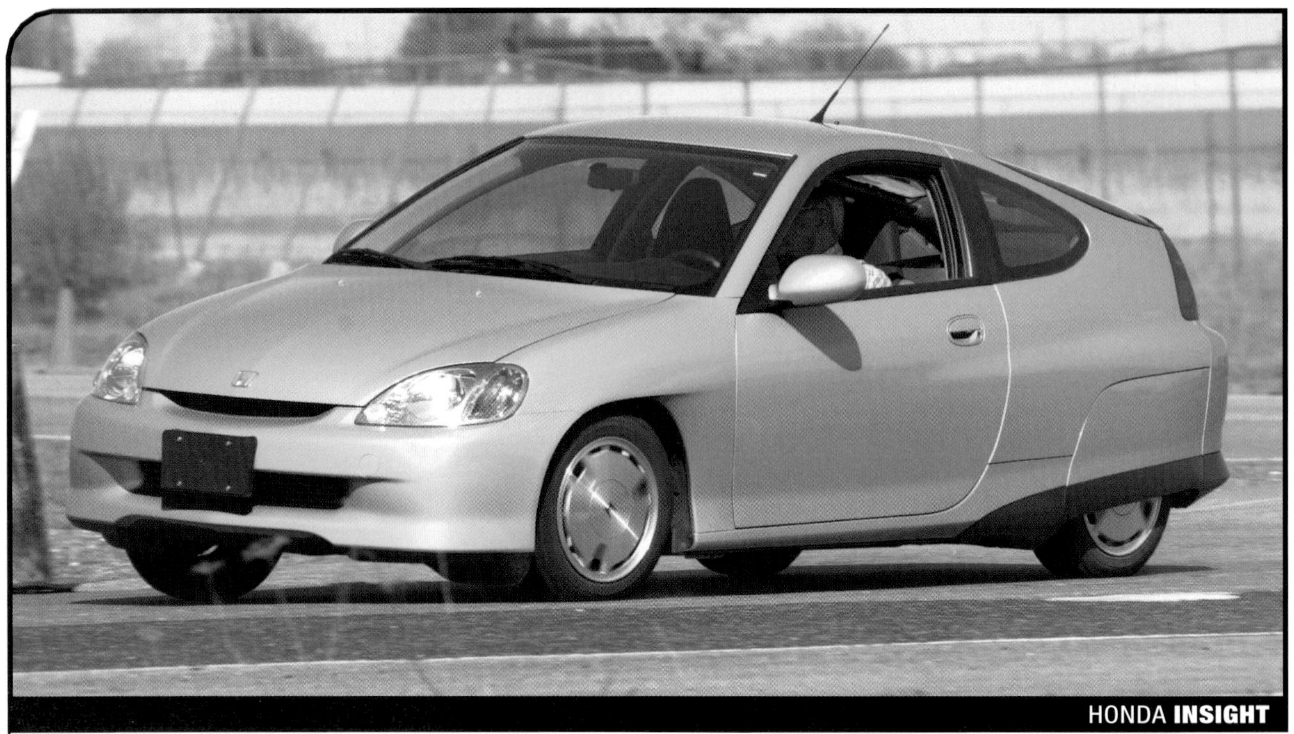
HONDA **INSIGHT**

Where are the Buyers?

Now that we desperately need them, where are all those eloquent defenders of the planet who never get tired of protesting against automobile pollution? That's a personal question, but it might as well have come from Honda, on behalf of its gasoline-electric hybrid car, the ecologically-friendly Insight. As far as the Insight – and, for that matter, its more practical "colleague," the Toyota Prius – is concerned, the anticipated support from potential "green" buyers has amounted to little more than lip service. Is the Insight's poor sales record simply a reflection of an environmental snub, or are there other factors at play?

To get to the bottom of such seeming indifference, we "borrowed" one of the first Insights ever to hit the market and we gave it an extended road test spanning an entire year. After roughly 12,500 miles (20,000 km), and despite our nagging doubts about the car's mechanical reliability, we're pleased to report there were no nasty surprises of any kind, whether under the hood or anywhere else inside the car.

Integrated Motor Assist (IMA)

At the heart of the Insight's power is the Honda-designed Integrated Motor Assist (IMA), combining a 67-hp 1.0-liter 3-cylinder VTEC-E gas engine with a 6-hp permanent-magnet electric motor/generator, itself powered by 16 nickel-metal hydrid batteries located under the rear floor. The electric motor serves as a backup for the gasoline engine, the exact opposite of the system used in the Toyota Prius. In other words, the Insight scoots forward with the help of its 3-cylinder engine, eventually using the electric motor further along the road. The Prius, on the other hand, gets going thanks to its 288 volts before "sipping" the first drop of fuel from its tank. As a result, the Prius is more economical in city traffic while the Insight does better on the highway.

Fuel economy has its own cost

Our test Insight delivered a whopping 46 mpg on average, and we could have done even better had we practiced "economy-conscious" driving. Impressive though it may sound, this figure shouldn't overshadow the fact that a lightened and more streamlined Honda Civic can perform just as well, without having to resort to the complexity and extra cost of a hybrid powertrain.

▲ PROS

- Adequate performance • Easy to drive
- Excellent engine start in winter • Fun to drive
- Fuel economy • Reliable mechanicals

▼ CONS

- High price • Ill-adapted front suspension
- Limited rear visibility • Poor pickup (acceleration)
- Spartan comfort • Worrisome dimensions

But the cost of driving what essentially amounts to a 2-seater includes more than just its purchase price, high as it is already. You see, the Insight isn't exactly well adapted to harsh winters, and its small size doesn't inspire confidence in a landscape over-crowded with 4X4s and similar motorized mastodons. "I feel extremely vulnerable aboard this mini Honda," wrote a test driver in the car's logbook.

Nor is comfort the Insight's strong point. The front suspension is incredibly stiff, as another test driver observed. His logbook entry: "The suspension is utterly ill-adapted. It pounds against the road, drags, and bounces around. After some 9,000 miles (15,000 km), the noise becomes so loud you'd think the whole thing was falling apart. The system needs work, from A to Z." To be fair, though, the suspension problem was compounded by the pressure of the front tires, which was found to be too high after the car had been on the road for thousands of miles. On the other hand, once the pressure problem was corrected, another problem cropped up – the shock absorbers froze solid in cold weather.

And as if all this were not enough, the car's enormous doors and very low seats make it tricky to get in and out. And don't rely on the Insight's rear visibility when parking, because there is practically none, especially in winter.

Good engine, bad car

Despite this storm of criticism, Honda is to be commended for the technological *tour*

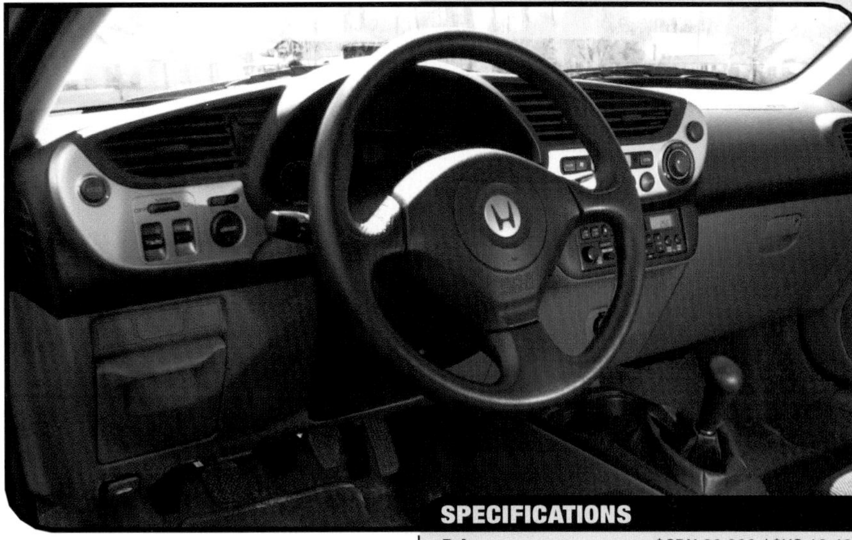

de force that is its Integrated Motoring Assist (IMA) system. Despite all its sophistication, the system consistently performed like a Swiss clock. The engine was perhaps a tad rough, but it never stalled, glacial weather notwithstanding. Performance, though not dazzling, was respectable, and so was roadholding. As a bonus, the car was actually fun to drive on snowy roads.

In a nutshell, those were the impressions of the members of *The Auto Guide* who shared in the Insight's 12,500-mile road test. Our collective verdict: Good engine, bad car. Let's hope that Honda will find a way to apply this first-rate hybrid engine technology to more practical models, so it can meet the everyday needs of the majority of its customers.

Jacques Duval

SPECIFICATIONS	
Price	$CDN 26,000 / $US 19,420
Warranty	3 years/ 36,000 miles (60,000 km)
Type	2-seat coupe / front wheel drive
Wheelbase / Length	95.5 in / 155.1 in
Width / Height	53.3 in / 66.7 in
Weight	1878 lb (852 kg)
Trunk / Fuel tank	5.0 cu. ft / 11 gallons
Air bags	front
Front suspension	independent
Rear suspension	semi-rigid rear axle
Front brakes / Rear brakes	disc / drum ABS
Traction control	no
Steering	rack-and-pinion, elect. assist
Turning circle	31 feet
Tires (front/rear)	P165/65R14

PERFORMANCE	
Engine	3L 1.0-liter + permanent-magnet
Transmission	electric motor
Horsepower	5-speed manual
Torque	67 hp at 5700 rpm + 6 hp (el. motor)
Other engines	66 lb-ft at 4800 rpm
Other transmission	none
Acceleration (0-60 mph)	11.2 sec
Maximum speed	109 mph (175 km/h)
Braking (60-0 mph)	n.a.
Fuel consumption	44.5 mpg (5.1 L/100 km)

COMPETITION

- Toyota Prius

NEW FOR 2002

- One new color (blue)

RATING	(out of 5 stars)
Driveability	★★★
Comfort	★★
Reliability	★★★★
Roominess	★★
Winter driving rating	★★
Safety	★★★
Resale value	★★★★★

HONDA ODYSSEY

HONDA **ODYSSEY**

The Benchmark

Last year, the strong comeback registered by a new generation of Chrysler minivans was reason enough to assume that the Detroit automaker was finally going to steal the thunder back from the increasingly popular Honda Odyssey. After all, both the Dodge Caravan and the Chrysler Town & Country boasted several interesting innovations, not to mention the irresistible option of owning the most powerful engine ever offered in the minivan market. As it turned out, none of the fuss put a dent in the public's enthusiasm for the Odyssey.

Honda's popularity didn't just grow out of thin air. If the carmaker enjoys some of the highest ratings in each category, it's because of its quality automobiles, whose proven reliability, good road manners and driving pleasure turn their owners into convincing Honda boosters. During a comparison test of minivans in 1999, for instance, a participating couple were so impressed by the overall quality of the Odyssey that their opinions about the other entries were seriously affected.

And yet this particular minivan, the biggest model in the Honda stable, is not without flaws.

Nondescript styling

With the possible exception of the Civic Hatchback, most of Honda's automobiles marketed in North America sport unexciting silhouettes. The Accord is known for its "drab" profile, the Prelude's proportions look out of whack, while the Civic becomes "gentrified" with each new generation. The Odyssey is nothing to write home about either.

Its silhouette is standard and subdued, with flat sidewalls, relatively angular wings and a protection strip separating the upper and lower body halves. Yet the general effect exudes character, thanks to the plunging hoodline, the grille lower down, and the wrap-around rear lights which confer an imposing and dignified air. After three years, the minivan still manages to look refreshing.

Ever reliable

Same thing for the cabin, although some would say it looks far too straightforward. But it's the sort of straightforwardness that you never get tired of. The dashboard looks plain with its array of display panels arranged in the shape of an inverted, roundish U. In the center are the climate and sound insulation con-

▲ PROS

• Powerful engine • Flawless finish • Predictable road manners • Comfortable suspension • Versatile interior

▼ CONS

• Dull looks • Infiltration of road noise inside the cabin • Slow power side doors • High price • Noisy engine

trols. Almost everything is easy to see and reach, the exceptions being the control for the exterior mirrors, which is blocked by the steering wheel; the storage compartment and the 12-volt electrical plug, which are located too far down and hard to reach – in fact, the plug is partly obstructed by the carpet. The portable car desk between the front seats can be eliminated to facilitate access to the rear, although to do so, you'll have to find another spot for the cupholders.

In the rear, the middle bench is only moderately comfortable. Even though you can convert it into two bucket seats by sliding it apart, that's easier said than done. (Mazda incorporated the idea into its MPV model with better results.) The third-row bench can be folded into a recess in the floor – a neat idea, although this configuration causes road noise to infiltrate the cabin. Storage space for the headrests, too, needs some rethinking.

Hot contender

As expected from Honda, the Odyssey's performance is above average in terms of steering precision as well as handling and stability during cornering. Also typical of Honda, however, the engine is noisier than average, braking spongy, and the automatic transmission sluggish when shifting from 3rd to 4th gear. On the other hand, the gearbox's "downshift logic" – a feature that detects uneven road conditions and reacts accordingly – remains the industry standard.

If only one person is on board, suspension may seem a little firm. But such firmness is greatly appreciated when the Odyssey is loaded down with passengers and their luggage. The suspension absorbs all bumps in stride and doesn't jerk around corners. The Odyssey's hauling capabilities, on the other hand, are less impressive.

Despite its snail-pace automatic side doors, stark cabin and austere overall looks, the Honda Odyssey is equipped with countless mechanical qualities and features that make it a hot contender in the race for best minivan in the market.

Denis Duquet

SPECIFICATIONS	
Price	$CDN 31,900-34,900 / $US 24,340-28,840
Warranty	3 years / 36,000 miles (60,000 km)
Type	minivan / front wheel drive
Wheelbase / Length	118 in / 201.2 in
Width / Height	75.6 in / 70 in
Weight	4288 lb (1945 kg)
Trunk / Fuel tank	25.1 cu. ft / 20 gallons
Air bags	front
Front suspension	independent
Rear suspension	independent
Front brakes / Rear brakes	disc / drum ABS
Traction control	yes (EX)
Steering	rack-and-pinion, power assist
Turning circle	38 feet
Tires (front/rear)	P215/65R16

PERFORMANCE	
Engine	V6 3.5-liter
Transmission	4-speed automatic
Horsepower	210 hp at 5200 rpm
Torque	229 lb-ft at 4300 rpm
Other engines	none
Other transmission	none
Acceleration (0-60 mph)	10.4 sec
Maximum speed	118 mph (190 km/h)
Braking (60-0 mph)	139 feet (42.4 m)
Fuel consumption	21 mpg (10.8 L/100 km)

COMPETITION

• Chevrolet Venture/Pont. Montana • Dodge Caravan • Ford Windstar • Toyota Sienna • VW EuroVan

NEW FOR 2002

• 5-speed automatic transmission • More powerful engine • Rear disc brakes • Softened suspension

RATING	(out of 5 stars)
Driveability	★★★
Comfort	★★★★
Reliability	★★★★
Roominess	★★★★½
Winter driving rating	★★★½
Safety	★★★★
Resale value	★★★★

HONDA S2000

HONDA **S2000**

Athletic Two-Seater

A roadster is, almost by definition, not for the faint of the heart. The feelings aroused by road-testing one of these speedy cars release a powerful rush as the driver puts the S2000 through its impressive paces. Here is a personal report on one such occasion.

The styling is rather conservative, ditto the construction. Nothing revolutionary. No super-sophisticated materials. But what an engine! The only mass-produced car engine with a red line at around 9000 rpm. No turbo or turbocharger, but a mere little 2.4-liter just like the Ford Focus or the Daewoo Nubira. But instead of 120 or 130 hp, this little Honda number churns out 240 hp. How? Aluminum, four valves per cylinder, twin overhead cams, variable timing control (VTEC). But above all, the know-how of one of the best engine makers in the world, an experience drawn from motorcycle and car racing at the highest levels.

Heavy metal

On first contact, after having depressed the red starter button located left of the (non-adjustable) steering column, the "small" 4-cylinder doesn't reveal anything unusual. It even sounds ordinary. A rather banal rumble. You depress the clutch; a light pressure. First gear. Ah ha! I feel something happening. Gearshift throw is short and feels "very direct." It's even better than my Miata. I increase speed normally. Click, click goes the shifter. The next gear comes easily, a mere flick of the wrist.

A few minutes later, the engine has reached operating temperature, I choose a small winding road leading up to a ski resort. I get into third, and floor the accelerator – 4000, 5000, 6000 rpm. Suddenly, the engine comes alive. The rumble is now a screech. It is like a superbike. It's now 8000 rpm, I slip into fourth. I glance at the digital speedometer to realize that the speed has soared perilously. Fifth gear, I back off just before the curves. Superb, but careful now, the steering is diabolically precise. Finesse is a must. So is concentration.

What an engine!

I turn around in the ski resort's parking lot and come down the hill. Not as fast this time, but just enough to test

▲ PROS

- Exceptional engine • Excellent braking
- Great shift lever feel • Remarkable roadholding
- Stiff chassis

▼ CONS

- Limited use • Poor bottom-end torque
- Tight space

the braking. And what braking! It's effective, immediate and reassuring. And as a sign of good breeding, the ABS intervenes only at the very limit.

This morning gallop is followed by a more easy-going drive in the countryside plus a few miles of highway. Steady, with little sensitivity to lateral wind, the Honda roadster reveals some shortcomings: wind noise, a soft-top which flaps if a window is open, a very firm ride.

Yielding to critics, Honda has fitted the power soft-top with a heated rear window for 2002. Bravo! Also, the two bucket seats give excellent support, but if you're an XL size, perhaps you ought to look elsewhere – or go on a diet. Interior space is snug and the engine, mounted further to the rear than normal in a front-engined car, means that the bell housing encroaches heavily inside the cockpit, covered by an unfortunate choice of carpet. As for the sparse storage space, the 2002 edition has two extra nets on the inside door. Effectively, the trunk is the carryall, where you'll also find the semi-rigid soft-top cover that is supposed to hide the soft-top when it's not in use. The moral of this story: travel light.

As a test of Honda's mechanical capability, it's a success. No other carmaker offers such power per cubic inch. Torque, however, is much too low at low rpm, hampering throttle response. This may be a serious handicap in the face of the German roadsters, and detracts from driving enjoyment. One must constantly flog this Honda engine to bring out its power and torque, a pain in the neck after a while. Don't forget that you'll need to store the car in winter, because without a limited slip differential, stability control, or the $4,000+ hardtop, the S2000 should really be classified as WG (winter garaged).

Finally, if your heart is really set on a Honda S2000 and you want your money's worth, you better join a sports car club and attend all the track days you can find. Only in that setting will you fully enjoy, in complete safety, this athletic two-seater with the powerful personality.

Alain Raymond

SPECIFICATIONS	
Price	$CDN 48,000 / $US 32,740
Warranty	3 years / 36,000 miles (60,000 km)
Type	roadster / rear wheel drive
Wheelbase / Length	94.5 in / 162.2 in
Width / Height	68.9 in / 50.4 in
Weight	2809 lb (1274 kg)
Trunk / Fuel tank	5.4 cu. ft / 13 gallons
Air bags	front
Front suspension	independent
Rear suspension	independent
Front brakes / Rear brakes	disc
Traction control	no
Steering	rack-and-pinion, power assist
Turning circle	35 feet
Tires (front/rear)	P205/55R16 / P225/50R16

PERFORMANCE	
Engine	4L 2.0-liter
Transmission	6-speed manual
Horsepower	240 hp at 8300 rpm
Torque	153 lb-ft at 7500 rpm
Other engines	none
Other transmission	none
Acceleration (0-60 mph)	6.8 sec
Maximum speed	149 mph (240 km/h)
Braking (60-0 mph)	120 feet (36.5 m)
Fuel consumption	21.2 mpg (10.7 L/100 km)

COMPETITION

• Audi TT Roadster • BMW Z3
• Mercedes-Benz SLK320 • Porsche Boxster

NEW FOR 2002

• Glass window with defogger • More powerful stereo system • New colors • New wheels

RATING	(out of 5 stars)
Driveability	★★★★
Comfort	★★★½
Reliability	★★★★½
Roominess	★★
Winter driving rating	★
Safety	★★★
Resale value	★★★★

HYUNDAI ACCENT

HYUNDAI **ACCENT**

Getting Better All the Time

As Hyundai automobiles evolve, their quality, style and technical concept improve at a pace that surprises even their most ardent defenders. If it's true that the first Hyundai models were more rustic than elegant, and more fragile than even 1960s British cars, then the constant progress achieved by the automaker during the past two decades seems even more remarkable.

Take the Accent. It has come a long way from the lackluster Pony and the Excel models. Back then, all those small economy cars from the Hyundai stable had going for them was their low price, which undersold all the competition. The arrival of the first-generation Accent in 1995 signaled a "new and improved" philosophy in terms of mechanical refinement and manufacturing. And these improvements have continued unabated, as the Accent's 2000 model demonstrates.

As designers set about transforming the Accent, they managed to give it a more sophisticated allure without sacrificing its qualities as a sub-compact. The GSi coupe, a hatchback, is a far cry from the Accent GT it replaces. Aerodynamic headlights, an egg-shaped grille and imposing rear spoiler contribute to its smart new look and emphasize its sporty aspirations. The cabin is well appointed, made even smarter-looking by improved quality material and finish. While the rear seats are comfortable enough, they are hard to get into.

With its leather-covered shift knob, its instrument panels displayed against a white background and sporty seats, the GSi really looks the part. Climate controls are a fair size and easy to reach; but the radio has tiny buttons that are hard to read. The oversized steering hub stores the car's only airbag; the fact that the passenger is not entitled to such protection is an unforgivable omission in the 2002 model.

Experience talks

The GSi boasts a 4-cylinder,1.6-liter engine producing 106 horsepower, whereas the standard GS hatchback comes with a 1.5-liter engine producing 92 hp that should deliver better performance. All versions come with the standard 5-speed manual transmission, while the automatic is optional.

On the road, this little Korean number defends itself respectably. The engine is relatively noisy, but not unpleasantly so.

▲ PROS

- 1.6-liter engine • Good road manners
- Precise steering • Decent finish
- Excellent quality/price ratio

▼ CONS

- Listless 1.5-liter engine • Sluggish automatic gearbox • Nondescript tires • No passenger-side airbag • Difficult to use radio

The manual gearbox shifts quickly and smoothly, with good spacing between ratios, unlike the automatic transmission, which is slow and listless. Some say the automatic gearbox is adaptive, I say it needs improving. In any case, it doesn't suit the 1.5-liter engine, and hampers performance. It is naturally enough better suited to the 1.6-liter engine.

Without being overly sporty, the Accent GSi offers an above-average mix of comfort, performance and driving pleasure. Steering is precise, letting the driver thoroughly exploit the car's driveability. The rigid chassis ensures good road manners while not quite allowing all-out sports-car driving. Body roll during cornering is much better controlled in the GSi than in its weaker cousins. Braking is adequate, although ABS is unfortunately not available.

Overall, the Accent GSi is a worthy contender in the small economy car category, especially considering its low price and the fairly complete equipment you'll get in return. All you need to do next is upgrade the silly radio buttons, install a passenger–side airbag and add ABS brakes, and the car will be as good as any in its class.

Don't forget the sedan!

While hatchback models are often more popular in this category, they shouldn't overshadow the Accent Sedan, one of the most economical cars in its class. Time was when its only rival was the Suzuki Esteem. Today, the Accent Sedan also has to contend with Daewoo Lanos and Kia Rios.

Equipped with the 106 hp engine, a 5-speed manual transmission as standard, the Accent Sedan is an honest car whose quasi-complete equipment and modern lines should attract buyers. But then Hyundai has been on the market for less than 20 years, a clear advantage over its main competitors.

Given Hyundai's perpetual evolution, the two Accent models have a lot going for them.

Denis Duquet

SPECIFICATIONS	
Price	$CDN 12,395-14,495 / $US 9,494-10,394
Warranty	3 years / 36,000 miles (60,000 km)
Type	hatchback / front wheel drive
Wheelbase / Length	96 in / 166.5 in
Width / Height	65.7 in / 54.7 in
Weight	2187 lb (992 kg)
Trunk / Fuel tank	13.2 cu. ft / 12 gallons
Air bags	front
Front suspension	independent
Rear suspension	independent
Front brakes / Rear brakes	disc / drum
Traction control	no
Steering	rack-and-pinion, power assist
Turning circle	32 feet
Tires (front/rear)	P185/60R14

PERFORMANCE	
Engine	4L 1.6-liter
Transmission	5-speed manual
Horsepower	106 hp at 5800 rpm
Torque	107 lb-ft at 3000 rpm
Other engines	4L 1.5-liter 92 hp
Other transmission	4-speed automatic
Acceleration (0-60 mph)	10.5 sec
Maximum speed	112 mph (180 km/h)
Braking (60-0 mph)	142 feet (43.2 m)
Fuel consumption	28.7 mpg (7.9 L/100 km)

COMPETITION

- Daewoo Lanos • Honda Civic • Suzuki Swift
- Toyota Echo

NEW FOR 2002

No major change

RATING	(out of 5 stars)
Driveability	★★★
Comfort	★★★
Reliability	★★★
Roominess	★★★
Winter driving rating	★★★★½
Safety	★★★
Resale value	★★★

HYUNDAI ELANTRA HYUNDAI ELANTRA GT

HYUNDAI **ELANTRA**

Getting Better All the Time

Last year, Hyundai presented an all-new version of the Elantra, whose launch in 1992 demonstrated that the South Korean company was more than just a maker of budget cars for the lower end of the market. The new Elantra is quieter and displays greatly improved road manners, along with a slicker and more refined exterior – as befits Hyundai's tradition of providing significant improvements to each new automobile generation.

At the revamped Elantra's unveiling, Hyundai announced its intention to bring out a hatchback version – the Elantra GT – in 2002. The new model shares the same platform, dashboard and a few other mechanical components with the Elantra sedan, but it also boasts many distinctive elements of its own.

The most obvious difference is the tailgate, which blends in nicely with the GT's design, thanks mainly to the longer-than-usual side glass panels. Other distinctive characteristics include the black-colored grille and moldings and the streamlined rear glass window. However, this same rear glass panel offers a deformed view of what's behind the driver, making the cars appear bigger than they really are.

In the cockpit, both the steering wheel and the gearshift knob are leather-wrapped, while the dashboard sports a magenta-colored background light. Instruments are easy to read in daytime or at night, but not the analog information center located below the speedometer. The numbers are infuriatingly tiny and the control button is positively Lilliputian. Small, too, are the GT's radio buttons, which must have been specifically designed for a baby's fingers. The radio itself leaves much to be desired, a "corporate" variety that's also offered in several other Hyundai models. It's so complicated that you need a degree in electronics to operate it.

Happy compromise

The front seats are adequate for grownups of all sizes, and the rear bench comfortable and easy to get to. Headroom, however, is on the snug side if you're more than six feet tall. And by the way, the quality of the materials used is excellent for a car in this price range.

▲ PROS

• ABS brakes • Adequate suspension • Competitive price • Nice exterior • Practical tailgate

▼ CONS

• Clutch sometimes hard to use • Illegible trip odometer • Inadequate headroom (rear) • No side-impact airbag • Hard-to-use radio

The GT's 140-hp 2.0-liter DOHC engine is user friendly, perfectly competent and has a nice, comforting sound. With a manual gearbox, however, watch out for the clutch, which isn't always willing to cooperate. On the other hand, gear changing is precise and the leather-wrapped shift knob is a pleasure to handle. As for its road manners, the GT falls a tad short of its overblown GT appellation. All the same, the Elantra GT is a decent car, quite capable of fulfilling individual and family needs. No doubt you'll find it fun to drive, especially with its European-tuned, fully independent suspension.

What about the sedan?

No, I haven't forgotten the sedan. It's just that the GT and its tailgate are such big news for 2002. Who knows, the year 2003 might even witness the return of the station wagon!

Entirely revamped in 2001, the 4-door Elantra exhibits no major change for 2002. Its exterior, inspired by both British and German styling, is congenially refreshing, yet instinctively recognizable.

But the Elantra's premier quality is its overall balance. Its 140-hp 2.0-liter engine is smoother, more durable and user friendly than in the previous-generation model. You may find fault at highway speeds or when passing, but all in all it performs reasonably well. The 4-speed automatic gearbox has dramatically improved, so that shifting is smoothness personified.

True to Hyundai's philosophy of offering customers more for less, the Elantra has been largely responsible for the South Korean automaker's spectacular market grab over the past two years. The new Elantra GT has already revealed itself as following faithfully in the sedan's "footsteps," virtually ensuring Hyundai's further growth.

Denis Duquet

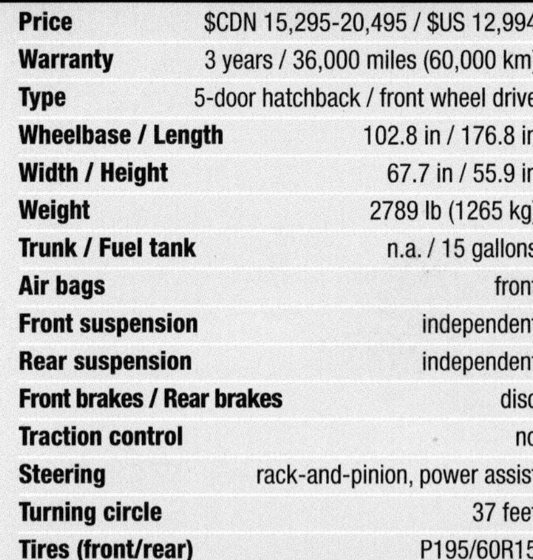

SPECIFICATIONS	GT
Price	$CDN 15,295-20,495 / $US 12,994
Warranty	3 years / 36,000 miles (60,000 km)
Type	5-door hatchback / front wheel drive
Wheelbase / Length	102.8 in / 176.8 in
Width / Height	67.7 in / 55.9 in
Weight	2789 lb (1265 kg)
Trunk / Fuel tank	n.a. / 15 gallons
Air bags	front
Front suspension	independent
Rear suspension	independent
Front brakes / Rear brakes	disc
Traction control	no
Steering	rack-and-pinion, power assist
Turning circle	37 feet
Tires (front/rear)	P195/60R15

PERFORMANCE	
Engine	2.0-liter DOHC 16 valves
Transmission	5-speed manual
Horsepower	140 hp at 6000 rpm
Torque	133 lb-ft at 4800 rpm
Other engines	none
Other transmission	4-speed automatic
Acceleration (0-60 mph)	10.7 sec
Maximum speed	118 mph (190 km/h)
Braking (60-0 mph)	n.a.
Fuel consumption	27.7 mpg (8.2 L/100 km)

COMPETITION

- Cavalier/Sunfire • Civic • Corolla • Focus • Neon • Protegé • Saturn SL • Sentra • Spectra

NEW FOR 2002

- New GT model

RATING	(out of 5 stars)
Driveability	★★★½
Comfort	★★★½
Reliability	★★★★
Roominess	★★★½
Winter driving rating	★★★
Safety	★★★
Resale value	★★★½

HYUNDAI **SANTAFE**

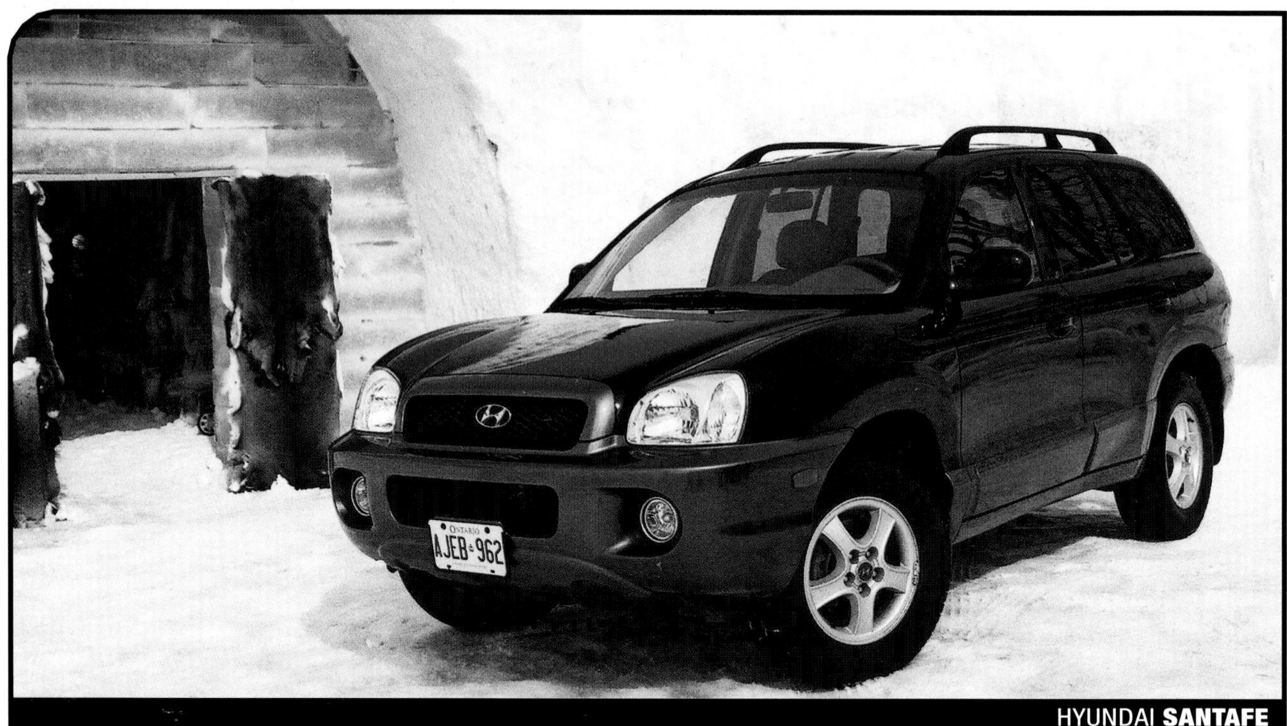

HYUNDAI **SANTAFE**

Be Careful Off the Beaten Track

If you're in the market for a 4X4 look-alike, the Hyundai SantaFe is for you. Trendy looks aside, this model lacks the usual SUV qualities while inheriting some of its flaws. On the other hand, its roadholding capability is more like that of an ordinary car, and as such provides better overall comfort than its SUV competitors.

And take heart, because we really know what we're talking about here. The SantaFe was the subject of an *Auto Guide* in-depth test-drive for more than 6000 miles. The first 5000 miles went well enough, but beyond that it was another story. First, oil started to leak from the front axle, quickly turning into a thick white smoke as it came in contact with the exhaust pipe. Once the gasket had been replaced, another leak developed – this time in the area of the differential – which required the addition of a gasket where none had been before. Our test drivers all noticed body rattles on rough roads. The noise, though hard to pinpoint, seemed to come from the rear seat area.

All-Wheel-Drive Station Wagon

In terms of overall reliability, our SantaFe was not without flaws, but that's to be expected since it is Hyundai's first venture into the specialized world of SUVs. Still, there's no escaping the fact that the Korean 4X4 felt more like a big station wagon car than an SUV.

That said, the most serious shortcoming in our test model (GLS) was unquestionably its lack of a limited slip differential, now available and – trust me – absolutely essential. Without it, and especially if you're an intrepid cross-country type who enjoys venturing off the beaten track, make sure your cell phone is handy, along with the number of the nearest towing company.

Not there yet!

As for driveability, the SantaFe is an all-wheel-drive vehicle, boasting a double viscous coupling that normally splits power 60/40 between the front and rear axles. This percentage varies according to driving conditions. Even so, our test model seemed ill-equipped for slippery surfaces. Following a big snowstorm, it could hardly make it up a gentle slope because one of the wheels kept spinning

▲ PROS

• Affordable price • Trendy looks • Above-average overall comfort • Independent rear suspension • Spaciousness

▼ CONS

• Limited traction • Poor power-to-weight ratio • Gas guzzler • Body rattles • Sub-par radio

aimlessly. In winter or on bumpy roads, the SantaFe isn't quite in its element. Worse, it guzzles gas, with only 17 mpg (13.6 L / 100km). That would have been fine if the car's 2.7-liter V6 engine, mounted transversely, and its automatic transmission had been a little more cooperative as we tried to pass another car. Instead, the 181 horsepower engine did not seem quite up to the task, as we couldn't even scoot 0-60 mph in less than 10 seconds. I guess with a total weight of 3719 lbs (1687 kg) to propel, the V6 certainly had "its hands full."

Flaws as qualities

The SantaFe's shortcomings as an SUV can in fact turn into advantages as a touring car. Built on a car platform (the same as the Sonata), the SantaFe is more comfortable to drive than its competitors and has better roadholding than other cars in its class. Its independent rear suspension certainly helps when it comes to roadholding. The SantaFe's generous dimensions allow up to 2209 liters of cargo space once the rear seat is folded. Incidentally, the trunk is accessible through a tailgate equipped with a practical handle and a protection rack for stowing the rear windshield wiper.

But there's nothing smart about the abominably complex radio. Just look at the tiny control buttons to see what I mean. They were impossible to manipulate without taking my eyes off the road. That's really the pits. Other not-so-good ideas include the driver's seat, which cannot be pushed back far enough to accommodate taller drivers. Access to the car is another negative point and on the passenger side, the grab handle can be a hazard in case of an accident. As for the grey-on-black dashboard, well, to each his own. Some liked it, others found the colors too funereal.

To recap, our extensive SantaFe test-drive allows us to say that Hyundai hasn't quite mastered the double-challenge of building a new model in a new category. The "package" looks attractive enough and the price is certainly right, but it badly needs fine-tuning, something the Korean maker will surely take care of in the coming years.

Jacques Duval

SPECIFICATIONS	GLS
Price	$CDN 21,060-29,250 / $US 16,994-22,494
Warranty	3 years / 36,000 miles (60,000 km)
Type	sport utility / all wheel drive
Wheelbase / Length	103 in / 177 in
Width / Height	72 in / 66 in
Weight	3719 lb (1687 kg)
Trunk / Fuel tank	30.5 – 78 cu. ft / 17 gallons
Air bags	front
Front suspension	independent
Rear suspension	independent
Front brakes / Rear brakes	disc ABS
Traction control	no
Steering	rack-and-pinion, power assist
Turning circle	37 feet
Tires (front/rear)	P225/70R16

PERFORMANCE	
Engine	V6 2.7 liter
Transmission	4-speed automatic
Horsepower	181 hp at 6000 rpm
Torque	171 lb-ft at 4000 rpm
Other engines	4L 2.4 liter
Other transmission	5-speed manual (4 cyl)
Acceleration (0-60 mph)	10.8 sec
Maximum speed	108 mph (174 km/h)
Braking (60-0 mph)	122 feet (37,2 m)
Fuel consumption	16.7 mpg (13.6 L/100 km)

COMPETITION

• Ford Escape/M. Tribute • Honda CR-V • Jeep Liberty • Subaru Forester • Suzuki G. Vitara • Toyota RAV4

NEW FOR 2002

• 2.4L 4 DOHC engine • 5-speed manual transmission • Front wheel drive system

RATING	(out of 5 stars)
Driveability	★★★½
Comfort	★★★½
Reliability	★★
Roominess	★★★★½
Winter driving rating	★★★½
Safety	★★★½
Resale value	★★½

HYUNDAI SONATA

HYUNDAI **SONATA**

The Japanese Model

If you're interested in the world of automobiles, you're probably aware of the strategy adopted by Japanese automakers since the late 1960s: copy the best of what European and North American automakers have to offer, build them better and then sell them for less. The next step, invade world markets with low-end models, gradually moving up to mid-level and then into the ultimate luxury-car category. Turnaround time: 20 years.

That's precisely the formula adopted by South-Korean automakers, most notably by Hyundai. From humble origins – remember the unfortunate Pony? – Carving out a viable niche for itself in North America. Hyundai's market share jumped a few points thanks in large measure to the Accent, the most widely sold subcompact in the country. And while all this is going on, major automakers are busy feeding off the truck-and-SUV market. Let's bet that a rude awakening could be just around the corner.

Dramatic increases in sales like Hyundai's can only mean that buyers are satisfied with their products and service. At least, that's what the results of a survey conducted last year by J. D. Power and Associates seemed to indicate. On the other hand, you need only take a look at the new, improved and slightly bigger Sonata to be convinced of Hyundai's steady progress.

If you look at it from the side, the 2002 Sonata bears some resemblance to a Jaguar, while its sculpted sealed-beam headlights remind you of a certain Mercedes model. Well, if you're determined to copy, then you may as well copy from the best. The overall design is indeed pleasant and well proportioned, which should please Hyundai's loyal customers, and might even appeal to some devotees of Japanese makes.

Nice equipment, but no ABS

The Sonata comes in three trim levels: GL (4-cylinder, 2.4 liters), GLV6 and GLX (V6, 2.7 liters). All feature power windows and locks, heated mirrors, air conditioning and a CD player. In addition, the mid-level GLV6 gets 16-inch alloy wheels, and four-wheel disc brakes. Finally at the top end, the GLX

▲ PROS

- Decent comfort • Good equipment/price ratio
- Nice styling • Roominess • Well-appointed cabin

▼ CONS

- No manual transmission • No standard ABS
- Sub-standard radio • Underperforming engines

gets imitation-wood trim, sunroof, cruise control, heated front seats, leather seating and driver adjustable power seat. But no ABS, except as an option or in the GLX version only. That's a regrettable – no, make it bad – decision on Hyundai's part.

Comfortably installed in the leather bucket seat of my test GLX, I quickly found a good driving position, thanks to the multi-adjustable power seat and tilt steering wheel. Incidentally, the Sonata's front seats are borrowed from the high-end XG300 model, which may explain the awkward position of the driver seat's power control.

The front passenger, on the other hand, can't find much comfort at all, because the seat bottom is non-adjustable and tilted forward too steeply. Rear passengers fare better with their excellent bench seat, whose 60/40 split backrest can be folded down to access an adequate trunk.

On the road, the 2002 Sonata is quiet, almost peaceful. No wonder, because according to Hyundai, the one-piece dashboard was specifically designed to eliminate all the rattling that tends to occur as you drive on rough roads.

Supple, but not very "muscular"

The 2.7-liter V6 engine that powers the new Sonata, replacing the previous-generation's 2.5-liter engine is the same V6 that propels the Hyundai SantaFe, developing 181 horsepower and 177 lb-ft of torque. It's coupled to a 4-speed automatic transmission with Shiftronic manual mode.

Compared with the Honda Accord's V6 generating 200 hp, the Korean engine feels decidedly sluggish, especially when going up a hill. I know, I know, the Honda is more expensive and its V6 displaces 3.0-liters. But still…

The Sonata's suspension system consists of double wishbones in front and a multi-link setup in the rear, a reasonably sophisticated arrangement that provides both overall comfort and sound handling. Sound but, not sporty, but that's a perfectly acceptable compromise. The same thing can be said about the Sonata itself, considering its competitive sticker price.

Alain Raymond

SPECIFICATIONS	**GLX**
Price	$CDN 21,195-25,695 / $US 15,494-18,819
Warranty	3 years / 36,000 miles (60,000 km)
Type	sedan / front wheel drive
Wheelbase / Length	106.3 in / 187 in
Width / Height	71.7 in / 55.9 in
Weight	3254 lb (1476 kg)
Trunk / Fuel tank	14.1 cu. ft / 17 gallons
Air bags	front
Front suspension	independent
Rear suspension	independent
Front brakes / Rear brakes	disc
Traction control	no
Steering	rack-and-pinion, power assist
Turning circle	37 feet
Tires (front/rear)	P205/60HR16
PERFORMANCE	
Engine	V6 2.7-liter
Transmission	4-speed automatic
Horsepower	181 hp at 6000 rpm
Torque	177 lb-ft at 4000 rpm
Other engines	4L 2.4-liter 149 hp
Other transmission	none
Acceleration (0-60 mph)	9.5 sec
Maximum speed	120 mph
Braking (60-0 mph)	133.5 feet
Fuel consumption	22.7 mpg (10 L/100 km)

COMPETITION

- 626 • Accord • Altima • Camry
- Malibu/Alero/Grand Am • Leganza • Sebring

NEW FOR 2002

- New model

RATING	**(out of 5 stars)**
Driveability	★★★½
Comfort	★★★½
Reliability	★★★★
Roominess	★★★★
Winter driving rating	★★★
Safety	★★★
Resale value	★★

HYUNDAI XG350

HYUNDAI **XG350**

Not as Bad as Expected

The Hyundai XG already had two strikes against it when it arrived last year. First, it was lambasted by some members of the automobile fraternity who had test-driven it in Korea; and the pre-production models made available to a few car journalists the year before hadn't impressed either. So we all waited with trepidation. Would this high-end Hyundai really be as bad as the early reports claimed?

Let's admit that the critics overreacted. The Hyundai XG is not in the same league as the Passat 1.8 or the Acura TL, but will give the other cars in the luxury compact sector – the Honda Accord V6, the high-end Toyota Camry and the Nissan Maxima – a run for their money.

Too sluggish

The XG350 (formerly 300) is not without its strengths, but I see it more as Hyundai's way of promoting its name and retaining the converts, so those who had already graduated from Elantra to Sonata would stay in the family and buy an XG350. Happy Hyundai owners will probably not be disappointed by this high-end sedan model, which is offered at an attractive price and comes remarkably well equipped. About $31,000 will buy you a long list of impressive "standard" accessories including automatic air conditioner, power sunroof, leather seats, a simple trip computer, heated exterior mirrors, heated seats and just about every comfort item associated with quasi-luxury cars. But I'd gladly do without the "keyless remote entry" feature which also lowers the side windows, if you press the button too long. I found this gadget more of a safety hazard than convenience.

Built in an ultra-modern plant in Asan, South Korea, the XG350 this year boasts a 3.5-liter V6 engine which channels its 194 horsepower to the front axle through a 5-speed automatic transmission. According to Hyundai's press kit, this transmission utilizes neuro-fuzzy logic control technology. I haven't the faintest idea what this is, but I can tell you that XG350's transmission has a manual shifting mode which lets you select the various gears as you please. I'm told that this will gain you half a second – what they didn't say, is that the automatic transmission is exasperatingly slow.

A hard sell

Suspension, however, is first-rate (double wishbones in front, multi-link system

▲ PROS

• Comfortable seats • Standard equipment • Efficient traction control • Pleasant steering • Roominess • Quiet engine

▼ CONS

• Dull engine • Poor restarts • Slow automatic transmission • Simplistic trip computer • Overcomplicated keyless remote entry (see text)

in rear). Also standard on every XG 350 are four-wheel disc brakes with ABS as well as electronic traction control system.

That's nice, but what kind of performance can a potential buyer expect from the XG350? We took it on a week-long test drive.

The car's looks, which Hyundai described as "European-styled," seem more North American to me, but that's a matter of taste. The roadholding capability also corresponds more to American taste than European. If your idea of a good drive is a quiet engine at work, a degree of comfort and adequate performance, you'll enjoy driving this Hyundai.

But if you prefer a dynamic engine, then you'll be less impressed with the XG350's lethargic acceleration, especially while trying to overtake another vehicle. At 60 mph, for instance, the engine turns only 2000 rpm. It's one thing to settle for a 0-60 mph time of 9 seconds, but if you need to pass another vehicle, such listless response can be a serious handicap.

The XG350 performs well at average speeds but the front suspension tends to grow limp and let the car lean excessively while cornering. And it handles potholes just as abruptly. On the other hand, rough road conditions help you appreciate the XG350's sturdy body. On smoother roads, the car is comfortable to ride in, and the ride is impeccable. Test-driven on slippery winter surfaces, the "quasi-luxury" Hyundai behaved correctly, benefiting from a good traction control system.

Seats are superb and easily adjustable. Visibility deserves an A minus while the dashboard displays good ergonomics with easy-to-read instruments. Hyundai paid attention to the tiniest details, from the extendable sunvisors to the spacious center console. Except for a fragile vent grill, every feature is generally well finished and the interior is handsome, save for the excessive amount of fake wood trim. The rear is reasonably spacious, made somewhat "inhospitable" by a large bump on the floor.

Although the Hyundai XG 350 is not as hapless as last year's reviews made it sound, its competitors, especially European, can relax. It's a perfectly okay car, whose lower price doesn't really carry much weight in this segment of the market. Hyundai's sales force is going to have to work hard.

Jacques Duval

SPECIFICATIONS	
Price	$CDN 31,995 / $US 25,494
Warranty	3 years / 36,000 miles (60,000 km)
Type	4-seat sedan / front wheel drive
Wheelbase / Length	108.3 in / 191.5 in
Width / Height	72 in / 56 in
Weight	3600 lb (1633 kg)
Trunk / Fuel tank	14.5 cu. ft / 18 gallons
Air bags	front and side
Front suspension	independent
Rear suspension	independent
Front brakes / Rear brakes	disc ABS
Traction control	yes
Steering	rack-and-pinion, power assist
Turning circle	35 feet
Tires (front/rear)	P205/65VR15

PERFORMANCE	
Engine	V6 3.5-liter 24-valve DOHC
Transmission	5-speed automatic
Horsepower	194 hp at 5500 rpm
Torque	216 lb-ft at 3500 rpm
Other engines	none
Other transmission	none
Acceleration (0-60 mph)	9 sec
Maximum speed	124 mph (200 km/h)
Braking (60-0 mph)	143 feet (43.7 m)
Fuel consumption	20.6 mpg (11 L/100 km)

COMPETITION

- Acura TL • Chrysler Sebring • Honda Accord V6
- Nissan Maxima • Olds. Intrigue • Toyota Camry V6

NEW FOR 2002

- 3.5 liter engine

RATING	**(out of 5 stars)**
Driveability	★★★
Comfort	★★★½
Reliability	★★★
Roominess	★★★½
Winter driving rating	★★★½
Safety	★★★½
Resale value	★★

INFINITI G20 INFINITI I35

INFINITI I35

Infiniti in Transition

We brought together these two Infiniti models because the G20 is its replacement. The I35 is about to be released.

We were saying that the good old G20 is now on its last lap. Just slightly bigger than a Nissan Sentra, but with the price of a base model Maxima, the G20 is still on the "unwanted" list. Built on the excellent chassis of the Nissan Primera, European version, the G20 has suffered from its ordinary lines, a lack of interest from Infiniti and an engine which does not justify the price tag. However, the G20 does have some great qualities, particularly as far as roadholding and riding comfort are concerned. Certainly, this 145 hp 2.0 litre 4-cylinder does not compare with some of its rivals; however, the dynamic efficiency of this vehicle is such that the engine manages to sustain very high average speeds on winding roads. The steering is lively and responsive, easy to control and can direct the car on a dime, all this with surprising comfort. But, rather than keeping up its interest in the pathetic case of the G20, Infiniti will drop that model in 2002, putting instead a new entry vehicle, the G35 2003 which is based on the very smart XVL prototype and which will be propelled (yes, yes, rear traction!) by a 3.5-liter V6. Note, another anti-BMW prospect!

Power present and correct

Main difference for 2002: the Infiniti I35 is fitted with the excellent 3.5-liter V6 which it also shares with the upscale Altima. With 260 hp and the non-insignificant 246 lb-ft of torque (33 hp more and 29 lb-ft more than the old 3.0-liter), this engine with variable valve timing is destined for a brilliant future. The new I35 is also equipped with a 4-speed automatic gearbox (how about a 5-speed box?) and a standard stability control system. Also improved are the brakes (with standard ABS) which are now fitted with an electronic brake management system and an emergency braking amplifier.

Hello ... and goodbye!

As far as styling is concerned, the weak spot of the Infiniti, most changes affect its snout, which has a grille very similar to that of the Q45 and a lighting cluster unit with xenon. The rear look still reminds one of the Maxima with which

▲ PROS

• Brilliant engine • Excellent soundproofing
• Proven reliability • Roominess • Excellent finish

▼ CONS

• Mundane styling • 4-speed automatic transmission
• No manual gearbox • No sporting temperament

the I35 shares the same platform. A remodeled trunk top, which is more harmonious, multi-purpose lights and a chrome exhaust pipe (hurrah!) take care of the rear. And of course, there are three new colors in the 2002 catalog. In other words, a rather timid evolution which does not really address the lack of personality in the overall styling.

Inside, the 2002 Infiniti I352 is fitted with new leather seats, the trademark Infiniti clock, the instrument cluster with electro-luminescent lighting, a new leather-covered semi-wood steering wheel, a new Bose sound system with seven loud speakers and an AM-FM radio-cassette and an in-dash 6-CD changer, all of which promise some very pleasant moments.

The Sports version of the Infiniti I35 comes with a sliding roof, sport suspension, 17-inch wheels, a stability control system, bottom sill protection, chrome-rimmed options with heated steering-wheel, front and rear seats and outside mirrors.

Predictable road behavior

The basic elements of the car is the same as those in the previous version! One can expect that the I35 will also have well-balanced roadholding, and a quiet but not sporty ride. You can also expect established reliability and overall riding comfort. The increase in power and torque will guarantee a better performance but the weight emphasis on the front does not enable it to measure up to the benchmarks in this luxury mid-size sedan slot: the BMW 3 Series, the Mercedes-Benz C Class and the Audi A4. If it has to be taken further, one should think in terms of a rear wheel drive system.

Alain Morin/Alain Raymond

INFINITI **G20**

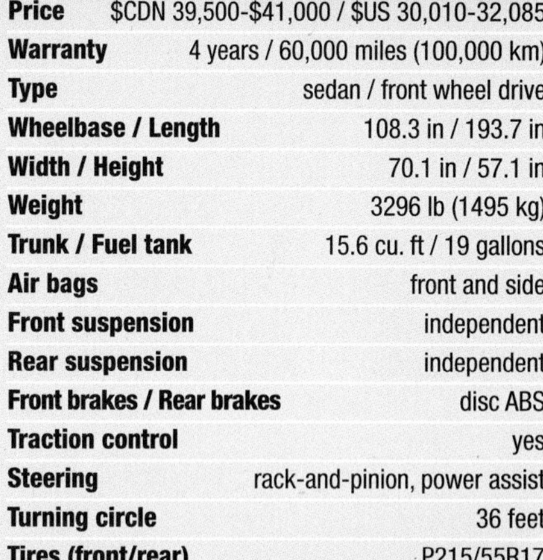

SPECIFICATIONS	
Price	$CDN 39,500-$41,000 / $US 30,010-32,085
Warranty	4 years / 60,000 miles (100,000 km)
Type	sedan / front wheel drive
Wheelbase / Length	108.3 in / 193.7 in
Width / Height	70.1 in / 57.1 in
Weight	3296 lb (1495 kg)
Trunk / Fuel tank	15.6 cu. ft / 19 gallons
Air bags	front and side
Front suspension	independent
Rear suspension	independent
Front brakes / Rear brakes	disc ABS
Traction control	yes
Steering	rack-and-pinion, power assist
Turning circle	36 feet
Tires (front/rear)	P215/55R17

PERFORMANCE	
Engine	V6 3.5-liter
Transmission	4-speed automatic
Horsepower	260 hp at 5800 rpm
Torque	246 lb-ft at 4400 rpm
Other engines	none
Other transmission	none
Acceleration (0-60 mph)	8.7 sec
Maximum speed	134 mph (215 km/h)
Braking (60-0 mph)	127.6 feet (38.9 m)
Fuel consumption	17.2 mpg (13.2 L/100 km)

COMPETITION

• Acura TL • Audi A4 • BMW 3 Series • Cadillac Catera • Chrysler 300 M • Lexus ES 300

NEW FOR 2002

• New model

RATING	(out of 5 stars)
Driveability	★★★★
Comfort	★★★★★
Reliability	★★★★★
Roominess	★★★★
Winter driving rating	★★★★
Safety	★★★★
Resale value	New model

INFINITI Q45

INFINITI **Q45**

Excellent Car Seeks Designer

Out of the limelight ever since its 1990 debut, the Infiniti Q45 might as well stay there a while longer if styling is the only thing to lure upscale buyers away from its rivals. In fact, the third-generation model is saddled with a design so common that nothing short of high-pressure salesmen will persuade buyers to opt for the 2002 Q45 rather than the Mercedes-Benz E430, the BMW 540i, or even the Lexus LS430. Those are just a few of the models that Infiniti's standard-bearer is stacked up against. Looks aside, does the new, entirely revamped Q45 boast any other attributes with which to enlarge its owners' circle?

To hear the Infiniti people talk, the new Q45 has been developed to "transform the act of driving," as opposed to the BMW's familiar theme, which is to provide pure driving pleasure. To this end, the Q45 boasts, among other features, the most powerful engine in its class – a 4.5-liter V8 producing 340 horsepower. That's 62 hp above the BMW 540i, and 50 above the Lexus LS 430. This gorgeous engine features titanium valves, and is race-car bred. In other words, the engine was taken apart for a second balancing of its components. What's more, it comes with a 5-speed automatic transmission – the only one listed in the catalog.

Infiniti sales hype further claims that the Q45 is the quickest accelerating car in its class, and has a better weight/power ratio than the Lexus LS430 or the BMW 540i. On the road, however, I was unable to achieve the promised acceleration. My stopwatch showed 0-60 mph in 7 seconds, not the 6.3 seconds touted by Infiniti.

Big headlights, small problem

Too late!

Another troubling feature of the Q45 is its lighting, provided by the oversized seven-lens xenon headlights. Touted as the most powerful headlight system in the world for a production automobile, it certainly lets you dispense with fog lights. However, our experience with night-driving wasn't especially pleasant. The xenon headlights did provide excellent illumination, but they proved blinding for other motorists. Whether driving behind another vehicle, or traveling in the oppo-

▲ PROS

• Quality build • High-tech engine • Praiseworthy comfort • Good road behavior • Advanced passive safety features • Good equipment

▼ CONS

• Cumbersome shape • Blinding headlights • Disappointing handling • Exaggerated performance claims • Questionable price/value ratio

site direction, we were the target of angry protests from drivers disturbed by the overly powerful lights. Since our test-car was a pre-production model, we made sure to test the definitive version of the Q45, which was virtually rid of this problem.

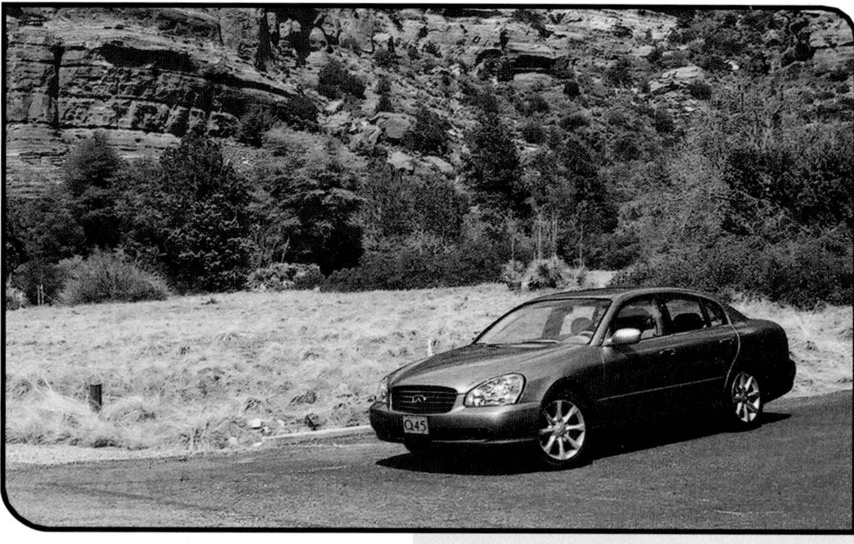

An impressive CV

In order to qualify for the upper luxury class, the Infiniti Q45 leaves nothing to chance. If you don't mind its so-so looks and the fact that its engine is affected by high altitudes, the Q45 has all you could wish for in a car of its class. In some respects, it's true that the Q45 has simply followed in the footsteps of its rivals, but at least all the desired features are there. Namely: disc brakes with a brake-assist system for emergency stops (a technology borrowed from Mercedes-Benz) and a multi-link suspension system – inspired by that of the Nissan Skyline GTR, the not-for-America high-performance model – with adjustable shock absorbers, antiskid and stability control. Standard alloy wheels are 17 inches, but you have the option of getting the18-inch variety with .45 aspect ratio tires.

Although the same size as its predecessor, the 2002 Q45 is lighter and the sveltest in its class, with the exception of the Mercedes-Benz E430. Its drag

INFINITI Q45

coefficient has been reduced from 0.32 to 0.30.

Have a seat!

If technical prowess leaves you unmoved, this Infiniti has plenty of other impressive features once you get behind the wheel. Unless, like me, you're overwhelmed by accessories which often complicate life rather than make it easier. I'm talking about the voice recognition system, which was developed by Visteon and enables the driver to "talk" to his car, to control functions like the air conditioner and the stereo system. To me, it's nothing more than a gadget – albeit a sophisticated one – which you'll soon tire of.

The small 5.8-inch display screen in the middle of the dashboard simply imitates what Mercedes-Benz has done for the last few years. The Q45 screen is perhaps slightly more user-friendly but it, too, belongs in the "gadget" category.

But I dig the interior's lush and high-quality finish, where plush leather and pale-colored maple are used to beautiful effect. The retro-style clock of the very first Q45 is still there and the quality of the Bose 8-speaker audio system is A-one. This Infiniti doesn't skimp on safety measures either, offering front and side air bags as well as a front-and-back curtain for head protection. Rounding out the Q45 array of equipment are an electronic ignition key, a tire-pressure monitor and, on the "Premium" version, heated, power-reclining rear seats as well as an "intelligent" cruise control device to maintain the distance between your car and the vehicle ahead.

A spin through the canyons

Infiniti had chosen Sedona, a small town about 125 miles north of Phoenix, to unveil its new Q45. This middle-size "Grand Canyon" offers road variety and a breathtaking landscape. Those majestic, wind-sculpted rocks the color of ochre stood out in a light so intense that they looked surreal, as if we were on a movie set.

On this striking plateau, the Q45 had trouble distinguishing itself with its impersonal design that reminded me of a Hyundai or a Ford Crown Vic. But the seats were remarkably comfortable and the dashboard pretty cool. According to data published by Infiniti, the Q45 offers more legroom, both front and back, than any of its rivals. The same data, however, prove that the skimpy headroom in the back is not an illusion. In this department, the Q45 doesn't compare favorably with its rivals. Trunk space is ade-

■ STANDARD EQUIPMENT

• Xenon headlights • Tire-pressure monitor
• Emergency power brake
• Side-impact curtain airbags

■ OPTIONAL EQUIPMENT

• Premium package (18-inch wheels, activated suspension, heated rear seats with reclinable backrests, rear radio and climate controls)

quate, but no better than average. Although smooth and silent, the engine doesn't exactly reflect its touted 340 hp. Acceleration is adequate, but fails to match the published data. With the suspension adjusted to sport-mode and 18-inch alloy wheels, roadholding is satisfactory. Tire grip is excellent, and body roll minimal although, as a colleague judiciously pointed out, the Q45 doesn't quite give you the urge to sport-drive – the very quality to which it so proudly lays claim. Steering assistance is just right and the steering wheel never feels too light. The suspension's rather stiff shocks don't really affect the car's overall comfort, but the tires proved noisy on some surfaces.

Last word

The mere fact that the Infiniti Q45 is still in production proves all too clearly the determination of the Japanese automobile industry. Just when we thought the car's demise was imminent due to poor demand, the Japanese manufacturer tried to give it a new lease on life. The result is a remarkable car in search of a good designer. With its rather bland looks, the Q45's qualities risk passing unnoticed. The Japanese are no doubt aware of the old adage: "If at first you don't succeed, try, try again!"

Jacques Duval

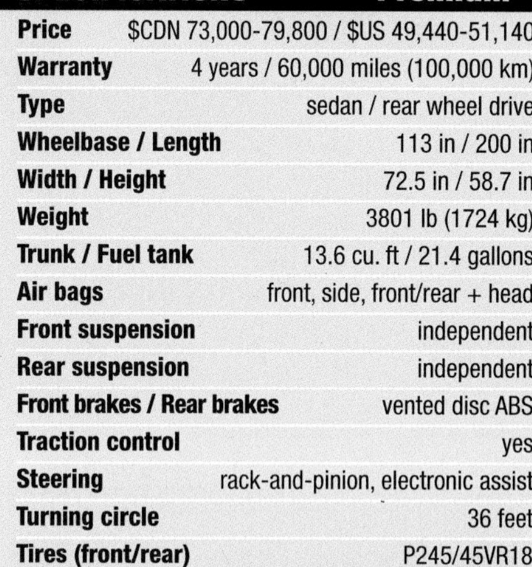

SPECIFICATIONS	**Premium**
Price	$CDN 73,000-79,800 / $US 49,440-51,140
Warranty	4 years / 60,000 miles (100,000 km)
Type	sedan / rear wheel drive
Wheelbase / Length	113 in / 200 in
Width / Height	72.5 in / 58.7 in
Weight	3801 lb (1724 kg)
Trunk / Fuel tank	13.6 cu. ft / 21.4 gallons
Air bags	front, side, front/rear + head
Front suspension	independent
Rear suspension	independent
Front brakes / Rear brakes	vented disc ABS
Traction control	yes
Steering	rack-and-pinion, electronic assist
Turning circle	36 feet
Tires (front/rear)	P245/45VR18

PERFORMANCE	
Engine	V8 4.5-liter 32-valve SOHC
Transmission	5-speed automatic
Horsepower	340 hp at 6400 rpm
Torque	333 lb-ft at 4000 rpm
Other engines	none
Other transmission	none
Acceleration (0-60 mph)	7 sec
Maximum speed	155 mph (250 km/h)
Braking (60-0 mph)	141 feet (43 m)
Fuel consumption	14.7 mpg (15.4 L/100 km)

COMPETITION

- Audi A8 • BMW 540i • Cadillac Seville
- Lexus LS 430 • Mercedes-Benz E430

NEW FOR 2002

- New model

RATING	**(out of 5 stars)**
Driveability	★★★★
Comfort	★★★★
Reliability	New model
Roominess	★★★★
Winter driving rating	★★★½
Safety	★★★★
Resale value	New model

ISUZU RODEO ISUZU TROOPER

ISUZU **RODEO**

Workhorses

Once strictly confined to the countryside, all-terrain and other sport-utility vehicles are now very much a part of the urban automotive landscape. Therefore it's not in the least surprising to see Isuzu play the versatility card with its Rodeo and Trooper models, touting both their on- and off-road capabilities. In fact, both models prove to be better suited to farmwork than a leisurely excursion through city traffic.

Redesigned in 1998, the Rodeo sports a stylish allure which makes it look smaller than it really is. Once the rear seats are folded, its cargo space amounts to a whopping 81 cubic feet! With an almost 4200-lb mass to propel, the Rodeo's modern 205-hp V6 engine is hardly a luxury, but certainly it's a clear necessity. It will never turn the Rodeo into a fiery charger, but the torque it generates at low rpms is enough to take care of your slightest whims. All this comes at a price, however, in the form of high fuel consumption, especially when you switch from rear-wheel drive to low range 4X4 mode.

With high ground clearance and plates protecting its bottom, the Rodeo is solidly equipped to venture off road. On paved roads, it rides more like a truck than a car, pitching and wallowing as it bounces off each and every bump and pothole in the road. Did you ever wonder why it was called Rodeo in the first place? At cruising speed, the variable-assist power steering proves to be reasonably precise, but its low gearing, combined with the wide turning circle, is a nuisance. As expected of a 4200-lb vehicle, stopping distances are longer than average, and I suspect the brakes won't last very long under hard use.

Marginal at best

The flat seats are quite comfortable in front, less so in back, but at least rear-seat occupants can recline their backrest, and enjoy ample legroom. While the driving position is excellent, the spare tire, placed in the back (versions S and LS), hampers visibility (in fact, the problem has been corrected in the 2002 model). The dashboard get high marks for the layout of various controls and instruments, but both the antiquated design and quality of the plastic used leave a great deal to be desired. With a base price of $33,000, customers deserve

▲ PROS

• Excellent off-road capabilities • Generous cargo space • Modern engines • Roominess • Simple and efficient 4X4 system

▼ CONS

• Dated interior • High fuel consumption • Limited distribution network • Too low gearing of steering • Stiff, unsophisticated suspensions

better. For an extra $10,000, you'll get the top-of-the-line version, the LSE, which includes a power sunroof, leather seating, automatic transmission and "Intelligent Suspension Control" that automatically adjusts shock absorbers to optimize ride and handling.

Trooper

The Trooper shares more or less the same attributes with the Rodeo, except it's a good 10 inches longer – resulting in 10% more cargo space – and 285 lbs heavier. Propelling this mass is a 3.5-liter V6, which does the job respectably, although its horsepower is a tad too low, compared to the V8 that powers many of its rivals.

The Trooper is not only bigger than the Rodeo, but its character traits also seem more pronounced. Handling is positively unctuous on smooth surfaces, but drive the vehicle on rough roads, and it struggles like a fish out of water. The Trooper's high center of gravity tends to make it lean on curves, a fact that makes many an unsuspecting driver nervous.

Another major difference with the Rodeo is the Trooper's Torque on Demand system – offered with the Limited version. It automatically directs more engine torque to the wheels with the most traction, thus limiting wheelspin.

Other than the torque system, both the Rodeo and Trooper clearly come from the same family: both are versatile SUVs, although they seem better suited to a country driver who needs to visit the city than the other way around. Both models are fairly reliable, but the fact that Isuzu dealerships are few and far in between may create a problem for owners. Besides, Isuzu is not yet a household name, and this may have an effect on the vehicles' resale value.

Jean-Georges Laliberté

SPECIFICATIONS	**Rodeo**
Price	$CDN 31,935-44,565 / $US 16,235-35,333
Warranty	3 years / 36,000 miles (60,000 km)
Type	sport utility / rear wheel drive/4X4
Wheelbase / Length	106.3 in / 177.6 in
Width / Height	70.4 in / 69.3 in
Weight	4167 lb (1890 kg)
Trunk / Fuel tank	33 cu.ft / 20 gallons
Air bags	front
Front suspension	independent
Rear suspension	rigid axle
Front brakes / Rear brakes	disc ABS
Traction control	no
Steering	rack-and-pinion, variable assist
Turning circle	38 feet
Tires (front/rear)	P225/70R16

PERFORMANCE	
Engine	V6 3.2-liter
Transmission	4-speed automatic
Horsepower	205 hp at 5400 rpm
Torque	214 lb-ft at 3000 rpm
Other engines	no
Other transmission	5-speed manual
Acceleration (0-60 mph)	9.2 sec
Maximum speed	112 mph (180 km/h)
Braking (60-0 mph)	144 feet (44 m)
Fuel consumption	16.2 mpg (14 L/100 km)

COMPETITION

• Chevrolet Blazer/GMC Jimmy • Ford Explorer • Jeep Liberty • Nissan Pathfinder • Toyota 4Runner

NEW FOR 2002

• Rodeo: new model SE • Spare tire under the floor • Larger front discs • Trooper: minor changes

RATING	**(out of 5 stars)**
Driveability	★★★
Comfort	★★★
Reliability	★★★★
Roominess	★★★½
Winter driving rating	★★★★★
Safety	★★★
Resale value	★★½

ISUZU **TROOPER**

JAGUAR **S-TYPE**

JAGUAR **S-TYPE**

A Pioneer

When Ford acquired Jaguar in 1989, many people feared that the American giant was going to "cannibalize" the prestigious British firm whose automaking tradition dated back to the 1930s. As it turned out, those fears were unfounded since Ford's idea was to provide Jaguar with the means to develop its own original and up-to-date models.

The S-Type sedan was developed in Jaguar's newly built plants, taking advantage of Ford's advanced product development tools and methods. Launched in 2000, it was the first all-new model to come off the Jaguar assembly line in decades and the first to be offered in a lower price range. To keep production costs low, Jaguar based the S-Type on the same platform as the Lincoln LS, and thus was able to "borrow" a few of its mechanical components. But the S-Type's modern suspension (unequal-length arms in front and double wishbones in back) and its 4.0-liter 281 hp V8 engine are pure Jaguar. The model is also available with a 3.0-liter V6 engine, the first ever to power the famed "leaping cat." In fact, the V6 is a variation of the Ford Duratec, though extensively refined at Jaguar's Whitley Engineering Center in Coventry, England. Both the V6 and V8 engines are paired to a 5-speed automatic transmission featuring Normal and Sport modes.

In order to keep up with the competition in its select field, which includes such illustrious models as the Mercedes-Benz E Class, BMW 5 Series, Audi A6 and Lexus GS300, the S-Type is adorned with all sorts of high-end technical amenities: self-adjustable suspension, dynamic stability control, optional sport suspension (CATS) with Pirelli P-Zero 17-inch low-profile tires, satellite navigation system, rain-sensing wipers, and a myriad of other features worthy of its class.

On the fence

Elegance and comfort

The designers wanted to make a major impact, so they decided to evoke Jaguar's glorious past, retaining the distinctive elliptical grille with vertical flutes as well as the circular headlights that graced the midsize Jaguar sport sedans of yore – the 1959 Mark II and 1964 S-Type, both direct ancestors of the new 2000 S-Type. As a result, although it's been a long time coming, Jaguar's all-new sedan is instantly recog-

▲ PROS

- Prestigious past • Sophisticated engines
- Interesting sport suspension • User-friendly dashboard • Exemplary sound insulation

▼ CONS

- Snug rear seats • Controversial silhouette
- Finish needs work • Average performance

nizable. But the rear end looks as if the designers had trouble deciding between the XJ sedan styling and an all-new contemporary concept.

The interior features lots of leather and wood trim, as befits a deluxe British automobile. The dashboard, however, represents a genuine departure from the past. Controls are logically laid out, all within easy reach and easy to read, even the ventilation and A/C system. In fact, everything is so clearly indicated that you don't need to consult the owner's manual. It's a pity that some of the switches look tacky, as if borrowed from humbler Ford models – an affront, really, to such a classy car. On the other hand, the wood-rimmed, leather-wrapped steering wheel gets high marks for its elegant look and comfortable feel.

Also worth noting is the S-Type's voice-command system. By simply "talking" to the radio, for example, you can switch stations or adjust the volume. Ditto for the cell phone and climate control. The highly sophisticated system is programmed not only to recognize and memorize the driver's voice, but also several regional accents.

Silent performance

Jaguars are renowned for their smooth, quiet rides, and the S-Type is exceptional in this area. It also boasts an irreproachable driving position. That said, not everything works smoothly: there's a constant ticking noise emanating from the dashboard and the climate control has trouble demisting the windshield. Oh well, there's always room for improvement.

The car is stable and predictable during hard cornering, especially at high speeds. But turn off the stability control system and this Anglo-American machine becomes capricious and unpredictable. Moreover, in at least two test cars, the brakes tended to overheat. And do opt for the V8 engine, because the 5-speed automatic gearbox tends to emasculate the V6. It's a pity no manual transmission is offered, which would have been ideal for the V6.

All in all, this midsize sedan leaves us longing for more. But there's always the Lincoln LS, which shares the same mechanics, and costs less.

Denis Duquet

SPECIFICATIONS

Price	$CDN 59,960-70,950 / $US 44,250-49,950
Warranty	4 years / 48,000 miles (80,000 km)
Type	sedan / rear wheel drive
Wheelbase / Length	14.6 in / 191.3 in
Width / Height	71.7 in / 55.9 in
Weight	3770 lb (1710 kg)
Trunk / Fuel tank	13.1 cu. ft / 18 gallons
Air bags	front and side
Front suspension	independent
Rear suspension	independent
Front brakes / Rear brakes	disc ABS
Traction control	yes
Steering	rack-and-pinion, power assist
Turning circle	37 feet
Tires (front/rear)	P225/55HR16

PERFORMANCE

Engine	V8 4-liter
Transmission	5-speed automatic
Horsepower	281 hp at 6100 rpm
Torque	287 lb-ft at 4300 rpm
Other engines	V6 3-liter 240 hp
Other transmission	none
Acceleration (0-60 mph)	7 s; 9 s (V6)
Maximum speed	130 mph (210 km/h) (limited)
Braking (60-0 mph)	126 feet (38.5 m)
Fuel consumption	18.9 mpg (12 L/100 km)

COMPETITION

• Audi A6 4.2 • BMW 5 Series • Lexus GS 430 • Lincoln LS • M-B E430 • Saab 9[5] • Volvo S80

NEW FOR 2002

No major change

RATING	**(out of 5 stars)**
Driveability	★★★
Comfort	★★★★½
Reliability	★★★
Roominess	★★★
Winter driving rating	★★★½
Safety	★★★★
Resale value	★★★

JAGUAR XJ8 JAGUAR XJR JAGUAR VANDEN PLAS

JAGUAR XJR

An Athlete in Motion!

The rush of power registers quickly in the driver's mind. Not so the concept of torque. It's unfortunate that power is at the top of any list describing a car's selling points, at the expense of torque, a more important factor in everyday driving.

So I'm sorry to disappoint you, but it's torque and not horsepower that makes things feel so exhilarating as your foot presses the accelerator when changing up to fourth gear. The torque pushes the car forward, hard, and you as well, into the back of your seat. In automobile matters, torque depends principally on the engine's cubic capacity, as attested by that oh-so familiar sensation provided by the large and powerful V8. But torque can also be enhanced by juicing up the engine, either by using a turbocharger or a supercharger.

A touch of class, old chap

Under her finely sculpted hood, this updated "English rose" conceals a fine 4-liter V8 that has been boosted by an Eaton supercharger. The 387 lb-ft of torque thus obtained are available at 3600 rpm, but even at 1600 rpm, it surpasses the maximum torque generated by the same, unboosted V8 engine. Once underway, car behavior is magnificent. Endowed with a 5-speed automatic gearbox, this large sedan speeds up as gracefully and nimbly as a ballerina to music, accompanied by the soft minor-key lament of the supercharger blowing air into the twin air liquid intercoolers, thus cooling it on its way to the cylinder intake.

Test-driving at the Willow Springs, California, race course we found the XJR easier to drive than its more youthful cousin, the XK8. Wearing an imperturbable air, well seated on its mighty 18-inch Pirelli P Zero low-profile tires, this Jag is the real McCoy, offering matchless driving despite its 3960 lbs (1800 kg). Admittedly it's neither a Miata nor a Boxster, but its braking performance would put many so-called sports cars to shame. While its calm, British-to-the-core appearance will make those automakers who have tried for years to give their sadly nondescript luxury models an air of dignity, green with envy.

Prestige revisited

As befits its sporty legacy, the XJR benefits from well-shod wheels plus a

▲ PROS

- Gorgeous lines • Runaway performance
- Prestigious touring car • Comforting roadholding

▼ CONS

- Restricted roominess • Annoying gear lever
- A little overweight • End-of-line model

firmer – though not hard – suspension than that of the XJ8 sedan. Its rear-wheel drive system is well adapted for winter use with anti-skid, anti-slip and anti-lock brake controls. Despite so much care given to the mechanicals, Jaguar didn't cut corners on equipment, which covers the entire spectrum. Worth noting are the high-fidelity sound system, power-heated front and rear seating, automatic climate control and power-assisted steering with electric tilt and telescopic adjustment.

The car's profile reaches back to the purest traditions of its Coventry origins, presenting a timeless elegance. Despite the fact that its automotive industry has been virtually swallowed up by Ford, GM, BMW, VW, etc., we are reminded that Great Britain was the birthplace of the world's most prestigious marques.

The body in question

Appearances may be deceptive. While the fragrant leather seats evoke richness and opulence, XJ8 comfort is not all it should be. As for headroom, well, let's just say I was relieved to be under six feet tall. The trunk is also short on space and legroom is limited in the rear, at least in the standard version. That's not a problem in the Vanden Plas version with its longer wheelbase. Then there is still the J-shaped gear selector that Jaguar has obstinately preserved in the face of constant criticism over the years.

The lack of roominess reflects the fact that the design of the large Jaguar sedans – however elegant and well-performing – is based on the XJ6, which came off the production line in...you guessed it, 1988! Defects such as the above can be overlooked, thanks to the modern engine, constant upgrading of the brakes and suspension, improved reliability, and a cockpit and overall lines of rare elegance. But ultimately the body structure will have to be recast before these drawbacks can be eliminated. Let's hope that under Ford's shrewd leadership, Jaguar can renew the XJ series, retaining that excitement; inspiring the mantra of so many fans: "One day I will drive my own Jaguar!"

Alain Raymond

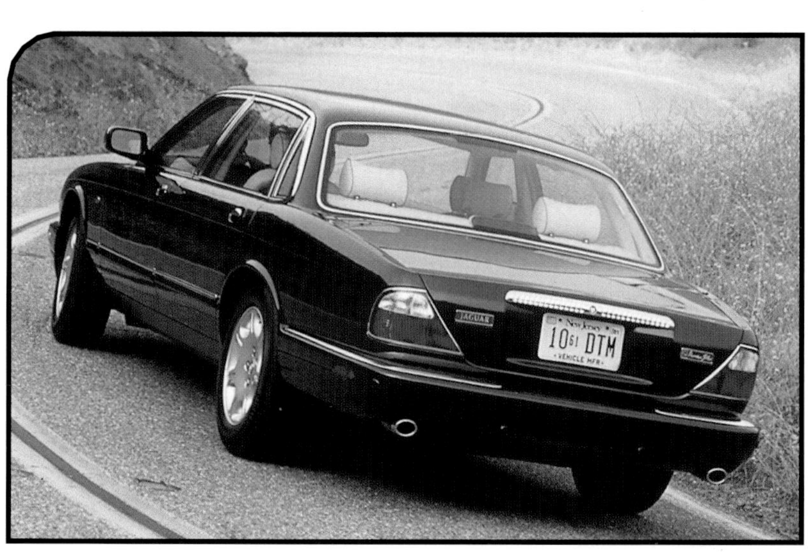

SPECIFICATIONS	XJR
Price	$CDN 82,950-91,950 / $US 56,950-86,145
Warranty	4 years / 48,000 miles (80,000 km)
Type	sedan / rear wheel drive
Wheelbase / Length	113 in / 197.6 in
Width / Height	71 in / 53 in
Weight	4050 lb (1837 kg)
Trunk / Fuel tank	12.7 cu. ft / 23 gallons
Air bags	front and side
Front suspension	independent
Rear suspension	independent
Front brakes / Rear brakes	disc ABS
Traction control	yes
Steering	rack-and-pinion, variable assist
Turning circle	41 feet
Tires (front/rear)	P255/40ZR18

PERFORMANCE	
Engine	V8 4-liter boosted
Transmission	5-speed automatic
Horsepower	370 hp at 6150 rpm
Torque	387 lb-ft at 3600 rpm
Other engines	V8 4-liter 290 hp, normally aspirated
Other transmission	none
Acceleration (0-60 mph)	5.6 sec
Maximum speed	155 mph (250 km/h)
Braking (60-0 mph)	125 feet (38.2 m)
Fuel consumption	13.4 mpg (17 L/100 km)

COMPETITION

• Audi A8 • BMW 7 Series • Infiniti Q45
• Lexus LS 430 • Mercedes-Benz S Class

NEW FOR 2002

No major change

RATING	(out of 5 stars)
Driveability	★★★★
Comfort	★★★★
Reliability	★★★★
Roominess	★★★½
Winter driving rating	★★★★
Safety	★★★★
Resale value	★★★

JAGUAR XK8 JAGUAR XKR

JAGUAR **XKR 100**

Waiting for the E-Type's Heir

It's difficult to discuss the Jaguar without invoking the incomparable E-type, which recently celebrated its 40th birthday. Inheriting its predecessor's exquisite lines, the XK8 has a twofold agenda: to erase the unhappy memory of the hideous XKS and recapture the timeless looks that made the E-type one of the most illustrious sports cars of the latter half of the 20th century.

The XK120 roadster, XK8's ancestor, first saw the light of day in 1948, marking Jaguar's arrival in North America, today its most important market. Thirteen years later, in 1961, the company unveiled the E-Type, the decade's cult car that was inspired by the models that Jaguar raced to victory at the 24 Hours of Le Mans. For Jaguar lovers, the pure lines of the E-Type roadster and coupe have never been surpassed. Then came the long "drought" during which Jaguar almost disappeared, a victim of government nationalization and the unrest which for years afflicted employers and labor unions. It wasn't until 1984 that Jaguar, finally freed itself from labor problems, and was able to stage a gradual comeback. Success soon followed, thanks largely to the company's purchase by Ford in 1989.

Back to basics

Unveiled in coupe and roadster versions at the 1996 Geneva Motor Show, the XK8 – styled by the late designer Geoff Lawson and his team – finally restored the essence of the Jaguar style. Looks aside, the XK8 doesn't have what it takes to be regarded as a true sports car. Based on an aging platform derived from that used by the XKS, the XK8's imposing weight and dimensions, lack of manual transmission and spongy suspension hardly lend themselves to the kind of nimble performance characteristic of a Porsche 911, for example. Factor in the XK8's appeal to the silver-haired retirees in Florida and California, and you've got the picture: a car blessed with docile mechanics and "civilized" road manners, that demands no special skills on the driver's part. It's a Grand Touring model, performing honorably and quite capable of transporting its two occupants in grand style.

GT-class

Despite their similarities, the XK8 is no E-Type. In 1998, Jaguar introduced the XKR, a modified version of the XK8, much like a specialized tuning house would have

▲ PROS

• Exuberant engine (XKR) • Classic lines • Cockpit well-appointed and equipped • Reassuring road handling • Marque's top contender

▼ CONS

• Aging platform • Non-retractable top (roadster) • Heavy weight • No manual transmission

done. Jaguar wanted to safeguard its hard-earned reputation – garnered in the 1950s when Jaguar faced tough competition from Ferrari and other glamorous marques. The XKR's superb 4.0-liter V8 engine is fitted with a supercharger incorporating two intercoolers, boosting its power to 370 horses and torque to an even more remarkable 387 lb-ft. Moreover, to mark its return to Formula-1 racing, the company brought out a limited series last year: the XKR Silverstone, named after the British racing circuit. Although this variation is not listed in the 2002 catalog, you can reproduce it by opting for specific equipment, in particular 20-inch BBS alloy wheels fitted with Pirelli P Zero low-profile tires, large Brembo brakes as well as speed-sensitive steering and CATS-controlled suspension. Incidentally, the last two features are the secret behind the XKR coupe and roadster's exceptional handling capabilities, as they go head to head against their German competitors.

On the Willow Springs, California, racetrack the XKR clearly demonstrated the importance of braking in sport driving. The combination of high-performance tires and brakes, speed-sensitive steering and the CATS-controlled suspension give you a better chance to exploit the substantial power and torque generated by the monster engine. With a few pounds shed (on the car, that is) and a manual gearbox, you'd think it was the E-Type all over again.

Today, the Jag embodies more than just superb performance. The ever-present wood and leather trim reflects that quintessential British tradition, while luxury accessories abound in the cockpit. The soft-top is first-class, both in terms of quality and sound insulation, as one has come to expect of its manufacturer, Karman, one of the industry's finest. Too bad this same top doesn't retract completely when it's folded up because it ruins the roadster's profile. Maybe that's why I prefer the XK8 coupe, which has the advantage of a more rigid chassis and even more predictable road-handling.

Finally, I have the great pleasure of announcing that Jaguar has decided to bring out its successor. It will be called, yes, that's right, the F-Type.

Alain Raymond

SPECIFICATIONS	**XKR coupe**
Price	$CDN 95,950-116,950 / $US 70,545-75,545
Warranty	4 years / 48,000 miles (80,000 km)
Type	coupe 2+2 / rear wheel drive
Wheelbase / Length	102 in / 187.4 in
Width / Height	72 in / 50.4 in
Weight	3785 lb (1717 kg)
Trunk / Fuel tank	10.9 cu ft / 20 gallons
Air bags	front and side
Front suspension	independent
Rear suspension	independent
Front brakes / Rear brakes	disc ABS
Traction control	yes
Steering	rack-and-pinion, variable assist
Turning circle	36 feet
Tires (front/rear)	P245/45ZR18 / P255/45ZR18

PERFORMANCE	
Engine	V8 4-liter boosted
Transmission	5-speed automatic
Horsepower	370 hp at 6150 rpm
Torque	387 lb-ft at 3600 rpm
Other engines	V8 4-liter 290 hp, normally aspirated
Other transmission	none
Acceleration (0-60 mph)	5.4 sec
Maximum speed	155 mph (250 km/h) (limited)
Braking (60-0 mph)	125 feet (38.2 m)
Fuel consumption	16.6 mpg (13.7 L/100 km)

COMPETITION

• BMW Z8 • Mercedes-Benz SL
• Porsche 911 Turbo

NEW FOR 2002

No major change

RATING	**(out of 5 stars)**
Driveability	★★★★
Comfort	★★★★
Reliability	★★★★
Roominess	★★½
Winter driving rating	★★★
Safety	★★★
Resale value	★★★

JAGUAR X-TYPE

JAGUAR **X-TYPE**

A Healthy Baby Cat

There's a new rival for the BMW 3 Series, Audi A4 and Mercedes-Benz C Class – the Jaguar X-Type. It's a tall order for the "British debutante," even though it comes equipped with desirable credentials: a prestigious name; compact sport sedan; standard all-wheel drive; and the lowest base price ever for a Jaguar. In return, the X-Type is expected to double Jaguar's current worldwide sales.

For the second time in three years, Jaguar has expanded its automotive lineup downward. After the S-Type, it's now the X-Type's turn to attract a broader, less affluent customer base. So far, Jaguar's projections are on target. The S-Type sales have doubled – from 50,000 units to 100,000 – and the same is expected of the new "Baby Jag." "That's the only way we can raise funds for the F-Type," said Mike O'Driscoll, president of Jaguar-North America. Due in 2005, the F-Type will be based on a prototype that has been making the rounds of various auto shows, and is slated to compete against the Porsche Boxster, both in terms of price and performance.

While Jaguar's plans seem ambitious in today's volatile economy, the company insists that its targets are on the conservative side, especially when compared with the competition. BMW 3 Series, for example, sells roughly half a million units per year, while Mercedes C Class clears a quarter-million units. But is it realistic to expect the X-Type to compete in this select group? To showcase their latest "cat," Jaguar invited us all to test- drive the X-Type in Burgundy, France – on a race track in Pouilly-en-Auxois, as well as a roughly 200-mile-long route (300 km) through the region's picturesque vineyards and sunflower fields.

Off to a great start

Impressive specs

Given the fact that Jaguar's corporate master is headquartered in a Dearborn, Michigan building emblazoned with the Ford oval, there are grounds for concern about potential parts-sharing between Ford and Jaguar. While Jaguar acknowledged that the X-Type shared a basic body structure with the German-built Ford Mondeo, it made sure that both the platform and engines were considerably modified beforehand. The most

▲ PROS

- Competitive price • Decent comfort
- Excellent road manners • Quality build
- Roominess • Standard all-wheel drive

▼ CONS

- Annoying gear lever (automatic) • Disappointing performance (automatic-2.5 V6) • Poor rear visibility
- Slow automatic gearbox • Too many options

important change involved the X-Type's viscous-coupling central differential, which allows for a 40/60 power distribution between the front and rear axles, a percentage that provides the balanced feel of a rear-drive car – as is the case with the BMW Xi 3 Series – and unlike the Audi A4, an all-wheel drive car that feels more like a front-driver. When the going gets heavy, the visco-coupling automatically transfers power to the wheels with the best traction.

Plenty of options

The X-Type is powered by the 24-valve Ford Duratec V6 engine, with aluminum block and cylinder heads. There are two versions: the 2.5-liter with 194 hp and the 3.0-liter with 231 hp, both of which, interestingly enough, achieve 90% of their maximum torque between 2500 and 6000 rpm. Also worth mentioning is the choice the customer can make between a manual transmission and a 5-speed automatic with either engine version. Better still, the 3.0-liter engine can be paired with an automatic gearbox at no extra charge. Acutely aware that driving pleasure is a high priority for this customer group, Jaguar offers a wide array of models and options. The sport package, for instance, includes 17-inch alloy wheels (instead of 16-inch), Dynamic Stability Control, performance-tuned suspension and Connolly leather sport seats – all accompanied by superb visual touches like a body-colored grille, leather-wrapped shift knob, dashboard adorned with dark wood trim, not to mention a little fin sitting prettily atop the trunk.

Speaking of options, Jaguar really went to town! The list of extra accessories and equipment runs on forever. I can understand paying extra for a navigation system, but not for a split-folding rear seat. Sensibly, the manufacturer didn't skimp on safety features, offering front and side air bags, as well as head and side curtain. Other specifications include tried and true features such as multi-link rear suspension and electronic braking force distribution.

Car versus train

I had the good fortune to test-drive the entire X-Type line through rain and shine –

JAGUAR **X-TYPE**

on a racetrack as well as a variety of roads – and was thus able to formulate a quasi-complete assessment of the new Jaguar. Since I'm partial to sport sedans, I'd opt for the 3.0-liter engine with manual transmission, plus the optional sport package. But each version has its own validity and appeal. In my view, the 2.5-liter/manual combination offers the best deal, in terms of quality/price. The automatic gearbox, however, doesn't quite mesh with the 2.5-liter engine. Reaction time is slow and keeps hunting for the correct gear to be (and stay) in at any given time. Needless to say, acceleration leaves much to be desired. Jaguar claimed it took nine seconds to go from 0-60 mph, but no matter how hard I tried, I couldn't do it in less than 11. The J-shaped lever movement is no piece of cake either. Once you're in "man-

■ STANDARD EQUIPMENT

- Heated mirrors and washer fluid
- Fog lamps front and rear
- automatic climate control

■ OPTIONAL EQUIPMENT

- Sport package • Xenon headlights
- Automatic wipers • Reverse-gear beeper

ual mode," it's very hard to get back to "automatic." Even with a manual transmission, the 2.5-liter engine isn't exactly punchy, although it's easier to get used to.

Apart from these minor (or major) details, the X-Type is particularly nimble, thanks to its compact size. The body/chassis unit is remarkably rigid, steering is pleasant, and road manners are on a par with its rivals. Body roll on curves is barely noticeable and grip is spectacular. Frankly, you can't go wrong with this car. Despite its compact size, the X-Type is surprisingly comfortable, made all the more enjoyable by the low noise level. Of the two brands of tires offered, the Continental Contact-Sport tires fared much better than the Pirelli P Zero variety on the varied test-track and road conditions.

Well behaved

The 3.0-liter engine took care of all the flaws exhibited by the 2.5-liter, even though its response time, too, was on the slow side, and that in turn affected acceleration. With the manual gearbox, coordinating accelerator and clutch movement took some getting used to. Still, the X-Type behaved just as smartly as the BMW Xi, as demonstrated during an impromptu race with a TGV – France's legendary high-speed train – and on a wet road surface to boot. Needless to say, the TGV quickly outsped me due to heavy traffic, but at least I had a chance to experience first-hand the X-Type's Dynamic Control Stability in action. And it lived up to its reputation, efficiently intervening at the slightest hint of a slide. When pushed closer to the limit on a track, however, the front wheels tend to give way first, causing slight understeer. In this situation you'll appreciate the X-Type's superbly precise steering, as well as its efficient brakes.

The art of seduction

Visually, the X-Type's lines (and grille) are closer to classic Jaguar limousine models than the S-Type. Inside, genuine leather (unscented, alas) and exquisite maple trim confirm that sense of luxuriousness associated with Jaguar's high-end models. The cabin features plush seats, a superb driving position, and larger rear seats and trunk than the competition's. Some people may fault the poor rear visibility or the hard-to-reach button that adjusts the driver's seat. But all in all, the X-Type seems more appropriate to its targeted audience than the S-Type. Even the preproduction- or test models exhibited a quality build that belied the horror stories associated with older Jaguar models.

For an "entry-level" luxury sedan, the X-Type is more than competent, capable of taking on its "well-bred" rivals on the strength both of its own qualities and the prestige of driving a Jaguar at an astonishingly low price.

Jacques Duval

SPECIFICATIONS	**X-Type 3.0 liter**
Price	$CDN 42,950-$49,950 / $US 30,545-36,545
Warranty	4 years / 48,000 miles (80,000 km)
Type	5-seat sedan / all wheel drive
Wheelbase / Length	106.7 in / 183.9 in
Width / Height	70.4 in / 54.8 in
Weight	3428 lb (1555 kg)
Trunk / Fuel tank	17.1 cu. ft / 16 gallons
Air bags	front, side front/rear + head
Front suspension	independent
Rear suspension	independent
Front brakes / Rear brakes	disc ABS
Traction control	yes
Steering	rack-and-pinion, variable assist
Turning circle	36 feet
Tires (front/rear)	P205/55VR16
PERFORMANCE	
Engine	V6 3.0-liter
Transmission	5-speed automatic
Horsepower	231 hp at 6800 rpm
Torque	209 lb-ft at 3000 rpm
Other engines	V6 2.5-liter, 194 hp
Other transmission	5-speed manual
Acceleration (0-60 mph)	7.6 s; 10.8 s (2.5 automatic)
Maximum speed	149 mph (240 km/h)
Braking (60-0 mph)	n.a.
Fuel consumption	18 mpg (12.8 L/100 km)

COMPETITION

• Audi A4 • BMW 3 Series • M-Benz C Class
• Saab 9^3 • VW Passat 4Motion • Volvo S60

NEW FOR 2002

• New model

RATING	**(out of 5 stars)**
Driveability	★★★★
Comfort	★★★½
Reliability	New model
Roominess	★★★½
Winter driving rating	★★★★
Safety	★★★★
Resale value	New model

JEEP GRAND CHEROKEE

JEEP **GRAND CHEROKEE**

The Trendsetter

Some vehicles are destined to lead and establish themselves as the industry standard guarding their status against all upstarts. The DaimlerChrysler group boasts two such beacons: the Dodge Caravan minivan and the Jeep Grand Cherokee. Even though other models perform just as well – better in some cases – those two remain the benchmark in their respective categories.

When the Grand Cherokee made its debut 10 years ago, the competition was limited to a couple of American rivals (Blazer/Jimmy, Explorer) and two or three Japanese SUVs (sport-utility vehicles). Several prestigious marques have since entered the fray, like Acura, Infiniti, Lexus, Mercedes and BMW, not to mention the imminent arrival of Volkswagen and Porsche.

Today, models abound to suit every taste, provided you've got a fat wallet, because there aren't many midsize SUVs under $40,000. Blame it on the Grand Cherokee, the forerunner of luxury SUVs. But its immense popularity vindicates the thinking heads at Jeep, and continues to do so now that the second generation, launched three years ago, has taken up the torch as successfully as the first generation. What is the Grand Cherokee's secret?

Mechanical prowess

As before, the new Grand Cherokee comes with two engine options. The base version (Laredo) sports the standard 4.0-liter six-cylinder engine that generates 195 horsepower. But don't turn your nose up simply because it's not a V8. This standard engine has got plenty of power to propel the beast in a suitably dashing manner.

If you long for the vanished era of muscle cars, the Limited's 4.7-liter V8 will bring back pleasant memories. As strong as a horse and as fast as a sprinter, the V8 is awesome, and has a matching appetite. For environmentalists, that's a big strike against the vehicle, but fuel consumption is the last thing that SUV owners or makers worry about. The former go for the vehicle's trendy looks, while the latter only see the dollar signs. Perhaps gas-price hikes will bring these folks down to earth, in order to better protect it...

Uneven quality

To manage its raw power, the V8 is fitted with a robust gearbox, which has no trouble carrying out its heavy-duty job. Reliability may not be Jeep's main selling point, but

▲ PROS

- Cool exterior • Excellent handling • Impressive V8 engine • Luxurious and functional cabin
- Superior off-road capability

▼ CONS

- Body rattling • High fuel economy
- Old-fashioned seats • Iffy reliability
- Vague, overassisted steering

their engines and transmissions are more robust than other mechanical features.

Amusement park, anyone?

The less spongy brake pedal suggests improvements in the braking system, although abrupt stopping can still be worrisome. It plunges forward and tends to weave from side to side. Furthermore, if a roller coaster ride makes you feel queasy, then Grand Cherokee may not be for you. It lurches about in every direction as if its body were tied to the axles by elastic bands. The vehicle's height doesn't help, either. And to top it all off, power steering is fuzzy and overassisted: as a result, you have to correct it constantly. That's too bad, because the steering is otherwise precise and boasts a gorgeously tight turning circle. And on the matter of off-road ability, the Grand Cherokee is truly one of a kind.

Considering how it tosses about, it takes a certain courage to try driving the Grand Cherokee like a sports car. But take heart – its suspension effectiveness is excellent. It handles body roll on twisting roads remarkably well and keeps the vehicle stable.

Styling wise, the second-generation Grand Cherokee is a carryover from its predecessor, both inside or outside. The consensus out there is still that the beast is so ruggedly handsome... What more can I say? It's just a guy thing.

In addition to its opulent feel, the cabin is roomy, comfortable and has good ergonomics. The dashboard is fairly complete, well appointed and eye-pleasing. Controls are easy to reach and storage space abounds.

But the seats remind you of those huge American sedans of long ago – over-padded, and offering poor support. The competition does a much better job. But I've seen worse, like the school bus-like seats in the Mercedes ML320. A real horror show.

Despite a decent overall finish, material quality is not up to snuff. The leather, for example, looks and feels more like leatherette. At $50,000 a crack, you deserve better.

But that's the Grand Cherokee for you: Its major qualities manage to disguise its flaws. In any case, Grand Cherokee fans usually lease – rather than buy – their vehicle. That's probably the way to go. And while you're at it, make sure the lease period doesn't exceed the duration of the basic guarantee.

Jacques Duval

SPECIFICATIONS	Limited
Price	$CDN 39,095-51,850 / $ US 27,900-35,695
Warranty	3 years / 36,000 miles (60,000 km)
Type	sport utility / all wheel drive
Wheelbase / Length	106 in / 181.5 in
Width / Height	72.4 in / 69.3 in
Weight	4167 lb (1890 kg)
Trunk / Fuel tank	39 cu. ft / 21 gallons
Air bags	front
Front suspension	rigid axle
Rear suspension	rigid axle
Front brakes / Rear brakes	disc ABS
Traction control	no
Steering	recirculating balls, power assist
Turning circle	37 feet
Tires (front/rear)	P235/65R17

PERFORMANCE	
Engine	V8 4.7-liter
Transmission	5-speed automatic
Horsepower	235 hp at 4800 rpm
Torque	295 lb-ft at 3200 rpm
Other engines	6L 4-liter 195 hp
Other transmission	4-speed automatic
Acceleration (0-60 mph)	7.8 sec
Maximum speed	115 mph (185 km/h)
Braking (60-0 mph)	132 feet (40.2 m)
Fuel consumption	13.8 mpg (16.5 L/100 km)

COMPETITION

• Acura MDX • Explorer • Infiniti QX4 • Pathfinder • 4Runner • TrailBlazer/Envoy

NEW FOR 2002

• New high-performance engine
• Adjustable pedal system • New wheels

RATING	(out of 5 stars)
Driveability	★★½
Comfort	★★★
Reliability	★★★
Roominess	★★★
Winter driving rating	★★★★
Safety	★★★★
Resale value	★★★

JEEP LIBERTY

JEEP **LIBERTY**

Battleground Savior

The Jeep Cherokee is dead! Long live the Jeep Liberty! At first glance, DaimlerChrysler's decision to abandon the model name that gave birth to the SUV craze seems strange. Stranger still is the name of the new vehicle – Liberty – chosen to memorialize the exploits of those first Jeeps on the battlefields of World War II. It's a curious choice, to say the least, especially since the very same vehicle will be marketed in Europe under the name Cherokee.

Different theories surround the new name. In the official version, "Liberty" was the popular choice to honor the vehicle that helped save Europe from the Third Reich. The unofficial, but perhaps more credible, version is that this model was not really slated to replace the Cherokee, hence its newly minted name. Still another theory claims that financial considerations forced the company to change its product plans.

Whatever the truth of the matter, it can't top the irony apparent in the speech by DaimlerChrysler group president Dieter Zetche during the official Jeep Liberty launch at the North American International Auto Show in Detroit. "The new Liberty, Jeep," intoned Herr Zetche, "the machine that saved Europe." It was eerie to have a German executive remind us that the Jeep had played a role in defeating Germany in 1945, while videotaped war scenes played out in the background. The irony surfaced again later at Chrysler, when it was announced that the all-terrain vehicle will keep the Cherokee name when it is marketed in Europe, perhaps as a bow to political correctness.

But there's more to the Jeep Liberty than semantics. It's the company's aim to use this all-new model to propel Jeep to the forefront of the compact-SUV category, one of the most active segments of the automotive market.

Masterstroke

From the very beginning, designers conceded that concocting a new style for such a well-established off-road vehicle would be an uphill battle. What's more, "the new model has to be distinctly Jeep, easy to spot as such," as a company executive put it. So how could the designers possibly have altered the vertical

▲ PROS

• Rigid platform • Excellent all-terrain • Powerful V6 engine • Comfortable cabin • Elegant dashboard

▼ CONS

• 4-cylinder engine • Manual transmission with 4-cylinder • Badly placed footrest • Vulnerable to side wind • High fuel consumption (V6)

grille with the seven vertical openings, the round headlights, the square silhouette, and countless other unmistakable Jeep features without alienating Jeep's hard-core fans? The result turns out to have been nothing short of a masterstroke.

The rear and sides were derived from the Dakar, a Chrysler concept vehicle unveiled in January 1997, while the front, with its round headlights following the curving hoodline, were borrowed from the Jeepster, another prototype introduced in 1998.

When the Liberty was unveiled on a show platform, some critics believed that the front's dramatically curved shape would affect the vehicle's overall visual balance. They needn't have worried. As seen on the road, proportions are just fine. What's more, the Cherokee's more notorious weaknesses have all been corrected. The rear doors, for example, are larger, making for easier access. Rear seats are firm yet comfortable, offering excellent thigh support, while both legroom and headroom are adequate. The spare tire, which occupied too much space in the Cherokee's luggage compartment, is now mounted on a swing-out rear gate. The luggage compartment is smaller than Cherokee's, but becomes considerably larger once the backrest is lowered. But you can't fold the backrest completely flat, and that might annoy some passengers. Moreover, if you want to lower the backrest while the headrests are in place, you have to first slide the front seats forward so as to make room to maneuver.

To accommodate the spare tire, engineers had to transform the old tailgate into a swing-out variety that could be hinged on the side, like that of the Honda CR-V, or the Toyota Rav4. It's a two-step procedure: You need to lift the rear glass before you can pull the swing-gate open. But don't worry, unlike the Honda CR-V, all you need to do here is pull on the handle and the glass will automatically flip up, and a further pull opens the gate. Simple but ingenious! Whether customers prefer this feature to the traditional tailgate remains to be seen, although owners of the Honda CR-V and the Toyota Rav4 don't seem unhappy about it.

JEEP LIBERTY

The dashboard is a thing of beauty, featuring nifty details like a round-dialed instrument cluster with black-on-beige graphics and round air-conditioning outlets. On the Limited model, the module bearing the radio and climate controls is smartly fitted onto a brushed-aluminum appliqué. The driver's seat is well appointed, though a tall driver might find the available space too confining. Models fitted with manual transmission lack space for the left foot next to the clutch pedal. Some people might also dislike the fact that buttons for the power windows are placed on the center console.

New technology

Traditionally, the Jeep is fitted with front and rear solid-axle suspension, recirculating-balls steering, a uniframe chassis with integral frame rails, and a tried and true engine dating back to time immemorial. That's pretty much how the Grand Cherokee is engineered, except that it is powered by a more modern 4.7-liter V8 engine. The Liberty's specifications don't exactly follow the same approach. In effect, engineers opted for an independent upper/lower arm front suspension, which they say will improve comfort and provide sturdier support for the rigors of off-roading. At the rear is a multi-link solid-axle with coil springs practically identical to the Grand Cherokee's. Precise rack-and-pinion steering improves directional stability, providing excellent on-road dynamics.

There are two engine options. First is the all-new 3.7-liter V6 producing 201 horsepower – a version of the 4.7-liter V8 that powers the Grand Cherokee. The second is a 2.4-liter 4-cylinder engine that generates 150 hp and is similar to the one installed in the PT Cruiser. What is surprising, at least for a North American vehicle, is that both engines are offered as standard equipment, and come with a 5-speed manual transmission. The 4-speed automatic is optional.

In Canada, only 4X4 models are available. The Sport model comes with the standard part-time Command Trac four-wheel-drive system, and the Limited with the full-time SelecTrac. The latter is optional on the Sport model.

"True Jeep"

A drive in the Cherokee is like a trip down memory lane: the narrow doors, flat side walls, boxy body, rustic looks, stiff suspension on bad roads, so-so handling at best. In other words, elements that betray the Jeep's ancient origins.

From the first few turns at the wheel of the Liberty, I've become impressed with its

■ STANDARD EQUIPMENT

- 5 gear manual gearbox • 2.4-liter engine
- Under-body protection • 16-inch wheels
- All-wheel drive CommandTrac wheel train

■ OPTIONAL EQUIPMENT

- 3.7-liter V6 engine • Side curtain air bags
- Air conditioning • 6 CD disk player
- SelecTrac system • TracLoc differential

steering, which is not only nicely balanced but transmits feedback from the road surface remarkably well. In fact, the response is so direct for an American vehicle that I wondered if drivers with more traditional tastes will enjoy the improvement.

The chassis is more rigid than either the Cherokee's, or the Grand Cherokee's for that matter. Comfort is further enhanced by the full 8 inches of suspension travel. Although the Liberty is relatively high, direction changes and body roll are particularly well controlled. It's definitely not a sports car, but as an SUV, the Liberty is quiet, comfortable and demonstrates excellent road manners. The V6 engine ensures good performance and acceleration packs a lot of punch. But fuel consumption is disappointing: only 14 mpg. The manual transmission, however, is subpar – its shifting is not not precise, making it difficult to find the right gear. As for the 4-cylinder engine, acceleration is timid, and you'll need to be careful and think ahead before you pass another car.

You can't really compare the Cherokee with the Liberty. The former was a fine vehicle in 1984, but you have to move on, and its replacement has all it takes to give the competition a run for its money. To find out more about this subject, take a look at our comparison test at the beginning of this guide.

In order to uphold the "true Jeep" tradition – "Go anywhere, do anything" – engineers asked off-road driving experts to test the Liberty on the legendary Rubicon Trail. Their verdict: Definitely a Jeep. Public reaction remains to be seen. As for me, after a test drive over an intermediate circuit, I'm convinced that the Liberty has all-terrain capabilities, in addition to comfort and mechanical refinement. Purists will appreciate the part-time CommandTrac four-wheel-drive system, while on-road drivers will dig the full-time SelecTrac. Curiously, the sideways pitching motion that this system caused on the Grand Cherokee seems less pronounced on the Liberty.

It's hard to find fault with the Liberty. The price is competitive, it's fun to drive, and it retains all the traditional off-road Jeep qualities.

Denis Duquet

SPECIFICATIONS

Price	$CDN 22,880-26-680 / $US 17,035-23,305
Warranty	3 years / 36,000 miles (60,000 km)
Type	compact sport utility / all wheel drive
Wheelbase / Length	104 in / 174.4 in
Width / Height	71.6 in / 71 in
Weight	4116 lb (1867 kg)
Trunk / Fuel tank	29 cu. ft (68.9 cu. ft) / 18 gallons
Air bags	front and side
Front suspension	independent
Rear suspension	rigid
Front brakes / Rear brakes	disc / drum (ABS optional)
Traction control	no
Steering	rack-and-pinion, power assist
Turning circle	39 feet
Tires (front/rear)	P215/75R16

PERFORMANCE

Engine	V6 3.7-liter
Transmission	4-speed automatic
Horsepower	210 hp at 5200 rpm
Torque	225 lb-ft at 4000 rpm
Other engines	4L 2.4-liter 150 hp
Other transmission	5-speed manual
Acceleration (0-60 mph)	10.4 sec (V6 automatic)
Maximum speed	115 mph (185 km/h)
Braking (60-0 mph)	126 feet (38.5 m)
Fuel consumption	14.3 mpg (15.8 L/100 km)

COMPETITION

• Ford Escape • Honda CR-V • Nissan Xterra • Suzuki XL7 • Toyota RAV4

NEW FOR 2002

• New model • New body
• New front suspension

RATING (out of 5 stars)

Driveability	★★★★
Comfort	★★★
Reliability	New model
Roominess	★★★½
Winter driving rating	★★★★★
Safety	★★★★
Resale value	New model

JEEP TJ

JEEP **TJ**

The Real Thing

Once strictly reserved for use by prospectors, campers and hunters, 4X4s have grown increasingly popular with city-dwellers and suburbanites. As a result, these vehicles have become more and more sophisticated and gentrified, so as to meet the new demands placed on them. Today, more people use SUVs for daily commuting than for off-road activities.

Until recently, these robust vehicles were designed exclusively for rough terrain. Driving an SUV on the highway for any length of time would have felt like torture. Given current market trends, however, most SUVs are today better adapted to use on paved roads.

Not the Jeeps, however. The Jeep TJ (called Wrangler in the U.S.), for instance, clings stubbornly to its off-road "calling." With its short wheelbase, generous ground clearance and spartan cockpit, its natural habitat is a boulder or rock-strewn terrain. Accordingly, the TJ is fitted with the original rigid-axle front suspension, recirculating-balls steering and a rear axle capable of absorbing every conceivable shock. In 1997, a new version came on the market, incorporating a chassis that was given better lateral and transversal rigidity. But the highlight is the Quadra-Coil rear suspension: hello comfort, and goodbye to all that jolting along rough roads as well as the occasional kicking and pitching stemming from the rear axle. All in all, there have been huge improvements in comfort as well as in cockpit presentation.

What's especially impressive is the fact that despite the "makeover," the TJ has still not lost its rock-crawling capabilities. While more comfortable on the highway, it's off the beaten track that the TJ really proves its mettle.

Its natural habitat

Romantic? Sure, but it's mostly practical

TJ commercials typically show a wholesome young woman driving the Sahara model along a California beach at sunset, blonde hair blowing in the wind... Romantic? You bet! But if you believe that at the expense of the TJ's true nature, you're in for a rude surprise.

▲ PROS

- Manual transmission
- More efficient ventilation
- Multitude of options
- Real all-terrain
- 6-cylinder engine

▼ CONS

- Poor rear seats
- Limited road comfort
- Top difficult to retract
- Specialized use only
- Useless 5th gear

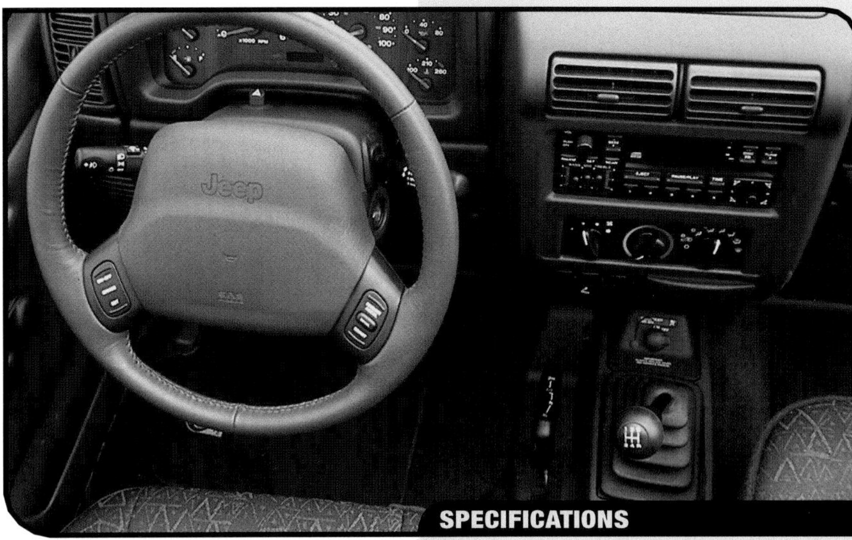

I say rude deliberately because the TJ is one tough machine. The cabin is so narrow that even with the soft top retracted, you have to contort your body to avoid banging your head against the roll bar. The rear seats are poorly padded – even uncomfortable – and difficult to reach. And once you're finally seated, there's not much room for your legs. The front section is better, but not by much. The doors are flimsy and the dashboard, while more up-to-date, doesn't amount to much. With the soft top on, it's less noisy than before, although the overall noise level is still very high. The optional hard top is recommended for drivers living in places where winter is harsher than average.

"Mountain goat"

On the road, the short wheelbase and somewhat vague steering take some getting used to. The most economical powerplant is the 2.5-liter 4-cylinder engine with 120 horsepower – borderline for a 3300-lb vehicle (1482 kg). The manual gearbox is smooth and gearshifting is excellent. However, the fifth gear seems virtually useless. It's so long that to avoid vibration, you need to drive over 80 mph. Incidentally, the 3-speed automatic transmission is optional on all models equipped with the 4.0-liter 140 hp inline-6 engine. Though hardly sophisticated, this gearbox is robust and reliable. On the other hand, the 6-cylinder engine and the manual transmission make for an interesting match, despite that dubious fifth gear.

In the hands of an expert driver, the Jeep TJ is capable of taking on the toughest driving conditions with aplomb. And therein lies the secret of this bona fide "mountain goat": to appreciate it you must really need it. Otherwise, it's better to stay behind on the beach with that blonde bombshell ...

Denis Duquet

SPECIFICATIONS

Price	$CDN 19,975-28,120 / $US 15,475-23,020
Warranty	3 years / 36,000 miles (60,000 km)
Type	sport-utility / part-time 4X4
Wheelbase / Length	93.3 in / 150 in
Width / Height	66.5 in / 70.9 in
Weight	3267 lb (1482 kg)
Trunk / Fuel tank	11.5 cu. ft / 19 gallons
Air bags	front
Front suspension	rigid axle
Rear suspension	rigid axle
Front brakes / Rear brakes	disc / drum (ABS optional)
Traction control	no
Steering	recirculating-balls, power assist
Turning circle	33 feet
Tires (front/rear)	P225/70R15

PERFORMANCE

Engine	6L 4-liter
Transmission	5-speed manual
Horsepower	190 hp at 4600 rpm
Torque	235 lb-ft at 3200 rpm
Other engines	4L 2.5-liter 120 hp
Other transmission	3-speed automatic
Acceleration (0-60 mph)	10.8 sec
Maximum speed	103 mph (165 km/h)
Braking (60-0 mph)	139 feet (42.3 m)
Fuel consumption	15.5 mpg (14.7 L / 100 km)

COMPETITION

- Chevrolet Tracker/Suzuki Vitara
- Kia Sportage

NEW FOR 2002

- New speakers
- New alloy wheels in all models

RATING (out of 5 stars)

Driveability	★★
Comfort	★★
Reliability	★★★
Roominess	★★
Winter driving rating	★★★½
Safety	★★★
Resale value	★★★

KIA MAGENTIS

KIA **MAGENTIS**

A Better Buy?

The Auto Guide **hasn't exactly been gentle with Kia automobiles ever since they hit the market. Indeed, the models that the company allowed us to test didn't quite hit the bull's eye, at least as far as the competition was concerned. The South Korean automaker is principally known for its budget-pricing policy which, in our opinion, amounts to little more than a popular myth. At the time of writing, for example, a Kia Sportage EX sells for $23,745 while a Toyota RAV4 can be purchased for $23,260. So tell me, which one is the better buy? Furthermore, compared to the Japanese 4X4, the Sportage is positively antique! But let's talk instead about the Magentis, a luxury car that has recently been added to the steadily growing Kia lineup.**

In order to dispel our doubts about the short-term reliability of its vehicles, Kia made a high-end Magentis available to us so that we could test it over a period of several months. The V6 SE is Kia's most luxurious model, retailing for $27,995, or $3000 less than either a Honda Accord or Toyota Camry, both equipped with V6 engines.

The most common mistake that any buyer makes is the one that I have just committed, and that is to compare the Magentis with the Accord and Camry – the two most popular mid-size cars on the market. In any such comparison test, there's not much anyone can expect the Magentis to do except bring up the rear. In all fairness, it should be pitted against American-made cars like the Chevrolet Malibu, Ford Taurus or Chrysler Sebring – even the Hyundai Sonata, the car from which the Magentis was derived. In this kind of company, the Kia can compete on a more even keel, bearing in mind that its handling is "Americanized" in a way – characterized by a too-supple suspension and over-light steering. You might imagine that you were behind the wheel of a good old-fashioned Buick from the recent past.

Getting there

Hang on tight

Regarded in this context, I'm sure the Magentis will acquit itself fairly well. Steering is so unresponsive that the driver gets no feedback from the road. At high speeds, the car's supple suspension makes it lean too much in corners, so that you need to hang on firmly to the steering wheel. If the seats offered more

▲ PROS

- Decent cabin space • Excellent visibility
- Good equipment/price ratio • Noteworthy comfort
- Quiet engine

▼ CONS

- Painful access • Suspension too supple
- Unresponsive steering • Weighty hood
- Wind noise

in the way of lateral support, you wouldn't need to – but they don't.

That's frustrating because it would have taken very little to make the Magentis fun to drive. It's simply a matter of firming up the suspension, and retuning the steering.

Otherwise, the engine is quite up to the job: displacement has been increased from 2.5 liters to 2.7 liters, and horsepower boosted from 170 to 178. Paired to a decent 4-speed automatic gearbox, it proves to be silky-smooth and remarkably crisp. The hood does a good job of muting engine noise, and that's probably why it ends up weighing a ton! The engine's quiet functioning is sometimes marred by wind noise, however. And if the Magentis soaks up bumps and potholes seamlessly to the delight of its occupants, it does so at the expense of handling. Roadholding is good, though there's not much point in stepping on the gas in a car like this. Braking (disc brakes front and rear, incidentally) is under-assisted and on the long side, as I discovered when simulating an emergency stop. So you need to really push down hard on the pedal.

The interior is the place where the Magentis SE shines – it's spacious and features a complete range of equipment such as air conditioning, traction control, 8-speaker stereo system with CD player and side-impact airbags. Kia also offers a base version of the Magentis, with fewer accessories and a weaker 4-cylinder engine.

Ouch! All the test drivers, regardless of size, had a painful experience to relate – in bold letters in the logbook – about getting in and out. The door opening is not terribly high in the first place, and there's an absolutely useless overhead grab handle on the driver's side which is the spot on which everybody banged their heads. The cupholder cover on the center console opens from the wrong side, making it awkward to use. The broad windshield provides excellent visibility in front, but the rear is hampered by a number of blind spots due to the three headrests.

During our entire 3750-mile test period (6000 km), the Magentis never had a mechanical problem, except for the little button controlling the power-adjustable seats that fell off. Arguably, 3750 miles isn't an especially demanding test, but considering its close ties with the Hyundai Sonata, this new-generation Kia could set the South-Korean automaker well on its way.

Jacques Duval

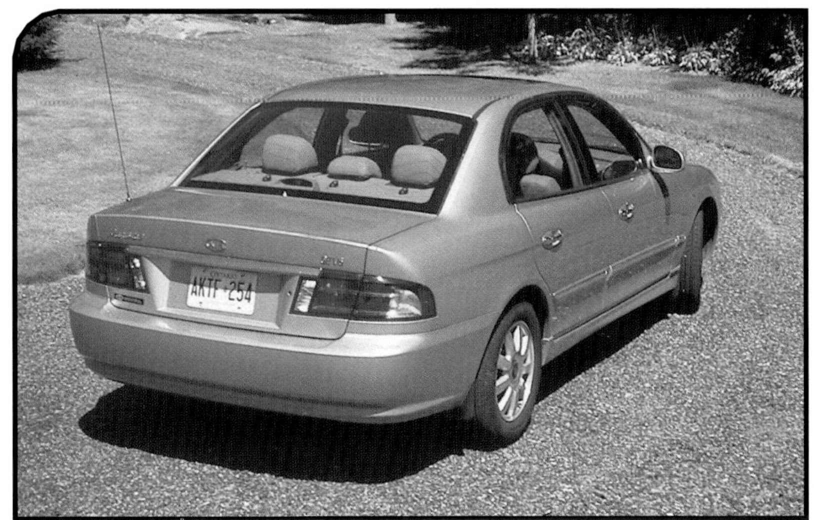

SPECIFICATIONS	**2.7 SE V6**
Price	$CDN 21,295-29,095 / $US 15,794-20,444
Warranty	5 years/ 36,000 miles (60,000 km)
Type	sedan / front wheel drive
Wheelbase / Length	106.3 in / 185.8 in
Width / Height	71.5 in / 55.5 in
Weight	3285 lb (1490 kg)
Trunk / Fuel tank	13.6 cu. ft / 17 gallons
Air bags	front and side
Front suspension	independent
Rear suspension	independent
Front brakes / Rear brakes	disc ABS
Traction control	yes (optional on LX)
Steering	rack-and-pinion, variable assist
Turning circle	34 feet
Tires (front/rear)	P205/60R15

PERFORMANCE	
Engine	V6 2.7-liter
Transmission	4-speed auto. with manual mode
Horsepower	178 hp at 6000 rpm
Torque	181 lb-ft at 4000 rpm
Other engines	4L 2.4-liter 149 hp
Other transmission	4-speed automatic
Acceleration (0-60 mph)	9 sec
Maximum speed	122 mph (195 km/h)
Braking (60-0 mph)	140 feet (42.7 m)
Fuel consumption	20.6 mpg (11 L/100 km)

COMPETITION

• Chevrolet Malibu • Chrysler Sebring • Daewoo Leganza • Hyundai Sonata • Mazda 626

NEW FOR 2002

• More powerful 2.7-liter engine
• 5-year warranty

RATING	**(out of 5 stars)**
Driveability	★★
Comfort	★★★★
Reliability	New model
Roominess	★★★½
Winter driving rating	★★★
Safety	★★★½
Resale value	★★

KIA RIO

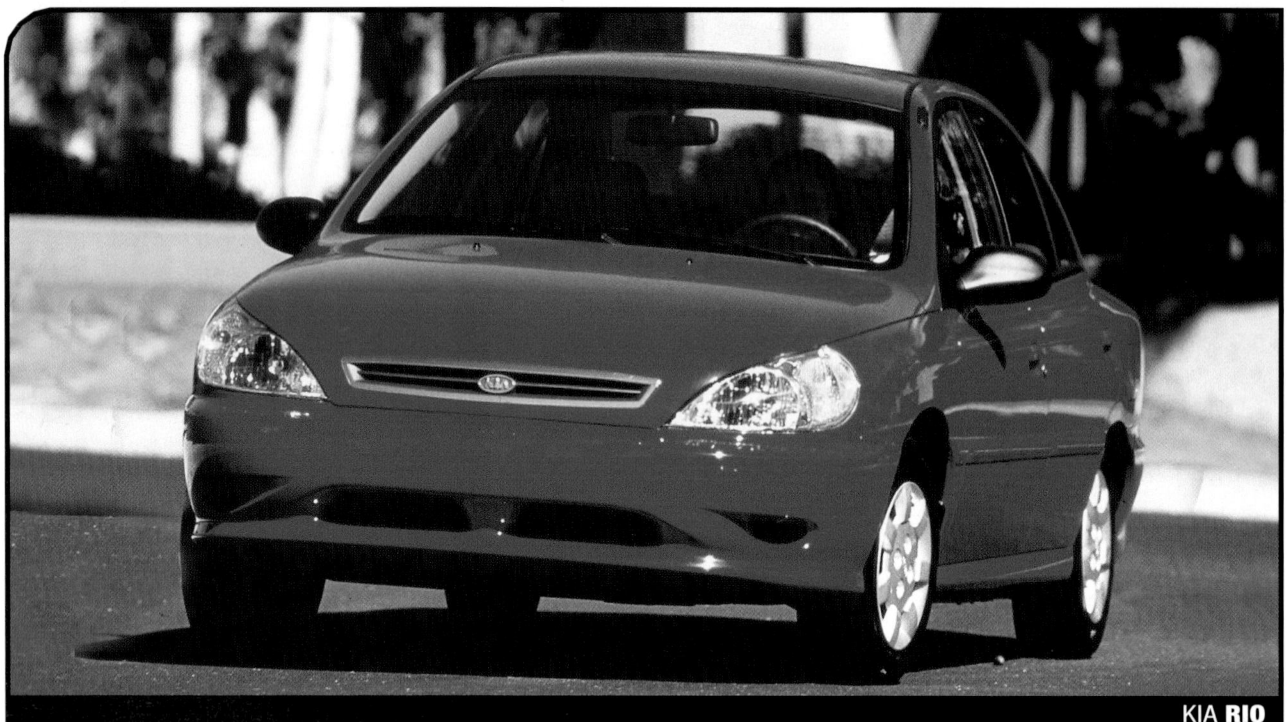

KIA **RIO**

Low Expectations

There's something inherently unsatisfying about evaluating a low-end car whose main asset is its cheap price. After all, no one can work a miracle. Despite the best intentions in the world, an automaker simply cannot make a product for less money than the competition without compromising either quality or performance.

The Kia Rio is a case in point. Realistically speaking, a critic can't expect it to have been built according to the same quality standards as other more established subcompacts.

Not bad

This year, the Kia Rio has added a station wagon to its lineup, based on the sedan's platform. Interestingly enough, the wagon looks more appealing than the sedan, whose outmoded lines remind you of the Hyundai Accent. The assembly process, especially of the various body panels, leaves a lot to be desired, even though I've seen much worse in some American-made cars.

The interior was designed in the same vein. The plastic feels hard and the dashboard looks stripped and utterly nondescript, although I must admit it's neat and easy to read. The commands are few and far between, but at least they're conveniently placed. Storage bins, too, are scarce and tiny, except for the glove compartment, which is a decent size and practical.

The front seats are comfortable enough, though they don't offer much in the way of lateral support. The driver's bucket seat is height-adjustable manually in the RS and LS trims, and provides a practical, pull-down right armrest, very similar to certain minivans.

In the rear, the bench is very low, so that passengers have to sit with their knees apart to avoid banging them against the front backrests. But there's ample headroom. The trunk is just average, and you can't fold down the bench's backrest for more cargo space. The trunk's opening is an odd shape as well, limiting the size of objects you can store there. The station wagon contains an extra 1.4 cubic feet of cargo space, but if you're thinking of using it to moonlight as a mover, forget it.

To be continued...

▲ PROS

- Adequate power • Comfortable suspension
- Reasonable fuel consumption
- Satisfactory ergonomics • Up-to-date engine

▼ CONS

- Dubious price • Funny-shaped trunk
- Inadequate tires • Suspensions too soft
- Unproven reliability

Noisy engine

The Kia Rio is powered by a relatively up-to-date DOHC engine with 96 horsepower. Power kicks in only at 4000 rpms, and maximum torque, at 4500 rpms! So expect a lot of engine noise. The car works fine with two people on board, but add one or two heavier passengers and the weight/power ratio goes right out of whack.

The manual gearbox doesn't exactly encourage you to fully exploit the last vestiges of the available horsepower – the gear stick feels as if it were mired in a bucketful of golf balls. The automatic box acquits itself efficiently enough, if somewhat curtly. Fuel consumption is average for the category. The rudimentary suspension was tuned more for comfort than "enthusiastic" driving. The car leans heavily in corners, and bounces whenever it hits bumps and potholes on the road. Handling is predictable, although steering is annoyingly vague. The disc/drum brakes show no sign of premature heating, but braking distances are on the long side for a car so light – a direct result of the poor quality of the tires. ABS doesn't figure in the catalog.

Waiting game

The sedan comes in three trim levels: S, RS and LS. The base model, at $12,000, is so utterly bare-boned – deprived even of power steering – it must have been intended for the ascetics among us. The LS, at $16,000, comes with automatic transmission, hub cabs, tachometer, CD player, air conditioning and some power-assisted features. The RS falls somewhere between the two. As ever, climate control and automatic transmission are on offer.

Now comes the "million-dollar" question: Is the Rio worth buying? The Norman-French in my blood says ... unequivocally: "Hmm ... We'll see!"

Jean-Georges Laliberté

KIA **RIO RX-V**

SPECIFICATIONS	RX-V
Price	$CDN 12,095-16,095 / $US 9,390
Warranty	3 years / 36,000 miles (60,000 km)
Type	sedan / front wheel drive
Wheelbase / Length	94.9 in / 165.9 in
Width / Height	65.9 in / 56.7 in
Weight	208 lb (944 kg)
Trunk / Fuel tank	10.2 cu. ft / 12 gallons
Air bags	front
Front suspension	independent, MacPherson struts
Rear suspension	rigid axle
Front brakes / Rear brakes	disc / drum
Traction control	no
Steering	rack-and-pinion, power assist (except S)
Turning circle	n.a.
Tires (front/rear)	P175/65R14
PERFORMANCE	
Engine	4L 1.5-liter DOHC
Transmission	5-speed manual
Horsepower	96 hp at 5800 rpm
Torque	98 lb-ft at 4500 rpm
Other engines	none
Other transmission	4-speed automatic
Acceleration (0-60 mph)	11.9 sec
Maximum speed	103 mph (165 km/h)
Braking (60-0 mph)	148 feet (45 m)
Fuel consumption	33.3 mpg (6.8 L / 100 km)

COMPETITION

- Daewoo Lanos • Hyundai Accent • Saturn SL1
- Toyota Echo

NEW FOR 2002

- New wagon
- 5-year warranty

RATING	(out of 5 stars)
Driveability	★★½
Comfort	★★★
Reliability	★★★
Roominess	★★★
Winter driving rating	★★★
Safety	★★★
Resale value	★★½

KIA SEDONA

KIA **SEDONA**

A Korean Coup

If you belong to a certain generation, you will never forget the Russian hockey team who came to Canada allegedly to learn the finer points from their North American counterparts, and who would have gone home with the Stanley Cup, if they had decided to play out the entire season. I have the distinct feeling that the Kia team in Korea is quietly doing just that – in an automotive context, that is – with their Sedona minivan, this time around at the expense of the Americans and Japanese.

Sporting two side doors, the Sedona is ranked in the mid-range of the long-wheelbase minivan category – theoretically capable of accommodating seven people plus baggage. The body design, though pleasant, is far from original. Here and there, you'll find visual characteristics obviously lifted from both the Toyota Sienna and Ford Windstar.

Nice interior

The front seats, wide and flat, offer a decent driving position. The gearshift lever is conveniently mounted on the nearby console storage compartment between the seats, like the Honda Odyssey. The base LX version gets a comfortable and foldable second-row bench seat, while the EX version gets even cushier captain's chairs – a sea-going reference that I've always found bizarre and whose significance totally escapes me. The third-row three-seat bench is so snug it should be reserved for the kids, or else consenting adults who have no objection to sitting in intimate proximity. On the other hand, it can be adjusted fore and aft, or easily removed thanks to very functional wheels. The baggage area is generous, even when all the seats are in place.

A place in the sun

As we've come to expect of any Korean vehicle, the Sedona's complete range of equipment is one of its strongest selling points. The LX comes with all the principal power-assist features, body-colored bumpers, heated mirrors, front and rear air conditioning (electronically controlled, to boot), and CD player. In addition, EX buyers get ABS (disc/drum), cruise control, power rear quarter windows, contrasting-colored bumpers, alloy wheels (15-inch only), some leather trim, adjustable power front seats (eight-way for the driver, four-way for the passenger), and AM/FM/cassette/CD stereo. As a mat-

▲ PROS

- Complete range of equipment
- Exceptional warranty • Modern design
- Quiet ride • Unbeatable price

▼ CONS

- Dealerships few and far between
- Sluggish acceleration • Shock absorbers too soft
- Substantial weight • Unknown reliability

ter of fact, the equipment is so complete that the only options on offer are the power roof and leather seats (first-rate quality). Needless to say, the quality of materials used and their assembly is beyond reproach.

Ultramodern drivetrain

Kia devoted equal attention to the Sedona's drivetrain, starting with a 3.5-liter V6 engine with 24 valves, perfectly paired to a smooth and well-spaced 5-speed automatic gearbox, a first in the minivan segment. It later transpired that both engine and transmission (minus the Sequential Shift) were "borrowed" from the Sedona's distant relative, the all-new Hyundai XG350 (formerly XG300).

The sum total of all these components makes for a very satisfying ride. The engine's 195 horsepower has little trouble pulling the Sedona's substantial bulk. At 4709 lbs (2136 kg), the machine is way overweight – roughly 440 lbs (200 kg) more than the larger-sized Honda Odyssey, currently the heaviest in its class.

Although I wasn't able to conduct a thorough road test, I suspected that the Sedona's powerplant might have to work a little harder than normal to propel the car in everyday driving conditions. At cruising speed, there was very little engine, road or wind noise. In fact, it was eerily quiet, except for some minor rattles around the location of the outside mirrors. Braking was fine under normal driving conditions – the pedal is satisfyingly firm and easy to modulate. The classical suspension system does its job competently, but I expected more effective dampening. Also, body roll was quite pronounced when cornering. Finally, as is the current standard in this segment, storage areas abound in the Sedona – cupholders too – satisfying everyone's expectations.

"That's all very nice, but will it hold up over the long run?" I don't have answer, except to say that the vehicle's components are up-to-date, and its construction seems rigorous. What's more, it comes with a reassuring 5-year warranty, or 60,000 miles (100,000 km), whichever comes first – no doubt the clincher that this very satisfying Sedona needs as it tries to establish its own place in the sun.

Jean-Georges Laliberté

SPECIFICATIONS	EX
Price	$CDN 24,595-29,595 / $US n.a.
Warranty	5 years / 60,000 miles (100,000 km)
Type	minivan / front wheel drive
Wheelbase / Length	114.6 in / 194.1 in
Width / Height	74.4 in / 68.1 in
Weight	4709 lb (2136 kg)
Trunk / Fuel tank	21.8 / 70.6 cu.ft / 20 gallons
Air bags	front
Front suspension	MacPherson struts
Rear suspension	rigid axle
Front brakes / Rear brakes	disc / drum ABS
Traction control	no
Steering	rack-and-pinion, variable assist
Turning circle	41 feet
Tires (front/rear)	P215/70R15

PERFORMANCE	
Engine	V6 3.5-liter 24-valve DOHC
Transmission	5-speed automatic
Horsepower	195-hp at 5500 rpm
Torque	218 lb-ft at 3500 rpm
Other engines	none
Other transmission	none
Acceleration (0-60 mph)	12.5 sec (est.)
Maximum speed	n.a.
Braking (60-0 mph)	148 feet (est.) (45 m)
Fuel consumption	17.7 mpg (12.8 L/100 km)

COMPETITION

- Chevrolet Venture/Pontiac Montana • Ford Windstar • Honda Odyssey • Mazda MPV • Toyota Sienna

NEW FOR 2002

- New model

RATING	(out of 5 stars)
Driveability	★★★½
Comfort	★★★★
Reliability	New model
Roominess	★★★★
Winter driving rating	★★★½
Safety	★★★½
Resale value	New model

KIA SPECTRA

KIA **SPECTRA**

The Shadow of the Sephia

Last year, the Kia Sephia received an unflattering road report and was given bad marks by our testers. We simply encouraged you to look elsewhere. Is the Spectra any better?

The bad old Sephia's bodywork induced a fit of yawning. On the other hand, the Spectra does create an impression of liveliness that moves it up to a better group of cars. Although it is impossible to identify its designers by name, they do, however, deserve respect. Like their associates from Hyundai, the creators of this transformation also introduced a five-door GS-X model, which fits half-way between a sedan and a traditional wagon. Its trunk space is a little bigger than the others, while still being the smallest in its category, and it is also more practical and easier to use. The sedan's rear backrests can also be folded. The impression is that some manufacturers want to push this type of arrangement on North America, where the buying public just doesn't share the European enthusiasm for this type of car. Whatever the preference, both cars are assembled with great care.

A basic base model

You would think that in view of the rather awful working conditions at Kia the Spectra would reach our shores full of the accessories which are normally offered as options by its rivals. Contrary to this thinking, the base model is just that, with only really basic features for a price of almost $15,000. You must choose the LS if you want air conditioning, standard power systems, and even a rev counter or a simple CD player. With the automatic gearbox, the price comes close to $18,000. The GS-X is $1000 more expensive, but comes with a hatchback, small 14-inch alloy wheels and a few useless leather accessories. Not a good deal, in my opinion.

Inside the cockpit, the plastics have better padding and seem to be of a better quality, the cloth seat covers are thicker and seem likely to last longer. The seats are a little longer and wider, height adjustable, and provide very comfortable seating. Two passengers can sit in the back comfortably, even if the rear window of the GS-X is very close to the back of their heads. But, there is still room for

▲ PROS

- Lively bodywork • Practical GS-X
- Improved materials • Less wind noise
- Exceptional warranty

▼ CONS

- Weak engine • Gearbox needs improvement
- Spongy road behavior • Awful tires
- Price too high

improvement. For example, the aluminum bits on the dashboard of the GS-X seem to have been sprayed on with aerosol paint, and the top of the dashboard seems coated with a bad quality emery paper. As for the rest, the available space and ergonomics are the same as those found on the Sephia – that is, quite acceptable. After a detailed examination one arrives quickly at the conclusion that the improvements are mere bandaids, not serious medicine.

Unsatisfactory engine and gearbox

Just as in a bad movie, uncovering the new Spectra one discovers the spectre of the Sephia with all its mechanical shortcomings. The engine, for example, in spite of promising specifications (16-valve double overhead cam) seems to have been transplanted directly from the older model and it shouts its disapproval beyond 4000 rpm. When you realize that the rather feeble maximum torque of 108 lb-ft only appears a further 500 rpm up the scale, you must resign yourself to making energetic use of whichever gearbox you have chosen. Unfortunately, the automatic gearbox brings us a few years back, with harsh gear changes, while the shift linkage of the manual option is vague and hardly confidence-inspiring.

The Spectra reveals road manners shared by most Korean cars, the springing is too soft and the shock absorbers do not quite manage to control the unsprung weight. The tires don't help matters either, ruining all the efforts made by the designers and engineers to improve the roadholding of their creation. The tires stick to the road like open-toe sandals would stick to the ice, and braking efficiency suffers greatly from the poor tires, even more so as ABS is not available. However, wind and road noise levels are much better when you stay within legal speed limits. As the miles piled on, I had the impression that I was driving a first-generation Elantra. Perhaps it wasn't just a coincidence, if you consider the more and more obvious collusion between these two companies. And in spite of the very strong warranty, five years or 60,000 miles, I would prefer waiting for a complete redesign before investing my money in this car.

Jean-Georges Laliberté

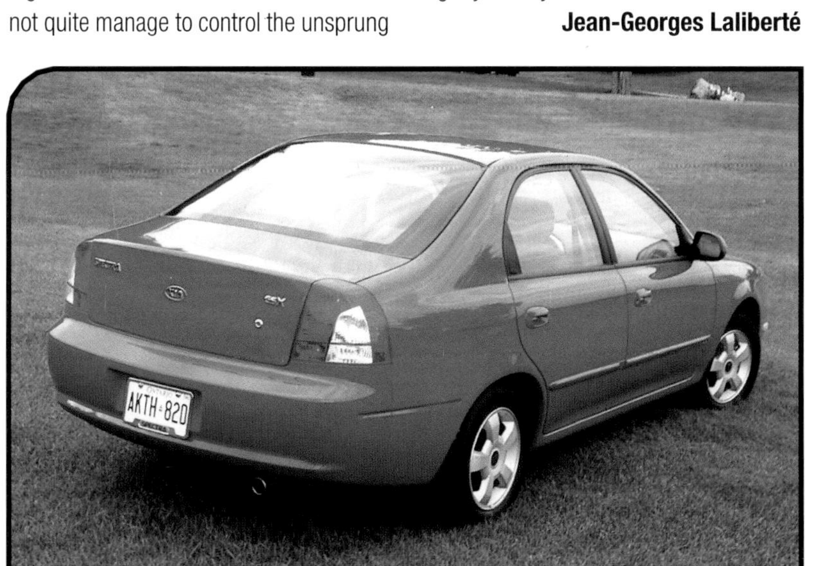

SPECIFICATIONS	**GS-X**
Price	$CDN 14,595-17,595 / $US 11,740-13,940
Warranty	5 years / 60,000 miles (100,000 km)
Type	5-door sedan / front wheel drive
Wheelbase / Length	100.8 in / 178 in
Width / Height	67.7 in / 55.9 in
Weight	2751 lb (1248 kg)
Trunk / Fuel tank	11.6 to 18.6 cu. ft / 13 gal.
Air bags	front
Front suspension	independent, MacPherson struts
Rear suspension	independent, multi-link
Front brakes / Rear brakes	disc / drum
Traction control	no
Steering	rack-and-pinion, power assist
Turning circle	32 ft
Tires (front/rear)	P195/65R14

PERFORMANCE	
Engine	L4 1.8-liter DOHC 16 valves
Transmission	4-speed automatic
Horsepower	125 hp at 6000 rpm
Torque	108 lb-ft at 4500 rpm
Other engines	none
Other transmission	5-speed manual
Acceleration (0-60 mph)	12.5 sec (estimated)
Maximum speed	103 mph (165 km/h)
Braking (60-0 mph)	148 feet (45 m)
Fuel consumption	24.9 mpg (9.1 L/100 km)

COMPETITION

• Cavalier/Sunfire • Civic • Corolla • Elantra • Focus • Neon • Nubira • Protegé

NEW FOR 2002

• New model

RATING	**(out of 5 stars)**
Driveability	★★½
Comfort	★★★
Reliability	New model
Roominess	★★★
Winter driving rating	★★½
Safety	★★★
Resale value	New model

KIA SPORTAGE

KIA **SPORTAGE**

Two Steps Forward...

If sport-utility vehicles were sold on the basis of their looks alone, the Kia Sportage would have an edge over its competitors. In fact, even though this model has been available in North America for five years, it has lost none of its visual appeal. Its roundish looks are still refreshing while other less appealing details are astutely concealed by the use of such contemporary artifices as contrasting-colored strips, alloy wheels and an integrated roof rack.

The same styling approach has been applied to the interior. The dashboard looks positively up-to-date thanks to the go-go, sensible vertical arrangement of the air conditioner and radio controls. And the relatively fat steering wheel certainly enhances the overall effect, conferring an atmosphere of sturdiness and reliability.

In the meantime, since you must "render unto Caesar the things that are Caesar's," the body and platform as well as the quality of finish and assembly have been steadily improved over the past three years. The body panels fit together more snugly as a result, greatly reducing the presence of body noise. As the familiar saying goes, you can always find some room for improvement, but taken all in all, the Sportage has come a long way. Unfortunately, the engineers appear to have spent the greater part of their time and effort on assembly, at the expense of removing one of the vehicle's major irritations: the spare tire is mounted on a bracket blocking the rear liftgate.

As you might suspect, operating the liftgate is a major production. To reach the gate in the first place, you have to begin by swinging the spare tire bracket out of the way. A lever must be pulled to release the rack from its closed position. It then locks in the open position. You can then use your key to open the liftgate. Closing the liftgate involves another serious physical effort because the gate's pneumatic supports are very firm, and you have to push hard to slam it shut. After that, pull the spare tire bracket back into position and you are done. What a chore!

Fine-tuning would help

Don't push your luck

There was no major upset during *The Auto Guide* 4X4 comparison test – certainly not

▲ PROS

- Comfortable rear seats • Elegant exterior
- Finish quality improving • Exceptional warranty
- Off-road prowess

▼ CONS

- Body roll • Cumbersome spare tire
- Wheezy engine • Tailgate too heavy to operate
- Vibration (sideview mirrors)

so far as the Kia Sportage was concerned. But that's really no surprise given the Sportage's run-of-the-mill technical specs. In short, it's a body-on-frame all-terrain vehicle propelled by a 2.0-liter 4-cylinder rated at 130 horsepower, paired to a manual gearbox. An electronically controlled automatic transmission is available as an option. Although made by the legendary German manufacturer Getrag – of BMW fame – the manual gearbox proved to be a disappointment, making constant vibrations that became irritating over the long run. The automatic transmission delivers even flabbier acceleration and passing power, but at least it's smoother. Unfortunately, the box shows some slippage on upshifts, and acceleration suffers as a result. Even in Power mode, the Sportage does poorly in this department, taking just under 14 seconds to go from 0-60 mph.

Poor acceleration might be a good thing, however, since the Sportage's handling is unpredictable at best. First off, it bounces hard on rough road surfaces. And even though steering is far more precise than it used to be, you still have to approach corners with care: body roll is pronounced, and the Sportage's high center of gravity is cause enough for concern. Fortunately, the vehicle is also wide, which helps to some extent. Still, better not push your luck.

The vehicle redeems itself once it forsakes the beaten track, where it proves to be pretty agile and easy to drive. Its part-time all-wheel drive system is rudimentary, but acquits itself fairly respectably in the main. On the other hand, the transfer case lever is not always easy to use.

The Sportage has increasing trouble keeping abreast of the competition, which is often more up-to-date and more powerful, but not necessarily more expensive. Let's hope that the company will continue fine-tuning both its quality and finish.

Denis Duquet

SPECIFICATIONS

Price	$CDN 22,095-25,595 / $US 15,640-19,840
Warranty	3 years / 36,000 miles (60,000 km)
Type	compact SUV / 4X4
Wheelbase / Length	104.3 in / 170.1 in
Width / Height	68.1 in / 65 in
Weight	3373 lb (1530 kg)
Trunk / Fuel tank	26.9 cu. ft / 16 gallons
Air bags	front
Front suspension	independent
Rear suspension	rigid axle
Front brakes / Rear brakes	disc / drum (ABS optional)
Traction control	no
Steering	recirculating balls, power assist
Turning circle	37 feet
Tires (front/rear)	P205/75R15

PERFORMANCE

Engine	4L 2.0-liter
Transmission	5-speed manual
Horsepower	130-hp at 5500 rpm
Torque	127 lb-ft at 4000 rpm
Other engines	none
Other transmission	4-speed automatic
Acceleration (0-60 mph)	14.6 sec
Maximum speed	109 mph (175 km/h)
Braking (60-0 mph)	143 feet (43.7 m)
Fuel consumption	20.5 mpg (11.2 L/100 km)

COMPETITION

• Chevrolet Tracker/Suzuki Vitara • Ford Escape/ Mazda Tribute • Honda CR-V • Toyota RAV4

NEW FOR 2002

No major change

RATING (out of 5 stars)

Driveability	★★
Comfort	★★★
Reliability	★★★
Roominess	★★★
Winter driving rating	★★★★
Safety	★★★½
Resale value	★★★

LAND ROVER DISCOVERY II

LAND ROVER **DISCOVERY II**

Country Chic

Given the current sport-utility craze, automakers seem unanimous in subscribing to the same formula: all-wheel drive and high ground clearance in order to give their vehicles an "all-terrain" illusion when in fact they're intended for smooth, flat, paved roads.

The Land Rover Discovery II, on the other hand, has gone in the opposite direction. Originally conceived for off-road excursion, it's been "dressed up" to blend in with those handsome highway toys you can't help noticing on your weekend outings. But there's a vast difference between a Sunday all-terrain and an all-terrain in its Sunday best, if you catch my drift.

British to the core

Compared with its predecessor which resembled a gigantic roller skate, the Discovery II displays smartly harmonious lines. Thanks to its lengthened body, the cabin is roomier and therefore cosier. Overall ergonomics are satisfactory, and the instrumentation layout looks as British as ever – straightforward, discreet, purposeful. And to think the Rover marque was bought by BMW in 1994, then by Ford only last year!

The front seats are comfortable, if a tad shallow, and the leather upholstery seems of good quality. Passengers may have some trouble getting through the rear's narrow opening, but once inside, the seats are relaxing and offer excellent visibility. The base model comes with 5 seats, to which you can add two optional jump seats, part of a package that includes self-leveling suspension (SLS) and a hydraulic rear step.

The Discovery II comes in three trims: SD, LE and SE. Standard in the base SD model are air-conditioning, cruise control, power windows and locks, leather seating, power-adjustable front seats, 100-watt stereo system and 16-inch alloy wheels. The higher-end models come with the more luxurious accessories.

Cheers for Series II

Something old, something new

The Discovery II stands tall over other SUVs thanks to its original and sophisticated full-time all-wheel drive. In addition to three differentials, it's equipped with Electronic Traction Control (ETC), which applies braking force to wheels that have

▲ PROS

- Complete equipment • Prestigious brand
- Impressive off-road capability • Pleasant design
- Sophisticated all wheel drive

▼ CONS

- Archaic engine • Difficult access to rear seats
- Fragile mechanical components
- Limited production • Stiff price

lost traction as it transfers torque to those with the better grip; Hill Descent Control (HDC) which, as the name suggests, exerts both engine and wheel braking to direct the vehicle gently down a steep descent; Active Cornering Enhancement (ACE), which uses roll-control bars fitted with hydraulic actuators to maintain the vehicle on an even keel in a corner or on rough surfaces. The car can be ordered with 18-inch wheels and 4-season tires.

Unfortunately, the Discovery II's 4.0-liter V8 doesn't match such sophisticated driving aids. It's an all-aluminum overhead-valve engine, developed by GM back in the 1960s – antiquated, if you ask me. Despite its valiant efforts, it generates barely enough power and torque to propel the huge mass at hand. Fortunately, it's supported by an excellent adaptive automatic transmission.

Like Captain Kirk aboard the starship *Enterprise*, you can go where "no man has gone before," behind the wheel of Discovery II. Its sophisticated all-wheel drive system will take you a long way, well, as far as the quality of your tires will allow. The 18-inch Pirelli tires perform honorably enough on paved roads and in the snow but they don't take muddy mires very well, tending to slide around like a wet bar of soap.

On the highway, the Discovery II is less comfortable to ride. Even though the ACE system protects passengers from motion sickness, the stiff suspension will jolt them around ceaselessly. The low steering ratio forces the driver to crank the wheel like a bus driver trying to maneuver his vehicle into a tight parking spot. And let's not even talk about acceleration. If it's any consolation, there's no danger of spilling your tea.

The Discovery Series II shows a marked improvement over its predecessor, although it could use a more up-to-date engine. And the reliability of its mechanical components is not yet proven. Driving a Land or Range Rover still says more about status than it does about practicality.

Jean-Georges Laliberté

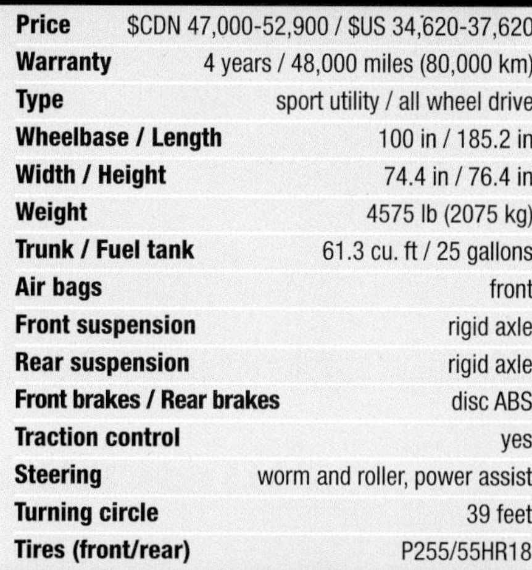

SPECIFICATIONS	
Price	$CDN 47,000-52,900 / $US 34,620-37,620
Warranty	4 years / 48,000 miles (80,000 km)
Type	sport utility / all wheel drive
Wheelbase / Length	100 in / 185.2 in
Width / Height	74.4 in / 76.4 in
Weight	4575 lb (2075 kg)
Trunk / Fuel tank	61.3 cu. ft / 25 gallons
Air bags	front
Front suspension	rigid axle
Rear suspension	rigid axle
Front brakes / Rear brakes	disc ABS
Traction control	yes
Steering	worm and roller, power assist
Turning circle	39 feet
Tires (front/rear)	P255/55HR18

PERFORMANCE	
Engine	V8 4.0-liter
Transmission	4-speed automatic
Horsepower	188 hp at 4750 rpm
Torque	250 lb/ft at 2600 rpm
Other engines	none
Other transmission	none
Acceleration (0-60 mph)	11.8 sec
Maximum speed	106 mph (170 km/h)
Braking (60-0 mph)	150 feet (45.8 m)
Fuel consumption	15.1 mpg (15 L/100 km)

COMPETITION

• BMW X5 3.0 • Ford Expedition • Jeep Grand Cherokee • Mercedez-Benz ML 430

NEW FOR 2002

• Front seat row widened by 2 inches (52 mm)
• New cupholders with rubber trim (WOW!)

RATING	(out of 5 stars)
Driveability	★★
Comfort	★★★
Reliability	★★
Roominess	★★★★
Winter driving rating	★★★★★
Safety	★★★★
Resale value	★★

LAND ROVER FREELANDER

LAND ROVER **FREELANDER**

An American Adventure

For the past few years, Land Rover has been traveling not just over rough roads, but the company has been going through rough some economic times at the same time. First the automaker was bought by BMW, which wanted to carve out a niche for itself in the luxury-SUV market. Unable to turn the venerable marque around financially, the Munich-based automaker threw in the towel and subsequently sold it to the Ford Motor Company. One of the consequences of these developments is the delayed arrival of the Freelander on our shores. Launched in Europe in 1997, Land Rover's compact SUV finally made its North American debut this year.

At first glance, the Freelander reminds you of the Honda CR-V. And that's not a coincidence because Honda and Land Rover were partners before BMW acquired the British firm. But beyond a few similar design characteristics, the pair has virtually nothing else in common.

Like Jeep vehicles, the British-made Freelander has a unibody construction, combining the rigidity of a monocoque body and the sturdiness of an independent chassis. For the time being, only the 2.5-liter V6 version, with a 5-speed automatic transmission, is available in North America. While the Japanese-made gearbox inspires confidence, the Rover-made engine doesn't, considering that automaker's less than stellar reputation for reliability. Be that as it may, its 175 horsepower won't be a waste of energy since the Freelander is heavy for its class, tipping the scales at 3585 lbs (1626 kg), 660 lbs (300 kg) heavier than the Honda CR-V. The reason for the extra weight is simple: the Freelander is a genuine all-terrain vehicle, and not just any compact four-wheel-drive vehicle. Just take a quick glance under the Freelander and you'll see proof of its genuine pedigree: thick skid plates and sturdy suspension components.

All-terrain pedigree

As dictated by the current trends for vehicles in its class, the Freelander features a permanent all-wheel-drive system with a viscous center coupling whose purpose is to transfer torque to the wheels with the best traction. Under normal driving conditions, almost 90% of torque is directed to the front wheels.

▲ PROS

• Comfortable cockpit • Complete equipment • Efficient all-wheel drive • Numerous accessories • Solid platform

▼ CONS

• Average performance • Body roll (when cornering) • Steep price • Limited distribution • Uncertain reliability

In the event of loss of traction in the front, the viscous coupling unit (VCU) automatically "locks" the coupling, increasing torque to the rear wheels. Some purists have often criticized this approach, but it is efficient nonetheless and will certainly be adopted in virtually all SUVs in the future.

In fact, like its bigger brother, Discovery II, the Freelander is equipped with the Hill Descent Control (HDC) which, as the name suggests, exerts wheel braking force to help direct the vehicle gently down a steep slope. This feature replaces the "Lo" low range in more traditional vehicles.

Familiar sensation

The Freelander's cockpit is smaller and less austere than the Discovery II's. Controls are also easier to read and operate, except the button for the rear window, which has an air of mystery about it. For the rest, the quality of finish is seriously good, seats are comfortable and storage areas abound. On the other hand, the driving position is on the high side, so watch your head before you step down, in case you bang it against the door frame.

Driving the Freelander feels remarkably like driving any other Land Rover. So, sporty drivers, consider yourselves warned. Like other Land Rover vehicles, the Freelander is securely attached to its wheels and tends to lean hard each time you tackle a corner. What's more, the engine feels like it's being taxed to the limit, taking more than 11 seconds to go from 0-60 mph, for example. And it also has to contend with the Freelander's high center of gravity. Fortunately, steering is more precise than with the Discovery, so you won't have to rotate the wheel so furiously.

Interested buyers should give the Freelander a careful road test before committing themselves. It's an all-terrain vehicle worthy of its name, but its road manners may disappoint some drivers. As for Land Rover's less-than-stellar reputation for reliability, let's just wait and see whether this most recent version will fare any better than its predecessors.

Denis Duquet

SPECIFICATIONS	
Price	$CDN 34,800-38,800 / $US 29,000-34,000
Warranty	4 years / 48,000 miles (80,000 km)
Type	compact SUV / all wheel drive
Wheelbase / Length	100.8 in / 175.2 in
Width / Height	70.9 in / 69.3 in
Weight	3585 lb (1626 kg)
Trunk / Fuel tank	19.1/46.6 cu. ft (seats down) / 16 gal
Air bags	front
Front suspension	independent
Rear suspension	independent
Front brakes / Rear brakes	disc / drum ABS
Traction control	yes
Steering	rack-and-pinion
Turning circle	38 feet
Tires (front/rear)	P215/65R16 (P225/55R17 opt.)

PERFORMANCE	
Engine	V6 2.5-liter DOHC
Transmission	5-speed automatic
Horsepower	175 hp at 6250 rpm
Torque	177 lb-ft at 4000 rpm
Other engines	none
Other transmission	none
Acceleration (0-60 mph)	11.2 sec
Maximum speed	112 mph (180 km/h)
Braking (60-0 mph)	n.a.
Fuel consumption	16.4 mpg (13.8 L/100 km)

COMPETITION

• Ford Escape/Mazda Tribute • Jeep Liberty

NEW FOR 2002

• All-new model • All wheel drive
• Hill Descent Control • 2.5-liter V6

RATING	(out of 5 stars)
Driveability	★★★½
Comfort	★★★
Reliability	New model
Roominess	★★★½
Winter driving rating	★★★★½
Safety	★★★★
Resale value	New model

LAND ROVER RANGE ROVER 4.6 HSE

RANGE ROVER

Aging Revolutionary

Is anybody really surprised that baby boomers feel so attached to Land Rovers? After all, the automaker – which began producing cars in 1948 – is, in a very real sense, their contemporary. Mind you, the first vehicle that came off the production line had nothing in common with today's Range Rover. In fact, the early vehicle was so rough-and-ready that even doors were considered optional. Still, like everything else, even a vehicle had to start somewhere.

The first Range Rover was launched in 1970, and it became Europe's first ever luxury all-wheel-drive vehicle. Over the next three decades, the model continued to evolve, incorporating many innovations and refinements, mechanical and otherwise, some of which are still exclusive to the Rover name. But the fact remains that the Range Rover continues to be based on the original platform, which helps to explain the many contradictions in its style, genre and mechanical concept.

Innovations

The Range Rover's platform may sound conventional enough today, but 30 years ago, the idea of using flat-aluminum body panels on a boxed-steel ladder-style frame was a strikingly innovative concept. The configuration helps keep the vehicle firmly on the ground, despite its high center of gravity. Another Range Rover development worth noting is the oversized windows, a feature that improves overall visibility especially during off-road activities.

Range Rover's most spectacular innovation, however, involves the use of electronics. Its full-time four-wheel-drive system – currently one of the most sophisticated on the market – consists of three differentials, a two-stage transfer case and a visco-coupling – all linked up to an electronic traction control system. The system works in concert with the four-channel antilock brake system specially calibrated for off-road driving.

Fit for a country squire

In 1993, the Range Rover replaced helicoidal springs with air springs, eventually paving way for an electronic air suspension system that automatically adjusts the vehicle's height to suit every driving situation. Normal mode is for driving in the

▲ PROS

• Air suspension • Aluminum body
• Complete range of equipment • Guaranteed luxury • Off-road capabilities

▼ CONS

• Ancient engine • Exorbitant price
• High fuel consumption • Suspect reliability
• Unclear controls

city and at low speeds. On the open road, the vehicle lowers itself for better stability and less wind resistance. For off-road situations, it raises itself for extra ground clearance, and at a complete stop, it lowers again to accommodate ingress and egress.

Also worth noting are the Range Rover's messaging system and super-powerful audio system – something to inform and entertain its occupants.

Contradictions

The Range Rover's elaborate list of electronic aids alone is enough to impress the most jaded motorists. But the vehicle runs the risk of disappointing them with its ancient overhead-valve engine, probably developed so long ago that Elvis was still learning to play the guitar. Its 222 horsepower has to work hard to propel this 4965-lb mass (2252 kg) and, needless to say, is certain to run up a fuel bill as high as the asking price for this gorgeous English off-roader. Let's just hope that Ford, Rover's owner since 2000, will replace its powerplant soon. At least, during the six years it spent under BMW's ownership, from 1994 to 2000, the Range Rover received an up-to-date automatic transmission.

Unfortunately, that was the extent of BMW's contribution. The Range Rover's dashboard looks as if it had been designed by the British scientists who had deciphered the Enigma machine during World War II. While the cockpit abounds in leather and wood trim and other luxurious features worthy of a vehicle in this price range, the overall presentation suggests it would be more at home in a London club than the cockpit of a state-of-the-art all-terrain vehicle.

Finally, despite all the electronic whizz-bang stuff, driving this mastodon on wheels proves to be an unsatisfying experience. Steering is on the vague side, body roll is pretty pronounced and the engine tends to simply follow the traffic at the rate of 13 mpg (18 L/100 km).

A contradictory vehicle, whose long-term reliability is still unproven, the Range Rover is little more than an oversized conveyance for buyers with oversized, deep pockets.

Denis Duquet

SPECIFICATIONS	4.6 HSE
Price	$CDN 98,000 / $US 63,290-69,290
Warranty	4 year / 48,000 miles (80,000 km)
Type	Sport utility / all wheel drive
Wheelbase / Length	108.3 in / 185.4 in
Width / Height	74.4 in / 71.7 in
Weight	2 252 kg / 4965 lb.
Trunk / Fuel tank	19.5 / 57.9 cu. ft / 25 gallons
Air bags	front and side
Front suspension	rigid axle, air suspension
Rear suspension	rigid axle, air suspension
Front brakes / Rear brakes	disc ABS
Traction control	yes
Steering	recirculating balls, power assist
Turning circle	39 feet
Tires (front/rear)	P255/55HR18

PERFORMANCE	
Engine	V8 4.6-liter ACC 16 valves
Transmission	4-speed automatic
Horsepower	222 hp at 4750 rpm
Torque	300 lb-ft at 2600 rpm
Other engines	none
Other transmission	none
Acceleration (0-60 mph)	10.5 sec
Maximum speed	109 mph (175 km/h)
Braking (60-0 mph)	157 feet (48 m)
Fuel consumption	12.6 mpg (18 L/100 km)

COMPETITION

- BMW X5 • Cadillac Escalade • Lexus LX 470
- Lincoln Navigator • Mercedes-Benz M Class

NEW FOR 2002

- Leather/wood steering wheel with audio controls
- New colors • SE model discontinued

RATING	(out of 5 stars)
Driveability	★★★½
Comfort	★★★½
Reliability	★★½
Roominess	★★★½
Winter driving rating	★★★★★
Safety	★★★★
Resale value	★★

LEXUS GS 300/430

LEXUS **GS 430**

Steady Course

Have you ever tried to pick the winner in a Miss Universe competition? How can you possibly make up your mind between the ravishing Miss Japan, the adorable Miss Germany or the equally exquisite Miss Bavaria? After a little practice, though, you'll just instinctly know what to look for.

Well, that's more or less the procedure *The Auto Guide* took when it considered the Lexus GS. This luxury sport sedan is an excellent car, no question about it, but since each of its competitors possesses its own irresistible features, we decided to scrutinize the flaws, such as they were. The Lexus passed muster, we're happy to report, but that doesn't mean it's absolutely flawless.

A question of balance

The Lexus GS comes in two trim levels, GS 300 and GS 430 that, as their respective numerals indicate, are equipped with 3.0-liter and 4.3-liter VVT-i engines (variable valve timing with intelligence). The first engine is an inline-6 generating 220 horsepower, and the second, a ULEV-certified 8-cylinder (for Ultra Low Emission Vehicle). Introduced in 2000, the 8-cylinder engine produces 300 hp and 325 lb-ft of torque at 3400 rpm. The inline-6 is not short of power by any stretch of the imagination, but by comparison, the 4.3-liter is a genuine big cat, taking barely 6 seconds to do the 0-60 mph. At high revs, it emits a reassuring growl – both throaty and smooth as syrup – which turns into a soft purr as the tachometer needle eases off.

Torque is transferred to the rear wheels via an electronically controlled 5-speed transmission (Super ETC). The gearbox does its job predictably enough, although I detected the occasional, slight hesitation as it hunted for the appropriate ratio. A manual transmission would no doubt suit the GS 300 better, despite the availability of sequential mode on the automatic, which becomes tiring after a while.

Nobody's perfect

Its controls are mounted on the steering wheel and can be awkward to get to, especially when cornering. Surely Lexus can – and should – do something about this.

The suspension system, on the other hand, is firm and supple at the same time – just ideal for a car like the GS 300. The GS 430 doesn't fare as well, its shock absorbers proving to be a tad too harsh for comfort. Furthermore, when pushed to the limit, the GS

▲ PROS

- **Exemplary reliability • Handling (GS 300)**
- **Luxurious and complete range of equipment**
- **Quality assembly and finish • V8 performance**

▼ CONS

- **Cramped cabin space for 5 • Impractical trunk**
- **Poor rear visibility • Unsatisfactory sequential mode on automatic gearbox**

430 starts to behave somewhat unpredictably. We're discussing sporty driving here, and the ever vigilant Vehicle Skid Control system does it job competently, no question about it, but it's equally clear that the engineers haven't quite managed to strike the right balance between comfort and handling, considering the GS 430's extraordinary engine power, which sometimes seems excessive when approaching the cornering limits of the car.

Having got that out of the way, both the 300 and 430 ride smoothly under normal driving conditions. The variable-assist steering doesn't always transmit road feel, but it's quick and precise, and all you need to worry about is resisting the temptation to doze off in the quiet, cushy cabin. But even if that happens, you'll be protected by the powerful disc brakes and their ABS, ever ready to intervene, delivering safe and short stopping distances. And if worst comes to worst, extra protection is at hand in the form of side curtain air bags, added last year to the existing front and side air bags.

Complete range of equipment

The GS's luxury /sport sedan dual nature is plainly visible in its silhouette. And that's not necessarily a compliment. The car's streamlined body looks sporty, but in a somewhat boring way. And not even the optional rear spoiler can help matters. If anything, it further limits the poor visibility that exists in the first place.

The trunk is spacious, but its incongruous shape won't hold cumbersome items. Cabin space, too, is decent – for four people, that is. Despite the central headrest, I can't see how three adults can sit comfortably in the back. The front seats, tautly upholstered in leather, provide excellent comfort and support. The cockpit brims with accessories and commodities. The higher-end 430 gets a few additional luxury items including a superb stereo system, offered as an option, but nothing that justifies the extra $10,000 Lexus charges.

In short, unless you're a diehard sport-minded driver, the GS 300 represents the logical choice. Its proven reliability is promise enough of an enduring love affair – a little devoid of passion perhaps – but that's a small price to pay, since passion is ephemeral at the best of times.

Jean-Georges Laliberté

SPECIFICATIONS	**GS 300**
Price	$CDN 61,600-71,600 / $US 39,150-47,950
Warranty	4 years / 48,000 miles (80,000 km)
Type	sedan / rear wheel drive
Wheelbase / Length	110.2 in / 189.2 in
Width / Height	70.9 in / 56.7 in
Weight	3682 lb (1670 kg)
Trunk / Fuel tank	14. 8 cu. ft / 20 gallons
Air bags	front, side and curtain
Front suspension	independent
Rear suspension	independent
Front brakes / Rear brakes	disc ABS
Traction control	yes
Steering	rack-and-pinion, variable assist
Turning circle	37 feet
Tires (front/rear)	P225/55VR16
PERFORMANCE	
Engine	6L 3-liter
Transmission	5-speed automatic (sequential)
Horsepower	220 hp at 5800 rpm
Torque	220 lb-ft at 3800 rpm
Other engines	V8 4.3-liter 300 hp
Other transmission	5-speed automatic
Acceleration (0-60 mph)	7.9 sec
Maximum speed	143 mph (230 km/h)
Braking (60-0 mph)	129 feet (39.4 m)
Fuel consumption	20.6 mpg (11 L/100 km)

COMPETITION

- BMW 5-Series • Cadillac Seville STS • Infiniti Q45
- Jaguar S-Type • Mercedes-Benz E-Class

NEW FOR 2002

- New navigation system (optional)

RATING	**(out of 5 stars)**
Driveability	★★★★
Comfort	★★★★
Reliability	★★★★½
Roominess	★★★
Winter driving rating	★★★★
Safety	★★★★½
Resale value	★★★★

LEXUS IS 300

LEXUS **IS 300**

Lexus vs. BMW

Last year, the *Auto Guide* published an article headlined "In hot pursuit of BMW" describing the particular niche Lexus had chosen to launch its luxury sports sedan. In its second year on the North American market, the Lexus IS 300 has cranked up its pursuit of BMW with a sexy 5-door version and a manual transmission for its sedan, just as we suggested when it appeared on the scene. I hasten to add that Lexus claims it is not trying to make this little sports sedan into a BMW clone.

Our flaming red Lexus IS 300 sedan had only a few kilometers on the clock when we took possession of it. Our impression after a few turns at the wheel? The same as with the 2001 version and its automatic gearbox: a compact car, pleasant looking but nothing to write home about, easy to handle and particularly well built. The doors made a reassuring "clunk" when we slammed them shut. The suspension was remarkable, if perhaps a little abrupt.

We felt all ruts, potholes and other crevices aboard our IS 300, no doubt amplified by the low-profile tires and the slightly firmer suspension that graces this manual-gearbox model. At the risk of repeating ourselves, we'd like to point out that while these tires improve handling on smooth surfaces, they shake the car on rough roads. So really, is enhanced handling on smooth surfaces worth all this constant knocking about?

At the same time, though, thanks to the favorable fore and aft weight distribution that comes with rear-wheel drive, the IS 300 handling is excellent, and provides the sort of driving pleasure that's impossible to reproduce with front-wheel drive. Body roll is minimal when turning and steering is so precise it's easy to correct the trajectory. The steering wheel, by the way, couldn't be better positioned – it literally falls into your hands. What's more, with a manual transmission, you can play with the accelerator and modulate the level of power that you send to the rear wheels.

The hunt continues

The joy of a manual transmission

As with the doors, the "mechanical" rush you feel when handling the 5-speed manual gearbox (some were hoping for 6) attests to Lexus' thorough engineering work. Naturally, the box is placed right

▲ PROS

- Quality construction • Guaranteed driving pleasure
- Comfortable seats • Complete equipment
- Good-looking station wagon

▼ CONS

- Limited trunk opening (sedan)
- Abrupt suspension (17-inch tires) • No anti-skid
- Slippery pedals • Limited space in the rear

under the lever, thus eliminating wires and other links which often cause the kind of sponginess one feels when handling the manual box of a front-wheel drive car. Final gearing, too, seems to have been chosen to enhance performance.

Thus, in 5th gear at 60 mph, the tachometer hovers near 3000 rpm, near maximum torque, eliminating the need to downshift to pass a car on the road. This instant engine reaction is sheer delight and gives you the impression that the engine is even more powerful than it really is. Not that you need more than 215 horses, but let's just say that the Bimmer's 3.0-liter engine produces even stronger sensations during acceleration.

Another difference with the BMW is the Lexus' lack of anti-skid control, something that makes the BMW more reassuring to drive in winter. But the brakes (with ABS) are up to the job and seem much improved, while traction control prevents you from ruining your 17-inch tires.

While the 2002 sedan is a carryover from 2001, except for the manual gearbox, the IS 300 SportCross is entirely new. The arrival of this hatchback-style station wagon confirms a new trend: specialized wagons offering buyers both driving pleasure and sufficient space as alternatives to minivans and SUVs. SportCross is aimed at those with "an active lifestyle," say the marketing folks.

A discreet and graceful little wing sits atop the rear of the SportCross. Worth noting are a cargo-area "false floor" for storing – or hiding – small items, a backrest that doubles as a table, a folding passenger seat in the front and flat-folding backrests in the rear. What's more, the two front seats are height-adjustable, and the perforated suede covering the middle part of the seats enhances comfort and keeps you well positioned in your seat. And on the subject of slippage, watch out for the "metalized" pedals.

All in all, the IS 300 line – which has yet to include a convertible – will be sure to appeal to a larger public. The ball is now in BMW's court. Let's see if the German maker will "retaliate" by bringing its 3-Series station wagon to North America.

Alain Raymond

LEXUS **IS 300 SPORTCROSS**

SPECIFICATIONS

Price	$CDN 37,820-49,450 / $US 31,350
Warranty	4 years / 48,000 miles (80,000 km)
Type	sedan / rear wheel drive
Wheelbase / Length	105 in / 177 in
Width / Height	68 in / 55.7 in
Weight	3274 lb (1485 kg)
Trunk / Fuel tank	13.8 cu. ft / 18 gallons
Air bags	front and side
Front suspension	independent
Rear suspension	independent
Front brakes / Rear brakes	vented disc / disc ABS
Traction control	yes
Steering	rack-and-pinion, variable assist
Turning circle	36 feet
Tires (front/rear)	P215/45R17 (optional)

PERFORMANCE

Engine	6L 3-liter
Transmission	5-speed manual
Horsepower	215 hp at 5800 rpm
Torque	215 lb-ft at 3800 rpm
Other engines	none
Other transmission	5-speed automatic
Acceleration (0-60 mph)	7.8 sec
Maximum speed	143 mph (230 km/h)
Braking (60-0 mph)	1221 feet (36.8 m)
Fuel consumption	20.3 mpg (11.2 L/100 km)

COMPETITION

• Audi A4 2.8 • BMW 3 Series • Infiniti I35 • Mazda Millenia • M-B C320 • Saab 9³ • Volvo S60

NEW FOR 2002

• 5-speed manual transmission (sedan)

RATING (out of 5 stars)

Driveability	★★★★
Comfort	★★★
Reliability	★★★★★
Roominess	★★★
Winter driving rating	★★★
Safety	★★★★
Resale value	★★★★

LEXUS LS 430

LEXUS **LS 430**

Fantastic Combo

Until the LS 430's arrival in 2001, the bigger Lexus models had never really impressed anyone, other than those who judge an automobile by its reliability and the smoothness of its drive. After a spectacular debut, Lexus sales stagnated for a few years, prompting the Japanese carmaker to rethink its luxury-car strategy if it was going to penetrate a market dominated by the three German greats – Mercedes-Benz, BMW and Audi. The third-generation Lexus model proves that its engineers and designers keenly appreciated the challenge they were facing. The LS 430 has all it takes to challenge the German establishment, which it does by focusing on a more traditional approach to their car.

It's no exaggeration to say that the Lexus LS 430 has become the Cadillac of Mercedes-Benzes or the Mercedes-Benz of Cadillacs. However you look at it, the LS 430 is a terrific combination of American and German ideas of luxury.

Its exterior is inspired by the older Mercedes-Benz S Class while its quiet, smooth performance reminds me of a Cadillac. It all adds up to genuine driving pleasure. At the very least, the LS 430 is a great deal more pleasant to drive than its predecessor, a taxi cab compared to this new European-styled sedan.

LS 430's secret

How did Lexus do it? The answer lies in two main areas: the suspension and the (more rigid) chassis. For the front suspension, Lexus continues to use the double-wishbone layout. But what's interesting here is that the buyer can choose between normal suspension, sport suspension (with low-profile, 17-inch tires, European tuning) or air suspension (for maximum smoothness). Special attention, too, is paid to the forged aluminum chassis, which has been considerably strengthened (by 40%), further enhancing the car's passive safety and roadholding capability. Despite its massive exterior, the LS 430 has a drag coefficient of only 0.25, a remarkable figure under the circumstances.

A matter of taste

Among features worth mentioning are the Dynamic Laser Cruise Control, a system like Mercedes-Benz's "Distronic," which helps maintain a safe distance from the car ahead in bumper-to-bumper traffic, power-heated rear seat with vibro-massage and climate-

▲ PROS

- Outstanding performance • A-1 audio system
- Good roadholding • Excellent engine
- Impeccable brakes

▼ CONS

- Traction control too sensitive • Fragile leather
- Slow response by the automatic transmission
- Impersonal styling

controlled front seats. And music lovers, take heart: the LS 430 boasts a high-end Mark Levinson audio system complete with an in-dash six-CD changer and large, user-friendly control buttons.

Break from the past

Once on the road, the LS 430 quickly asserts itself with steering effort that's just right and an even tighter turning circle than the Mercedes-Benz S Class, giving the driver lots of parking maneuverability. Despite its extra 300 cubic centimeters, the 4.3-liter V8 engine produces the same 290 horsepower as before, but with more torque. Acceleration and passing maneuvers are impressive and discreet without affecting fuel consumption. However, I find the 5-speed automatic transmission a tad slow in responding to the accelerator's demands.

Where the LS 430 breaks from the past is in its roadholding capability. Despite the limitations of the Pirelli snow tires in dry conditions, the LS 430 seems nimble with good control of body roll and relatively neutral roadholding ability. Pushed to the limit, the car oversteers slightly – a loss of adhesion that is quickly corrected by the lateral-stability control system. The car's roadholding capability seemed all the more impressive since our test model didn't even boast the sport-suspension option.

The one problem that I saw was the LS 430's Vehicle Skid Control (VSC) feature, whose too-quick intervention almost caused an accident. Wanting to avoid a yellow light, I stepped hard on the accelerator, but because the road was somewhat slippery the car simply didn't budge, resulting in my being stuck at a red light in the middle of traffic.

For driver and passengers, the cockpit of the LS 430 is a veritable little sitting room with comfortable seats, beautiful leather and wood trims and perfect acoustics. Visibility is impeccable except perhaps when the power rear sunshade is deployed. Exterior mirrors can be electronically collapsed in tight situations. There's so much legroom in the rear, you'd think you were in a limo. Headroom, however, is limited. The trunk is slightly larger than that of the Mercedes-Benz S430.

In sum, the Lexus LS 430 measures up fairly well against its German rival while boasting comfort features a Cadillac driver would enjoy. The rest is a matter of taste.

Jacques Duval

SPECIFICATIONS

Price	$CDN 81,900-94,600 /$US 54,750
Warranty	4 years / 48,000 miles (80,000 km)
Type	5-seat sedan / rear wheel drive
Wheelbase / Length	115.2 in / 196.7 in
Width / Height	72 in / 58.7 in
Weight	3957 lb (1795 kg)
Trunk / Fuel tank	16 cu. ft / 22 gallons
Air bags	front, side and ceiling
Front suspension	independent
Rear suspension	independent
Front brakes / Rear brakes	disc, ABS + brake assist
Traction control	yes
Steering	rack-and-pinion, variable assist
Turning circle	35 feet
Tires (front/rear)	P225/60R16

PERFORMANCE

Engine	V8 4.3-liter
Transmission	5-speed automatic
Horsepower	290 hp at 5600 rpm
Torque	320 lb-ft at 3400 rpm
Other engines	none
Other transmission	none
Acceleration (0-60 mph)	6.8 sec
Maximum speed	155 mph (250 km/h)
Braking (60-0 mph)	131 feet (39.8 m)
Fuel consumption	17.5 mpg (13 L/100 km)

COMPETITION

• Audi A8 • BMW 740i • Cadillac DeVille • Infiniti Q45 • Jaguar XJ8 • Mercedes-Benz S430

NEW FOR 2002

• Navigation system available on Premium and Ultra Premium packages

RATING (out of 5 stars)

Driveability	★★★★
Comfort	★★★★
Reliability	★★★★★
Roominess	★★★★
Winter driving rating	★★★½
Safety	★★★★★
Resale value	★★★★

LEXUS **LX 470**

LEXUS **LX 470**

An Inside Look

In a hangar, bathed in the surreal orange of the sodium-vapor lamps, a group of people are gazing at the huge chassis of a large 4-wheel-drive vehicle. An imposing V8 engine dominates the front end while participants in the event are busy poking and tweaking "the exposed beast." They are Lexus division engineers who are laying bare the innards of the new Lexus LX 470 to the journalists in attendance.

It was in December 1999, just a few days before Christmas, that Lexus unveiled the RX 300 and the LX 470. While the first quickly became hugely popular with the "in crowd," the LX 470 proved to be a status symbol for the "rich and famous." With a hefty price tag it's hardly surprising that its production is limited.

The point of that rather unusual bare-bones examination was to demonstrate the highly rigid mechanical components that made up the LX 470's frame, even though they weren't hydroformed as is the case with its rival, the Cadillac Escalade. On the other hand, the LX 470 features a height-adjustable suspension system, which is ideal for either off-road, or highway/city driving. And while it's true that these mechanical components were more or less borrowed from the new-generation Toyota Land Cruiser, the LX 470 boasts countless features that are its very own.

Since the 1999 unveiling, the technical specifications of this luxury sport ute have not changed much, although a few accessories have been added to enhance the luxury level. The LX 470 is still powered by the original 4.7-liter V8 engine, with the same as yet unequalled smoothness. Its 230 hp – no doubt perfectly adequate at the time – now seems meager next to the 345 hp cranked out by the Escalade. While the Cadillac's look is quite an eye-catcher with its unusual grille and provocative stance, it's obvious that no one is going to buy a Lexus LX 470 to see how many heads will turn. Worse still, it could be mistaken for a Toyota Sequoia, or even a Highlander, by someone not too familiar with the art of grille or insignia recognition.

Status Symbol

▲ PROS

• Height adjustable suspension • High quality materials • Incomparable reliability • Meticulously constructed • Super smooth engine

▼ CONS

• Bland design • Elephant sized • High price • Thirsty engine • Token third bench

But step inside the vehicle and you'll discover the level of luxury hidden behind its rather bland shape. The high quality of the materials alone is a distinctive hallmark. The seats are not just remarkable because of the superior leather quality, they're also super comfortable and can be adjusted in every conceivable direction. Ditto the suspension which features compressed air springs to raise or lower it by two inches, to respond to changing driving conditions or simply for ease of entry.

A nimble hippo

It's physically impossible for a vehicle weighing more than 5000 lbs (2450 kg) with an overall length of 192.5 inches (489 cm) to perform as nimbly as a Toyota RAV4 or an RX 300. A quick glance at the specifications and you expect the worst. You have visions of driving a V8-propelled hippopotamus. Yet despite its sumo wrestler size, this 4WD is surprisingly nimble. Road manners are very good considering the mass and high center of gravity. Following a gently winding road without easing up on the gas pedal is quite feasible, and you don't need to shut your eyes and say your prayers. Moreover, if you just can't control the urge to step on the gas, the brakes are effective and resist quite well to overheating.

Those who dare expose the fine machinery and exquisite paint job of this upscale vehicle to off-road driving will be pleasantly surprised, because it handles itself capably in those conditions even though the tires aren't always efficient in mud. Still, you'll get more out of the LX 470's balance and efficient all wheel drive system over snowy or icy roads than studying tree forms in the boreal forest.

Quiet as a cat, with an engine that rarely expresses more than a gentle purr, the LX 470 is beautifully put together which should provide all those who ride in it with a reassuring but boring sense of efficiency.

Denis Duquet

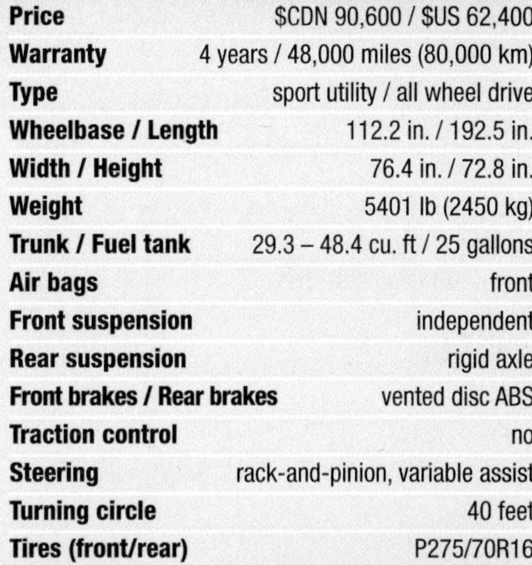

SPECIFICATIONS	
Price	$CDN 90,600 / $US 62,400
Warranty	4 years / 48,000 miles (80,000 km)
Type	sport utility / all wheel drive
Wheelbase / Length	112.2 in. / 192.5 in.
Width / Height	76.4 in. / 72.8 in.
Weight	5401 lb (2450 kg)
Trunk / Fuel tank	29.3 – 48.4 cu. ft / 25 gallons
Air bags	front
Front suspension	independent
Rear suspension	rigid axle
Front brakes / Rear brakes	vented disc ABS
Traction control	no
Steering	rack-and-pinion, variable assist
Turning circle	40 feet
Tires (front/rear)	P275/70R16

PERFORMANCE	
Engine	V8 4.7-liter
Transmission	4-speed automatic
Horsepower	230-hp at 4800 rpm
Torque	320 lb-ft at 3400 rpm
Other engines	none
Other transmission	none
Acceleration (0-60 mph)	10.4 sec
Maximum speed	112 mph (180 km/h) (electron. lim.)
Braking (60-0 mph)	144 feet (44 m)
Fuel consumption	12.2 mpg (18.5 L/100 km)

COMPETITION

• BMW X5 • Cadillac Escalade/Lincoln Navigator
• Mercedes-Benz ML430 • Range Rover

NEW FOR 2002

No major change

RATING	(out of 5 stars)
Driveability	★★
Comfort	★★★★
Reliability	★★★★½
Roominess	★★★★
Winter driving rating	★★★★★
Safety	★★★★
Resale value	★★★★½

LEXUS RX 300

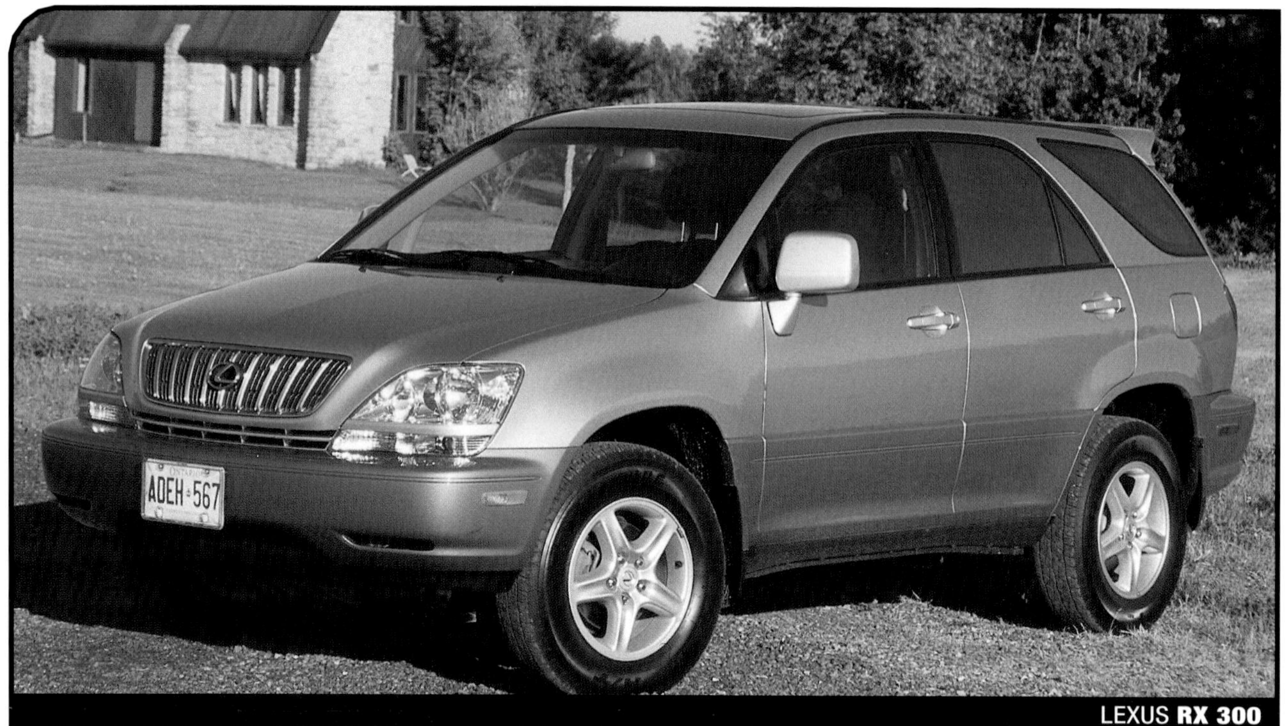

LEXUS **RX 300**

Still the Benchmark

Over the years, the Lexus division has not experienced only commercial successes. Some models bombed so badly that the company would rather forget about them. These days, however, Lexus folks are more than eager to brag about the RX 300, a model so successful year after year that it's become the benchmark in its category.

No one had anticipated such an enthusiastic response from the public. In fact, when the Canadian model was unveiled, it was in the form of a quick, unpublicized test-drive of a prototype scheduled just a few days before Christmas. While the Lexus badge was clearly visible at the center of the grille, the prototype was in fact a refined version of the Toyota Harrier, itself derived from the Camry platform. The engine was the ubiquitous 3.0-liter V6 with 220 hp – 20 more than in the ES 300. Finally, its all-wheel drive shared many components with the old Camry AWD.

The new RX 300 sports a distinctive, attractive silhouette, something between an SUV and a station wagon, except for the front fascia, which appears sedan-like. The rear is definitely station-wagon material, complete with a triangular-shaped window and a thick C pillar.

Surprisingly, the RX 300 is 11 inches (28 cm) taller than the ES 300, and 10 inches (25 cm) shorter than the sedan. It's this rearrangement of mass that makes the vehicle look like a big SUV, although in fact it's nothing more than a taller-than-average station wagon with all-wheel drive.

Another secret of the RX 300's success is the cockpit, which is second to none. Get into its comfortable front bucket seats and you'll discover a dashboard like no other on the market. The highlight is the vertical console that divides the dash in two parts. The top part includes a liquid-crystal display screen (LCD) framed by two vents. In models lacking a satellite navigation system, the screen displays status information concerning the audio and climate control systems which are located directly below it. This arrangement may seem impressive at first glance, but is not exactly user-friendly. I kept activating the wrong button, increasing the radio's volume when in fact what I wanted

The compromise

▲ PROS

- Flexible V6 engine • Comfortable interior
- Adequate handling • Impeccable finish
- Unique styling

▼ CONS

- Sluggish steering • Some controls need work
- Slow automatic gearbox • Rudimentary all-wheel drive • End-of-line model

to do was to turn down the air conditioner. Like the LCD, the shift lever is mounted on the center dashboard, freeing up some floor space for a movable console between the seats. As for the CD player, look in the glove compartment. This arrangement may have been interesting a few years ago, but no longer makes sense today, what with the advent of the CD changer (up to 6 CDs) that is integrated in the audio system.

Passengers will appreciate the generous leg and headroom provided by the rear seats. You can even slide or recline the various sections of the 60/40 bench individually. Cargo space, however, is just average.

An ideal compromise

On the road, the RX 300 performs quite adequately. All in all, it's nicely responsive to the public's driving demands – a macho-looking all-terrain vehicle, the feeling of safety provided by all-wheel drive, comfortable suspension and reasonable fuel economy. Its road behavior is similar to that of a big station wagon, exhibiting some body roll during cornering, and steering is sluggish. The four-wheel independent suspension is relatively soft and soaks up road irregularities efficiently. In fact, it's only when you make a tight turn that you discover that the car is taller than average. The V6 engine is supple and quiet thanks in large measure to its continuously-variable-valve-timing system.

Despite the fact that the RX 300 has been on the market for more than four years, it remains the benchmark. The Acura MDX has what it takes to topple Lexus, and would have done so had it not been for its rather harsh suspension, noisier engine and rudimentary sound insulation. Admittedly, the Acura's all-wheel drive is superior, but I doubt that drivers buy these vehicles to go play in the woods.

Even though it has reached the end of the line, this Lexus is still an ideal compromise. Its equipment – superior to the Toyota Highlander – and the prestige of the Lexus marque make sure of that.

Denis Duquet

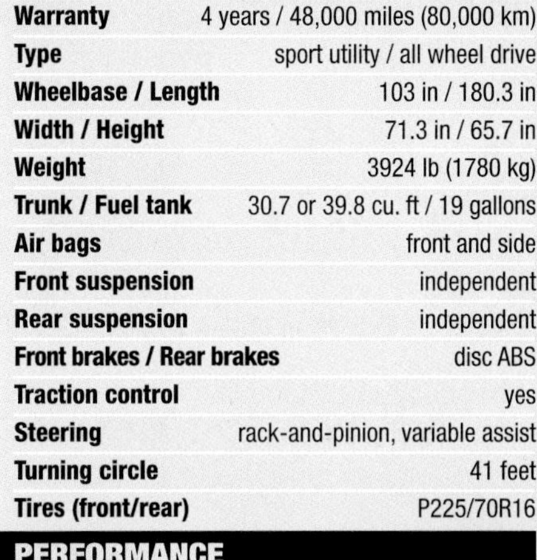

SPECIFICATIONS	
Price	$CDN 48,000 / $US 34,500-36,250
Warranty	4 years / 48,000 miles (80,000 km)
Type	sport utility / all wheel drive
Wheelbase / Length	103 in / 180.3 in
Width / Height	71.3 in / 65.7 in
Weight	3924 lb (1780 kg)
Trunk / Fuel tank	30.7 or 39.8 cu. ft / 19 gallons
Air bags	front and side
Front suspension	independent
Rear suspension	independent
Front brakes / Rear brakes	disc ABS
Traction control	yes
Steering	rack-and-pinion, variable assist
Turning circle	41 feet
Tires (front/rear)	P225/70R16

PERFORMANCE	
Engine	V6 3-liter
Transmission	4-speed automatic
Horsepower	220 hp at 5800 rpm
Torque	222 lb-ft at 4400 rpm
Other engines	none
Other transmission	none
Acceleration (0-60 mph)	9.1 sec
Maximum speed	112 mph (180 km/h) (limited)
Braking (60-0 mph)	131 feet (40 m)
Fuel consumption	17.9 mpg (12.7 L/100 km)

COMPETITION

- Chev. TrailBlazer/GMC Envoy • Ford Explorer
- Infiniti QX4 • Jeep Gr Cherokee • MB ML320

NEW FOR 2002

No major change

RATING	(out of 5 stars)
Driveability	★★★½
Comfort	★★★★½
Reliability	★★★★
Roominess	★★★★
Winter driving rating	★★★★★
Safety	★★★★½
Resale value	★★★★★

LEXUS SC 430

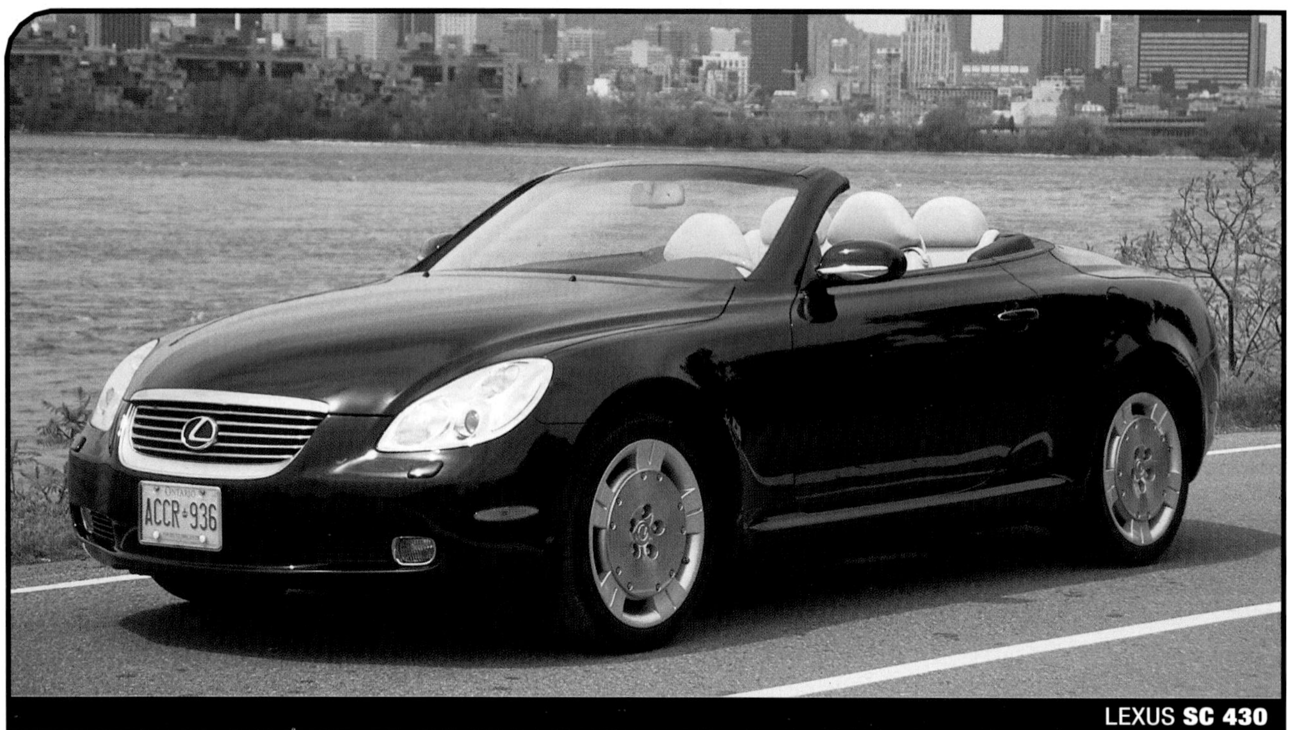

LEXUS **SC 430**

Daring to Be Different

Say whatever you like about the new Lexus SC 430's fantastic all-aluminum V8 and its 300 hp, the sophisticated vehicle skid control, or the big run-flat tires. What makes this "Coupe-vertible" truly amazing, is none of the above. In fact, you ain't see nothin' until you witness the little magic trick this Lexus performs when eight little motors come to life and begin to retract the roof. Like a nimble contortionist, the roof lifts up, reclines, then disappears seamlessly into the trunk.

Japanese automakers have invariably been criticized for their lack of imagination and style. Well, no more, and hats off to Lexus for daring to be different. Even though its styling has yet to win unanimous approval, at least we can agree that the SC 430 Coupe-vertible has the advantage of being unique. For many people, including myself, this car is an ode to esthetics. Its 18-inch alloy-wheels look unusually attractive and the art-deco interior is reminiscent of those luxury yachts that ply the deep blue Mediterranean – just as the Lexus brochure pretends. From the aluminum door-sills that illuminate at night to the bird's-eye-maple trim that adorns the dashboard, this model reeks of exclusivity. Incidentally, the bird's-eye-maple trim didn't pass unnoticed by the people I met in Madawaska, where my test-drive took place. They wasted no time telling me about the rarity as well as prohibitive cost of this precious material. Like the Audi TT, the SC 430 Coupe-vertible is the kind of car you can't help but stop to admire before finally slipping behind the wheel.

Between sport and Grand-Touring

Lexus' market research shows that every seven seconds, a new 50-something is "born" in North America. It's precisely this clientele that the company had in mind when it developed the SC 430. Which explains why the model is more like a grand-touring car than a sports number. After a 1,200-mile test-drive, I'll say that the SC 430 comes to rest somewhere between these two interpretations. The car doesn't exhibit the nimbleness of a Boxster, but it's not sluggish like its main competitor – the Jaguar XK8 – either. Its big low-profile tires are the reason for all the knocking about on rough roads, but, on the other hand, they stick to the road like Velcro, especially through corners. The one drawback is the

Hats off to Lexus!

▲ PROS
- Superb engine • Tenacious road manners
- Excellent construction quality
- Low engine noise • Luxurious equipment

▼ CONS
- Sluggish automatic transmission
- Harsh tires • Narrow trunk (convertible)
- Poor rear visibility

all-too-obvious body roll. But any mature driver with a taste for sporty driving will appreciate the unobtrusive intervention of the vehicle skid control (VSC) feature.

Braking is up to snuff, as you might expect from the vented front disc brakes with electronic brake distribution (EBD). The 4.3-liter 32-valve V8 engine is exceptionally smooth and quiet, with enough horsepower to achieve a top speed of 156 mph, with matching torque. The same can't be said of the automatic transmission, which is a tad slow in responding to the accelerator's demands. As a result, the car takes an unimpressive 6.6 seconds to go from 0-60 mph.

Exception to the rule

Like the Mercedes SLK, the Lexus Coupevertible avoids almost all the shortcomings associated with a convertible. With its roof in place, wind noise is practically non-existent, allowing you to appreciate the exquisite sound quality of the Mark Levinson AM/FM/6-CD in-dash changer with nine speakers. That much said, there's one weakness: If the roof retracts in 25 seconds, it takes exactly the same length of time to reduce the trunk capacity by half!

On the road, the car exhibits some body noise. Its body is acceptably rigid, but not enough to make the car behave like a genuine fixed-roof coupe. At least the fact that the top is not made of canvas makes it more pleasant to drive in winter than a sedan.

The SC 430's sumptuous standard equipment justifies the steep price. Worth noting is the built-in tire-pressure monitoring system that's intended to gauge tire pressure every 15 seconds. Still, I was driving for a good distance at 120 mph before the system kicked in to notify me that the tires were not properly inflated to sustain that sort of speed. By the way, at 150 mph, directional stability is impeccable. At dusk, however, the sunshades are either too high or too low. The same goes for the invisible remote controls for the trunk and the fuel tank.

Lucky the 50-something who can afford this Lexus SC 430. Behind the wheel, he'll be able to recapture the thrills of his youth – with the additional comfort and peace of mind that he has come to appreciate.

Jacques Duval

SPECIFICATIONS	
Price	$CDN 84,000 / $US 59,000
Warranty	4 years / 48,000 miles (80,000 km)
Type	2+2 coupe-convertible / rear wheel drive
Wheelbase / Length	103 in / 177.8 in
Width / Height	72 in / 53 in
Weight	3843 lb (1743 kg)
Trunk / Fuel tank	8.8 cu. ft / 22 gallons
Air bags	front and side
Front suspension	independent
Rear suspension	independent
Front brakes / Rear brakes	disc ABS
Traction control	yes
Steering	rack-and-pinion, power assist
Turning circle	35 feet
Tires (front/rear)	P245/405ZR18

PERFORMANCE	
Engine	V8 4.3-liter
Transmission	5-speed automatic
Horsepower	300-hp at 5600 rpm
Torque	325 lb-ft at 3400 rpm
Other engines	none
Other transmission	none
Acceleration (0-60 mph)	6.6 sec
Maximum speed	155 mph (250 km/h)
Braking (60-0 mph)	120 feet (36.6 m)
Fuel consumption	18.1 mpg (12.5 L/100 km)

COMPETITION

- Jaguar XK8 • Mercedes-Benz SL500

NEW FOR 2002

- New model

RATING	(out of 5 stars)
Driveability	★★★★
Comfort	★★★
Reliability	New model
Roominess	★★½
Winter driving rating	★★★
Safety	★★★
Resale value	New model

LINCOLN CONTINENTAL

LINCOLN **CONTINENTAL**

American-Style Luxury

The Lincoln division has recently been integrated into the Premier Automotive Group (PAG) – created by Ford to ensure that the luxury-car brands gathered under its corporate umbrella are properly differentiated. In addition to Lincoln, PAG includes Aston Martin, Jaguar, Land Rover and Volvo. The message seems clear enough – Lincoln has absolutely no intention of emulating the Europeans. Its mission remains the same to build American-style luxury cars.

This rather vague description can signal both the best and worst of what is meant by American automobile luxury. The Lincoln LS is an example of American luxury at its finest: a well-rounded sport sedan, incorporating high-level road performance and unabashedly American sophistication. At the opposite end of the spectrum is the Lincoln Town Car – a caricature in almost every respect, confirming all the excesses that earmark an American luxury car.

The Lincoln Continental falls somewhere in between, in terms of performance and style. By trying too hard to avoid mistakes, engineers and designers seemed to have lost their bearings. The result of their combined efforts is a less than exciting luxury sedan, doubly handicapped by a performance that can optimistically be described as average, and by a total lack of personality.

Not to the manor born

For years, Lincoln Continentals were so huge they looked like road versions of ocean liners. Redesigned for the first time in 1988, the car's size and weight were considerably reduced, and it went from rear-wheel to front-wheel drive. Mechanicals were thus brought up-to-date, but the styling grew blander.

Needs work!

After going back to the drawing board in 1995, the Continental was treated to a 4.6-liter V6 engine, but was saddled with an even more forgettable appearance. The 2002 model is a slightly updated version of this earlier generation, and as suspected, it looks as ho-hum as its predecessors of the past 15 years.

The bland leading the bland

Curiously, Lincoln engineers were mandated to develop a super luxury sedan: rigid

▲ PROS

- Comfortable rear seats • Powerful engine
- Quiet ride • Superb finish

▼ CONS

- Body roll on turns • Baffling electronics
- Nondescript appearance • Poorly tuned suspension
- Seats lack side support

chassis, four-wheel independent suspension, sophisticated 4.6-liter 32-valve DOHC "InTech" V8 engine with 275 hp, coil-on-plug electronic ignition system, the whole works. They did just that, only to sabotage the effort with a consistently anonymous chassis.

In fact, when was the last time you actually spotted a Continental on the road? I'll bet no one remembers. The Continental is the elusive car. It's well proportioned and all that, but the general effect is so indifferent it's scary. The blandness extends to the interior. The dashboard is functional enough, but looks like a bare wall decorated with a handful of random buttons. Finally, the front "armchairs" look as if they'd been borrowed from a conference room. Adjustable in any position you like, they're also super soft and conducive to snoozing, rather than piloting the car. On the other hand, the finish and the quality of the materials used are first class, and the rear cabin gets top marks: comfortable bench and excellent head and legroom, even for tall adults.

So here we are, behind the wheel of a mediocre-looking car – inside or outside – but one whose mechanical components are among the most advanced. It's therefore possible to hope that, beneath the nondescript appearance is a car that's a pleasure to drive, capable of competing with the best. After all, it's so sophisticated that you can even electronically adjust the steering's assistance or the firmness of the suspension.

Alas, the Continental fails us once again. All those electronic controls turned out to be completely useless because neither the steering nor suspension responded properly to the commands. This particular Lincoln would be right at home in a funeral procession, in bumper-to-bumper traffic or as a car to take grocery-shopping with you. Unfortunately, it rapidly loses its bearings if you step too hard on the accelerator. Body roll is pronounced while turning and the zero-pressure tires tend to squeal if you turn the least bit energetically. The driver has to hang on tight to the steering wheel so he won't slide out of his seat, which offers no side support whatsoever.

Denis Duquet

SPECIFICATIONS

Price	$CDN 51,920 / $US 40,405
Warranty	4 years / 48,000 miles (80,000 km)
Type	sedan / front wheel drive
Wheelbase / Length	109. in / 208.7 in
Width / Height	73.6 in / 55.9 in
Weight	3836 lb (1740 kg)
Trunk / Fuel tank	18.4 cu ft / 20 gallons
Air bags	front and side
Front suspension	independent
Rear suspension	independent
Front brakes / Rear brakes	disc ABS
Traction control	yes
Steering	rack-and-pinion, variable assist
Turning circle	41 feet
Tires (front/rear)	P225/60R16

PERFORMANCE

Engine	V6 4.6-liter
Transmission	4-speed automatic
Horsepower	275 hp at 5750 rpm
Torque	275 lb-ft at 4750 rpm
Other engines	none
Other transmission	none
Acceleration (0-60 mph)	8.3 sec
Maximum speed	134 mph (215 km/h)
Braking (60-0 mph)	136 feet (41.5 m)
Fuel consumption	16.3 mpg (13.9 L/100 km)

COMPETITION

• Acura RL • Buick Park Avenue • Cadillac Seville

NEW FOR 2002

• Improved message center

RATING (out of 5 stars)

Driveability	★★½
Comfort	★★★★
Reliability	★★★½
Roominess	★★★★
Winter driving rating	★★★★
Safety	★★★★
Resale value	★★

LINCOLN LS

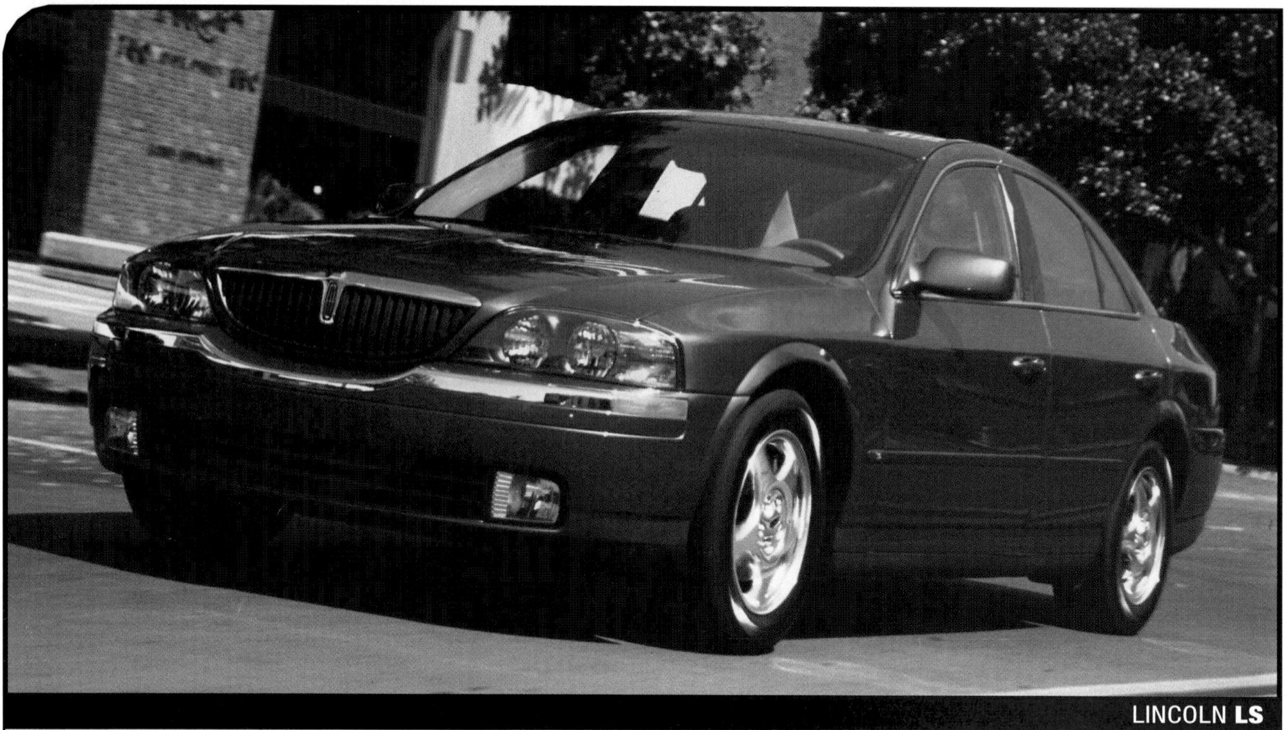

LINCOLN **LS**

On the Right Path

North American automakers today face a serious demographic challenge: their regular customers are aging and the younger ones – not to say the young at heart – tend to gravitate toward foreign makes in at least two important automobile categories: the low-end models on the one hand, and high end on the other. Born in the last century, the Lincoln LS is now trying to play its part in reversing the situation.

That's a tall order as far as the Big Three are concerned, because their combined market share has been steadily eroding during the past 30 years. Come to think of it, following Chrysler's highly publicized defection into the arms of Daimler Benz, it may well be more appropriate to refer to the group as the "Truck Two." After all, it was to energetically promote the truck and sport-utility market that North American automakers chose to neglect other less profitable niches.

A good base

Ford's counterattack – at least, attempted counterattack – rests squarely on the wheels of the Lincoln LS, American cousin of the Jaguar S-Type, both sharing the same platform. Since front-wheel drive no longer suits this category of automobile, the new LS is a rear-driver, with independent four-wheel suspension – a prerequisite if you want both driving pleasure and acceptable handling. With 50/50 weight distribution front and rear, handling is indeed predictable and sound – pleasant even – despite the car's hefty 3693-lb (1675 kg) weight.

Good start

Steering is disappointing, however, Not that it's imprecise, but because it feels heavy. What's more, the steering wheel kicks each time you hit a bump or pothole in the road, a flaw I find unacceptable in a car this expensive. The problem was worse in the test car, I might add, because the front wheels were improperly balanced.

Braking, too, is not quite up to standard. The brakes themselves are efficient, but the pedal feels spongy. The LS redeems itself considerably with its 5-speed automatic transmission, which

▲ PROS

• Comfortable seats • Complete equipment • Good value/price ratio • Sound handling

▼ CONS

• Boring V6 • Poor acceleration • Nondescript styling • Small trunk • Steering vibration

proves to be a perfect match for the 3.9-liter V8 engine. Shifting is so smooth it's imperceptible. As is the norm today, the gearbox comes with a manual mode, which is neither particularly useful, nor widely used.

Performance-wise, the LS doesn't quite make the grade. Given its unfavorable power/weight ratio, the car takes almost 9 seconds to go from 0-60 mph. That's a long time for a car of this class. But take heart, downshifting is swift, and that enhances passing power: 6 seconds to go from 50-75 mph.

Polished and comfortable, but dull

There's no point in carping over the rather non-style style of the youthful Lincoln. However, the cabin is both polished and luxurious. Seats are comfortable front and back, multi-way adjustable in front. If it weren't for the hard-to-reach controls, the cockpit would have scored a perfect 10. The rear seats can flip forward for extra cargo space – a blessing, since the trunk's floor had to be raised to make room for the rear axle underneath. So forget that big suitcase, or the cooler for your picnic. They won't fit.

The dashboard looks classic and understated, and the superb sound wafting from the Alpine stereo system – with 6-CD changer, to boot – will make you forget the ergonomically-challenged center console, brimming with controls of one kind or another. Nifty features abound: heated seats and mirrors, automatic air conditioner, tilt and telescopic steering column, automatic rain-sensing wipers, easy-to-reach ignition. A few storage areas would have completed the picture nicely.

Let's finish up with a few stats. The fuel mileage of 19mpg on the highway decreases to 16 mpg in the city. We're obviously talking about the V8 engine. The V6, paired to a 5-speed manual gearbox, delivers such mediocre performance that it's really not worth considering. As for pricing, the test model for example – V8, traction control, sport package (17-inch chromed wheels, sunroof, leather trim etc.) – retails for less than $53,000, which represents one of the car's selling points. It's a good car, all in all, but there's still much work to be done.

Alain Raymond

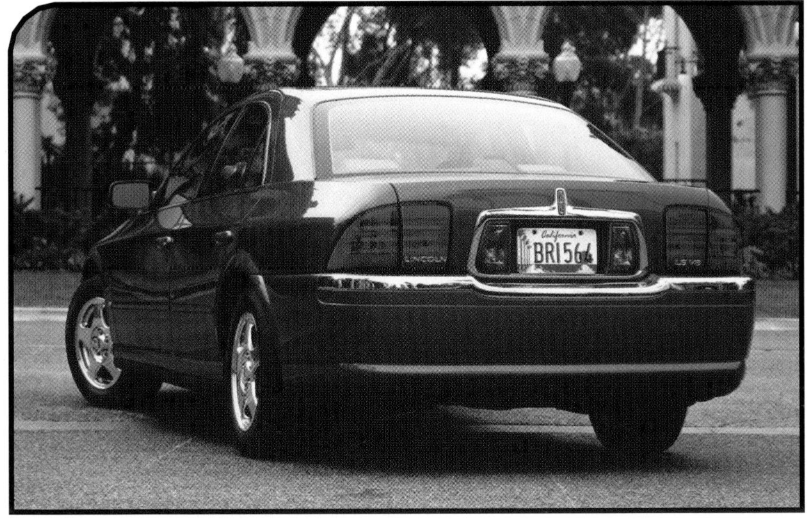

SPECIFICATIONS

Price	$CDN 40,870-49,195 / $US 32,700-36,730
Warranty	4 years / 48,000 miles (80,000 km)
Type	sedan / rear wheel drive
Wheelbase / Length	114.2 in / 193.7 in
Width / Height	73.2 in / 56.1 in
Weight	3693 lb (1675 kg)
Trunk / Fuel tank	13.5 cu. ft / 18 gallons
Air bags	front and side
Front suspension	independent
Rear suspension	independent
Front brakes / Rear brakes	disc ABS
Traction control	yes
Steering	rack-and-pinion, variable assist
Turning circle	38 feet
Tires (front/rear)	P235/50R17

PERFORMANCE

Engine	V8 3.9-liter
Transmission	5-speed automatic
Horsepower	252-hp at 6100 rpm
Torque	267 lb-ft at 4300 rpm
Other engines	V6 3.0-liter 210-hp
Other transmission	5-speed manual
Acceleration (0-60 mph)	8.8 sec
Maximum speed	137 mph (220 km/h)
Braking (60-0 mph)	135 feet (41 m)
Fuel consumption	18.6 mpg (12.2 L/100 km)

COMPETITION

• Jaguar S-Type • Infiniti I35 • Lexus GS
• M.-Benz C Class • Volvo S80

NEW FOR 2002

No major change

RATING (out of 5 stars)

Driveability	★★★½
Comfort	★★★★
Reliability	★★★
Roominess	★★★½
Winter driving rating	★★★½
Safety	★★★★
Resale value	★★★

LINCOLN TOWN CAR

LINCOLN **TOWN CAR**

Car, Limousine or Hearse?

According to its order book, the Lincoln Town Car comes in three categories: touring car, commercial limousine or hearse. This should give you a good idea about its customer base which consists mainly of fleet buyers and limo-and-hearse service companies. It should come as no surprise, then, that regular customers rarely buy Lincoln Town Cars.

While there's no accounting for taste and color, it's a relief to see that the Town Car is not exactly popular with individuals or families. After all, who would want to drive their kids around in such a nondescript, sinister-looking sedan unless you wished to scar them for life? Besides what would the neighbors think? They'd probably wonder about the kind of company you keep, or imagine you're an underworld bigshot with an army of bodyguards ready to spring into action. If that sounds too distasteful, how about being taken for a banker, an undertaker or a chauffeur? Seriously, let's just leave the TC to airport transportation professionals or those about to depart this world for a better place.

Separate chassis

Lincoln cars – at least the biggest among them – can be adapted to so many configurations because they have a separate chassis. All it takes is frame rails and reinforcement parts, and you've got a suitably modified wheelbase. And since it's a rear-wheel drive, the car's overall balance is not affected. Lincoln itself got into the "modifying" act last year by bringing out the Executive model with a wheelbase extended by 15 cm at the factory, providing more legroom in the rear.

That said, the technical specifications of this huge American car are far from sophisticated. It's still fitted with solid-axle rear suspension and recirculating-balls steering. You would think some mechanical features haven't been changed for ages. At least the engine is up to date, since it's a 4.6-liter V8. Curiously, both the Executive and Signature models are fitted with the single-overhead-camshaft version of this engine, which produces only 220 horsepower, while the Touring and Cartier models, as well as those destined for the limo-and-hearse market, get slightly more with 235 hp. The Continental, on the other hand, is given the dual-overhead camshaft version, which generates an extra 40 hp. All models come with 4-speed automatic transmission.

A car for "The Sopranos"

▲ PROS

- Reliable mechanics • Solid body
- Complete equipment • Predictable road manners
- Spaciousness

▼ CONS

- Uneven finish • Not fun to drive
- Arguable aesthetics • Inadequate dashboard
- Rear suspension not quite up to the task

Not bad, but...

Until its redesign in 1998, the Town Car was a highway dinosaur sporting every flaw associated with oversized American cars. The chassis has since been improved, offering better performance and handling worthy of its name. Although it hasn't turned into a Mercedes-Benz S Class or a BMW 7 Series, you can still tackle turns at reasonable speeds without worrying about scraping the fenders on the road. Moreover, the steering has lost that notorious dead zone straight ahead that gave the impression you were at the controls of a landing craft. Braking, too, is more powerful and heat-resistant.

But mechanical changes seem minor compared to the elaborate makeover of the interior, namely a wealth of electronic gadgets – from sound system to sound insulation. Clearly, Lincoln has paid more attention to the "gold package" on its Cartier model than fine tuning its suspension or braking systems. They probably have a point. How important are good suspension and brakes anyway when the car is leading a funeral procession or stuck in downtown traffic?

If you're a serious car nut, your enthusiasm might get a jolt if you ever find yourself behind the wheel of this humongous sedan. Installed in a bench seat which offers little lateral support and placed in front of a dashboard directly borrowed from 1970s models, you're going to need all your reflexes and instincts because steering response from the road surface is virtually zero. Thank goodness for the power-adjustable accelerator and brake pedals!

And while you're behind the wheel, bear in mind the car's size, weight and braking capabilities. In this regard, the Town Car can really thumb its nose at other sport utilities.

If you like a traditional North American car, if you have to transport a bevy of passengers even though you're not a limo driver, and if you're one of those for whom supple suspension means luxury and comfort, then the Lincoln is your kind of car. And take heart, its reliability is considered better than average. If you're none of the above, the only Town Cars that you'll ever need to use in your lifetime will either take you to the airport or the cemetery.

Denis Duquet

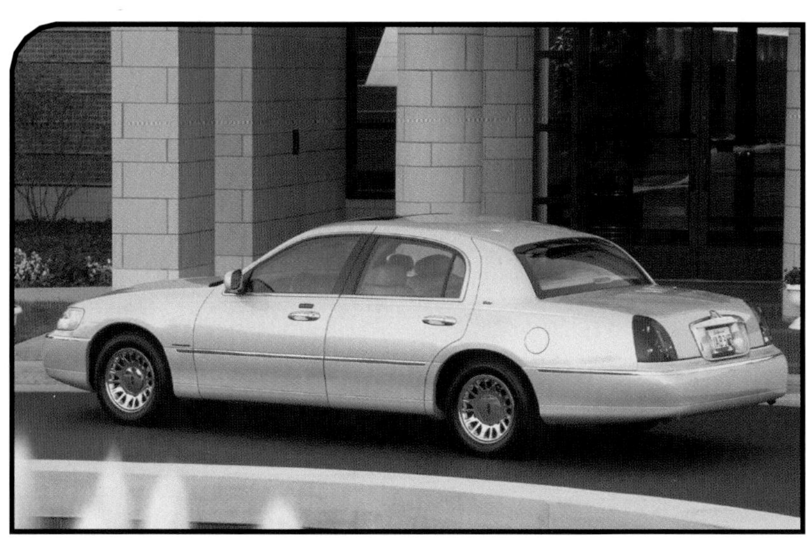

SPECIFICATIONS	
Price	$CDN 50,700-66,415 / $US 40,290-49,355
Warranty	4 years / 48,000 miles (80,000 km)
Type	sedan / rear wheel drive
Wheelbase / Length	118 in / 215 in
Width / Height	78.3 in / 58 in
Weight	4045 lb (1835 kg)
Trunk / Fuel tank	20.6 cu. ft / 20 gallons
Air bags	front and side
Front suspension	independent
Rear suspension	rigid axle
Front brakes / Rear brakes	disc ABS
Traction control	yes
Steering	recirculating balls, variable assist
Turning circle	42 feet
Tires (front/rear)	P225/60R16

PERFORMANCE	
Engine	V8 4.6-liter
Transmission	4-speed automatic
Horsepower	235 hp at 4750 rpm
Torque	265 lb-ft at 4000 rpm
Other engines	V8 4.6-liter 220 hp
Other transmission	none
Acceleration (0-60 mph)	9 sec
Maximum speed	112 mph (180 km/h)
Braking (60-0 mph)	(electronically limited)
Fuel consumption	129 feet (39.4 m)
	15.3 mpg (14.8 L/100 km)

COMPETITION

- Acura RL • Buick Park Avenue • Cadillac DeVille
- Infiniti Q45 • Lexus LS 400

NEW FOR 2002

- More sophisticated message center

RATING	**(out of 5 stars)**
Driveability	★★½
Comfort	★★★★★
Reliability	★★★★
Roominess	★★★★½
Winter driving rating	★★½
Safety	★★★★½
Resale value	★★½

MAZDA 626

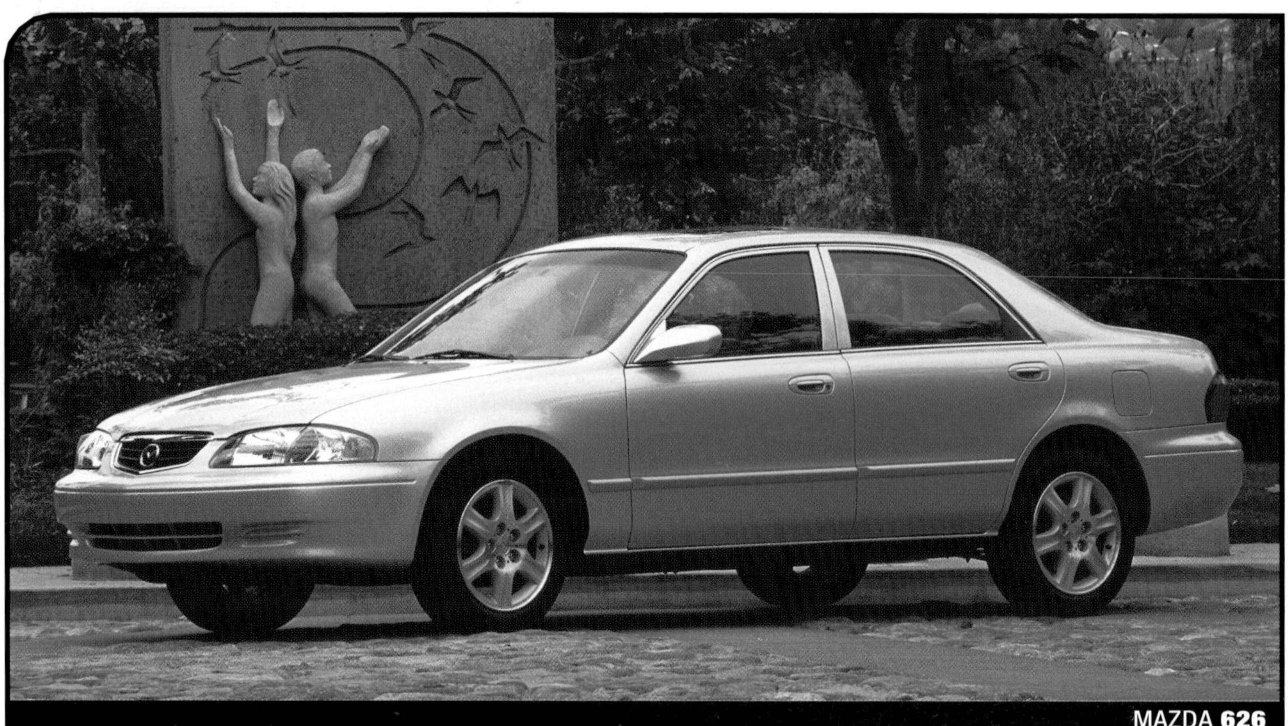
MAZDA **626**

Last Call

The Mazda 626 is at the end of its life cycle and will be just going through the motions this model year. Instead, Mazda has chosen to channel its energies toward the production of the next generation.

Except for a few minor details, the 2002 Mazda 626 remains practically unchanged. And these details are two new color options (Galaxy Blue and Silver Desert) and an in-dash six-CD changer now offered as standard equipment on the ES model.

Still misunderstood after all these years

When your direct competition is Honda Accord or Toyota Camry, all you can hope for is a third-place finish. These two Japanese products have become benchmarks in a market segment where there are many upstarts, but none yet really capable of reaching their high level.

Despite its genuine efforts, including a major revamping three years ago, the Mazda 626 still hasn't managed to catch up with its more popular rivals, nor has it succeeded in attracting new buyers. On the contrary, its target market seems to be drawing further away. Yet, this very pleasant sedan is really worth paying some attention to.

If you can get pass the Mazda 626's rather mundane bodywork, you'll be charmed by its qualities, not least of which is its excellent interior, so comfortable you'll want to go for long drives.

Space is generous, and the very spacious rear seating arrangement offers more that its fair share of legroom. Front-seat occupants could use a little more lateral support, however, a suggestion that Mazda promises to implement in the revamped model, due to appear next year. Incidentally, the new-generation 626 will have a different name.

Bye-Bye! (Buy-Buy!)

The 626 was assembled in the United States but, contrary to popular belief, this is by no means a drawback. Workmanship and construction are beyond reproach.

V6 Advantage

The 626 comes with either a 4- or 6-cylinder engine. But which one to choose? The difference between the two is significant. If you have a limited budget and consider the 626 as just a modest mode of transportation to take you from place to place

▲ PROS

- Interior space • Impeccable workmanship
- Predictable road manners • Manual gearbox with V6 • Spacious trunk space

▼ CONS

- Bland 4-cylinder engine • Confusing shiftgate
- End-of-line model • Light steering
- Mundane look

without any other expectations, then the 4-cylinder LX is for you. Still, ask to test-drive both versions before putting your John Henry on the contract.

A simple road test may be all it takes to convince you to spend the extra dollars for the more responsive V6. And if you want more, go for the manual gearbox. It allows you to take full advantage of the engine's performance, which otherwise lacks a bit of punch, particularly during acceleration.

The automatic gearbox should be seriously considered for the 4-cylinder engine. It provides the best compromise between performance and economy. Unfortunately, this gearbox is not without its own drawbacks. The shiftgate is annoyingly confusing and should be addressed by Mazda next year.

As for its road behavior, the 626 lays no claims to being a talented sports machine. However, it's generally predictable and reacts well to the demands of winding roads. In this regard, the 626 has nothing to learn from its direct rivals whose criteria are no more demanding. Steering still feels light, too light.

Great expectations

Thus, the Mazda 626 will be replaced in about a year's time by the M6 which raises great expectations. Here's a sneak preview.

The new mid-size Mazda model will not only be bigger, but also more attractive. It will be offered in various configurations: 4-door sedan and 5-door hatchback for sure, and perhaps even a wagon. Unfortunately, only the sedan will be available in North America. And despite rumors to the contrary, all-wheel drive will not be offered either.

But first Mazda has to develop a better way to promote its product. Perhaps the fact that the 626 hasn't succeeded in reaching as many consumers as its more aggressive rivals is due to Mazda's lack of decisiveness in its marketing strategy.

Louis Butcher

SPECIFICATIONS

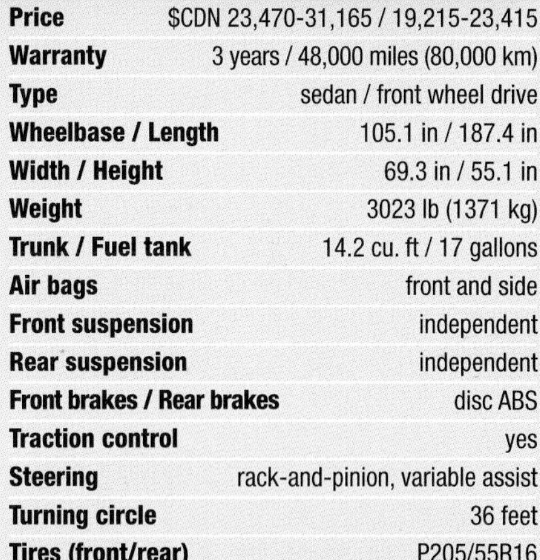

Price	$CDN 23,470-31,165 / 19,215-23,415
Warranty	3 years / 48,000 miles (80,000 km)
Type	sedan / front wheel drive
Wheelbase / Length	105.1 in / 187.4 in
Width / Height	69.3 in / 55.1 in
Weight	3023 lb (1371 kg)
Trunk / Fuel tank	14.2 cu. ft / 17 gallons
Air bags	front and side
Front suspension	independent
Rear suspension	independent
Front brakes / Rear brakes	disc ABS
Traction control	yes
Steering	rack-and-pinion, variable assist
Turning circle	36 feet
Tires (front/rear)	P205/55R16

PERFORMANCE

Engine	V6 2.5-liter
Transmission	5-speed manual
Horsepower	165 hp at 6000 rpm
Torque	161 lb-ft at 5000 rpm
Other engines	4L 2.0-liter 125 hp
Other transmission	4-speed automatic
Acceleration (0-60 mph)	8.9 sec
Maximum speed	134 mph (215 km/h)
Braking (60-0 mph)	137 feet (41.7 m)
Fuel consumption	20.2 mpg (11.2 L/100 km)

COMPETITION

- Ford Taurus • Honda Accord • Hyundai Sonata
- Nissan Altima • Toyota Camry

NEW FOR 2002

- Standard 6-CD changer (ES model)
- Two new body colors

RATING (out of 5 stars)

Driveability	★★★½
Comfort	★★★★
Reliability	★★★½
Roominess	★★★★
Winter driving rating	★★★★
Safety	★★★★
Resale value	★★

MAZDA M6

MAZDA **M6**

First steps toward a new life

After coming close to financial disaster, the Mazda organization is now in better shape, and in order to avoid further risk, management has devised a restructuring plan that involves the development of new models, each one more sophisticated than the last. The first car in this renewal process is the M6, which will replace the 626 in Fall 2002.

At the present time, 626s aren't exactly overcrowding our highways and byways. Not that this sedan is fundamentally flawed, it's simply regarded as just another Japanese car. But you can bet your bottom dollar that the problem is going to be fixed by Mazda's new management.

The Hiroshima-based stylists have established a set of visual parameters – dubbed "Emotions in Action" – which will be applied to all new Mazdas, starting with the M6. They include the five-point grille, the living area resting on a wider platform, no exterior chrome, four-lamp clusters in front and wrap-around taillights. Inside, the titanium-colored dashboard features a center console housing the air conditioning and radio controls, while the three-spoke steering wheel sports the cruise control buttons on its hub. Storage areas abound. Front legroom is far better than average and tall people will find themselves at ease in the rear benchseat.

Only the sedan version will be marketed in North America, while Japanese and European markets will also have access to the wagon and the hatchback.

Ambitious

Although the current Mazda 626 boasts all "must-have" features, the designers of the new M6 are aiming much higher. Among the target vehicles that served as benchmarks were the BMW 3-Series, Ford Mondeo, Volkswagen Passat and Honda Accord. According to statements made by company representatives, the new M6 outclasses them all in technical specifications and in measurable features such as space, performance, etc.

Renewal

The all-new platform is clearly very rigid, which enables the engineers to develop a more efficient yet supple suspension. Up front, the double wishbones are attached high on the chassis in order

▲ PROS

• Elegant seat-covers • Improved platform • Modern engines • Refined styling • Roomy interior

▼ CONS

• All-wheel transmission not available • No wagon or hatchback • Obtrusive handbrake level • Unknown reliability

to reduce understeer. In the back, engineers have redesigned the multi-link suspension which was originally used on the Luce 18 years ago. At the time, this old 929 was one of the most technically refined Japanese cars. The new and improved version of this suspension used on the M6 gives it a solid, well-planted feel at the rear. Moreover, it is quite low and does not encroach into the cargo space.

Since Mazda's mandate is to develop 4-cylinder engines for use throughout the Ford empire, the company decided to start with its own M6, equipping it with an all-aluminum 2.3-liter 4-cylinder engine rating 150 hp. It can be paired to a 5-speed manual transmission, or a 4-speed automatic. With balancing shafts eliminating all vibrations, the engine is silky smooth, and fuel-efficient to boot. The second engine option is a 3.0-liter V6 which can be linked to a 5-speed manual or a new 5-speed automatic box.

New bodywork includes an exclusive Triple H structure that provides better protection in case of lateral collision, while the pedals recess into the floor in case of a frontal impact. In addition to the four-wheel disk brakes, the ABS system and stability controls, curtain air bags will be offered as options.

I was lucky enough to take the wheel of this new M6 during a preview in Japan. My driving impressions are under embargo until mid-summer 2002, but I can assure you that the M6 measures up to the best cars in its class. The tested cars were only pre-production prototypes. Production models should be even better.

Denis Duquet

SPECIFICATIONS

Price	$CDN n.a. / $US n.a.
Warranty	3 years / 36,000 miles (60,000 km)
Type	mid-size sedan / front wheel drive
Wheelbase / Length	105.1 in / 186.6 in
Width / Height	56.7 in / 70.1 in
Weight	3009 lb (1365 kg)
Trunk / Fuel tank	15.2 cu.ft. / 20 gallons
Air bags	front, side and head
Front suspension	independent
Rear suspension	independent
Front brakes / Rear brakes	disc ABS
Traction control	yes
Steering	rack-and-pinion, variable assist
Turning circle	39 feet
Tires (front/rear)	P205/60R16

PERFORMANCE

Engine	4L 2.3-liter
Transmission	5-speed manual
Horsepower	150-hp at 6500 rpm
Torque	152 lb-ft at 4000 rpm
Other engines	V6 3.0-liter 219-hp
Other transmission	4-speed automatic; 5-speed automatic (V6)
Acceleration (0-60 mph)	9.1 sec; 8.2 sec (V6)
Maximum speed	130 mph (210 km/h)
Braking (60-0 mph)	121 feet (37 m)
Fuel consumption	26.1 mpg (8.7 L/100 km)

COMPETITION

• Honda Accord • Nissan Altima • Toyota Camry • VW Passat

NEW FOR 2002

• New 2003 model (Launch Fall 2002)
• New chassis • New engines

RATING (out of 5 stars)

Driveability	★★★★
Comfort	★★★★½
Reliability	New model
Roominess	★★★★½
Winter driving rating	★★★★
Safety	★★★★★
Resale value	New model

MAZDA MIATA

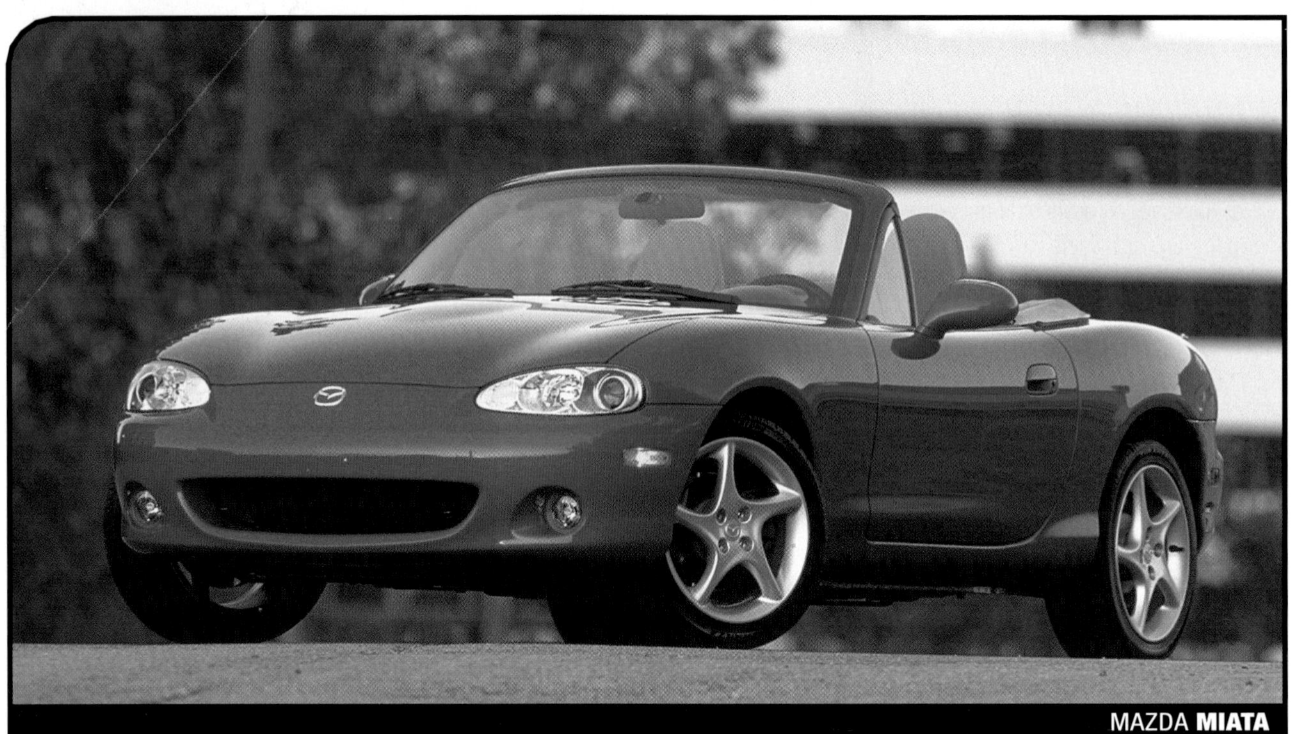
MAZDA **MIATA**

Spirited Beauty

Last fall, Mazda triumphantly announced that, with the aid of its variable-valve-timing (VVT) system, its little 1.8-liter 4-cylinder engine would generate an extra 15 horsepower. I imagined my esteemed colleague Alain Raymond – who tinkers with Miatas in his spare time – would be overjoyed by the news. Instead, he just shrugged it off. Because like many election promises, the much ballyhooed extra power amounted to a meager 2 horses!

Now, this kind of mistake can happen to anyone. But a promise is a promise. And so Mazda decided to make amends by offering Miata owners two options: full repurchase or free factory-scheduled maintenance for the length of the Miata's 3-year warranty. Too bad about those costly missing ponies – which must have drowned somewhere in the Pacific, between Japan and North America – but I can assure you, the promised driving fun is all there.

Eye-pleasing

Pure pleasure from every angle – the Miata team's overriding objective. Visually speaking, the Miata is gorgeous – its curvy lines, refined over the years, exude a particular, "androgynous" charm, blending grace and energy. The appearance is further enhanced by the front air dam and rear spoiler, optional with the aero/sport package. Mazda's trademark "pop up" headlights have been replaced by fixed ones, integrated on each side of the front grille. Better yet, the new headlights are lighter and impossible to jam in winter.

Redesigned in 1999, the Miata is 130 lbs (60 kg) heavier and its overall dimensions are larger. The cabin certainly can use the extra inches, although tall drivers still need to push their seat back all the way. The minuscule trunk, too, gains in capacity. Believe me, any extra cubic inch counts in the Miata!

Pure pleasure

The instrument panel is logically laid out and the gauges are easy to read, unobstructed by the steering wheel that, unfortunately, is not height adjustable. Controls are generally within easy reach, except for the button controlling the mirrors, which has been placed behind the steering wheel. The soft top is light, watertight, and easy to retract and put up. The old plastic rear window is now made of glass and comes

▲ PROS

• Elegant styling • Driving fun • Exemplary road manners • Perfect manual transmission • Affordable price and maintenance

▼ CONS

• Cramped cabin • Dubious horsepower • Flat performance

equipped with a defogger. To face long winter months, there's always the hard-top option, although that will detract from the Miata's charm.

Standard equipment includes 15-inch wheels and many power-assisted features. In addition to the front air dam and rear spoiler, the sport package offers 16-inch wheels, 6-speed manual transmission, a sport suspension and the Torsen limited-slip differential (this option group is expensive, but very efficient). The leather package consists of chamois coverings for the seats and soft top, as well as cruise control, air conditioner, Bose audio system, a windblocker placed behind the bucket seats, power door locks and ABS.

Driving fun

Under the hood a 4-cylinder 1800cc engine generates 142 horsepower at 7000 rpm. Maximum torque is 125 lb-ft. Although last year's engine modifications failed to deliver the promised power, torque is now more linear, providing for smoother power delivery.

Though it's no powerhouse, the Miata is nimble on the road, accompanied by a gorgeous grumble that's music to my ears. The gearbox is a real gem, as precise as a Swiss watch. The joystick is indeed a joy, shifting swiftly and smoothly from one gear to the next. There's also the 4-speed automatic transmission, available as an option with the leather package. But don't brag about it, lest you compromise the car's resale value. Handling is beyond reproach, thanks to the Miata's excellent weight distribution and traction. The revised suspensions are better tuned and more adaptive, while the disc brakes inspire confidence with their power and endurance.

The Miata is fun to drive. Hop in it for a two-hour spin on country roads, and you'll feel instantly re-energized – the effect is as good as a dose of Viagra, or a two-week vacation. Horsepower notwithstanding.

Jean-Georges Laliberté

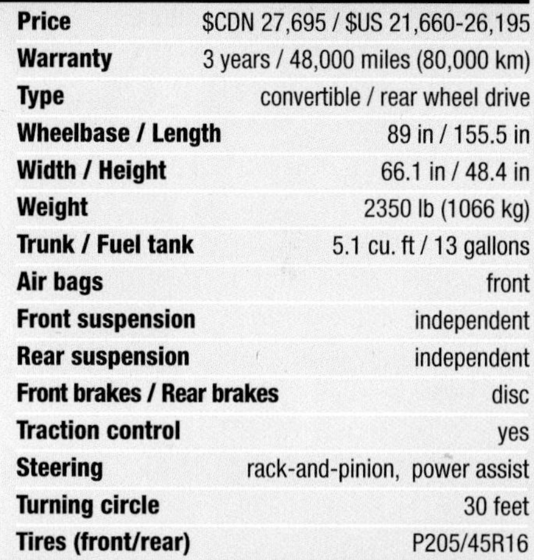

SPECIFICATIONS	
Price	$CDN 27,695 / $US 21,660-26,195
Warranty	3 years / 48,000 miles (80,000 km)
Type	convertible / rear wheel drive
Wheelbase / Length	89 in / 155.5 in
Width / Height	66.1 in / 48.4 in
Weight	2350 lb (1066 kg)
Trunk / Fuel tank	5.1 cu. ft / 13 gallons
Air bags	front
Front suspension	independent
Rear suspension	independent
Front brakes / Rear brakes	disc
Traction control	yes
Steering	rack-and-pinion, power assist
Turning circle	30 feet
Tires (front/rear)	P205/45R16

PERFORMANCE	
Engine	4L 1.8-liter DOHC
Transmission	6-speed manual
Horsepower	142 hp at 7000 rpm
Torque	125 lb-ft at 5500 rpm
Other engines	none
Other transmission	5-speed manual, 4-speed automatic
Acceleration (0-60 mph)	8.1 sec
Maximum speed	127 mph (205 km/h)
Braking (60-0 mph)	125 feet (38 m)
Fuel consumption	25.2 mpg (9 L/100 km)

COMPETITION

- Chevrolet Camaro / Pontiac Firebird
- Ford Mustang

NEW FOR 2002

• Bose audio system • OBD II (to detect component or system malfunctions) • Standard fog lights

RATING	(out of 5 stars)
Driveability	★★★★½
Comfort	★★★
Reliability	★★★★★
Roominess	★½
Winter driving rating	★
Safety	★★★½
Resale value	★★★★★

MAZDA **MILLENIA**

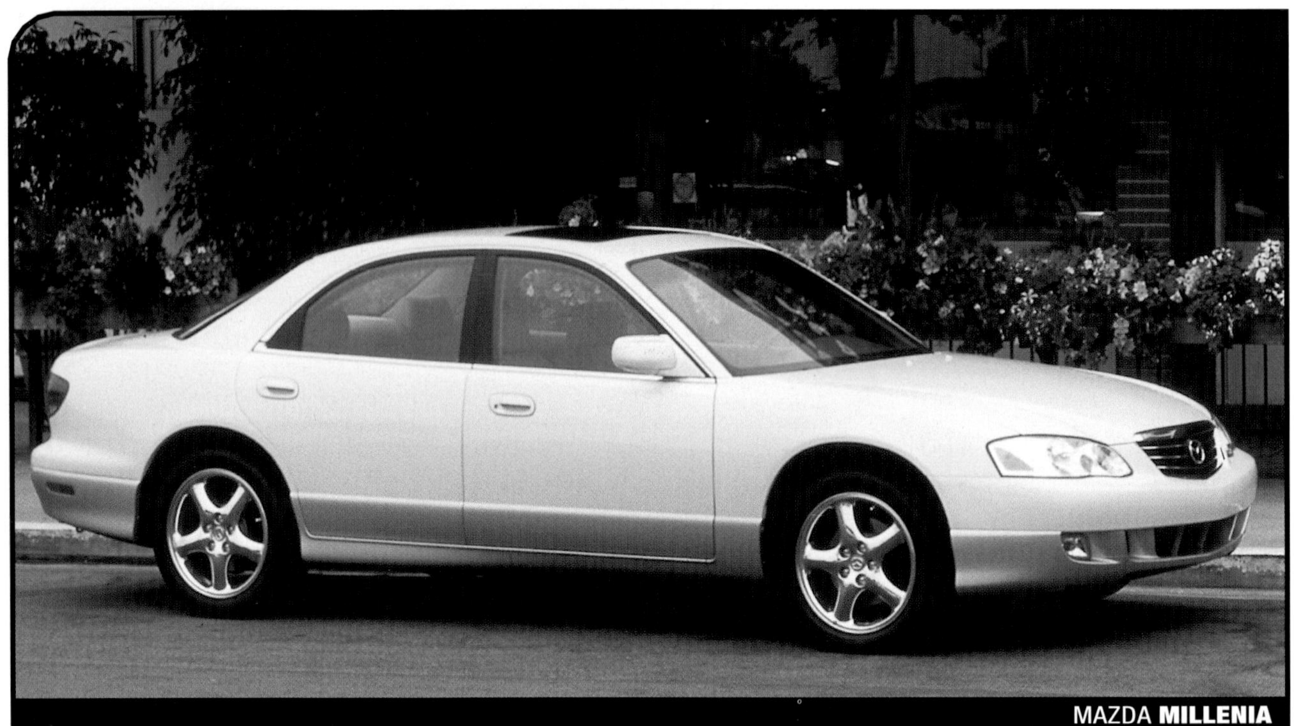
MAZDA **MILLENIA**

A Sweet Dream

Imagine a slice of mouth-watering chocolate cake, still warm and whose luscious icing is torturing your taste buds. Your mouth opens wide and, as you're about to capture the cake... the alarm goes off!

With its large 17-inch wheels and low-profile tires, the Mazda Millenia is as appealing as that dream-like piece of cake, exuding luxury, comfort and sportiness. As luck would have it, the last ingredient ran out just as the cake was being prepared.

Launched in 1995, the Millenia's superb design continues to make heads turn wherever the car happens to turn up. Its unique Miller-cycle engine is another key factor in its claim to fame. Not that the Millenia runs on hops, mind you – the name refers instead to Ralph A. Miller, the American engineer who pioneered the use of delayed intake valve closing and a compressor in order to extract more power and torque than would normally be available from a regular engine. In point of fact, Mazda managed to obtain the same performance from the Millenia' 210-hp 2.3-liter V6 as that produced by a 3.0-liter engine. But strictly between you and me, all this extra power doesn't really amount to very much. In the first place, the Millenia's fuel mileage – 19 mpg (12.4 liters per 100 km) – is equivalent to that of a big V6 engine. And in the second, when you lift the Millenia's hood – getting your fingertips burned in the process – you'll be astonished to see how much room all this high-tech gadgetry actually takes up. A bigger old-fashioned V6 (perhaps even a carversion of the Mazda Tribute's engine) would have done the job just as well without discouraging what few potential customers there are for this model.

Unsuccessful formula

Having got all that off my chest, don't think that the engine isn't up to snuff. On the contrary, you'd imagine it was a turbocharged engine with turbo lag down to nothing. And as you depress the accelerator, it emits a barely discernible whistling sound, courtesy of the Lysholm turbo rotors. Unfortunately, only a 4-speed automatic transmission is available.

If you try to really drive the Millenia – as opposed to just going along for the ride – you're sure to spoil everything. On the straightaway, it does a splendid job. On twisty roads, you'll even enjoy the ride –

▲ PROS

- Decent performance • First-rate air conditioning
- Guaranteed reliability • Timeless design
- Ultra-comfortable

▼ CONS

- So-so ergonomics • Suspension hardly sporty
- Unnecessarily complex drivetrain
- Weighty hood and trunk

and the attendant body roll – but only if you maintain a more discreet speed all the way. Push the Millenia the least bit too hard, and it'll quickly strike back. The suspension is too supple and despite the electronic traction control, you may find yourself off the road in no time at all. The powerful brakes with ABS come in handy at moments like these, even though they're noisy.

Deceptive appearance

Inside, storage pockets abound, and all are very deep. They also have covers, which make them awkward to reach when you're driving. The glove compartment, on the other hand, is ridiculously small, and tricky to open because the button is located on the inside of a door; ditto the button for the fuel-tank cover. The button activating the cruise control is also awkwardly placed – on the dashboard this time. And while I'm in a recriminatory mood, I may as well mention the excessively heavy trunk lid, the absence of a retention net (a shame really, for a car in this price range), and the fixed rear bench seat. All you'll find there is a small trap door to give more room for your skis.

At least the supple suspension provides decent comfort for the occupants of the car, and there is the additional pleasure of superb leather seating. The steering wheel looks a bit odd, but it falls nicely into your hands, and steering response is adequate. On the other hand, there's some torque steer and the turning circle is on the wide side. The automatic climate control system

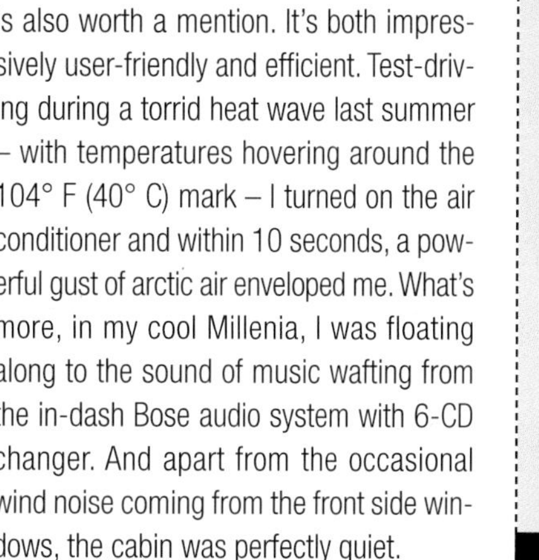

is also worth a mention. It's both impressively user-friendly and efficient. Test-driving during a torrid heat wave last summer – with temperatures hovering around the 104° F (40° C) mark – I turned on the air conditioner and within 10 seconds, a powerful gust of arctic air enveloped me. What's more, in my cool Millenia, I was floating along to the sound of music wafting from the in-dash Bose audio system with 6-CD changer. And apart from the occasional wind noise coming from the front side windows, the cabin was perfectly quiet.

Mazda claims that most Millenia buyers are in the 35-55 age bracket, but I'm skeptical. The Mazda Millenia is not a bad car, not by a long shot, but it's still hard to reconcile its sporty air and handsome design with its "unsportsmanlike" handling.

Alain Morin

SPECIFICATIONS	
Price	$CDN 41,450 / $US 31,505
Warranty	3 years / 48,000 miles (80,000 km)
Type	sedan / front wheel drive
Wheelbase / Length	108.3 in / 191.7 in
Width / Height	69.7 in / 54.7 in
Weight	3488 lb (1582 kg)
Trunk / Fuel tank	13.3 cu. ft / 18 gallons
Air bags	front and side
Front suspension	independent
Rear suspension	independent
Front brakes / Rear brakes	disc ABS
Traction control	yes
Steering	rack-and-pinion, variable assist
Turning circle	37 feet
Tires (front/rear)	P215/50R17

PERFORMANCE	
Engine	V6 2.3-liter Miller-cycle
Transmission	4-speed automatic
Horsepower	210 hp at 5300 rpm
Torque	210 lb-ft at 3500 rpm
Other engines	none
Other transmission	none
Acceleration (0-60 mph)	8.8 sec
Maximum speed	143 mph (230 km/h)
Braking (60-0 mph)	141 feet (43 m)
Fuel consumption	18.3 mpg (12.4 L/100 km)

COMPETITION

- Acura 3.2 TL • BMW 325 • Lexus ES 300
- M-B C240 • Toyota Avalon • Volvo S60 • VW Passat

NEW FOR 2002

- New color (Pearl white)
- Standard chromed alloy wheels

RATING	(out of 5 stars)
Driveability	★★★½
Comfort	★★★★
Reliability	★★★★★
Roominess	★★★½
Winter driving rating	★★★½
Safety	★★★★
Resale value	★★½

MAZDA MPV

MAZDA **MPV**

A Solid Competitor

The first-generation MPVs remained unchanged far too long. The minivan was finally – and thoroughly – redesigned last year and performed well, give or take a few exceptions. And it's precisely these flaws that Mazda management has decided to correct this year.

While the testers praised the driving comfort and practical nature of the MPV, they also pointed out that the 170 hp cranked out by its 2.5-liter V6 fell short of what was really needed. You had to constantly floor the pedal simply to accelerate under normal conditions, let alone try overtaking. Although drivers with a patient and easygoing style rarely complained about any power shortcomings, many wished for a little more muscle to this minivan. Which is precisely what the company has done this year by replacing the 2.5-liter V6 with a 200-hp 3.5 liter with better torque. The difference is immediate, catapulting the MPV into the same league as such leaders such as the Honda Odyssey and various Chrysler minivans.

Since the entire Mazda model line will be replaced during the course of the next two years, stylists have jumped the gun and modified the grille of this minivan to give it a little more emphasis. Other modifications to the bodywork give it a more balanced look. The interior, very well designed from the start, remains more or less the same, except for the dashboard which has been slightly revised.

The features that make the MPV one of the most practical minivans in its class have been retained. Thus, the second-row seats are still mounted on rails so that they can slide laterally and be set up as a bench or as independent bucket seats. Moreover, the third bench can be stowed into the floor. Finally, the two lateral doors still feature windows that open vertically much like those of a conventional vehicle. These are mere details, but sometimes they're much appreciated.

Mostly nimble

One day, as I was interviewing a minivan owner about the pros and cons of his vehicle, he mentioned that this was his third minivan, but the first to have a longer wheelbase. Although he appreciated the extra cargo space, he wasn't too happy about the road behavior of this lengthened model. He then declared that "the 12 extra

▲ PROS

- More powerful engine • Solid roadholding
- Multi-purpose interior • Handy in town
- Competitively priced

▼ CONS

- Uncomfortable third bench • DX model insufficiently equipped • Difficult to access spare tire
- Narrow interior • Heavy removable seats

inches can make the difference between a minivan and a truck." In short, the overall balance is not always ideal in some minivans with a lengthened wheelbase, especially if it means greater lateral wind sensitivity.

However, even though the short-wheelbase minivan is a more logical choice, not every driver is convinced of it. The Mercury Villager disappeared after failing to attract buyers, just like its twin sister the Nissan Quest. While the public shied away from them, the MPV continues to find favor.

Like some of its rivals, the MPV essentially behaves like a car – or a large station wagon, at worst – while providing minivan advantage. Driving through curves in quick succession doesn't upset its stance and its steering response is on a par with that of many sedans. Moreover, on the open road, although the power steering could provide a little less assistance, directional stability is impeccable. The MPV has practically the mobility of a compact in traffic and parking is not too difficult. The fact that this Mazda is the shortest minivan on the market may explain its nimbleness in city driving. With the V6 engine's new additional power, we expect that responsiveness and acceleration will be improved. Finally, if you need to stop quickly, braking distance is similar to that of the 626 sedan.

All these different features, the esthetic qualities, the practicality and performance, serve to explain the success of this all-purpose Mazda. What's more, the model lineup is well thought out and prices are competitive, considering the range of its standard equipment. If Mazda is listening, an all-wheel drive option in the near future will be welcome.

Denis Duquet

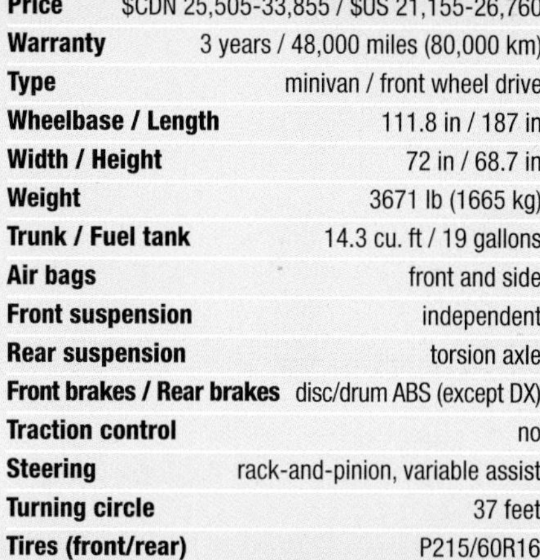

SPECIFICATIONS

Price	$CDN 25,505-33,855 / $US 21,155-26,760
Warranty	3 years / 48,000 miles (80,000 km)
Type	minivan / front wheel drive
Wheelbase / Length	111.8 in / 187 in
Width / Height	72 in / 68.7 in
Weight	3671 lb (1665 kg)
Trunk / Fuel tank	14.3 cu. ft / 19 gallons
Air bags	front and side
Front suspension	independent
Rear suspension	torsion axle
Front brakes / Rear brakes	disc/drum ABS (except DX)
Traction control	no
Steering	rack-and-pinion, variable assist
Turning circle	37 feet
Tires (front/rear)	P215/60R16

PERFORMANCE

Engine	V6 3.0-liter DOHC 24 valves
Transmission	4-speed automatic
Horsepower	200 hp at 6000 rpm
Torque	200 lb-ft at 4750 rpm
Other engines	none
Other transmission	none
Acceleration (0-60 mph)	10 sec
Maximum speed	109 mph (175 km/h)
Braking (60-0 mph)	135 feet (41 m)
Fuel consumption	19.6 mpg (11.6 L/100 km)

COMPETITION

- Chevrolet Venture • Dodge Caravan
- Toyota Sienna

NEW FOR 2002

- Modified dashboard • Modified grille
- New 3.0-liter engine

RATING (out of 5 stars)

Driveability	★★★½
Comfort	★★★½
Reliability	★★★★
Roominess	★★★
Winter driving rating	★★★
Safety	★★★½
Resale value	★★★½

MAZDA PROTEGÉ

MAZDA PROTEGÉ5
MAZDA MP3

MAZDA **PROTEGÉ**

Continually Improving

It's hard to believe, but the nondescript Mazda Protegé sedan is one of the best-selling cars in North America. And the trend keeps right on growing because the Japanese carmaker continues to polish its popular subcompact line. For 2001, for example, the sedan has been revised and improved, and fitted with a new 2.0-liter 130-hp engine. A few months later, its hatchback cousin, the Protegé5, joined the lineup. The year 2002 welcomes the arrival of the flashiest Protegé model of them all – the MP3, a sporty subcompact intended to give every GTI and Si of this world a run for their money.

At this point in their history, all Protegés have reached a stage of maturity and development that is reassuring for consumers, making them popular choices among various consumer groups. This is what you can expect from the 2002 Mazda Protegé line.

First off, the sedan has been given several styling changes – a new grille as well as redesigned headlights and bumpers. Inside, the seats are more comfortable, a new CD player is standard equipment, the ignition key now lights up at night, and the console has been subtly touched up.

On the road, stability has been vastly improved, steering provides better feedback, and the brakes are more powerful. Moreover, the car benefits from better sound insulation. The sedan comes in three trim levels: SE, LX and ES – the first fitted with an anemic 4-cylinder engine producing a mere 103 horsepower.

Timid horses

The 2002 Protegé was launched in Los Angeles. My test-drive took place in the Mulholland Drive area, on narrow roads winding their way through the canyons. The new 2.0-liter engine wasn't overly powerful with its 130 horsepower. On the other hand, it performed effortlessly at high revs and stayed quiet all the way up to its 7000 rpm limit, working well with its user-friendly 5-speed manual gearbox.

Gets better with age

The car's behavior felt rather neutral and nimble, thanks in large measure to a sensitive steering mechanism. On twisting roads, the Protegé was pleasantly "sporty," although its modest horsepower left me longing for a livelier performance. The MP3 will certainly fare better (check out its performance listed in *The Auto Guide*'s mid-size comparison test).

▲ PROS

- Attractive styling • Excellent handling
- Low engine noise • Practical car
- Tried-and-true components

▼ CONS

- Average brakes • Modest base model (sedan)
- Steering exhibits torque effect
- Timid performance

Star Protegé5

Launched last summer, the Protegé5 hatchback is unquestionably the star in the 2002 Mazda lineup. Its less-than-$20,000 price, cool and cute silhouette (especially in yellow), excellent standard equipment and other amenities are the ideal ingredients for success. The model is essentially fitted with the same features as the Protegé ES sedan: 2.0-liter engine, 4-disc brakes with ABS and 16-inch alloy wheels.

A glance under the hood reveals the presence of a red crossbar, designed to strengthen the car's torsional rigidity, especially in turns. In other words, the hatchback won't surrender its sporty claim just because it has a luggage compartment capable of storing between 18.6 and 22.9 cubic feet of cargo.

On rough road surfaces, this Mazda stayed rock solid and eerily quiet. Engine noise – even at speeds as high as 90 mph – was so faint that there was no need to turn up the radio volume. Headlights and fog lamps (standard on Protegé5) provided ample illumination at night, and I loved the dashboard's soothing reddish glow, borrowed from Audi. The interior is attractively appointed, with a carbon fiber center console and a few silvery touches here and there. Instrument displays are smartly set against a beige background. And the gorgeous Miata-style three-spoke steering wheel feels wonderfully comfortable to hold. The front seats offer solid support and an excellent driving position thanks to the adjustable cushion. The rear bench can accommodate two adults, and offers plenty of legroom. Headroom, however, is on the snug side.

Even though this model is slightly heavier than the sedan, it is just as much fun to drive thanks to a quasi-neutral road behavior and highly precise steering. If only the engine had more horsepower. That said, the Protegé5 is the most versatile "all-purpose car" I've ever laid my hands on. And I'm willing to bet that its sales will help maintain Mazda's rank in the best-selling chart.

Jacques Duval

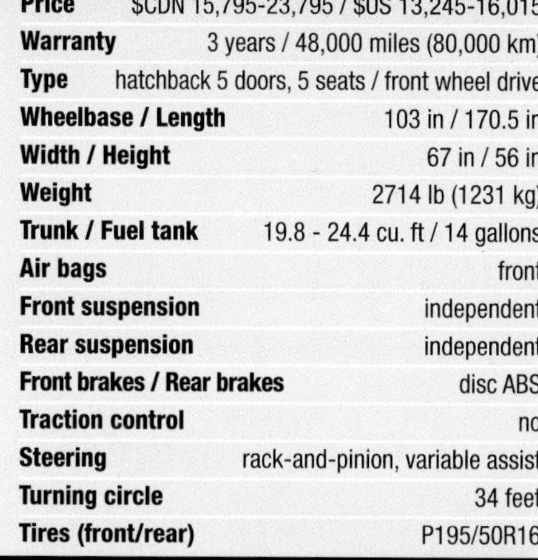

SPECIFICATIONS	**Protegé5**
Price	$CDN 15,795-23,795 / $US 13,245-16,015
Warranty	3 years / 48,000 miles (80,000 km)
Type	hatchback 5 doors, 5 seats / front wheel drive
Wheelbase / Length	103 in / 170.5 in
Width / Height	67 in / 56 in
Weight	2714 lb (1231 kg)
Trunk / Fuel tank	19.8 - 24.4 cu. ft / 14 gallons
Air bags	front
Front suspension	independent
Rear suspension	independent
Front brakes / Rear brakes	disc ABS
Traction control	no
Steering	rack-and-pinion, variable assist
Turning circle	34 feet
Tires (front/rear)	P195/50R16

PERFORMANCE	
Engine	4L 2-liter
Transmission	5-speed manual
Horsepower	130 hp at 6000 rpm
Torque	135 lb-ft at 4000 rpm
Other engines	4L 1.6-liter 103 hp (sedan SE)
Other transmission	4-speed automatic
Acceleration (0-60 mph)	9.3 sec
Maximum speed	122 mph (195 km/h)
Braking (60-0 mph)	140 feet (42.7 m)
Fuel consumption	26.7 mpg (8.5 L/100 km)

COMPETITION

- Chrysler PT Cruiser • Ford Focus
- Subaru Impreza Outback • VW Jetta

NEW FOR 2002

- New model

RATING	**(out of 5 stars)**
Driveability	★★★★
Comfort	★★★½
Reliability	★★★★
Roominess	★★★
Winter driving rating	★★★½
Safety	★★★½
Resale value	★★★½

MAZDA TRIBUTE

MAZDA **TRIBUTE**

For Well-informed Consumers Only

Winner of the 2001 Auto Guide award in the compact SUV category, the current Mazda Tribute proves worthy of the title, except for its excessive fuel consumption. During a test last fall aboard an already "broken-in" Tribute, we averaged 17 mpg (13 liters per l00 km). But the new model provided for our extended road test – fitted with a V6 engine – revealed a substantially heartier appetite, and some Tribute owners have complained that their experience was worse – 11 mpg (20 liters per 100 km)! That's a lot of gas, and a disappointing record, because the Tribute oozes quality in many other respects.

When they were informed about this voracious appetite, Mazda put the blame squarely on Ford, which provided the V6 Duratec engine used in the Tribute. Incidentally, Ford also produced its own version of the same V6, for the Ford Escape. According to various sources, this powerplant's high consumption diminishes over time, as the vehicle's mileage accumulates. But our own experience showed an average consumption of roughly 16 mpg (15 liters per 100 km). Alas, that's the price you have to pay for a 3.0-liter engine with 200 hp, one that in return provides ample acceleration power. The price is raised even higher in the form of engine noise, especially when you sprint from 0-60 mph. Add pronounced wind noise at highway speed, and the Tribute's cockpit is not exactly the place to carry on a serious conversation. Incidentally, a Ford Escape test, conducted around the same time as its Mazda twin brother's, revealed that its noise level was even worse. I should add that the Ford was equipped with Firestone Wilderness tires, while the Mazda benefited from the Michelin's 4X4 Alpin varieties.

A little guzzler

Getting back to the Tribute's extended road test, it's worth mentioning that we experienced absolutely no mechanical problems throughout the Auto Guide's 8000-mile (13,000-km) winter-driving journey, apart from two relatively minor incidents. The anti-freeze nozzle froze, for instance, and the heating was inadequate. We soon traced the latter problem to the stuck air vents. We adjusted them back to "normal" and bingo, the cabin took next to no time to warm up. Driving in winter also allowed us to fully appreciate the central differential's locking ability, which estab-

▲ PROS

- Adequate performance • Decent comfort
- Excellent off-road capabilities • Solid handling

▼ CONS

- Badly placed gearshift lever • Difficult entry and exit • Excessive fuel consumption • Noisy V6
- Suspension sometimes harsh

lishes a firm connection to the two axles. On snowy and slippery roads, the Tribute fared much better than the Hyundai Santa Fe, which also spent the winter with us (see assessment elsewhere in the Guide).

For those who don't have to contend with harsh weather conditions, the Tribute also comes equipped with front-wheel drive only. A 4-cylinder 130 hp engine is available, although it may not be ideal – or powerful enough – for such a heavy vehicle.

When asked what they liked most about the Tribute, the majority of our test drivers mentioned its handling – not as comfortable as a car's, granted, but not as heavy-going as a truck's either. Suspension is pleasant on the whole, but it can get unsettled over rough roads. On the other hand, road holding is excellent thanks to the Tribute's reasonable dimensions.

Hidden key

Ratings for the interior range from the sublime to the ridiculous. First off, access to the vehicle is seriously hampered by a completely useless running board. Its only purpose, as far as I can see, is to drum up business for dry-cleaners by soiling the pant cuffs of anyone attempting to get behind the Tribute's wheel. And once there, you'll be faced with a gearshift lever that's mounted on the steering column, just like the old days. That would have been okay, I suppose, if it didn't severely obstruct access to the radio and climate controls. The ignition key, too, is concealed under the steering wheel, making it tricky to locate at night. Finally, it's surprising that the Tribute doesn't come with heated seats, not even the top-of-the-line ES version.

The reverse of the coin, happily, is shinier. The driving position is excellent, although the seats could use better padding.Visibility is good from every angle, provided you clean your rear window frequently. Storage space abounds and I especially like those grab handles mounted on the A pillars. Cabin space is generous and the tailgate is both light and easy to operate.

All through our extended road test, the Mazda Tribute conducted itself competently, despite a couple of "youthful indiscretions."

Jacques Duval

SPECIFICATIONS	ES V6
Price	$CDN 22,415-33,870 / $US 17,750-23,970
Warranty	3 years / 48,000 miles (80,000 km)
Type	compact sport-utility / all wheel drive
Wheelbase / Length	103.1 in / 173 in
Width / Height	70.9 in / 67.2 in
Weight	3455 lb (1567 kg)
Trunk / Fuel tank	33.1 – 64.3 cu. ft / 16 gallons
Air bags	front and side
Front suspension	independent
Rear suspension	independent
Front brakes / Rear brakes	disc / drum ABS
Traction control	no
Steering	rack-and-pinion, variable assist
Turning circle	37 feet
Tires (front/rear)	P235/70R16

PERFORMANCE	
Engine	V6 3-liter
Transmission	4-speed automatic
Horsepower	200 hp at 6000 rpm
Torque	200 lb-ft at 4750 rpm
Other engines	4L 2 liter 130 hp
Other transmission	5-speed manual (4L)
Acceleration (0-60 mph)	10.3 sec
Maximum speed	118 mph (190 km/h)
Braking (60-0 mph)	141 feet (42.9 m)
Fuel consumption	15.1 mpg (15 L/100 km)

COMPETITION

• Ford Escape • Honda CR-V • Jeep Liberty • Nissan Xterra • Subaru Forester • Toyota RAV4

NEW FOR 2002

No major change

RATING	(out of 5 stars)
Driveability	★★★
Comfort	★★★
Reliability	★★★½
Roominess	★★★★
Winter driving rating	★★★★
Safety	★★★½
Resale value	★★★

MERCEDES-BENZ C CLASS

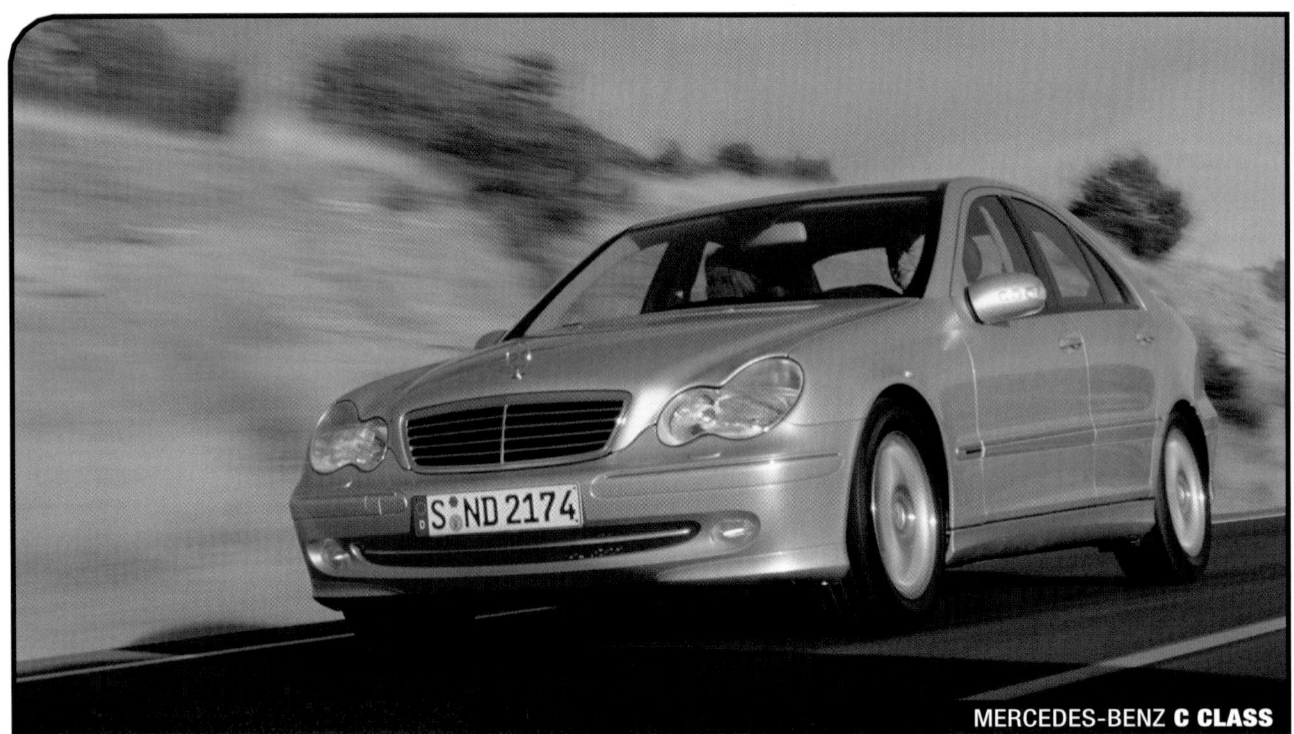

MERCEDES-BENZ **C CLASS**

Excellent Entry-Level Line

The Mercedes-Benz C Class line has never been so chock-full of goodies. This year, the prestigious German automaker has added a wagon and a sport coupe (see separate text) to the C240 and 320 sedans launched a year ago, not to mention a high-performance version – the C320 – which is featured in the "Exotic Sports Cars" section. The following impressions are focussed on the C240 Elegance (manual gearbox), as well as the C320 wagon (automatic).

A quick spin in the C240 Elegance, equipped with a manual gearbox, was all it took to understand why Mercedes-Benz has always been reluctant to send models with manual transmissions to North America. Putting the matter as courteously as we can, let's say simply that Mercedes' automotive mastery lies elsewhere.

And it's all the more regrettable that Mercedes decided to pit its latest C Class model against the BMW team, renowned for creating unsurpassed driving pleasure. Frankly, all the 6-speed manual gearbox accomplished was to spoil the otherwise remarkable performance by the C240's 2.6-liter V6 engine. Gearshift travel course was excessively long, making it difficult to shift seamlessly – a flaw that might have been avoided had Mercedes paired the engine to a twin-mode automatic transmission. Another irritant is the fact that 6th gear is too long to be useful, especially when you drive at less than 55 mph. And adding insult to injury, the manual C240's fuel mileage is barely higher than the automatic C320 – 21 mpg vs 20 mpg. Also, you might as well not have a reverse gear, because where it's located is anyone's guess!

Both the C240 and C320 engines, on the other hand, are smooth and pleasingly sonorous. Despite its misleading numerical appellation, the C240 is powered by a 2.6-liter V6, which generates 165 hp, whereas the C320 is endowed with a 3.2-liter V6, producing 215 hp.

Auto-matic, please!

In the Elegance version, the C240 has neither the kind of tires nor suspension necessary to compete with other genuine sport sedans. Body roll is fairly pronounced and the rear axle tends to "switch off" for no apparent reason. Nevertheless, the car proves to be pleasant to drive in most circumstances, even though it takes two seconds longer than the C320 to sprint from 0-60 mph. Braking is irreproachable, and so is steering, although we found the C320's power steering unpleas-

▲ PROS

- Excellent comfort/handling ratio
- Low noise level • Optimal safety
- Practical wagon • Remarkable engines

▼ CONS

- Heavy steering (C320) • Ill-fitted original tires
- Optional CD player • Some problematic accessories • Unpleasant manual gearbox

antly heavy. Despite its apparent firmness, the suspension absorbs bumps and potholes reasonably well, and the body confers a reassuring sense of safety that's further enhanced by the presence of 4 side-impact air bags as well as an inflatable curtain for head protection.

The first C Class models suffered from a variety of small inconveniences, mainly stemming from the accessories. Let's hope the problems have been fixed for 2002 versions.

The big old Mercedes steering wheel, for example, has been scaled down over time, so that now it's just the right size. In both the C240 and C320, the steering wheel is height- and reach-adjustable, and feels particularly nice to hold. It also incorporates the radio and cell-phone controls. Orthopedically designed, the lightly padded seats are super comfortable. Legroom is at a premium in front, while the narrow rear doors make access difficult. To make up for the tiny glove compartment, Mercedes provides ample storage space elsewhere, particularly on the center console where a deep and height-adjustable tray doubles as an elbow rest.

Wagon

The arrival of the Mercedes compact wagon speaks volumes about the strong comeback of this category. And the new C320 is one of the rare station wagons that rides like a sedan, and capable at the same time of hauling a huge amount of cargo.

Our test drive, of the C320 wagon with a 218-hp 3.2 liter V6 engine coupled to an adaptive 5-speed automatic gearbox, carried out mostly on mountainous surfaces, showed a 0-60 mph time of 8.1 seconds, and an average fuel mileage of 18 mpg (12.4 liters per 100 km).

This multi-purpose C Class wagon represents a viable alternative for those who are beginning to realize that sport-utility vehicles are not the answer to all their dreams.

Drawing inspiration from its S Class limousines, Mercedes has successfully developed an excellent line of entry-level models. The C320 wagon is no doubt the most desirable of these little Benzes, although the C240 Elegance acquits itself respectably, even without the automatic transmission it badly needs!

Jacques Duval/Denis Duquet

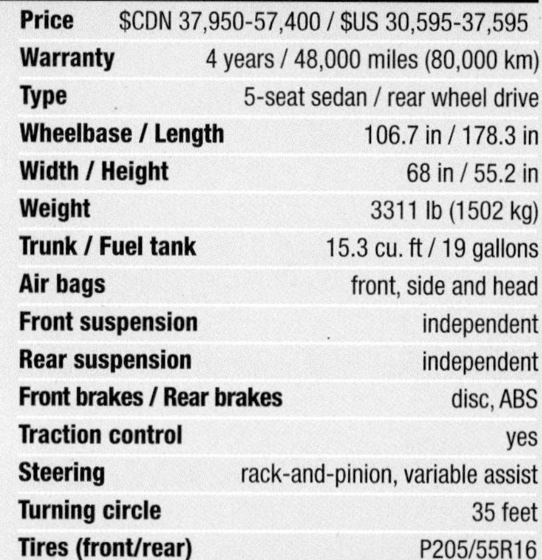

SPECIFICATIONS	C240 Elegance
Price	$CDN 37,950-57,400 / $US 30,595-37,595
Warranty	4 years / 48,000 miles (80,000 km)
Type	5-seat sedan / rear wheel drive
Wheelbase / Length	106.7 in / 178.3 in
Width / Height	68 in / 55.2 in
Weight	3311 lb (1502 kg)
Trunk / Fuel tank	15.3 cu. ft / 19 gallons
Air bags	front, side and head
Front suspension	independent
Rear suspension	independent
Front brakes / Rear brakes	disc, ABS
Traction control	yes
Steering	rack-and-pinion, variable assist
Turning circle	35 feet
Tires (front/rear)	P205/55R16

PERFORMANCE	
Engine	V6 2.6-liter
Transmission	6-speed manual
Horsepower	168-hp at 5500 rpm
Torque	177 lb-ft at 4500 rpm
Other engines	V6 3.2-liter 215-hp
Other transmission	5-speed automatic
Acceleration (0-60 mph)	9 sec; 6.8 sec (C320)
Maximum speed	140 mph (225 km/h)
Braking (60-0 mph)	138 feet (42 m)
Fuel consumption	20.6 mpg (11 L/100 km)

COMPETITION

- Audi A4 • BMW 3 Series • Jaguar X-Type
- Lexus IS 300 • Volvo S60

NEW FOR 2002

- Wagon version • AMG version
- 2 new colors

RATING	(out of 5 stars)
Driveability	★★★★
Comfort	★★★★
Reliability	★★★
Roominess	★★★½
Winter driving rating	★★★½
Safety	★★★★½
Resale value	★★★★

MERCEDES-BENZ C CLASS COUPE

MERCEDES-BENZ **C CLASS COUPE**

Fountain of Youth

To really appreciate the scope of Mercedes-Benz's efforts to reach a younger market, you have to watch the videos and photographs used to promote its new C Class Sport Coupe. The commercials show attractive and energetic 20-somethings crowding around a cluster of lime green and flaming red cars – colors so striking they would make Karl Benz and Gottlieb Daimler, founders of the venerable German brand, twirl in their graves.

Welcome to phase two of Operation Youth! Phase one, which saw the introduction of the SLK roadster in 1995 and the SUV ML two years later, brought a measure of success – sales at the German division of DaimlerChrysler have doubled since 1993, although most buyers remain in the same middle-aged bracket. Mercedes-Benz is now aggressively going after a new generation of buyers who, it hopes, will stay with the brand for life.

To boost sales, the C Class Sport Coupe will be offered at just under $40,000, marking the first time ever that a Mercedes-Benz coupe costs less than the sedan from which it's derived. It's a lot of money for sure, but it's still the most economical way to own such a prestigious marque.

Atypical silhouette

The C Class Sport Coupe has nothing in common with what Mercedes-Benz has designed until now. If the front looks familiar, the rear – truncated and turned up – is most unusual. The Sport Coupe distinguishes itself with its large all-glass tailgate that provides perfect visibility – a rare quality for this body type. If you opt for the panoramic glass roof, the glassed-in ceiling surface will extend from the windshield to the trunk spoiler, not to mention the clear plastic panel just underneath the rear spoiler.

Rejuvenation treatment

▲ PROS

- Excellent roadholding • Remarkable comfort
- Good performance • Attractive price
- Genuine four-seater

▼ CONS

- Light steering • Dodgy panoramic roof
- Engine somewhat coarse
- Tail-design not quite there

Seven inches (18 cm) shorter than the C Class sedan, the sport coupe is compact; its dimensions are comparable to those of the Volkswagen Jetta or the Honda Civic.

What's under the hood?

Curiously, when they handed out the information kits to the international press corps gathered in Nice for the sport coupe's launch, the engine came last in the model's specifications list. Is Mercedes-Benz embarrassed about the 197-hp supercharged 4-cylinder engine under its hood? First introduced in the SLK roadster, this engine has since been fine-tuned to get rid of its antiquated sound, although it still hasn't got the refinement of the fantastic V6 that propels many other Mercedes-Benz models. Nevertheless, its performance is adequate for a self-avowed sports car. Of the two kinds of transmission offered, the 5-speed automatic seems far preferable to the 6-speed manual, the latter being a type that Mercedes-Benz hasn't been able to master quite as well. In any case, both accelerations are practically identical (8 and 8.1 seconds) and, for once, the "Speedtronic," which offers manual gear changes, is user-friendly.

Mechanicals apart, construction quality is up to par and performance "feel" is as expected, and worthy of Mercedes-Benz. Steering is a tad fuzzy, but roadholding is irreproachable, as is overall comfort, even with the low-profile 17-inch tires (P-0s, which are part of the Evolution sport package). The latter, however, strip the car of the kind of tight turning circle for which most Mercedes-Benzes are admired.

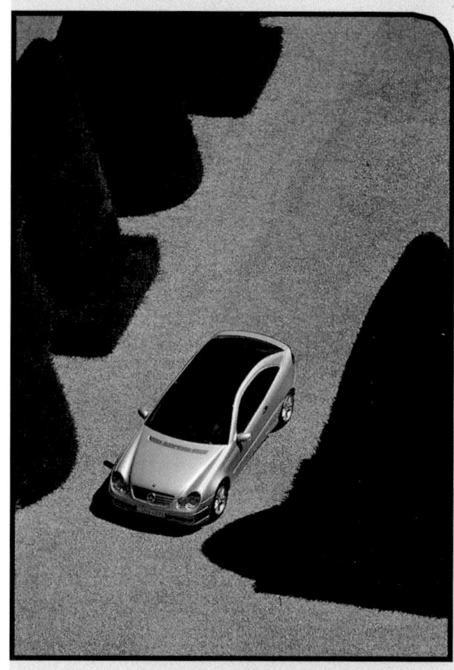

MERCEDES-BENZ **C CLASS COUPE**

Genuine four-seater
The C Coupe's interior is not a sedan clone but boasts its own dashboard with three-spoke steering, anti-glare instrument cluster and smart aluminum trim around the center console. The rear is spacious enough to accommodate two average-size adults. The rear bench can be collapsed to further enlarge the luggage compartment, which can accommodate 10.8 to 38.8 cubic feet of luggage. Despite its compact dimensions, there's civilized roominess inside the new Mercedes-Benz Coupe.

Despite the model's reasonable price, there's been no skimping on safety measures. A Scandinavian colleague owes Mercedes-Benz big time when he unwittingly experienced the full force of air bags from practically every direction, including the roof, after his car repeatedly hit a wall at different angles. The car was ready for the scrap yard after the accident, but it was the great columnist's pride that was really hurt.

Iffy panoramic roof
As attractive as it is with green-tinted safety glass and a 30% larger opening than the conventional sunroof, the panoramic roof remains iffy until the car has racked up a few thousand miles. The same accessory from the same maker caused problems for the first Porsche Targas in 1996. The generous glass surface (covering the entire roof) may weaken the structure's rigidity, producing grating noises on bad roads. Naturally, Mercedes-Benz claimed

■ STANDARD EQUIPMENT
- Power-assisted emergency brakes
- Stability system • Trip computer
- Head air bags

■ OPTIONAL EQUIPMENT
- Panoramic sunroof • Navigation system
- Speedtronic transmission

there was no reason for concern, but let's just wait and see. Besides, the option costs about $2000, too expensive for what it offers.

With its reasonable price, youthful looks and prestigious heritage, the C Class Sport Coupe places the tri-star in a new orbit. Will it be able to lure the much-coveted young clientele in today's fiercely competitive marketplace? For Mercedes-Benz, it's a risky venture, for if the C Class Coupe misses its target, it's not the company's traditional customer base that will pick up the pieces.

Jacques Duval

SPECIFICATIONS

Price	$CDN 33,950-35,450 / $US n.a.
Warranty	4 years / 48,000 miles (80,000 km)
Type	4-seat coupe / rear wheel drive
Wheelbase / Length	107 in / 171 in
Width / Height	68 in / 55.4 in
Weight	3307 lb (1500 kg)
Trunk / Fuel tank	10.9 to 38.9 cu. ft / 16 gallons
Air bags	front, side and ceiling
Front suspension	independent
Rear suspension	independent
Front brakes / Rear brakes	disc, ABS and ESP
Traction control	yes
Steering	rack-and-pinion, power assist
Turning circle	35 feet
Tires (front/rear)	P225/45R17

PERFORMANCE

Engine	4L 2.3-liter
Transmission	5-speed automatic
Horsepower	197 hp at 5500 rpm
Torque	207 lb-ft at 2500 - 4800 rpm
Other engines	none
Other transmission	6-speed manual
Acceleration (0-60 mph)	8 sec
Maximum speed	147 mph (237 km/h)
Braking (60-0 mph)	n.a.
Fuel consumption	22.9 mpg (9.9 L/100 km)

COMPETITION

• Acura CL Coupe • Audi TT Coupe • BMW 330Ci
• Chrysler Sebring Coupe • Toyota Solara Coupe

NEW FOR 2002

• New model

RATING (out of 5 stars)

Driveability	★★★½
Comfort	★★★½
Reliability	New model
Roominess	★★★½
Winter driving rating	★★★
Safety	★★★★
Resale value	New model

MERCEDES-BENZ E CLASS

MERCEDES **E CLASS**

A Farewell Tour

Introduced six years ago, the Mercedes-Benz E Class (E320, E430, E55) is currently making its farewell tour. The final version of these sedans and wagons (both 2- and 4-wheel drivers) will be unveiled soon as 2003 models (in North America).

I remember how long it took us all back in 1996 to get used to those new round headlights that seemed such a direct clash with the German automaker's habitually conservative approach. And yet, in a relatively short period of time, Mercedes brushed off its traditional image in favor of an infinitely more dynamic style, because the E Class cars looked utterly different from other Mercedes models.

Once again I can give you first-hand proof of the quality of these mid-size sedans and wagons, thanks to an opportunity to drive an E320 4MATIC in mid-winter so that I could fully check out – and appreciate – its all-wheel-drive system. At first, I wasn't that keen to test this model because I didn't think it would be the first choice for E Class buyers. However, the marketing team at Mercedes quickly convinced me, telling me that the E320 4MATIC accounted for 50% of total E Class sales, at least in Canada. In hindsight I can see why, not only does the car boast Mercedes' legendary passive safety features, it also offers the bonus of four-wheel drive.

Accident detector

At the 2001 Frankfurt Auto Show, Mercedes-Benz unveiled an electronic active security system-in-progress that may well become an integral part of the next generation of E Class models. Called "PRE-SAFE," it's a sophisticated accident detector that will automatically activate all the vehicle's safety systems – extensible bumpers, "survival cells" in the front end of the car, and mobile doors – just fractions of a second before an eventual impact.

In the meantime, thanks to their relatively young age, E Class models can benefit from both Mercedes Benz reliability and the carmaker's many up-to-date developments. Just consider for a moment the fact that despite its weight, all-wheel drive and extensive array of equipment, the E320 4MATIC is actually well served by its 3.2-liter V6 engine. The V6, according to official stats, produces 221 hp, only 6 ponies

▲ PROS

- Peerless drivetrain • Sophisticated safety features • Sound handling • Spacious and comfortable cabin

▼ CONS

- CD player optional • End-of-line model
- Fixed rear bench seat

more than that generated by the C Class engine, although the way it performs makes you imagine that it's really much more powerful. Acceleration is crisp and passing power is reassuring. And the fact that it delivers a generous 21-mpg fuel mileage is almost unbelievable. Unbelievable, but true, and all the more so given the fact that our test drive took place in the thick of winter!

Active security

I was half "sport-driving" the car, and the way it handled convinced me that engineers in Stuttgart took the principle of active security very seriously indeed. Suspension was firm, and body roll virtually non-existent when cornering. What's more, the rough roads I traveled on never once caused even the least body noise.

If you're a serious sport-driver, you might want to consider buying the E55 AMG (see the AMG special report in this guidebook). Finally the 2002 E55 comes with a CD player, perhaps because the automaker was embarrassed by our frequent criticism of Mercedes' stinginess for failing to include one in a $100,000 car. The other major addition in the 2002 E Class models are 6-spoke alloy wheels on the E320 and E320 4MATIC models.

What I don't like

The thing that I dread most after testing a car is the sudden realization that there is nothing much to say about the car in question. That's the situation today and I almost feel like apologizing for the fact that this report reads like a press release. After thinking long and hard, however, I've decided that what I don't like about this E320 is its ordinary silhouette, the beige (or mustard) color of the interior, the fixed rear-bench backrest, and, of course, the fact that buyers have to fork over an extra $840 for an in-dash CD player (installation not included). By comparison, you can buy an all-wheel-drive Audi 2.7 T for slightly under $60,000. But when you come right down to it, a Mercedes is a Mercedes and the E320 4MATIC is unquestionably one of the finest cars in the world. And that's worth something.

Jacques Duval

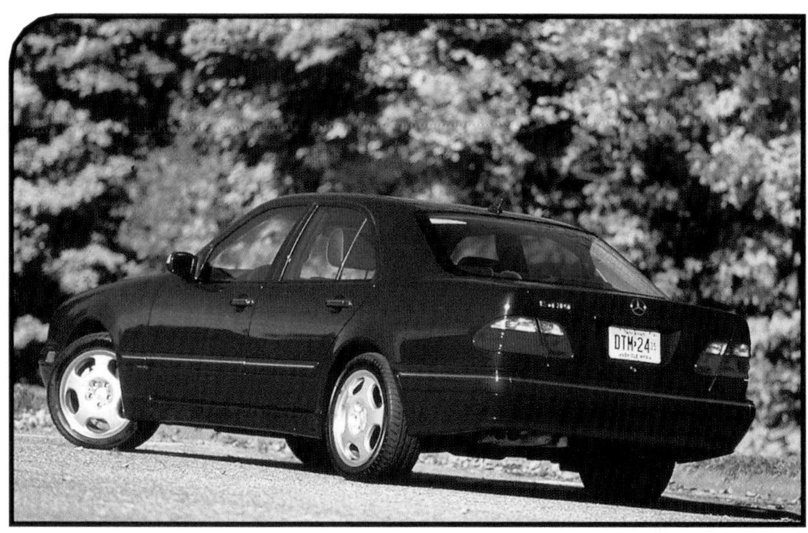

SPECIFICATIONS	E320 4MATIC
Price	$CDN 73,250-101,600 / $US 48,495-70,945
Warranty	4 years / 48,000 miles (80,000 km)
Type	sedan / all wheel drive
Wheelbase / Length	111.4 in / 189.4 in
Width / Height	70.9 in / 56.7 in
Weight	3688 lb (1673 kg)
Trunk / Fuel tank	15.3 cu. ft / 21 gallons
Air bags	front, side and head curtains
Front suspension	independent
Rear suspension	independent
Front brakes / Rear brakes	disc ABS
Traction control	yes
Steering	rack-and-pinion, variable assist
Turning circle	37 feet
Tires (front/rear)	P215/55R16

PERFORMANCE	
Engine	V2 3.2-liter
Transmission	5-speed automatic SpeedShift
Horsepower	221-hp at 5500 rpm
Torque	232 lb-ft at 3000-4600 rpm
Other engines	V8 4.3-liter 275-hp; V8 5.5-liter 349-hp
Other transmission	none
Acceleration (0-60 mph)	7.9 sec
Maximum speed	130 mph (210 km/h)
Braking (60-0 mph)	127 feet (38.7 m)
Fuel consumption	20.4 mpg (11.1 L/100km)

COMPETITION

• Audi A6 • BMW 5 Series • Cadillac Seville
• Jaguar S-Type V8 • Lexus GS 430 • Volvo S80

NEW FOR 2002

• New wheels (320) • Personalized interior (on request) • Two new colors

RATING	(out of 5 stars)
Driveability	★★★★
Comfort	★★★★
Reliability	★★★★
Roominess	★★★★
Winter driving rating	★★★★½
Safety	★★★★½
Resale value	★★★★

MERCEDES-BENZ M CLASS

MERCEDES-BENZ **M CLASS**

Proving Critics Wrong

Ever since it was introduced in 1998, the M Class sport-utility series has attracted its fair share of criticism. While it's true that these vehicles took a while to break in properly and show off their legendary Mercedes-brand workmanship, others questioned the appropriateness of their sport-utility character in an urban context. But the M Class series' success speaks for itself. Is it simply a passing trend? Entirely probable, but then any explanation at all deserves consideration, including the possibility that Mercedes may have created a vehicle that has met the expectations of many motorists.

In the M Class, the numerals refer to the models' engine displacement. The ML320 comes with a 3.2-liter V6; the ML55, launched in 2000, offers a 5.5-liter engine. Between the pair comes the ML430, whose engine was replaced this year by a 5.0-liter V8 borrowed from the S Class. It's been renamed ML500.

Modifications in 2002 also include a redesign of both the exterior and interior, as well as upgraded accessories and amenities. Taken together, 1100 components have either been added or modified. Among the new features are inflatable curtains, joining the existing six air bags, a new automatic climate control and a redesigned center console.

The ML55 is the most energetic of the trio, and the series' standard bearer. With 342 horsepower and 376 lb-ft of torque, the vehicle leaps forward so powerfully that the outline of the stitching decorating its excellent seats will be imprinted on your back. The ML500 also gains its share of attention with a new powertrain, generating an extra 20 ponies – bringing it to 288 hp – enough to propel it from 0-60 mph in just over seven seconds. Next to these two powerhouses, the ML320 seems like a poor relation, taking 9.4 seconds to execute the same exercise – a relatively poor showing for a vehicle whose price starts in the $50,000 range.

Almost perfect

Decent handling

Yet that's the model you'll encounter most often on the road. Not only because it's the least expensive of the three, but it has the kind of characteristics that most drivers want or need. Intended mostly for use between the city and the destination of

▲ PROS

• Prestigious brand • Comprehensive engine choices • Efficient all-wheel drive • Predictable handling • Spacious interior

▼ CONS

• Brakes hard to modulate • Excessive fuel consumption (ML500 and 55) • High maintenance cost • Steep prices (ML500 and 55) • Stiff steering

the moment, the ML320 handles rather like a touring car, providing a comfortable and smooth means of transportation. The independent four-wheel suspension is highly versatile, displaying firmness on sharp curves and absorbing every shake, rattle and roll with ease and aplomb. Handling is equally smooth in city traffic, thanks to the well-integrated 5-speed automatic transmission with manual mode (Touch Shift) and the powerful and long-wearing brakes. Mind you, the pedal feels spongy at times and is therefore difficult to modulate. Steering is fine at cruising speeds, but feels a tad too stiff for maneuvering in and out of parking spaces. In off-road situations, just set the all-wheel-drive system at low range and see how easy it then becomes to deal with any obstacle, big or small, that nature places in your way. That is, so long as you don't get carried away. To test the vehicle's sport-ute function, offer to drive your teen-age son and his pals, plus pads and equipment, to the arena. The ML, needless to say, will readily oblige with its generous cargo space – a cavernous 40.4 cubic feet. And with the 60/40 rear bench seat, things can only get better on this front.

The seats are comfortable and provide solid support. From the majestically high driving position, you can lord it over your environment. The base model – ML320 Classic – comes with a relatively complete range of standard equipment. But if you want leather seats, you'll have to go up a notch and get the ML320 Elegance. The 2002 M Class models prove that Mercedes has addressed most buyers' complaints about inferior finish quality and ergonomic flaws. But not quite all of them. You're still more than likely to activate the cruise control lever when in fact what you were looking for was the turn signal.

Having got that out of the way, the ML is an all-purpose vehicle capable of meeting the differing needs of a family of four or five. It's comfortable and practical, and has that shiny star perched in the middle of the grille – a little something to stroke your ego.

Jean-Georges Laliberté

SPECIFICATIONS	**ML 320 Elegance**
Price	$CDN 55,600-92,850 / $US 36,445-66,545
Warranty	4 years / 48,000 miles (80,000 km)
Type	sport utility / all wheel drive
Wheelbase / Length	111 in / 180.7 in
Width / Height	72 in / 70.1 in
Weight	4586 lb (2080 kg)
Trunk / Fuel tank	40.4 cu.ft / 22 gallons
Air bags	front, side and curtain
Front suspension	independent
Rear suspension	independent
Front brakes / Rear brakes	disc ABS
Traction control	yes
Steering	rack-and-pinion, variable assist
Turning circle	37 feet
Tires (front/rear)	P275/55R17

PERFORMANCE	
Engine	V6 3.2-liter
Transmission	5-speed automatic Touch Shift
Horsepower	215-hp at 5500 rpm
Torque	233 lb-ft at 3000 rpm
Other engines	V8 5.0-liter 288 hp; V8 5.5-liter 342 hp
Other transmission	none
Acceleration (0-60 mph)	9.4 sec
Maximum speed	117 mph (188 km/h)
Braking (60-0 mph)	131 feet (40 m)
Fuel consumption	17.4 mpg (13 L/100 km)

COMPETITION

• Acura MDX • BMW X5 3.0i • Infiniti QX4 • Land Rover Discovery • Lexus RX 300

NEW FOR 2002

• 5.0-liter engine (ML500) • New safety accessories • Slight design modification (body and interior)

RATING	**(out of 5 stars)**
Driveability	★★★★
Comfort	★★★★
Reliability	★★★½
Roominess	★★★★
Winter driving rating	★★★★
Safety	★★★★½
Resale value	★★★½

MERCEDES-BENZ S CLASS

MERCEDES-BENZ **S CLASS**

NASA on Four Wheels

"Our high-end models boast more electronic gadgets than an F1 single-seater," the communications officer of the F1 McLaren-Mercedes team told me. And I thought, probably even more than the space shuttle.

As a matter of fact, almost every device aboard the "starship" Mercedes-Benz is electronically controlled, whether we're talking about passive safety and its numerous array of air bags, or active safety and its many "anti" features (antilock, antiskid, antislip), or the automatic climate control, transmissions, navigation or engine-management system.

And why not, because as a result Mercedes' reliability has been greatly improved. It has certainly come a very long way since those ancient mechanical systems of yore. But aren't we in danger of forsaking driving pleasure in the process? Are electronics about to supplant human beings themselves in the automotive field? The answer is a resounding yes. In fact, it already has. For example, road safety management has made great strides during the past 30 years, thanks to the various electronic devices designed to compensate for human flaws and weaknesses.

Shedding weight

But philosophy and electronics aside, let's scrutinize the supreme S Class series. It consists of four models, which means four different engines and four vocations. First, there's the S430 with its 275-hp V8. Next comes the S500 with its 302-hp 5.0-liter engine, capable of propelling its roughly 4000-lb mass (1800 kg) from 0-60 mph in 7.3 seconds. Go another notch and you'll find the devilish S55 AMG, powered by a superb 5.5-liter V8 with 349 hp, whose thunderous acceleration and passing power rivals the sleekest and most powerful sports cars in the world. And if it's supremacy you're after, check out the 5.8-liter V12 engine under the hood of the divine S600 (5.8-liter, 362 hp). Its suppleness and torque will leave you stunned. Another detail: the S430 comes in either short or long wheelbase, while the S500 and S600 only come in long wheelbase.

Electronic extravaganza

Needless to say, this high-class mechanical extravaganza is accompanied by the kind of luxury accoutrements that contribute to the renown of the celebrated three-point star: multi-directional adjustable steering wheel and front seats, supple

▲ PROS

• Choice of models and engines • Excellent active and passive safety • High-level handling and braking • Quality workmanship • Rigid body

▼ CONS

• Certain complex controls • Limited trunk space • Plain silhouette • Steep prices

leather, lush floor covering, exquisite wood trim, quality plastic material, and power everything else. So far so good. It's only when you decide to turn the radio on that things start getting complicated. Since the stereo functions are displayed on the complex navigation-system monitor, you'll have to concentrate on each and every step so as not to activate anything else by mistake. The entire process seems a little excessive, not to say frustrating. And if you want some music, you've got to go to the trunk, because that's where the CD player – finally offered as standard equipment in 2002 – is located.

But let's move on to something more cheerful, like handling. The new S Class generation, introduced in 2000, is hundreds of pounds lighter than the previous one, with the extensive use of aluminum and other lighter materials. Even so, the smallest model still weighs a significant 4090 lbs (1855 kg). Yet on the road, the electronically-controlled AIRMATIC pneumatic suspension system is so efficient that it makes you forget all about the weight. The ride is as nimble and smooth as anyone could wish.

Double assistance

And to control your own enthusiasm, you can rely on the doubly assisted disc brakes. I say "doubly," because in addition to the regular brake assistance, the S Class' system boasts an extra feature designed to detect an emergency braking situation from the speed of the driver's foot as it's applied to the brake pedal. In response, it automatically builds up the maximum brake force, thus decisively reducing the braking distance.

The power-assist rack-and-pinion steering system is highly precise, and with all those electronic driving aids, it's virtually impossible to make the car slide sideways, no matter how hard you try. And that's the point I'm trying to make. Driving this car is not as thrilling as driving a sports car in the1960s when you could work with the steering wheel and the accelerator when cornering near the limit. Still, considering the tremendous benefits of active and passive safety, comfort and reliability, such a comparison seems self-indulgent and no longer makes sense.

Alain Raymond

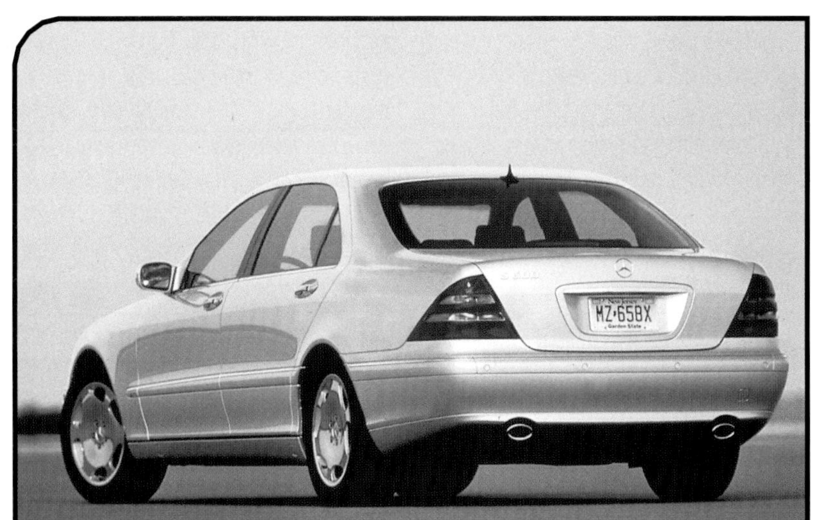

SPECIFICATIONS

Price	$CDN 101,850-171,100 / $US 71,445-114,645
Warranty	4 years / 48,000 miles (80,000 km)
Type	sedan / rear wheel drive
Wheelbase / Length	116.5 in / 198.4 in
Width / Height	73.2 in / 56.7 in
Weight	4090 lb (1855 kg)
Trunk / Fuel tank	15.4 cu. ft / 23 gallons
Air bags	front and side
Front suspension	independent
Rear suspension	independent
Front brakes / Rear brakes	disc ABS
Traction control	yes
Steering	rack-and-pinion, variable assist
Turning circle	38 feet
Tires (front/rear)	P225/60R16

PERFORMANCE

Engine	V8 4.3-liter
Transmission	5-speed automatic
Horsepower	275 hp at 5750 rpm
Torque	295 lb-ft at 3000 - 4400 rpm
Other engines	V12 5.8-liter 362 hp; V8 5.0-liter 302 hp; V8 5.5-liter 355 hp
Other transmission	none
Acceleration (0-60 mph)	7.1 sec
Maximum speed	130 mph (210 km/h)
Braking (60-0 mph)	121 feet (37 m)
Fuel consumption	16.6 mpg (13.7 L/100 km)

COMPETITION

• Audi S8 • BMW 750i • Jaguar XJR
• Lexus LS 430

NEW FOR 2002

• Designo • New colors • Standard CD player

RATING	**(out of 5 stars)**
Driveability	★★★★
Comfort	★★★★½
Reliability	★★★★
Roominess	★★★★½
Winter driving rating	★★★★
Safety	★★★★★
Resale value	★★★★

MERCEDES-BENZ CLK 320/430 55 AMG

MERCEDES-BENZ **CLK320**

Just to indulge

Slotted somewhere between the E Class and C Class, Mercedes-Benz has in the last few years created some very fine coupes and convertibles, bearing the designation CLK. In some ways, they have replaced the expensive E320 coupes and convertibles which were derived from the old E Class. These new models are less expensive and a little less elaborate, but they have quickly acquired an important following which was immediately seduced by their attractive lines. And besides, they're also very enjoyable cars to drive.

The CLK model line includes three coupes and a convertible with several different engine options: the CLK320 with a 3.2-liter V6, the CLK430 with a solid 4.3-liter V8, the CLK 55 AMG propelled by the rocket-type 5.5-liter V8 specially tuned by AMG, which is the subject of another article. Despite its excellent rigidity, the convertible's chassis may be the worst for wear over a period of time when equipped with the aggressive 5.5-liter V8 engine.

One word about the reliability or, if you prefer, the workmanship. Some drivers have had to contend with various mechanical or electrical problems, and personally we had an unfortunate incident with the roof power system on a convertible 430. It's not the end of the world, but it's a nuisance coming from such a pricey car. I'd admit that the quality you perceive at first glance is very impressive, but over a period of time, some Mercedes models seem to suffer from the strains imposed by increased production figures over the last few years. Take, for example, the small rattle from the passenger seat of the coupe that was lent to me for this test.

Heart struck

Having said this, it's difficult not to fall in love with a CLK. First, its elegant and well-proportioned lines, then its excellent road manners. You really have to push very hard to get the car to roll a little or show some of its built-in understeer near the limit. Anyway, its stability control system is tuned to intervene before you can embarrass yourself. Aware of the slightest loss of grip, the automatic power reduction and smart braking quickly brings the car back on the straight and narrow. Steering follows your every whim and keeps you well informed as to road conditions and available grip, which greatly enhances driving pleasure. Braking effec-

Good compromise

▲ PROS

- Attractive lines • Comfortable seats
- Good engine selection • Quiet convertible
- Stimulating road manners

▼ CONS

- Difficult winter driving • Quality on the lax side
- Rear seating impractical • Redundant middle V8 engine option • Restricted trunk space (convertible)

tivenes, while not spectacular, is well up to the task. You'd have to push the car very hard before they'd show any sign of weakness.

The three engine options range from a 215-hp V6 base motor to a 342-hp V8 for the CLK AMG. Between the 4.2-liter V6 and the middle option, a 4.3-liter V8 with 60 more horsepower, I'd be happy with the V6, which I've always found suitable for my needs. I think the $10,000 extra for the V8 engine is not justified, unless a few tenths of a second from 0-60 mph are of vital importance to you. And on a snow-covered road, I would rather prefer the V6, with its smoother power delivery. Whatever the engine option, the transmission remains the same: a 5-speed automatic with selectable manual shift override.

Open skies

Riding comfort and suspension effort are what you would expect from a Mercedes and buyers of the convertible need not lose any sleep over the soft-top's waterproofing or even windproofing. Wind noise does increase above 60 mph, but that's the lot of all convertibles. Rear visibility is not what it should be. However, knocks and rattles just don't exist in CLK convertibles, at least not in low mileage samples.

Despite its size, the CLK coupe's rear seats are not exactly hospitable. The rear bench amounts to little more than a temporary refuge for adolescents or average-sized adults. Moreover, in order to get to the back seats, you have to fold the front backrest, powered by an electric motor which performs incredibly slowly. You'd almost have time to read your paper. On the other hand, the front seats are well designed and their comfort is worthy of note. As for trunk space, let's just say that it is best to "travel light" with a CLK, particularly if it's a convertible.

The coupe offers 11.2 cubic feet of trunk space, the convertible has 9.6 cubic feet with the top up and only 4.9 cubic feet if you decide to let the wind in your hair. But don't worry, standard equipment includes a windbreak in the shape of a mosquito net which will keep your hair curlers in place while you go for a drive under the open skies. Enjoy the drive!

Jacques Duval

SPECIFICATIONS	**CLK320**
Price	$CDN 59,900-107,500 / $US 42,595-68,055
Warranty	4 years / 48,000 miles (80,000 km)
Type	4-seat coupe / rear wheel drive
Wheelbase / Length	105.9 in / 180.3 in
Width / Height	67.7 in / 53.9 in
Weight	3212 lb (1457 kg)
Trunk / Fuel tank	11.2 cu. ft / 19 gallons
Air bags	front and side
Front suspension	independent
Rear suspension	independent
Front brakes / Rear brakes	disc ABS
Traction control	yes
Steering	recirculating-ball, variable assist
Turning circle	35 feet (10.7 m)
Tires (front/rear)	P205/55R16
PERFORMANCE	
Engine	V6 3.2-liter
Transmission	5-speed automatic
Horsepower	215 hp at 5700 rpm
Torque	229 lb-ft at 3000 - 4600 rpm
Other engines	V8 4.3-liter 275 hp; V8 5.5-liter 342 hp
Other transmission	none
Acceleration (0-60 mph)	7.3 sec
Maximum speed	130 mph (limited) (210 km/h)
Braking (60-0 mph)	115 feet (35 m)
Fuel consumption	19.7 mpg (11.5 L/100 km)

COMPETITION

• Audi A4 cabriolet • BMW 330Ci • Saab 9³ • Volvo C70

NEW FOR 2002

• AMG convertible • New color • Sport package (CLK 320)

RATING	**(out of 5 stars)**
Driveability	★★★★
Comfort	★★★½
Reliability	★★★
Roominess	★★½
Winter driving rating	★★½
Safety	★★★★
Resale value	★★★★½

MERCEDES-BENZ **SLK**

MERCEDES-BENZ **SLK**

More Power, More Pleasure

An innocent roadster when it was born in 1996, the SLK Class coupe-convertible has been transformed into a genuine hod rod in its latest AMG-tuned incarnation – the SLK 32 AMG. It's now fitted with a 3.2-liter supercharged V6 developing 349 horsepower – far removed from the meager 190 hp cranked out by an unworthy 2.3-liter 4-cylinder compressor engine. The 0-60 mph time is now 5 seconds, down from 8.5 seconds.

Just a year ago, the SLK was given Mercedes' newly developed modular V6 engine generating 215 hp. This year's revision can mean only one thing: the German automaker has every intention of letting the car end its career with a bang.

I can't say for sure whether the SLK 32 AMG will allow the popular roadster to shed its "women's car" label, but I would dearly like to see the expression on the face of a Corvette driver after he's been "eaten alive" by a lady-driver behind the wheel of her SLK 32. Incidentally, you'll find our impressions of this AMG version in the article "Six Mercedes on the Loose" in the first section of this guidebook.

Best buy

But we shouldn't let the AMG version overshadow the excellent SLK 320 that came out last year. Its modular V6 was a huge improvement over the original industrial-sounding 4-cylinder *mit kompressor* engine. For roughly $5000, you'll get not just 25 extra horsepower, but more torque in the bargain and the privilege of using one of the best V6s currently available on the market anywhere. Compared with the 230 Kom pressor, the SLK 320 gets exclusive alloy wheels, power seats, leather and wood trim and a stiffer anti-roll bar in the rear.

With this in place, driving pleasure increases enormously, even with a 5-speed automatic gearbox with TouchShift manual shifting mode. As a matter of fact, the automatic transmission is just as effective as the 6-speed manual which, despite Mercedes' many efforts to improve it, isn't the best example of its kind. Without being a genuine sports car – that role being reserved for the AMG version – the SLK 320 still handles itself with panache. Its supple engine readily obliges the slightest demand from the accelerator.

Status quo

Suspension is tuned rather more for comfort than handling, and the car's occupants benefit from excellent dampening,

▲ PROS

• Above-average comfort • Excellent handling • Retractable hard top • Wonderful V6 engine

▼ CONS

• Boring 4-cylinder engine • Rear-wheel drive suspect in winter • Tiny trunk • Unpleasant manual gearbox

despite the car's short wheelbase. The chassis is remarkably rigid, which means that you can have fun with the car without having to worry about having the rear end come around at the least provocation. In any case, that's what the standard Electronic Stability Program (ESP) is there for. What's unclear, however, is the SLK's limited capabilities in harsh winter driving conditions.

Steering is precise and the steering wheel has a nice feel to it. The brakes too are efficient, and prove highly durable. On the other hand, a number of owners complained about electrical problems.

The retractable-top battle

With the exception of the old Ford Skyliner, the SLK coupe convertible was the first car to offer a retractable hard top. In fact, during the initial demonstration, Mercedes made a big hullabaloo over the fact that it took a mere 25 seconds either to retract the top or put it back. This year, Lexus managed the same feat with its SC 430 roadster, but the German automaker surged ahead once again with its 2003 SL 500, whose top can be retracted or put back in only 16 seconds. It all sounds very fine and dandy, except that precious trunk space will be used to store the top. In the SLK, for example, trunk space will be reduced from 9.5 cubic feet to 3.6 cubic feet when the top is down, making for the tiniest of trunks.

Despite limited cabin space, the SLK offers comfortable seats and excellent storage areas. The dashboard is both efficient and esthetically pleasing.

The next step

It will come as no surprise to anyone to learn that the SLK is on the verge of a major overhaul. Reading between the lines, the fact that the 2002 models were deprived of any significant change or technical improvement is a clear signal, so far as Mercedes-Benz is concerned, that the company intends to save its innovations for the following year. The year 2002 will belong instead to its big sister, the SL (see separate text), and we can assume that it won't be long before the SLK itself will go back to the drawing board. Meanwhile, SLK devotees will have to settle for a new color or the possibility of personalizing the interior of their car, as offered through Mercedes' Designo program. And that's it. There's nothing further to report.

Jacques Duval

SPECIFICATIONS	AMG
Price	$CDN 55,100-76,900 / $US 39,545-44,545
Warranty	4 years / 48,000 miles (80,000 km)
Type	2-seat coupe-convertible / front wheel drive
Wheelbase / Length	94.5 in / 157.9 in
Width / Height	67.3 in / 50.4 in
Weight	3097 lb (1405 kg)
Trunk / Fuel tank	3.7 - 9.6 cu. ft / 16 gallons
Air bags	front and side
Front suspension	independent
Rear suspension	independent
Front brakes / Rear brakes	disc ABS
Traction control	yes
Steering	recirculating-balls, power assist
Turning circle	34 feet
Tires (front/rear)	P205/55R16-225/50R16

PERFORMANCE	
Engine	V6 3.2-liter
Transmission	5-speed automatic
Horsepower	215 hp at 5700 rpm
Torque	229 lb-ft at 3000 – 4600 rpm
Other engines	4L 2.3-liter (compressor) 190 hp
Other transmission	6-speed manual
Acceleration (0-60 mph)	7.2 sec
Maximum speed	140 mph (electron. lim.) (225 km/h)
Braking (60-0 mph)	125 feet (38.2 m)
Fuel consumption	19.9 mpg (11.4 L/100 km

COMPETITION

- Audi TT Roadster • BMW Z3 • Honda S2000
- Porsche Boxster

NEW FOR 2002

- AMG version • Designo option (interior)
- New color

RATING	(out of 5 stars)
Driveability	★★★½
Comfort	★★★½
Reliability	★★★½
Roominess	★★
Winter driving rating	★★★
Safety	★★★★
Resale value	★★★★

MERCURY COUGAR

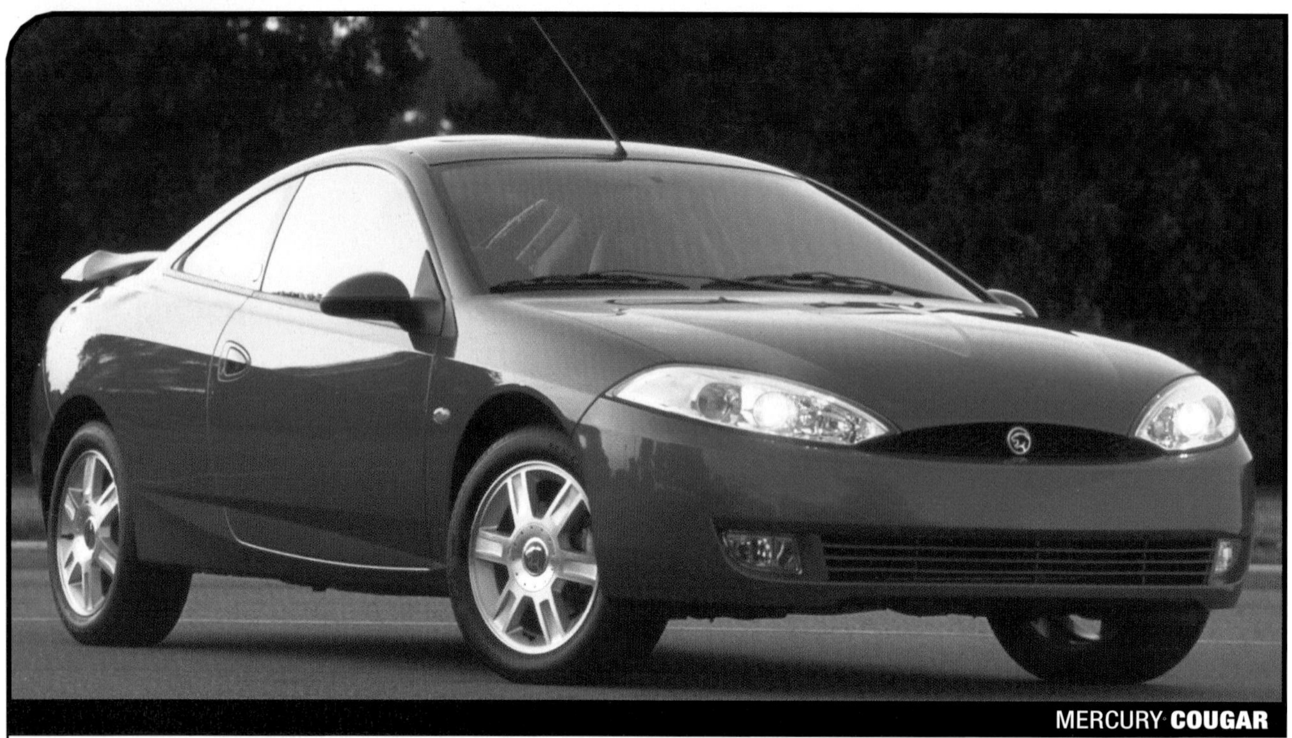

MERCURY COUGAR

Cat with Nine Lives

Born in 1967 as a Ford Mustang clone, the Mercury Cougar evolved over the years into many shapes and forms before settling down as a "companion" of the Thunderbird – a luxury coupe known more for its large, sloppy size than its agility. In 1999, the Cougar was redesigned yet again based partly on the European-engineered Ford Mondeo.

Following this latest transformation, the Cougar went from "rear-wheel" status to front-wheel drive. Its dimensions were also reduced. Still, the changes didn't go far enough, and this has evidently not been fixed on the 2002 model.

"New Edge" look

It's an eye-catching design, combining smooth, curvy body lines and sharp-edged geometric features. Whether you like it or not is beside the point, the so-called New Edge Cougar certainly looks original – a refreshing change from the common look that invariably afflicts cars of this nature. But I dislike its sloping roofline, which hampers rear visibility.

Presented as a 2+2 coupe, the Cougar can theoretically seat four adults. But frankly, the rear cabin is so cramped it can accommodate two kids, or at best, two very young adults, if they don't mind traveling with their heads squashed between their knees. Front-cabin passengers have more legroom, although they have to put up with seats that are so hard they rattle your bones.

The trunk is impressively spacious for a sport coupe. With the backrest flipped forward, cargo space is a whopping 24 cubic feet (680 liters), although its high opening doesn't make loading any easier. The ergonomics of the Euro-look dashboard give the interior a simple, elegant appearance.

Too little, too late

One engine

Eye-catching looks may be fine and dandy, but can the car perform? The 125-hp 4-cylinder engine of yore is gone, leaving the 2.5-liter V6 with 170 hp to do the job. It does perform respectably, but owners of Camaros or similar sport coupes have little to fear. No fire-

▲ PROS

- Adequate braking • Eye-catching design
- Good roadability • Sound drivetrain
- Spacious trunk

▼ CONS

- Cramped rear cabin • Inadequate engine power
- Rear visibility • Transmissions need work
- Uncomfortable seats

ball, the Cougar sorely needs more horsepower – an extra 40 would be just about right – if it wants to compete, let alone excel. The lazy 4-speed automatic transmission makes matters even worse. So, if you insist on buying a Cougar, go for the 5-speed manual. However stubborn and imprecise it may be, it's your best bet.

Worth mentioning, however, is the fact that the V6 engine has finally shed its annoying habit of not slowing down once the accelerator has been released. For those who drive Cougars still affected by this problem, there are many websites devoted to the subject, offering good, simple advice on how to correct it.

In general, the Cougar is a decent car, both comfortable and roadworthy. Its superbly rigid chassis is a shade too heavy, making it less nimble on the road, but it handles well enough, exhibiting little evidence of understeer. Thanks to its all-independent suspension, derived from the Ford Mondeo, and 16-inch tires (optional), the Cougar sticks tenaciously to the road. The disc brakes, too, perform admirably, and won't overheat.

The Cougar's base price is fairly competitive, and includes air-conditioning, cruise control as well as all the regular power-assisted features. For an extra $1500, you'll get the Sport package which offers four-wheel disc brakes, 16-inch wheels and a couple of "cosmetic" features, but no ABS or traction control, for which you'll have to shell out even more.

In the final analysis, however, the new Cougar has yet to reach the finish line. To be the kind of high-performance car that Lincoln-Mercury has in mind, it needs to go back to the drawing board.

Jean-Georges Laliberté

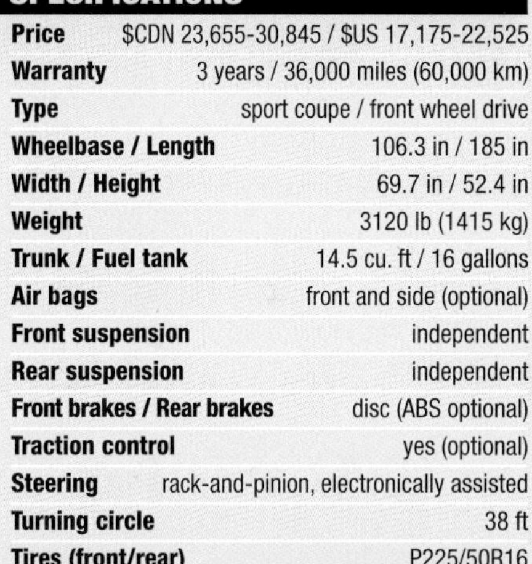

SPECIFICATIONS

Price	$CDN 23,655-30,845 / $US 17,175-22,525
Warranty	3 years / 36,000 miles (60,000 km)
Type	sport coupe / front wheel drive
Wheelbase / Length	106.3 in / 185 in
Width / Height	69.7 in / 52.4 in
Weight	3120 lb (1415 kg)
Trunk / Fuel tank	14.5 cu. ft / 16 gallons
Air bags	front and side (optional)
Front suspension	independent
Rear suspension	independent
Front brakes / Rear brakes	disc (ABS optional)
Traction control	yes (optional)
Steering	rack-and-pinion, electronically assisted
Turning circle	38 ft
Tires (front/rear)	P225/50R16

PERFORMANCE

Engine	V6 2.5-liter
Transmission	4-speed automatic
Horsepower	170 hp at 6200 rpm
Torque	165 lb-ft at 4250 rpm
Other engines	none
Other transmission	5-speed manual
Acceleration (0-60 mph)	7.9 sec
Maximum speed	134 mph (216 km/h)
Braking (60-0 mph)	130 feet (39.7 m)
Fuel consumption	18.9 mpg (12 L/100 km)

COMPETITION

- Chrysler Sebring • Honda Prelude
- Hyundai Tiburon • Saturn SC • Toyota Celica

NEW FOR 2002

- Commodity package now standard on all models
- Feature car on MACH station

RATING (out of 5 stars)

Driveability	★★★½
Comfort	★★★
Reliability	★★★★
Roominess	★★
Winter driving rating	★★★
Safety	★★★★
Resale value	★★½

MERCURY GRAND MARQUIS MERCURY MARAUDER

MERCURY **GRAND MARQUIS**

A Very Fit Dinosaur

With its retro lines, old mechanicals and road manners worthy of a wobbly bowl of jelly, you'd think the Grand Marquis might soon be a car for the history books. Logically, this highway dinosaur should disappear through lack of interest. But there's a small ray of hope. The car is gaining in popularity as it heads into the millennium and a number of new models have recently been unveiled by Mercury.

Yet more proof that logic and the world of cars seldom mesh. Theoretically, the Mercury division no longer exists in Canada yet this Mercury Grand Marquis has replaced the Ford Crown Victoria in the same market. Logical? Whimsical? We may as well expect anything!

So, far from heading into the sunset, the largest of the Mercurys will offer an even sportier 2003 model in summer 2002. It's called the Marauder, named after a former Mercury that came off the production line in 1963. Back then it was powered by a big 406-cubic-inch V8 engine producing a whopping 405 hp (gross). Such statistics weren't considered suitable for a family sedan and soon the Super Marauder burst on the scene. Its 427-cubic-inch 425-hp engine promised to make its proud owner wary of twisting roads.

With that wild period in mind, the Mercury division's thinking heads dreamed up a Marauder for the new millennium. It will be more powerful than its forerunner, promising a minimum of 300-hp from a 4.6-liter dual overhead cam V8 engine. Its 18-inch wheels, low-profile tires and sport suspension system should guarantee satisfactory road handling. And, of course, it will sport a specialized exterior worthy of its glorious past: extra-dimensional alloy wheels, lowered suspension, dark-colored grille. The interior will feature bucket seats and instrument dials sporting black letters set against a white background.

Back to the future

All in all, a car that should please both retired members of the police force or those still on duty who need a speedy unmarked pursuit vehicle. Still, I doubt that the Marauder will appeal to younger buyers.

If only grandpa had known...

It's easy to thumb your nose at these Grand Marquis. The shape's old-fash-

▲ PROS

- Comfortable suspension • Excellent sound insulation• Reassuring reliability • Roominess
- Tried and true engine

▼ CONS

- Large size • Roll and pitch
- So-so handling • Trunk needs rethinking
- Uncomfortable front seats

ioned, road handling is so so, the car feels sluggish and the steering is imprecise, all features that will set it apart for people who have one taste in common: a horror of fun cars. Perhaps it means that Marquis owners understand and appreciate its characteristics only too well...

First of all, they love the separate chassis, which in their minds gives the car "stature." And stature translates into comfort. Yet it also means a good deal of roll and pitch on any kind of road and at any speed. On the other hand, this chassis, as well as the ruggedness of the various suspension components, guarantees sturdiness. And that explains why its twin, the Ford Crown Victoria, is so popular with police forces and taxicab companies. In a city like New York, for example, they're among the few that can withstand the tough conditions.

Other positive points include the car's above-average roominess, its remarkably quiet ride and a very spacious luggage compartment. The trunk even has a luminous handle that might come in handy if you're ever stuck inside, accidentally or on purpose!

While this sedan may appeal mostly to parents, I'll bet the younger set will appreciate its roomy one-piece front seat, which has some fringe benefits when you're at, say, a drive-in movie theater with your sweetheart. And if you should veer off the main road to admire the city lights on a starry summer night, the large and comfortable rear bench beckons – who knows...

But let's return to the car's road-handling capabilities. Despite its fantastic size, it rides and handles admirably, thanks to an engine that generates 225 to 235 hp, depending on the version. The 16-inch wheels are just right to keep this colossus lined up straight and true on the road. After all, it's 197 inches (5 m) long and weighs a tad under four tons.

So, those who look forward to the Grand Marquis's demise may be in for a long wait. Its renewed popularity is another sign that the general population is getting on a bit.

Denis Duquet

MERCURY **MARAUDER 2003**

SPECIFICATIONS

Price	$CDN 34,125-35,490 / $US 23,685-25,585
Warranty	3 years / 36,000 miles (60,000 km)
Type	sedan / rear wheel drive
Wheelbase / Length	114 in / 212 in
Width / Height	78 in / 57 in
Weight	3951 lb (1792 kg)
Trunk / Fuel tank	20.6 cu. ft / 19 gallons
Air bags	front
Front suspension	independent
Rear suspension	rigid axle
Front brakes / Rear brakes	disc ABS
Traction control	yes (optional)
Steering	recirculating balls, variable assist
Turning circle	39 feet
Tires (front/rear)	P225/60R16

PERFORMANCE

Engine	V8 4.6-liter
Transmission	4-speed automatic
Horsepower	220 hp at 4500 rpm
Torque	290 lb-ft at 3000 rpm
Other engines	V8 4.6-liter 235 hp
Other transmission	none
Acceleration (0-60 mph)	8.9 sec
Maximum speed	103 mph (166 km/h) (electron. lim.)
Braking (60-0 mph)	129 feet (39.4 m)
Fuel consumption	16.5 mpg (13.8 L/100 km)

COMPETITION

• Buick LeSabre/Park Avenue • Chrysler Intrepid

NEW FOR 2002

• LSE and Limited models • Marauder in 2003
• 235 hp engine in LSE

RATING (out of 5 stars)

Driveability	★★★
Comfort	★★★★
Reliability	★★★★
Roominess	★★★★½
Winter driving rating	★★½
Safety	★★★★
Resale value	★★½

MINI COOPER

MINI **COOPER**

Cool, Nimble and Fun to Drive...

Those were the impressions of Paul Frère, the dean of the international automotive press, as he described the reincarnated MINI Cooper. I bumped into Frère at the launch of the latest entry in the BMW stable.

First off, let me just say that only two versions of the MINI (note the capital letters, which distinguish the new model from the Mini of yore) will be shipped to North America: Cooper and Cooper S. The base model, MINI One, equipped with a 90-horsepower engine, is available only in Europe.

A roaring success

My road test, behind the wheel of a red-and-white MINI Cooper, took me along the mountainous roads and highways wending and winding through Italy's picturesque Umbria region. My first contact with the MINI, however, took place at the 2001 Detroit Auto Show where I was instantly seduced by this superb reinterpretation of Sir Alec Issigonis' creation. The current MINI retains many of the original features, like the two-door design, square top, super-short snout, truncated and roundish tail end, upright windshield, and wheels mounted at the far corners. The designers even managed to recreate the distinctive grille, complete with the chrome bars that remind me of old-fashioned bumpers. There's one noticeable difference, and that's the tailgate, which replaces the fixed glass window and tiny trunk lid. The new MINI is significantly bigger than the original model, measuring 142.9 inches (363 cm) in length, versus 120 inches (305 cm) for the old Mini, and weighing 2315 lbs (1050 kg), as opposed to 1460 lbs (662 kg). All the same, it's still the smallest car in the North American market.

MINI to the max

If it was the nostalgic exterior that seduced me, the interior stole my heart. To have succeeded in creating a cockpit so enchanting from the minimalist design of the original Mini is nothing short of a stroke of genius. The inner doors, the speedometer smack in the middle of the dashboard, the old-fashioned toggle switches aligned in the center console, the tachometer perched on the steering column – all smartly set off by silver-colored plastic moldings – everything's been well thought out and executed. The overall effect is simply exquisite, a harmonious

▲ PROS

- Flawless roadholding • "Flirtatious" design
- Remarkably nimble • Rigid chassis

▼ CONS

- Unsatisfactory engine • Tight rear seats
- Tiny trunk • Too many options

blend old and new. A coup de foudre, as the French say.

Seated behind the wheel, you'll notice at once that the windshield is only slightly tilted, but the driving position is nowhere near the "trucker" position of old. Ergonomics are impeccable: telescoping steering wheel, height-adjustable seats, logically arranged controls. In the back, however, space is definitely at a premium, seriously impeded by the wheel wells (the days of 10-inch wheels are long gone). As a result, the seat bottoms are very narrow. What's more, the same rear wheels are attached to a suspension which takes up considerably more room under the floor than the original design, drastically limiting trunk space. It's now barely enough to accommodate a couple of grocery bags. If you're carrying luggage, you'll have to make room for it somewhere else – collapsing the rear backrests, for instance. In the end, the MINI is like any other 2+2 coupe, or most 2-door models – minus a trunk, that is.

A many-colored MINI

So I tell myself: forget the MINI for moving house. But let's see how it actually performs. Contact. The little 1.6-liter 4-cylinder starts to breathe. Discreetly. No vibrations, excellent sound insulation. But that's because the car has barely moved, you'll say. Okay, okay, but you've got to start somewhere! First gear. I accelerate. Second, third. I accelerate some more. Nice, very nice, indeed. I like it. I keep accelerating. No noise. Maybe I should push a little harder. Still very little noise. What a pity, it would have been nice to hear a little *vroom vroom*, some small hint to remind me of the old Mini. And what's that slack between 2000 and 4000 rpms? Not much of an engine, I finally decide, although it does come alive at high revs. Still, this first date leaves me cold.

The little Brazilian-made Chrysler/BMW engine is like a sauce without piquancy. So take me to the samba! "Ah, but you have to wait for the Cooper S if you want to dance," the boffins at BMW will advise me later. But in the meantime, don't think that I'm not enjoying myself. On the contrary. Turning off the highway, I leap into the twisting lanes of the Italian countryside, and

that's where I meet up with my old Mini. Flat cornering, barely discernible body roll, even roadholding. The car's perfectly comfortable with those 16-inch wheels, and braking is up to snuff. Then the road gets bumpy (just like back home), and that's when I start smiling again. The chassis proves to be exceptionally rigid. You'd think it was a bank vault on wheels. What can I say? It's a BMW product, after all. You can almost feel the suspension at work. As for steering, it feels a little odd at first, but as the road continues to wind and twist, the smile on my face grows wider. Kart-like precision! What a treat!

Then come the mountains. Oh how I love them! Completely deserted. Not even a stray cat. But tons of turns, one after another, guardrails on one side, mountainsides on the other. I'm totally transported. Second gear, I press all the way, and the little engine revs and revs until the redline becomes visible between the steering spokes. I shift to third for a short distance, then brake before downshifting. The four-wheel disc brakes are powerful and progressive and the pedal is set at just the right height. So there's no danger of twisting my ankle. To test the car to the limit, I turn over the steering wheel hard at the next turn. The tires screech. I feel a gentle jolt. The traction control is at work, applying brake force to the inside rear wheel so as to bring the MINI back on its course.

I remember what a MINI engineer had said the night before: "No other car in this category offers so many electronic gadgets," namely, anti-lock, anti-slip, traction control, electronic brake force distribution, four standard airbags and two optional head airbags for front-seat occupants. Six airbags in total. And if you think all that is not enough, you'll be pleased to learn that the MINI will be the first car in this category – and many others, for that matter – to include a standard flat-tire indicator as well as optional tires that continue to function even when flat (with 16- and 17-inch wheels), thus eliminating the need for carrying spares.

But let's get back to our endlessly twisting road. The car makes so many turns it gives me vertigo. Maybe I'm getting old. I stop for some fresh air and to take a couple of photographs. Italy is truly gorgeous. An ancient farm tractor goes by. It's not that big, but still, I'm glad I stopped the car.

At noon, I stop for an *al fresco* lunch at a Corys restaurant, near Cortona. You don't know where that is? Neither did I until now. There, I find many other MINIs in every color imaginable. There will be 14 in total, it seems. Colors, that is. But I can tell you my favorite, and that's the colors of my test car – red with a white top. Green and white is also pretty nice.

An *autostrada* excursion

Having refreshed my spirits, I hit the road again, looking for the highway leading to Perugia. The MINI's press kit indicates a top speed of 125 mph (200 km/h). I try 110, 115, 120... after I've lifted my foot, the engine continues to rev briefly. So the publicity is all true, the MINI engine is perfectly capable, although in terms of the sound it makes, I still prefer my Miata.

Acceleration is respectable, with a 0-60 mph time of slightly less than 9.2 seconds. But it'll take you 10.5 seconds to go from 50 to 75 mph in fourth gear. "Wait for the Cooper S," I keep hearing the MINI engineer's voice in my head. I know, but in the meantime, you could have added a couple of extra pounds for the torque at low rpms. "Wait for the Cooper S." Obviously with the promised 164 horsepower, a supercharger and 6-speed gearbox, the Cooper S is bound to give its twice-as-expensive rivals a serious run for their money.

My idyllic Italian interlude ends on an afternoon near Perugia airport, without an opportunity to test the MINI's as yet unavailable continuously variable transmission (CVT). That will have to wait until next time, I promise myself. With a twinge in my heart, I return the keys of the MINI 136. *Ciao, bella. Grazie.* Or should I say: *Danke schön* or simply thank you? I'm totally confused. There are so many nationalities involved here.

Alain Raymond

SPECIFICATIONS	
Price	$CDN 25,000-$30 000 / $US n.a.
Warranty	n.a.
Type	2-door sedan / front wheel drive
Wheelbase / Length	97.2 in / 142.9 in
Width / Height	66.5 in / 55.5 in
Weight	2315 lb (1050 kg)
Trunk / Fuel tank	5.7 cu.ft / 13 gallons
Air bags	front, side, overhead (opt.)
Front suspension	independent
Rear suspension	independent
Front brakes / Rear brakes	disc / disc ABS
Traction control	optional
Steering	rack-and-pinion, electro-hydraulic assist
Turning circle	35 feet
Tires (front/rear)	P175/65R15

PERFORMANCE	
Engine	4 L 1.6-liter 16-valve
Transmission	5-speed manual
Horsepower	115 hp at 6000 rpm
Torque	110 lb-ft at 4500 rpm
Other engines	160 hp (Cooper S)
Other transmission	CVT; 6-speed man. (S)
Acceleration (0-60 mph)	9.2 sec
Maximum speed	124 mph (200 km/h)
Braking (60-0 mph)	n.a.
Fuel consumption	32.4 mpg (est.) (7 L/100 km)

COMPETITION

- Chrysler PT Cruiser • Honda Civic Si
- Nissan Sentra SR • VW New Beetle

NEW FOR 2002

- New model

RATING	(out of 5 stars)
Driveability	★★★★½
Comfort	★★★½
Reliability	New model
Roominess	★★
Winter driving rating	★★★★
Safety	★★★★
Resale value	New model

NISSAN ALTIMA

NISSAN **ALTIMA**

Dawn of a New Era

Following their merger in 1999, the Renault-Nissan alliance made many promises and unveiled scores of prototypes, but nothing concrete has ever been offered to customers until now. The new and improved Altima is the first serious indication of renewal to suggest that the new Franco-Japanese company really means business.

Admittedly, many of us were skeptical at the time. We'd heard it all before from Nissan – revolutionary design concept and all that jazz – only to be continually disappointed by new cars that bore little resemblance to the entrancing models that had been advertised.

But that was yesterday. With the advent of the new Altima, complete with a design that suggests a dramatic break with the past, today and tomorrow suddenly seem more enticing. Not only does this mid-size sedan look positively modern and graceful, its drivetrain practically guarantees a more spirited performance than the modest 150-horsepower four-cylinder engine that accompanied the previous generation. From now on, the name Nissan Altima means more than just "tried-and-true reliability" and "excellent leasing terms." It also has design, power and performance going for it, more than enough to catapult the car to the top of its class.

Inspired silhouette

Whether you talk about the first- or second-generation, the Altima has always been a reliable car – "reliable" as in predictable handling and deeply boring design. The second-generation model looks slightly more refined, but it still has that "ma-and-pa" feel to it, especially when you see it parked next to the slick new Altima. The third-generation silhouette, as I mentioned, is a complete departure from the first two models, and that's a good thing. It reminds me just a little bit of the Volkswagen Passat. The front end isn't terribly exciting, looking more like a compromise between the Nissan Sentra and the Nissan Maxima. In marked contrast, the tail end is far more original, with its taillights – each incorporating three round lamps – covered by crystalline lenses. For the first time in many years,

A run for your money

▲ PROS
- Competitive price • Excellent finish
- Exemplary roadholding • Sensational engines
- Successful design

▼ CONS
- Automatic gearbox shift gate • Illegible "data cent
- Radio and stereo displays fade in direct sunlight
- Speedometer reading display • Torque effect (V6)

here's a Nissan sedan that actually makes heads turn.

The stylists also worked hard to give the interior the kind of uncluttered design that's contemporary and ergonomically sensible. The dashboard features a high-tech "cockpit" three-gauge instrument panel as well as a practical center unit housing the audio system and climate controls – a neat row of three round switches and two push buttons. The gauges are brightly illuminated and easy to consult at all times. On the other hand, the speedometer's rectangular "data center," set against an orange colored background, is almost impossible to read accurately. The problem is further compounded by the infuriatingly tiny numbers on the dial.

In the higher-end models, both the controls for the radio and trip computer are mounted on the rim of the steering hub. All in all, the cabin is spacious, seats are comfortable, finish is impeccable, although the plastic used for the dashboard could have been a little less shiny. But I have a particular bone to pick: the displays for the radio and climate controls tend to wash out in direct sunlight, making them difficult to read.

All-new suspension

In the past, Nissan was often accused of giving its engineers too much leeway, and not enough to its designers and marketing staff. This time around, the last two groups were given free rein, but definitely not at the expense of the engineers, who also had ample opportunity to showcase their mechanical know-how.

The new Altima is longer, taller and wider. In fact, its dimensions are practically identical to those of the Maxima, which belongs to a more upscale category. With increased measurements, you might suspect that the platform would be less rigid. Yet the opposite is the case here. In fact, rigidity has increased by a solid 65%, thanks to Nissan's use of a unibody structure, transversal reinforcement frames and more rigid body mounts. Remarkably, all these positive results were achieved without the drawback to significant weight increase. The secret? Aluminum, which

was used for, among other components, the hood, trunk lid, and various suspension parts.

And speaking of suspension, the Altima features an all-new system. Up front, a cradle-frame provides better handling and riding performance, reducing the side loads that act on the front suspension by 30%. The multi-link independent rear suspension with stabilizer bar is derived from the Skyline supercar, Nissan's fastest sedan.

Finally, after having long been criticized for failing to equip the Altima with a V6, Nissan engineers made amends by offering a 240-horsepower 3.5-liter V6, far and away the most muscular in its class. It may be ordered either with a 5-speed manual transmission, or a 4-speed automatic. Both gearboxes are also available with the other engine being offered: the 180-hp 2.5-liter 4-cylinder.

The silhouette and ultrasophisticated technical specs of the new Altima certainly score high marks. Now let's see if it delivers the goods.

A conclusive test

My test car was a 3.5 SE model, equipped with the standard V6 coupled to the 4-speed automatic transmission. Needless to say, with 240 horsepower under the hood, acceleration was utterly dazzling. The car scooted from 0-60 mph in 7.4 seconds. With a manual transmission, I would probably have done it in less than 7 seconds. The only sour note here was the pronounced torque steer that I felt through the steering.

All the same, this sedan proves to be an excellent touring car, quite capable of

■ STANDARD EQUIPMENT

• 16-inch wheels • Cruise control • Manually controlled air conditioning • Four-wheel disc brakes

■ OPTIONAL EQUIPMENT

• 3.5-liter V6 engine • ABS brakes • 17-inch wheels • Visual information center • Leather seats • Power driver's seat

going head to head with other, more expensive cars. Braking is progressive and powerful. Steering is precise, making the Altima very nimble, especially on twisting roads. On the other hand, even though the Altima's dimensions are similar to those of the Maxima, handling is more direct and less "polite."

And if you think that models equipped with a 4-cylinder engine are not as peppy, think again! I can assure you right off the bat that the Altima's 180-hp 2.5-liter engine can take on any rival anytime, even leaving it in the dust. But before talking about performance, let's see how this model differs from the V6 version. First off, the 2.5 appears to be more manageable and road feedback is unimpeded. What's more, torque effect is barely discernible. On the other hand, the V6 has bigger tires, which allow for quicker transitions.

Now on to the key question of performance. The 4-cylinder Altima accelerates from 0-60 mph in a respectable 8.5 seconds. Roll-on acceleration is also better than average. Excellent results like these are due to the manual gearbox's short and precise shifter travel. The automatic transmission is not to be sniffed at either, despite its unnecessarily complex shift gate. And unless Nissan has radically transformed its production methods, its mechanical components should be more reliable and durable than the competition's.

The new Altima deserves our attention, not just for its contemporary silhouette and exquisitely designed cockpit, but also because it's a first-rate touring car, whether on the open road or twisting back-country lanes. For once, powertrain, style and performance meet in perfect harmony, providing the Altima with potent ammunition as it confronts its fiercest rivals – the Honda Accord and Toyota Camry – head on.

And believe me, the Nissan will not be ignored this time around. In the bad old days the company's motto may have been, "After you, ladies and gentlemen of the competition." But now, it's "Get out of the way everybody!"

Denis Duquet

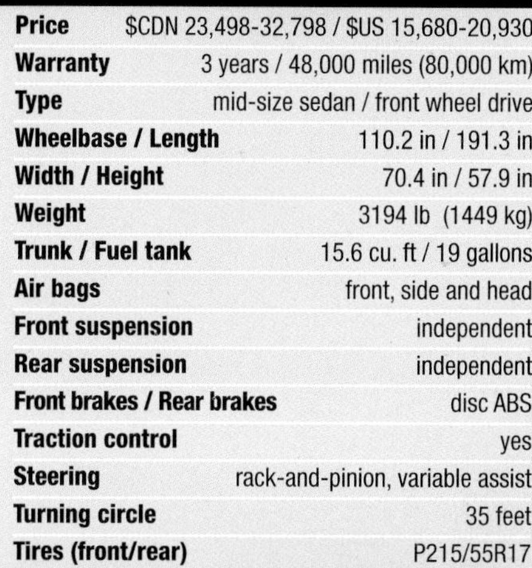

SPECIFICATIONS	3.5 SE
Price	$CDN 23,498-32,798 / $US 15,680-20,930
Warranty	3 years / 48,000 miles (80,000 km)
Type	mid-size sedan / front wheel drive
Wheelbase / Length	110.2 in / 191.3 in
Width / Height	70.4 in / 57.9 in
Weight	3194 lb (1449 kg)
Trunk / Fuel tank	15.6 cu. ft / 19 gallons
Air bags	front, side and head
Front suspension	independent
Rear suspension	independent
Front brakes / Rear brakes	disc ABS
Traction control	yes
Steering	rack-and-pinion, variable assist
Turning circle	35 feet
Tires (front/rear)	P215/55R17

PERFORMANCE	
Engine	V6 3.5-liter
Transmission	5-speed manual
Horsepower	240 hp at 5800 rpm
Torque	246 lb-ft at 4400 rpm
Other engines	4L 2.5-liter 180 hp
Other transmission	4-speed automatic
Acceleration (0-60 mph)	6.9 s (V6 man.); 7.4 s (auto.); 8.5 s (2.5-liter)
Maximum speed	137 mph (220 km/h)
Braking (60-0 mph)	n.a.
Fuel consumption	23 mpg (V6) 27 mpg (2.5 l) (10.4 L/8.6/100km)

COMPETITION

- Honda Accord • Mazda 626
- Toyota Camry

NEW FOR 2002

- New model • New platform and chassis
- 3.5-liter V6 engine

RATING	(out of 5 stars)
Driveability	★★★★
Comfort	★★★½
Reliability	New model
Roominess	★★★★
Winter driving rating	★★★½
Safety	★★★
Resale value	New model

NISSAN MAXIMA

NISSAN **MAXIMA**

Luxury, and Then Some

For more than a decade, the mid-size Maxima has been Nissan's most luxurious and powerful sedan – its flagship car, in other words, helping to maintain the brand's fortunes, not forgetting its prestige, as its younger siblings, the Sentra and Altima, struggled to attract buyers.

Undertaking a concerted effort to revive its flagging fortunes, Nissan has recently come up with many intriguing new initiatives. The all-new 2002 Altima is one of them, endowed with a new platform, bodywork, and a powerful 245-hp V6 engine. This practically amounts to high treason, as far as the Maxima is concerned. Its own 222-hp 3.0-literV6 was until recently one of the most muscled in its field. Nissan therefore had no choice but to equip the Maxima with the same 3.5-liter V6, plus superior horsepower.

As things turned out, the VQ35 engine that turns under the hood of the new Maxima cranks out 260 hp – 15 hp over and above the Altima. As if to accommodate – and exploit – the whopping new horsepower, the Maxima also gets a larger air intake and an equal-length tuned exhaust system with a variable-capacity muffler, not to mention thicker stabilizer bars, firmer suspension and 17-inch wheels (SE and GLE). The base GXE model gets 16-inch aluminum-alloy wheels.

Besides increasing the engine displacement, engineers modified the engine block, introduced molybdenum-coated pistons, a resin intake collector and a host of other similar mechanical refinements. What's more, the performance SE model comes with a new standard 6-speed manual transmission, and none too soon – I seriously doubt that anyone will mourn the previous year's 5-speed box.

Success story

Needless to say, Nissan also mobilized their stylists and sent them into battle. The front end was modified and given a new grille, new fascia, modified side-sill spoilers, and high-intensity discharge (HID) xenon headlights. The rear was treated to new taillights with clear lenses and dual chrome exhaust tip finishers (SE and GLE). The modifications were subtle, but the new Maxima looks much more dynamic than it used to.

Inside, the cabin received its own share of improvements including new, more supportive seat designs and titanium-colored

▲ PROS

• 6-speed manual gearbox • Enhanced driving pleasure • More powerful V6 engine • Quiet and smoother ride • Reliability and quality assembly

▼ CONS

• Impractical raised armrest • Nondescript dashboard • Some controls badly located • Sound insulation needs work • Torque effect (steering wheel)

gauge faces with black numerals. Ergonomics are not consistently practical, however, what with all those controls mounted on – or should I say, hidden by – the leather-wrapped steering wheel, especially the control for the outside mirrors.

Split personality

At first, it looked as if the Maxima was going to be eclipsed by the new Altima with its powerful V6 engine, dynamic silhouette, equally spacious cabin, and, most importantly, lower sticker price. Still, even without staging a head-to-head showdown between the pair, I'm convinced that you can easily feel the difference. Despite their almost identical dimensions, the cars "drive" differently. The Maxima has better sound insulation and its ride is smoother, especially so far as the mid-level SE model is concerned. In short, you instinctively feel that you're driving a bona fide luxury car, the kind of sensation that you don't experience behind the wheel of the Altima.

All this doesn't mean that the Maxima is nothing more than a bland deluxe town car. Despite its substantial dimensions, it negotiates twisting roads with ease, aided by precise steering and an ultra smooth and highly responsive engine. Perhaps steering could have been less assisted and the brakes more powerful, but taken all in all performance was fine.

On the open road, the base GXE model handles itself respectably enough, but doesn't exactly sparkle. It's a very good car, no doubt about it, much less soporific than it used to be, but I wish all Maximas were like the SE model, the sportiest of the lot. Its 6-speed manual is a dream come true for every serious driving enthusiast. But a word of caution: while gear spacing is tight and lever travel short, shifting itself is rough.

Nissan's initiatives in 2001 have been impressive on every front. You can bet your bottom dollar that the new and improved 2002 Maxima will help keep the company's momentum going.

Denis Duquet

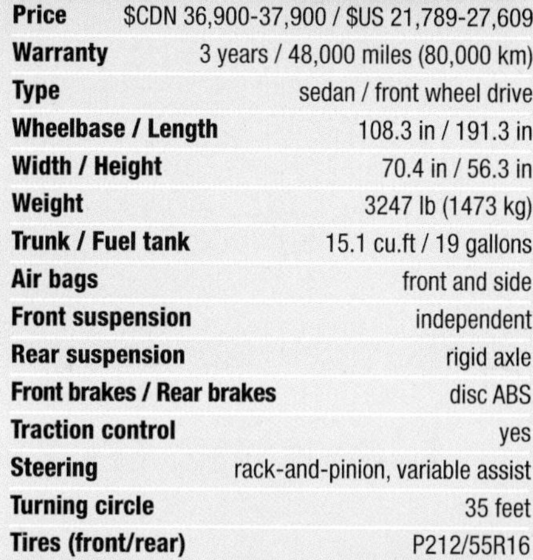

SPECIFICATIONS	GXE
Price	$CDN 36,900-37,900 / $US 21,789-27,609
Warranty	3 years / 48,000 miles (80,000 km)
Type	sedan / front wheel drive
Wheelbase / Length	108.3 in / 191.3 in
Width / Height	70.4 in / 56.3 in
Weight	3247 lb (1473 kg)
Trunk / Fuel tank	15.1 cu.ft / 19 gallons
Air bags	front and side
Front suspension	independent
Rear suspension	rigid axle
Front brakes / Rear brakes	disc ABS
Traction control	yes
Steering	rack-and-pinion, variable assist
Turning circle	35 feet
Tires (front/rear)	P212/55R16

PERFORMANCE	
Engine	V6 3.5-liter
Transmission	4-speed automatic
Horsepower	260-hp at 5800 rpm
Torque	246 lb-ft at 4400 rpm
Other engines	none
Other transmission	6-speed manual (SE only)
Acceleration (0-60 mph)	9.1 s; 8.5 s (SE manual)
Maximum speed	122 mph (195 km/h)
Braking (60-0 mph)	127 feet (38.7 m)
Fuel consumption	16 mpg (14.2 L/100 km)

COMPETITION

• Acura TL • Buick Regal/Olds Intrigue • Honda Accord • Mazda Millenia • Toyota Avalon V6 • VW Passat

NEW FOR 2002

• 3.5-l 260 hp V6 eng. • 6-speed manual gearbox (SE) • Modified silhouette • More powerful brakes

RATING	(out of 5 stars)
Driveability	★★★★
Comfort	★★★★½
Reliability	★★★★★
Roominess	★★★★
Winter driving rating	★★★★
Safety	★★★★
Resale value	★★★★★

NISSAN PATHFINDER INFINITI QX4

NISSAN **PATHFINDER**

Caught in Between

When a company is drifting toward the brink of financial disaster, it's very difficult for it to change its entire model line. Some models must be modernized where needed, while others must remain competitive to keep their popularity. The Pathfinder was once Nissan's most popular model, before losing ground to its more up-to-date, powerful and attractive rivals. The crisis was serious enough, although a catastrophe was averted, to Nissan's relief, given the unabated popularity of SUVs during the past five years.

To remedy this situation, Nissan pulled out all the stops last year, fitting a 250-hp V6 engine under the Pathfinder's hood, which pushed it ahead of many of its rivals. Coupled with a 5-speed manual gearbox, it's one of the few vehicles in its class to offer such a combination. However, with the 4-speed automatic option, the engine is limited to 240 hp. Finally, starting from last year, you can choose either a part-time 4-wheel drive system which can be engaged below 50 mph or a full-time all-wheel drive system that can switch from Auto to 4Hi or 4Lo mode at the flick of a knob.

These mechanical improvements came along with many other styling and equipment changes. First, the front was redesigned. The dashboard was refurbished, then was fitted with a 6-CD changer as standard equipment on the SE and LE models, with controls mounted on the steering wheel.

Following these major changes and improvements in 2001, the 2002 edition is practically unchanged. Which is understandable. However, although the mechanicals and the looks have been revised, the fact remains that the platform is beginning to feel dated and its rigidity needs to be increased. We were actually expecting a little more when driving the Pathfinder. The engine and the transmission are among the best in their category, but once behind the wheel, you very soon realize that the vehicle comes with a few blemishes. Steering is getting a little lazier than average, changes in direction are not as lively as they could be and the suspension can't always cope with the conditions and demands from the driver. Nothing very serious, but a lot of small things which add up and lead to the conclusion that the company should impose the same treatment on the

Redesigned

▲ PROS

- 4-wheel drive options • Manual gearbox
- Powerful engine • Reassuring reliability
- Well equipped

▼ CONS

- Average cargo space • Ergonomics needs work
- Inappropriate tires • Needs a new chassis
- Uncomfortable rear seats

Pathfinder that it had with the Altima earlier this year: that is, to start from scratch and rebuild a new model from the ground up.

Infiniti QX4

Until last year, the QX4 was in a lead position over the less expensive Nissan Pathfinder. The QX4, a luxury SUV, was the only one of the two with an all-wheel drive system. Since the Pathfinder now offers this type of drivetrain, the only advantages of the Infiniti model are its more luxurious accessories and the prestige of a make which traditionally spares no effort to satisfy its clients. What's more, reliability is far above average. And, I almost forgot, the QX4 is the only one of the two to provide as standard equipment a gold-rimmed analog clock while Pathfinder must make do with a very conservative digital clock.

The two share the same body, which means that the cargo space in the Infiniti is rather limited and rear legroom is at best just average. However, the Infiniti has noticeably better sound insulation and the quality of the materials is better than that found on its smaller sister. The wood trim on the QX4 steering wheel points to a more elevated status. However, ergonomics could be improved, and some controls are difficult to reach. For instance, the wing mirror controls are obstructed by the steering wheel.

Despite the more solid equipment and better sound insulation, driving impressions on the road are still that the vehicle needs a new platform. There's plenty of power, braking is above average, but then again, as it goes around a corner, or while changing lanes or on a bad surface, you notice a few little things and then you see the differences between this pair and some of the more modern vehicles. For instance, the Ford Explorer, although not without its own drawbacks, has a more rigid, better performing chassis and road behavior; the GMC Envoy is also superior, in addition to featuring an even more powerful engine.

This tandem is still competitive but needs to be improved to keep up with the competition.

Denis Duquet

SPECIFICATIONS	
Price	$CDN 35,900-48,000 / $US 29,889-32,339
Warranty	3 years / 48,000 miles (80,000 km)
Type	sport utility / 4X4
Wheelbase / Length	106.3 in / 182.7 in
Width / Height	71.7 in / 68.1 in
Weight	4250 lb (1928 kg)
Trunk / Fuel tank	38/85 cu. ft (seats down) / 21 gal.
Air bags	front and side (optional)
Front suspension	independent
Rear suspension	rigid axle
Front brakes / Rear brakes	disc / drum ABS
Traction control	no
Steering	rack-and-pinion, power assist
Turning circle	37 ft
Tires (front/rear)	P245/70R16

PERFORMANCE	
Engine	V6 3.5-liter
Transmission	5-speed manual
Horsepower	250 hp at 6000 rpm
Torque	240 lb-ft at 3200 rpm
Other engines	V6 3.5-liter 240 hp (automatic)
Other transmission	4-speed automatic
Acceleration (0-60 mph)	9 sec
Maximum speed	103 mph (165 km/h)
Braking (60-0 mph)	143 ft (43.7 m)
Fuel consumption	17.1 mpg (13.3 L/100 km)

COMPETITION

• Chevrolet TrailBlazer/GMC Jimmy • Ford Explorer • Jeep Grand Cherokee • Toyota 4Runner

NEW FOR 2002

No major change

RATING	**(out of 5 stars)**
Driveability	★★★★
Comfort	★★★★
Reliability	★★★★★
Roominess	★★★★½
Winter driving rating	★★★★½
Safety	★★★★½
Resale value	★★★★

NISSAN SENTRA

NISSAN **SENTRA**

Unfairly Neglected

Only a few years ago, the Nissan Sentra was one of the most underestimated cars on the market. But today, it seems a worthy contender in the race for gold in the sub-compact category. Since the 2001 model was launched in the spring of 2000, Sentra sales have grown steadily.

This Nissan has always been known for its reliable drivetrain and its competent handling. Still, it has two strikes against it: a nondescript exterior and an ever-increasing sticker price.

To fix the problem, Nissan built a huge plant in Aguascalientes, Mexico, where production costs are lower. The automaker is therefore able to pass the savings on to buyers. Although the current Sentra is longer and wider than the model it replaces, it is less expensive. Moreover, it's apparent that the quality of workmanship is beyond reproach.

What's more, Nissan's designers in California were given the go-ahead by head office in Tokyo to jazz up the car's overall appearance. Unfortunately, the new look – inspired by the Altima and the Maxima, both of which were intended for an older clientele – is not much to write home about. The "young and dynamic" Sentra looks more suitable for a 40-something than the recent college graduate it wants to attract. Fortunately, the interior looks better. The cabin, for example, is remarkably roomier, given the unchanged length of the wheelbase. Head and elbow rooms are beyond reproach and the front seats more comfortable. In fact, the new Sentra's roominess is such that the U.S. Department of Motor Vehicles (DMV) classifies it as a compact car, not a subcompact as was the case previously. Unfortunately, the driver's seat in the XE model is not height adjustable, and it's on the low side. This version doesn't come with intermittent windshield wipers either: a surprising omission.

Down Mexico way

But the dashboard is well appointed, with a center console that makes for easy access to the knobs and buttons for the climate control and radio, and to the dual cupholders smartly placed directly below them. There's also an overhead storage compartment for valuable objects. High marks also go to the 60/40 fold-down rear seat, standard on all models.

▲ PROS

- Reliable drivetrain • Comfortable interior
- Good handling • SE-R model
- Well-appointed dashboard

▼ CONS

- High price for SE-R model • Boring exterior
- Sluggish steering • XE model too basic
- So-so sound insulation

"Zoom Zoom"

Even though this snappy slogan is henceforth associated with the ad campaign of another subcompact, it suits the Sentra to a tee, considering the fact that it comes in three engine options. The standard model is fitted out with a 1.8-liter 4-cylinder engine producing 126 horsepower. With a manual gearbox, the car charges forward from 0-60 mph in a very respectable 10.3 seconds. In 2002, the SE model and its 145-hp engine are no longer listed in the catalog. But don't despair: it will be replaced by the SE-R model with a 2.5-liter engine 165 horsepower (175 hp on the SE-R SpecV), much to the delight of sport drivers. Incidentally, the Sentra was one of the models included in *The Auto Guide*'s comparison test. The results appear in the first part of the *Guide*.

Easy to drive

But it's the XE and GXE that prove to be the most popular models. In fact, it's very difficult to find fault with either of them. Acceleration is excellent and fuel consumption – at 23 mpg (10 liters per 100 km) – is reasonable even when driving with enthusiasm. The 1.8-liter engine is noisy during acceleration, but the noise level is tolerable.Even though the Sentra's cockpit is more spacious than average, the wheelbase is relatively short, making the car easy to park or change direction. On the other hand, directional stability suffers as a result and the steering feels sluggish. That much said, this Mexican-made Nissan is easy to drive. The ride is smooth on rough roads, thanks to the solid chassis and excellent front and rear suspension. The standard disc/drum brakes are adequate, but it's too bad that only the SE comes with four disc brakes. ABS is optional on any model.

Despite a nondescript exterior, the fifth-generation Sentra is among the best buys from a price/quality point of view.

Denis Duquet

SPECIFICATIONS	**XE**
Price	$CDN 15,598-21,198 / $US 12,189-15,439
Warranty	3 years / 48,000 miles (80,000 km)
Type	sedan / front wheel drive
Wheelbase / Length	99.6 in / 177.2 in
Width / Height	67 in / 55.5 in
Weight	2568 lb (1165 kg)
Trunk / Fuel tank	11.6 cu. ft / 13 gallons
Air bags	front
Front suspension	independent
Rear suspension	semi-independent
Front brakes / Rear brakes	disc / drum (ABS op)
Traction control	no
Steering	rack-and-pinion, power assist
Turning circle	34 feet
Tires (front/rear)	P185/65R14

PERFORMANCE	
Engine	4L 1.8-liter
Transmission	5-speed manual
Horsepower	126 hp at 6000 rpm
Torque	129 lb-ft at 2400 rpm
Other engines	4L 2.5-liter 165 hp; 4L 2.5-liter 175 hp
Other transmission	5-speed automatic; 6-speed manual (SR-R SpecV)
Acceleration (0-60 mph)	10.3 s; 8 sec (SE-R man.); 7.3 sec (SE-R SpecV)
Maximum speed	115 mph (185 km/h)
Braking (60-0 mph)	135 feet (41.2 m)
Fuel consumption	31.9 mpg (7.1 L/100 km))

COMPETITION

• Civic • Corolla • Elantra • Focus • Golf • Neon • Nubira • Protegé • Saturn SL

NEW FOR 2002

• SE-R with 170-hp engine • SE-R SpecV with 180-hp engine • 16-in wheels • Modified grille

RATING	**(out of 5 stars)**
Driveability	★★★½
Comfort	★★★½
Reliability	★★★★★
Roominess	★★★★
Winter driving rating	★★★½
Safety	★★★½
Resale value	★★★

NISSAN XTERRA

NISSAN **XTERRA**

Faulty DNA

These days, there isn't a carmaker spokesperson who doesn't revel in DNA talk about their product, promoting its "intrinsic qualities" or its famous lineage, or its technical, commercial or mechanical antecedents. In this case, the Nissan Xterra's DNA is at the root of its shortcomings. In fact, the vehicle's good looks when it came out soon made it one of the most popular in its group, yet its old-fashioned drivetrain has brought it to a premature old age.

A little like Dolly, the first sheep to be cloned, it is aging very rapidly, and is losing ground against rivals which feature better, more up-to-date mechanical components. As an example, an Xterra with a normally aspirated 170-hp V6 took part in The *Auto Guide* comparison test, the results of which are in the first part of this book. Compared to a test from barely two years ago, the Xterra lost four places to the competition.

Nevertheless the styling is still attractive. This year, the changes to the front grille and valence have even improved its looks. The cockpit has also been revised; the controls are new and the instrument cluster has contrasting colors. The glove compartment is bigger and cupholders more practical. The Xterra really takes advantage of the improvements made to the Frontier model, which should not be surprising, as both models share almost all the same mechanical and interior features. And, the big news is that the emergency brake is no longer that devilishly hard-to-use pull-out lever under the dashboard, but a foot pedal positioned as it is in most vans, along the left forward panel. Following this common approach to engine sharing, the Xterra can be ordered this year with the supercharged 210-hp 3.3-liter V6, which the Frontier had available last year. This is an improvement well worth mentioning as the 170 hp of the normally aspirated engine is somewhat short of what this type of vehicle really needs. More powerful, this supercharged V6 has an unpleasant sound which some may find annoying.

Until then!

The cockpit of the Xterra is roomy and practical. The cargo area is big and liberally sprinkled with various anchor points where all sorts of odds and sods or acces-

▲ PROS

• Modern dashboard • More powerful engine • Nimble off the road • Original lines • Roominess

▼ CONS

• Lazy steering • Noisy supercharged V6 • Old-style road behavior • Primitive rear suspension • Wind sensitive

sories can be stationed. In brief, this 4-wheel drive vehicle is very practical and its macho looks serve it well. However, the mechanical DNA is less impressive. This explains the drop in ranking after our comparison test.

No longer a novelty item

I must admit I fell to the charms of the Xterra upon its introduction. Its imaginative looks, roomy interior, and the availability of a V6 with a manual transmission were very attractive. The vehicle seemed to have everything needed to handle difficult road conditions, and its part-time 4-wheel drive system was simple and effective. Moreover, the high ground clearance could handle very difficult terrain. These "roughrider" characteristics made up for the so-so roadholding. After all, for a sport-ute based on the Frontier pickup, the results weren't too bad.

Unfortunately when the Xterra was unveiled, the platform, suspension and drivetrain originated from a utility vehicle that had last been modified and updated in 1998. Therefore, as other models appeared on the market, the Xterra lost ground. It was a real shocker, when during the spring of 2001, I drove the Nissan after having driven the new Jeep Liberty. Never was the aging process so obvious in terms of driving impressions, responsiveness and roadholding. If the innovative lines managed to cover up some weaknesses when it was launched in spring1999, then 24 months later, it was way out of it. Moreover, its high center of gravity and a very basic rear suspension will have you wish that you had chosen another by-road, where the side winds are less likely to push the car around.

It is a fact though, that this year's improvements have made the Xterra a better machine, but now, the chassis is in need of attention.

Denis Duquet

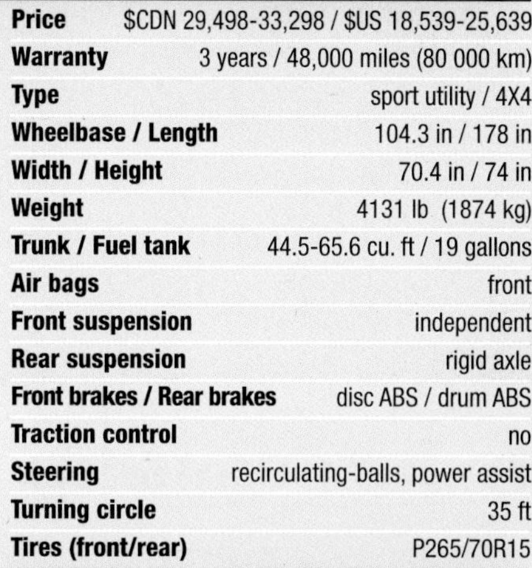

SPECIFICATIONS	
Price	$CDN 29,498-33,298 / $US 18,539-25,639
Warranty	3 years / 48,000 miles (80 000 km)
Type	sport utility / 4X4
Wheelbase / Length	104.3 in / 178 in
Width / Height	70.4 in / 74 in
Weight	4131 lb (1874 kg)
Trunk / Fuel tank	44.5-65.6 cu. ft / 19 gallons
Air bags	front
Front suspension	independent
Rear suspension	rigid axle
Front brakes / Rear brakes	disc ABS / drum ABS
Traction control	no
Steering	recirculating-balls, power assist
Turning circle	35 ft
Tires (front/rear)	P265/70R15

PERFORMANCE	
Engine	V6 3.3-liter
Transmission	4-speed automatic
Horsepower	170 hp at 4800 rpm
Torque	200 lb-ft at 2 800 rpm
Other engines	V 6 3.0-liter 210 hp (compressor)
Other transmission	5-speed manual
Acceleration (0-60 mph)	12 sec
Maximum speed	99 mpg (160 km/h)
Braking (60-0 mph)	155 ft (47.3 m)
Fuel consumption	16.2 mpg (14 L/100 km)

COMPETITION

• CR-V • Escape/ Tribute • Hyundai SantaFe • Jeep Liberty • Subaru Forester • Suzuki Vitara

NEW FOR 2002

• 210-hp supercharged engine • New dashboard • New exterior lines

RATING	(out of 5 stars)
Driveability	★★★
Comfort	★★★
Reliability	★★★★
Roominess	★★★★
Winter driving rating	★★★★½
Safety	★★★½
Resale value	★★★½

PONTIAC BONNEVILLE BUICK LESABRE

PONTIAC **BONNEVILLE**

Interesting Car, Limited Interest

I remember it well. In the early 1960s, the Pontiac Bonneville had the fastest acceleration of any car on the market. And this, despite its humongous proportions and road manners worthy of a funeral procession. Then, a little while later, the GTO became the Pontiac family's sports car.

This family car was named after the Bonneville Salt Flats in Utah. The Great Salt Lake was the rendezvous for high-speed auto racers who convened every year to set new land-speed records on the hard salt surface. But that was long ago. Today, the race is not as popular as it used to be because the surface has deteriorated badly.

The same can be said of the Bonneville. Despite its sporty claims and Pontiac's desire to continue appealing to thrill-seekers, times have changed. It's difficult to get excited about a car whose measurements nudge it closer to a limousine than a sports sedan. Even though this juggernaut is still reasonably popular, it's not exactly sports-car material.

But since it's supposed to be a sports car, designers couldn't resist adorning it with flashy rocker panels, a garish grille and huge fog lamps to give it a "sports" look. The dash got the same treatment: controls and buttons large and small are arranged in a rather untidy cluster. The orange light emanating from the display panel is supposed to bring out a little "atmosphere."

Whether or not you go for this styling approach, ergonomics are not bad, seats comfortable and the cabin irreproachable.

Healthy road manners

It's too bad that Bonneville's designers chose such a garish look, which deflects attention from its intrinsic handling qualities. No wonder many people turn thumbs down at the Bonny's technical specs, which they claim are unworthy of a sports sedan. Yet, although the two variants of the Bonny's 3.8-liter pushrod V6 engine have been around for ages, their reliability is time-tested, with the kind of performance that is clearly superior to its competitors's overhead camshaft engines. And though the automatic transmission lacks a 5th gear, as is the case with many European and Japanese models, it is reliable and shifting is smooth.

Vestige of the past

Despite perceptible understeer, this huge American car is impressive all the same. Its

▲ PROS

- Reliable engines • Predictable road manners
- Spaciousness • Complete equipment
- Competitive price

▼ CONS

- Garish silhouette • Big size
- Untidy dashboard
- Understeer on sharp curves

road manners inspire confidence, its rigid body ensures a uniformly smooth drive on all road surfaces and braking is well modulated, despite an occasionally spongy pedal. Unfortunately, the variable-ratio power steering is sluggish and overassisted, removing all the driving fun and making the Bonny's "sport package" irrelevant.

A good touring car, the Bonneville should drop its sporty pretentions and be content with its role as a large-sized suburban family sedan – like the Buick LeSabre.

Drab elegance

I'm willing to bet that had the LeSabre not been so popular, the Buick division would have packed up a long time ago. In fact, the LeSabre is Buick's best-selling car and the most reliable in its category, making its owners among the most satisfied consumer groups in the market.

This is hardly surprising since the LeSabre shares its platform and mechanical features with the Bonneville, although the latter doesn't share its cousin's stellar reputation. The main difference between the two is that the LeSabre doesn't pretend to be anything other than a big North American sedan bent on comfort and a quiet drive.

The redesigned LeSabre sports a graceful exterior, clean-looking lines and a curved rear fascia – a look that is little-changed from the previous generation. Clearly, the designers did little besides trying to fine-tune the previous model – and it looked better, in my opinion.

Sitting comfortably in front of the soft-hued dashboard, nicely enhanced with wood trim, the driver will have no trouble locating all the controls. The display panel, too, is user friendly. However, the gearshift, which is mounted on the steering column, is hard to reach and shifting is erratic.

Unlike Bonneville's sports-car pretentions, the LeSabre's ambition is to ensure a smooth collaboration between suspension and handling. Overall results are good, although the shock absorbers are too supple and the steering too isolated from the road surface. The Touring model with its 16-inch wheels will help correct matters.

Despite its aerodynamic limitations, the LeSabre is an elegant and reliable sedan. Excellent value.

Denis Duquet

SPECIFICATIONS	**SLE**
Price	$CDN 32,365-42,805 / $US 24,915-33,215
Warranty	3 years / 36,000 (60,000 km)
Type	sedan / front wheel drive
Wheelbase / Length	112.2 in / 202.4 in
Width / Height	74 in / 56 in
Weight	3638 lb (1650 kg)
Trunk / Fuel tank	18 cu. ft / 18 gallons
Air bags	front and side
Front suspension	independent
Rear suspension	independent
Front brakes / Rear brakes	disc ABS
Traction control	yes
Steering	rack-and-pinion, variable assist
Turning circle	39 feet
Tires (front/rear)	P235/55HR17

PERFORMANCE	
Engine	V6 3.8-liter boosted
Transmission	4-speed automatic
Horsepower	240 hp at 5200 rpm
Torque	280 lb-ft at 4000 rpm
Other engines	V6 3.8 liter 205 hp (LeSabre and SE)
Other transmission	none
Acceleration (0-60 mph)	7.9 sec; 9.6 sec (LeSabre)
Maximum speed	118 mph (190 km/h)
Braking (60-0 mph)	123 feet (37.4 m)
Fuel consumption	16 mpg (14.2 L/100 km)

COMPETITION

• Chrysler Intrepid • Infiniti I30
• Toyota Avalon

NEW FOR 2002

• 17-inch chromed wheels (Bonneville) • New front and rear fascia (Bonneville) • New radios

RATING	**(out of 5 stars)**
Driveability	★★★½
Comfort	★★★★
Reliability	★★★½
Roominess	★★★½
Winter driving rating	★★★★
Safety	★★★★
Resale value	★★★

PONTIAC **GRAND AM**

PONTIAC **GRAND AM**

Bold and Bolder

"Style is the man." wrote the great 18th-century French naturalist Georges Louis Leclerc Buffon. No doubt the same may be said of cars. In any case, the Pontiac people certainly won't pooh-pooh the notion. For years, the Grand Am's sales have exceeded those of Buick Skylark and Oldsmobile Achieva, even though both the Skylark and Achieva were built on the same Grand Am platform. It all boils down to style.

Even today, the Grand Am shares a number of components with the Oldsmobile Alero. But while the Alero is aimed at a rather more conservative clientele, the Pontiac goes after a brash, young and extrovert crowd, in whose eyes the racier the style, the better.

Distinctive style

You either love the Grand Am's appearance or you don't. According to some people, it's sporty and dynamic; for others, it's all flash and little class. One thing is certain: the latest styling modifications won't put an end to the debate.

The Grand Am's cockpit features bold styling too. Display panels, knobs and buttons all sport unusual – even tortured – shapes, including the two huge cavities housing the tachometer and speedometer. The cramped style, however, is ergonomically sound. All controls are within reach and easy to read, particularly the radio and climate controls, which are mounted on a panel angled toward the driver. What's more, the plastic used for various features looks and feels better than in previous-generation models.

Cabin dimensions are standard for an intermediate car. The front seats are big, well padded on the sides, ensuring good lateral support and the driving position ensures excellent visibility. In the back, legroom is ample, but the rear seat is still too low for tall passengers. The trunk is spacious and can be made even bigger thanks to the collapsible backrest, except in the SE base model.

Style is the car

A variety of options

The Grand Am comes in two body styles: two-door coupe and four-door sedan. Each style is available in four trim levels: SE (base), SE1, GT and GT1. Standard features on the SE base model are decent, including

▲ PROS

- Attractive price • Interesting equipment
- Racy styling (for some) • Rigid chassis
- Improved road manners

▼ CONS

- Archaic 6-cylinder engine • Odd dashboard
- Outrageous styling (for some) • Rear seats too snug • Rough 4-cylinder engine

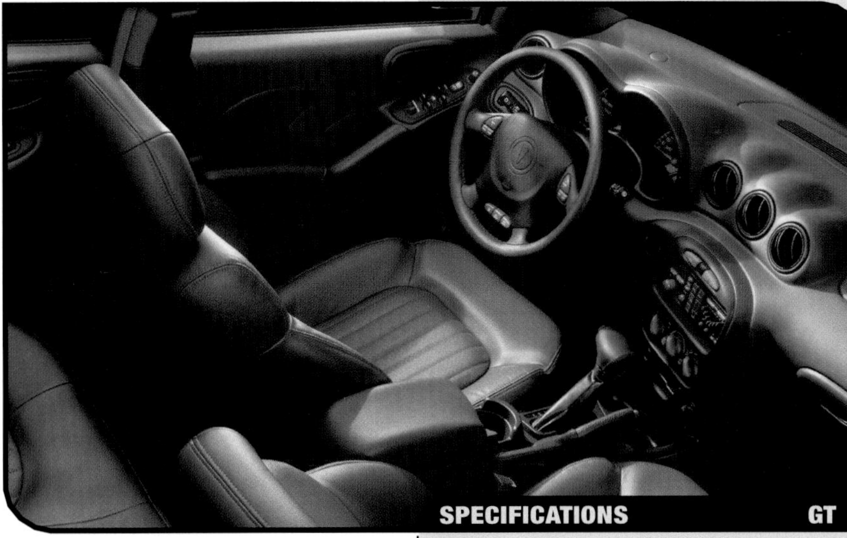

a radio/cassette stereo system with four speakers, air conditioning, 15-inch wheels and disc/drum brakes with ABS. At the other end of the spectrum, the top-of-the-line GT1 offers radio/CD with eight speakers, 16-inch alloy wheels, 4-wheel disc brakes, cruise control and countless power-assisted features. Between the two extremes, the buyer is faced with a puzzling maze of options.

The buyer's final decision could very well depend on mechanical components. The SE is powered by a 2.5-liter 4-cylinder DOHC engine, coupled to a 5-speed manual transmission, whereas the GT "imposes" the use of a 3.4-liter V6, fitted with a 4-speed automatic gearbox. I say "impose" because that's the only configuration offered with the GT. The SE can be equipped with a V6 and automatic transmission.

The 4-cylinder behaves itself respectably enough, if matched with a manual gearbox, but it tends to come up a bit short when mated to the automatic. Incidentally, GM announced it will bring out a new 2.2-liter aluminum DOHC engine, with 138 horsepower, which would eliminate that rough aspect of the antiquated Quad Four. Until that happens, I'd recommend the V6 that, despite its "archaic" configuration, does its job efficiently and consumes hardly more fuel than the 4-cylinder. And believe me, being "archaic" in this situation is not a bad thing.

Granted, driving the Grand Am isn't like fooling around with a slick European car, but it's satisfying all the same. On the SE base model, the suspension – MacPherson-strut in front and multi-link in back – was tuned for the car's overall comfort, but certainly not at the expense of its balance on right corners. The plusher GT model boasts sport suspension and tires that offer even better grip. Steering is precise, if a tad inconsistent in terms of transmitting road feel. Braking on the SE is adequate under normal driving conditions, excellent and evenly distributed on the GT, thanks to the all-disc system.

So, for the moment at least, the Grand Am continues as best it can to maintain its position near the top of its class. Sooner or later though, GM should give the car what it truly deserves: a better chassis and more engine power worthy of its devastatingly handsome looks.

Jean-Georges Laliberté

SPECIFICATIONS	**GT**
Price	$CDN 21,405-27,830 / $US 16,790-22,540
Warranty	3 years / 36,000 miles (60,000 km)
Type	sedan / front wheel drive
Wheelbase / Length	107.1 in / 186.2 in
Width / Height	70.4 in / 55.1 in
Weight	3120 lb (1415 kg)
Trunk / Fuel tank	14.6 cu. ft / 14 gallons
Air bags	front
Front suspension	independent
Rear suspension	independent
Front brakes / Rear brakes	disc ABS
Traction control	yes
Steering	rack-and-pinion, electronically assisted
Turning circle	38 feet
Tires (front/rear)	P225/50R16

PERFORMANCE	
Engine	V6 3.4-liter 12 valves
Transmission	4-speed automatic
Horsepower	175 hp at 4800 rpm
Torque	205 lb-ft at 4000 rpm
Other engines	L4 2.4-liter DOHC 150 hp (SE)
Other transmission	5-speed manual (4L)
Acceleration (0-60 mph)	9.1 s; 10.4 s (4L)
Maximum speed	115 mph (185 km/h)
Braking (60-0 mph)	138 feet (42 m)
Fuel consumption	20.3 mpg; (11.2 L/100 km)

COMPETITION

- Honda Accord • Chrysler Sebring • Mazda 626
- Nissan Altima • Oldsmobile Alero • VW Jetta

NEW FOR 2002

- 4L 2.2-liter engine • 16-inch alloy wheels
- Redesigned console

RATING	**(out of 5 stars)**
Driveability	★★★
Comfort	★★★
Reliability	★★★
Roominess	★★★½
Winter driving rating	★★★½
Safety	★★★
Resale value	★★★

PONTIAC GRAND PRIX

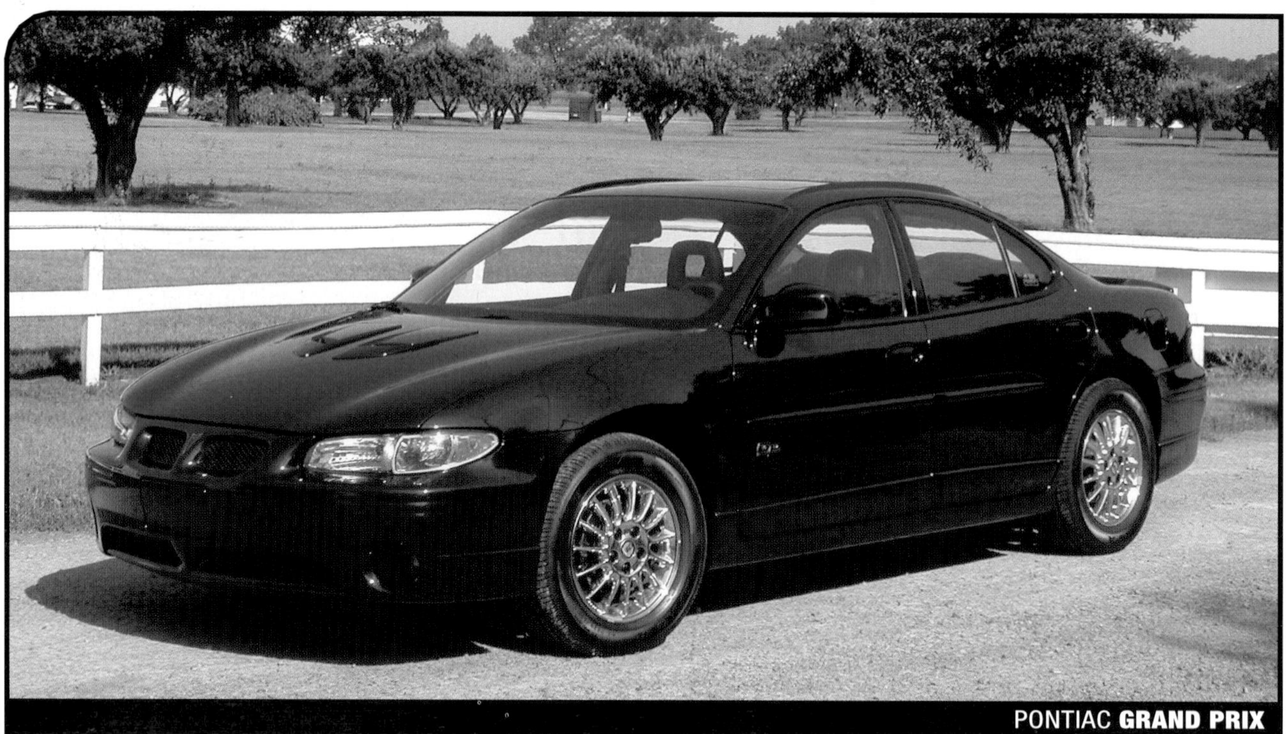

PONTIAC **GRAND PRIX**

The Young and the Restless

For some people, the words Grand Prix stand for the most sophisticated type of racing on this planet. For others, Grand Prix is synonymous with one of the most popular brand-name cars in America. And this stylish Pontiac celebrates its 40th birthday this year.

As befits the occasion and as basic marketing principles dictate, Pontiac has come up with a special 40th-anniversary version of the Grand Prix. The changes are strictly cosmetic, however, amounting to little more than a new shell. It would have been nice had Pontiac equipped it with the Oldsmobile Aurora's 4.0-liter V8, in lieu of the 3.6-liter V6 – an engine that's almost as old as the Grand Prix itself. An electronically controlled suspension, like the one in the Corvette, would have spiced things up, too. Instead, we have to contend with a hideous rear spoiler and hood-mounted air inlets – all "exclusive" to the Grand Prix – as well as various roof-mounted aerodynamic elements, similar to those you see on Nascar's Winston Cup entries. In case you've forgotten, it was the great Bobby Labonté who won that famous cup in 2000, behind the wheel of a Grand Prix.

That said, let me admit that the exterior looks trendy enough, tastefully painted in cherry red. But the dual-tone interior – graphite and dark red – is suspect. Finally, the commemorative version comes in only two trim levels: GT and GTP.

Good touring car

Appearances aside, the Grand Prix is a remarkable touring car, excelling in cornering and able to change lanes rapidly with predictable agility. When pushed, it makes a terrific racket – the tires squeal in unison – but control is good and the average speed surprisingly high for a car of its size.

Four decades later

Oddly enough, the most "high-performance" model isn't necessarily the most fun to drive under normal conditions. The SE, with its 3.1-liter V6 engine, is not as fast as models equipped with the more powerful 3.8-liter variety, but its suspension is more compliant and its higher-profile tires provide markedly better comfort. In terms of performance and handling, the

▲ PROS

- Flexible engines • Excellent handling
- Growing reliability • Precise steering
- Trendy silhouette

▼ CONS

- Average rear seats • Busy dashboard
- Stiff suspension (GT and GTP) • Uneven finish
- Redundant 40th anniversary version

GT and GTP versions win hands down, but on bad roads their very stiff suspension makes it hard on your posterior, and causes constant body noises for miles on end. Still, the Grand Prix's reliability has greatly improved over the years, so take heart.

But let's return to the engines. Both the 3.8-liter V6 and its turbocharged version are competent under all circumstances. They deliver enough torque at low rpms to provide better-than-average acceleration. The GT scoots from 0-60 mph in slightly more than 9 seconds, while the GTP takes less than 7 seconds. The turbocharged version proves to be more energetic at high rpms than its normally-aspirated cousin.

The Grand Prix doesn't just look sporty, its performance is also among the best in its category. But I can't say I like the dashboard – the plethora of buttons and gauges makes it look like a complicated video game. It certainly doesn't leave people indifferent: either you love or hate it. The front seats are comfortable and offer decent lateral support, but if you're tall and have to sit in the back, you'll be the first to complain about poor headroom, and having the back of your neck fry in the burning sun.

The quality of finish and the materials used is decidedly subpar, but that's a small price to pay, I suppose, since the Grand Prix has more than proved itself for 40 years, and counting.

Denis Duquet

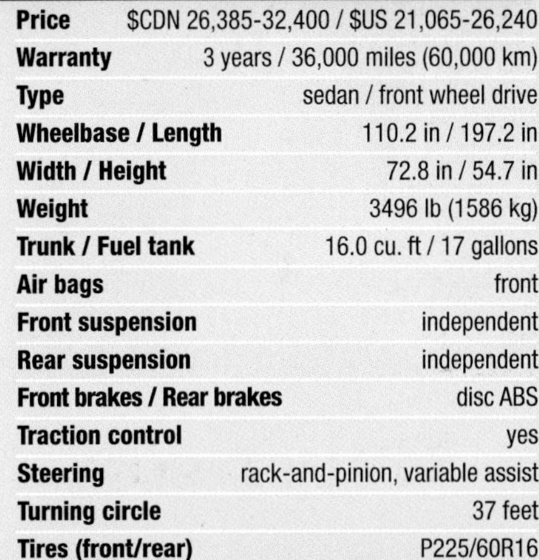

SPECIFICATIONS	**GTP**
Price	$CDN 26,385-32,400 / $US 21,065-26,240
Warranty	3 years / 36,000 miles (60,000 km)
Type	sedan / front wheel drive
Wheelbase / Length	110.2 in / 197.2 in
Width / Height	72.8 in / 54.7 in
Weight	3496 lb (1586 kg)
Trunk / Fuel tank	16.0 cu. ft / 17 gallons
Air bags	front
Front suspension	independent
Rear suspension	independent
Front brakes / Rear brakes	disc ABS
Traction control	yes
Steering	rack-and-pinion, variable assist
Turning circle	37 feet
Tires (front/rear)	P225/60R16

PERFORMANCE	
Engine	V6 3.8-liter turbocharged
Transmission	4-speed automatic
Horsepower	240 hp at 5200 rpm
Torque	280 lb-ft at 3600 rpm
Other engines	3.1-liter V6 175 hp;
Other transmission	3.8-liter V6 200 hp
Acceleration (0-60 mph)	none
Maximum speed	6.9 s (GTP) ; 9.3 s
Braking (60-0 mph)	112 mph (180 km/h)
Fuel consumption	140 ft. (42.6 m)
	17.7 ; 15.9 mpg (GTP)
	(12.8 ; 14.3 L/100 km)

COMPETITION

• Chevrolet Impala • Chrysler Intrepid • Ford Taurus • Honda Accord • Toyota Camry

NEW FOR 2002

• 40th anniversary version • More complete standard equipment • New colors

RATING	**(out of 5 stars)**
Driveability	★★★½
Comfort	★★★½
Reliability	★★★½
Roominess	★★★★
Winter driving rating	★★★½
Safety	★★★★
Resale value	★★★½

PORSCHE 911 PORSCHE CARRERA 2/4S/TARGA

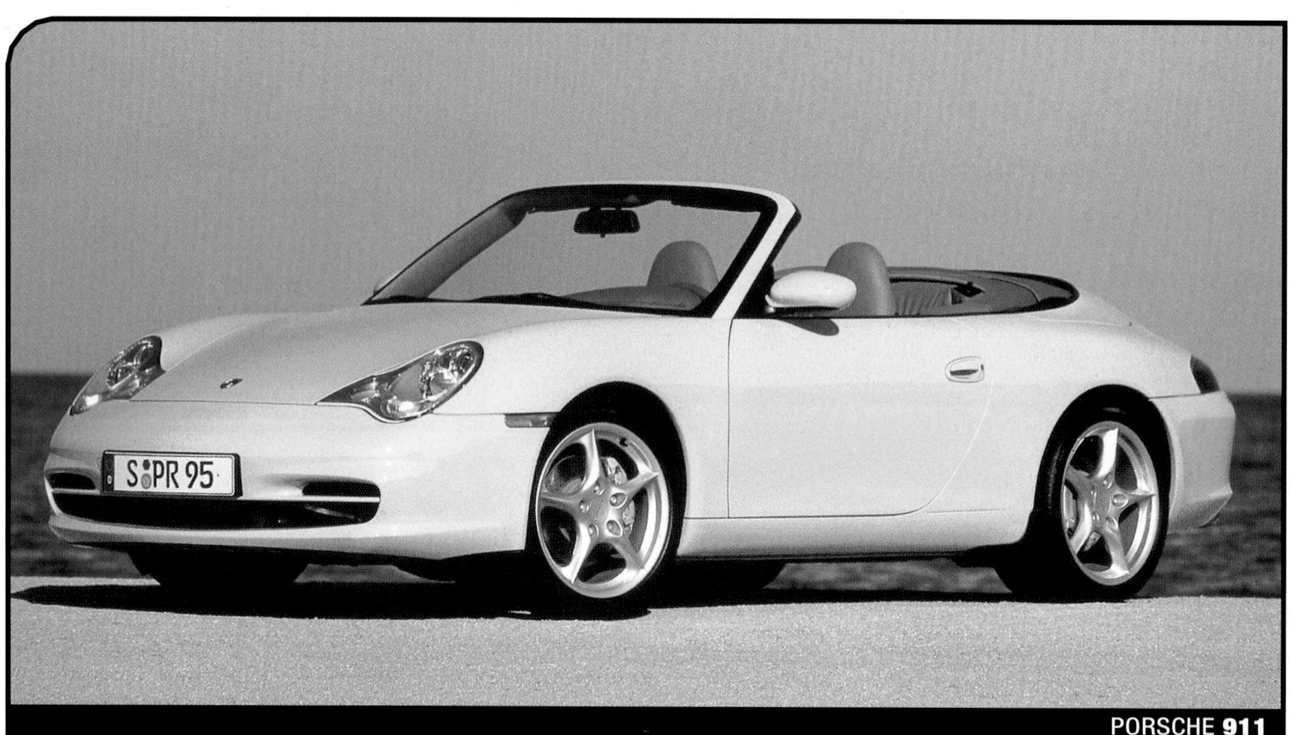

PORSCHE **911**

New Look, New Engine

The sky's the limit **at Porsche, I thought to myself after testing the 2002 Porsche Carrera 2 and 4 in Germany recently. I liked both models, which was surprising, given my aversion to anything 996. A Porsche 911 die-hard – and I mean the original model – I had trouble warming up to the new lines, as did scores of other car writers around the world. But Porsche seems to know what it's doing, as demonstrated by the latest sales figures – and profits. To be sure, the Boxster contributed heavily to those positive numbers, but the 911 wasn't that far behind, judging from its well-filled order book.**

Right after the Porsche 996's launch in 1997, the Stuttgart-based automaker began walking on eggshells. Would the car enjoy the same success as its predecessor? The answer took a long time in coming, four years to be exact. As far as Porsche is concerned, it's definitely *mission accomplished*, judging by the just-released second-generation 996, which has beefed up horsepower and greater agility.

Car enthusiasts may wonder why a new look for the latter-day 911 at this early stage in its career. The reason is obvious – it's to differentiate it from its lower-rung companion, the Boxster.

What's new?

In my judgment, Porsche shot itself in the foot by restyling the 911 along the same lines as last year's 911 Turbo version. This might annoy Turbo owners who are adamant that their sacred machine sports a look all its own. Unfortunately for Turbo fans, no modification has been planned for the 2002 model. They'll have to wait at least another year.

Off you go!

And so, the Carreras – both 2 and 4 – use the same light clusters, front bumper and instrument pod found on the Porsche 911 Turbo. On the mechanical front, they feature VarioCam Plus, a system combining continuous camshaft adjustment and valve lift switchover. Finally, some suspension components were "borrowed" from the Turbo/GT2 line, so that there's precious little separating the Carreras from their big Turbo sister.

▲ PROS

- Active safety • Exceptional handling
- Remarkable performance • Turbo look
- Winter driveability

▼ CONS

- Expensive options • So-so comfort (18-inch wheels) • Steering wheel too low
- Subpar finish • Tiny trunk

Acceleration to spare

What's more, the new Carreras get remodeled air scoops, which help increase the throughput of cooling air by 15%, and spoiler lips, which significantly reduce front and rear axle lift forces, by 25% and 40% respectively.

The Carrera is powered by a 3.6-liter flat-6 engine rating 320 hp, 20 more than the 3.4-liter engine it replaces. Top speed is 178 mph (285 km/h), and acceleration is stupefying, taking exactly 5 seconds from 0-60 mph (5.2 seconds for the convertible). Incidentally, despite the increased horsepower, the car's combined city/highway fuel mileage is higher than before – 20 mpg (11.3 liters per 100 km). Not that this detail ranks high on Porsche buyers' list of priorities, but it's impressive nonetheless. Finally, the 6-speed manual gearbox is still available, while the old Tiptronic transmission has given way to the Turbo version, which can better accommodate the new engine's extra ponies.

The cabriolet gets an all-new heated rear window, made of real glass, as opposed to the plastic variety in the previous model. And none too soon, as far as winter-driving Porsche fans are concerned. As always, the top can be retracted and replaced easily and quickly. Incidentally, all Porsche convertible models take unkindly to rough surfaces, producing a lot of body noise.

Porsche finally succumbed to customer pressure and installed an all-new glove compartment and a redesigned cupholder in the cockpit – a sacrilege, if you ask me. The nice touch here is the three-spoke steering wheel, which now comes as standard equipment. In the rear, the oval tailpipes are another sign of distinction from the previous model, while new light alloy wheels – featuring ultra slender spokes – reduce unsprung masses by 8 lbs (3.6 kg) in the case of 17-inch wheels, and 22 lbs (10 kg) in the case of 18-inch wheels. In our opinion, the 18-inch wheels should be reserved strictly for smooth road surfaces, or a racetrack.

On the Bavarian Autobahn

The new models were unveiled in Munich, where I had my first outing on

CARRERA **4S**

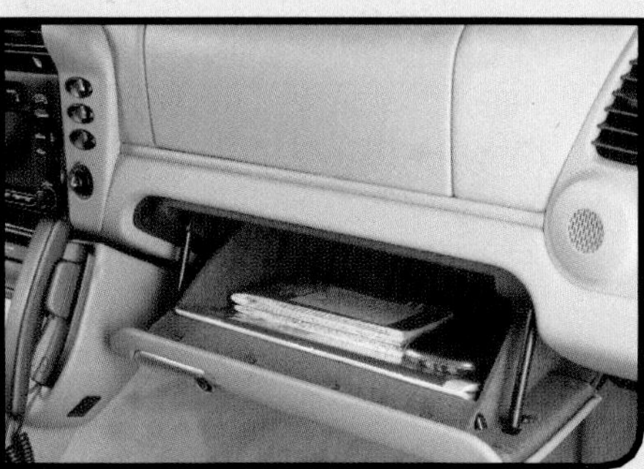

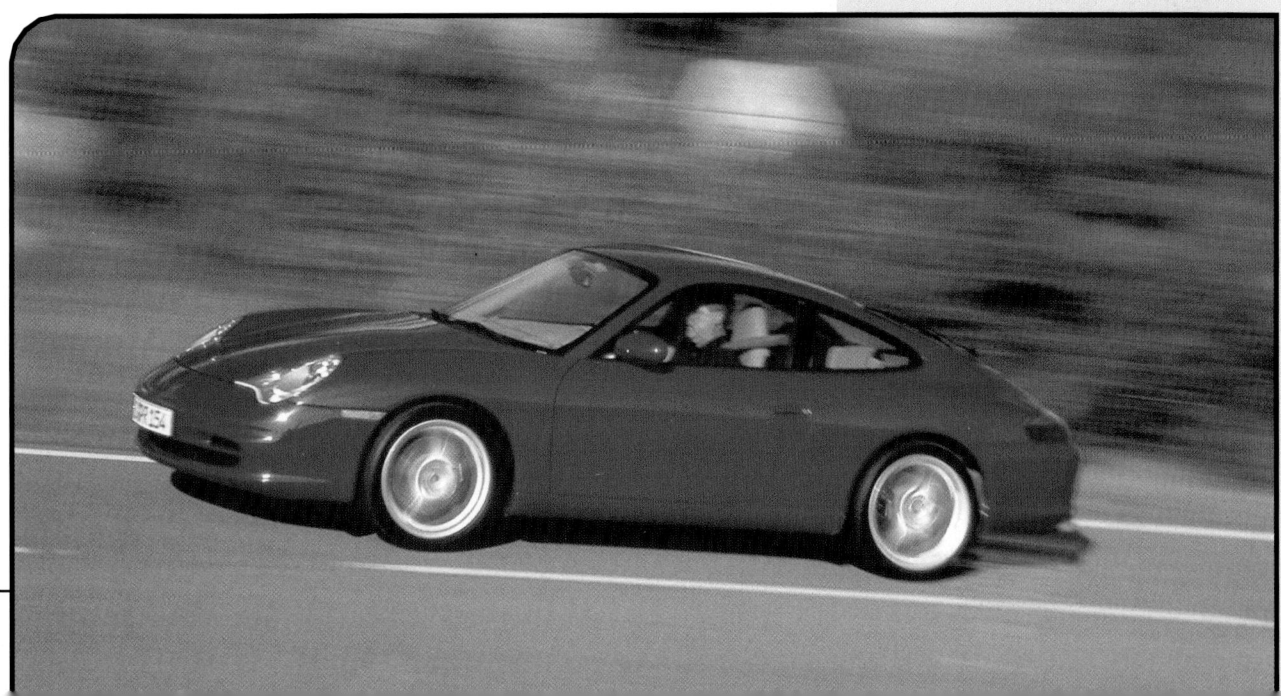

PORSCHE 911/CARRERA 2/CARRERA 4S

911 **TARGA**

the famous, or infamous, no-speed-limit Autobahn – an ideal venue to test the 911, especially when the weather cooperates. As I pressed the accelerator, I could feel the rush of full-force engine power, accompanied by the unmistakably flat-6 rumble that was pure music to my Porsche-diehard ear. Acceleration was quick and with VarioCam Plus, you could feel engine torque throughout the rev range. At 4000 rpm, however, I noticed a slight response lag.

The Carrera 4 (now 4S) was far and away my favorite model. It's solidly built and boasts impeccable 4-wheel drive power, thanks to the combination visco-coupling/PSM (Porsche Stability Management). The car feels immensely secure and exhibits perfect neutrality on turns. The Carrera 2 requires a little more effort from the driver. At high speeds, the front end feels significantly lighter and you have to make a conscious effort to keep the car on track before tackling a turn. On the other hand, handling in both Carreras is greatly enhanced by the new bumper system, especially at high speeds. Despite increased rigidity (25% for the coupe, and 10% for the cabriolet), the car remains particularly flexible and easy to handle. As for the brakes, there's not much to say. As always, they're Porsche-graded, and that sums it up nicely.

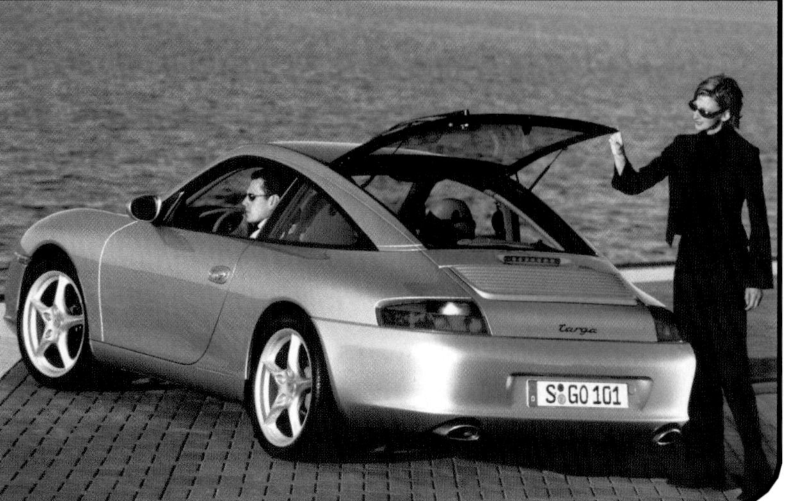

911 **TARGA**

If I have to say something critical about the 911, I'd quibble about the quality of finish, which has yet to reach the level of the old 993 models; a couple of controls that can't quite resist the test of time; the "subpar" interior design, considering a car in this price range; and the all-new dashboard that looks too much like the Boxster's. I also find the long list of exorbitant options a bit extravagant.

Targa and 4S

Porsche unveiled the Targa versions of its latest 911 models at the 2001 Frankfurt Auto Show. The first version features a glass top that's twice as large as the 911 coupe's. The 2002 model differs from the previous version (1996-1998) with its removable glass rear window, which facilitates baggage loading when the rear backrests are folded down. The glass surface is bigger than before and the two motors required to operate the top adds 155 lbs (70 kg) to the 911 coupe's weight. As for structural rigidity, mediocre in the first Targas back in 1996, you can't really tell until the miles have had a chance to add up.

Another piece of good news to report is the return of the Carrera 4S, replacing the regular Carrera 4. Like the 911 Turbo, it features wider brakes and a widened rear track. Porsche specialists and fans will spot it by the red lamp strip across the back of the car.

François Duval

SPECIFICATIONS

Price	$CDN 99,300-121,900 / $US 67,265-82,265
Warranty	4 years / 48,000 miles (80,000 km)
Type	coupe 2 + 2 / all-wheel drive
Wheelbase / Length	92.5 in / 174.4 in
Width / Height	69.7 in / 51.3 in
Weight	3098 lb (1405 kg)
Trunk / Fuel tank	3.5 cu. ft / 17 gallons
Air bags	front and side
Front suspension	independent
Rear suspension	independent
Front brakes / Rear brakes	vented disc ABS
Traction control	yes (PSM)
Steering	rack-and-pinion, power assist
Turning circle	36 ft
Tires (front/rear)	P205/50ZR17 / P25540ZR17

PERFORMANCE

Engine	Flat-6 3.6-liter
Transmission	6-speed manual
Horsepower	320 hp at 6800 rpm
Torque	273 lb-ft at 4250 rpm
Other engines	none
Other transmission	Tiptronic S
Acceleration (0-60 mph)	5 sec
Maximum speed	178 mph (285 km/h)
Braking (60-0 mph)	121 feet (37 m)
Fuel consumption	20.1 mpg (11.3 L/100 km)

COMPETITION

• Acura NSX • Corvette Z06 • Dodge Viper GTS • Jaguar XKR • Mercedes-Benz SL

NEW FOR 2002

• More powerful engine • New front bumper

RATING (out of 5 stars)

Driveability	★★★★½
Comfort	★★★
Reliability	★★★½
Roominess	★★
Winter driving rating	★★★★
Safety	★★★★
Resale value	★★★★½

PORSCHE **BOXSTER S**

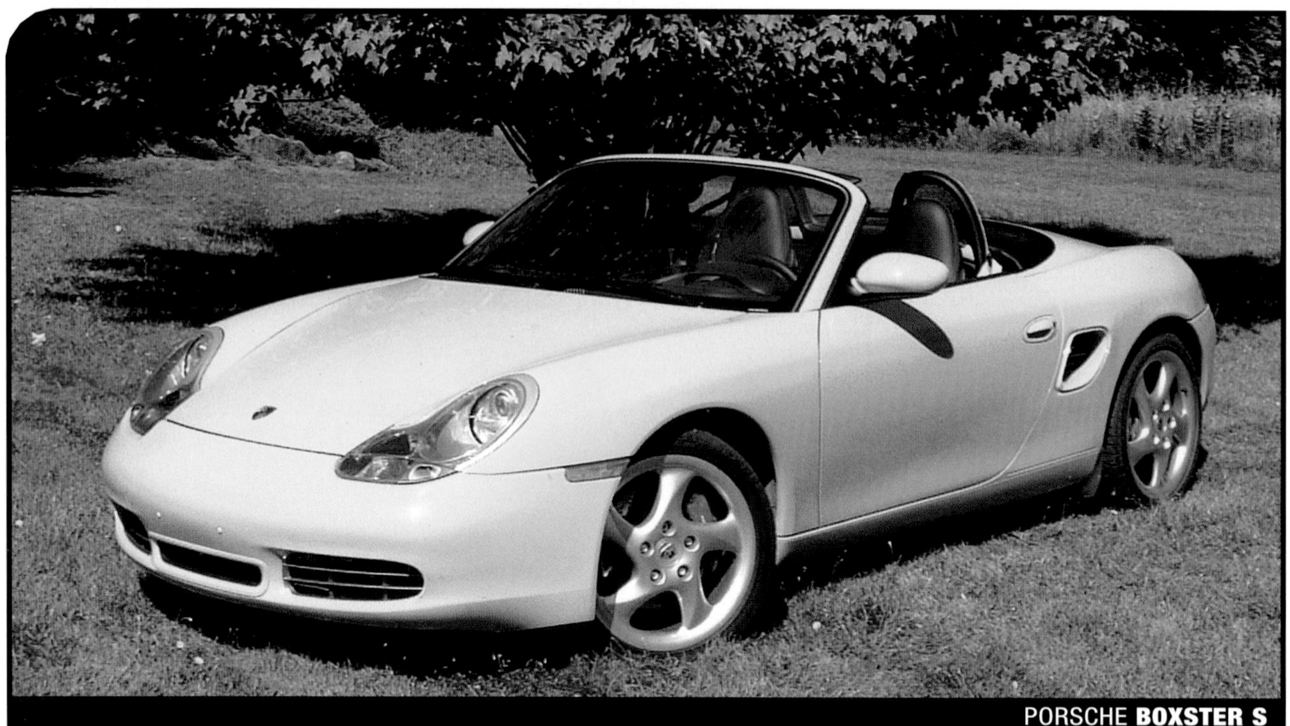

PORSCHE **BOXSTER S**

With a Capital S

S is for satisfaction. S stands for suppleness. S is for sensual. S means sexy. Or quite simply, S equals sport. The real McCoy. No half measures, no false claims, no hood-mounted flame or eagle. Instead, "sport" defined in terms of engine power, great handling, overwhelming brakes. Meaning sport as in genuine sports car – for its own sake, its own pure pleasure. However irrational that may sound, or be.

Launched in 1996, the Porsche Boxster has reclaimed its rightful place as a bona fide sports car, a claim that its predecessor – the venerable Porsche 911 – had gradually abandoned, forsaking the "sport" label in favor of "GT" as a concession to the vitally-important American market. Indeed, in recent years, more and more Porsche 911 buyers went after the prestige and glamorous image of the brand, as opposed to the sport-oriented character of the car itself. Understandably, the automaker obliged.

Taking its cue from the 550 Spyder of the 1950s, the Boxster picked up where the 911 left off, as it began to assume its GT personality.

Balance

Two-seater, convertible, mid-engine. A well-known but little-used formula that guarantees excellent front/rear weight distribution. As luck would have it, the memory of the odd 914 model, launched in the 1970s, was still fresh in the minds of Porsche designers, who made sure to keep the trademark Porsche look with the new Boxster. As a matter of fact, the Boxster inherits the 911's classic nose – much to the consternation of many 911 owners – while the tail end is inspired by the legendary Spyder, the car that actor James Dean immortalized with his fatal crash in 1955.

YESSSS!

And so, the Boxster is a handsome creature. Handsomely virile, without undue flourish or artifice, and with a formidable drivetrain to boot, starting with the engine.

Torque galore

The Boxster S is equipped with a 3.2-liter flat-6 engine developing 250 hp – 33 more than that cranked out by the standard Boxster's 2.7-liter engine. Worthy horsepower, to be sure, but what's remark-

▲ PROS

- **Efficient engine • Excellent chassis**
- **Fun to drive • Remarkable brakes**

▼ CONS

- **Nondescript dashboard • Plastic window**
- **Radio needs work • Too many options**

able here is the amazing 225 lb-ft of torque at 4500 rpm – 80% of which is already there at 2000 rpm. Thus equipped, the Boxster S scoots from 50-75 mph in seven seconds. Effortlessly and smoothly, as befits all German-made engines, at least as far as Porsche, BMW and Mercedes-Benz are concerned.

Other satisfying features include the 6-speed manual transmission (a paragon of smoothness), the superbly rigid chassis (for a convertible) and ever-so-discreet traction control. Handling is a joy, aided in this case by the 18-inch wheels that graced my test model. To my surprise, the sport-tuned suspension actually delivered decent comfort on rough surfaces. Only one apparent weakness: the car tended to hop around and hunt while in a straight line. So one strike for directional stability.

While the engine is a thing of beauty, and handling is a joy forever, the brakes are the real stars here. Borrowed directly from the 911, the cross-drilled disc brakes deliver remarkable stopping distances, capable of rivaling the very best anywhere. A word of caution, however: the front brakes tend to lock when they're cold. So, brake if you must, but not too abruptly or too hard, at least until the brakes are properly warmed up.

But sad to say, not everything is fine aboard the Boxster S. The plastic rear window, no doubt of good quality, is prone to scratching and collecting dirt. The stereo system, too, leaves something to be desired. Those tiny Hyundai-style buttons definitely need work. Ditto the utterly unoriginal central part of the dashboard, a refugee from the 911. Something along the lines of the Audi TT's dashboard would be nicer.

For the rest, the Boxster S is pretty much standard for a coupe or convertible: whether in terms of storage space (no glove compartment, instead there are pockets under armrests), trunk space (front and rear), or the ease with which the top is retracted and put back. The price? Not cheap, especially when you start tinkering with the endless combination of options, a practice that German automakers favor, as opposed to the "all inclusive" policy adopted by the Japanese, Swedes, and a few others.

Alain Raymond

SPECIFICATIONS

Price	$CDN 60,500-73,300 / $US 42,865-50,965
Warranty	4 years / 48,000 miles (80,000 km)
Type	roadster / rear wheel drive
Wheelbase / Length	95.1 in / 169.9 in
Width / Height	70.1 in / 50.8 in
Weight	2855 lb (1295 kg)
Trunk / Fuel tank	9.2 cu. ft / 17 gallons
Air bags	front and side
Front suspension	independent
Rear suspension	independent
Front brakes / Rear brakes	vented disc ABS
Traction control	yes
Steering	rack-and-pinion, power assist
Turning circle	36 feet
Tires (front/rear)	P225/40ZR18 / P265/35ZR18

PERFORMANCE

Engine	6H 3.2-liter
Transmission	6-speed manual
Horsepower	252 hp at 6250 rpm
Torque	225 lb-ft at 4500 rpm
Other engines	6H 2.7-liter 219 hp
Other transmission	Tiptronic 5-speed
Acceleration (0-60 mph)	6 sec
Maximum speed	162 mph (260 km/h)
Braking (60-0 mph)	120 feet (36.5 m)
Fuel consumption	17.2 mpg (13.2 L/100 km)

COMPETITION

• Audi TT Roadster • BMW Z3 • Honda S2000
• Mercedes-Benz SLK 320

NEW FOR 2002

No major change

RATING (out of 5 stars)

Driveability	★★★★½
Comfort	★★★½
Reliability	★★½
Roominess	★★½
Winter driving rating	★★★
Safety	★★★★
Resale value	★★★★½

SAAB 9^3

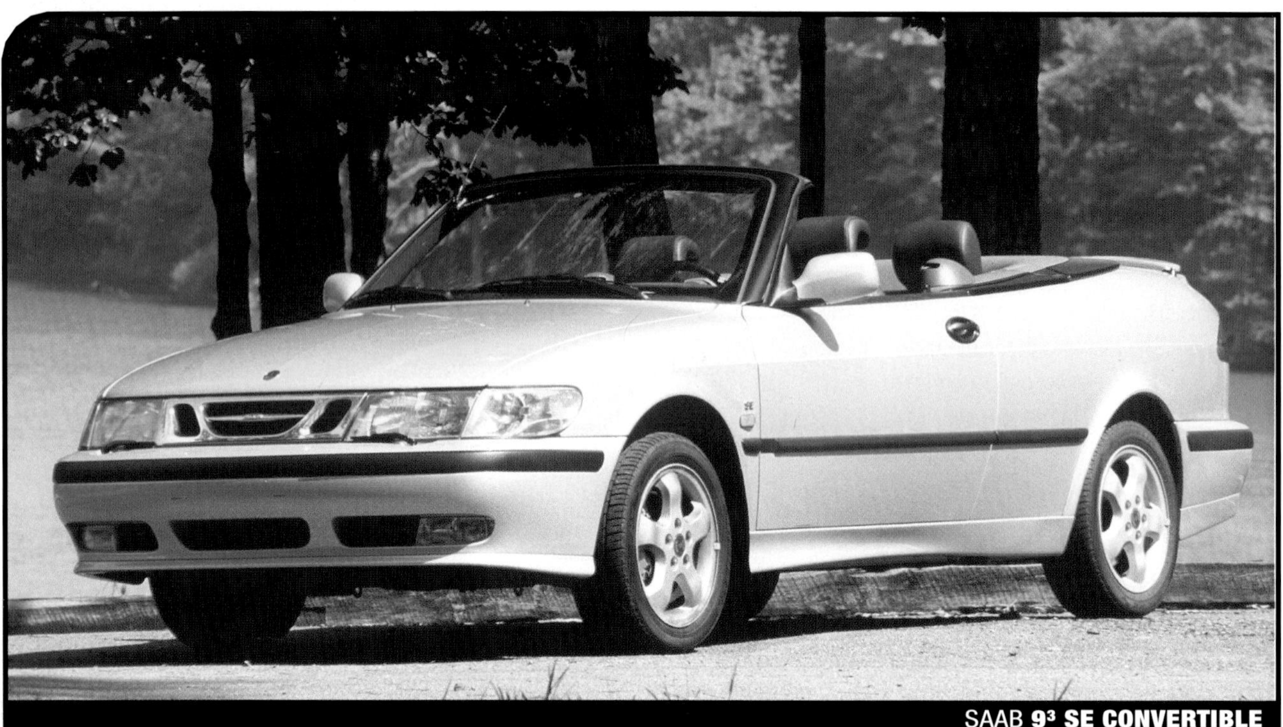

SAAB **9^3 SE CONVERTIBLE**

Behind the Times

Having paid a lot for the Swedish marque, General Motors must now make its investment pay off by modernizing the Saab line. That's exactly what the Ford Motor Company did when it resuscitated – and the word is not too strong – the fortunes of the moribund Jaguar. Saab's future is on the line.

My test drive took place behind the wheel of a superb Saab 9^3 convertible, a vehicle oozing style and richness. Whether the soft top is down or up, the car looks as elegant as its leading contemporaries, and that's saying a good deal because the 9^3 sedan doesn't quite capture the same charm, at least in my eyes.

But the compliments stop right there. As I wheeled the test model out of the GM dealership, I had a strange feeling: the steering column shook each time I hit a bump.

Later, driving along the highway, the shaking persisted, not just the steering column, but the windshield also shook and soon the rearview mirror. In fact, the entire chassis vibrated over every bump and pothole in the road. Granted, I didn't expect the car to be as rigid as a tank – it's a convertible after all – but that's not saying it should tremble like a leaf swirled around by the wind! Since the suspension uses flexible bushings, handling and comfort deteriorate on rough road surfaces, spoiling the pleasure of driving with the top down.

My research over, I realized that the 9^3 was launched back in 1994, and despite various upgrading efforts over the intervening years, the car's basic structure has never been altered. The Saab 9^3's body is seriously out-of-date.

Wanted: a makeover

Cabin to the rescue

Not everything is bleak behind the wheel of this "topless" belle, however. The power-assisted soft top is easy to operate and, once deployed, provides reasonable cargo space in the trunk. Another positive feature is the multi-way adjustable front seats, comfortable and heated. The exterior mirrors, too, are heated and the driver's-side mirror boasts a bifocal lens designed to enlarge the field of vision. A very practical touch (other automakers, please take note). Also worth mentioning are the active headrests that protect the

▲ PROS

• Comfortable front seat • Cool appearance • Decent trunk for a convertible • Good passive safety • Supple and powerful engine

▼ CONS

• Average reliability • Blatant lack of rigidity (convertible) • Steep price • Torque effect in steering wheel

back of your neck in case of a rear-end collision, side airbags and headlight wipers, perfect for bad weather conditions. It's a pity that Saab totally neglected rear visibility, which might as well be non-existent, owing to the tiny rear window.

Other nifty details include the OnStar system, functional ergonomics (except the radio button), excellent quality of both finish and materials used and last but not least, the floor-mounted ignition key. It seemed disconcerting at first, but I grew to like the idea, finding it very practical. On the other hand, there's almost no room for the driver's left foot, the central elbowrest is way too low, and the noise from the ventilation system is disconcerting.

Danger warning

There's a 2.0-liter 4-cylinder turbocharged engine under the hood that develops 205 hp and 184 lb-ft (automatic) or 207 lb-ft (manual) of torque. The car accelerates briskly, leaping from 50 to 75 mph in 7 seconds. Turbo takes next to no time to kick in. But this ideal situation only occurs when you drive in a straight line. Things can deteriorate quickly if you decide to accelerate in a corner as violent torque steer kicks in – a safety hazard serious enough for the *Auto Guide* to strongly sanction the Saab 9^3 Viggen last year. The Viggen's 258 lb-ft of torque produced a violent torque effect.

So whether we're talking about chassis rigidity or torque effect, the Saab 9^3 can no longer hide its age. A makeover is long overdue. If you can ignore the shaking and don't intend to make the engine do its job, you'll probably dig this cute convertible. But if you're serious about cars, look elsewhere. At the asking price, you can certainly do better.

Alain Raymond

SPECIFICATIONS	SE CONVERTIBLE
Price	$CDN 32,000-65,000 / $US 27,070-45,570
Warranty	4 years / 48,000 miles (80,000 km)
Type	sport convertible / front wheel drive
Wheelbase / Length	102.6 in / 182.3 in
Width / Height	67.3 in / 55.9 in
Weight	3296 lb (1495 kg)
Trunk / Fuel tank	10.1 cu. ft / 17 gallons
Air bags	front and side
Front suspension	independent
Rear suspension	semi-independent
Front brakes / Rear brakes	disc ABS
Traction control	yes
Steering	rack-and-pinion, variable assist
Turning circle	34 feet
Tires (front/rear)	P205/50R16

PERFORMANCE	
Engine	4L 2 liter Turbo
Transmission	4-speed automatic
Horsepower	205 hp at 5500 rpm
Torque	184 lb-ft at 1900 rpm
Other engines	4L 2 liter turbo 185 hp; 2.3 liter turbo 235 hp
Other transmission	5-speed manual
Acceleration (0-60 mph)	9.1 sec (auto)
Maximum speed	140 mph (225 km/h)
Braking (60-0 mph)	139 feet (42.3 m)
Fuel consumption	19.1 mpg (11.9 L/100 km)

COMPETITION

• Audi S4 • BMW 3 Series • Mercedes-Benz 320A cabriolet • Volvo C70 cabriolet

NEW FOR 2002

• 25th Anniversary version, Turbo
• Two new colors

RATING	(out of 5 stars)
Driveability	★★½
Comfort	★★★
Reliability	★★½
Roominess	★★★½
Winter driving rating	★★
Safety	★★★
Resale value	★★

SAAB 9^5

SAAB 9^5

Onward and Upward

The Saab 9^5 represents an enormous improvement over the 9^3, perceived by many drivers as a model that has seen its best days. Part of the reason for this perception is the excessively supple chassis and pronounced torque steer.

Still even the best that Saab has to offer is not quite there yet. These Swedish cars have always been burdened with ungainly silhouettes in the eyes of most people, and designers had been anxious to make the 9^5 look more conventional. All they came up with, however, was a bland-looking car that would have a hard time standing out in a crowd. Certainly there are some changes this year, but they're only visible to the most penetrating eye. To wit, new bumpers and self-cleaning headlights. The rear end is given a number of minor touch-ups.

The cabin remains unaltered, except for the different materials specific to each of the three trim levels. The Linear version comes with the Ecopower 2.3-liter 4-cylinder engine developing 185 hp and 16-inch wheels, cloth seating and in-dash wood appliqués. The Arc version comes with a 3.0-liter V6 producing 200 hp, paired to a 5-speed automatic transmission. It gets leather seating and in-dash wood slats. Finally, there's the Aero version, the fastest of the three, powered by a performance-oriented 2.3-liter Turbo engine developing 250 hp. As it happens, this is the most powerful European front-driver ever offered in North America. It comes with 17-inch alloy wheels, specially tuned suspension (lowered by roughly half an inch), extra-supportive leather seating and a brushed aluminum dashboard.

More horsepower

Slow progress

Styling changes may have been few and subtle, but the 9^5's new mechanical components are anything but. First of all, there's a 5-speed automatic gearbox, robust enough to withstand the extra 20 ponies cranked out by the performance-oriented 2.3-liter engine. This is important because it will allow the Saab to compete head-on with its German rivals.

Unlike Porsche's Tiptronic transmission, the Saab gearbox doesn't boast a manual-shifting feature, consisting instead of three distinct modes: Normal, Sport and Winter.

▲ PROS

• 5-speed automatic gearbox • More powerful Aero model • Practical wagon • Reliability on the rise • Roominess

▼ CONS

• Dealers few and far between • Hard-to use air conditioner • Imprecise manual gearbox shifter • Poor resale value • Substandard ergonomics

In Sport mode, the computer-controlled drive-by-wire throttle system becomes more sensitive to the driver's foot pressure.

Other mechanical improvements include lateral stability control – a first for Saab – a firmed-up suspension and modified steering linkage. The front sub-frame, too, has been lightened and reinforced.

The die is cast

Despite its extra power and better handling capabilities, the Aero is still saddled with its same old irritants – namely, the ignition key, awkwardly mounted on the console and a bad-tempered climate control. You simply can't adjust it. The only thing to do is to set it at "Auto" and let it go at that.

With the extra 20 horsepower, acceleration is convincing. The automatic gearbox is absolutely "businesslike" – electric kick-down is instant and gear-spacing adequate. Torque steer, however, is pronounced, although not as bad as the kind that the Saab Viggen used to inflict on us. The manual gearbox would have benefited from a more precise shift lever linkage and better gear spacing.

The suspension feels a tad firm on bad roads, but that's easy to take when you consider the car's otherwise predictable handling, excellent directional stability and powerful brakes. The lateral stability control system, however, must have been designed more as a preventive rather than corrective measure, as demonstrated by its meek and mild intervention.

There's no denial that the 9.5 is a better car than it used to be. But that's just a first step in the right direction, as Saab plans to expand its lineup with new models.

Denis Duquet

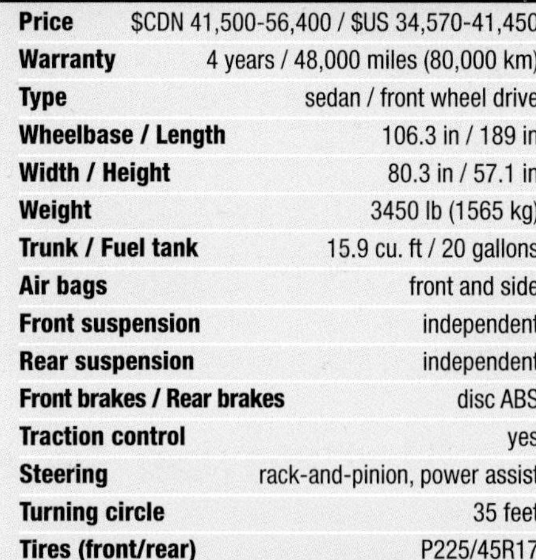

SPECIFICATIONS	9⁵ Aero
Price	$CDN 41,500-56,400 / $US 34,570-41,450
Warranty	4 years / 48,000 miles (80,000 km)
Type	sedan / front wheel drive
Wheelbase / Length	106.3 in / 189 in
Width / Height	80.3 in / 57.1 in
Weight	3450 lb (1565 kg)
Trunk / Fuel tank	15.9 cu. ft / 20 gallons
Air bags	front and side
Front suspension	independent
Rear suspension	independent
Front brakes / Rear brakes	disc ABS
Traction control	yes
Steering	rack-and-pinion, power assist
Turning circle	35 feet
Tires (front/rear)	P225/45R17

PERFORMANCE	
Engine	4L 2.3-liter Turbo
Transmission	5-speed automatic
Horsepower	250 hp at 5500 rpm
Torque	258 lb-ft at 2 500 rpm
Other engines	4L 2.3-liter Turbo 185 hp
	V6 3.0-liter Turbo 200 hp
Other transmission	5-speed manual (except V6)
Acceleration (0-60 mph)	6.8 sec
Maximum speed	149 mph (240 km/h)
Braking (60-0 mph)	133 feet (40.6 m)
Fuel consumption	17 mpg (13.4 L/100 km)

COMPETITION

• Audi A6 2.7T • BMW 530i • Jaguar S-Type V6 • Lexus GS 300 • Lincoln LS • Olds Aurora • Volvo S80

NEW FOR 2002

• 5-speed automatic gearbox • HPT 250-hp engine • Lateral stability system • Modified Aero model

RATING	(out of 5 stars)
Driveability	★★★★
Comfort	★★★★
Reliability	★★★½
Roominess	★★★★
Winter driving rating	★★★★
Safety	★★★★½
Resale value	★★

SAAB 9⁵ **AERO**

SATURN LS

SATURN LW

SATURN **LS**

Patience Is a Virtue

Every time I get behind the wheel of a Saturn, my initial reaction is unfavorable. The engine is as noisy as ever, the driving position is unusual and the front end tends to weave about. Then, after driving it a while things start to fall into place and I gradually grow accustomed to its unusual manners.

Almost everything about this American-made car is different: from its composite body panels to the unique, down-home-style marketing approach GM reserved for it.

Even the most up-to-date Saturn model – the LS, launched two years ago – exhibits the same bothersome traits I noticed during my first Saturn road test 10 years ago, at the wheel of the SL model. Still, the L300 sedan provided for my test drive certainly looked impressive with its 3.0-liter 180-hp V6 and a full complement of standard equipment.

As I left the dealer's parking lot, I deliberately chose a notoriously bumpy road to begin the test drive. Sure enough, I felt torque steer in the wheel almost immediately and the suspension tended to hop about more than the situation warranted. Moreover, the driver's backrest felt inflated, making it hard to find a comfortable driving position. The engine, on the other hand, behaved in an exemplary fashion, offering enough oomph for a smooth, incident-free return journey.

Finally, after 20 minutes or so, my seat felt more comfortable and I was able to find an acceptable driving position. So here's yet another Saturn that becomes more congenial as you add on the miles. Although the front suspension remained stiff, it gradually became more bearable. If you only try the car for a short time, you may find the ride unpleasant. It wouldn't be such a bad idea if Saturn dealers decided to lobby the municipal authorities in their area to improve road conditions.

Serious, but...

The LS proved to be a far superior car to the SL. Still, it could use a better-tuned front suspension. And while they're at it, Saturn might want to revise the dashboard, which looks as if its designers had spent the bulk of their careers at Trabant in the former East Germany, or working for Yugo in the former Yugoslavia. The little notched vent buttons, in particular, have simply got to go. They look all right by themselves, but

▲ PROS

- Complete equipment • Engine options
- Excellent visibility • Large trunk
- Roominess

▼ CONS

- Anonymous appearance • Average tires
- Dull dashboard • Poorly-tuned front suspension
- Some controls need work

don't fit in with the rest of the decor. Ditto for the faux-wood trim, which does absolutely nothing to improve the dash.

In fact, the LS is a quality car handicapped by a host of minor irritants the collective effect of which diminishes the pleasure of driving it. Its look, too, is bland, resembling a Saab designed for the Third World.

Ideal format

The current trend among automakers is to add wagon models to their lineups, especially those in the intermediate category. Saturn, for instance, brought out the LW model two years ago. Unlike its dull-looking sedan sibling, the LW looks decidedly more distinctive with its bold, truncated rear end that compensates for the generic front end.

The LW's format is ideal in terms of size and cargo space. What's more, it's nimble in city traffic and a pleasure to drive on the open road. But, as with everything else in this world, there's room for improvement – namely, the sound insulation and the same annoying problems that saddled the sedan. The V6 engine seems to suit the wagon better, although the base 2.2-liter 4-cylinder with 135 hp is one of the best engines in its category. The manual gearbox, too, is one of the best, except that gearshifting can get hesitant at times.

All in all, both the LS and LW are generally good vehicles, if handicapped by a couple of minor – but easily fixable – mechanical and styling flaws. Now, if only Saturn would go that extra mile and spruce up the cars' looks.

Denis Duquet

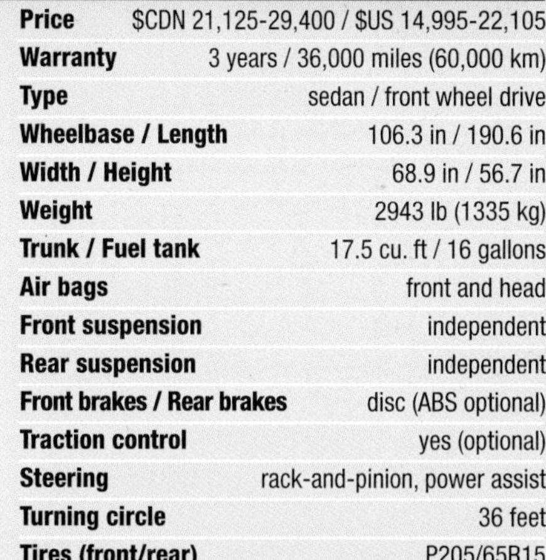

SPECIFICATIONS	**LS1**
Price	$CDN 21,125-29,400 / $US 14,995-22,105
Warranty	3 years / 36,000 miles (60,000 km)
Type	sedan / front wheel drive
Wheelbase / Length	106.3 in / 190.6 in
Width / Height	68.9 in / 56.7 in
Weight	2943 lb (1335 kg)
Trunk / Fuel tank	17.5 cu. ft / 16 gallons
Air bags	front and head
Front suspension	independent
Rear suspension	independent
Front brakes / Rear brakes	disc (ABS optional)
Traction control	yes (optional)
Steering	rack-and-pinion, power assist
Turning circle	36 feet
Tires (front/rear)	P205/65R15

PERFORMANCE	
Engine	4L 2.2-liter
Transmission	5-speed manual
Horsepower	182 hp at 6000 rpm
Torque	184 lb-ft at 3600 rpm
Other engines	4L 2.2-liter 135 hp
Other transmission	5-speed manual
Acceleration (0-60 mph)	10.1 sec
Maximum speed	112 mph (180 km/h)
Braking (60-0 mph)	142 feet (43.4 m)
Fuel consumption	22.7 mpg (10 L/100 km)

COMPETITION

• Honda Accord • Hyundai Sonata • Kia Magentis • Mazda 626 • Nissan Altima • Toyota Camry

NEW FOR 2002

• Head curtain airbags standard • On Star available mid-year • Automatic headlamps standard

RATING	**(out of 5 stars)**
Driveability	★★★
Comfort	★★★½
Reliability	★★★
Roominess	★★★★
Winter driving rating	★★★
Safety	★★★½
Resale value	★★

SATURN **SC**

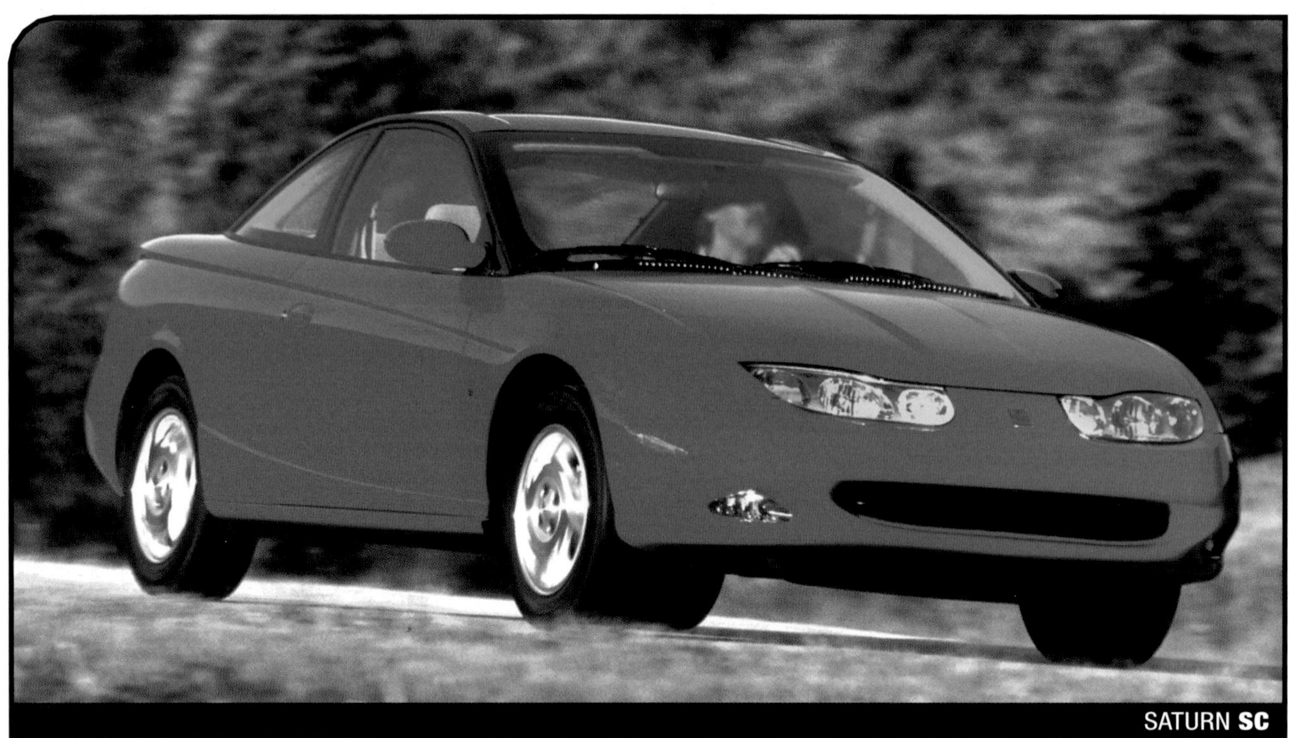

SATURN **SC**

The Case of the Third Door

After a career spanning more than a decade, the venerable Saturn line – both the SL sedan and the SC coupe – will finally be replaced. And none too soon either, although the SC still looks as elegant as ever, disguising its flaws better than the SL. But both cars are starting to show their age and need serious attention.

At this stage of the game, if buyers continue to clamor for more Saturns, it's largely thanks to the automaker's extraordinary after-sales service record. Surveys show that even with its aging models, the Saturn marque consistently ranks number one in terms of customer satisfaction.

Still, all you need to do is get behind the wheel of any SL or SC to realize how hard Saturn's sales force must need to work to please and then hang on to their clients – the cars don't exactly inspire you to go for a spin. On the other hand, the SC does *look* appealing, and is the only coupe with a third – driver-side – door. Granted, the door doesn't make the rear bench any more spacious or comfortable, but it's a practical device for loading up with luggage or for installing your baby in the infant car seat. I'm convinced that the main reason many parents keep their SC rather than replace it with the sedan is because of this door.

Bad vibes

On paper at least, the Saturn sounds fantastic: rigid steel space frame with no-rust polymer body panels, independent four-wheel suspension, up-to-date overhead-camshaft engines with all-aluminum blocks and cylinder heads. But these specifications aren't as impressive as they sound.

Watch your head!

The engines, for example, are incredibly noisy and cause vibrations in the cockpit. Both have the same displacement – 1.9 liters – although the base engine, an SOHC with 100 horsepower, is downright inadequate for a 2-door coupe with sporty aspirations. High revs are an absolute must, but even then engine noise is far more apparent than the level of performance. Things are decidedly better with the 124-hp DOHC version, although engine noise still is a dominant and annoying factor.

Driving a Saturn in a rally or even on a track is a trying experience, especially for

▲ PROS

- Elegant silhouette • Exceptional after-sales service
- Ingenious third door • 124-hp engine
- Polymer body panels

▼ CONS

- Body roll • Dashboard needs work
- Noisy engines • Poor rear visibility
- Uncomfortable front seats

the uninitiated. The car is certainly capable of delivering higher performance levels than others in its category, but you have to "row" hard to get there. You also have to contend with a perfunctory suspension, pronounced body roll and less-than-precise steering.

Come to think of it, the car exhibits pretty much the same kind of behavior on just about any kind of road, namely body roll and pitching. And watch out if you feel in the mood to drive fast and the road is bumpy. The car isn't exactly stable and might even jolt you right out of your seat.

In my opinion, the SC's sole redeeming features are its sporty look and unique third door. However, Saturn also offers a special – in other words, sportier – version, thanks to an accessory package that includes a less restrictive exhaust system, firmer springs and other similar useful upgrades. As promising as it may sound, this version is strictly a temporary measure while you wait for the new generation to come along.

Fortunately, the sport suspension has a relatively supple feel and is a definite asset on rough roads. But cabin comfort is still marginal. Given the coupe's low stance – 2 inches (5 cm) lower than the sedan – you have to bend over before you can slide into the car. Seating room is not exactly generous, especially if you're tall. Added to all this are the dashboard's lackluster gauges and cheap-looking plastic. It's not a pretty sight.

Denis Duquet

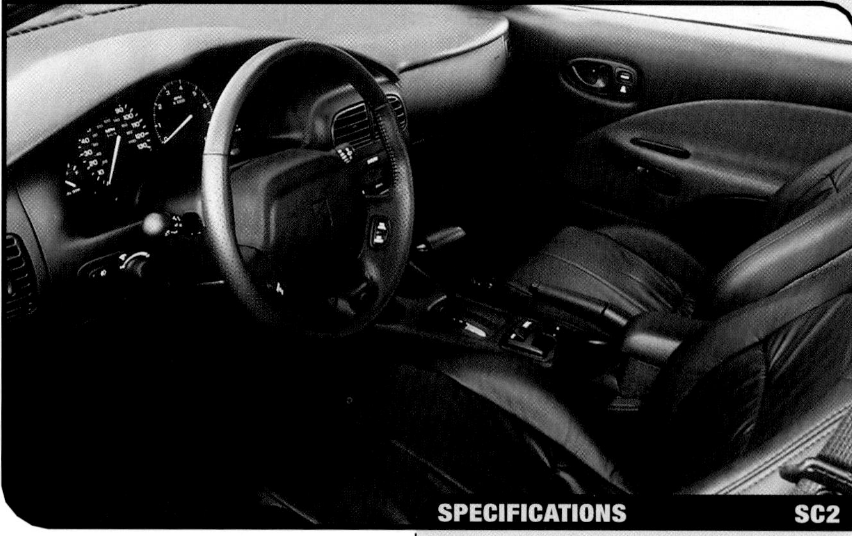

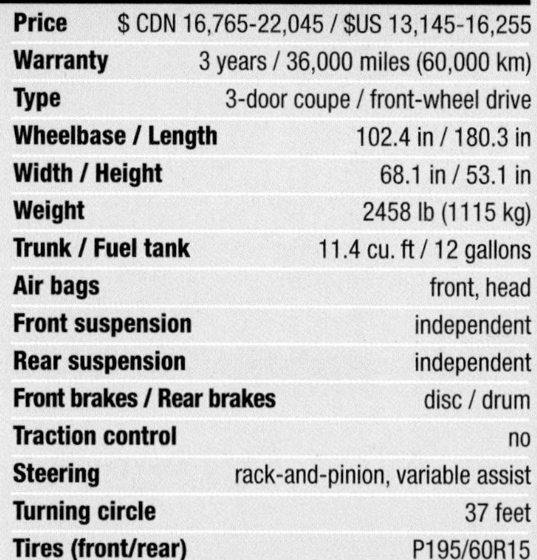

SPECIFICATIONS	**SC2**
Price	$ CDN 16,765-22,045 / $US 13,145-16,255
Warranty	3 years / 36,000 miles (60,000 km)
Type	3-door coupe / front-wheel drive
Wheelbase / Length	102.4 in / 180.3 in
Width / Height	68.1 in / 53.1 in
Weight	2458 lb (1115 kg)
Trunk / Fuel tank	11.4 cu. ft / 12 gallons
Air bags	front, head
Front suspension	independent
Rear suspension	independent
Front brakes / Rear brakes	disc / drum
Traction control	no
Steering	rack-and-pinion, variable assist
Turning circle	37 feet
Tires (front/rear)	P195/60R15

PERFORMANCE	
Engine	4L 1.9-liter DOHC
Transmission	4-speed automatic
Horsepower	124 hp at 5600 rpm
Torque	114 lb-ft at 2400 rpm
Other engines	4L 1.9-liter 100 hp
Other transmission	5-speed manual
Acceleration (0-60 mph)	10.1 sec
Maximum speed	122 mph (195 km/h)
Braking (60-0 mph)	134 feet (40.7 m)
Fuel consumption	25.2 mpg (9 L/100 km)

COMPETITION

• Chevrolet Cavalier / Pontiac Sunfire • Honda Civic coupe • Hyundai Tiburon • Mercury Cougar

NEW FOR 2002

• Dual-tone leather seats in SC2 • New alloy-wheel on SC2 • New body colors • New carpets

RATING	**(out of 5 stars)**
Driveability	★★½
Comfort	★★½
Reliability	★★★½
Roominess	★★★
Winter driving rating	★★★
Safety	★★★
Resale value	★★★

SATURN SL

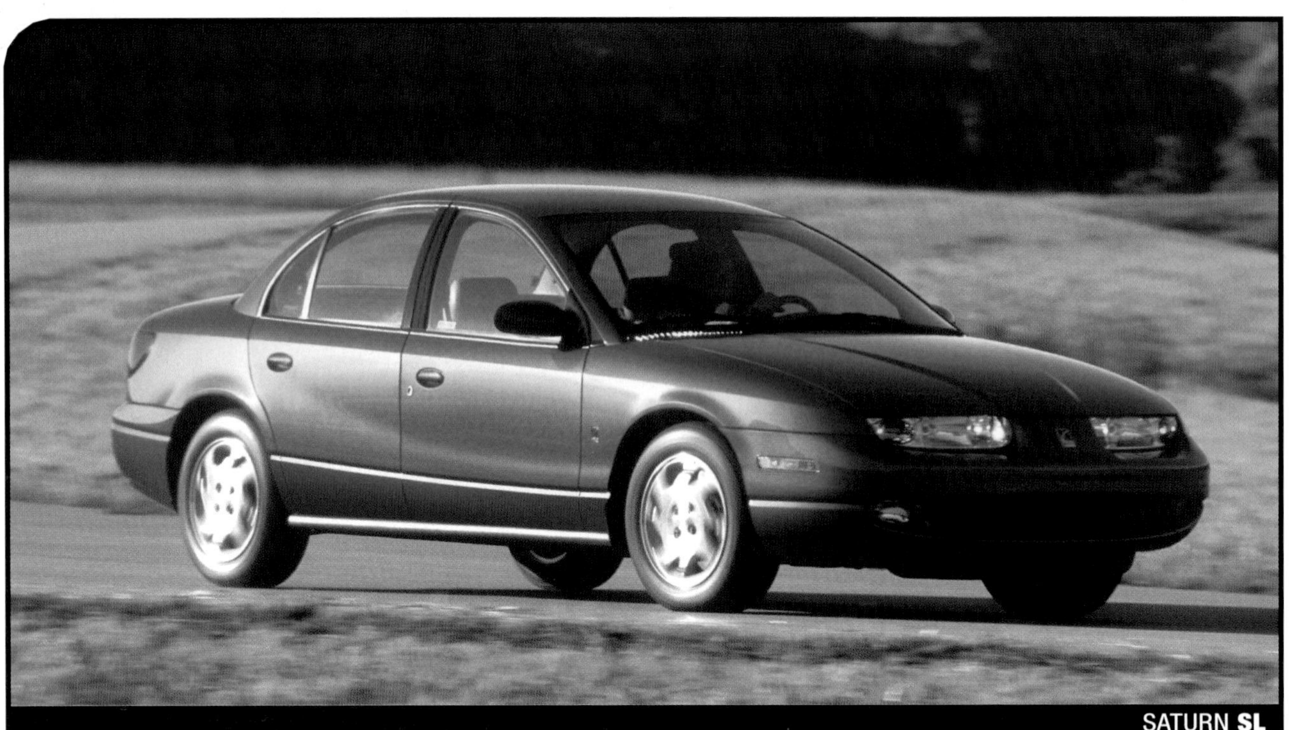

SATURN **SL**

The New-Age T Ford

In his inimitably headstrong way, Henry Ford once declared that because the Model T was perfect as it was, there was no reason ever to change it. This may have been true in 1908, but over the years competition has made giant leaps forward. And the T Ford really looked like a museum piece when production stopped in 1927.

Somewhere at Saturn, a General Motors offspring, a stubborn fellow also seems convinced that the SL models are perfect as they stand. Just like the Model T, the SL series, introduced in 1992, was perfectly adapted to the American market at the time. However, you have to admit that the Saturn SL is no longer in the running. The base engine acquired a few more horses in 1995, the bodywork was revised the following year, and it finally acquired a new dashboard in 2000. All well and good.

But in order to survive in a market dominated by Japanese quality and standards, you have to look for an edge. Particularly so if the asking price is at the same level. I admit that the lines of the S series still manage to hold their own, that the roadholding is quite surprising, and even that the riding comfort is acceptable. However, you can no longer ignore the mediocre performance of the base 1.9-liter SOHC engine, especially the scream of pain that emerges when it's asked to show its stuff. Acceleration from 0-60 mph takes 12 seconds and during that time you wonder if a piston is going to burst though the hood. Strangely, acceleration from 50-75 mph is not bad, and if the volume on the radio (which deserves an honorable mention) is turned up, no one will notice the ruckus. There's another engine on option for the "upscale" (strange word associated with the Saturn) model, which is the SL2. Although sporting the same cubic displacement, it's fitted with two overhead cams and its greater refinement allows it to put out 125 hp, fully 24 horsepower more than its impoverished sibling. Smoother and less noisy, it's the best option.

Thank goodness for the SL2

The automatic gearbox fitted to our test car didn't show the habitual perfection you'd expect from gearboxes built by GM. It would sometimes upshift needlessly, especially when accelerating up a hill. The braking without ABS is acceptable but does overheat when asked to work a little harder. If you want the ABS as standard equipment,

▲ PROS

• Competent and friendly dealers • Great resale value • Rust-resistant bodywork • Surprising roadholding • Truck-like safety in frontal collision

▼ CONS

• Dated look • Poor workmanship • Strange interior design • Third-world base engine • Unusual driving position

you have to go for the SL2. Driving enjoyment increases, but so does the price!

The best feature of the SL is without a doubt its suspension. It's comfortable and roadholding is comforting. It's a pity that the power steering system is a little overassisted and doesn't provide enough feedback. At least, steering is precise. I can imagine that driving an SL with quality tires would be rather pleasant. When pushed to the limit, the SL shows considerable initial roll, but then acquires a set and sticks solidly to the road before developing noticeable understeer. This behavior is more than satisfactory for buyers who are not looking for a sports car.

The interior is nothing to write home about. The top of the dashboard is flat as a plank and, in my humble opinion, really ugly. Not as ugly as the steering wheel, but not far behind. The front seats are set too low for a good driving position and create the impression that the steering wheel is off-center. But, you can get used to it. However, it's much more difficult to accept the poor workmanship. What happened to all these assembly-line workers who ten years ago kept talking about "the Saturn pride"? Some rubber joints were badly installed in our car and a bit of plastic was just hanging there under the dashboard on the passenger's side, the console seemed about ready to drop, sometimes to the right, sometimes to the left.

Not enough time

What's most surprising though, is this lack of refinement, as if it were some pre-production model the design department hadn't had time to finish completely. It's true that the SL has only been in production for ten years, yet no one has found the time to put a cap on the screws that hold the armrests to the doors. And no one has yet noticed that the rubber fitted around the door locks really looks rather crude.

For many people, the main attraction of a Saturn is its polymer bodywork, which can resist small knocks and rust. Furthermore, in spite of being made of plastic, Saturns have proved to be solid and have scored maximum points (10/10) in frontal collision tests. The resale value makes the SL worthy of a closer look.

Yep, in the end, the T Ford had an end. It's alleged that the Saturn S Series will be completely redesigned in 2003. Let's wait and see.

Alain Morin

SPECIFICATIONS

Price	$CDN 14,245-18,125 / $US 11,035-14,755
Warranty	3 years / 36,000 miles (60,000 km)
Type	sedan / front wheel drive
Wheelbase / Length	102.3 in / 178 in
Width / Height	66.5 in / 55.1 in
Weight	2377 lb (1078 kg)
Trunk / Fuel tank	12.1 cu. ft / 12 gallons
Air bags	front
Front suspension	independent
Rear suspension	independent
Front brakes / Rear brakes	disc / drum (ABS opt.)
Traction control	yes (optional)
Steering	rack-and-pinion, variable assist
Turning circle	37 feet
Tires (front/rear)	P185/65R14

PERFORMANCE

Engine	4L 1.9-liter
Transmission	4-speed automatic
Horsepower	100 hp at 5000 rpm
Torque	114 lb-ft at 2400 rpm
Other engines	4L 1.9-liter 124 hp
Other transmission	5-speed manual
Acceleration (0-60 mph)	12 sec
Maximum speed	103 mph (165 km/h)
Braking (60-0 mph)	141 feet (43 m)
Fuel consumption	28.7 mpg (7.9 L/100 km)

COMPETITION

- Civic • Corolla • Elantra • Focus • Neon
- Nubira • Protegé • Sentra

NEW FOR 2002

- New colors • New hubcaps (SL2)

RATING (out of 5 stars)

Driveability	★★★
Comfort	★★★★
Reliability	★★★½
Roominess	★★★½
Winter driving rating	★★★½
Safety	★★★★
Resale value	★★★★

SATURN VUE

SATURN **VUE**

A Latecomer

Saturn, a division of General Motors, has always been slow to change and introduce cars. For instance, more than a decade slipped by before it launched a mid-size companion to its sub-compact model, the SL, which was itself long overdue for an overhaul by then. And despite the nearly unanimous public clamor for sport-utility vehicles that's been raging for years, it's only now that Saturn has decided to enter the fray.

Too little, too late? Better late than never? Only time will tell. Still, let's take a positive approach and applaud the arrival of the Saturn VUE, only two years after the LS. That's an improvement! Predictably, the new all-terrain vehicle also shares a particular characteristic with all other Saturn cars, past and present: the use of dent-resistant polymer body panels.

Assembled in Spring Hill, Tenn., the VUE has its own, exclusive platform, according to the Saturn folks. But other sources claim that it's based on the new Pontiac Vibe compact wagon. We decided to find out for ourselves, and after a quick glance at the LW's technical specs, we were convinced that Saturn was indeed exclusive.

The VUE comes in two engine versions: the standard 2.2-liter inline-4 DOHC engine with 138 hp and a 5-speed manual transmission (front-wheel and all-wheel drive configurations), or a 3.0-liter V6 with 181 hp coupled to a 5-speed automatic (all-wheel-drive only). Incidentally, the 2.2-liter engine is one of the most efficient in its category and has been used in several Saturn models over the years, most recently in the LS and LW.

Furthermore, Saturn went one up on all its rivals by offering the first ever continuously variable transmission (CVT) in a North American sport-utility vehicle. Available only with the 2.2-liter engine, CVT can be ordered either with front-wheel or all-wheel drive.

A good bet

And speaking of all-wheel drive, it's none other than the ubiquitous Versatrak system, used in several 2002 GM models. Somewhat similar to the system that's employed in the Ford Escape/Mazda Tribute, Versatrak is noted for its use of an internal hydraulic pump, providing a faster reaction time. Boasting independent four-wheel suspension, the VUE is guaranteed

▲ PROS

- All wheel drive • Polymer panels
- Renowned customer service
- SVTi transmission • Up-to-date engines

▼ CONS

- Rear 70/30 split bench • Trunk space limited by wheel wells • Uncomfortable front seats • Unproven reliability

to provide adequate comfort for long trips. Its closest rivals in this SUV corner of the market, incidentally, are the Honda CR-V and Toyota RAV4.

Standing out in a crowd

Although Saturn cars have shattered all records in terms of popularity, customer satisfaction and sales over the years, design has never been a strong selling point. In fact, except for its station wagons, Saturn's sense of style has always been debatable. Until the VUE, that is. It has the kind of looks that will appeal to a great many car buffs.

Indeed, the VUE's exterior shows that the Spring Hill, Tenn., design team have done their homework carefully and thoroughly. It's instantly recognizable as a Saturn, yet has its own visual personality, featuring a body-colored horizontal bar between large rectangular headlamps, strong flares over the wheels and a subtle swoosh along the lower body sides.

The cockpit is a far cry from that of the Saturn L series, and that's an excellent thing. Gauges and controls are sensibly placed and displayed for quick and easy access. And thanks goodness Saturn has finally done away with the jagged-wheel vent control that drove so many drivers mad. The front seats come with bulging backrests and so comfort is not their strong suit. At least the passenger side backrest folds flat and features a durable scuff-resistant surface, so objects like a ladder or surfboard can be carried inside the vehicle. The rear bench seat is a 70/30 fold-down design, so you can tailor the space exactly as you see fit, although I'm personally convinced that a 60/40 configuration would have been more practical. Finally, if it hadn't been for the wheel wells, trunk space would have been vast. Still, it's generous enough as it is.

The new Saturn VUE has all it takes to carve out its own niche in the increasingly crowded SUV field: tried-and-true drivetrain (inherited from the successful SL/SW line), appealing design, various engine and transmission options, and versatility.

Denis Duquet

SPECIFICATIONS

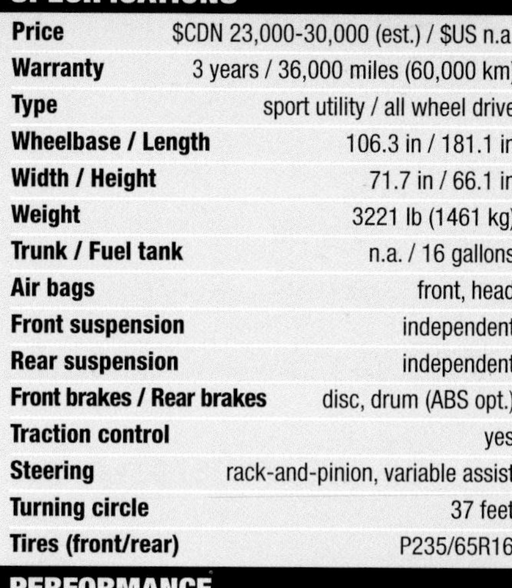

Price	$CDN 23,000-30,000 (est.) / $US n.a.
Warranty	3 years / 36,000 miles (60,000 km)
Type	sport utility / all wheel drive
Wheelbase / Length	106.3 in / 181.1 in
Width / Height	71.7 in / 66.1 in
Weight	3221 lb (1461 kg)
Trunk / Fuel tank	n.a. / 16 gallons
Air bags	front, head
Front suspension	independent
Rear suspension	independent
Front brakes / Rear brakes	disc, drum (ABS opt.)
Traction control	yes
Steering	rack-and-pinion, variable assist
Turning circle	37 feet
Tires (front/rear)	P235/65R16

PERFORMANCE

Engine	4L 2.2-liter
Transmission	5-speed manual
Horsepower	138 hp at 5600 rpm
Torque	145 lb-ft at 4000 rpm
Other engines	V6 3.0-liter 181 hp
Other transmission	5-speed automatic; CVT (4-cylinder)
Acceleration (0-60 mph)	10.8 sec
Maximum speed	112 mph (180 km/h)
Braking (60-0 mph)	n.a.
Fuel consumption	22.2 mpg (4-cyl.) (10.2 L/100km)

COMPETITION

- Chevrolet Tracker/Suzuki Grand Vitara
- Honda CR-V • Jeep Liberty • Toyota RAV4

NEW FOR 2002

- All-new model • CVT with 2.2-liter engine

RATING (out of 5 stars)

Driveability	Insufficient data
Comfort	
Reliability	
Roominess	
Winter driving rating	
Safety	
Resale value	

SUBARU FORESTER

SUBARU **FORESTER**

Category Leader

Since its launch in fall 1997, the Subaru Forester has raised the bar in its category, thanks to an engine that's more powerful than the competition's.

The Forester has twice beaten its rivals to scoop first place in *The Auto Guide* comparison tests, in 1998 and 2000. But things change rapidly in this ultracompetitive field, and today new players – some sporting 4- to 6-cylinder engines – have entered the fray (Ford Escape/Mazda Tribute, Hyundai SantaFe, Jeep Liberty), while others have been thoroughly revised (Toyota RAV4), so much so that the Forester has lost its edge.

In order to stand out, Subaru plays the hybrid card – a term that crops up regularly in the auto industry these days. But the Forester should rather be seen as a cross between a car and a traditional SUV. Some say it's closer to the former and they're not all wrong – the Forester is based on the Impreza platform and has the lowest ground clearance in its class.

But all this is a double-edged sword. Critics now fault the Forester for its low ground clearance. Not that it needs to be higher – it never ventures off the beaten path anyway. When you ask these same critics what the problem is, the argument is pretty lame: "For me, a 4X4 has to be high up."

Another common response: "Oh yeah, the Forester, sure, but it doesn't look so hot!" An assessment that is by no means unanimous, but in a competitive field, such remarks can make all the difference at decision time.

The blandness

What the creators of the Forester set out to do was to make it feel and ride like a car. They certainly did this by focussing on a lower center of gravity and a car-based platform. Cabin comfort and car-like road manners, not usually SUV strong points, are what the Forester is noted for.

In first place

As for the drivetrain, the Forester has proven its reliability. Redesigned last year, the model retains all the main mechanical features and boasts subtle styling changes that only a pair of very sharp eyes can discern (new body panels and grille).

Unfortunately, Subaru has also succumbed to the blandness trap that has wreaked havoc throughout the Japanese auto industry. Take steering feel and response, for example. Until recently, it was a model for others to follow. Today, it lacks

▲ PROS

• Balanced handling • Efficient all-wheel drive • Overall comfort • Tried and true mechanicals • Well-conceived vehicle

▼ CONS

• Body roll • High fuel consumption for a 4-cylinder • Lackluster interior • Overassisted steering • Unstable in crosswinds

precision and feels as if it were encased in molasses! The suspension, which Subaru claimed to have firmed up, is anything but, as demonstrated by the body lean in corners.

Nevertheless the suspension provides first-class comfort and the Forester rides as smoothly as a comfortable sedan, showing off exemplary road manners. No surprise here, really, since the Legacy and the Impreza – both Forester's cousins – are brilliant performers. Superior pedigree simply will not be denied.

An old acquaintance lurks under the hood, the Subaru all-purpose 2.5-liter 4-cylinder boxer engine, whose opposed-piston design is one of the Forester's major assets. Although its performance is best described as adequate, the engine offers enough power and torque to keep its class lead. Only a few V6-equipped rivals provide superior performance. Fuel consumption, however, is closer to that of a V6 rather than a 4-cylinder.

As for those who hope to find the Outback's 6-cylinder under the Forester's hood, they can forget about it, at least until the next redesign, scheduled for 2004.

Happy medium

As noted earlier, there's no consensus regarding the Forester's look. Moreover, its square shape makes it vulnerable to side winds. The interior isn't much to look at either, though the cabin has been redecorated. The high end Limited model is better, thanks to leather and wood trim on the dashboard and center console.

Be that as it may, connoisseurs among buyers can look past esthetic considerations and admire the cabin's practical qualities: flawless ergonomics, ample storage space as well as above-average roominess. As expected from Japan, overall finish and assembly quality more than compensate for the interior's lack of originality.

Beyond its prestigious pedigree, the Forester is brilliantly conceived: half-car, half-SUV, it ranks halfway between the mini and the midsize SUVs in terms of size, cabin and engine. The happy medium (see comparison match).

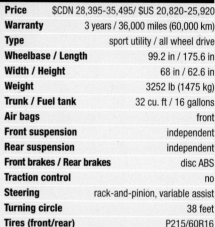

SPECIFICATIONS	**S Limited**
Price	$CDN 28,395-35,495/ $US 20,820-25,920
Warranty	3 years / 36,000 miles (60,000 km)
Type	sport utility / all wheel drive
Wheelbase / Length	99.2 in / 175.6 in
Width / Height	68 in / 62.6 in
Weight	3252 lb (1475 kg)
Trunk / Fuel tank	32 cu. ft / 16 gallons
Air bags	front
Front suspension	independent
Rear suspension	independent
Front brakes / Rear brakes	disc ABS
Traction control	no
Steering	rack-and-pinion, variable assist
Turning circle	38 feet
Tires (front/rear)	P215/60R16

PERFORMANCE	
Engine	4H 2.5-liter
Transmission	4-speed automatic
Horsepower	165 hp at 5600 rpm
Torque	162 lb-ft at 4000 rpm
Other engines	none
Other transmission	5-speed manual
Acceleration (0-60 mph)	9.8 sec
Maximum speed	109 mph (175 km/h)
Braking (60-0 mph)	133 feet (40.6 m)
Fuel consumption	18.9 mpg (12 L/100 km)

COMPETITION

- CR-V • Grand Vitara • Liberty • RAV4
- Tribute/Escape • XTerra

NEW FOR 2002

- Optional Sport package

RATING	**(out of 5 stars)**
Driveability	★★★½
Comfort	★★★★
Reliability	★★★★
Roominess	★★★½
Winter driving rating	★★★★★
Safety	★★★★
Resale value	★★★★

SUBARU IMPREZA SUBARU OUTBACK SPORT

SUBARU **IMPREZA 2.5TS**

Trademark Revival

Subaru's jewel in the crown for 2002 is unquestionably the WRX Turbo, a much anticipated model whose reputation clearly preceded its arrival – judging from the huge crowd at the Subaru stand at the latest Detroit Auto Show. But the new Impreza lineup also includes a number of lesser models and they, too, teem with interesting features. What follows is an account of our week spent behind the wheel of the new Impreza 2.5 TS Sport Wagon.

The popularity of compact wagons is nothing new so far as Subaru is concerned. After all, the Japanese automaker has been producing them for a long time. For 2002, in addition to the WRX Turbo, Impreza comes in two wagon versions (2.5 TS Sport Wagon and Outback Sport) and a 4-door sedan (2.5 RS). All three models are fitted with a 2.5-liter flat-4 engine and, of course, full-time all-wheel drive, Subaru's trademark.

Boxer engine: versatile but greedy

Revised and toned up last year, Subaru's boxer engine provides plenty of power and torque, as our test model demonstrated with its peppier starts and more vigorous acceleration – more than usual for cars in this price range (50 to 75 mph in 8.5 seconds). Moreover, given the considerable torque, manual transmission is well suited to this Sport Wagon model, enhancing its remarkably versatile flat-4 engine still further. The only discordant note here is the high fuel consumption: 21 mpg. While it's better than it used to be, thanks in large measure to torque distribution – which favors the front wheels in normal driving conditions – it's still higher than what other same-sized front-drivers consume. But that's the price you have to pay for the extra safety provided by full-time all-wheel drive.

More desirable than ever

I have yet to meet an automobile journalist who hasn't been happy singing the praises of Subaru's all-wheel drive system: "Superior motor function on slippery surfaces," they all write, "better handling and, as a result, greater active safety," and, of course, the all-important detail – the possibility of wandering off to places where most front- and rear- drivers fear to tread. The 2002 model includes all these qualities and more, such as a more rigid body and even better-tuned suspensions, which make Impreza's handling capabilities stand out in even starker contrast in comparison

▲ PROS

- Versatile and powerful engine • Excellent active safety • Fun to drive • Improved brakes • Affordable price

▼ CONS

- Some accessories need work
- Above average fuel consumption
- Useless armrest • Some body rattles

with its front-drive rivals. Despite the excellent rigidity, however, we did detect some body rattling in our test Impreza, although we couldn't quite pinpoint exactly where the noise was coming from.

Steering is precise and the wheel, which literally floated into my hands, made the Wagon more fun to drive, even inspired me to try ... dare I utter the word ... sport-driving it. Even the brakes – considered a weak point in the previous version – were up to the job. It was a pleasant surprise to see that all Imprezas come with vented front disc/rear drum brakes with ABS as standard equipment, a rare situation in this category. And whoever tells you that rear drum brakes make no difference doesn't know what he, or she, is talking about.

Aluminum look

Inside, we can report that Impreza designers have done their best to jazz up the dashboard with plastic trim painted to look like aluminum. The rest is pretty much traditional stuff, except for the driver's seat, which is height-adjustable – a good thing. The front seats are decent and have good support. The rear looks comfortable and roomy enough, though the seats are still a little on the high side.

Equipment-wise, all essential features are present: power windows, locks and mirrors (with de-icer, but no remote control), air conditioning, tilt-adjust steering wheel, intermittent windshield wipers front and rear. If I had a personal wish list, I'd ask for larger buttons for the AM/FM/CD sound system, a cargo-area tray, and a remote control for operating the tailgate. I'd also remove the central armrest, which seems to have no practical value.

Styling is typically Subaru: not so bad, but not great either. Fortunately, the big, fake air intake in the previous model has been removed from the normally aspirated Imprezas. But can someone please do something about that disgraceful muffler that droops conspicuously from beneath the back end of the car?

If you decide to buy the Impreza 2.5 TS, I'd suggest you pay extra to have fog lamps installed, if only to get rid of those humongous "Tupperware-looking" covers. No doubt about it, the Impreza 2.5 TS is one of the most desirable station wagons on the market today.

Alain Raymond

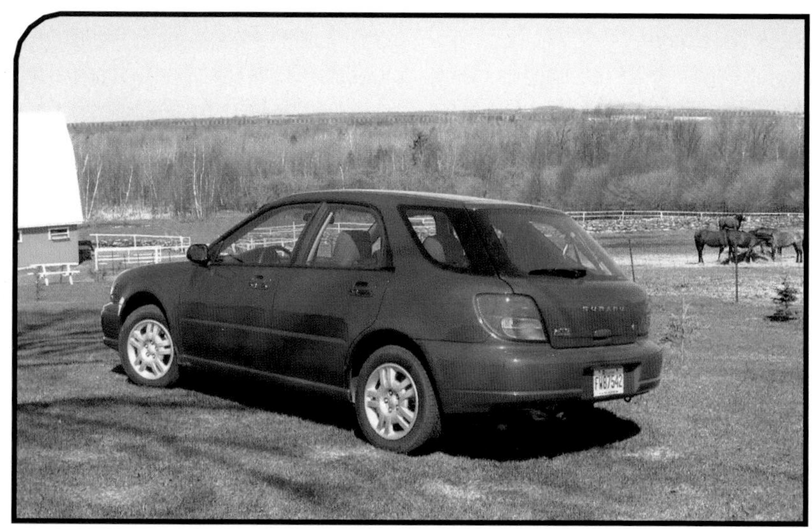

SPECIFICATIONS	**2.5TS**
Price	$CDN 21,995-22,995/ $US 18,020-19,220
Warranty	3 years / 36,000 miles (60,000 km)
Type	wagon / all wheel drive
Wheelbase / Length	99.2 in / 173.4 in
Width / Height	66.7 in / 58.5 in
Weight	3045 lb (1381 kg)
Trunk / Fuel tank	23.8 to 61.6 cu. ft / 16 gallons
Air bags	front
Front suspension	independent
Rear suspension	independent
Front brakes / Rear brakes	disc / disc ABS
Traction control	no
Steering	rack-and-pinion, variable assist
Turning circle	33 feet
Tires (front/rear)	P195/60R15

PERFORMANCE	
Engine	4H 2.5-liter 16-valve
Transmission	4-speed automatic
Horsepower	165 hp at 5600 rpm
Torque	166 lb-ft at 4000 rpm
Other engines	none
Other transmission	5-speed manual
Acceleration (0-60 mph)	9.5 sec
Maximum speed	118 mph (190 km/h)
Braking (60-0 mph)	133 feet (40.6 m)
Fuel consumption	21 mpg (10.8 L/100 km)

COMPETITION

• PT Cruiser • Nubira wagon • Focus ZX5 • CR-V
• Protegé5 • Saturn SW2 • Esteem wagon • RAV4

NEW FOR 2002

New model

RATING	**(out of 5 stars)**
Driveability	★★★★
Comfort	★★★½
Reliability	★★★★★
Roominess	★★★★
Winter driving rating	★★★★½
Safety	★★★★
Resale value	★★★★★

SUBARU IMPREZA WRX

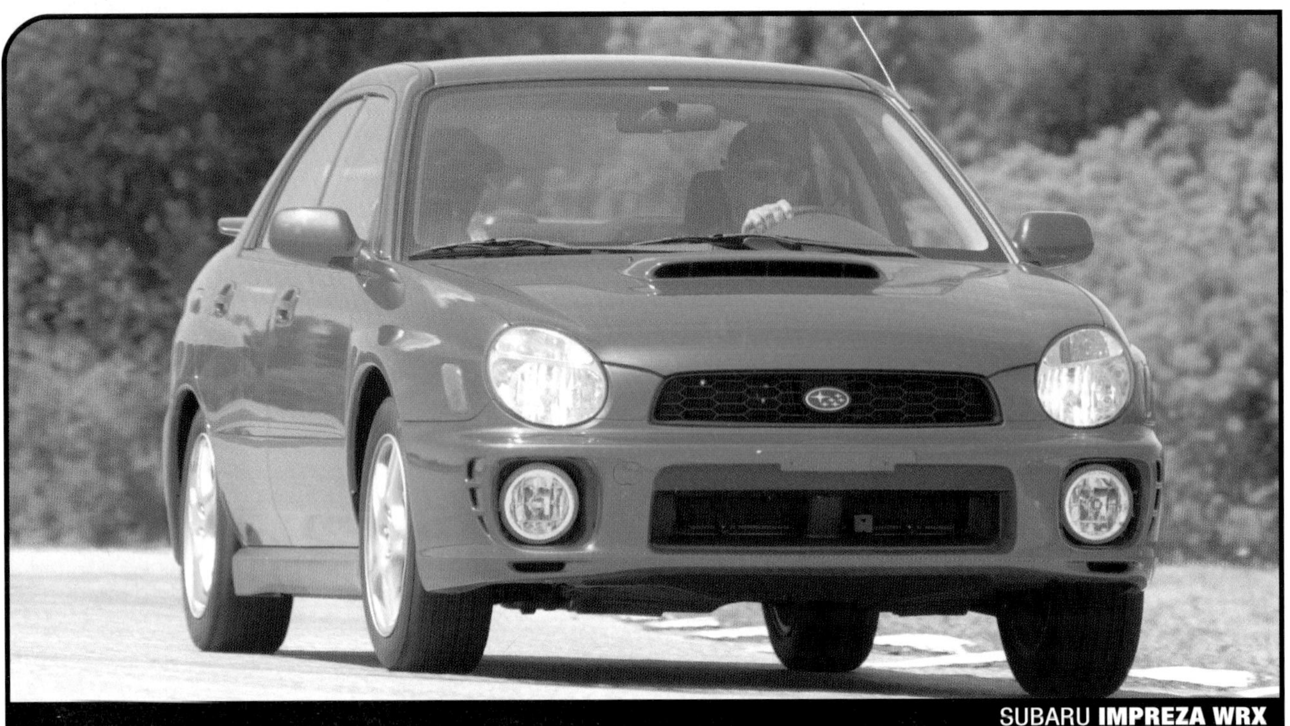

SUBARU **IMPREZA WRX**

Bye Bye Boxster

God knows I enjoy thumbing my nose at BMW drivers while driving my innocent little Subaru. The new Subaru Impreza line includes five distinct models – three wagons and two sedans. At the bottom of the list are the RS sedan, as well as the TS and Outback wagons – all three fitted with a 2.5-liter flat-4 engine producing 165 hp. But it's the remaining two models that got me excited – the WRX sedan and wagon, both basking in World-Rally-Championship glory, which Subaru has won three times with a rally version of the WRX.

For 2002, not only has the Japanese maker revitalized its Impreza line with totally revamped cars, but in the process has managed to shed its reputation as carmaker for the wannabe rural crowd. Ironically, it's the rough and tough back country – the favored venue for major international car rallies – that gave birth to the road version of the WRX Turbo. Drawn from those blue with gold trim Subies that racked up victory after victory on various back roads scattered around the globe, the WRX sedan and wagon are probably the brashest sub-compacts ever sold on the free market.

Slick little baby

Now that the Audi S4 has found its match, what about the BMW 330i and all those sports cars without the all-wheel drive they need to showcase their performances? Take note, this WRX can take on the Porsche Boxster anytime, or a slew of other contenders, all the while saving you big bucks – say, 30 grand and up. At first glance, though, the WRX looks distinctly umimpressive, since its 2.0-liter flat-four engine has to work its way up the rev range before its 227 hp kicks in, and the turbocharger is a little slow in responding. But pull out your stopwatch, and what you'll see will boggle your mind! With a ravishing vroooom, the slick WRX spools up past 7000 rpm in no time, and propels you from 0-60 mph in roughly 6 seconds. In fact, things start to get interesting at 4000 rpms. The car's all-wheel drive really puts the power to the ground without the slightest protest from the tires. All this can be a little hard on the clutch, so don't try too many explosive starts in a row. The shift lever, too, can get a bit stiff, though not enough to make me switch to the automatic gearbox which, along with traction control, is optional.

Enjoy it while you can

▲ PROS

• Fantastic engine (WRX) • Incredible road manners • Solid chassis • Excellent seats • Seasoned sports car

▼ CONS

• Stiff shift lever • Uncomfortable suspension • Cheesy interior • Flimsy sheetmetal • Brakes need improvement

Steering is responsive, making it easy to exploit the WRX's driveability and appreciate its excellent road manners. Caught in a snowstorm at one point, I tackled an exit ramp much faster than normal and let the car do all the work. Any novice could turn into a rally champ in that car. There was no body roll and the tire grip was amazing. The suspension is firm, but it is the limited amount of up-and-down wheel travel that makes driving on bad roads a trying experience. Your spine will take a painful beating as the car bottoms in major heaves while the potholes will finish off the job by crushing your vertebrae. Thank goodness for the bucket seats, which are comfortably snug and provide excellent lateral support during cornering.

If the WRX seems glued to the road, it's partly thanks to the rigid chassis, whose torsional rigidity has been increased by a whopping 147%. The car could use higher rated tires for better handling on the road or track. Braking, while adequate under normal driving conditions, could use a little upgrading to reduce the rather long stopping distances at speeds of 60 mph and up.

With its big round eyes, this Subaru is nothing much to look at and its rear deck spoiler adds nothing to the overall appearance. But the rocker panel and the enormous aluminum air intake on the hood are serious stuff. The latter feeds fresh air into the air-to-air intercooler, thus energizing the little 2.0-liter engine.

Inside, the cute Momo steering wheel and the aluminum racer-type pedals look smart, but the effect is spoiled by the cheap trim around the plastic center console painted gray to resemble aluminum. The dash, too, could look a little less cheesy, and should include an oil-pressure gauge and, most of all, a turbo boost pressure gauge indicator.

Finally, only when I closed the trunk's lid did I discover a less than heartening aspect of this WRX: the sheet metal felt so flimsy it made me wonder about its long-term resistance.

For now, however, the little Subaru Impreza WRX is to sport sedans what the Corvette is to sports cars. The hands-down winner of the price/value ratio award.

Jacques Duval

SPECIFICATIONS	**WRX**
Price	$CDN 34,995 / $US 24,020-24,520
Warranty	3 years / 36,000 miles (60,000 km)
Type	5-seat sport sedan / all wheel drive
Wheelbase / Length	99.4 in / 173.4 in
Width / Height	68 in / 57 in
Weight	3084 lb (1399 kg)
Trunk / Fuel tank	11 cu. ft / 16 gallons
Air bags	front and side
Front suspension	independent
Rear suspension	independent
Front brakes / Rear brakes	disc (vented, front) ABS
Traction control	yes (automatic only)
Steering	rack-and-pinion, variable assist
Turning circle	34.1 feet
Tires (front/rear)	P205/55R16

PERFORMANCE	
Engine	4H 2-liter turbo
Transmission	5-speed manual
Horsepower	227 hp at 6000 rpm
Torque	217 lb-ft at 4000 rpm
Other engines	4H 2.5-liter 165 hp (see other text)
Other transmission	5-speed automatic
Acceleration (0-60 mph)	6.8 sec
Maximum speed	140 mph (225 km/h)
Braking (60-0 mph)	133.2 ft (40.6 m)
Fuel consumption	19.7 mpg (11.5 L/100 km)

COMPETITION

• Audi S4 • BMW 330Xi • VW Passat 4-Motion

NEW FOR 2002

• New model

RATING	**(out of 5 stars)**
Driveability	★★★★½
Comfort	★★★½
Reliability	New model
Roominess	★★★
Winter driving rating	★★★★
Safety	★★★★
Resale value	New model

SUBARU LEGACY

SUBARU **LEGACY GT Limited**

Bring on the blizzard!

I hate winter. There's no two ways about it. During the first five or six years of my life, Santa Claus used to work things out for me. But after that, it's been all downhill. Now, 35 years later, I find myself longing for a snowstorm just to see how far I can go with a Subaru Legacy.

It's too bad that the general public seems to favor the Outback (the subject of an independent test) at the expense of the Legacy, a capable all-wheel-drive car worthy of serious attention.

Legacys are available as wagons or sedans. Both models come in three trim levels – the wagon as Brighton (a lovely name that's wasted on a base model, in my opinion), L and GT; the sedans as L, GT and GT Limited.

Mud and slush: what fun!

Normally, 70% of the power is routed to the front wheels. But this percentage changes as soon as a wheel begins to lose traction. Both the GT and GT Limited feature a self-locking rear differential, which is a big plus in difficult road conditions. A drive around a sand pit convinced us of the advantages of the system. Admittedly, as the Legacy's ground clearance is just slightly higher than that of a two-wheel-drive car, there is no point trying to compete with a Jeep. Still, the Legacy was able to get through where a "normal" automobile would have bogged down. The torque is there when you need it, and I can imagine that, with a good set of winter tires, Legacy's capabilities must be impressive. Let it snow, anytime!

And reliable, to boot

The word Subaru is often associated with the "boxer" engine; that is, with cylinders horizontally opposed, giving it a lower center of gravity than an in-line or V-shaped engine. This engine type has never been known either for smoothness or high performance. Worse, the Legacy's 165-hp 2.5-liter 4-cylinder has to contend with a 3500-lb mass (1590 kg), and its fuel consumption suffers as a result – 18 mph (12 liters per 100 km). Acceleration is barely adequate, and responsiveness unspectacular at best. An extra 20 horsepower would not be too much! The automatic transmission seems to work well, but it tends to hunt around for a gear when going up a hill, and the zigzag selector gate proves to be more of a nuisance than a practical aid.

▲ PROS

• Excellent winter car • Good roadholding • Guaranteed reliability • Superior riding comfort • Well-equipped

▼ CONS

• Barely adequate power • Difficult driver access • High fuel consumption • Some body noises • Wind noise

Maybe there is a Santa Claus after all?

The ABS disk brakes – improved this year – are impressive, both in terms of smoothness and the ease with which you can modulate braking effort. The steering system gave good feedback despite a slight lack of tautness when centered. Add to all this a rigid chassis and a well-balanced suspension and you'll feel the urge to drive it more spiritedly. How things have changed! Now, it's a joy to push a Subaru around a curve, which it negotiates with remarkable aplomb. Body roll is extremely well controlled: there is no collapsing or diving of the suspension and the roll angle is not excessive. At the limit, slight understeer occurs, but it's easily controlled.

Driving a Legacy is a pleasant experience. The cabin is well sound-proofed, seats are firm but comfortable, plastic fixtures are of a good quality and the radio, though modest, produces excellent sound. But, as always, there's a minus column: the frameless windows could be a little more watertight, access to the driver's seat is a little tricky, the rear backrests cannot be lowered (there's just a ski storage opening), the trunk and fuel cap opening controls are difficult to reach and the front left-hand door gives off a noticeable rattle.

Still, these are minor details. If you like to drive and you detest winter, then a Legacy must be on your wish list. It's more refined, safer and more coherent than many pseudo sport-utilities.

Alain Morin

SPECIFICATIONS	GT Limited
Price	$CDN 24,295-34,395 / $US 19,790-24,890
Warranty	3 years / 36,000 miles (60,000 km)
Type	sedan / all wheel drive
Wheelbase / Length	104.3 in / 184.6 in
Width / Height	77.2 in / 55.9 in
Weight	3399 lb (1542 kg)
Trunk / Fuel tank	12.4 cu. ft / 17 gallons
Air bags	front
Front suspension	independent
Rear suspension	independent
Front brakes / Rear brakes	disc ABS
Traction control	no
Steering	rack-and-pinion, power assist
Turning circle	37 feet
Tires (front/rear)	P205/55R16

PERFORMANCE	
Engine	4H 2.5-liter
Transmission	4-speed automatic
Horsepower	165 hp at 5600 rpm
Torque	166 lb-ft at 4000 rpm
Other engines	none
Other transmission	5-speed manual
Acceleration (0-60 mph)	8.5 sec
Maximum speed	127 mph (205 km/h)
Braking (60-0 mph)	139 feet (42.3 m)
Fuel consumption	18.9 mpg (12 L/100 km)

COMPETITION

• Audi A4 1.8T • Volkswagen Passat

NEW FOR 2002

• Improved brake system • Standard brakes with ABS in Brighton • Two new colors • Minor changes in cabin

RATING	(out of 5 stars)
Driveability	★★★½
Comfort	★★★★
Reliability	★★★★
Roominess	★★★½
Winter driving rating	★★★★★
Safety	★★★★
Resale value	★★★

SUBARU OUTBACK

SUBARU **OUTBACK**

A winning formula

Once upon a time, Subaru cars looked bland and unattractive, but over the years they've become the "in" thing. Their inherent sturdiness and 4-wheel drive combined with a few marketing ploys have rescued them from virtual anonymity. In 1995, one of the Subaru's better strategic decisions was to bring out a new line called Outback, accurately aimed at a need for adventure, leisure and driving relaxation.

It's hardly surprising that Subaru is still focussing on this steadily growing market segment. Based on the Legacy, the Outback line now includes seven distinct sedan and wagon models, two of which are recent entries – the H6 3.0 and H6 3.0 VDC sedans. The acronym stands for Vehicle Dynamics Control, an impressive system that works harmoniously with variable torque distribution, all-wheel drive and traction control, as I discovered during a climb up a muddy ski slope. Of course, the heavy-duty fully independent suspension, M & S (mud and snow) tires, and high ground clearance are also assets in such conditions. In addition to the 212-hp flat-6 engine that was introduced last year on both the sedan and wagon, the Outback line includes two other wagon models and a sedan, powered by a flat-4 engine rating 165 hp.

In good company

Our most vocal criticism of the new Outback H6 last year was its steep sticker price, which placed it in the company of such high-end models as the Audi A4, Jaguar X-type and BMW 325i. To find out how our gutsy little Subaru sedan measured up to such formidable competition, see our comparison test in Part I of the *Auto Guide.*

Winter carnival queen

Let's concentrate on the H6 3.0 VDC wagon instead, which we also tested. Despite its extra 47 hp, the new engine didn't feel any more powerful than the 4-cylinder, and it was only with the aid of a stopwatch that we were able to measure the increased acceleration. What we did notice was how rough the engine was – a flaw that was more than compensated for by a pleasing, deep-throated rumble. But our biggest surprise was the gas mileage, a whopping 21 mpg, unusual for an all-wheel driver.

On the highway it was hard to find fault with anything in this all-weather

▲ PROS

• Excellent legroom (rear) • Good overall comfort • Impressive active safety • Proven reliability • Sophisticated audio system

▼ CONS

• Average performance • Awkward look (sedan) • Moderate steering response • Steep prices • Wind noise

Subaru. Spacious, practical, luxurious, comfortable and sure-footed, it offered a welcome peace of mind. The Bridgestone Blizzak Studless tires really bite into the snow and if some people don't appreciate its particular driving style, well it's all a matter of taste.

Concert hall

Other than its on and off-road qualities, the 6-cylinder models treat their passengers as bona fide music lovers, providing one of the best stereo sound systems ever installed in an automobile. Built by McIntosh, the 200-watt 11-speaker system also includes woofers and tweeters and a CD player.

I'm not convinced that the H6 sedan will be as popular as the wagon. It doesn't look as attractive and the road manners associated with a higher suspension and semi off-road tires are more in keeping with a sport-utility vehicle. As with the wagon, you wonder where the 212 hp of this flat-6 3.0-liter went.

Driving on the open road at around 70 mph (110 km/h), I could hear wind noise and it seemed to be coming from the roof rack. But that wasn't the case, as it turned out. The noise was caused by the car's tall stance, a factor that makes it sensitive to the wind. Riding comfort is generally good, although the shock absorbers feel rather stiff on rough road surfaces.

This Subaru has more space than its European rivals, particularly for its rear passengers. Trunk space may be smaller than the wagon's but on the other hand, it comes with a storage trap for skis. This is important as the Subaru Outback is ideal for skiers, and is the queen of our winter carnivals.

Jacques Duval

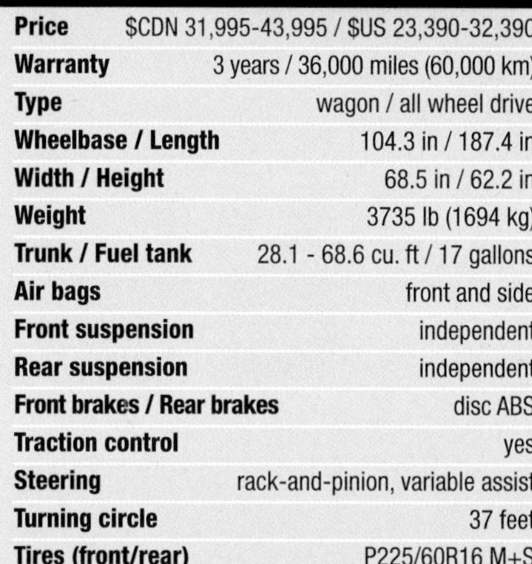

SPECIFICATIONS	**H6 VDC**
Price	$CDN 31,995-43,995 / $US 23,390-32,390
Warranty	3 years / 36,000 miles (60,000 km)
Type	wagon / all wheel drive
Wheelbase / Length	104.3 in / 187.4 in
Width / Height	68.5 in / 62.2 in
Weight	3735 lb (1694 kg)
Trunk / Fuel tank	28.1 - 68.6 cu. ft / 17 gallons
Air bags	front and side
Front suspension	independent
Rear suspension	independent
Front brakes / Rear brakes	disc ABS
Traction control	yes
Steering	rack-and-pinion, variable assist
Turning circle	37 feet
Tires (front/rear)	P225/60R16 M+S
PERFORMANCE	
Engine	6H 3.0-liter 24 valves
Transmission	4-speed automatic
Horsepower	212 hp at 6000 rpm
Torque	210 lb-ft at 4400 rpm
Other engines	4H 2.5-liter 165 hp
Other transmission	none
Acceleration (0-60 mph)	8.5 sec
Maximum speed	130 mph (210 km/h)
Braking (60-0 mph)	137 feet (41.8 m)
Fuel consumption	21 mpg (10.8 L/100 km)

COMPETITION

• Audi A4 • BMW 325Xi • Jaguar X-Type • Volkswagen Passat 4Motion • Volvo S60 AWD

NEW FOR 2002

• Illuminated ignition • Intermittent wipers (variable speed) • Time-delay ceiling light

RATING	**(out of 5 stars)**
Driveability	★★★½
Comfort	★★★½
Reliability	★★★
Roominess	★★★★
Winter driving rating	★★★★
Safety	★★★★★
Resale value	★★★½

SUZUKI ESTEEM

SUZUKI **ESTEEM**

Appearances Are Deceptive

There must be something at least a little bit exclusive about the Suzuki Esteem sedan, because how often does anyone actually see one on the road? And even then, like spotting rare birds, you have to be lucky, or else move, dare I say it, in exclusive neighborhoods of town. The Esteem wagon, on the other hand, is more ubiquitous, thanks in large measure to its generous cargo space (see text on the *Auto Guide* compact wagon comparison test).

Even so, the Esteem wagon has been unable to break away from its many rivals, which are just as roomy but offer much more in terms of performance, handling and driving fun. Its 122-hp 1.8-liter engine is fuel-efficient, but performance is average at best. The car's biggest handicap is the absence of value: a steep sticker price in return for an unappealing and austere interior.

Be that as it may, buyers in the market for a compact model with surprisingly generous cargo space should check out the Esteem, despite its run-of-the-mill handling, and the fact that it's beginning to show its age. Introduced in 1995, the car is still being sold in its original version while the rest of the market is flooded with the latest-flavor models. Fortunately, the most recent word from Suzuki is that a new model is on its way, announced for next year, to be precise. And you can bet your bottom dollar that it will be more competitive.

It's easy to see why Suzuki took so long to revamp the Esteem. The automaker had understandably, and sensibly, devoted all its resources to developing its full-size SUVs – the Grand Vitara and XL7 – which turned out to be hugely popular.

Exterior, interior

Help wanted

Suzuki stylists deserve a round of applause for the Esteem sedan's exterior styling. The lines are subtly understated, and I particularly like the front grille with its horizontal slats. It's all pretty mild-mannered, mind you, but it does exude a certain charm.

I wish I could say the same thing about the interior, but unfortunately I can't. It looks so tedious that it makes you wonder if there was a designer in charge in the first place. The plastics look and feel cheap, and the steering wheel is utterly nondescript – that is, except for the fact that it

▲ PROS

• 1.8-liter engine (wagon) • Comfortable suspension • Decent fuel economy • Neat silhouette • Reliable drivetrain

▼ CONS

• Anemic 1.6-liter engine • Average tires • Cockpit presentation • "Condemned" model • Vulnerable to side wind

contains an airbag in its hub. Ingenious! The seats are poorly padded and elegant is not an adjective I'd use to describe their cloth cover. In short, the Esteem tries to entice us with its silhouette, only to let us down with a substandard cockpit.

Things don't get a whole lot better on the road either. Quite the contrary, I'm sorry to say. Unlike the Esteem wagon, which is aided by a decent 122-hp 1.8-liter engine, the sedan has to contend with an overworked 95-hp 1.6-liter, hence the need to use the gearbox constantly to maintain a respectable pace. And you had better be dexterous, because gearshift travel is annoyingly imprecise. An automatic transmission would have been a useful solution, except that it would require more power than the engine has to offer in the first place. The result is that the car takes 14 seconds to go from 0-60 mph, and another second and a half with an automatic gearbox – all accompanied by engine noise so ominous you'd imagine something was about to explode under the hood. It doesn't help the situation either if the car is fully loaded with passengers and baggage.

If the Esteem's compact size is an asset in city traffic, it's a liability on the open road. You need to hang on tight to the steering wheel, especially if there's a side wind blowing.

To attract buyers, the Esteem sedan will need more than just a handsome silhouette. It'll have to do something about its bare-bones cockpit, lackluster handling and steep sticker price.

Denis Duquet

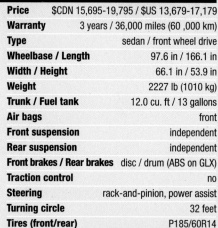

SPECIFICATIONS

Price	$CDN 15,695-19,795 / $US 13,679-17,179
Warranty	3 years / 36,000 miles (60 ,000 km)
Type	sedan / front wheel drive
Wheelbase / Length	97.6 in / 166.1 in
Width / Height	66.1 in / 53.9 in
Weight	2227 lb (1010 kg)
Trunk / Fuel tank	12.0 cu. ft / 13 gallons
Air bags	front
Front suspension	independent
Rear suspension	independent
Front brakes / Rear brakes	disc / drum (ABS on GLX)
Traction control	no
Steering	rack-and-pinion, power assist
Turning circle	32 feet
Tires (front/rear)	P185/60R14

PERFORMANCE

Engine	4L 1.6-liter
Transmission	5-speed manual
Horsepower	95 hp at 6000 rpm
Torque	99 lb-ft at 3000 rpm
Other engines	4L 1.8-l 122 hp (wagon)
Other transmission	4-speed automatic
Acceleration (0-60 mph)	13.8 s (1.6-liter); 10.7 s (wagon)
Maximum speed	103 mph (165 km/h)
Braking (60-0 mph)	148 feet (45 m)
Fuel consumption	27.6 mpg (8.2 L/100 km)

COMPETITION

• Daewoo Nubira • Ford Focus
• Huyndai Elantra

NEW FOR 2002

No major change

RATING (out of 5 stars)

Driveability	★★½
Comfort	★★★
Reliability	★★★
Roominess	★★★
Winter driving rating	★★★½
Safety	★★★
Resale value	★★★

SUZUKI VITARA

SUZUKI GRAND VITARA
CHEVROLET TRACKER

SUZUKI **GRAND VITARA**

Woodsman in a Tuxedo

The Suzuki car division had a tough debut in North America. Remember its Forza and Samurai 4X4, both now defunct? But don't count this Japanese automaker out just yet, because it's full of surprises. The Vitara and Grand Vitara, introduced in 1999, are living proof of that.

In fact, we're dealing with a trio. The Grand Vitara is the top of the line, followed by the Vitara and the Vitara convertible. The latter two are also members of the Chevrolet line-up with no differences other than the front badge and a few minor fittings.

Contrary to what the name suggests, the Grand Vitara is not much bigger than the Vitara. Its main advantage is the fact that it's the only Suzuki model equipped with a V6 engine – a smooth and quiet aluminum 155-hp 2.5-liter rating 155 hp. Acceleration and responsiveness are genuine but at high speeds the V7 could clearly use a little more power. It can be paired to either a 4-speed automatic gearbox or a 5-speed manual.

The Vitara has no reason to feel shy alongside its big brother. The look is a little less refined but the attractive features are still there. If anything, the lower body panels overdressing the sills of the Grand Vitara are gone, leaving only well integrated anti-scrape protection. There is only one engine on offer: a 2.0-liter 4-cylinder rating 127 hp – obviously less of a performer than the V6. The good news is that it's also 25% less thirsty. Maximum torque is reached at lower revs than with the V6, which is better for off-road driving. If you want to climb trees with your Suzuki, than this is the one you need.

The black sheep

If you think that the 2.0-liter's performance is borderline, then you can imagine what the Vitara convertible's1.6-liter 4-cylinder with 97 ponies is like. It's just good enough for cruising along the main drag with the top down. At least Suzuki had the decency to fit this power pack – fit for a lawn mower, if you ask me – with a manual gearbox.

Compact, but sturdy

All three Vitara models share the same platform, even though the convertible's wheelbase has been shortened to 86.6 inches (220 cm) – a good 9 inches (28 cm) less than its siblings. But we're dealing with a separate and very solidly assembled chassis here.

▲ PROS

- **Convivial V6 • Good looking design**
- **Good off-roader • Priced to move**
- **Tough chassis**

▼ CONS

- **Barely average comfort • 1.6-liter and 2.0-liter engines short-winded • Tailgate opens on the wrong side • Wind noise**

When the 4-wheel feature is disconnected, the Vitara and Grand Vitara are capable rear-wheel drivers. you can switch back to 4-wheel drive without stopping. Roadholding is on a par with other vehicles in their category, without some of the jerky, bouncy characteristics associated with 4X4s. Directional stability is good, although not perfect, and gives a secure feeling. With an 8-inch (20 cm) ground clearance, good forward visibility and decent low-end torque, hills are a breeze. Downhill, however, the ABS intervenes a little too quickly.

Genuine 4X4

A major irritant in many compact off-road vehicles – both Vitaras among them – is getting the tailgate open, especially when it swings the wrong way, that is, toward the curb. This may seem picky, but when it's –10 °F (-23 °C) and you've got two grocery bags to load in the back, the problem suddenly becomes acute. The same tailgate also carries the spare tire which seriously obstructs the driver's rear visibility. Things are better in the cabin. The instrument cluster is functional, if on the boring side. The sliding controls for the heating system seem old-fashioned, but at least they work. The driving position is quite acceptable in spite of the seats, whose backrests are a little too high, and don't give the legs enough support. For the busy collector, there are lots of storage places. Trunk space is incredibly tiny when the seats are up, but fold them down and the rear compartment becomes a convenient flush-bottomed space.

The Grand Vitara and Vitara are loaded with attractive features at a very realistic price. These are genuine 4-wheel drive vehicles, pleasant to drive even if a little unrefined. You can't have everything!

Alain Morin

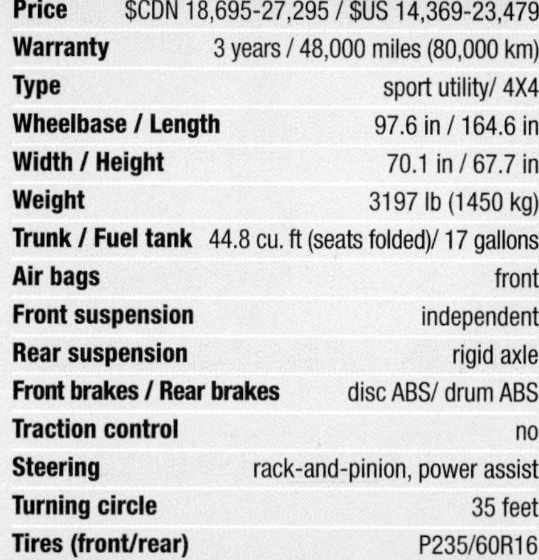

SPECIFICATIONS	
Price	$CDN 18,695-27,295 / $US 14,369-23,479
Warranty	3 years / 48,000 miles (80,000 km)
Type	sport utility/ 4X4
Wheelbase / Length	97.6 in / 164.6 in
Width / Height	70.1 in / 67.7 in
Weight	3197 lb (1450 kg)
Trunk / Fuel tank	44.8 cu. ft (seats folded)/ 17 gallons
Air bags	front
Front suspension	independent
Rear suspension	rigid axle
Front brakes / Rear brakes	disc ABS/ drum ABS
Traction control	no
Steering	rack-and-pinion, power assist
Turning circle	35 feet
Tires (front/rear)	P235/60R16

PERFORMANCE	
Engine	V6 2.5-liter
Transmission	4-speed automatic
Horsepower	155 hp at 6500 rpm
Torque	160 lb-ft at 4000 rpm
Other engines	4L 2.0-liter 127 hp (incl. conv.)
Other transmission	4L 1.6-liter 97 hp (convertible)
Acceleration (0-60 mph)	5-speed manual
Maximum speed	9.2 sec
Braking (60-0 mph)	106 mph (170 km/h)
Fuel consumption	139 feet (42.3 m)
	18.4 mpg (12.3 L/100 km)

COMPETITION

- Ford Escape • Honda CR-V • Kia Sportage
- Subaru Forester • Toyota RAV4

NEW FOR 2002

- ABS standard in all Grand Vitaras

RATING	(out of 5 stars)
Driveability	★★½
Comfort	★★★
Reliability	★★★½
Roominess	★★½
Winter driving rating	★★★
Safety	★★★★
Resale value	★★½

SUZUKI XL7

SUZUKI **XL7**

The Art of Compromise

Even though Suzuki is principally in the business of selling cars and motorbikes, the company's SUVs have done more than anything to contribute to its expansion in North America. It all started modestly with the Samurai, a vehicle that was minimalist to the extreme. But over time, Suzuki 4X4s have evolved and gained in both power and size. The Vitara was the first real model of its era, setting the stage for the Grand Vitara, from whose platform the current XL7 has been derived.

Suzuki's latest venture is the answer to the current North American craze: a 4X4 with third-row seating. Knowing that it couldn't compete with full-size vehicles such as the Ford Expedition and Chevrolet Tahoe/GMC Yukon, the Japanese carmaker shrewdly decided to produce the smallest 4X4 ever to offer third-row seats. XL7 stands for, yes, you've guessed right, "eXtra Long" and the capacity of accommodating seven people.

Even though its wheelbase has gained 12.5 inches (32 cm), and overall length a total of 19 inches (48 cm), the XL7 isn't any wider than the Grand Vitara. This posed quite a challenge for the engineers, who started out by placing the second-row seats on tracks so that they could slide forward to facilitate access to the third bench – so low that passengers literally have to sit with their heads between their knees. Fortunately, the backrest can be leaned back. Except for the front seats, the others are all relatively uncomfortable, due to the lack of proper legroom. There's no question that the XL7 can accommodate seven people, but only for a short period of time. Incidentally, once all the seats and headrests are in place, you begin to feel as if you were driving with an entire sports-team in the back.

Still evolving

On the other hand, thanks to the extended wheelbase and overall length, the XL7's luggage compartment looks immense beside the Grand Vitara's. To make use of this cargo space, remove the headrests, then fold the rear backrest forward. But take heart, it's easier than it sounds.

The dashboard is first and foremost practical, but completely devoid of style. On the other hand, the cabin teems with side pockets. The quality of materials used is decent enough, even though the plastic texture strikes me as being on the cheap

▲ PROS

• Complete equipment • Good finish • 170-hp engine • Rear tailgate • Well-balanced exterior

▼ CONS

• Average legroom • Difficult access to third bench • Mediocre stereo system • Old-fashioned dashboard • So-so off-road capabilities

side: a flaw in a vehicle that costs upwards of $30,000.

Reversal of fortune

While the Grand Vitara performs competently off-road, the XL7's larger size proves counter-productive. Its longer wheelbase combined with a ground clearance identical to the Grand Vitara's make the XL7 particularly vulnerable if there's a hump on the road. The lower beams tend to scrape against the surface, thus damaging the finish, not to mention the risk of catching – rather than "gliding" over – an obstacle on a straightaway. Clearly, Suzuki wants to aim this model at an urban clientele in search of a robust all-wheel drive capable of transporting people and luggage on paved roads, rather than off the beaten track. Besides, the greater distance between the front and rear wheels allows the use of a softer suspension while reducing the front-to-back pitching motion on uneven roads – an advantage for any "urban cowboy" who is normally content to drive on the main arteries.

The 2.7-liter V6 proudly displays its 170 horsepower, especially during acceleration, although it's somewhat dampened by the automatic gearbox's slow upshifts. Given the fairly recent origins of the XL7, Suzuki should have done better than fitting it with a part-time 4X4 engaged by a lever located between the front seats.

All in all the XL7 proves to be a competent enough touring vehicle, powered by an engine capable of meeting the needs of most drivers. Its only handicap is the price, a little steep for its category. You must really have a good reason to justify paying so much money. Obviously, for some people the reason might be that they simply couldn't resist the XL7's understated and stylish exterior

Denis Duquet

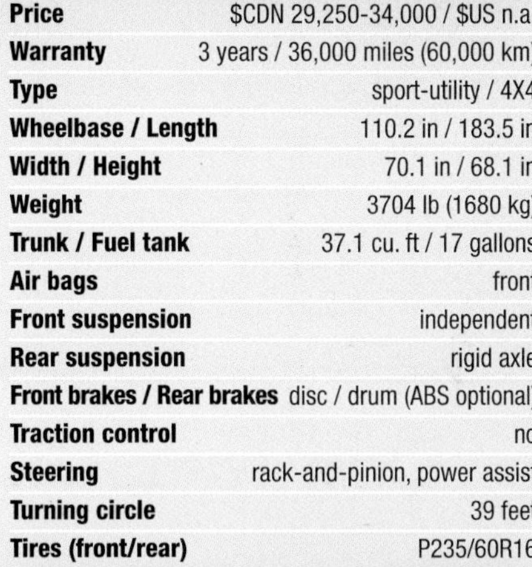

SPECIFICATIONS	
Price	$CDN 29,250-34,000 / $US n.a.
Warranty	3 years / 36,000 miles (60,000 km)
Type	sport-utility / 4X4
Wheelbase / Length	110.2 in / 183.5 in
Width / Height	70.1 in / 68.1 in
Weight	3704 lb (1680 kg)
Trunk / Fuel tank	37.1 cu. ft / 17 gallons
Air bags	front
Front suspension	independent
Rear suspension	rigid axle
Front brakes / Rear brakes	disc / drum (ABS optional)
Traction control	no
Steering	rack-and-pinion, power assist
Turning circle	39 feet
Tires (front/rear)	P235/60R16

PERFORMANCE	
Engine	V6 2.7 liter
Transmission	5-speed manual
Horsepower	170 hp at 5500 rpm
Torque	178 lb-ft at 4000 rpm
Other engines	none
Other transmission	4-speed automatic
Acceleration (0-60 mph)	9.2 sec
Maximum speed	109 mph (175 km/h)
Braking (60-0 mph)	132 feet (40.3 m)
Fuel consumption	16.4 mpg (13.8 L/100 km)

COMPETITION

- Ford Escape • Jeep Liberty • Mazda Tribute
- Nissan Xterra • Kia Sportage

NEW FOR 2002

- New model in 2001

RATING	**(out of 5 stars)**
Driveability	★★★
Comfort	★★★
Reliability	★★★
Roominess	★★★★
Winter driving rating	★★★★
Safety	★★★★
Resale value	★★★★★

TOYOTA AVALON

TOYOTA **AVALON**

Comfort Guaranteed

There are two classes of motorists: those who are willing to withstand the most aggravating discomfort in return for the thrill of driving a super-fast sports car; and then there are all those people who swear only by a vehicle's downy, quiet comfort on the one hand, and solid and dependable engine and drivetrain on the other. For them, an automobile is a tranquil, cosy oasis far removed from the vagaries of daily life.

If you belong in the second camp, the Toyota Avalon has got everything needed to satisfy your every whim and desire, and then some. Take its mechanical reliability for a start. At a time when it costs an arm and a leg each time a mechanic lifts your hood, it's reassuring to know that, save for a few very minor irritations, this Japanese mid-size sedan simply will not let you down. In fact its machinery is so dependable that that it will readily give other more prestigious models a run for their money. So carefree buyers – mechanically speaking that is – this car's for you. Especially if you're the sort of driver who prefers not to have to worry about what makes your car tick.

You can't possibly ask for a more user-friendly interior: Body-hugging bucket seats, as comfortably firm as any top-quality home furniture you'll find anywhere; controls are so clearly indicated and logically placed you'll never need to bother with the owner's manual. Besides, there's an in-dash digital compass and calendar with big, clear lettering and figures that tells you the exact time and date – even the direction in which you're heading. It must be comforting, for example, to know that the nearest shopping mall is south of your house and the medical clinic is northeast!

Dull sophistication

Cosy oasis

If you're still reading this report, that's because the Avalon's cosy, sitting-room character hasn't put you off! So let's continue our test and get behind the wheel. Comfortably installed inside this quiet oasis-on-wheels, you'll be reassured by what you see. Everything is exquisitely assembled, the quality of the materials used is first-rate, no question about it, ditto the wood trim adorning the dashboard. Not unlike what you'd find in a Mercedes. Oops! Excuse the slip of the tongue! I meant to say Lexus. And if you're the least bit claus-

▲ PROS

- Flawless reliability • Generous cabin space
- Impeccable finish • Super quiet cabin
- Ultra smooth engine

▼ CONS

- Body noise • Body roll • Heavy steering
- Nondescript silhouette • Zero driving fun

trophobic, you'll feel right at home in this roomy sedan. By the way, the Avalon was originally developed so that it could compete with the Mercury Grand Marquis and Chrysler Intrepids of this world, which explains its above-average roominess. The front seats are so generous they can comfortably accommodate two slightly overweight occupants, while three tall adults can sit side by side on the rear bench without sticking their elbows into one another's sides.

And rest assured, not even the 210-hp engine can disrupt this tranquillity and comfort. In fact, everything is so velvety smooth that if it hadn't been for the movements of the tachometer needle, you wouldn't even realize that the 3.0-liter V6 engine is quietly purring under the hood. Set the gearshift lever to the D position, and you're on your tranquil, silky way. Like most top-selling full-size American-made sedans, the Avalon features fully independent suspension with anti-roll bars, and shock absorbers set at the "supple" position – the key ingredients for a smooth and effortless ride. And if the car leans a tad more than necessary into a turn, you'll know it's time to reduce your speed. In short, this is a sedan for relaxed driving. Nervous or impatient drivers, please step aside.

Conceived for a specific clientele, the Avalon is a quality car with a sticker price that puts it in a precarious position – that is, in direct competition with more prestigious models that are just as comfortable, but offer better handling and more driving fun. In fact, why would you opt for the Avalon when you can get a Lexus ES 300 for just a couple of thousand dollars more?

Denis Duquet

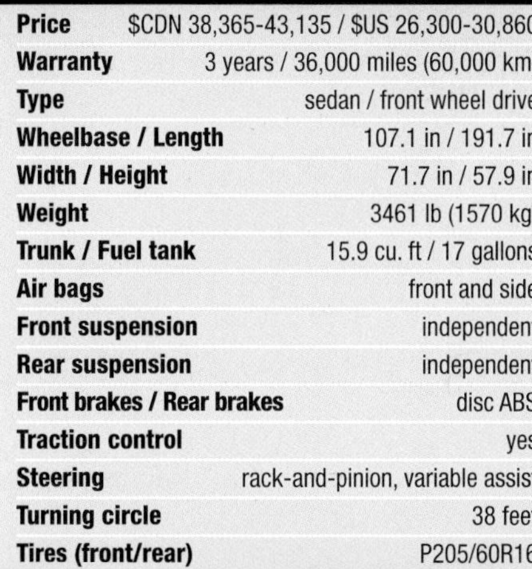

SPECIFICATIONS	**XLS**
Price	$CDN 38,365-43,135 / $US 26,300-30,860
Warranty	3 years / 36,000 miles (60,000 km)
Type	sedan / front wheel drive
Wheelbase / Length	107.1 in / 191.7 in
Width / Height	71.7 in / 57.9 in
Weight	3461 lb (1570 kg)
Trunk / Fuel tank	15.9 cu. ft / 17 gallons
Air bags	front and side
Front suspension	independent
Rear suspension	independent
Front brakes / Rear brakes	disc ABS
Traction control	yes
Steering	rack-and-pinion, variable assist
Turning circle	38 feet
Tires (front/rear)	P205/60R16

PERFORMANCE	
Engine	V6 3.0-liter
Transmission	4-speed automatic
Horsepower	210 hp at 5800 rpm
Torque	220 lb-ft at 4400 rpm
Other engines	none
Other transmission	none
Acceleration (0-60 mph)	9.7 sec
Maximum speed	130 mph (210 km/h)
Braking (60-0 mph)	139 feet (42.3 m)
Fuel consumption	18.9 mpg (12 L/100 km)

COMPETITION

• Buick LeSabre • Chrysler Concorde • Infiniti I35 • Mazda Millenia • Mercury Grand Marquis

NEW FOR 2002

No major change

RATING	**(out of 5 stars)**
Driveability	★★
Comfort	★★★★
Reliability	★★★★½
Roominess	★★★½
Winter driving rating	★★★½
Safety	★★★½
Resale value	★★

TOYOTA CAMRY/LEXUS ES 300

TOYOTA **CAMRY**

Added Value

When the time came to modify the wildly popular Camry in 1997, Toyota faced a dilemma. The competitively priced sedan was a best-seller in North America, and engineers knew they had to keep costs down without compromising the car's handling and overall qualities.

Their strategy paid off handsomely as the Camry continued to outsell all other mid-size sedans. After four years, however, the platform – by now a decade old – was starting to show its age. Once again, the engineers faced the challenge of updating the car while keeping an eye on costs, despite the fact that the Camry platform had been used over the years to develop other Toyota models – the Avalon coupe and convertible, for example, as well as the Lexus ES 300, the Highlander SUV and Sienna minivan.

This time around, Toyota hit the bull's eye and revamped the Camry in record time. The improvements are impressive: the car is bigger and better equipped, provides better handling and costs less! Needless to say, the more upscale Lexus ES 300, while boasting its own bodywork, also benefits from these improvements. But let's start with the Camry.

More space

Good value in North American automotive terms generally means more interior roominess and comfort, and the fifth-generation Camry readily obliges on this score. It features a higher roof and longer wheelbase (by two inches), providing more space all around – extra rear legroom (by an inch and a half) as well as overall head and shoulder room. Armrests and the height of the seats have also been modified for greater comfort.

Cornerstone

With the new, more rigid platform, cabin noise is greatly reduced. The ride is also more comfortable, thanks to the suppler, all-independent suspension featuring MacPherson struts in front and rear – a relatively modern technology that's straightforward, space-efficient and fairly inexpensive to produce.

New engine

It's not surprising that Toyota gave the fifth-generation Camry an all-new four-cylinder engine. After all, more than 75% of Camry buyers order the inline-4 en-

▲ PROS

- Competitive prices • Livelier exterior
- New and improved 4-cylinder engine
- Roomier cabin • SE version

▼ CONS

- Average tires • No manual gearbox with V6
- Sluggish steering (LE, XLE) • Suspension too supple (except SE)

gine. The new 4-cylinder displaces 2.4 liters, is 55 lbs (25 kg) lighter than the 2.2-liter engine it replaces, and features balancer shafts to reduce all piston vibrations. Horsepower has been increased by 15%, to 157 hp, and torque by 10%, to 163 lb-ft – just what it takes to pull the 3400-lb mass without effort. Aided by continuously variable valve timing with intelligence (VVT-i), acceleration is decent. My test car, a 4-cylinder LE version equipped with an automatic gearbox, took 9.8 seconds to go from 0-60 mph. The 2.4-liter engine can also be paired to a 5-speed manual transmission.

The optional 3.0-liter DOHC V6 is the same as the previous model's, and it will only be available with the 4-speed automatic box. But take heart, this is an all-new transmission, featuring a shift-logic system, which greatly reduces response lag when you're driving up or down hill.

Multiple choice

Stylists did a good job rejigging the Camry's exterior, which looks definitely livelier, though no one would mistake it for anything else but a Camry. It could have been a little bolder, I suppose. The interior is on the conservative side, but has a modern twist. The center stack is decidedly more dramatic, featuring flawlessly assembled controls. As befitting Camry's reputation, the seats are super comfortable, especially in the front, and on all versions.

The Camry comes in three trim levels: LE, SE and XLE. Even the base LE offers excellent standard equipment, such as air conditioning, cruise control, power windows and mirrors. Its overall balance will appeal to buyers who want a dependable car capable of transporting driver and passengers comfortably from place to place. The 4-cylinder engine is no powerhouse, but it's more than adequate to pull a fully loaded car.

I'd like to leave the SE for "dessert," so let's move right on to the top-of-the-line XLE, which offers all the optional features listed in the catalog as standard equipment. Its handling closely approximates the Lexus ES 300, with comfort-tuned suspension and excellent sound insulation. If you like luxury and comfort, this Camry is for you.

TOYOTA **CAMRY**

LEXUS **ES 300**

TOYOTA CAMRY/LEXUS ES 300

On the other hand, if you value driving pleasure above everything else, then go for the SE. It features firmer springs and shock dampings, performance-oriented 16-inch wheels and "underassisted" steering – in other words, all the ingredients necessary for an enjoyable spin through twisting roads. To be sure, the SE is no sports car, but it will allow you to appreciate Camry's new road capabilities. At the very least, it has the sport look: rear spoiler, blackened grille, fog lights, and stylish alloy wheels.

Finally, the biggest news about the 2002 Camry is that despite its better range of standard equipment, the new model is no pricier than last year's. The car certainly has a lot going for it, except for some disturbing noise that I heard each time I slammed the door shut. Call me picky, but it sort of made you doubt Toyota's claims about the car's solid build.

Lexus ES 300: Wise Evolution

The destinies of the ES 300 and the Toyota Camry are intimately linked. This shouldn't be surprising as the latter shares its platform and mechanical components with its big sister. But the Lexus has more to offer in terms of equipment, as well as look and finish, all of which are much more luxurious. Sound insulation is also more advanced. Like the Camry, the ES 300 has been entirely revamped this year. It's now longer, wider and higher, while the platform is more resistant to flexing and torsion. The suspension components work that much better as they're also fitted on more rigid sub-frames. Another option is the Adaptive Variable Suspension (AVS) which constantly modulates the shock-absorber dampening for each wheel. You can choose between Comfort and Sport modes, or the two intermediate settings. The optional AVS is designed to respond to changing road surfaces, vehicle speed, driver steering, braking inputs and even vertical movement.

The new ES 300 is powered by the same 3.0-liter V6 engine as the Camry, coupled to an electronically-controlled 5-speed automatic gearbox. Unlike the Camry, the ES 300 doesn't come with a 4-cylinder engine.

The standard four-wheel disk brake system features Electronic Brake Force Distribution (EBD), as well as a sophisticated Brake Assist which will add the force needed to engage ABS in case the driver hasn't pressed hard enough on the brake pedal. The Luxury and Premium packages include the Lexus Vehicle Skid Control (VSC) with integrated electronic traction control (TRAC).

As you might expect, Lexus has equipped the ES 300 with the same luxury features that are found on the LS 430 sedan – in particular, the dual-zone automatic climate control system. Both models also offer a sophisticated audio system as standard equipment, featuring a five-channel amplifier and seven speakers.

Hesitant suspension

Filled to the brim with luxury accessories, and endowed with an appearance that seems less subdued than before thanks to

■ STANDARD EQUIPMENT

- Air conditioning • CD player • Cruise control
- Power windows and locks

■ OPTIONAL EQUIPMENT

- ABS • Alloy wheels • Automatic transmission
- Dynamic Stability Program

a sculpted hood and Lexus' signature lighting clusters, the new ES 300 has indeed come a very long way and is far more exciting than ever. The engine is just as smooth, the automatic gearbox has almost completely eliminated its response lag and steering is even more precise. Unfortunately, all these improvements were sabotaged in our test car by the AVS suspension, which seemed totally out of sync with what the car was actually doing. The Sport mode seemed to turn the shock absorbers into rigid stalks while the Comfort mode was far too soft. This option is a waste. Best to stick with the standard suspension, which is at least more predictable, even though a little too soft.

It's really a shame that this Lexus is still handicapped by an unresponsive ride while the improved chassis allows us to hope for a lot better. Although the V6 engine offers adequate power, it may not be enough to face the all-new Infiniti I35 and its 260-hp engine.

Denis Duquet

SPECIFICATIONS	**ES 300**
Price	$CDN 23,750-34,940 / $US 32,050
Warranty	4 years / 48,000 miles (80,000 km)
Type	sedan / front wheel drive
Wheelbase / Length	107.1 in / 189 in
Width / Height	70.4 in / 58.7 in
Weight	3446 lb (1563 kg)
Trunk / Fuel tank	17.6 cu. ft / 19 gallons
Air bags	front, side and head
Front suspension	independent
Rear suspension	independent
Front brakes / Rear brakes	disc ABS
Traction control	yes
Steering	rack-and-pinion, power assist
Turning circle	37 feet
Tires (front/rear)	P215/60R16

PERFORMANCE	
Engine	V6 3.0-liter
Transmission	5-speed automatic
Horsepower	210 hp at 5800 rpm
Torque	220 lb-ft at 4400 rpm
Other engines	none
Other transmission	none
Acceleration (0-60 mph)	8.4 sec
Maximum speed	134 mph (215 km/h)
Braking (60-0 mph)	118 feet (36 m)
Fuel consumption	21.4 mpg (10.6 L/100 km)

COMPETITION

• Acura 3.2TL • Audi A6 • Cadillac CTS • Infiniti I35 • Lincoln LS • Saab 9.5

NEW FOR 2002

• Extended wheelbase • 5-speed automatic transmission • New model • Roomier cabin

RATING	**(out of 5 stars)**
Driveability	★★★★★
Comfort	★★★★★
Reliability	★★★★★
Roominess	★★★★½
Winter driving rating	★★★★
Safety	★★★★★
Resale value	★★★★★

TOYOTA CAMRY SOLARA

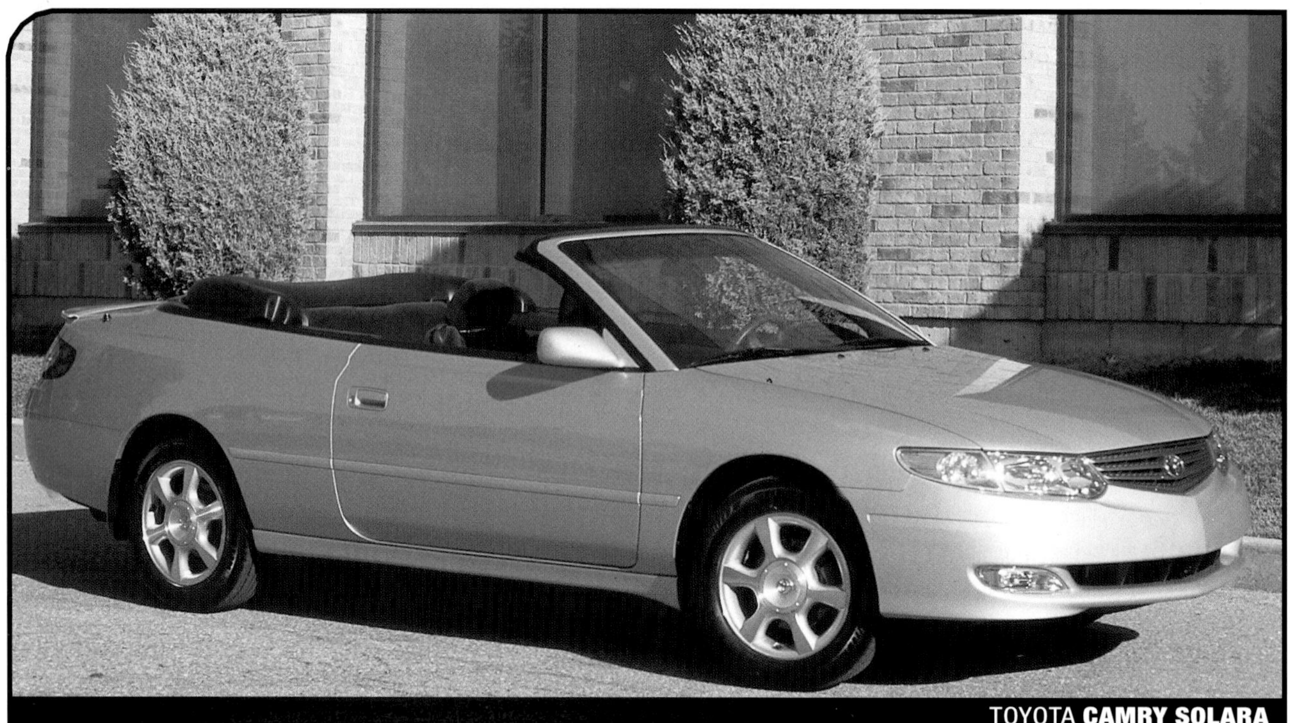

TOYOTA **CAMRY SOLARA**

Guaranteed Failure

While the Toyota Camry was redesigned for 2002, the Solara coupe and convertible – both derived from this wildly popular sedan – will have to wait a while longer for their own makeovers. And who can blame Toyota for this deliberate neglect, since the Camry continues to sell like hot cakes while the supposedly sporty Solaras sit idly by like bridesmaids.

Launched with much fanfare three years ago, the Solara coupe has never enjoyed the kind of success expected of it. The arrival of its convertible cousin a year later made little or no difference – sales figures stubbornly stayed in the doldrums and that's where they've been ever since. It's hard to be surprised, because apart from components borrowed from the Camry, the Solaras offered little more than an amputated 2-door body. The coupe fares reasonably well, but the convertible leaves a lot to be desired. Its chassis and body structure required many reinforcements – especially to restore the missing rigidity owing to the soft-top. But all to no avail, as it turned out. The suspension remains overly supple, the car itself feels heavy and vibrates when driven over rough roads, especially the dashboard and windshield.

Negligent subcontractor

What's hardest to understand is how Toyota, renowned for its impeccable quality and exemplary reliability, could have subcontracted the job of transforming the Solara coupe into a convertible to an outside manufacturer. The company concerned – American Sun Roof (ASR) – has a reputation for expertise, true, but they certainly messed up on this job. Admittedly, Toyota has every right to send the ball back to ASR's court, but as far as Solara buyers are concerned, the buck should stop with Toyota.

Lost cause

During my first test drive in Florida, a loud, whistling wind noise could be heard coming from the soft-top, although I was driving at low speeds. I assumed the top was improperly closed. Another test drive confirmed that the problem was confined to that particular car, because the second test car proved to be much less noisy. Nevertheless, new problems cropped up – the "check-engine" and "trac-off" lights, for instance, came on for no apparent reason. We were not terribly impressed.

▲ PROS

- Cosy comfort • Excellent seats
- Good engine • Quality finish
- Spacious trunk

▼ CONS

- Anemic 4-cylinder • Annoying manual gearbox
- Body not rigid enough • Botched convertible
- Wobbly handling

We were not the only ones, as it turned out. During a comparative test carried out by *Car and Driver* magazine, the Solara convertible came last among five models in the same category. The magazine's test drivers drew exactly the same conclusion as the *Auto Guide:* there simply was nothing sporty about the Solara, which felt rubbery and flabby, as though it were sitting in molasses. Suspension was so soft the car shook each time it hit a bump or pothole in the road, especially when cornering.

Roomy interior

No doubt the Solara convertible's chief quality is its roomy cabin. On this point, it beats the competition hands down (namely, the Chrysler Sebring and Ford Mustang), thanks to a rear seat so big it seats two adults easily. Even trunk space, usually cramped in convertible cars, is larger than average. Another plus is the heated rear window, excellent for winter driving conditions.

On the road, the 3.0-liter 200-hp V6 engine that powered our SLE test model was as smooth as BMW's 6-cylinder. We also found that it worked better with an automatic transmission, because of the excessively long throw of the clutch pedal and gear lever.

Fortunately, the Solara coupe exhibited none of the irritants we experienced with the convertible. Its performance, while not especially exciting, was perfectly acceptable, and comfort was first class. But I'd opt for the V6 version rather than the base 2.2-liter 4-cylinder with 135 hp.

That said, you may want to try both Solaras and make up your own mind. But in my opinion, neither model is terribly interesting, and those customers who have passed them up do have some justification. If you like flash and dash and you feel like renting a car while you're on vacation in Florida, then the Solara may be just the ticket. But I honestly don't understand their attraction. Or, put another way, they're the reason for their own lack of success.

Jacques Duval

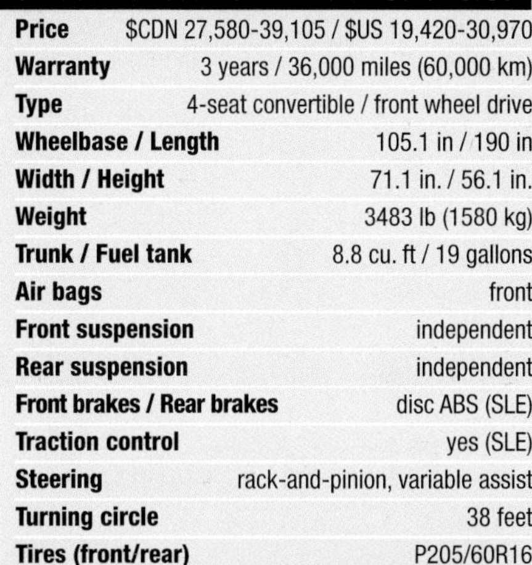

SPECIFICATIONS	SLE Cabriolet
Price	$CDN 27,580-39,105 / $US 19,420-30,970
Warranty	3 years / 36,000 miles (60,000 km)
Type	4-seat convertible / front wheel drive
Wheelbase / Length	105.1 in / 190 in
Width / Height	71.1 in. / 56.1 in.
Weight	3483 lb (1580 kg)
Trunk / Fuel tank	8.8 cu. ft / 19 gallons
Air bags	front
Front suspension	independent
Rear suspension	independent
Front brakes / Rear brakes	disc ABS (SLE)
Traction control	yes (SLE)
Steering	rack-and-pinion, variable assist
Turning circle	38 feet
Tires (front/rear)	P205/60R16

PERFORMANCE	
Engine	V6 3 liter
Transmission	4-speed automatic
Horsepower	200 hp at 5200 rpm
Torque	214 lb-ft at 4400 rpm
Other engines	4L 2.2 liter 135 hp (coupe only)
Other transmission	5-speed manual (4L)
Acceleration (0-60 mph)	10.8 sec
Maximum speed	122 mph (195 km/h)
Braking (60-0 mph)	131 feet (40 m)
Fuel consumption	19.1 mpg (11.9 L/100 km)

COMPETITION

- Chevrolet Camaro/Pontiac Firebird
- Chrysler Sebring • Ford Mustang

NEW FOR 2002

- New 157-hp 4-cylinder • Light styling touch-ups

RATING	(out of 5 stars)
Driveability	★★
Comfort	★★★½
Reliability	★★★½
Roominess	★★★
Winter driving rating	★★★
Safety	★★★½
Resale value	★★★

TOYOTA CELICA GT-S

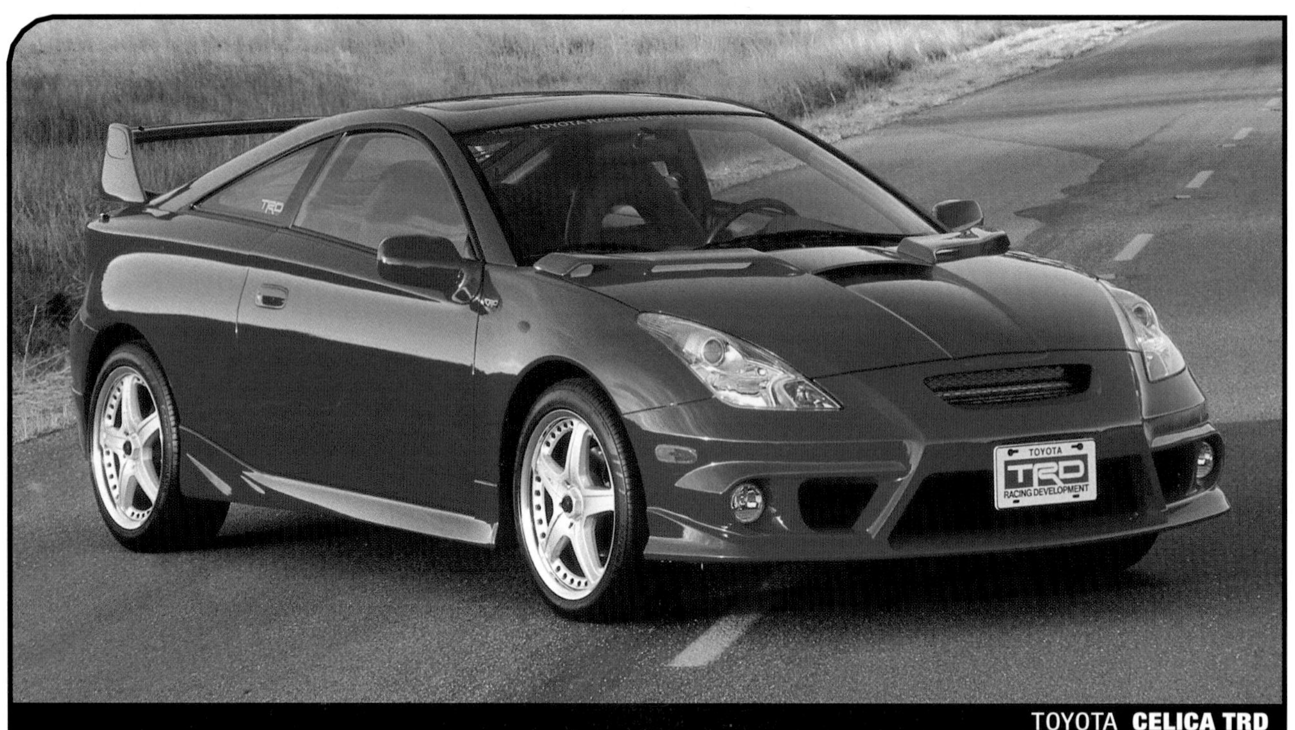

TOYOTA **CELICA TRD**

Nice Steering Wheel! Thank Goodness!

Entirely revamped in 2000, the 7th generation Celica has abandoned its whale-like outline for a decidedly angular design. The new look is attractive without being spectacular which explains the model's relative success and a welcome change from the disappointing record of its predecessor. But why "thank goodness"? Read on.

Last year, we drew attention to the incompatibility between the Celica's superb 180-hp engine and its 4-speed automatic transmission. Since the engine only really got going at 6000 rpm, the poor torque it generated at low rpm didn't mesh well with the automatic. Performance left a lot to be desired. And if you imagine that the pseudo-manual transmission with its cute little buttons mounted on the steering wheel will come to the engine's rescue, think again! If engines had stomachs, this one would be suffering from a bad case of indigestion.

Smooth is the operative word

To be fair, the Celica's 4-cylinder engine, with "intelligent" variable valve timing, is a gem that works wonders when it's allowed to do its job – between 6000 and 8000 rpm. Only you don't do that kind of driving in city traffic. Out on the open road, however, satisfaction is guaranteed, especially on sinuous corners, but only if the road surface is smooth. Otherwise, the firm – not to say stiff – suspension and low-profile tires mean that your posterior will painfully register every bump and pothole. The situation can get annoying, unless you try to drown out tire rumbling with the hi-fi rumble blasting from the 8-speaker stereo system.

Qualities, but flaws too

The incompatibility between the engine and the GT-S's automatic gearbox may be irreparable, but the cockpit definitely gets higher marks: an ergonomically-sound dashboard, comfortable bucket seats, and that magnificent three-spoke steering wheel. It's precise and a distinct pleasure to handle, a fact that's partly attributable to the suspension which is tuned for handling rather than comfort. And the Celica's handling is remarkable – but keep in mind that it does its job best only on smooth surfaces.

Half man, half beast

The four-wheel disc brakes with ABS are adequate, though nothing to write home about. Curiously, traction control

▲ PROS

• Excellent ergonomics • Fine performance (GT-S manual) • Generous trunk space • Good handling • Intriguing styling

▼ CONS

• Clumsy spoiler (GT-S and TRD) • Incompatible automatic gearbox (GT-S) • Limited headroom • Uncomfortable suspension (GT-S and TRD)

is not offered. But let's get back to the cockpit. As nice as it is, tall people are not welcome because the roof is on the low side. It's worse in the back where even an average-height passenger will find his or her head poking through the rear glass window. The trunk is impressively spacious, but the lid is saddled with a spoiler so badly located it virtually obscures any car traveling behind.

Jacques Duval tests the TRD

Wearing its Toyota Racing Development (TRD) outfit, the Celica GT-S certainly looks eye-catching, though not necessarily in good taste. And if its zany disguise won't make heads turn, the loud noise emanating from the tailpipe will. In fact, this sport muffler is the only component apt to improve engine performance; according to my stopwatch, the TRD package's extra 14 horses made no noticeable difference. And if you want to test the various aerodynamic appendages (like that grotesque spoiler), I suppose you'll have to drive the car at breakneck speed on a racetrack.

The modified suspension, on the other hand, combined with the special alloy wheels, will certainly help keep this sport coupe firmly attached to the ground or possibly turn it into a potential car-rally champion. It's nimble on corners and very easy to control, thanks to its precise steering. Alas, the cost (almost an extra $9000) and its negligible effect on the car's overall performance is hardly justifiable ***(JD)***.

To recap: interesting styling, excellent handling, automatic transmission with GT (140 hp), manual gearbox with GT-S. On the debit side are the cramped cabin (height) and limited comfort and visibility. But there's always Toyota's legendary reliability and the terrific steering wheel.

Alain Raymond

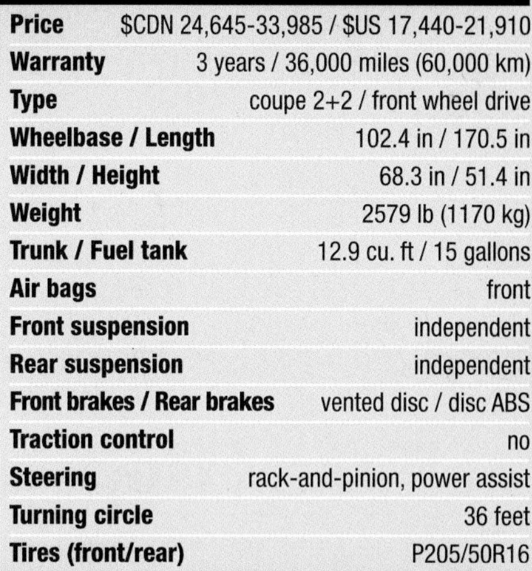

SPECIFICATIONS	**GT-S**
Price	$CDN 24,645-33,985 / $US 17,440-21,910
Warranty	3 years / 36,000 miles (60,000 km)
Type	coupe 2+2 / front wheel drive
Wheelbase / Length	102.4 in / 170.5 in
Width / Height	68.3 in / 51.4 in
Weight	2579 lb (1170 kg)
Trunk / Fuel tank	12.9 cu. ft / 15 gallons
Air bags	front
Front suspension	independent
Rear suspension	independent
Front brakes / Rear brakes	vented disc / disc ABS
Traction control	no
Steering	rack-and-pinion, power assist
Turning circle	36 feet
Tires (front/rear)	P205/50R16

PERFORMANCE	
Engine	4L 1.8-liter
Transmission	4-speed automatic
Horsepower	180 hp at 7600 rpm
Torque	130 lb-ft at 6800 rpm
Other engines	4L 1.8-liter 140 hp (GT); 194 hp (TRD)
Other transmission	6-speed manual / 5-speed (GT)
Acceleration (0-60 mph)	10.3 sec
Maximum speed	118 mph (190 km/h)
Braking (60-0 mph)	129 feet (39.3 m)
Fuel consumption	22.7 mpg (10 L/100 km)

COMPETITION

- Acura RSX • Honda Prelude • Hyundai Tiburon
- Mercury Cougar

NEW FOR 2002

- TRD model

RATING	**(out of 5 stars)**
Driveability	★★★
Comfort	★★½
Reliability	★★★★
Roominess	★★½
Winter driving rating	★★★
Safety	★★★
Resale value	★★★

TOYOTA COROLLA

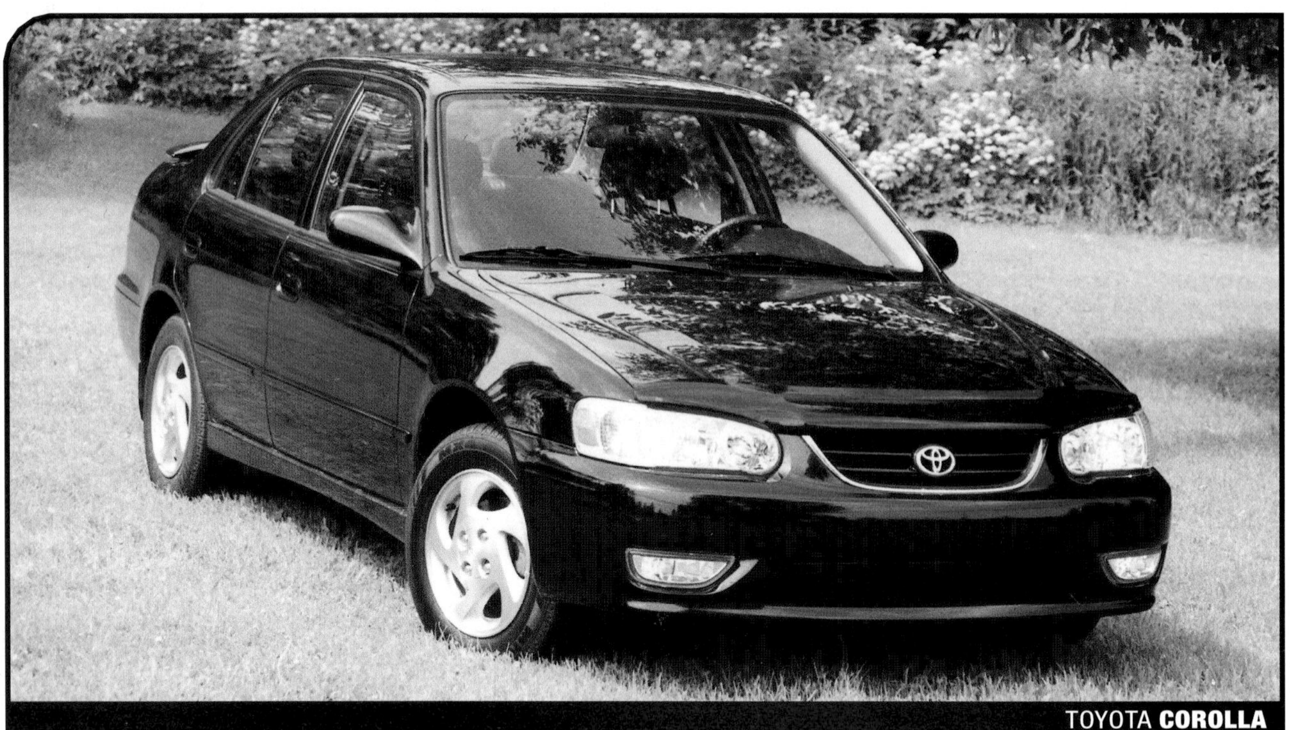

TOYOTA **COROLLA**

False Representation?

Last year, Toyota brought out a sport version of its Corolla, complete with rear-deck spoiler, alloy wheels, a proud "S" gracing the trunk lid, and red-over-black gauges on the dashboard. Unfortunately, the new version did not quite live up to its sporty aspirations, handling itself pretty much like any other Corolla. In other words, the Corolla sport sedan was sporty in name only, little more than a jazzed-up version of a sedan essentially designed for carrying out daily-driver tasks rather than performing dazzling movements on the open road.

So Toyota was trying to pull the wool over our eyes. But let's not pass judgment based on just one particular case.

I recently had an opportunity to drive an LE model for a whole week, and the experience led me to revise my opinion and it served to rehabilitate the Corolla in my eyes. If anything, my test demonstrated that in order to appreciate this sedan's full value, drivers need to select the appropriate version and equipment suited to his or her specific driving needs.

All dressed

In Toyota's case, they must have decided that gentrification was a much easier job to do than actually transforming a regular sedan into a sport sedan. And so, the LE, Corolla's top-end version, can be equipped to your heart's content, or the next best thing: remote door locks, power windows, climate control, tilt steering, more luxurious seats, CD player, larger wheels and automatic transmission.

It was behind the wheel of this virtual mini-limousine that I made a 350-mile return trip in a single day, long enough to find out that the car was ideally adapted to journeys such as this. The front seats were comfortable and the 4-cylinder engine, paired to a 4-speed automatic transmission, acquitted itself in respectable fashion. The car was equally easy to drive through busy city traffic and passing power was remarkable, especially considering its 1.8-liter engine.

Split personality

I remember testing other Corollas in the past – mostly the base versions – and I invariably found that their steering was too sensitive – yet it was fine in the LE, even though the folks at Toyota assured me that

▲ PROS

- Adequate engine • Impeccable finish
- Rock-solid body • Sound handling
- Spacious interior

▼ CONS

- Average tires • Light steering • Not much driving fun • Expensive high-end model
- Spongy brakes

no change at all had been made on this score. My test LE was perfectly stable, virtually unaffected by the very strong side winds I encountered on the road.

In fact, the only fault worth mentioning was the considerable wind noise I heard at highway speeds. And that surprised me, considering Toyota's significant efforts to insulate the cabin.

City slicker

I very much doubt that most drivers keep their Corollas, LE version or otherwise, just for long-distance trips. The cars are more likely used to get their owners to and from work, or for transporting groceries. In fact, many Corolla owners told us that they appreciated the way the car handled in busy traffic, and that its reasonable dimensions made it easy to park and to maneuver in and out of tight spots. What's more, fuel consumption is low, a not negligible factor in this age of volatile fuel supplies and prices.

My own city excursions confirmed all these assessments. The Corolla behaves very well indeed and its relative comfort enhances the driving pleasure. I also find that an automatic transmission is better adapted to city driving than a manual, helping the engine deliver more immediate acceleration, especially when you need to change lanes in congested traffic.

On twisting roads, the car performs less well. Handling is average a best, steering proves to be overly assisted, and body roll too pronounced. At least, the high-end LE model is more comfortable and less frustrating to drive.

Needless to say, the LE, Corolla's top-end model, is the most agreeable to drive. But its over-$20,000 sticker price may make you think twice. Let's hope that the new generation – scheduled to arrive in early 2002 – will retain all the car's current qualities, structural rigidity in particular, while providing a little more driving pleasure.

Denis Duquet

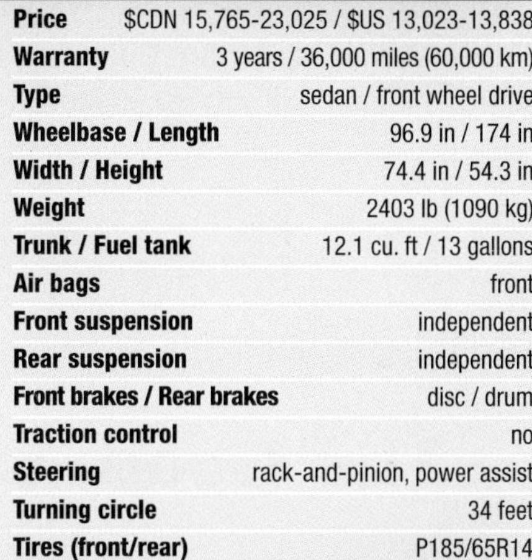

SPECIFICATIONS	**LE**
Price	$CDN 15,765-23,025 / $US 13,023-13,838
Warranty	3 years / 36,000 miles (60,000 km)
Type	sedan / front wheel drive
Wheelbase / Length	96.9 in / 174 in
Width / Height	74.4 in / 54.3 in
Weight	2403 lb (1090 kg)
Trunk / Fuel tank	12.1 cu. ft / 13 gallons
Air bags	front
Front suspension	independent
Rear suspension	independent
Front brakes / Rear brakes	disc / drum
Traction control	no
Steering	rack-and-pinion, power assist
Turning circle	34 feet
Tires (front/rear)	P185/65R14

PERFORMANCE	
Engine	4L 1.8-liter 16-valve
Transmission	4-speed automatic
Horsepower	125 hp at 5600 rpm
Torque	126 lb-ft at 4000 rpm
Other engines	none
Other transmission	5-speed manual
Acceleration (0-60 mph)	11.9 s; 12.5 s (automatic)
Maximum speed	112 mph (180 km/h)
Braking (60-0 mph)	138 feet (42 m)
Fuel consumption	29.8 mpg (7.6 L/100 km)

COMPETITION

- Cavalier/Sunfire • Civic • Elantra • Focus • Jetta • Neon • Nubira • Protegé • Sentra • Spectra

NEW FOR 2002

- New model in January 2002

RATING	**(out of 5 stars)**
Driveability	★★½
Comfort	★★★½
Reliability	★★★★★
Roominess	★★★½
Winter driving rating	★★★½
Safety	★★★
Resale value	★★★★½

TOYOTA ECHO

TOYOTA **ECHO**

The Good, the Ugly, the Cheap

Behind its unattractive exterior, there's more to the Toyota Echo than meets the eye. Its body looks as out of place in the North American automobile landscape as a blast of heavy-metal sound during a high mass. Yet it can't be dismissed, especially since its tall bodystyle has grown increasingly trendy. Even the Ford Focus now adopts the vertical stance, albeit with more finesse.

You either adore or despise the Echo. My 10-year-old daughter thinks it's the coolest car she's ever seen, while I believe a "cathedral" ceiling looks good in a house, not a car. At the very least, designers had the good sense to give the Echo lots of glass, providing excellent visibility, not to mention a generous luggage compartment and comfortable cabin. Much attention has been paid to the interior. Nooks and crannies abound for storing various items, all ingenious and within easy reach. Controls are ergonomically friendly, and are mounted on a – yes – centrally-positioned dashboard!

At first glance, the dash layout seems gratuitously eccentric – either that or a serious design mistake. But it turned out to be at least as user-friendly, if not more so, as the conventional arrangement. Hey, it took me a good four seconds to get used to it. On the other hand, I had trouble finding a decent driving position.

The cloth seat covers look cheap, something completely unlike Toyota, which is noted for the exquisite finish of its products. Radio reception could be better, and the control buttons less sensitive. Many times, I turned the radio off when all I wanted to do was adjust the volume. The buttons for folding the rear seats looked rather flimsy as well. Anyway, they do the job properly, I suppose, in case you want to fold the seats down and increase the already large trunk space still further.

A noisy powertrain

Odd bird

The Toyota Echo is powered by a 1.5-liter 4-cylinder engine producing 108 hp, accompanied by variable valve timing with intelligence (VVTi). Thanks to all that new "green" engine technology, the Echo knows exactly how to endear itself to drivers. Although Toyota claims that its fuel mileage is 40 mpg, the best I could manage was 30 mpg. But I must add that I test-drove the Echo in winter, during a week teeming with snowstorms.

At first, the 1.5-liter engine didn't appear overly lively, but acceleration was

▲ PROS

- Honest handling • Low fuel consumption
- Surprising roominess • Toyota reliability
- Well-adapted engine

▼ CONS

- Bizarre driving position • Noisy engine
- Not a sporty car • Susceptible to side winds
- Ugly styling

peppy, accompanied by a reassuring hum. When cornering, especially if I exceeded the speed limit, the Echo demonstrated serious body roll, without actually falling over – unless you wanted it to, of course. At times like this, understeer, too, was pronounced. At top speed, the front of the car felt annoyingly light and if I panic-braked, it settled down, although it didn't exactly stay pointed straight ahead. But don't get excited, it's not a problem worth reporting to your local consumers group. On the other hand, I would have been happier if the plastic storage bin had stayed where it was under the seat during panic braking, instead of sliding out and banging up under the dashboard. Obviously, the Echo doesn't lend itself to sporty-driving.

Not for the faint of heart

My test-car was fitted with 14-inch tires, standard on all Echos. And after driving it in winter, I'm absolutely convinced that snow tires are a must. Even in fine summer weather, the car is susceptible to side winds and tends to sway when riding beside big trucks. On snowy surfaces, the Echo shows signs of instability. Let me tell you, my stomach churned whenever the road was the least bit slippery. Steering, though highly precise, was a bit too low for my taste.

The 4-speed automatic transmission did a generally good job, although at times gearshifting felt hesitant. It may be that my test-car was the only one affected by this problem, since the other auto journalists uniformly praised the gearbox. Personally I prefer a manual shift, but I must admit that's not a popular choice for a city car like the Echo. On the open road, the car is comfortable and the suspension takes bumps and potholes in its stride. Obviously, we're not talking about the Lincoln Continental here, but let's not compare apples and oranges.

Although hardly an automotive masterpiece, the Toyota Echo acquits itself honorably, never pretending to be a sports car or a mini BMW. It's an excellent choice for low-budget customers whose chief concerns are reliability and resale value, rather than styling. I'm beginning to understand why there are so many of them on the road.

Alain Morin

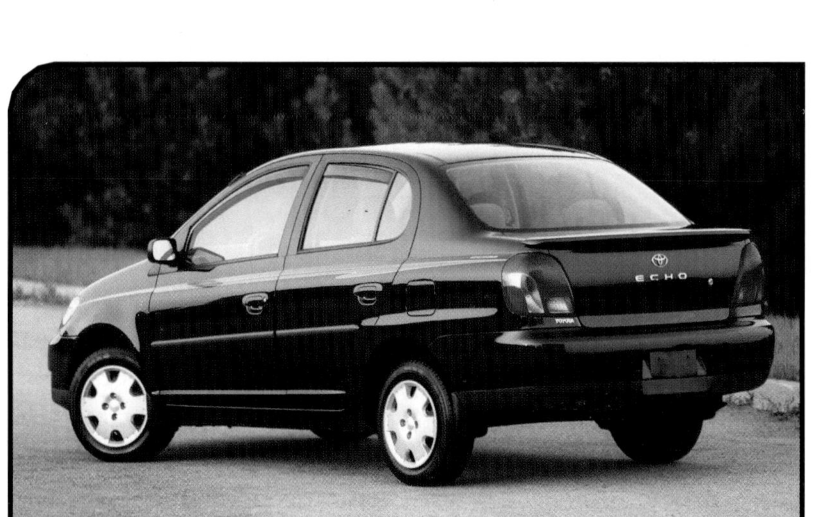

SPECIFICATIONS

Price	$CDN 14,085-16,760 / $US 10,450-10,980
Warranty	3 years / 36,000 miles (60,000 km)
Type	sedan / front wheel drive
Wheelbase / Length	93.3 in / 163 in
Width / Height	65.4 in / 59 in
Weight	2094 lb (950 kg)
Trunk / Fuel tank	13.6 cu. ft / 12 gallons
Air bags	front
Front suspension	independent
Rear suspension	semi-independent
Front brakes / Rear brakes	disc / drum
Traction control	no
Steering	rack-and-pinion, power assist
Turning circle	32 feet
Tires (front/rear)	P175/65R14

PERFORMANCE

Engine	4L 1.5 liter
Transmission	4-speed automatic
Horsepower	108 hp at 6000 rpm
Torque	105 lb-ft at 4200 rpm
Other engines	none
Other transmission	5-speed manual
Acceleration (0-60 mph)	9.5 sec
Maximum speed	106 mph (170 km/h)
Braking (60-0 mph)	161 feet (49.2 m)
Fuel consumption	34.9 mpg (6.5 L/100 km)

COMPETITION

• Hyundai Accent • Daewoo Lanos • Kia Rio
• Suzuki Swift

NEW FOR 2002

• APX package

RATING

	(out of 5 stars)
Driveability	★★
Comfort	★★★
Reliability	★★★★
Roominess	★★★★
Winter driving rating	★★
Safety	★★★★
Resale value	★★★

TOYOTA HIGHLANDER

TOYOTA **HIGHLANDER**

Fitting Compromise

From a distance, the Highlander looks like any other sturdy truck-based 4X4. But just as we should never judge a book by its cover, so we should not judge this sport-utility by its appearance. In the fall of 2000, the Highlander spearheaded Toyota's concerted efforts to improve its position in the light-truck and SUV market. But the Highlander's characteristics place it somewhere between "pseudo-trucks" like the RAV4 and the more ruggedly hardy 4Runner. The ranking sounds about right in view of the fact that this on- and off-road Toyota is car-based – a direct descendant of the Lexus RX 300, itself an upscale version of the Camry.

If "image is everything," then the Highlander's exterior resembles a *trompe l'oeil* façade. Its height, square shape and truck-style grille reek of adventure and invulnerability. Stylewise, though, I prefer the RAV4, but the Highlander does look more inspiring than the Sequoia, which reminds you of a hearse or a refrigerator on wheels.

If the exterior doesn't show the Highlander's affinities with the RX 300, the elegant cockpit betrays its lineage. Like the Lexus, the center console is integrated with the instrument panel, thus freeing-up floorspace and allowing a pass-through between the front and the rear. The shift selector juts out from the center console, just below the audio system and climate controls, both of which have oversized, easy-to-use buttons and knobs. The display dials, though pleasingly styled, are deeply set in an egg-shaped receptable, and therefore hard to read.

As befits a Toyota, both the materials and the quality of finish are first-rate. The front seats are comfortably firm, but just slightly contoured, offering little lateral support. On the other hand, the rear bench is mighty comfortable, a rare thing in this category of vehicle. The 60/40 backrest can recline backward or fold flat forward, without getting in the way of the headrests. Cabin space abounds, well above average. But unlike the Ford Explorer or the Toyota Sequoia, the Highlander doesn't offer third-row seating.

"Downscale" RX 300

Double duty

Toyota is aiming the Highlander straight at those customers who are keen on "the

▲ PROS

- **Reliable drivetrain • Elegant dashboard**
- **Comfortable seats • Well-tuned suspension**
- **Predictable roadholding**

▼ CONS

• High center of gravity • Limited model too expensive • No side air bags • Poor dampening of bumps • Barely efficient AWD

image and versatility of an SUV," as well as on Toyota's brand-name reliability and a virtually guaranteed resale value. The standard version is equipped with a 2.4-liter 4-cylinder engine with 155 horsepower, and is not available with all-wheel drive. This all-new powertrain is silent and soft, in great part because of the two counter-rotating balance shafts.

The most popular choice proves to be the 3.0-liter DOHC V6 engine with all-wheel drive, the same as the RX 300. The 220 horsepower will come in handy when driving in deep snow or on a muddy trail. Fuel economy is 15 mpg (15 liters per 100 km), only slightly better than the V8 engine. Despite the many modifications brought to it over the years, Toyota's all-wheel drive – developed in the early 1990s for the Camry and Celica – is beginning to show its age. Although the Highlander handles itself respectably on barely passable roads – snowy or icy – it's no Jeep Liberty.

Maximum comfort

This "compromise vehicle" – fitting in somewhere between the RAV4 and the 4Runner – handles like one, too. Its all-wheel drive conducts itself better on the open highway than off the beaten track. Under normal driving conditions, the Highlander behaves like a big station wagon, its center of gravity resting on a relatively soft suspension to ensure maximum overall comfort. Steering is not exactly precise, but perhaps that is the point, as engineers tried to mitigate the shocks caused by those annoying expansion joints in the road. And as we have come to expect from Toyota, sound insulation is excellent, braking and road-holding reliable, though a slight feeling of understeer is noticeable on sharp curves.

Finally, you will need a calculator to tabulate the total price list. Beware of the Limited model, whose price is markedly higher than the other models. Admittedly, it's the only model offering a V6 engine, traction and vehicle skid controls, but the rest of the package is on the expensive side.

Denis Duquet

SPECIFICATIONS	
Price	$CDN 31,990-36,190 / $US 23,995-26,975
Warranty	3 years / 36,000 miles (60,000 km)
Type	sport utility / all wheel drive
Wheelbase / Length	106.7 in / 184.3 in
Width / Height	71.7 in / 66 in
Weight	3880 lb (1760 kg)
Trunk / Fuel tank	32.1; 81.4 cu. ft / 20 gallons
Air bags	front
Front suspension	independent
Rear suspension	independent
Front brakes / Rear brakes	disc ABS
Traction control	yes (optional with V6)
Steering	rack-and-pinion, variable assist
Turning circle	41 feet
Tires (front/rear)	P225/70R16

PERFORMANCE	
Engine	V6 3-liter
Transmission	4-speed automatic
Horsepower	220 hp at 5800 rpm
Torque	222 lb-ft at 4400 rpm
Other engines	4L 2.4-liter 155 hp
Other transmission	none
Acceleration (0-60 mph)	8.6 sec; 11.3 sec (4L)
Maximum speed	112 mph (180 km/h)
Braking (60-0 mph)	130 feet (39.6 m)
Fuel consumption	15.1 mpg (15 L/100 km)

COMPETITION

- Acura MDX • Chev. TrailBlazer/GMC Envoy
- Ford Explorer • Subaru Forester

NEW FOR 2002

- No major change

RATING	(out of 5 stars)
Driveability	★★★
Comfort	★★★★
Reliability	★★★★½
Roominess	★★★★
Winter driving rating	★★★★
Safety	★★★½
Resale value	★★★★

TOYOTA MATRIX PONTIAC VIBE

TOYOTA **MATRIX**

Dynamic Duo

Car manufacturers are always on the lookout for the next big thing. Those who used to believe that the market would never respond favorably to sport utility vehicles paid dearly for their mistake. For their part, General Motors and Toyota are apparently convinced that compact wagons will be the next craze in the coming decade. They have therefore joined forces to develop a new compact wagon – something appealing and reasonably sized, which will provide good fuel economy and can carry bulky loads more efficiently than a sedan.

While you may wonder what GM and Toyota are doing in the same boat, it's not really that surprising. These two car-manufacturing giants have been working together for years on model development and production. The Prism, sold only in the United States, is an example of this collaboration. This time around, they have developed an elegant hybrid wagon combining the advantages of a sport utility with the affordable price of a compact. It will be available in Canada and in the United States under the Pontiac and Toyota banners. It will be known as the Vibe at Pontiac, and Matrix over at Toyota.

Toyota die-hards probably won't appreciate driving a vehicle with GM-built mechanical components. It's an open secret that the number one U.S. manufacturer doesn't exactly enjoy a good reputation among buyers of imported vehicles. Mindful that this could work against their joint project, managers decided that the mechanical aspect would be largely designed and developed by Toyota, whose reliability and sophistication in this area is legendary.

Sexy SUVs

However, in terms of style and bodywork design, Toyota has frequently been accused of being unduly conservative, while Pontiac vehicles are generally considered more dynamic and seem better equipped to attract buyers. Body styling was therefore assigned to the General Motors design studio. CALTY Design Research Inc., the Toyota design center in California, brought the necessary modifications that would give the Matrix a Toyota personality.

Although it's a joint undertaking, the two cars will be manufactured in two dif-

▲ PROS

- Attractive bodywork • Flat cargo space
- Optional all-wheel drive • Well chosen engines • Well-designed interior

▼ CONS

- Average rear seats • Busy dashboard
- Instruments difficult to read
- Unknown reliability

ferent plants. The Vibe will be assembled at the NUMI plant in California, while the Matrix will be built exclusively in Canada.

Everything for everyone

Although their mechanical components are essentially the same, these two vehicles aim to use the differences in their bodywork design to assert their individuality. And if you think that a compact wagon is just a utility vehicle, you're in for quite a surprise.

The two models will be available in front-wheel or all-wheel drive with a selection of engines and transmissions, in order to allow the greatest number of buyers to find the right combination of accessories and engines. The standard engine is a 1.8-liter 4-cylinder rating 130 hp. Acceleration to 60 mph should be around 10 seconds. This model is a direct rival to the Protegé5 whose engine has exactly the same horsepower. But the combined forces of Toyota and Pontiac currently have the edge, in the form of engine options as Mazda offers no such option at present.

Both the Matrix Sport version and the Vibe GT version feature ground-effect bodywork and 17-inch wheels. Under their hood is a 180-hp 1.8-liter VVTL-i engine – the same as the Celica GT-S – paired to a 6-speed manual gearbox.

All models offers excellent interior space, the kind of headroom and riding comfort you'd find in a five-seater, as well as the adaptability and cargo capacity of a sport utility. The rear cargo area is perfectly flat and there are numerous anchor points. The Matrix features running on rails in the cargo bay, similar to those of the Saab 9[5] wagon.

For once, the two companies have managed to use their respective strong points for the benefit of their buyers.

Denis Duquet

PONTIAC **VIBE**

SPECIFICATIONS

Price	est. $CDN 18,000-30,000 / $US 11,000-19,000
Warranty	3 years / 36,000 miles (60,000 km)
Type	wagon / all wheel drive
Wheelbase / Length	102.4 in / 171.7 in
Width / Height	69.7 in / 63 in
Weight	2976 lb (1350 kg)
Trunk / Fuel tank	58.7 cu. ft / 13 gallons
Air bags	front and side
Front suspension	independent
Rear suspension	independent
Front brakes / Rear brakes	disc ABS
Traction control	yes (4X2)
Steering	rack-and-pinion, power assist
Turning circle	n.a.
Tires (front/rear)	P265/40R18

PERFORMANCE

Engine	4L 1.8-liter
Transmission	6-speed manual
Horsepower	180 hp at 7600 rpm
Torque	130 lb-ft at 6800 rpm
Other engines	4L 1.8-liter 130 hp
Other transmission	4-speed automatic
Acceleration (0-60 mph)	7.1 sec (est.)
Maximum speed	130 mph (210 km/h)
Braking (60-0 mph)	125 ft (est.) (38 m)
Fuel consumption	27 mpg (8.4 L/100 km)

COMPETITION

- Ford Focus • Mazda Protegé5
- Volkswagen Jetta

NEW FOR 2002

- New model (available in Spring 2002)

RATING (out of 5 stars)

Driveability	Insufficient data
Comfort	
Reliability	
Roominess	
Winter driving rating	
Safety	
Resale value	

TOYOTA PRIUS

TOYOTA **PRIUS**

A Darker Shade of Green

It's going to be a while before the Toyota Prius starts competing in a production-vehicle contest or burning rubber on a racetrack. But while you're shedding fat crocodile tears over the idea of shelling out $80 each time you fill up your big, beloved SUV, save a small thought for the Prius, a car that will cost you $25 for the same distance traveled. And unlike the hefty Monsterwagon, the new Prius won't pollute the air you breathe in the process.

The dictionary defines the word "hybrid" as "consisting of two different types of components." The Toyota Prius is a hybrid vehicle, because it's propelled by an electric motor or an environmentally-conscious gasoline engine, or by both. The gas engine's very low rate of emission is achieved mainly because it relies on a non-polluting electric motor to intervene when fuel consumption is at its highest: during starts and acceleration or when you're driving at low speeds, say, in city traffic.

Waste not, recycle

With the Prius, the energy generated during braking – which would normally be lost as heat – is recovered by a regenerative braking system that converts it back into electricity, and then uses it to recharge the car's batteries. The batteries can also be recharged by an alternator powered by the gasoline engine. While the electric motor powers the front wheels via the car's continuously variable transmission, the purpose of the gasoline engine is to assist the electric motor when it's depleted, and as noted above, to power the alternator that recharges the batteries.

All these operations are electronically managed by the patented Toyota Hybrid System (THS). The result is an utterly seamless switch back and forth between the electric motor and gasoline engine. If if hadn't been for the display screen on the dashboard indicating what mode is being engaged, it would be almost impossible to tell.

The cutting-edge technology that makes the Prius stand out from other production cars is concealed under a modest automotive shell, whose nondescript shape is reminiscent of the Toyota Echo. We wouldn't say it's downright ugly, but at the same time, we'd be hard pressed to award it a prize for good looks.

So while the body may be nothing much to look at, the Prius' cockpit deserves high

▲ PROS

- Excellent sound insulation • Genuine 4-seater
- Low consumption and emissions
- Remarkable urban performances

▼ CONS

- Annoying highway driving • Nondescript body
- Poor overall performance • Steep price

marks if only for its originality. Instruments and commands are symmetrically arranged in the middle of the dashboard, making it easier and more practical for Toyota to configure both the left and right-hand driving positions for its various world markets.

The continuously variable transmission selector located on the dashboard is similar to that of the old Citroëns, very different from what we're accustomed to, though it doesn't take long getting used to it. The display screen that shows the functioning of the powertrain and other key data such as fuel consumption can be fun for a while, but the novelty soon wears off and you barely notice it anymore. Like the Echo, the Prius has a taller roofline than standard cars in its class, resulting in more upright seating than usual, extra comfort, easier exit and entry, and better visibility.

The Prius is also full of surprises. As you turn the key, the electric motor kicks in, which explains the complete absence of engine noise. You'll also be struck by the extra-powerful brakes, linked as they are to the regenerative system. Soon though, you'll get accustomed to the car and begin to appreciate its agility on city streets. It does less well on the highway, however, where it's sensitive to side winds and fuel consumption increases slightly. Also the hybrid powertrain tends to cause slight power surges which can be tiresome after a while.

Without question, the Prius does best in the city, where its hybrid powertrain makes most sense: consumption is modest – 60 mpg (4.5 liters per 100 km) for a sedan with four genuine seats – and emissions are ultra-low! That's a tribute to the Prius, a car unlike any other. Just think about it: if 25% of urban automobiles were built like the Prius, gas companies would have to find better excuses than the lame phrase "oil shortage" to justify their frequent price increases at the pump. And if you expect the government to encourage such behavior, you're in for a long wait. Besides gas companies, guess who benefits most from overconsumption brought on by our beloved gas-guzzling SUVs?

Alain Raymond

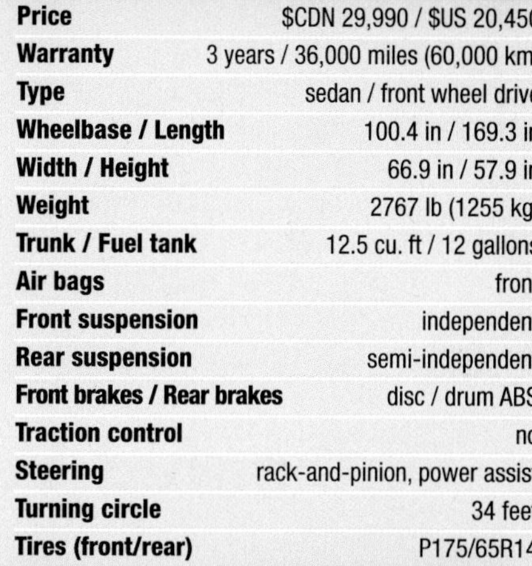

SPECIFICATIONS

Price	$CDN 29,990 / $US 20,450
Warranty	3 years / 36,000 miles (60,000 km)
Type	sedan / front wheel drive
Wheelbase / Length	100.4 in / 169.3 in
Width / Height	66.9 in / 57.9 in
Weight	2767 lb (1255 kg)
Trunk / Fuel tank	12.5 cu. ft / 12 gallons
Air bags	front
Front suspension	independent
Rear suspension	semi-independent
Front brakes / Rear brakes	disc / drum ABS
Traction control	no
Steering	rack-and-pinion, power assist
Turning circle	34 feet
Tires (front/rear)	P175/65R14

PERFORMANCE

Engine	4L 1.5-liter + electric motor
Transmission	automatic, variator
Horsepower	70 hp at 4500 rpm + 44 hp at 1000 rpm
Torque	82 lb-ft at 4200 rpm + 259 lb at 400 rpm
Other engines	none
Other transmission	none
Acceleration (0-60 mph)	12.8 sec
Maximum speed	93 mph (150 km/h)
Braking (60-0 mph)	138 feet (42 m)
Fuel consumption	50.1 mpg (city); 39.2 mpg (highway) (4.5 L; 5.8 L/100 km)

COMPETITION

• Honda Insight • VW Beetle TDI • VW Golf TDI • VW Jetta TDI

NEW FOR 2002

No major change

RATING	(out of 5 stars)
Driveability	★★½
Comfort	★★★★
Reliability	★★★★
Roominess	★★★★
Winter driving rating	★★★½
Safety	★★★
Resale value	n.a.

TOYOTA RAV4

TOYOTA **RAV4**

Older and Wiser

Now entering its second generation, the car-based Toyota RAV4 still ranks among the most popular compact SUVs. Its standing seems all the more assured for the present, given the unabating 4X4 craze, and at a time when the volatility at the gas pump causes full-size SUV enthusiasts to have second thoughts.

With most of its early flaws corrected in time for the second-generation launch last year, the 2002 model shows only minor changes.

The RAV4 is easily recognized by its sculpted lines, enhanced by a spoiler mounted atop the rear end of the roof. In front, the grille is flanked by two huge headlights, accompanied by fog lamps embedded in the wrap-around bumper. On the sides, a broad strip of molding efficiently protects the doors from potential knocks or scrapes. Despite constant carping from car columnists and drivers, the tailgate, designed for markets where they drive on the left-hand side of the road, continues to swing open from the curb side. Protected by a rigid cover, the spare tire is still mounted outside, but it's low enough not to hamper rear visibility.

"A" for effort

The RAV4's gorgeous styling extends to its interior. The well-designed dashboard is also ergonomically sound: the radio/CD is placed high, controls for heating and air conditioning are easy to reach and manipulate, cupholders solidly screwed in. There's room for improvement, however: the controls mounted on the steering wheel could be more readable; the front seats, though comfortable, are not heated, and rear visibility could be better. Still, the RAV4 stands out with its stylish three-spoke steering wheel, large heated exterior mirrors and numerous storage pockets. All in all, a far cry from the mediocre interior of the prior generation.

Well-rounded 4X4

In the rear, the 50/50 bench can slide, tumble, recline or be removed completely. Practical? Indeed. Spacious rear cabin? Not really, since there's still precious little headroom – or any kind of room to maneuver, for that matter.

▲ PROS

• Flexible rear cabin • Good ergonomics • Nimble vehicle • Pleasant silhouette and cockpit • Proven reliability

▼ CONS

• Badly designed rear door • Cramped rear cabin • Noisy engine during acceleration • Poor acceleration • Steep price (high end)

Straight to the top

With 148 hp and 142 lb-ft of torque, transmitted by a 4-speed automatic gearbox, you'd think the 2.0-liter engine would have no trouble propelling the RAV4 vigorously. But acceleration turned out to be ho-hum-0-60 mph in 11.4 seconds - and it takes 12 seconds to go from 50 to 75 mph. Clearly, the RAV4's weight – 2877 lbs (1305 kg) – is a factor. Don't even think about passing: it might prove to be hazardous. While its performance has clearly improved, the RAV4 still has a way to go. No doubt a 5-speed manual gearbox will make acceleration figures more respectable.

On the road, the power steering is excellent and proves more precise than the competition's. Braking force, barely adequate, would have been more efficient had the RAV4 been fitted with rear disc brakes rather than the antiquated drum variety. The four-wheel independent suspension ensures both comfort and decent handling. On patchy pavement, however, the big tires have a slight tendency to hop around.

Off-road, the RAV4 depends on its full-time all-wheel drive featuring a Torsen central differential and visco-coupling system – handy on slippery surfaces. This system is more efficient than the Honda CR-V's – the RAV4's main rival – where excessive front end wheel spin will hamper starts on a surface that's the least bit slippery. Our high-end test model also boasted a limited-slip rear differential, boosting its active-safety capabilities.

The improved second-generation RAV4 has catapulted Toyota to the head of the compact-SUV category. And it's easy to see why. Although not considered a genuine 4X4, the RAV4 harmoniously combines on- and off-road aptitudes. It's base price is certainly attractive and competitive, but beware, once all the options are factored in, the final amount can be steep.

Alain Raymond

SPECIFICATIONS

Price	$CDN 26,315 / $US16,845-18,245
Warranty	3 years / 36,000 miles (60,000 km)
Type	compact sport-utility / all wheel drive
Wheelbase / Length	98 in / 165 in
Width / Height	68.1 in / 66.1 in
Weight	2877 lb (1305 kg)
Trunk / Fuel tank	8.4 – 23.8 cu. ft / 15 gallons
Air bags	front
Front suspension	independent
Rear suspension	independent
Front brakes / Rear brakes	disc / drum (ABS optional)
Traction control	no
Steering	rack-and-pinion, variable assist
Turning circle	35 feet
Tires (front/rear)	P235/60R16

PERFORMANCE

Engine	4L 2 liter
Transmission	4-speed automatic
Horsepower	148 hp at 6000 rpm
Torque	142 lb-ft at 4000 rpm
Other engines	none
Other transmission	5-speed manual
Acceleration (0-60 mph)	11.4 s (automatic);
Maximum speed	10.6 s (manual)
Braking (60-0 mph)	106 mph (170 km/h)
Fuel consumption	134 feet (40.7 m)
	20.1 mpg (11.3 L/100 km)

COMPETITION

• CR-V • Escape • Forester • SantaFe
• Sportage • Tracker / Vitara • Tribute

NEW FOR 2002

No major change

RATING

(out of 5 stars)

Driveability	★★★½
Comfort	★★★½
Reliability	★★★★★
Roominess	★★★½
Winter driving rating	★★★★
Safety	★★★★½
Resale value	★★★★

TOYOTA 4RUNNER

TOYOTA **4RUNNER**

The Old Guard

Last year, Toyota launched a whole range of new SUVs. The RAV4 was redesigned from top to bottom and two new models appeared: the Highlander and the Sequoia. At the same time, the 4Runner's exterior was changed slightly. Moreover, its 4-wheel drivetrain was improved and several electronic systems were added.

But before getting into the mechanical details, it's important to emphasize that the modifications made to this Toyota's bodywork last year didn't satisfactorily rejuvenate the stout creature. In fact, the last time this vehicle was completely redesigned was in 1997. This time around, nothing terribly striking has been done with the aesthetics. To the point where a colleague of mine actually photographed an older model without realizing his mistake.

The vehicle has now reached a stage where it's trying to keep up with the competition with only evolutionary modifications, as and when it suits Toyota. The result is neither a coherent process nor a coherent vehicle. For a start, the design is dated. The cockpit looks okay, I suppose, but is nothing to write home about. The new color-contrasting strip on the console, which houses the radio and climate controls, does liven up the rather drab design. The sliding climate controls have been replaced by knobs, which are much more efficient and precise.

Switching over to 4-wheel-drive mode involves pressing a simple button while the central differential can be locked by means of a switch. The floor-mounted lever engages the 4-wheel drive system and selects 4Lo or 4Hi. It would have been a lot simpler if all these controls were mounted on the dashboard. But it's possible someone decided it was much more macho that way. Perhaps the system's mechanical configuration won't allow this possibility.

Modern retro

Whatever the reason, the cockpit appointments are well made, materials are high quality and the seats are comfortable. Unfortunately, ingress and egress can be tricky, as the vehicle is fairly high and the roofline fairly low. I can't even remember how many times I banged my head while getting in and out of the 4Runner. Moreover, this configuration makes the driving position a little awkward and

▲ PROS

- Electronically controlled driving assistance
- Quality materials • Reliable mechanicals
- Smooth V6 engine • Tough all-wheel drive

▼ CONS

- Average tires • Dated chassis • High price
- Imprecise steering • Wind noise

uncomfortable for tall people. Cargo capacity is good, however.

Modernization of the 4Runner, completed last year, essentially involved an electronic lateral stability control and an electronic braking force distribution system. Practically everything is electronically controlled now. The gas pedal is no longer controlled by a mechanical link but by an electric wire.

Old-fashioned approach

Despite a plethora of electronic controls over everything, the 4Runner can't hide a design that was inspired by an old philosophy, that of the true-blue four-wheel drive vehicle, relying more on the strength and sturdiness of its mechanical components in order to get itself out of trouble. In these vehicles, driving pleasure and comfort took second place. These days, the new models are designed to function so that the various electronic systems bear the brunt of the work.

To be fair, the 4Runner does have onboard electronics. The chassis is the component that lacks refinement, a fact that becomes all too obvious after a few miles. Ride and suspension are a tad firmer than average, steering is relatively imprecise, resulting in poor road feedback. Let's put it another way, despite all the add-ons and modifications made over the years, the 4Runner remains true to its truck origins. And while the 4-wheel drive system works particularly well thanks to active traction control, the tires are not completely up to the job.

The 4Runner is not without qualities. Its on and off-road behavior is well within the average. But because of the various modifications made over time, it lacks coherence, amounting to little more than just the sum of its parts.

Denis Duquet

SPECIFICATIONS	
Price	$CDN 36,250-49,465 / $US 26,815-36,585
Warranty	3 years / 36,000 miles (60,000 km)
Type	sport utility / 4X4
Wheelbase / Length	105.1 in / 178.7 in
Width / Height	70.9 in / 69.3 in
Weight	5249 lb (2381 kg)
Trunk / Fuel tank	44.6 cu. ft. / 19 gallons
Air bags	front
Front suspension	independent
Rear suspension	rigid axle
Front brakes / Rear brakes	disc / drum ABS
Traction control	yes
Steering	rack-and-pinion, variable assist
Turning circle	37 feet
Tires (front/rear)	P265/70R16 (LTD)

PERFORMANCE	
Engine	V6 3.4-liter
Transmission	4-speed automatic
Horsepower	183 hp at 4800 rpm
Torque	217 lb-ft at 3600 rpm
Other engines	none
Other transmission	none
Acceleration (0-60 mph)	11.7 sec
Maximum speed	106 mph (170 km/h)
Braking (60-0 mph)	152 feet (46.3 m)
Fuel consumption	15.2 mpg (14.9 L/100 km)

COMPETITION

• Chev. Blazer • Ford Explorer • Isuzu Rodeo • Jeep Grand Cherokee • Nissan Pathfinder • M-Benz ML320

NEW FOR 2002

• New hood (Renegade) • Compressor offered as an accessory

RATING	**(out of 5 stars)**
Driveability	★★★
Comfort	★★★
Reliability	★★★★★
Roominess	★★★★½
Winter driving rating	★★★★★
Safety	★★★★
Resale value	★★★½

TOYOTA SEQUOIA

TOYOTA **SEQUOIA**

A 240-HP Refrigerator

Even the most independent automakers must eventually yield to market forces. If Toyota wants to compete on an equal footing with its North American rivals, for example, it's obliged to think big, and bigger still if it wants to produce a quality SUV. Given the success of the Ford Expedition, Dodge Durango and Chevrolet Tahoe/GMC Yukon, the Japanese automaker knew it would have to join the race for supremacy in large-size vehicles. It decided to pursue the Ford Expedition, deeming the Chevrolet Suburban too cumbersome and the Tahoe too small.

The fact that Toyota had brought out a new full-size pickup truck in 2000 made the decision easier. It had a big, modern platform at its disposal on which to build a full-size SUV. They dubbed it Sequoia, after the tree that grows more than 150 meters high.

Timid designers?

Toyota's "visionaries" claim that styling is what sells SUVs. But looking at the Sequoia, it's hard to believe that style was high a priority. No doubt they had good intentions, but the results are disappointing. Next to even the models it emulates – which generally sport a somewhat conventional roundish exterior – the Sequoia looks more like a huge refrigerator on wheels. Toyota designers appear to favor the household-appliance look, which they've used on other models.

From the side, the Sequoia doesn't look all that bad. From the front, however, its curved lines are nondescript and retro, negating any visual impact Toyota designers hoped to achieve. That's too bad because they've demonstrated that they can be highly imaginative – the handsome RAV4 is a case in point. The Sequoia's nondescript "personality" is also an indication of its target clientele: the Grecian Formula crowd.

Think Big!

Fortunately, the cockpit looks good and is easy to enter thanks to a doorsill that's a good 5-cm lower than that of the Ford Expedition. It's also bigger than the Ford's cockpit. The front seats are comfortable: those in the middle row are reasonable, but third-row seating is for small passengers only or bigger people with a high tolerance for pain. Even with the seven-passenger configuration, the luggage compartment is a hefty size.

▲ PROS

• Excellent engine • Sophisticated 4X4 system • Spaciousness • Flawless finish • Comfortable suspension

▼ CONS

• Cumbersome dimensions • Retro looks • Control for rearview mirrors badly located • Imprecise steering • Third-row seats uncomfortable

The dashboard might have looked run-of-the-mill if it weren't for the triangular module with grey plastic trim holding the two ventilation outlets and buttons for the radio and climate control. Even claustrophobics will feel totally at ease aboard the Sequoia, the biggest Toyota ever sold in Canada. Second-row passengers have their own climate controls.

Ultra-sophisticated electronics

In the past, any self-respecting car columnist would have regaled you with the mechanical subtleties of the 240 hp 4.7-liter V8 engine, the multi-link solid-axle rear suspension – which ensured an above-average ground clearance – and four-wheel disc brakes. All that seems par for the course today. Unlike the Tundra pickup on which it is based, the Sequoia can switch between rear-wheel drive, all-wheel drive and low range. A button on the dashboard allows the driver to select the desired mode, while a floor-mounted shift lever automatically locks the central differential and switches to low range.

But there's more to the Sequoia, such as the panoply of electronic features for maintaining a more efficient all-wheel drive, a lateral stability control and the A-Trac system – an ultra-sophisticated anti-skid system for off-road driving.

A-Trac made it easy for me to descend steep hills or drive straight up a rough escarpment. All the features worked beautifully in sync: the automatic torque distribution, selective braking forces as well as power reduction. But I did wonder about the brakes' heat-absorption capabilities under constant use during lengthy off-road excursions.

On the road, the Sequoia is surprisingly nimble despite its imposing size and slight tendency to roll while cornering. The engine is remarkably quiet for a full-size SUV. The Sequoia inherits many qualities from the Tundra, whose platform it was based on, but proves nimbler still and more civilized in off-road driving.

I wonder, though, just who really needs a vehicle like this.

Denis Duquet

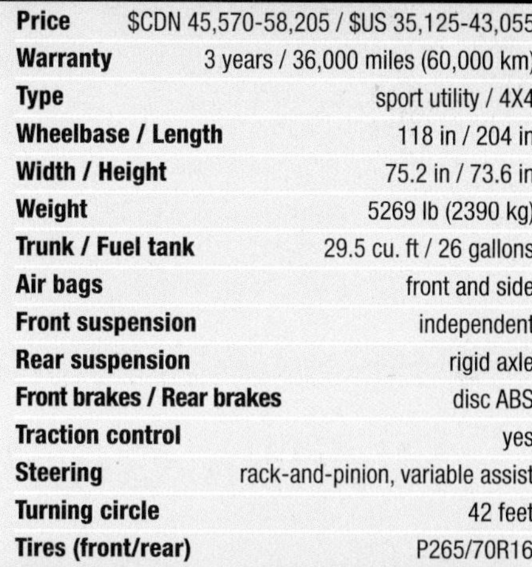

SPECIFICATIONS	**Limited**
Price	$CDN 45,570-58,205 / $US 35,125-43,055
Warranty	3 years / 36,000 miles (60,000 km)
Type	sport utility / 4X4
Wheelbase / Length	118 in / 204 in
Width / Height	75.2 in / 73.6 in
Weight	5269 lb (2390 kg)
Trunk / Fuel tank	29.5 cu. ft / 26 gallons
Air bags	front and side
Front suspension	independent
Rear suspension	rigid axle
Front brakes / Rear brakes	disc ABS
Traction control	yes
Steering	rack-and-pinion, variable assist
Turning circle	42 feet
Tires (front/rear)	P265/70R16

PERFORMANCE	
Engine	V8 4.7-liter
Transmission	4-speed automatic
Horsepower	240 hp at 4800 rpm
Torque	315 lb-ft at 3400 rpm
Other engines	none
Other transmission	none
Acceleration (0-60 mph)	8.5 sec
Maximum speed	118 mph (190 km/h)
Braking (60-0 mph)	141 feet (43 m)
Fuel consumption	18.6 mpg (12.2 L/100 km)

COMPETITION

- Chevrolet Tahoe/GMC Yukon • Dodge Durango
- Ford Expedition

NEW FOR 2002

No major change

RATING	**(out of 5 stars)**
Driveability	★★★½
Comfort	★★★★
Reliability	★★★★★
Roominess	★★★★½
Winter driving rating	★★★★★
Safety	★★★★
Resale value	★★★½

TOYOTA SIENNA

TOYOTA **SIENNA**

Hidden Qualities

The Toyota Sienna minivan was introduced in 1998 as a replacement for the exuberant and very different Previa. Based on the Camry platform, the Sienna obviously takes after the sedan's steady and predictable road manners, so much so that Toyota officials readily dubbed it the "Camry of minivans."

Styling-wise, this minivan has a lot in common with such benchmark models as the Dodge Caravan, Ford Windstar, Honda Odyssey and others. But the Sienna's best qualities are hidden under the hood. The environmentally-friendly and sophisticated 3.0-liter V6 engine with VVTi (Variable Valve Timing with intelligence), for example, generates a whopping 210 horsepower and is mated to a superb 4-speed electronically controlled "smart" gearbox (ECTi). Acceleration is unfailingly peppy and gear changes are silky smooth. Like all other Toyotas – with the exception of the Echo – sound insulation is so good that you forget there's actually an engine at work... and working hard! Torque is adequate, and at 20 mpg (12 liters per 100 km), fuel mileage is average for a vehicle of this category.

Don't push too hard

The Sienna's road manners are appropriate for its intended purpose in life, as long as you don't push the vehicle too hard. Remember that the suspension was tuned for comfort, not for sporty driving.

What's more, the leather seats are as slippery as the road itself during an ice storm. So make sure you don't do anything to "provoke" the vehicle when cornering. In a tight turn, the very ordinary standard tires will squeal and cause the minivan to lean even more. But rest assured, the Sienna will stay firmly on the road. In a longer bend, where you feel the urge to experience Formula-1 cornering, forget about it, because if you push it, you'll be penalized with severe understeer. Worse yet, steering is so overassisted and vague that it can't properly transmit road feel. In the same vein, the Sienna doesn't like it when you change lanes too quickly. So be careful of weight transfer.

Strong contender

On the other hand, the vehicle has a lot of good things to offer. It's so comfortable you look forward to taking long trips. Though it's not brilliant, braking power is more that adequate, except for an odd and worrisome noise that emanated from the

▲ PROS

• Exceptional reliability • Good engine performance • Ingenious cupholders • Overall comfort • Quality finish

▼ CONS

• Criminally high price • Overassisted and vague steering • Slippery leather seats • Suspension (not conducive to sporty driving)

ABS after I abruptly stepped on the brake pedal. It just goes to show, don't push the Sienna too hard...

Passengers are spoiled in this big vehicle. Finish is Toyota-perfect and you get the reassuring feeling that it's a solid car. The driving position is excellent, although the height-adjustable seat in my test model wasn't always in a cooperative mood. Neither was the gearshift lever, for that matter. It was hard to move and I often mistook it for the windshield-wiper lever. On the other hand, the radio and climate control buttons are big and easy to reach. No confusion on that score. Speaking of climate control, the one in the test model was quite noisy.

It's a pity that the rear is not as comfortable as it might be. The seat bottoms are too narrow and the armrests too short and tilted. Still, the seats are far better than the Hyundai Accent's rear bench. Visibility is adequate in front but less so in back – a potential problem when you're parking.

A driver's prayer

I find it hard to understand how a company like Toyota can spend zillions of dollars to develop super-sophisticated engines, yet fail to hire competent engineers to look after the other aspects of its vehicles. While the power side door on the right (you can get both through a complex and expensive option package) is an ingenious feat of engineering, the captain's chairs prove to be the exact opposite. With each weighing 59.5 lbs (27 kg), removing and putting them back isn't as simple an operation as it should be. In fact, it's more likely to tear bits of skin off your fingers. To end that afternoon in style, I amused myself by removing the spare tire from underneath the vehicle. It was an experience that finished me off completely. It is my most earnest and devout prayer that you will never get a flat tire on a rainy Sunday, on a deserted gravel road.

Despite these nagging irritations, the Toyota Sienna has everything to go head to head with the competition. With more precise steering, improved road manners and a more realistic price, it will undoubtedly rack up yet more sales.

Alain Morin

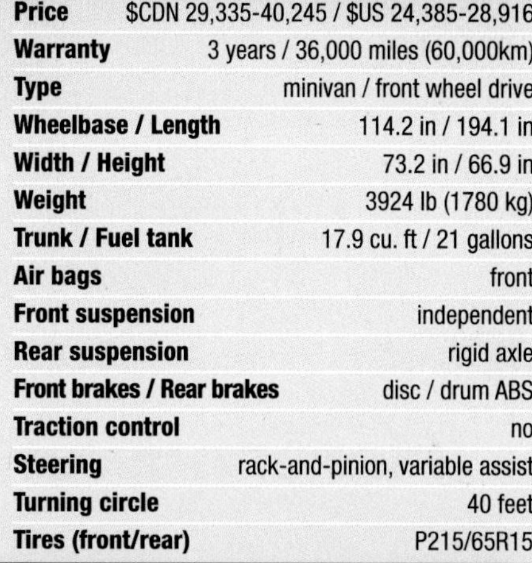

SPECIFICATIONS

Price	$CDN 29,335-40,245 / $US 24,385-28,916
Warranty	3 years / 36,000 miles (60,000km)
Type	minivan / front wheel drive
Wheelbase / Length	114.2 in / 194.1 in
Width / Height	73.2 in / 66.9 in
Weight	3924 lb (1780 kg)
Trunk / Fuel tank	17.9 cu. ft / 21 gallons
Air bags	front
Front suspension	independent
Rear suspension	rigid axle
Front brakes / Rear brakes	disc / drum ABS
Traction control	no
Steering	rack-and-pinion, variable assist
Turning circle	40 feet
Tires (front/rear)	P215/65R15

PERFORMANCE

Engine	V6 3.0-liter
Transmission	4-speed automatic
Horsepower	210 hp at 5800 rpm
Torque	220 lb-ft at 4400 rpm
Other engines	none
Other transmission	none
Acceleration (0-60 mph)	10.1 sec
Maximum speed	112 mph (180 km/h)
Braking (60-0 mph)	139 feet (42.4 m)
Fuel consumption	18.9 mpg (12 L/100 km)

COMPETITION

• Chevrolet Venture/Pontiac Montana • Dodge Caravan • Ford Windstar • Honda Odyssey • Mazda MPV

NEW FOR 2002

• Revamped option packages

RATING (out of 5 stars)

Driveability	★★★
Comfort	★★★★
Reliability	★★★★½
Roominess	★★★★
Winter driving rating	★★★★
Safety	★★★½
Resale value	★★★★

VOLKSWAGEN EUROVAN

VOLKSWAGEN **EUROVAN**

Horsepower Up, Price Down, News Good

While the North American minivan market is the world's most active, Volkswagen hasn't done particularly well in this sector in the past decade. Sales of the EuroVan, for example, have been sporadic right from the start in 1992 – a situation that's all the more surprising since it was the VW "Microbus" itself that literally created this vehicle category back in the 60s.

No one disputes the fact that Volkswagen is a household name in North America, but the German giant has never quite managed to adapt its minivan to the demands of this market. In Europe, it's considered a commercial vehicle and sold as the Volkswagen Caravelle. In fact, the Caravelle has been competing forever with the Ford Transit for customers in the construction trades as well as other small or family businesses. The Caravelle's passenger version is most often found outside various bed-and-breakfast establishments or country inns, where it's used as a taxi or airport limousine.

That makes it a little tricky to adapt the EuroVan to North American requirements. Its uncommon dimensions don't help matters: tall, narrow, and several inches shorter than the popular Honda Odyssey. But the two most awkward factors affecting EuroVan sales are its sub-par engine power and steep price. Despite the widespread, not-too-subtle protests from dealers and (potential) customers alike, the company stubbornly insisted on charging top dollar for a large minivan incongruously equipped with a 109 hp 5-cylinder engine.

Getting the message

In 1998, Volkswagen buckled under pressure and "awarded" its long-suffering EuroVan fans the same 2.8-liter VR6 engine as the Jetta's. To the fans' great disappointment, however, this VR6 could generate only 140 hp, not 174 as the Jetta was able to do. Still, the extra horses were welcome. Less welcome was the higher price that Volkswagen charged, seemingly commensurate with the extra engine power.

Temporary solution

But the German automaker has finally got the message, as the 2002 model amply demonstrates. Not only has the VR6's horsepower been bumped up to 201, but the suggested retail prices have been reduced by an average of 10% in Canada, and 15% in the United States. Another possible motive for Volkswagen's renewed

▲ PROS

• Above-average roominess • Performance on the rise • Quality materials • Reduced price • Weekender package

▼ CONS

• CD player not standard • Stiff suspension • Limited footroom in front • No glove compartment • No left-side sliding door • Greater height than width

interest in the EuroVan is its desire to establish a customer base for its Microbus (see Prototypes) that it hopes will hit the market within the next 5 or 6 years, assuming the project is approved.

In addition to the extra horsepower and lower price, the new EuroVan gets a few cosmetic changes: a modified grille, new air intake incorporated into the front bumper, revamped air conditioner with a more user-friendly control panel. Also new are 16-inch alloy wheels as standard equipment, as are ABS, traction control and the Electronic Stability Program (ESP).

EuroVan comes in two standard-wheelbase models: the GLS with three rows of seats, and the MultiVan – or MV – offering rear-facing second-row seats and a bench that can be converted into a bed. The Camper version is no longer offered, replaced by a longer-wheelbase camper made by Winnebago, and available only in the United States. The MultiVan model can also be fitted with the optional Weekender package – pop-up canopy top, sliding windows with screens, left-side rear-facing chair, refrigerator under a seat, auxiliary battery and alternator.

Much improved, but still...

There's no question that the new EuroVan is a huge improvement over the previous models. Backed up by 201 horsepower, it accelerates respectably, going from 0-60 mph in just under 12 seconds. The gearbox is well adapted to the vehicle, even though it seems hesitant at times, especially between 2nd and 3rd gears. Steering is more precise than average, if slightly hampered by a super-straight driving position combined with a non-adjustable steering wheel. This problem is exacerbated in the MultiVan, where the driver's backrest can't recline because there's a fixed rear-facing seat directly behind it.

EuroVan's overall height makes it susceptible to crosswinds, and the overly firm suspension doesn't really provide a smooth ride on bumpy roads. But the problem has been alleviated substantially thanks to the new EuroVan's more rigid body and better brakes.

All in all, the 3rd-generation EuroVan is more pleasant to drive than its predecessors. But its dimensions, cockpit configuration and price confine it to a more specialized clientele.

Denis Duquet

SPECIFICATIONS	GLS
Price	$CDN 41,795-44,190 / $US 26,815-28,315
Warranty	4 years / 48,000 miles (80,000 km)
Type	minivan / front wheel drive
Wheelbase / Length	115 in / 188.6 in
Width / Height	72.4 in / 76.4 in
Weight	4348 lb (1972 kg)
Trunk / Fuel tank	17.7 cu. ft / 21 gallons
Air bags	front
Front suspension	independent
Rear suspension	independent
Front brakes / Rear brakes	disc ABS
Traction control	yes
Steering	rack-and-pinion, power assist
Turning circle	43 feet
Tires (front/rear)	P225/65R16

PERFORMANCE	
Engine	V6 2.8-liter
Transmission	4-speed automatic
Horsepower	201 hp at 6200 rpm
Torque	181 lb-ft at 2500-5500 rpm
Other engines	none
Other transmission	none
Acceleration (0-60 mph)	11.4 sec
Maximum speed	118 mph (190 km/h)
Braking (60-0 mph)	152 feet (46.4 m)
Fuel consumption	16.6 mpg (13.7 L/100 km)

COMPETITION

• Chevrolet Astro/GMC Safari • Ford Econoline • GMC Savana

NEW FOR 2002

• Reduced price • 16-inch alloy wheels • 201 hp engine • Improved warranty

RATING	(out of 5 stars)
Driveability	★★
Comfort	★★★
Reliability	★★★
Roominess	★★★★★
Winter driving rating	★★★
Safety	★★★
Resale value	★★

VOLKSWAGEN GOLF

VOLKSWAGEN **GOLF**

Keeping it in the Family

The practice of sharing is an admirable virtue, and the Volkswagen Golf has a lot to be thankful for. Although no major change has been planned for 2002, its 1.8 turbocharged engine will benefit from the improvements made in its higher-end cousins, the Passat and Audi A4. These include an automatic 5-speed Tiptronic transmission, and a new 24-valve cylinder head for the GTI VR6.

The Golf is available as a base 2- or 4-door GL, 4-door GLS, or sporty GTI. The standard 115-hp 2.0-liter engine with an 8-valve cylinder head is now considered outdated, especially in light of the optional Turbo Direct Injection (TDI) diesel engine capable of generating 90 horsepower and a remarkable 155 lb-ft of torque at only 1900 rpm. Better still, diesel fuel mileage amounts to a whopping 45 mpg (5 liters per 100 km). The GL offers an impressive range of standard equipment, including ABS and front and side airbags.

In addition to the base equipment, the GLS includes air conditioning, cruise control, various power assistances and a swankier interior. Seats are comfortable enough, but taller passengers won't feel completely at ease sitting on the rear bench. Trunk space is on the plus side, capable of carrying big, cumbersome items with ease.

The GTI gets all the above-mentioned equipment, plus a 1.8-liter turbocharged engine to keep it zipping along.

In addition to the various Golfs, Volkswagen also offers the Cabrio, available, like the others, in three trim levels: base GL, mid-level GLS and top-of-the-line GLX. The GL comes with a manually-operated vinyl top and without the customary power assisted components – an unusual offering for a sub-compact car costing $28,500. The high-end GLX comes with heated leather front seats and an electrically controlled cloth top.

Think before you drive

Golf-based, the Cabrio offers a solid and comfortable ride despite its relatively small 14-inch wheels, thanks to a well-sorted suspension system (MacPherson struts and anti-roll bar in front and torsion-bar sprung rear axle) that provides ample straight-line stability and, unfortunately, a little too much body roll when cornering hard. It's a dream vacation car

▲ PROS

• Appealing silhouette • Excellent safety equipment • High-performance engines • OK handling • Practical trunk

▼ CONS

• Limited base warranty • Obsolete 2.0-liter engine • Steep price • Narrow rear seats • Unproven reliability

for two, if you ask me. And if you want to invite another couple to tag along, you needn't worry about the rear seats, which are just as comfortable. Trunk space, however, is limited, since half of the available area is needed for storing the 3-ply top.

Strong performance, steep price

A new sport-tuned suspension system, as well as an Anti-Slip Regulation System (ASR) and Electronic Differential Lock (EDL) come standard with the GTI. It's available in two trim levels: GLS and GLX. The GLS uses the superb 1.8-liter engine whose turbo readily kicks in at 2000 rpm. In 2001, horsepower was rated at 150, enough to deliver perfectly acceptable performance. With this year's 180 hp, things have obviously improved dramatically.

The GTI GLX serves up a 6-cylinder 24-valve VR6, capable of generating 201 horsepower. Paired to an exclusive 6-speed gearbox, it offers excellent acceleration. The suspension, however, is on the supple side and steering is a tad too light, a situation that doesn't favor "spirited" driving. Still, these are minor details, considering the car's generally solid handling and performance.

What is hardly a minor detail, however, is the $31,500 price tag that accompanies the GTI GLX. It's a splendid idea to have a leather interior, sunroof and trip computer. But do you really need all this equipment? Or is it mainly an attempt to justify the suspiciously steep asking prices for the entire Golf line? And although Volkswagen has made great strides in terms of reliability, the base warranty it offers is one of the most limited on the market. So, there you are: a little more food for thought as you consider your options.

Jean-Georges Laliberté

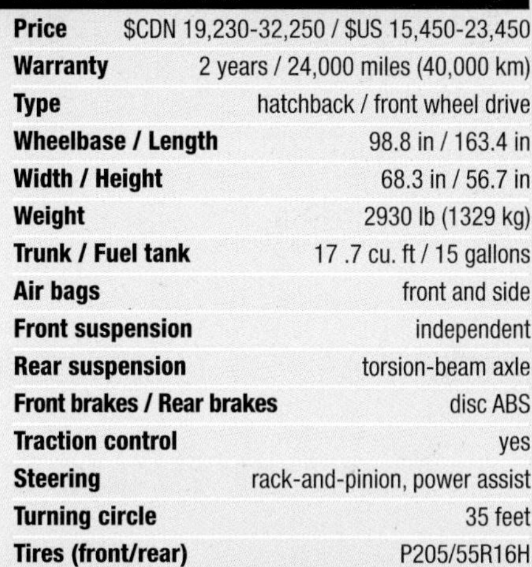

SPECIFICATIONS	**VR6**
Price	$CDN 19,230-32,250 / $US 15,450-23,450
Warranty	2 years / 24,000 miles (40,000 km)
Type	hatchback / front wheel drive
Wheelbase / Length	98.8 in / 163.4 in
Width / Height	68.3 in / 56.7 in
Weight	2930 lb (1329 kg)
Trunk / Fuel tank	17 .7 cu. ft / 15 gallons
Air bags	front and side
Front suspension	independent
Rear suspension	torsion-beam axle
Front brakes / Rear brakes	disc ABS
Traction control	yes
Steering	rack-and-pinion, power assist
Turning circle	35 feet
Tires (front/rear)	P205/55R16H
PERFORMANCE	
Engine	V6 2.8-liter
Transmission	5-speed manual (6 in 2002)
Horsepower	174 hp at 5800 rpm (201 hp in 2002)
Torque	181 lb-ft at 3200 rpm
Other engines	4L 2.0-liter; 4L 1.9-liter; TDI, 4L 1.8-liter turbo
Other transmission	4-speed automatic (except GTI GLX)
Acceleration (0-60 mph)	7.6 sec
Maximum speed	137 mph (220 km/h)
Braking (60-0 mph)	112 feet (34 m)
Fuel consumption	22.7 mpg (10 L/100 km)

COMPETITION

- Chrysler Neon • Ford Focus • Honda Civic
- Mazda Protegé • Toyota Corolla

NEW FOR 2002

- Improved warranty • New sport seats

RATING	**(out of 5 stars)**
Driveability	★★★★
Comfort	★★★½
Reliability	★★★
Roominess	★★★½
Winter driving rating	★★★½
Safety	★★★★
Resale value	★★★½

VOLKSWAGEN JETTA

VOLKSWAGEN **JETTA**

Turbo Muscle

The Jetta is Volkswagen's most popular model. In fact, it was the car's success in the United States that allowed Volkswagen to make a spectacular comeback in North America, where it is the top-selling European carmaker. In the old days, management would have rested comfortably on its laurels for several years before realizing that it had been overtaken by the competition as it was relaxing. But that was yesterday. Today, the decision-makers at Volkswagen are more aware than ever that they have to constantly fine-tune their products in terms of the needs and expectations of the driving public.

In 2002, the proof of that proposition is demonstrated by the overhaul of the complete Jetta lineup, and especially so with the arrival of the most powerful four-cylinder engine ever offered by Volkswagen: the 1.8 T developing 180 hp – 30 more than the previous year, and 6 more than the 2.8-liter V6, offered with the mid-level GLS and top-of-the-line GLX. Incidentally, starting in the spring of 2002, the V6's horsepower will be boosted to 201.

Even with 150 hp, the 1.8 T was already one of the more interesting engines on the market. A flat power curve guaranteed that the driver always had something in reserve, as it were, under his foot. By increasing turbo pressure and overhauling both the engine's control module and the exhaust system, Volkswagen was able to increase the 1.8 T's horsepower to 180.

Except for the 1.8 T, which gets a Tiptronic 5-speed automatic transmission, all other Jettas – namely the models equipped with 2.0-liter, 1.9 TDi and VR 6 engines – come with a 4 speed automatic gearbox. Also worth noting is the fact that, unlike the Passat's, the Jetta's Tiptronic gearbox was adapted for use with a transversal engine, and it has been reprogrammed to deliver "sportier" performance.

Steady progress

The arrival of the supercharged 1.8 T is good news indeed, but there's more. This year, for instance, Volkswagen has increased its warranty to 4-year/48,000-mile (80,000 km), a welcome change from the miserable 2-year/15,000-mile (24,000 km). Option packages have also been beefed up and a standard CD player will be added (finally!) later in the year. What's

▲ PROS

- **5-speed automatic gearbox • Large trunk**
- **Longer warranty • More powerful 1.8 T engine**
- **Wagon model in Spring 2002**

▼ CONS

- **Average rear seats • Badly located cupholders**
- **Dated and noisy 2.0-liter engine • GLX model too expensive • Torque steer**

more, prices for some models have been reduced.

Power and torque steer

It goes without saying that the 180-hp engine gives the Jetta much more pep. Equipped with a manual transmission, it takes 7.9 seconds to go from 0-60 mph. Passing power is just as effective. On the other hand, my test car exhibited pronounced torque steer each time I floored the accelerator, and that is unusual for a Volkswagen. The fact that our test drive took place on a rainy day might partly explain this phenomenon, as one tends to keep the revs low, well into the fat part of the torque curve, in such conditions. If you treat the accelerator more gently, however, the problem goes away.

The pleasure of driving the 1.8 T is further enhanced because it's the most interesting engine in the entire Jetta line, which also includes a 1.9 TDi turbo diesel. Even though the showers spoiled part of our test drive, I could tell that the modified suspension ensured better cornering, while the directional stability proved to be even more precise. The rear suspension gets better-quality shocks this year, which help stabilize the rear axle and reduce hopping on rough roads. The 1.8 T's suspension is also a little firmer than before, but less so than the Golf GTI.

As for the rest, nothing much has changed. The driving position is excellent and the control layout is, as always, practical. The planned arrival of the standard CD player later this year means that Volkswagen needs to rethink the location of the cupholders between the air vents and the radio. Finally, the center armrest is still in the way when the time comes to buckle up.

The automatic transmission changes gears more quickly than in past versions, but this seems irrelevant since the Tiptronic transmission shifts gear automatically, even when in manual mode, which is illogical in my view.

With this new Jetta lineup, Volkswagen has taken measures to attract a wide clientele by improving its products and by offering a genuine warranty. If only the automaker could improve reliability by a few more degrees, things would be even better.

Denis Duquet

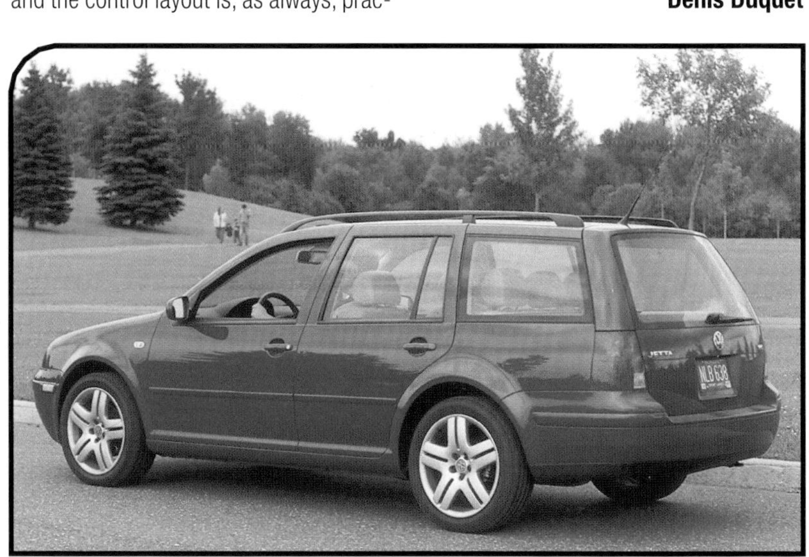

SPECIFICATIONS	**1.8T**
Price	$CDN 21,490-33,875 / $US 17,250-25,950
Warranty	4 years / 48,000 miles (80,000 km)
Type	sedan / front wheel drive
Wheelbase / Length	98.8 in / 172.4 in
Width / Height	68.3 in / 57.1 in
Weight	2873 lb (1303 kg)
Trunk / Fuel tank	16.1 cu.ft. / 15 galUS
Air bags	front, side and head
Front suspension	independent
Rear suspension	semi-independent
Front brakes / Rear brakes	disc ABS
Traction control	yes
Steering	rack-and-pinion, power assist
Turning circle	33 feet
Tires (front/rear)	P195/65R15

PERFORMANCE	
Engine	4L 1.8-liter Turbo
Transmission	5-speed automatic
Horsepower	180 hp at 5700 rpm
Torque	155 lb-ft at 1750 rpm
Other engines	4 L 2.0-liter 115 hp; 4L 1.9-liter TDi 90 hp; V6 2.8-liter 201 hp
Other transmission	5-speed manual; 4-speed automatic
Acceleration (0-60 mph)	7.8 sec (1.8-liter turbo)
Maximum speed	122 mph (195 km/h)
Braking (60-0 mph)	129 feet (39.4 m)
Fuel consumption	27 mpg (8.6 L/100 km)

COMPETITION

• Ford Focus • Honda Civic • Mazda Protegé • Nissan Sentra • Subaru Impreza • Saturn LS2 • Toyota Corolla

NEW FOR 2002

• Improved warranty • Lower price • 180-hp 1.8-liter engine • Sport suspension • Standard CD player

RATING	**(out of 5 stars)**
Driveability	★★★½
Comfort	★★★½
Reliability	★★★½
Roominess	★★★
Winter driving rating	★★★½
Safety	★★★★
Resale value	★★★½

VOLKSWAGEN NEW BEETLE

VOLKSWAGEN **NEW BEETLE**

A Fishbowl

Cool, funky, different, the New Beetle has done wonders for Volkswagen's solemn image ever since its unveiling four years ago, accompanied by classic 60's tunes and daisies adorning its dashboard. And the "bug" continues to amuse young and old with its unique charm – a bud vase on the dash and its strange yet familiar curved lines.

But this Golf in party clothes is more than the sum of its looks. Its main asset is hidden under the hood, namely, the 1.8-liter turbocharged engine.

Viva Turbo!

My test model was a high-end GLX, powered by a superb 1.8 turbocharged engine. It took no more than a couple of miles to discover that this made-in-Mexico Beetle really meant business. The supple 1.8 T engine moves effortlessly up the rev range, accompanied by a subtle hissing sound. But what impressed me most was the generous torque it developed without straining itself at low rpms. With the exception of the Subaru Impreza's turbo engine, VW's 1.8 T is easily the most satisfying 4-cylinder currently available.

Just imagine, it delivers a full head of steam, as it were, at 2000 rpm, enough to propel the Bug from 50 to 75 mph in 6.6 seconds in fourth gear, so there's no need to crank it up to 7000 to get things cracking. The Toyota Celica (180 hp), and the Honda S2000 (240 hp) can certainly burst out of the blocks faster, but unless your idea of fun is to speed down a race track everyday on your way to the office, the Beetle wins hands down in terms of driving enjoyment – and that includes several of the hottest V6s around.

A word of advice: if the 1.8 Turbo leaves you cold, go for the turbo-diesel, but for goodness' sake, don't spoil the fun by getting that antiquated, insipid and noisy 2.0-liter.

Serious drivers

Mounted on 17-inch alloy wheels (optional) and low-profile Michelin XSR tires, the test-Beetle takes corners in stride, keeping body roll and understeer under firm control. Braking force abounds, enhanced by a pedal that's both firm and easy to modulate. Steering is precise and

▲ PROS

• Comfortable front seats • Efficient brakes • Excellent handling • Great 1.8-liter turbo engine • Refreshing lines

▼ CONS

• Average reliability • No CD player • Short warranty period • Steep price • Unstable in crosswinds • Symbolic rear seats and trunk

responsive, making the car even more driveable. But I found fault with the brake and gas pedals – too far apart – and also with the Beetle's sensitivity to crosswinds, no doubt owing to its shape. But here again, the ingenious Bug will surprise you, automatically closing the sunroof and thereby improving aerodynamics, then, at highway speed, deploying the little spoiler located atop the rear window, designed to stabilize the car. The spoiler can also be activated manually by tinkering with the switch located under the dashboard. What more is there to say? The Germans do take their driving seriously.

A fishbowl

The interior is full of surprises, too. You feel as if you're inside an aquarium. There's glass everywhere – a huge windshield framed by curved pillars that impede visibility in tight corners; more glass on the side and rear windows; and in the sunroof. In short, a veritable fishbowl.

The fully loaded GLX comes with leather seats, heated and height-adjustable. The adjustable for tilt and height steering column makes it easy to find a suitable driving position. But if you want to recline your backrest, good luck, because that knob is a disgrace – frustrating. The rear bench and trunk, too, are laughable. You can cram in two 8-year-olds in the former, and keep your gloves in the latter. And if you collapse the teeny-weeny bench, there'll be just enough space for a weekend bag.

If you're single or a childless couple, the New Beetle is the car for you, assuming you go for the exciting turbo gasoline engine or thrifty turbodiesel (forget the 2.0-liter). For 2002, Volkswagen will add a new sporty Turbo S model to the lineup, boasting 180 horsepower and 6 speeds. In the final analysis, nostalgia is only a state of mind, because in fact the New Beetle is all new: fantastic performance, deluxe equipment – and price – and alas, only average reliability. In a nutshell, everything that the old Bug was not.

Alain Raymond

SPECIFICATIONS	GLX 1.8T
Price	$CDN 21,950-30,765 / $US 16,450-21,725
Warranty	4 years / 48,000 miles (80,000 km)
Type	coupe hatchback / front wheel drive
Wheelbase / Length	98.8 in / 161 in
Width / Height	67.7 in / 59.4 in
Weight	2866 lb (1300 kg)
Trunk / Fuel tank	10.6 cu. ft / 15 gallons
Air bags	front and side
Front suspension	independent
Rear suspension	semi-independent
Front brakes / Rear brakes	disc ABS
Traction control	yes
Steering	rack-and-pinion, power assist
Turning circle	36 feet
Tires (front/rear)	P225/45HR17

PERFORMANCE	
Engine	4L 1.8-liter Turbo
Transmission	5-speed manual
Horsepower	150 hp at 5800 rpm
Torque	162 lb-ft at 2200 rpm
Other engines	2.0 l 115 hp; 1.9 l turbodiesel 90 hp
Other transmission	4-speed automatic
Acceleration (0-60 mph)	7.8 s; 11.2 s (2 L); 11 s (diesel)
Maximum speed	124 mph (200 km/h); 106 mph (170 km/h) (diesel); 112 mph (180 km/h) (2 L)
Braking (60-0 mph)	134 feet (40.8 m)
Fuel consumption	21 mpg (10.8 L/100 km)

COMPETITION

• Acura RSX • Chrysler PT Cruiser • Honda Civic Si • Mini Cooper S • VW Golf • Toyota Celica GT

NEW FOR 2002

• 1.8T 180-hp version • 6-speed gearbox
• Improved warranty

RATING	(out of 5 stars)
Driveability	★★★★
Comfort	★★★½
Reliability	★★
Roominess	★★
Winter driving rating	★★★½
Safety	★★★★
Resale value	★★★★

VOLKSWAGEN PASSAT VOLKSWAGEN VR6

VOLKSWAGEN **PASSAT**

Of Horses and Chromium

How times have changed! Three decades ago, lots of chrome and V8 engines were the hallmark of big American cars. In 2002, such distinguished features are associated with a German intermediate sedan, the Volkswagen Passat. Its latest version, sparkling with chrome, is fitted with a 4.0-liter 8-cylinder engine that moves it up a giant notch in the luxury-car hierarchy. These days, Passats are anything but economy cars.

Apart from the overwhelming chrome moldings that set off its contour, the new W8's styling appears unchanged from its previous version, at least to the naked eye. But let's proceed chronologically, starting with its unveiling last fall in Sardinia – a few vigorous breaststrokes south of Corsica (see following pages for a full description of the Passat W8).

Destination: Olbia

Volkswagen graciously made it an important affair, chartering us automotive journalists from Rome to Olbia, in northeastearn Sardinia, so that we could take the pulse – not to mention the steering wheel – of its new and improved Passat. On this Mediterranean island, once the playground of the Aga Khan and Europe's aristocrats, I was finally able to test the car.

The fact that the new model didn't seem terribly different from its predecessor is not a bad thing, since the Passat is still one of the best cars in its class. On the other hand, tinkering with a winning formula must have been both tricky and risky.

That said, the latest Passat sedans and wagons positively gleam with chrome, adorning the grille and contouring the side windows, as well as the various gauges on the dashboard. It's all quite odd, because this kind of artifice was heavily criticized when it was first used on big American cars in their heyday. Other styling changes include the headlights, now covered with clear lenses; and the fog lamps, embedded in the bumpers.

Subtle differences

Volkswagen's media service was quick to point out that no fewer than 2313 parts had been replaced or modified in the new Passat. However, in the eyes of mere mortals – or even those of a car columnist – these changes were barely apparent. In fact, my notebook remained largely blank at the end of a 45-minute press conference that took place in a hotel on the Costa Smeralda.

▲ PROS

- Excellent comfort • Prolonged warranty
- Solid platform • Spacious rear seats
- Superb traction (4Motion)

▼ CONS

- Modest performance • Noisier wagon version
- Slow shifting transmission • Soft suspension
- Steep price • Vague steering

What I did notice, however, was the improved rigidity of the Passat's body, that the 1.8-liter turbo engine could now generate an extra 20 horsepower, and that passive-safety features included the new so-called head airbags. As for the other 2309 changes, I'm still searching. The press kit further mentioned that the hood, the trunk lid, the taillights and alloy wheels had been improved, but I couldn't honestly tell.

V6 and turbo

Introduced in mid 2001 as 2001.5 models, these "new and improved" Passats come with two engine options: a 2.8-liter V6 with 190 horsepower, and a 4-cylinder 1.8 turbo engine with 180 hp. The latter is by far the most interesting model. However, the 4Motion option (four-wheel drive) is only offered with the V6. Although the new Passat closely resembles the older version, its road manners and cabin fare better. In my judgment, the major difference between the two lies in the chassis. Its improved torsional rigidity provides a better balance between comfort and handling. On first impression, the suspension seems too soft (especially in the front), but after a couple of high-speed turns, you'll find out that the soft shock absorber settings hardly hamper handling. Although its suspension tends to "float" over humps in the road, Passat's four-wheel drive version adheres tenaciously to the surface.With 10 horses fewer than the V6, the 4-cylinder 1.8T still has a better weight/power ratio because the car is 220 lbs lighter. Road manners are thus sportier. It's a pity that steering doesn't transmit better road feel.

The 2001.5's cabin is pleasant. Its rear seats are more spacious than the old Audi A4's, the quality of finish is superb, equipment refined and visibility excellent – unhampered by any blind spots.

Introduced in its current shape in 1997, the Volkswagen Passat has done its job well, and has contributed to the company's restored fortunes in a special way, the car's reputation having been badly damaged by misadventures in the early 1990s.

Pending a thorough redesign, scheduled for 2003, the current rejuvenation will doubtless allow the Passat to maintain its position as leader in the mid-sedan category.

Jacques Duval

SPECIFICATIONS	GLX 4Motion
Price	$CDN 29,550-43,305 / $US 22,300-32,925
Warranty	4 years / 48,000 miles (80,000 km)
Type	5-seat sedan / all wheel drive
Wheelbase / Length	106.4 in / 185.2 in
Width / Height	68.7 in / 57.5 in
Weight	3644 lb (1653 kg)
Trunk / Fuel tank	14.1 cu. ft / 16 gallons
Air bags	front and side
Front suspension	independent
Rear suspension	independent
Front brakes / Rear brakes	disc ABS
Traction control	yes (except 4Motion)
Steering	rack-and-pinion, variable assist
Turning circle	37 feet
Tires (front/rear)	P205/55R16 (optional)

PERFORMANCE	
Engine	V6 2.8-liter
Transmission	5-speed Tiptronic (automatic)
Horsepower	190 hp at 6000 rpm
Torque	206 lb-ft at 3200 rpm
Other engines	4L 1.8-liter 180 hp
Other transmission	5-speed manual
Acceleration (0-60 mph)	9.5 sec
Maximum speed	130 mph (210 km/h)
Braking (60-0 mph)	138 feet (42 m)
Fuel consumption	18.1 mpg (12.5 L/100 km)

COMPETITION

• Audi A4 • BMW 325Xi • Jaguar X-Type • M-Benz C240 • Saab 9³ • Subaru Outback H6 • Volvo S60

NEW FOR 2002

• Improved warranty
• Handle inside the trunk

RATING	(out of 5 stars)
Driveability	★★★½
Comfort	★★★★
Reliability	★★★★
Roominess	★★★★
Winter driving rating	★★★★
Safety	★★★★
Resale value	★★★★

VOLKSWAGEN PASSAT W8

VOLKSWAGEN **PASSAT W8**

Summit Meeting

The reason why Volkswagen chose Les Diablerets, a village atop Glacier 3000, near Gstaad in the Swiss Alps, to launch their new Passat W8 was symbolic, though hardly subtle. It was the company's way of signaling the W8's flagship position in the VW lineup to the automobile press corps. Other than this little extravagant touch and the challenge of transporting the car up the 3000-meter-high mountain (it was hung from the base of the funicular), what else is there for Volkswagen to brag about, so far as its high-end luxurious sedan is concerned? The car clearly wants to insinuate itself into the prestigious trio of German tenors – namely the Mercedes-Benz C Class, BMW 3 Series and Audi A4.

Even though its time in the limelight risks being short-lived (a yet more luxurious VW is currently in the works), the W8 remains a flagship car teeming with interesting features, notably the one hidden under its hood – Volkswagen's first ever 8-cylinder engine, and in a novel configuration, to boot.

"W" engine

Contrary to popular belief, the W in this context has nothing to do with the initials VW, but refers to the special disposition of the engine's eight cylinders – in fact, two narrow angle V45 (15 degrees) side by side, sharing a common crankshaft. The angle between the outside banks of each V4 is 72 degrees, and the angle between the inner banks of the two V4S is – wait for it – 72 minus (2x15) = 42 degrees. Presto, an 8-cylinder engine as short as the 2-cylinder variety. In addition to its four overhead camshafts, this 4.0-liter engine boasts two counter-rotating balance shafts to cancel out dynamic engine vibrations. The new engine is the first in a series of modular VW engines with cubic capacities ranging from 1.8 to 8 liters. Its unusual architecture has the advantage of being short and light (420 lbs, 190 kg) compared with a traditional V8, making the engine easy to install in compact cars like the Passat, where it's mounted longitudinally. The same engine – in a W12 version – will equip the upcoming, temporarily named D-Limousine, as well as the next Audi A8. Another version – the W16 turbo, capable of generating 1001 horsepower – will be produced for the Bugatti EB 16.4 Veyron, which Volkswagen plans to bring out

A people's car?

▲ PROS

• Well sorted transmission • All wheel drive • Avant-garde engine • Extensive range of standard equipment • Very comfortable

▼ CONS

• Average performance • Boring appearance • Confusing instruments • Steep price • Unproven reliability • Wide turning circle

within the next few years. The big advantage of modular engines is that they allow the use of identical components (valves, camshafts, pistons, etc.) in powerplants of various cubic displacements.

Despite its high-tech aspect, the W8's fuel consumption is unexceptional. With 275 horsepower (6 horses fewer than the Jaguar V8, which has the same cubic capacity), and a barely average torque at low rpms, the new Passat won't qualify as a sport sedan – despite a 6-speed manual gearbox (available only in Europe).

Where are the horses?

Weighed down by its 4Motion all-wheel-drive system, the robust and fast W8 is first and foremost a luxury touring car. However, its top speed of 155 mph (240 km/h) on the Autobahn is irrelevant in North American driving terms. Though limited in both power and torque, the W8 4Motion's engine has a throaty, gorgeous sound. For me the lack of a manual gearbox in North America is not a worry. The 5-speed automatic Tiptronic seems perfectly suited to the Passat's subdued road manners.

No doubt about it, the W8 is an accomplished touring car, perfectly secure thanks to its all-wheel drive and sturdy road manners. It performs nimbly enough on mountain roads, even though the suspension tends to "float" slightly while cornering hard. Overall comfort is beyond reproach and the steering feels less "detached" from the road than the VR6's, but its wide turning circle might prove to be a handicap in tight situations. A 200-mile test run (300 km) convinced me that the Passat W8 has what it takes to face its rivals head on, even if it will never overtake them.

Apart from its W8 crest, twin chromed tailpipes and 17-inch alloy wheels, the car has no distinguishing features. Much the same can be said about the interior, which is indistinguishable from the VR6 GLX, except for its rather unusual, though confusing instrument panel, and seats with integrated back support. Fortunately, the W8's standard equipment is more substantial, including curtain airbags for head protection, Xenon headlights, an electronic stability program (ESP), traction control (TCS), and a panic braking system. Does this justify the steep price approaching $50,000? VW sales staff have their work cut out.

Jacques Duval

SPECIFICATIONS	4Motion
Price	est. $CDN 55,000 / $US 35,000
Warranty	4 years / 48,000 miles (80,000 km)
Type	5-seat sedan or wagon / all wheel drive
Wheelbase / Length	166.4 in / 185.2 in
Width / Height	68.7 in / 57.5 in
Weight	3783 lb (1716 kg)
Trunk / Fuel tank	14.1 cu. ft / 21 gallons
Air bags	front, side and head
Front suspension	independent
Rear suspension	independent
Front brakes / Rear brakes	vented disc ABS + EBV
Traction control	yes
Steering	rack-and-pinion, variable assist
Turning circle	38 feet
Tires (front/rear)	P225/45R17

PERFORMANCE	
Engine	W8 4-liter
Transmission	5-speed Tiptronic (automatic)
Horsepower	275 hp at 6000 rpm
Torque	278 lb-ft at 2750 rpm
Other engines	none
Other transmission	none
Acceleration (0-60 mph)	8.5 sec
Maximum speed	155 mph (250 km/h)
Braking (60-0 mph)	135 feet (41 m)
Fuel consumption	17.5 mpg (13 L/100 km)

COMPETITION

- Audi A6 • BMW 330Xi • Jaguar S-Type
- Mercedes-Benz C320 • Saab 9⁵ • Volvo S60T5

NEW FOR 2002

- New model
- Improved warranty

RATING	(out of 5 stars)
Driveability	★★★★
Comfort	★★★★
Reliability	★★★★★
Roominess	★★★★
Winter driving rating	★★★★
Safety	★★★★
Resale value	★★★★★

VOLVO C70

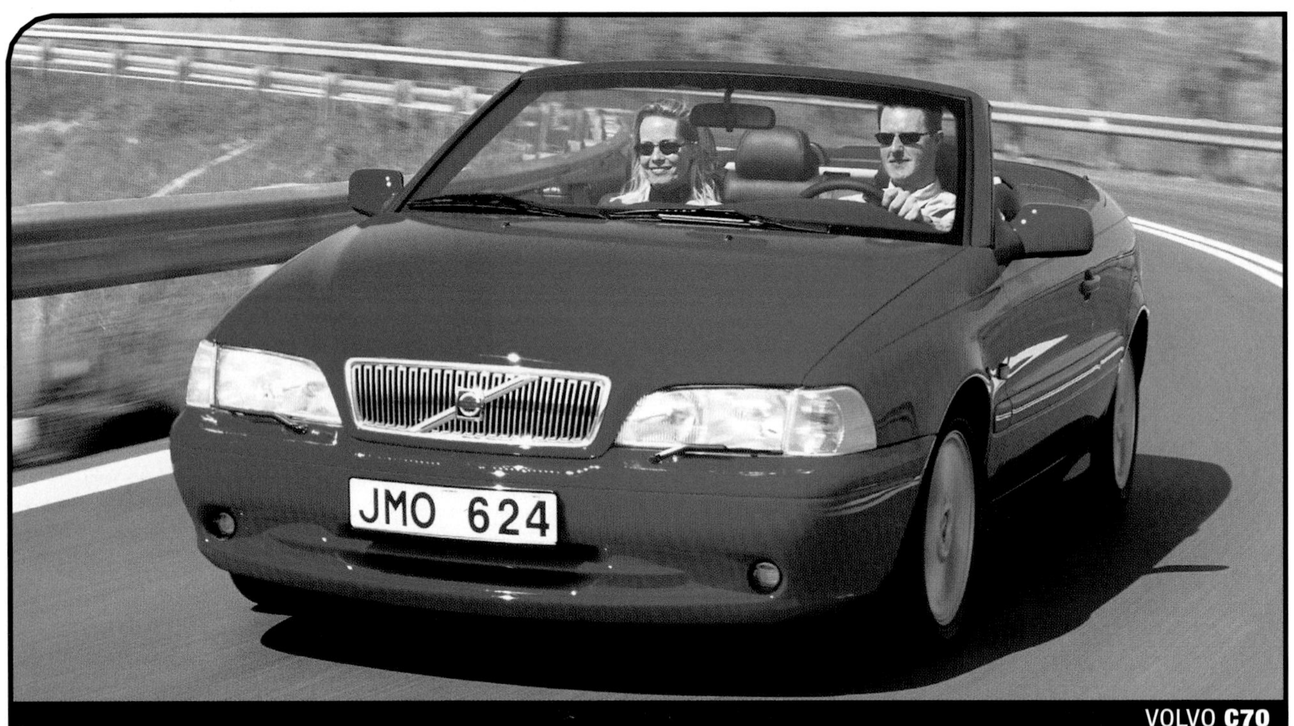

VOLVO **C70**

Elegance and Sportiness

Swedes think nothing of taking off their tops so they can take advantage of the occasional rays of sunshine that come their way. Four years ago, Volvo had the same idea and decided to take the top off one of its cars. Adding a convertible to the C70 line was the Göteborg-based automaker's way of underlining its intention to carve out its own niche in the luxury sports car segment of the market.

The C70 coupe and convertible are fitted essentially with the same mechanical components, although only the convertible gets the 2.5-liter low-pressure turbo engine. This 5-cylinder engine generates 190 horsepower at 5100 rpm, and an impressive amount of low-rpm torque – 199 lb-ft at 1600 rpm. Performance is perfectly acceptable, but if you insist upon more, you'll have to opt for the 2.3-liter high-pressure turbo engine, capable of cranking out 236 horsepower.

This engine is the only one offered with the coupe. Vigorous yet supple, it delivers crisp acceleration and passing power. But if you press the accelerator too abruptly, the front wheels will suffer from heavy torque effect. You might also find the slight turbo lag annoying, especially if you're one of those enthusiastic drivers who live for instant feedback! The standard 5-speed manual transmission is fairly user-friendly, although if you prefer, you can always get the optional 5-speed automatic (standard on the convertible with the 2.5-liter engine).

The C70 handles more like a grand-touring car than a sport model. If pushed hard, it will certainly rise to the occasion, and deliver a worthy performance, although that will be at the expense of road feel – not an ideal situation, either. Under normal driving conditions, the ride is smooth. You barely notice curves or bumps, proof of first-class structural rigidity and a well-tuned suspension. Steering is precise, making it easy to keep the car on the straight and narrow. But watch out for the ruts in the road, as they affect cars with wide tires such as this one. The cabin is quiet, that is except for the turbo's whistling sound.

Heads will turn

On the other hand, the noise from the convertible assaults your ears constantly, even though the thick top lining helps to insulate the cabin from road noise. The

▲ PROS

- Appealing style • Driving pleasure
- High-pressure turbo performance
- Overall comfort • Roomy cabin (for its class)

▼ CONS

- Difficult access to the back • Poor rear visibility • Pronounced torque effect • Turbo lag
- Unexciting performance (convertible)

rear-deck spoiler, too, helps on this score, especially when the top is lowered. This operation is accomplished by pressing a single button. In the event of a rollover, two hoops will instantly deploy the minute the sensors detect a potentially dangerous body lean angle. For the rest, Volvo's legendary array of safety gear includes four-wheel disc brakes with ABS, front and side airbags, and whiplash-reducing front seats, to name only a few.

Sexy and refined

Whether it's a coupe or convertible, the C70 invariably makes heads turn, although it has nothing in common with an eye-catching hot rod. Instead its seductively curving lines and slightly tapered tail end exude both elegance and sportiness. Inside, the heated leather seats are firmly contoured and supportive. And despite my own rather "healthy" weight, it took me next to no time to find my normal driving position. The rear seats are comfortable and provide more generous leg, hip and shoulder room than you'll find in most other coupes. In theory, the front seats can be moved back and forth electrically to make access to the back easier, but the operation proved to be a tricky one. There's lot of trunk space in the coupe, but storage room is seriously reduced in the convertible because of the folded top.

Optional equipment on models fitted with the high-pressure turbo engine include in-dash wood trim and the fabulous 12-speaker Dolby Prologic Surround Sound system. The quality of the materials used is first-rate, and both the instruments and controls are logically arranged and easy to read. It's a pity that rear visibility is seriously hampered by the narrow rear window, both in the coupe and convertible.

Volvo has every right to be proud of its coupe. It boasts everything to appeal to discriminating buyers for whom comfort and style take precedence over performance. Mission accomplished.

Jean-Georges Laliberté

SPECIFICATIONS

Price	$CDN 49,995-63,995 / $US 37,575-46,175
Warranty	4 years / 48,000 miles (80,000 km)
Type	coupe / front wheel drive
Wheelbase / Length	104.9 in / 185.7 in
Width / Height	71.5 in / 55.7 in
Weight	3199 lb (1451 kg)
Trunk / Fuel tank	13.1 cu. ft / 18 gallons
Air bags	front and side
Front suspension	independent
Rear suspension	semi-independent
Front brakes / Rear brakes	disc ABS
Traction control	yes
Steering	rack-and-pinion, variable assist
Turning circle	38 feet
Tires (front/rear)	P225/50VR16

PERFORMANCE

Engine	5L 2.3-liter high-pressure turbo
Transmission	5-speed manual
Horsepower	236 hp at 5400 rpm
Torque	243 lb-ft at 2400 rpm
Other engines	5L 2.5-liter low-pressure turbo (cabriolet)
Other transmission	5-speed automatic
Acceleration (0-60 mph)	7.2 sec
Maximum speed	145mph (234 km/h)
Braking (60-0 mph)	130 feet (39.6 m)
Fuel consumption	19.7 mpg (11.5 L/100 km)

COMPETITION

• Audi TT • BMW 330C • Mercedes-Benz CLK
• Saab 9^3 Viggen

NEW FOR 2002

No major change

RATING (out of 5 stars)

Driveability	★★★★
Comfort	★★★½
Reliability	★★★
Roominess	★★★
Winter driving rating	★★★½
Safety	★★★★½
Resale value	★★★

VOLVO S40 VOLVO V40

VOLVO **S40**

A Volvo by any Other Name

Though they'd been eagerly awaited by buyers, there was minimal interest when Volvo's S40 and V40 arrived last year. Despite an irresistible price that would have given potential customers access to one of the most sought-after makes, these compacts have remained on the sidelines. Is it possible they missed the mark?

Generally speaking, when a sedan and a station wagon share both a platform and mechanical components, the sedan prevails – it's more elegant and comfortable and usually more fun to drive. But as far as Volvo is concerned, the opposite is true. The S40 sedan has been left far behind by the V40 wagon.

It's not hard to figure out why. Even though both models were based on a platform developed in collaboration with Mitsubishi, the wagon was exclusively developed by Volvo. Mitsubishi was happy to leave the wagon market to the folks at Volvo, Europe's best wagon maker, while it concentrated on developing the Carisma 4-door version and the 5-door hatchback on the same platform.

Almost a Volvo

Public reaction to a new model is always interesting, sometimes disconcerting. For years, Volvo's boxy shape has been widely criticized. Drivers were unimpressed with the familiar square shape that was intended to emphasize the vehicle's functionality and comfort rather than superficial elegance. This time, the V40's design team wanted to round off all the sharp corners and present a less austere exterior. But Volvo is not beyond the critics' range just yet.

If the exterior is still not a crowd-pleaser, the cockpit is typically Volvo with its textured-plastic dashboard and vertical center console incorporating user-friendly radio and climate controls. The steering hub, however, is far too big. Thank goodness it doesn't block the instrument displays, which are quick and easy to read.

Shared genes

Like Volvos everywhere, the front seats are comfortable and simple to adjust. Upholstery quality is impeccable, although some people might find fault with it. There's not much headroom or legroom in the back and the rear 3/4 visibility is obstructed by a huge D pillar.

Cabin size is average, and this is the V40's main flaw, since the 1.9-liter tur-

▲ POUR

• Well-adapted engine • Excellent passive safety features • Comfortable seats • Precise steering • Adaptive automatic transmission

▼ CONTRE

• Cramped cabin • Pronounced understeer • Poor ¾ rear visibility • Some materials need rethinking • Too little room in the back

bocharged 4-cylinder engine produces 165 hp, with good acceleration capabilities (0-60 mph in about 9 seconds). What's more, the 5-speed adaptive automatic transmission is efficient. With long gearing, engine revs are in the low range even when you're going 60 mph, so it's easy to ignore the increasing speed until you suddenly realize you're driving at 100 mph. That's testimony to the V40's efficient sound insulation and great directional stability.

The V40 is a competent touring car but it doesn't like to be pushed to the limit in tight turns. Understeer is pronounced and the tires protest loudly. Fortunately the brakes are powerful and efficient. If you feel like driving the V40 like a sports car, don't forget that your passengers have no grab handles.

A shy sedan

If the V40 wagon is a winner, the S40 sedan won't exactly turn heads. Its style isn't all that bad, but it's impersonal. This car was designed in the mid-90s, and it shows. And if you think the V40's cockpit is cramped, it's not any better in the S40, which has a makeshift childseat in the rear, reducing precious legroom even more. And although the size of the S40's rear cabin is identical to that of the Audi 4, the former seems more cramped because of the seat's excessive width. This sedan was clearly built for families with very young children.

The S40 should be available with a manual transmission, thereby letting some enthusiasts sport-drive it, something that will make them forget the cramped cockpit and some of the subpar features like the B pillars. The latter are painted matte black which makes them look cheap. In the plus column are the S40's trunk, as spacious as the Volkswagen Passat's, and a panoply of passive-safety features worthy of Volvo's tough, straight-arrow image.

Despite those few favorable elements, Volvo should waste no time to develop replacement models since Passat introduced its new line in early 2001 and 2002 will bring us a revamped Audi A4.

Denis Duquet

VOLVO **V40**

SPECIFICATIONS

Price	$CDN 31,495-32,495 / $US 26,025-29,025
Warranty	4 years / 48,000 miles (80,000 km)
Type	wagon / front wheel drive
Wheelbase / Length	100.8 in / 178.7 in
Width / Height	67.7 in / 56 in
Weight	2855 lb (1295 kg)
Trunk / Fuel tank	16.6 cu. ft / 16 gallons
Air bags	front, side and rear (side)
Front suspension	independent
Rear suspension	independent
Front brakes / Rear brakes	vented disc ABS / disc ABS
Traction control	no
Steering	rack-and-pinion, power assist
Turning circle	35 feet
Tires (front/rear)	P195/60V15

PERFORMANCE

Engine	4L 1.9 liter turbo
Transmission	5-speed automatic
Horsepower	165 hp at 5250 rpm
Torque	177 lb-ft at 1800 – 4500 rpm
Other engines	none
Other transmission	none
Acceleration (0-60 mph)	9 sec
Maximum speed	134 mph (215 km/h)
Braking (60-0 mph)	146 feet (44.6 m)
Fuel consumption	24.7 mpg (9.2 L/100 km)

COMPETITION

• BMW 320 Touring • M-Benz C-Class wagon • Subaru Impreza • VW Jetta • VW Passat

NEW FOR 2002

No major change

RATING (out of 5 stars)

Driveability	★★★
Comfort	★★★
Reliability	★★★½
Roominess	★★
Winter driving rating	★★★
Safety	★★★★
Resale value	★★

VOLVO S60

VOLVO **S60**

Go – Go Volvo!

Until recently, the name Volvo was seldom associated with good looks. With their boxy and square lines, the Swedish sedans were automatically excluded from any automobile beauty contests. Little by little, however, the wind changed and Volvos began to draw admiration rather than derision. Witness the S60, which landed on our shores last year, replacing the discontinued S70, although the V70 – its station wagon model – is still available.

The S60 effortlessly exploits the rejuvenated lines of the S80, Volvo's top-of-the-line luxury sedan. Its sloping roofline inspires some to refer to it as a 4-door coupe, and rightly so. But such style concessions came with a price: If you want to get into the back seats without pain and a string of swear words, watch your head on the door frame. Visibility is also affected, since the new design creates a three-quarter blind spot in the rear. What's more, the A-pillar, or if you prefer, the windshield pillar is so wide that it blocks your view when you make a left turn.

Three engine options

Styling aside, the S60 comes in three front-wheel drive engine flavors: the 2.4 boasts a standard, transversely mounted 2.4-liter five-cylinder unit producing 168 horsepower; the mid-level 2.4 T has the same basic block with a low-pressure turbocharger and producing 197 hp; and the top end, the T5, with a 2.3-liter engine boasting the same number of cylinders but producing 247 hp, thanks to a high-pressure turbocharger. Our test model was a T5, fitted with a 5-speed automatic transmission. We could have chosen the manual gearbox version, but the 0-60 mph time of 7.4 seconds eloquently proved that the engine worked well with the automatic transmission. Discreet and dynamic, the engine was astonishingly frugal, averaging roughly 23 mpg (10 liters per 100 km).

Not sporty enough

Not quite there

By invoking memories of the old 544 or 122S models, Volvo clearly wants the S60 to be seen as a sporty car. But, despite the T5's enviable performance, it's not quite there yet as a sport sedan; the steering is both too light and vague and, worse, requires a too-large turning circle. Further-

▲ PROS

• Confidence-inspiring roadholding • Cool styling • Enviable performance • Impressive, powerful brakes • Spacious cabin

▼ CONS

• Difficult access to the rear • Excessive rolls in corners • Large turning circle • Light steering • Limited visibility

more, torque steer is way too pronounced, although not as bad as the Saab Viggen, where you really have to twist your arms. Suspension roll during quick cornering doesn't encourage sporty driving either. This is all the more regrettable since braking is uncommonly efficient, and, despite the model's propensity toward excessive lean in the corners, the Pirelli P-6, 17-inch tires provide reassuring road adherence. On bad roads, the S60 sometimes reacts a tad abruptly, although overall comfort is hardly affected. The chassis' rigidity, on the other hand, could be increased.

The Ford effect

Fortunately, the S60's interior doesn't look – ahem – "Fordized," as is the case with the Jaguar S-Type, for example, which clearly shows the mark of membership in the large Ford family. Nothing here smacks of Ford, neither the switches nor the textured plastic accessories. The smart combination of wood trim and brushed aluminum makes the S60's interior look as pleasant as its exterior. The steering wheel can be adjusted in two planes and the driver's seat is comfortable.

But I was rather surprised to find that even a safety-obsessed company like Volvo succumbed to the pressure to provide cupholders. Notwithstanding the awkward access, the rear seats provide ample legroom thanks to the front seats' hollowed-out backrests. Two can sit comfortably in the rear, separated by an armrest which doubles as a storage bin. The trunk is particularly large, if a little too deep to retrieve objects that might have slid to the front. There is a small tab conveniently located near the trunk lid to unlock the rear backrest for more storage space.

Except for a defective speaker, the quality of the construction of the test model is beyond reproach. However, only after tens of thousands of miles of road tests can we fairly attest to the sturdiness of the body, a weakness frequently criticized in earlier Volvo models. What's certain is that this S60 is the most pleasant of the Volvos that I have driven for a long time. Those who normally pay attention only to the BMW 3 Series, the Audi A4, the Mercedes-Benz C Class or the new Jaguar will do well to include the S60 in their shopping list.

Jacques Duval

SPECIFICATIONS

Price	$CDN 36,395-46,495 / $US 27,175-32,475
Warranty	4 years / 48,000 miles (80,000 km)
Type	5-seat sedan / front wheel drive
Wheelbase / Length	107 in / 180.3 in
Width / Height	71 in / 56.3 in
Weight	3146 lb (1427 kg)
Trunk / Fuel tank	13.9 cu. ft /18 gallons
Air bags	front and side
Front suspension	independent
Rear suspension	independent
Front brakes / Rear brakes	disc ABS
Traction control	yes
Steering	rack-and-pinion, variable assist
Turning circle	39 feet
Tires (front/rear)	P235/45ZR17

PERFORMANCE

Engine	5L 2.3-liter turbo
Transmission	5-speed automatic
Horsepower	247 hp at 5200 rpm
Torque	238 lb-ft at 1800 - 5000 rpm
Other engines	5L 2.4 168 hp; 2.4T 197 hp
Other transmission	5-speed manual
Acceleration (0-60 mph)	7.4 sec
Maximum speed	155 mph (250 km/h)
Braking (60-0 mph)	149 feet (45.4 m)
Fuel consumption	22.6 mpg (10 L/100 km)

COMPETITION

• Audi A4 • BMW 330i • Jaguar X-Type
• Lexus IS 300 • Mercedes-Benz C240

NEW FOR 2002

• AWD version • New "green" radiator (converting ozone into oxygen)

RATING (out of 5 stars)

Driveability	★★★½
Comfort	★★★½
Reliability	★★★
Roominess	★★★½
Winter driving rating	★★★½
Safety	★★★★½
Resale value	★★★★

VOLVO S80

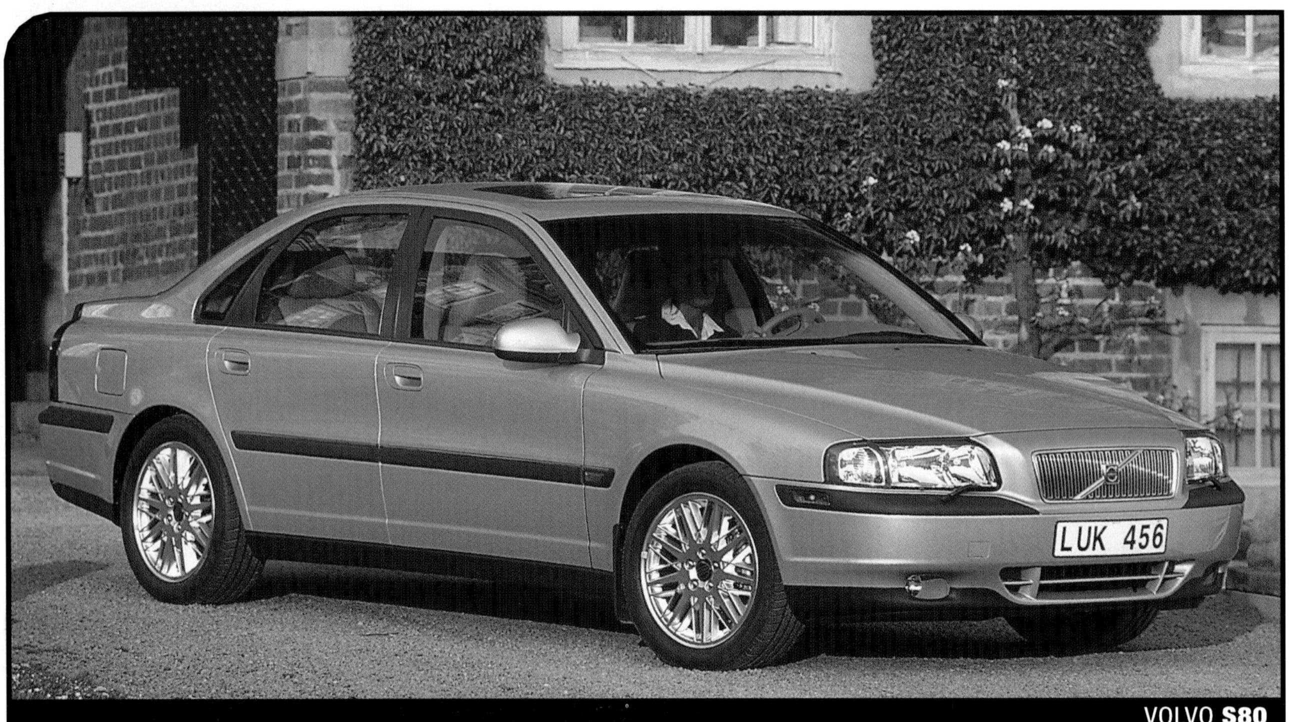

VOLVO **S80**

Luxury and Safety

As far as consumers are concerned, the Volvo image has always been characterized by sturdy quality and conservative lines. And that was especially the case with former models like the S90 and S70. The latest generation of Volvo cars seeks to alter that lingering perception, at least from the styling viewpoint.

Volvos have come a very long way from the days of those "boring square boxes on wheels." The 850 model, for example, managed to break out of that mold by virtue of its sportier handling. But the S80 is the model that represented a complete departure from tradition – in terms of styling, performance, luxury and refinement – and in the process, helped change the public's perception of the Göteborg company.

The one thing that will not change, however, is Volvo's legendary preoccupation with safety, a tradition that began back in the 1950s and earned the company worldwide recognition. It goes without saying that Volvo's latest lineup includes cars that are not only more agile, stylish and comfortable, but they also boast cutting-edge safety features. In point of fact, the S80 is the first automobile in the world to have swept the board with the best results in both European and American general crash tests. These tests are routinely conducted by three independent automobile-safety organizations: Euro-NCAP, US-NCAP and the Insurance Institute for Highway Safety. What's more, the S80 is the first car ever to score a perfect ten in a side-impact collision test. In plain language, it provides the best driver-and-passenger protection anywhere.

Overall reliability, however, is inconsistent. The S80's anti-roll bars are sometimes about as effective as a bowl of spaghetti, while the rack-and-pinion steering tends to fall apart over the long run.

Fragile Swede

Solid foundation

In the past, Volvo spent an average of 10 years in the process of developing a new product. In a clean break with tradition, the S80 took a mere few months to appear, but the company didn't cut corners. On the contrary, it spared no effort, as demonstrated by the more rigid platform – one of the few areas where Volvo didn't particularly shine in the past – and by the im-

▲ PROS

• Competitive price • Complete range of equipment • Exceptional trunk space • Sound handling • Peerless safety

▼ CONS

• Body noise • Over-assisted steering • Poor reliability • Torque steer (T6) • Wide turning radius

pressive new aluminum components that now make up the rear suspension. Incidentally, the S80's platform proved to be so satisfactory that it was later used as the basis for developing the V70 wagon and the S60 sedan. It's a pity that the company's own reliability and durability tests failed to detect the mechanical flaws mentioned above.

Volvo engineers managed to achieve another first by equipping the S80 with a transversely-mounted inline 6 engine as standard fare. With 197 horsepower, the atmospheric 2.9-liter is not only as capable as the 2.4-liter turbo engine that powered the previous-generation S70 sedan, it's also smoother and quieter. The mid-level S80 T6 gets a 2.8-liter inline 6, featuring two turbochargers configured to reduce response time while boosting horsepower to 268. Both engines are paired to a 4-speed automatic transmission. And to rein in all this power in case of poor road conditions, a dynamic stability control system is offered as an option.

Space and performance

If you like wide-open spaces, you'll appreciate the S80's interior, the roomiest in its category. And all that space is used to good effect. The front seats are comfortable, as is the case with all Volvo cars, while the rear boasts an extra two inches of legroom, another first for the Swedish brand. All told, the dashboard layout is practical and functional, though the radio controls could have been easier to understand.

On the road, the base model, powered by the 2.9-liter engine, exhibits perfect balance and feels reassuringly surefooted. But nothing sporty, mind you. The T6 with its 268 horsepower is faster and better equipped in terms of tires and suspension. But unfortunately, you must contend with pronounced torque steer and the ultrafirm suspension doesn't cope with bad roads very well. No wonder the anti-roll bars have a rough time. Doubtless the S80 was designed strictly for surfaces as smooth as a billiard table.

Denis Duquet

SPECIFICATIONS	
Price	$CDN 54,895-62,895 / $US 38,775-49,375
Warranty	4 years / 48,000 miles (80,000 km)
Type	sedan / front wheel drive
Wheelbase / Length	109.8 in / 189.8 in
Width / Height	72 in / 57.1 in
Weight	3283 lb (1489 kg)
Trunk / Fuel tank	14.2 cu. ft / 21 gallons
Air bags	front, side and overhead
Front suspension	independent
Rear suspension	independent
Front brakes / Rear brakes	disc ABS
Traction control	yes
Steering	rack-and-pinion, variable assist
Turning circle	36 feet
Tires (front/rear)	P225/50ZR17 (optional)

PERFORMANCE	
Engine	6L 2.8-liter biturbo
Transmission	4-speed automatic
Horsepower	268 hp at 5400 rpm
Torque	280 lb-ft at 2000 rpm
Other engines	6L 2.9-liter 201 hp
Other transmission	none
Acceleration (0-60 mph)	7.1 sec
Maximum speed	155 mph (250 km/h)
Braking (60-0 mph)	127 feet (38.7 m)
Fuel consumption	18.6 mpg (12.2 L/100 km)

COMPETITION

- Acura RL • Audi A6 • BMW 5 Series • Infiniti I30
- Lexus GS • Mazda Millenia

NEW FOR 2002

- New PremAir radiator (converting ozone into oxygen)

RATING	(out of 5 stars)
Driveability	★★★★
Comfort	★★★★★
Reliability	★★½
Roominess	★★★★
Winter driving rating	★★★★
Safety	★★★★★
Resale value	★★½

VOLVO V70 VOLVO XC

VOLVO **V70 XC**

Wide Range

It's always tough for any carmaker to make the distinction between two models with virtually the same mechanicals. Nearly identical features and an obvious price difference are enough ingredients to spoil the "sauce" and turn customers off one or both models. So Volvo faced a tall order last year when it launched replacements for its V70 and V70 XC station wagons. Their job was made even trickier since many people thought the first-generation XC was little more than a V70 to which a couple of features had been added to make it look more "macho" and justify its higher price. This time around, both the V70 and V70 XC (Cross Country) have been completely redesigned, and now constitute a separate unit since their sedan cousin, the S70, has evolved into the S60.

Each model has a different platform. The XC's front track is 2.36-inch (60 mm) wider than the V70, and the rear axle has been pushed back roughly half an inch (10 mm) to accommodate wider tires – the Pirelli Scorpion P215/65R16 – allowing the XC to tread confidently both on and off-road. Such versatility comes at a price, however: louder noise from the aggressive tread design. Only one engine is made available: a 197-horsepower, 2.4-liter, low-pressure turbocharged five-cylinder, paired with a 5-speed Geartronic automatic gearbox.

The Cross Country's exterior, too, differs noticeably from the V70. Its front fascia sports a black plastic "snout" and a bigger "valance." The fat wheel wells, painted a constrasting color, enhance the car's "macho" appearance. Other styling details worth mentioning are the black protective side moldings, hefty rear bumper and roof rack.

Dynamic duo

What the V70 and V70 XC have in common are the vertical taillights that frame the tailgate. The two cockpits, also, are virtually the same although the XC boasts a fold-down 40/20/40 rear seat. A third-row rearward facing seat is optional on both models.

More than just a fresh face

This essentially all-terrain Volvo deftly combines versatility, comfort and performance. Its 21 cm high ground clearance and efficient all-wheel drive make it

▲ PROS

- **Sophisticated AWD • Decent roadholding**
- **Guaranteed safety • Very comfortable cockpit • Adaptive engine**

▼ CONS

- **Slight vibrations in front disc brakes • Sound insulation needs work • Compromised tires**
- **Medium-sized rear seats**

stand out among other comparable vehicles in the under-$50,000 category. Moreover, the all-wheel drive is 22 lbs lighter following last year's revision and some components have been replaced for better durability. Finally, its traction control system TRACS now functions up to a maximum speed of 50 mph (80 km/h).

It would be wrong to regard the Cross Country as just another suitably dolled-up road car. On the highway, it's almost as nimble as the standard V70 despite its higher center of gravity and less suitable tires. But off-road, it'll surprise those who dare to try it out!

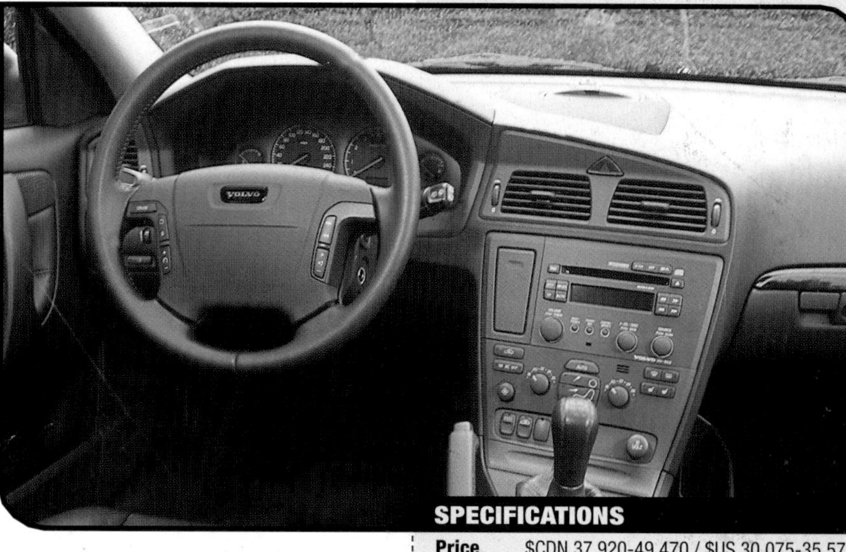

Sporty aspirations

When a company such as Volvo controls an entire market sector with its midsize station wagons, its customers should get a variety of choices. The older V70 came in three variants: family coach, sport-hybrid, and Cross Country. The new version continues to offer the three flavors. Thanks to a new, more rigid platform, a rear suspension borrowed from the S80 sedan as well as an up-to-date, even more practical cockpit, the 70 series can still be considered the benchmark in its field.

The most economical version is fitted with a normally-aspirated 2.4-liter 5-cylinder engine with 168 horsepower. Performance is average, commensurate with this type of engine. Taking it up a notch – the best compromise, in my opinion – you get a more powerful 2.4-liter engine light-turbo engine with an extra 29 horsepower. And finally, the T5 model is powered by a high-output turbocharged 2.3-liter engine with a whopping 247 horsepower. These impressive figures, however, don't quite manage to deliver the goods as they should, because the turbocharger's response time is too slow. The sporty wagon is an interesting idea, but Volvo needs to do something about the firm suspension, particularly in the T5, so as to spare its occupants the constant knocking about and vibration on rough roads.

That said, Volvo station wagons have proved their value time and time again, to which their legions of satisfied customers can attest.

Denis Duquet

SPECIFICATIONS

Price	$CDN 37,920-49,470 / $US 30,075-35,575
Warranty	4 years / 48,000 miles (80,000 km)
Type	hybrid sport utility / all wheel drive
Wheelbase / Length	109 in / 186 in
Width / Height	73 in / 61.4 in
Weight	3593 lb (1630 kg)
Trunk / Fuel tank	37.4 cu. ft / 21 gallons
Air bags	front and side
Front suspension	independent
Rear suspension	independent
Front brakes / Rear brakes	disc ABS
Traction control	yes
Steering	rack-and-pinion, power assist
Turning circle	39 feet
Tires (front/rear)	P215/65HR16

PERFORMANCE

Engine	5L 2.4 liter
Transmission	5-speed automatic
Horsepower	197 hp at 6000 rpm
Torque	210 lb-ft at 1800-5000 rpm
Other engines	5L 2.3 l 247 hp (V70 T5); 5L 2.4 l 168 hp (V70)
Other transmission	5-speed manual
Acceleration (0-60 mph)	8.2 s; 6.7 s (T5 manual)
Maximum speed	130 mph (210 km/h)
Braking (60-0 mph)	137 feet (41.7 m)
Fuel consumption	20.1 mpg (11.1 L/100 km)

COMPETITION

• Audi Allroad • Lexus RX 300 • Saab 9[5]
• Subaru Outback • Toyota Highlander

NEW FOR 2002

• PremAir radiator

RATING (out of 5 stars)

Driveability	★★★½
Comfort	★★★★
Reliability	★★★★
Roominess	★★★★
Winter driving rating	★★★★
Safety	★★★★★
Resale value	★★★★

Printed and bound in Canada
by Interglobe Inc.